WEST AFRICA

WEST AFRICA

An Introduction to its History, Civilization and Contemporary Situation

Eugene L. Mendonsa
University of Colorado

CAROLINA ACADEMIC PRESS
Durham, North Carolina

Library of Congress Cataloging-in-Publication Data

Mendonsa, Eugene L.
    West Africa : an introduction to its history, civilization and contemporary situation / Eugene L. Mendonsa.
        p. cm.
    Includes bibliographical references and index.
    ISBN: 0-89089-649-6
    1. Africa, West--Civilization. 2. Africa, West--History. 3. Africa, West--Politics and government--1960- 4. Africa, West--Economic conditions--1960- I. Title.

DT474 .M46 2002
966--dc21

2002071512

CAROLINA ACADEMIC PRESS
700 Kent Street
Durham, North Carolina 27701
Telephone (919) 489-7486
Fax (919)493-5668
www.cap-press.com

Printed in the United States of America
2017 Printing

This book is dedicated to two of my sons,
one of my loins, both of my heart—

Matthew Eugene Mendonsa

and

Nenkentie Badzongoly

Contents

List of Boxes

Chapter 2.

Chapter 3.

Chapter 4.

Chapter 9.

Chapter 11.

Chapter 16.

List of Figures

List of Maps

Chapter 10.

Chapter 11.

List of Photos

List of Tables

Chapter 18.

Chapter 19.

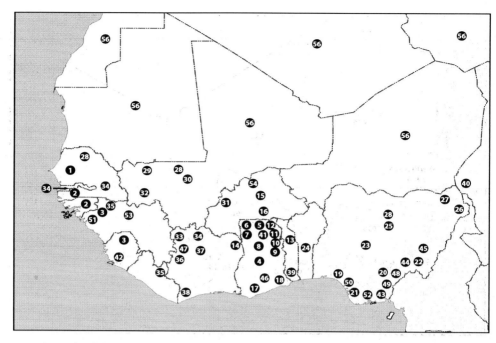

Location of Selected Ethnic Groups in West Africa.

1. Wolof	20. Igbo (Ibo)	39. Ewe
2. Mende	21. Kalabari	40. Sao
3. Temme	22. Tiv	41. Buisla
4. Asante	23. Nupe	42. Krios (Creoles)
5. Sisala (Grunshi*)	24. Fon (Dahomey)	43. Ogoni
6. Dagara	25. Hausa	44. Idoma
7. Wala	26. Kanuri	45. Jukun
8. Gonja	27. Caliphate of Sokoto	46. Akwapims (Akyem)
9. Dagomba	28. Fulani	47. Guro
10. Mamprusi	29. Soninke	48. Yakö
11. Tallensi	30. Dogon	49. Ekoi
12. Fra Fra (Grusi**)	31. Bobo	50. Efik
13. Kabre	32. Bambara (Djula)	51. Sherbro
14. Lobi	33. Senfo	52. Aja (Ijaw)
15. Mossi	34. Mandingo (Mandinka)	53. Koranko
16. Kasena (Grunshi)	35. Kpelle	54. Bwa
17. Fante	36. Dan	55. Susu
18. Gã	37. Baule	56. Tuaregs & Berbers
19. Yoruba	38. Kru	

* A pejorative term meaning "bush" or "hick."
** Similar to Grunshi. Most of the acephalous Voltaic peoples were called by a similar derogatory term.

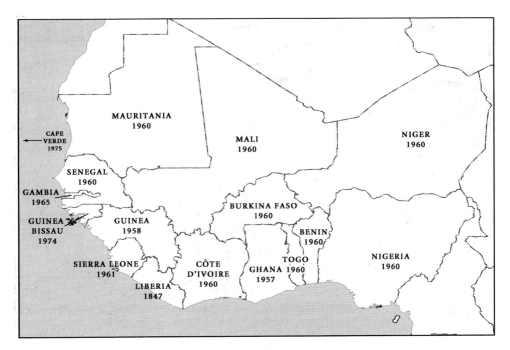

ECOWAS Countries with Their Dates of Independence.

Preface

In this textbook, I am going to tell a story. It is the story of the clash of two civilizations, one African, the other European. The first civilization has been compromised by contact with Europe, but it still survives through the customs and values of the people of West Africa. The second civilization is a global giant. It is overwhelming the world at present. It is the materially-based civilization of the Core (Western Civilization or the North), characterized by an economy based on capitalism, also referred to as the global economy.

This is a sad story, full of racism, conflict, slavery, exploitation and domination by members of European culture—the traders, sailors, missionaries, administrators, soldiers and adventurers who came to the shores of "Guinea." I write it in hopes that in some small way, when the student comes to understand the impact of history on the present, s/he will begin to understand what needs to be done now and in the future to begin to let the light of West Africa's indigenous civilization shine through the darkness of foreign oppression.

In a way, the saga of West Africa is a sad story. It is one of exploitation and domination; but it is also a story about a region filled with wonderful people. In my life I have had the opportunity to live in nearly twenty different countries in Africa, Asia, Europe and Latin America. In all my travels I have not found any people or region with more gracious people, with a culture I would rather be around. West Africa greatly impacted my consciousness when I first went there in 1970 as a young and naïve graduate student pursuing my first ethnographic field site, which became Sisalaland in Northern Ghana. Through the years I have been drawn back, again and again, not only by the opportunity to learn more about this fascinating region of the world, but also by the civility of its people, a warmth of friendship and relationship I have come to value of one of my most prized experiences as an anthropologist and human being.

The ending of this story I cannot write because it is being written by history, but what I want to do here is give the student an idea of how West African civilization developed and what its nature was and is. Secondly, I want to show the nature of European civilization, explain why Europeans came to West Africa and describe the immediate impact of that arrival. Then I want the student to understand that the historical clash between these two cultures has affected the nature of West Africa today, that the processes set in motion long ago resonate today in words like neocolonialism, underdevelopment, imperialism and dependency. West Africa's past is closely tied to the spread and power of European civilization beginning in the Age of Discovery and continued through centuries of contact and trade in the region. Similarly, West Africa's future is integrally connected to the spread and power of international capitalism. In other words, the dependency established at contact remains today.

Throughout the book, I will indicate how such intertwining began and how it has evolved. I begin with the setting, the geography, environment and languages of West Africa. I continue by showing how a civic way of life developed in West Africa, based on a fearful respect for nature and the spirits of the occult realm that were thought to be instrumental in the lives of the people. I will explicate the communalistic nature of this agricultural civilization that developed complex and humanitarian institutions to cope with nature, to make a living and provide a sense of community pride and warm security within their extended families and villages.

The advance of European civilization into West Africa encroached on the security of collectivist way of life. Little by little, Europeans moved down the Guinea coast from Portugal looking for riches. Their rapacious and materialistic appetites were to come face to face with the community-centered civilization of West Africa. Since West Africa already had an advanced regional trading system, what the French have called *economie de traite*, trade with the Europeans was a natural outgrowth. Ultimately, however, it had devastating consequences for West African communities. West African life was based on collectives designed to care for the weak and aged, and extended families focused on maintaining a mystic balance with nature and the ancestors. The acquisitive culture of the Northerners was to eventually dominate and transform the civilization of West Africa.

This book is about that transformative process.

Political Economy

I need to say a word here about the important concept of political economy that will figure so prominently in this work. The political economy is a tangle of institutions and relations involving political powers and related economic endeavors in a country or region. In most behavioral arenas, politics and economics go hand in glove. Politicians work with wealthy patrons and influential barons of trade or industry, each influencing the other. More and more social scientists are realizing the fundamental importance of this complex as driving force behind behaviors that heretofore were spoken of as separately political or economic, not both in combination.

In pre-contact times in West Africa, the kings and chiefs often controlled the political economy of states. With the coming of the Europeans a new political economy emerged, that of increasing European domination of trade. Control by these outsiders was gradually formalized over time, till the era of colonialism. When political independence was granted to the people of the region and Europeans ceremoniously withdrew, the economy remained in European hands. Europeans were able to manipulate the new holders of political office by persuasion, power plays and outright corruption. That political economy remains in place as of this writing.

How this Book is Organized

In chapter one, I will look at the geography, environment and language zones of West Africa to give the reader a perspective on what the region is like in terms of climate, vegetation, soils and language. I will also provide maps to acquaint the student with demographic divisions in the region.

Chapters two through seven present a detailed analysis of West African social organization. This section introduces kinship institutions and civic life that, together, form the foundation of West African culture. I go on to explain ritual institutions which are critical to any understanding of West African civic life. I also look at the traditional economic factors and political institutions that have shaped West African civilization and how these have changed over time in the region. The student is presented with a perspective called political economy that reflects the inter-relatedness of these two sets of institutions. This section ends with an excursion into the world of West African art and music and their place in ritual, social and political aspects of life.

In chapter eight, I present a short survey of the prehistory of West Africa as found in its meager archaeological record. I then turn to the pre-contact history of the region in chapter nine, focusing on the Great Sudanic kingdoms of Ghana, Mali and Songhai and the coming of Islam[1] to West Africa. At this juncture, I turn to the period of contact with the Portuguese and the effects of that collision on West Africans. In chapter eleven, we look at the all-important period of slave raiding and its consequences, especially those devolving from the discovery of the New World and the advent of the Atlantic Slave Trade. I move to a discussion in chapter twelve of how West Africans began to resist imperialism and the increasing shift toward hegemony by the Portuguese, British, French and Germans. In chapter 13, I chronicle the establishment of formal colonial status in the region. Chapter 14 is a discussion of the freedom movements and struggles for independence by West African intellectuals and their eventual attainment of political, if not economic, independence.

Chapter 15 covers the Postcolonial Period, its high expectations and the subsequent fall into underdevelopment. In chapter 16, I explain why West Africa can be considered a singular region and what the ECOWAS community is. I also provide a time line in this section with important events and other demographic information for each of the 16 West African countries. These final chapters cover the nature of dependent governance and lack of development today, urbanization, responses to modernity, the increasing integration of peasants and the economy into global capitalism, the nature of dept dependence, SAP's, NGOization, neocolonialism, underdevelopment and the spread of AIDS into the region.

Given this bleak picture, I end the book with a question: "Whither West African Civilization?" In this last chapter I will try to give the reader a sense of where West Africa is today, where it might be going, and my thoughts about how it might get there.

---

1. The dominant form of Islam practiced in West Africa is *Shi'ite*. Adherents believe that the law of Allah is superior to the law of the land. Fundamentalists who believe in *Shari'a* Law as supreme law.

Special Features in the Text

In this book, the important terms a student reader should know are in **boldface** in the text, and are repeated at the end of each chapter. I have bolded a few terms in this preface to give the reader an example, though these terms will appear many times throughout the textbook. Definitions can be found in the back of the book in the Glossary. There is a special glossary for West African People Cities, States & Empires. Since there are many acronyms in the text, I have included them in a special glossary.

At the end of each chapter, the reader will find *Critical Thinking Questions*, which can be used by the professor as essay questions or for purposes of class discussion. A section called *Key Concepts* includes all the bolded terms of that chapter. *Sources and Suggested Reading* contains the references used in creating the chapter and sources for further investigation.

Special Thanks

This book is a much better text because of the tireless and extremely efficient editing of Gretchen Jordan. Not only is she a great copy editor, but she is an anthropologist who helped me think through some of the main issues in this textbook.

WEST AFRICA

INTRODUCTION

Civilization is the humanisation of man in society

—Matthew Arnold
—*The Oxford English Dictionary*

*If the misery of our poor be caused not by the
laws of nature, but by our institutions, great is our sin.*

—*Charles Darwin,*
—*Voyage of the Beagle.*

> In this introductory chapter I want the reader to understand the essential contrast I make in this text between African culture and that imposed on them by the West. In this introduction I will only note the clash of cultures and some of the highpoints of the conflicts and transformations that resulted. These will be dealt with in more detail in subsequent chapters.
>
> One point is important—since 1434, when the Portuguese first arrived, West Africa has been under continual influence from European culture. At times this contact with the West, or what I will more frequently call the Core, led to economic and political domination, conditions that waxed and waned throughout the region's history, but ones that have not entirely gone away.
>
> This book is about the civilization of pre-contact West Africans and how it has been affected by contact with Europe and the world economy. Furthermore, it is about the various transformations of contact—trade, slaving, informal administration, formal colonialism and what will be defined as neocolonialism. It is also about how West Africans have perceived and reacted to these various manifestations of contact with the outside world

In this textbook I want to introduce the student reader to those historical forces that have altered the traditional culture and social organization of West African societies. As we move through the chapters I will try to show how historical forces and events of the past have continued, in transformed constructions, into the present. I will also try to show the reader why an understanding of ancient sociocultural formations, and how they have been altered, is crucial to the uncertain future of West Africa.

My fundamental thesis is that there was a commonality to West African culture and social organization, indeed, a strong similarity in the various ways of life throughout the entire African continent, something that has been called Africanity. Moçambique is about as far away from West Africa as one can get on the African continent, yet when I traveled there I found a strong resemblance to the village life I experienced in various parts of West Africa. Indeed, I have had the good fortune to travel throughout the continent over the last thirty plus years, and everywhere I have gone, I have found an

African-ness that is based on common assumptions of reality, and rooted in a common ancestral society.

What are these ideas and modes of living that make African cultures distinct from the European way of life? One key proposition of African culture is that human beings derive their identity and worth from being part of a group, most commonly a kinship group. Another is that the social group is part of a larger cosmic whole, which includes nature and the occult world. Thirdly, West Africans believe that influence and interaction occur between these three interlocked realms—society, nature and the supernatural. Fourthly, Africans suppose that divinity exists and has given humankind the ritual tools to induce inter-realm communication and influence. Fifthly, Africans assume that life in the present is the paramount realm and life should be lived in the here and now, rather than looking to some future idealistic condition like "heaven" (or fearing a terrible one, "hell").

These assumptions underpin a set of cultural ideas and patterns of behavior that have evolved out of a common existence in the African environment and a common ecology—that is, a similar relation to the material environment. Given this relational correspondence, African societies everywhere have produced similar imagined realities, or cosmological ideas about the nature of the universe and humankind's place within it.

As an anthropologist, I assume that all culture is a social construction, an imagined form that evolves out of symbolic interaction between human beings as they struggle to eat, protect themselves from harm and survive in a physical world. I speak of *imagined realities* because I believe sociocultural formations to be both fabrications, in the sense that they are created by human beings and *a priori* assumptions that, once created, are taken to be valid, true and unquestionable. As a shorthand I will refer to such constructions as a truth system.

In Africa such truths are embedded in myths and ancient tales that have been passed from generation to generation. The total body of lore constitutes a charter that tells people about the nature of life, explaining why things are and why things happen; and such stories also provide a behavioral charter, showing the proper and moral way to live life. As such, this knowledge base functions as a command system. It is used by the elders to organize others in accordance with the ways of the ancestors, those who have gone before, and who now reside in the occult realm. These ancestors are not dead, but are still volitional beings who retain an interest in their living kin. In accordance with ancestral beliefs, living kin also hold the idea that the moral order of the past is the proper one for the present and for the future. In this cosmology, the ancestors underpin the social order, asserting that the moral codes of the past should be passed on intact from generation to generation.

The great sociologist Max Weber believed "that man is an animal suspended in webs of significance he himself has spun". Truth systems provide meaning in life, giving individuals a sense of security and place. Humans everywhere have created such systems, albeit in diverse patterns. Yet in West Africa, because of migration and frequent interaction between groups, a similar way of life has emerged across the region. It focuses on sharing amongst related people, a fundamental humanism; and it also centers on communalism, a cultivated ideology of reciprocity and fairness. Furthermore, as I will show in this text, West Africans have experienced a common history of contact with outside forces, principally through a diffusion of ideas along Trans-Saharan trade routes and by way of the arrival of Portuguese traders who came by sea.

I am saying that West African cultures and social forms were relatively ordered and cohesive meaning systems (though I assume that no society is ever completely so). As such, they provided group members with social and psychological security. In the beginning, as the ancients hunted and foraged and began to work the soil, they developed assumptions and codes that were represented as coming from an otiose high god through a pantheon of spirit beings. These representations link up the divine with humanity through sacred rites, age-old procedures for getting information from deity and spirits, especially the ancestors. This connection with the occult world is thought to be crucial for the proper functioning of life on earth. Should a people lose their lifeline of communication to the ancestors, it is thought, they would forfeit the bonds that tie them together into a meaningful whole, into a moral system.

This early civilization was humanitarian and communalistic. By the former I mean that it was oriented toward people, putting the group before the individual, people before material goods. Personhood was expected to emerge out of continued and submissive involvement of the individual in a sacred set of ancestral codes. To be a true member of the community, the person should never violate the codes of sharing, reciprocity and interpersonal support so vital to group survival in Africa. By communalistic I mean that the individual, mighty or lowly, should put the needs of the community before his or her own needs. Where chiefs and kings evolved, communities developed checks and balances to prevent a despotic abuse of power and privilege. African leaders always had to respond to the wishes of the people or they were deposed or sometimes killed. Personal behavior, whether by king or commoner, was always subject to the democratic will of the majority. Big men, chiefs and kings—even emperors where they arose—were all commanders to the extent that they ruled according to ancestral principles; but they were also commanded by a variety of social institutions designed to limit their power. In fact, one of the defining traits of African civilization is the inherent distrust of power. Thus, everywhere, we find strong democratic institutions with checks and balances to limit the behavior of those in positions of authority.

This indigenous African civilization developed in relative isolation from Eurasia, except that from the 7th century on, Trans-Saharan traders carried goods back and forth and brought Islam to the region. To some extent there was a contrast of cultures between the Arabic-speaking world and West Africa, but a stronger transforming and disorganizing clash began when the Portuguese arrived on the western Guinea Coast in 1434. Their explorations were to bring West Africans into contact with two great mutating forces—an emerging international economy and Christianity. More profoundly, Africans were to be exposed to the evil of racism, which was applied to residents of the region as a justification of the material need for slaves. Africans were to become increasingly exposed to Western culture, which was individuating, that is, stressing individual needs and desires over and above that of corporate groups. Furthermore, it was a civilization that glorified material goods and their attainment as an end in itself. If West African civilization was distributive of material objects, Europe civilization was acquisitive and accumulative, displaying material goods as a sign of high status.

In Western civilization, identity and group solidarity are often created by exclusionary means, that is, ethnic or national groups are shored up by contrast with an opposing group—Protestants with Catholics in Northern Ireland, Serbs with Croats in the Balkans, capitalists with communists throughout the Cold War Era. Of course this is a panhuman tendency, but it is not a central characteristic of African civilization. If we can say that European politics have historically tended to be exclusionary; then we must say that African civilization inclines towards being inclusionary. Given a strong humanitarian strain, African culture leads members to include those who are strangers or different.

Let me give you a couple of examples of this. West African family members, like those in families everywhere, sometimes quarrel. At times this quarreling leads to a fissure in the group, a renting of the social fabric. Brothers get angry with brothers and move away, forming separate homesteads some distance away from the home compound. But they remain members of the clan family. They are still included in the important ancestral rites carried out on behalf of all members of the overarching clan.

And again, sometimes people are driven by environment, pressures or conflicts to wander afar looking for a new home. If such a stranger group arrives in the clan territory, they can ask for land and it will most likely be granted to them. People are usually welcomed into the group, first as strangers, then as in-laws and, sometimes, with the passage of time, their alien origins are forgotten and they are treated as a segment of the kinship group.

Did pre-contact tribes ever fight in West Africa? Did they in European history? Of course on both accounts, but there was a key difference between the two. In Africa tribes fought in spats or minor skirmishes. Even when the great states of the Western Sudan emerged—Ghana, Songhai and Mali—warfare was a limited part of their growth. Armies threatened peripheral peoples into submission to become tributaries of the central state, but they did not kill off many of the outlying peoples. Wealth in Africa was counted in personnel beholden to you, rather than dead combatants lying on the battlefield that you have just taken from them. In short, land was less valuable than people, so African wars were usually of a limited nature.

It was the other way round in Europe. Land was the means of production—it was a valuable asset to be taken in war and held by force of arms. Consequently, in their evolution Europeans developed a strong military capability. With much practice and many wars behind them, the Europeans who came to West Africa were experienced warriors with refined weaponry. Africans were no match for them in military tactics and firepower. It is important, however, for the reader to see that this does not mean that Africans were not civilized, unless you only define civilization in material or military terms. While the Europeans spent some of their time warring, conquering and sharply defining the boundaries between states, Africans were carefully developing a culture that focused on the value of life in community and sharing and cooperation between villages and clans. When they came into conflict with others, some fighting occurred, but it was minimized by the lack of advanced firepower and by the African tendency toward settling disputes by negotiation. When and where historico-material forces led to state development and expansion, again fighting was minimized. To paraphrase the old saw: Africans were not fighters so much as lovers of tranquility.

At this point I feel compelled to answer the criticism that has been leveled at the great Africanist Basil Davidson and others who have put forth a similar perspective on Africa. My critics may choose to follow a similar path claiming that my view is a "happy naked native" view, that I idealize pre-contact African civilization. In true postmodernist fashion, I must admit that having lived in various parts of Africa for nine years, most of that time in West Africa, I have developed a fondness for the African way of life. I have lived in some parts that I liked little, and would not want to return to; but in the main, I have found African life, even in the cities, to be "kinder and gentler" than what I have experienced in the West.

Before I talk about the changes brought about by the coming of the Portuguese along the Guinea Coast, let me point out one more key difference between these two civilizations. With the rise of Christianity, Europe began operating under a future-oriented religion that stressed a tie between sin and salvation. West African civilization lacked such a concept. Their relations were localized and focused on mandating behavior in the community according to an ancestral code. Misbehavior cannot be translated as "sin" in the European sense. In the traditional African context, behavior in this life had little to do with salvation in the next. The code of conduct did have a lot to do with adjusting power and property within the community to ensure a democratic way of life, one focusing on generalized reciprocity, on sharing and cooperation. In short, European religion was other-world-centered, whereas West African religion was this-world-centered.

Thus, when the ancient mariners sailed out of Portugal in their Caravels they were armed with two great weapons—the gun and salvation. They, and others who followed from the shores of Europe, used both to pit West Africans against each other, to convince some that their ancestral ways were wrong or sinful, mere fetishism or paganism. Europeans began to define West Africans as pagan savages. This was a convenient "otherizing" that gradually allowed Europeans to enslave millions of the inhabitants of Africa. It was the beginning of the history of racial prejudice against people of African descent, a racism that would only grow as the New World called for more and more laborers for the plantations there.

We will explore these issues in more depth later in this text. The point I want to make here is that African civilization began to be transformed, even disorganized, as the Europeans began to trade along the coast. Divisiveness was greatest among coastal peoples since Europeans were kept on the coast for centuries before eventually "conquering" the interior of Africa. The thin coastal strip was to become extremely important in West African history. It became the locus of Christianity, of European fortifications, and of a system of governance that would eventually develop into the nation-state. It was this heritage that would eventually be passed on to a later generation of West Africans who would regain their freedom from political repression by European interlopers. But it was not a healthy heritage. It infected Africa. It brought increased divisiveness to the region. It was a heritage of exploitation and extraction, an autocratic and violent way of life. This new legacy was to further rend the fabric of social cohesion in West Africa, and erode the self-confidence of those who lived there. Neither has fully recovered as I write these words.

I want the reader to understand that the problems of self-doubt, poverty, war and political turmoil that have plagued West Africa in the forty years since independence was regained are due largely, though not entirely, to contact with European imperialism, racism and avarice. This began in 1434 and continues today. Western civilization does not shine in my reading of West African history, nor do I think much of its present incarnation as expanding global capitalism, especially in its neoliberal incarnation. Nonetheless, fortune hunters and capitalists had and continue to have devastating impacts on the region. Since it appears that capitalism is a mighty force, at least for the immediate future of the world, West Africa will likely continue to feel is devastating impact in the coming decades.

What began in 1434 continues today as Western businessmen and foreign agents of International Financial Institutions step off airplanes onto African soil. Mistreatment of West Africans and exploitation of their resources began in the foggy mists of the 15th century, but also continue today in the lobbies of posh hotels where the power élite congregate to make deals continuing the cycle of dependence begun eons ago.

It seems that writing about Africa has gone through several stages. The earliest Islamic writers were interested in describing the social and political workings of African kingdoms, as well as presenting some interesting travel information and ethnographic detail from time to time. Generally, they marveled at the peace and benevolent governance they found in Sub-Saharan Africa (See Ibn Batuta's statement in Chapter 2).

European writers were enamored with the adventure of exploration in exotic and faraway lands. They generally portrayed Africans as backward and caught in a static state.

Early Thoughts on Progress and "Primitives"

In the main, Europeans saw West Africans as backward and mentally inferior. It is important to understand the background to the racist thoughts of these early adventurers, traders and political administrators who ventured into West Africa during the centuries following the 1444 landing of the Portuguese on the coast of what they called *Guiné*.

They were influenced by ideas that flowed out of the Enlightenment, or what the French call the *Siècle de Lumières* ("Age of the Enlightened"). This was a European intellectual movement of the 17th and 18th centuries in which ideas concerning God, reason, nature and man were synthesized into a narrow and skewed worldview that gained wide acceptance in European thought. The worldview instigated revolutionary developments in art, philosophy, and politics and gave intellectual justification for European domination of other societies around the world.

Central to Enlightenment perspectives were the use and the celebration of reason, the power by which humans understand the universe and improve the human condition through action based on reason.

Also coming out of the Enlightenment was a theory of evolutionary development from simple to complex. In the 18th century progress was thought to be universal. In other words, the innate rational capacity of all humans was emphasized. This was to change in the 19th century, especially in the influential writings of Herbert Spencer (1820–1903). He was a British sociologist and philosopher, an early advocate of the theory of evolution, who achieved an influential synthesis of knowledge, advocating the preeminence of the individual over society (the very opposite of African philosophy) and of science over religion. He wrote volumes on the principles of biology, psychology, morality, and sociology claiming that life is a struggle for existence and that the best approach is to allow unfettered free will and open competition, which he claimed would lead to survival of the fittest.

About the same time Darwin and others came to see biological organisms as evolving from uncomplicated organisms into complex ones. Social thinkers applied evolutionary theory to sociocultural change, leading to a perspective called Social Darwinism—the theory that persons, groups, and races are subject to the same laws of natural selection as Charles Darwin (1809–1882) had perceived in plants and animals. According to the theory, the weak were diminished and their cultures delimited, while the strong grew in power and in cultural influence over the weak. Social Darwinists held that the life of humans in society was a struggle for existence ruled by "survival of the fittest," a phrase proposed by the British philosopher and scientist Herbert Spencer.

The social Darwinists believed that the process of natural selection acting on variations in the population would result in the survival of the best competitors and in continuing improvement in the population. Based on the organic analogy, societies, like individuals, were viewed as organisms that also evolve in this manner.

These ideas were percolating in European society at a time when the exploration of the planet was bringing white Europeans into contact with many different kinds of peoples, most of whom did not have the technological sophistication of Europeans. This contact with exotic cultures and peoples of color led Europeans to ask the question: "why are societies at similar or different levels of evolution and development?"

One prominent answer to this question was the idea of unilineal evolution, which contained the concept of stages. Sir E. B. Tylor (1832–1917), the first academic anthropologist, wrote that there had been and was a single direction in evolutionary history and that it was away from simplicity and leading to ever increasing complexity or progress. Life was seen as full of competition and struggle, perhaps reflecting the Industrial Age in Europe and the rise of capitalism in the international marketplace.

The idea of stages of growth helped Europeans explain the sociocultural differences among the technologically inferior peoples they encountered in places like West Africa. The British Tylor and the American Lewis H. Morgan (1818–1881) proposed three stages in evolutionary history—savagery to barbarism to civilization. In the 19th century it was assumed that European civilization was the pinnacle of success in this competitive struggle for survival. Africans and other technologically backward peoples were placed on the lower rungs of the ladder.

Thus, the shift in thinking from the 18th to the 19th century was one from universal advancement to a graded system of classification, with White Europe at the top and people of color at the lower end of the scale. Arrogantly the West proclaimed itself to be superior and that peripheral peoples were inferior.

In terms of technology and military application, in most cases, this was correct. However, in public opinion and in the minds of many who went to West Africa to seek fame or fortune, the concept was extended to social, cultural and even mental matters. Along with many other peripheral peoples around the globe, West Africans were about to be classified as socially and culturally backward and intellectually inferior.

The 19th century saw many academics struggling with the concept of primitive mentality, as it was applied by Europeans to the various peoples they came to dominate in their Imperialist adventures. The Frenchman, Auguste Comte (1798–1857), for example, developed an evolutionary scheme claiming that mentality had progressed through three stages—theological (fictitious) to metaphysical (abstract) to positivistic (scientific). In other words, there had been progress in thinking and Europeans were defined as the best thinkers.

Comte, like other social theorists of the day, was struggling to deal with the revolutionary change in European society and with its spread imperialistically. In response to the scientific, political, and industrial revolutions of his day, Comte was essentially concerned with an intellectual, moral, and political reorganization of the social order. Adoption of the scientific attitude was the key to progress. Since non-Europeans were seen to lack science, they were classified as primitive thinkers.

If life was a competitive race to the top, Europeans declared that they had won the race and therefore had the right to rule "lower" peoples. In fact, most social scientists today reject this view. Rather it is felt that the Social Darwinists used their imagined ideas to justify the imperialistic expansion of European society, colonialism and the economic and political exploitation of peripheral peoples like those in West Africa.

First early travelers and traders, then later in reports sent between colonial administrators and to the home office European administrators described Africans as passive and submissive. They were characterized as "less than us."

Such racist views spawned a backlash among intellectuals and academicians. Many African writers objected to such stereotyping, as have some European writers e.g., Michael Crowder's *West African resistance; the military response to colonial occupation.* In these accounts Africans come across as anything but passive (See Chapter 12).

There are many writings that overstate the passivity and inability of Africans to combat the superior firepower and overwhelming force of early European invaders. In West Africa the reality was much more complex. Some peoples accepted Europeans because they were useful as trading partners and no one could foresee that centuries down the road they would become oppressors. Others fought the White Man right from the start. Still others resisted the imperialists later when their true exploitative colors began to show (for more details on this exploitation, See Chapter 11). There are sufficient references in accounts of colonial administrators to show that they had to deal much more African assertiveness than they wanted. Colonialism was not a total hegemony of civilization, one placed onto backward cultures. Indigenes found ways to insinuate themselves into the web of relations and exchanges that constituted the ongoing development of colonial rule.

While West African society tended toward inclusiveness, there were still alien tribes and even factions within the larger polities. Some sided with Europeans, others not. In spite of what resistance there was, the Europeans continued to come. They traded for centuries while manipulating local peoples, playing this faction of against that. The Africans did the same thing using the rivalries between European powers to maneuver themselves into a better commercial or bargaining position. West Africans were anything but passive, but they did not come to dominate the Europeans, it was the other way round. Some African writers today want to deny this fact of domination and stress the active resistance of their countrymen to the outside aggressor. I will try to present some of this perspective, but it must be said that the overwhelming force of history is on the side of colonial domination and the lingering effects of this in the postcolonial world. In short, West African countries find themselves labeled by International Financial Institutions as HIPCs (Highly Indebted Poor Countries). This is fundamentally because of Europe's imperialism in the past and the ongoing underdeveloping forces at work in West Africa today. These forces ensure the continuation of previously instituted unequal exchanges between international capital and West Africans. In short, the Core or World Economy began to dominate West Africa after the arrival of the Portuguese in 1434 and has done so ever since in a poleconomic sense.

Were there West Africans who struggled against the encroaching wave of Westernization and change? Of course. There are men and women in West Africa today who continue to do so. On the other hand, there are plenty who want more contact with the outside world, who clamor for "modernization." The particulars of individual lives are one thing, the forces of history are another. In the latter sense, the G-7 countries dominate Africa in economic terms, which allows much manipulation of politics in the region. I wish that I could report that Africa resistance worked or is working. But, sadly, it failed in the past and it is failing now. Will it continue to do so in the future? That is one of the subjects of this text.

≋ SOURCES & SUGGESTED READINGS ≋

Crowder, Michael (ed.). 1968. *West African resistance; the military response to colonial occupation.* New York: Africana.

1 GEOGRAPHY, ENVIRONMENT & LANGUAGE

This chapter looks at the ways in which the natural world in which West Africans live affects their way of life, both in history and today. The region is replete with disease-carrying insects, illness, inclement weather, poor soils and a lack of economic development. Reasons for this lack of growth are tied to the natural environment and conditions created in the political economy of West Africa.

In coping with the different environmental zones in West Africa, people have created many different forms of civilization in the region, giving rise to great diversity, albeit one united by some common threads. That diversity and linkage is also borne out by linguistic studies that show West Africa to be the homeland of many African languages, which were spread over the continent as early ancestors migrated to the east and south of the continent.

Explanations of Conditions in West Africa Today

West Africa covers an area roughly the size of the United States west of the Mississippi River (See Map 1.1). Most students of West Africa agree that the region is one of the poorest in the world. I will ask the reader to ponder why this is the case, and more widely, why Africa has fallen behind in economic development. This chapter will focus on the connection between geography, culture, history and development in the region. In short, it will say that much of life in the area has been a product of its harsh environment and that in terms of development, West Africa has been held back by disease, climate, poor soils and the like.

But this is only part of the answer. History, especially the coming of the Europeans with extractive and imperialistic designs, has played a large role. I will deal with this later in the text. Another factor, which cannot easily be extricated from its appearance in history, is the political economy that has evolved in the region. I will explain its negative impact on West Africa throughout the text, but, in short, the political economy of the region was and remains extractive, with wealth and power remaining in the hands of global capitalists and their supportive institutions, the International Financial Institutions of the **global economy.**

Again, these factors will be laid out in some detail in later chapters. Here I want the reader to be aware that the course of history and the development of the political economy in West Africa have been strongly influenced by topography, climate and the

Map 1.1 Size Comparison—U.S.A. and West Africa.

region's many diseases, just as have West African **civic culture** and the overall way of life in the village setting.

Environment and History in West Africa

More than most areas of the world, the climate and environment of West Africa have strongly influenced much of its long and illustrious history. Akin Mabogunje says of his homeland:

> much in the history of West Africa becomes understandable when set against the background of the character of the land on which the events took place. For while human ingenuity and resourcefulness are not space-bound, their manifestation

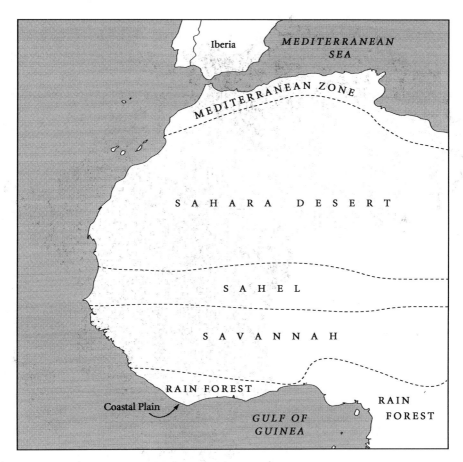

Map 1.2 Environmental & Vegetational Zones of Western Africa.

and development are often conditioned by the nature of the local material with which they have to work. The result is a close interaction between the people and their land, between the course of history and the elements of environment.

Put forthrightly, West African civilization was formed to meet the exigencies imposed on the people by a harsh environment e.g., poor soils, a lack of water to be used for irrigation and endemic and debilitating diseases. Secondly, it evolved to make use of the natural resources provided to humankind in the region, however sparse they might have been. Furthermore, it was a civilization designed to protect the whole community from extinction—thus, the civic culture of West Africans today still tends to emphasize the group over the individual. Put another way, local cultural values propound a sense of community for West Africans. Even in the 21st century, most West Africans have a profound attachment to their natal villages or urban wards. In this context, the individual is hardly ever alone or isolated from a sense of being a member in some organization larger than self.

The environment of West Africa is characterized by east-west climatic/environmental belts that contrast sharply from north to south (See Maps 1.2 & 1.6). Climate in

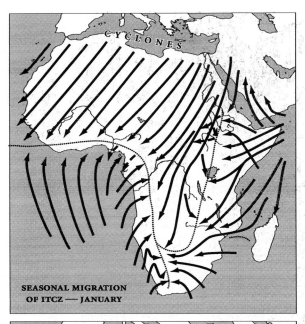

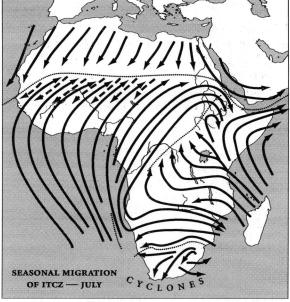

Map 1.3 Intercostal Convergence Zones.

West Africa is caused by its geographical location and by seasonal movement and pulsation of two air-masses. The first is a tropical continental air-mass commonly known as the Harmattan. This is a warm, dry and dusty air-mass that forms over the Sahara Desert. At its maximum extension in January, it covers the whole of West Africa from the desert to the coast. Alternating seasonally with the windy Harmattan period, is the tropical maritime air-mass that forms over the southern Atlantic Ocean. This is known as the Inter-tropical Front (ITF) or sometimes the ITCZ, or Inter-tropical Convergence Zone (See Map 1.3).

Photo 1.1   Elephant in Savannah Bush.

From its ocean formation the ITF moves inland progressively from January to July. Its presence allows a sufficient dept of humid air to form over most of the region, bringing rain to large parts of the land. Beginning in July, this front retreats southwards till December, when it begins its turnaround. In the southernmost parts of the rain-forested zone, rain falls virtually throughout the year, but with a disposition toward bifurcation—one season lasting from March to July, the other from September to December. There are two dry periods: a relatively long one from December to March and a short one in August.

This north-south oscillation of wind and rain underlines the latitudinal diversity which is so remarkable in West Africa. The interior or north tends to be hot and dry; while the south and coastal zone are more humid and less hot. This climatic variation shows up visually in the vegetational zoning of the region, from the Sahara Desert, through the thin **Sahel**, to the broader **Savannah** Zone (See Photo 1.1), into the rain forest and finally to a thin strip of Coastal Plain in some areas. Each vegetational zone extends from east to west, providing a longitudinal continuance that has framed much of West African history (See Maps 1.2 & 1.6).

Environmental Zones of West Africa

West Africa forms a bloc of states in a region that has a long history of human migration and interaction, and one that experienced contact with Europe before many of the other regions of Sub-Saharan Africa. It extends roughly from 5° to 25° north latitude and from 17° west to 15° east longitude. As a whole, it covers some 2.4 million square miles, or nearly five-sixths of the area of the United States. West Africa is the closest point to Europe in Sub-Saharan Africa (See Map 1.1). During the sad history of

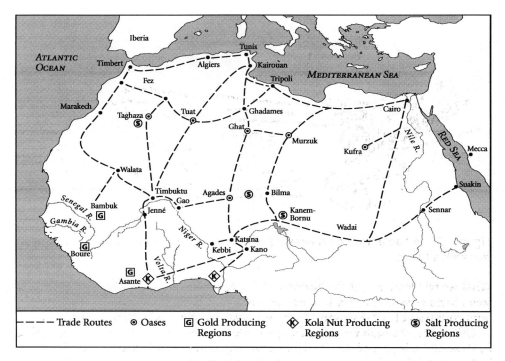

Map 1.4 Trans-Saharan Trade Routes and Raw Materials Sites.

slaving, the region supplied millions of persons to the plantations of the New World, probably more than any other area of Africa. It was also linked with many long-distance and regional trade routes and markets (See Map 1.4). This singularity has been amplified today as it is unified into an economic bloc, **ECOWAS** (See the glossary at the back of the book for all definitions of bolded terms).

The region was blessed with ample deposits of gold, with fields at Bambuk, Bure, Lobi and Asante or in the older terminology, Ashanti (See Map 1.4). These rich gold fields were a factor in the early establishment of **Trans-Saharan trade routes,** as Arab traders braved the long and arduous journey across the Sahara Desert to bring trade goods from Europe and the Levant to exchange for gold, ivory and other exotic goods of **Sub-Saharan Africa.** Thus, the region has a long-established history of trade with the outside world (See Figure 1.1). This started as a trickle and increased dramatically with the arrival of the Portuguese along the Atlantic Coast of what they called *Guiné* (See Map 1.5). Certainly from the 8th century onwards, West Africa has never been without economic and cultural exchanges with the world system, a fact that shaped and continues to shape the region today.

In this text we will learn of the effects of the Trans-Saharan trade routes along which goods and slaves have traveled for centuries. I say "have traveled" because the movement of goods and people continues today—some being migrants, but other are indentured servants or even true slaves taken away against their will. For example, Dirkou in Niger is the last Sub-Saharan stop on one of the continent's greatest and possibly most dangerous smuggling routes today. West Africa's steep and general economic and political decline in recent years leads thousands of its residents to risk this dangerous crossing to Tripoli in Libya to find jobs, and possibly a way to enter Europe.

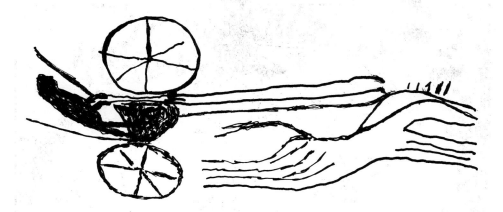

Figure 1.1   A Saharan Rock Engraving of a Horse-Drawn Chariot Driven by a Warrior with a Lance.

What we will learn about the history of West Africa, has present-day implications. In some basic ways in the relation between the rich **Core Countries** of Europe and the poor countries of Sub-Saharan Africa, not much has changed for centuries.

Other than the island nation of Cape Verde or *Cabo Verde* as the Portuguese called it, West Africa is part of the continent of Africa, a zone that is bounded on the north by the great Sahara Desert, on the west by the Atlantic Ocean and on the south by the waters of the Gulf of Guinea. On its eastern flank, West Africa butts up against Chad and Cameroon.

The climate and vegetation zones can be seen in Map 1.6. Along the coast of West Africa is a coastal plain, which normally slopes up toward the interior **rain forest** in most places, except for where the River Niger forms a vast drainage system of rivers and creeks in Nigeria, and along the coast of Mauritania (See Map 1.7).

It is likely that populations moved from the north or east into the rain forest later rather than sooner in West African history. Oral histories of present-day inhabitants tell of a north to south migration to live in the rain forest by hunter-gatherer groups. Except for the guinea-yam and oil palm, no significant cultivated plants were domesticated in this forested zone. True proliferation of peoples in the rain forest has come in historical times, after the introduction of new crops obtained through European contact.

It may have been that the rain forest was kind of a refuge zone, providing some degree of security for those seeking refuge from the aggressiveness of stronger, better organized groups in the grassland regions to the north.

The **Sahara Desert** has long been a travel barrier, though not an impenetrable one, as evidenced by the spider web of trade routes crisscrossing its arid wastes, nor was it always a barren wasteland. In the early Miocene (15–20 million years ago) probably more of the region was lush, but during the time of human evolution and migrations the Sahara Desert has called on human ingenuity to allow communications between the Mediterranean and Sub-Saharan Africa.

The Sahara was once a fertile area; grain was cultivated there over 8,000 years ago. We know this because archeologists have found traces of millet and the cave art of the area shows scenes of cultivation and village life. As conditions gradually became drier, however, and desertification set in, farmers abandoned their land.

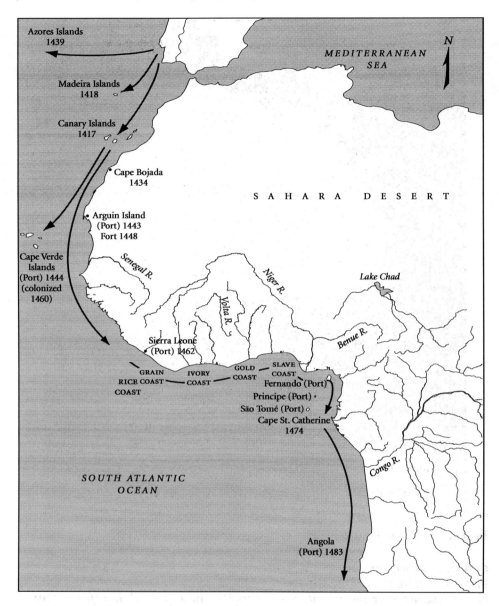

Map 1.5   Portuguese Voyages in West Africa.

The great desert area of northern Africa extends from the Atlantic Ocean eastward past the Red Sea to Iraq. The entire desert, the largest in the world, is about 1,610 km (about 1,000 mi.) wide and about 5,150 km (about 3200 mi.) long from East to West. The total area of the Sahara is more than 9,065,000 sq. km (more than 3,500,000 sq. mi.), of which some 207,200 sq. km (some 80,000 sq. mi.) consist of partially fertile oases. The boundaries are not clearly defined and have been shifting for millennia.

The barren land is almost entirely without rainfall or surface water, but possesses a number of underground rivers that flow from the Atlas and other mountains. Occa-

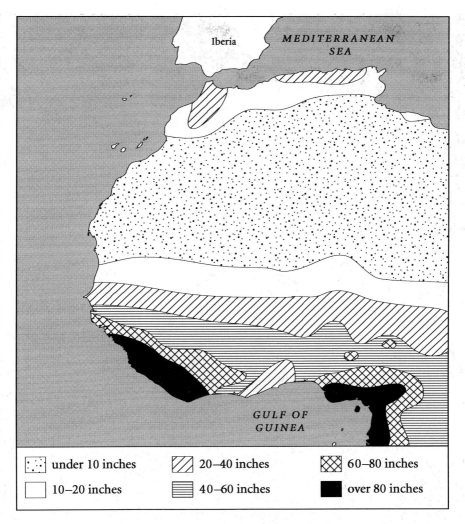

Map 1.6 Average Annual Precipitation in West Africa.

sionally the waters of these rivers find their way to the surface in naturally irrigated oases. The chief trees of the oases are the date palm and a form of acacia, a tree that also predominates in the Savannah to the south. The area is still inhabited by Tuareg and Berber tribesmen who are herders and traders.

The big environmental contrast within Sub-Saharan Africa, however, is between the Savannah and the rain forest, which is called "jungle" in popular parlance. These are two climatic and floral zones. The Savannah has one rainy season with limited and sporadic rains. The extreme northern edge of the Savannah is called the **Sahel**, meaning "coast" in Arabic—the coast of the great Sahara Desert. It becomes increasingly drier as you proceed toward the Sahara, wetter as you approach the rain forest.

The Sahel region of West Africa is a transition zone between the arid Sahara on the north and the wetter Savannah areas to the south. Relatively sparse orchard bush vegetation of grasses and shrubs predominates. Rainfall averages between 102 and 203 mm (40 and 80 inches) and falls mostly from June to September (See Map 1.6). Nomadic

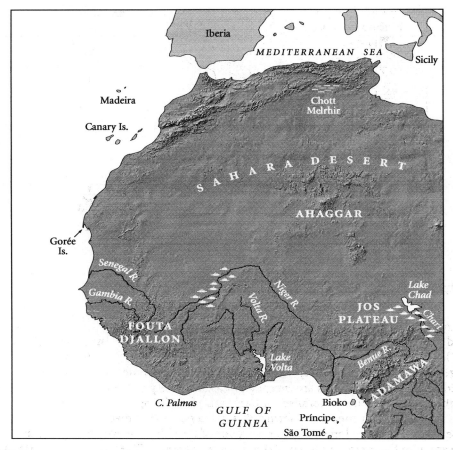

Map 1.7　Rivers of West Africa.

herding and limited cultivation of peanuts and millet are possible in most areas, but the zone is subject to periodic draughts, and there is some indication that the Sahara Desert may be moving southwards. An extended drought in the Sahel in the late 1960s, the 1970s, and the early 1980s, the worst in 150 years, suggested an increasingly arid regional climate.

Some of this climatic change may be humanly influenced e.g., the clearing of the rain forest and its replacement with such tree crops as cocoa, kola and rubber may have important implications for the apparent diminishment of the replenishing rains. Climatologists indicate that the rain forest of West Africa is responsible for inflating the southwesterly moist winds, without which the Savannah would have less rain, lower relative humidity and a shorter growing season. This would greatly harm already tenuous climatic and economic cycles in the region.

The population density tends to be low in the Savannah (See Map 1.8), leading to extensive farming and pastoralism as economic modes of production. Lacking the **tsetse fly** (which causes sleeping sickness in some large animals), this zone supports horses, donkeys and camels, all of which act as transportation, and are used for the transport of goods. The presence of the horse also allowed the development of cavalry in the early Sudanic Kingdoms and throughout the history of slave raiding.

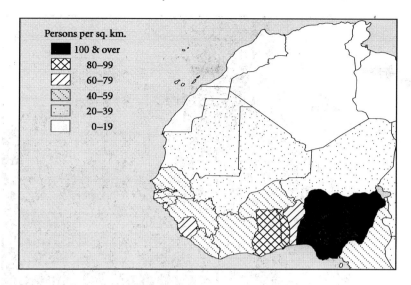

Map 1.8 Population Density in West Africa, ca. 2000.

Arab culture and **Islam** influenced this area more that European life or Christianity, and the dress and culture of the people of the region reflects that heritage (See Map 1.9). Crops in this zone are pearl millet, sorghum, maize, yams, calabash (gourds), indigenous cotton and a variety of legumes and vegetable crops. Cattle are commonly held as a wealth reserve, as are sheep, goats and a variety of fowls. Some people, such as the Fulani, practice pastoralism or herd cattle for a living.

In the Savannah zone many farm villages and pastoral nomads make their living in a severe land. It has long served as a crossroads, linking the Mediterranean and the Levant with the forest and seacoastal peoples to the south. The Great Sudanic States of Ghana, Mali and Songhai arose on the northern fringe of the Savannah by coming to dominate the Trans-Saharan trade.

Much of the Savannah is covered with Sudan Savannah Brushland or to the south Guinea Savannah Woodland, with scattered varieties of *Acacia*, baobab (*Adansonia digitata*), dawa dawa (*Parkia clappertoniana*), silk cotton (*Ceiba pentandra*) and shea (*Butryospermum paradoxum*) trees. Grasses are shorter in the northern Savannah, taller in the south. Rainfall in the northern extremities is less than 1,000 millimeters annually, while the southern edge of the Savannah may get up to 1,250 mm per year. This arid climate creates a very dry bush in the long rainless season from October to May and bush fires are common, thus many of the surviving trees are fire resistant.

Herders, such as the pastoral Fulani, have learned to keep cattle, goats and sheep in this land, moving to find grasses to feed their herds. Farmers have survived for thousands of years growing draught-resistant seeds—millet and sorghum. Maize was introduced by the Europeans and is commonly grown now. The storage of such grains allowed the accumulation of a surplus, a factor in the rise of the kingdoms of the Niger Bend area and in the rise of warfare and raiding that accompanied the emergence of storable wealth.

Traditionally there was little irrigation and most farmers practiced **rainfed horticulture** using slash-and-burn methods to clear the bush. Such shifting cultivation is

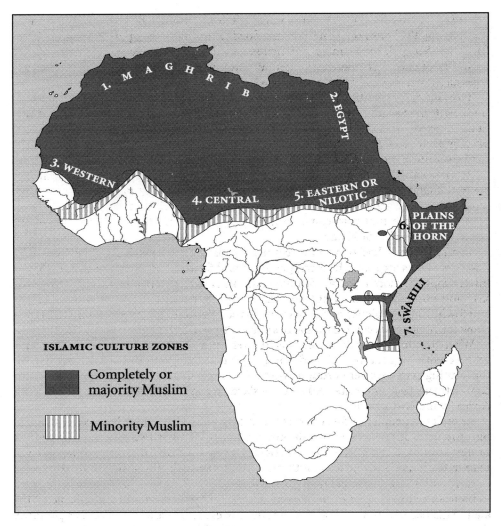

Map 1.9   Islamic Culture Zones of Africa.

still common in the area, though some peoples have intensified their farming. Scientists now realize that extensive farming methods were adaptive within the poor and fragile soil base. Agricultural intensification has sometimes caused erosion and depletion of soils. Furthermore, it has only been possible in some cases through the use of imported and expensive petrochemical fertilizers.

Environmentally, the lack of year-round streams, lakes and dependable rain makes life in the Sahel and Savannah quite precarious. In a given year the rains may be sparse, in another too heavy. In a different year, the rains may come at the wrong time, causing grain crops to wilt or become damaged. One farm may receive ample rains, while a farm a few km away will go dry. It is this variability of rainfall that makes farming difficult, as well as relatively poor soils that require farmers to move their fields frequently, especially since there is no strong and widespread tradition of manuring or composting in the region.

Of course, in this dry landscape, water is at a premium. Thus we find large settlements along the banks of the main rivers flowing through the region—the great Niger River, the Senegal, the Gambia, the Benue and the Volta (See Map 1.7). Well-known examples of such settlements were Jenné, Timbuktu and Gao, but many smaller villages and towns lay along these great flows of water.

The fact that Levantine traders had been able to use camels to cross the Sahara to trade with the Savannah peoples and get forest products such as gold, slaves and kola nuts, allowed for the coming of a world religion to Sub-Saharan Africa—Islam. It originated in 639 AD in Saudi Arabia and within four centuries that part of the African continent north of latitude 8° N had become largely Islamized.

At first, Islam was limited to a small number of traders and ruling élite in the Savannah kingdoms, where traveling merchants were given safe haven by the Sudanic kings. Today Islam is a widespread religion and a politco-religious force in West Africa. One new culture trait that came with Islam was literacy, as it is a "religion of the book"—the **Qur'an** or Koran.

The rain forest has two rainy seasons and is more tropical than the Savannah. Dwellers of this area were hunters, gatherers and farmers just as in the Savannah, but forest crops are more tropical with the addition of bananas, plantains, cocoyams, cassava and numerous fruits. Cattle are less common, though people keep goats, sheep and fowls. The prevalence of the tsetse fly in the rain forest led to a tradition of human conveyance of goods carried on the head, usually by women.

Whereas the Savannah is sparsely dotted with trees, the rain forest is thickly wooded with huge hardwoods and dense vegetation that made the clearing of this land for farming purposes very arduous work. For example, the Asante were only able to complete this task with imported labor—slaves brought into West Africa from Central Africa by the Portuguese.

As with the peoples of the Savannah, before the coming of world religions, the people were generally animistic, worshiping family and local deities, but with the coming of the Europeans some adopted Christianity, which is more prevalent along the coast than in the hinterlands. Just as southern peoples, especially those along the coast, were in early and frequent contact with Europeans and therefore became more acculturated to their ways; the peoples of the Savannah and interior hinterlands were less acculturated. This has led to a general perception in West Africa among many people today that southern = modernized and northern = "bush" or less modern or backward.

The kingdoms of the rain forest, such as the Asante, initially developed based on trading forest products and precious ore with both the peoples of the Savannah and those of the coast, passing the European goods coming across the Sahara along to the coastal peoples, who in turn bartered salt and fish to the middlemen of the forest.

Later, when the Europeans tried to conquer these kingdoms the dense forest and tropical climate were a strong barrier to Western penetration. White men died like flies in this zone, and they found it tough going to hack their way through the dense vegetation, or to engage in any kind of military operations. This also protected the hinterland peoples from European penetration, that is from all but a few brave White explorers, some of whom came to the Savannah across the Sahara, while others traveled inland from the coast.

In the 16th through the 18th centuries, because of their interstitial location, the forest kingdoms were able to capitalize on the business of slaving, trading slaves captured in the north or purchased from northern traders. These were sold to Europeans on the coast. When the kings got guns from the Europeans they also used these to dominate

Photo 1.2   A European Fort.

surrounding peoples of the forest, expanding local polities into states and kingdoms into empires.

As the slave trade diminished, peoples of the forest were able to expand production of forest products in demand in Europe for example, timber, rubber and especially oil palm products.

Because of their access to the sea, peoples of the coast have exploited the fish and other sea products for centuries, in addition to mining salt from seawater to trade with interior peoples.

Sometimes there is a wide coastal zone of lightly forested land leading into denser rain forest to the north or east, at other times the jungle grows right down to the water, as in the Axim area of modern-day Ghana. In other regions the coast is a tangle of creeks and rivers, as in the southern region of modern-day Nigeria.

The coastal plain or seacoast zone along the Gulf of Guinea and the Atlantic Ocean is variable in topography, but in general was the zone that permitted the greatest European presence. Where there were sufficient rock outcrops to build forts, the Europeans did so (See Photo 1.2). Where such was lacking, they traded from ships moored off the coast.

The Windward and Leeward Coasts

Some settlement of the coastal area was determined by geography. According to Fyfe, "Cape Palmas, the southern tip of Liberia, forms a geographical frontier between the Windward Coast and Leeward Coast of West Africa. Consequently, each has experienced a different history and plays different roles in the modern world. While the Windward Coast is exposed to the strong Atlantic, the Leeward Coast is a sheltered shore in the Gulf of Guinea. The Europeans tended to build their fortifications on the Leeward side, except where there was good harborage e.g., at Freetown in Sierra Leone. While the coast of modern-day Mauritania, Senegal, The Gambia and Guinea-Bissau were usually lumped together by early explorers as Upper Guinea, the present-day states of Guinea, Sierra Leone and Liberia constituted the Windward Coast. Early trading and slaving took place mainly in Upper Guinea, and when Europeans moved into the Windward Coast, they encountered hostile tribes. They did not ignore the area, but this hostility, together with a lack of natural harbors and a strong Atlantic current, largely led them on to the Leeward shores. In fact, much of the West African coastline was initially repellent to human contact by sea. For hundreds of miles, the surf-beaten coastline shows no indentation or natural harbors where ships could berth. These impediments necessitated the construction of artificial harbors at Takoradi, Tema and Cotonou, as well as artificial lagoon entrances at Abidjan and Lagos.

Not only Europeans were affected by West African topography, however. The coastal peoples of the Windward Coast were somewhat isolated from those in the interior as the rivers flowed fiercely to the sea and did not form long avenues of communication or travel. Rocks and rapids on their upland course prevent easy navigability. Because of the lack of maneuverability, travel was confined to paths along the rivers and transport was mainly by human portage. Also, on the Windward side, the rain forest tends to be thicker than to the east.

In fact, on a broader scale throughout West Africa, the rivers of the region, in spite of their length and number, have not been very significant as lines of human communication or movement. This is largely because of the existence of falls and rapids along their courses.

Just as the open Savannah allowed for frequent contact between the peoples of that region, from Tekrur to Kanem-Bornu, the peoples of the Windward Coast were influenced by a particularizing geography. The setting in which the peoples of the Windward Coast live affected their history. The forests and mountains insulated them from invasions by rulers of the vast Sahelian empires, just as the unappealing coastline put off European mariners. The difficulty of transport and movement through the dense jungle covering much of the terrain also compelled segregation. Linguistic evidence supports isolation. There are many languages implying that some must have been settled there, in the isolating forests, for many centuries, perhaps even millennia. This multiplicity of discrete languages probably came about through the process of language cleavage, migration and immigration in the context of a sequestering environment.

There is a difference in diet and botany between the Leeward Coast where yams and millet predominate and the Windward Coast where rice is the main diet of farming folk. Yams are also eaten a few miles beyond Cape Palmas in modern-day Ivory Coast at the Bandama River, which acts as sort of a rice barrier. On the west people eat rice; on the east yams dominate the diet.

There is also some serological evidence to show long-term isolation of some Windward Coast peoples e.g., the Kru people are devoid of the **sickle-cell trait** in their blood, which is found fairly universally in West Africa. This confirms that the Kru have long been a closed community who have not greatly intermarried with their neighbors.

Geography also affects political organization. Unlike the Savannah zone and the forests to the east, the Windward Coast shows no evidence of big empires; rather small communities who have apparently lived in relative isolation from each other populate the land. Fyfe notes a democratic pattern in these Windward kingdoms, however, not dissimilar from other democratic monarchies throughout the whole of West Africa:

Figure 1.2   Soapstone Nomoli Figurine from Sierra Leone. Possibly 16th Century.

Some were ruled by kings—but they were not absolute monarchies. The kings had councils to advise them, and could not disregard their council's advice. If a king wanted war and his council did not, there was no war. Thus, they were more democratic than the government of the Portuguese knew at home, where the king had far greater powers (indeed more democratic than most of the governments of sixteenth century Europe).

Another difference with the Savannah zone to the north is that Islam had not significantly penetrated the Windward forest at the time of European contact. The people remained largely animistic, with the widespread institution of the Poro secret society exercising many organizational functions—partly political, partly religious and partly educational.

When the Europeans came to the area they noticed ancient soapstone carvings called *nomoli* by the Bulom peoples and *pomta* by the Kisi (See Figure 1.2). The ancestors of these peoples likely created them. Carvers of that day too worked in soapstone, but also in ivory, as the forest were renown for large elephant and wild tusker (pig) populations. The Portuguese were greatly impressed with the skill of indigenous carvers and commonly commissioned them to manufacture the now well-known "Portuguese Ivories." These were delicately carved cups, spoons, salt boxes, hunting horns etc., that eventually made their way to many drawing rooms in Europe.

Thus, largely because of their isolating geography in the pre-European period, the Windward Coast peoples lived in small isolated communities and polities. Each had its own form of government that preserved the social order. They were wary of outsiders and innovation. They had bush schools and other educational institutions to instruct their children on proper moral comportment. They had sophisticated art. They traded with surrounding peoples and sometime went to war against them. In brief, the people had a civilization that was adapted to their region and influenced by its environment.

Geography also influences history. Compared to Upper Guinea to the north and *Mina* (The Gold Coast) to the east, Europeans found the small communities on the Windward Coast to be difficult and incomprehensible by European political consciousness. Consequently they largely avoided the area and no European power ruled any part of the Windward Coast until the end of the 18th century. The two British forts built on that side were built on islands—one on Bence Island in the Sierra Leone River, and another on York island in the Sherbro estuary south of it (See Map 10.1). These were attractive because of the deep anchorage of the Sierra Leone inlet. There they could put in safely for repairs, get supplies and get the famous King Jimmy fresh water that flowed down from high-mountain source and was sold to Europeans by a local potentate named—you guessed it, "King Jimmy."

As with other areas of West Africa, sovereignty remained with Africans and Europeans paid rent. Local politicos assiduously guarded the interior, keeping import-export commerce firmly in their hands, protecting their lucrative middleman status.

Europeans were considered by West Africans largely as merely new trading partners. They were useful in that they brought manufactured goods and carried away unwanted peoples as slaves—criminals could now be sold rather than exiled or put to death. Of course, to an extent, wars became more profitable. However, few slaves were taken from this area, it would seem, as gold was not plentiful. And, as ivory was purchased faster than natural reproduction, the elephant herds were soon greatly diminished. Two other products were prominent in trade—camwood from which red dye is made and Malagueta peppers.

Also, the men from Europe cohabited with local women and produced a small but influential Creole community. To this day several of the families descended from English fathers and African mothers rose to prominence in Sherbro country—namely the Caulker, Tucker and Rogers families.

Geography and Underdevelopment

There is a relationship between West Africa's **underdevelopment** and geography. The latter is very important in the analysis of West Africa, both from a need to understand its history, but also to understand why the region is so impoverished in comparison to other parts of the globe, even other parts of the developing world. Geographers seem to say that the diversity of environment creates a diversity of human responses to life. Anthropologists too say that we must focus on the ecological relation between culture and the fundamental reality of earth's natural processes. Culture cannot be divorced from ecology or the fact that it is formulated, enacted and changed in relation to foundational realities that stem from nature—from spatial, geological and climatic realities.

Having said this, West Africans have been born into a very difficult geography. It has largely determined their struggle and the type of civilization they produced to cope with the distinct but interlocking zones in their region—the Sahel, Savannah, rain forest and coastal plain. All of these have been, and continue to be, influenced by the great Sahara desert to the north and its continuing desiccation since about 7,000 years ago.

I am going to present a case to the reader to show that geography counts in the lives of real people. I am going to say that the tropical climate of West Africa limits economic advancement and makes the region fundamentally different in terms of how we need to think about it in developmental terms. Furthermore, it is incorrect to compare the lack of development in West Africa with so-called developing countries like Korea or Brazil, to name two places that are far more developed than any country in West Africa. To set the stage for this I am going to tell you a story of my old friend Gariba-Bein.

When I first met Gariba-Bein in 1970 he was a still lively man, but was an elder with a wife or two and several grown children, the youngest of which, an educated fellow named Bubachebe, was my research assistant. Bubachebe went blind in his mid-twenties from onchocerciasis and died before his thirtieth birthday. The father, Gariba-Bein, died as I was writing this book. In 1998 I returned to the village of my earlier fieldwork after a 25-year absence. When I saw him he was a virtual skeleton of a man lying naked on a skin mat in his mud hut. He was blind and feeble, but his mind was still lively and his heart still radiated the humanity and warmth so many researchers have noted in West Africans. Gariba was approximately 95 years old at this point. He had lived through an era when the world around West Africa got rich and perhaps rather fat. At the end he was a living skeleton and died childless, all his children having proceeded him into death.

I tell this story to put a human touch on the aggregate reality of death, disease and tropical debilitation that persists in West Africa. Statistics do not suffer and die—people do. West Africans, such as Gariba-Bein and Bubachebe, who suffered from disease and early death, were real people, ones who had hopes and dreams, who loved and danced, who farmed and fancied a better life and struggled against the odds to achieve it. Gariba-Bein would have liked to have died surrounded by his family and grandchildren. Instead he passed into eternity at the end of more than two decades sitting blind and feeble on a filthy cow skin mat. With his children and wives all gone, he was alone for much of the time. When I came upon him, he had not eaten in three days and was without clothing.

Gariba-Bein was alone in one sense, but he was part of a multitude of West Africans who suffered similar pain and suffering in the 20th century, while many others in the world lived in luxury, or at least improving conditions. I use the case of Gariba-Bein and his unfortunate children to represent the millions who have suffered and who continue to agonize today from poor economic conditions and political systems that do not meet their basic needs.

Toward the end of this text I will discuss development efforts in West Africa in more detail. But development is a misnomer in West African terms, because little has changed there for millions of people like Gariba-Bein and Bubachebe. Their lives, whether short or long, were, to paraphrase Hobbes, "nasty and brutish" though they were warm, humorous and loving human beings. I am better for having known these two people, but West Africa is not better off for having known the West. If Europeans defined Africa as "The Dark Continent", they brought little light to the matter. When I encountered Gariba-Bein, not only did I find him in the state I have mentioned, but also the only improvement to the village was the increase of the half-century old borehole from one to three. Many villages in the region aren't that fortunate. Americans had walked on the moon, but geography and environmental impediments to progress had left Gariba-Bein and Bubachebe behind. I present their cases as symbols of West Africa—overlooked, bypassed, underdeveloped and full of wonderful people who are suffering and dying needlessly.

This text will ask the question repeatedly, why are West Africans so poor? Some researchers answer with charts and figures. Economic or demographic statistics aggregate human realities, reifying them to a point of obfuscation. Even to say that a thousand children a day die worldwide for lack of potable water, many of them in West Africa, distances us from the reality of life's pain in these geographically backward areas of the world.

Again, the Libertarians and Neoliberals tell us that individuals can work themselves out of poverty if distant markets are opened to international **capitalism**. I would say that their optimism is ill founded, that it ignores the retarding influences people suffer from disease and isolation. Those environmental forces must be addressed, along with social matters such as education, before any real progress is going to be made in West African development. Will the most recent batch of policies by open-market advocates do the trick? That remains an empirical question, one to be answered in time. If they do change the lives of West Africans for the better, they will have to face the fact of geographical isolation in rural areas, and the widespread presence of debilitating diseases such as malaria, dengue fever, onchocerciasis, amoebic dysentery and a whole host of endemic infectious diseases that plague this tropical region.

The case of Gariba-Bein illustrates the downside of geographical isolation—he lived and died in a village without electricity, plumbing or a health center. He never had a chance to go to school. The village had little in the way of improvements during the colonial era or after Ghana gained its independence from the British. During that time, as today, most village farmers still scratch the unforgiving land with the centuries-old hand-held hoe. The more fortunate have oxen-plows.

In this isolation, villagers are subject to the debilitating effects of the many tropical diseases endemic to the region. Most elders are blind from simple cataracts that could be removed with laser surgery, but even basic first-aid-level health care is not available. Many people suffer from worms, bacteria and viruses that could be easily death with by modern medicine. None is available. Children die on a regular basis, at birth or shortly afterward. Mothers bear their children without medical care. Most villagers die before the age of fifty. It is not a healthy environment by any stretch of the imagination, yet these wonderful people persist and are capable of finding moments of real joy in the midst of material impoverishment. Living in the village opened to me the strength of the human spirit, the tenacity of humankind in the face of adversity.

But not all of Gariba-Bein's or his children's ills were environmental or geographical in origin. One son died of prolonged drug use. He routinely took uppers and downers available in the town market, but imported from the developed world— from the Core Countries of Europe and North America. This is an artificially created environment—the economy that makes it profitable to send manufactured drugs to such impoverished areas. His brother, Bubachebe, never took illegal drugs, but he died in his twenties from a lack of access to legal ones (See Photo 1.3). He died, in essence, from a political economy focused on developing the cities and providing the symbols of development for élites—automobiles, paved roads, electricity, indoor plumbing, supermarkets, cinemas and a house full of electronic gadgets.

Thus, when we look at environmental effects on development or its absence, we have to take into account two kinds of environment that work in tandem on human populations—the natural world and the humanly-constructed cultural, political and economic structures which have been created and shaped by historical forces as well as material conditions.

Languages and Migrations in West Africa

All the scientific evidence seems to point toward Africa as the original source of the human family. Sites in Eastern Africa as well as DNA studies both indicate this (See Map 1.10). While East Africa has extant sites of early hominids, it is uncertain where exactly humans originated within the continent. Nevertheless, it seems that people

Photo 1.3   Legal and Illegal Drugs in Open-Air African Market.

moved into West Africa from other parts of the African continent. Early cave sites in the Sahara Desert and in modern-day Mali at Rim Cave indicate that these early humans were hunters and gatherers.

Anthropologists recognize different African population grouping for example, Negroes, BaMbuti (Pygmies), San, Nilosaharans and Afroasiatics (Berbers and Cushites). It seems that Negroes originated in West Africa, most likely as a local population which adapted to that climatic zone. But Nilosaharans and Afroasiatics have been pushing westward and because of its extensive history of trade contacts with other parts of Africa, the **Maghrib** and the Levant (what we call the middle-east today), it seems reasonable that there has been an ongoing admixture of various types of Africans in the region. Anthropologists know that race is not fixed, if it exists as a demographic reality at all. Populations change in racial mixture through genetic processes as well as migration, contact and sexual exchange of genetic material.

Language also reflects such diversity and movement of peoples. Languages indigenous to the African continent number more than 1,500. Apart from Arabic, which is not confined to Africa, the most widely spoken African tongues are Swahili in East Africa and Hausa in West Africa, each with more than 10 million speakers. Several languages are spoken by only a few thousand people for example, Isaalang of the **Sisala** people of Northern Ghana who number around 100,000 (See Map 1.11). All West African languages were unwritten until some histories began to appear in Arabic and European languages, but all peoples of West Africa have a long tradition of remembering the past through oral histories and praise songs.

According to the most recent and widely accepted scholarly practice, the languages of Africa are grouped into four language families: Afroasiatic (or Hamito-Semitic),

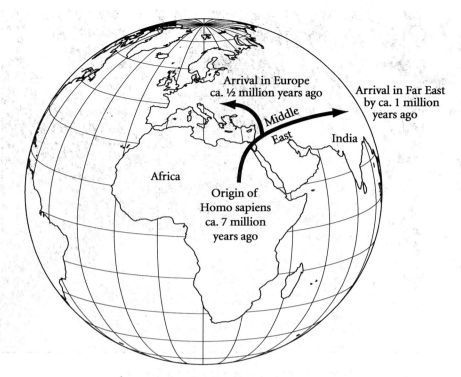

Map 1.10 The Spread of Humans out of Africa.

Nilosaharan, Khoisan, and **Niger-Congo** (some call it Niger-Kordofanian) (See Map 1.12). A language family is a group of related languages presumably derived from a common origin; a family is often further subdivided into branches composed of more closely related languages. At least some of the African linguistic families are believed to have a history of more than 5,000 years.

The dominant language family of West Africa is Niger-Congo, including Bantu. This family includes two subfamilies, Niger-Congo and Kordofanian. These latter languages number only about 30, all small; they are found in a tiny area of the Nuba hills in the Southern Sudan, surrounded by languages of the Nilosaharan family and by Arabic.

The Niger-Congo linguistic area, on the other hand, comprises almost all the African continent below the Sahara Desert. Although migrations presumably separated some branches of the Niger-Congo subfamily more than 5,000 years ago, languages in each of the branches have similar words for many common objects and actions and a striking resemblance in grammatical structure.

The Bantu languages do not constitute a separate family, but should logically be grouped with certain languages of Nigeria, such as Tiv and Birom. Bantu is a word meaning "the people" in many languages of the group. All these languages together are classified as the Benue-Congo branch of the Niger-Congo subfamily.

The Benue-Congo is by far the largest branch; the Bantu section alone numbers more speakers than all the rest of the Niger-Congo languages combined. North of the Bantu language area, in the northern Congo region and adjacent territory, is a second branch of the Niger-Congo subfamily, the Adamawa-Eastern branch. From Nigeria

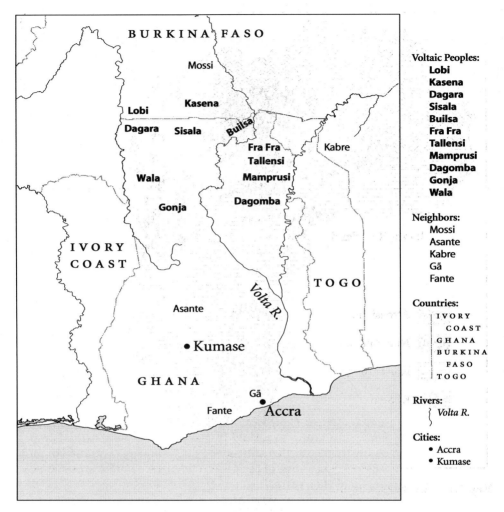

Map 1.11 Voltaic Peoples and Neighbors.

westward, five additional branches of the Niger-Congo family, which frequently have been called West Sudanic languages, are found. A group of three or four closely related languages in the Niger delta, which together are known as Ijo, constitutes one of the five branches of the subfamily.

In a strip along the West Coast from southeastern Nigeria to Liberia are found the languages of the Kwa branch. This branch includes such important languages as Efik, Igbo (Ibo), and Yoruba in Nigeria; Ewe in Togo and Ghana; Fante and Twi in Ghana; Anyi and Baule in *Côte d'Ivoire*; and Bassa and Kru in Liberia. North of the Kwa language region, extending from western Nigeria into much of Ivory Coast and Mali, are the languages of the Gur branch, including Moré in Burkina Faso.

Along the Atlantic coast, from Liberia to the desert north of Dakar, are several languages of the West Atlantic branch. These include Temne in Sierra Leone, Wolof in the vicinity of Dakar, and Fula (also known as Fulani, Fulfulde, or Peulh), by far the most widely spoken of the branch.

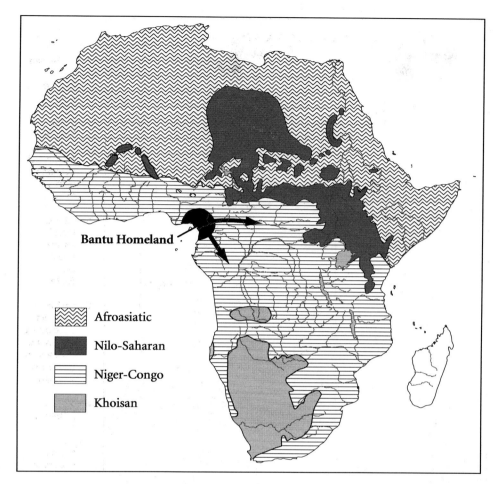

Bantu Homeland

Afroasiatic

Nilo-Saharan

Niger-Congo

Khoisan

Map 1.12   Language Families of Africa.

The two large concentrations of Fulani-speaking people are, on the one hand, located in Guinea; and in eastern Nigeria and Cameroon, on the other. Between these widely separated areas, Fulani-speaking people are spread out in numerous camps in which they raise cattle and sell meat, milk, and butter to neighboring tribes. They often act as cattleherds for farming peoples in the region.

Speakers of languages of the Mande branch inhabit most of the remaining portion of West Africa. One Mande language, known in various areas as Malinke, Maninka, Mandingo, Bambara, and Dyula, is spoken by some three million people from Senegal through much of Mali and northern Guinea and into northern Ivory Coast. Other important Mande languages are Mende in Sierra Leone and Kpelle in Liberia. Small islands of Mande-language speakers are also scattered through areas farther east, as far as western Nigeria.

The name Mandekan has recently been proposed as a name for the language as a whole and has gained substantial acceptance. The Mandekan languages are believed to be the oldest offshoots of the parent Niger-Congo language spoken more than 5,000 years ago.

Language studies have shown that West Africa played a pivotal role in the peopling of the rest of the African continent. Bantu is a name given to a linguistically related group of some 60 million people living in equatorial and Southern Africa. In all probability, the ancestors of Bantu-speakers migrated from West Africa, perhaps from the Nigeria/Cameroons area (See Map 1.12). Bantu-speaking peoples now occupy most of the continent south of the Congo River.

It therefore seems likely that much of the rest of Sub-Saharan Africa has been impacted by migrations out of West Africa and that language and culture have diffused southwards from there in the great Bantu migrations.

CRITICAL THINKING QUESTIONS

1. In what ways did the environment of West Africa influence the cultures that emerged there?
2. What was the effect on the tsetse fly on transport and warfare?
3. What is the relationship between geography and development?
4. What are the two kinds of environment discussed by the author and what is their causal relation to development?
5. What do language similarities in Africa tell us about migrations and origins of the Bantu?

KEY CONCEPTS

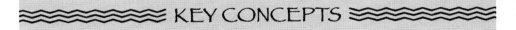

Capitalism
Civic culture
Core Countries
ECOWAS
Global economy
Guiné
Islam
Maghrib
Niger-Congo
Qur'an
Rainfed horticulture

Rain forest
Sahara Desert
Sahel
Savannah
Sickle-cell trait
Sisala
Sub-Saharan Africa
Tsetse Fly
Trans-Saharan trade routes
Underdevelopment

SOURCES & SUGGESTED READINGS

Alexandre, Pierre. 1972. *Languages and language in Black Africa*. Translated by F. A. Leary. Evanston: Northwestern University Press.
Binns, Tony. 1994. *Tropical Africa*. London: Routledge.
Funk & Wagnalls Standard encyclopedic college dictionary. 1968. New York: Funk & Wagnalls.
Greenberg, Joseph H. 1966. *The languages of Africa*. Bloomington: Indiana University

Greenberg, Joseph H. 1973. African languages. In: Elliott Skinner (ed.). *Peoples and cultures Africa: An anthropological reader.* Garden City, New York: Doubleday, 71–80.

Kasule, Samuel. 1998. *The history atlas of Africa.* New York: Macmillan.

Mabogunje, Akin. 1995. The land the peoples of West Africa. In: Ajayi, J. F. A. & Michael Crowder (eds.). 1972. *History of West Africa* (Vol. I). New York: Columbia University Press, 1–32.

McNulty, Michael L. 1995. In: Martin, Phyllis M. & Patrick O'Meara (eds.). *Africa* (Third edition). Bloomington: Indiana University Press, 8–45.

Oyebade, Adebayo. 2000. The study of Africa in historical perspective. In: Falola, Tony (ed.). *Africa: African history before 1885* (Volume 1). Durham, NC: Carolina Academic Press, 7–22.

Rand McNally. 1994. *Historical Atlas of the World.* Boston: Houghton Mifflin.

Welmers, Wm. E. 1973. *African language structures.* Berkeley: University of California Press.

2 TRADITION, CIVIC CULTURE & KINSHIP

In this chapter I want to inform the reader of the nature of West African traditional culture and social organization. While culture is a powerful influence on peoples' minds and behavior, it is not a perfect determinant. People conform, but they also deviate from cultural codes.

Furthermore, cultural ways become codified as tradition, but this amalgamation of cultural mores is never perfectly in harmony with the real past, which is remembered by people in imperfect ways and sometimes being put together with political agendas in mind. In other words, the discourse on tradition is often distorted by simple **slippage** or tinkering by political factions in the present-day.

Nevertheless, West Africa developed a strong civic culture based on the principles of kinship and affinity. This pre-contact West African civilization provided a relatively egalitarian, humanitarian, group-oriented and peaceful way of life throughout most of the region before the coming of Europeans.

In spite of a tendency to include all comers in community life, this was not an ideal world. Tribes warred against each other. Chiefs and kings arose to conquer weaker neighbors. In some ways, West Africans repeated the same processes found in the ancient world in **Eurasia**, yet their civilization and ethos of communalism allowed a high degree of cultural integrity throughout the region for most of its pre-contact history.

European Views of the African

On the eve of colonialism, Europeans assumed West Africans to be living in "darkness." The technological superiority of Europeans led them to assume that they were morally and racially superior to Africans. An hierarchical view of history put European civilization at the top and in the "light" of day. African "barbarism" was placed at the bottom, in the "heart of darkness." Armed with this slanted view, early imperialists slipped into a paternalistic posture in which Africans were seen as children that had to be cared for. From a religious perspective, it was considered that Christians had a sacred trust to enlighten such savages. This self-assumed responsibility was spoken of as the "**White Man's Burden.**"

This idea of a race in darkness was perpetrated by stories of early travelers, traders and adventurers who returned to Europe to spin tales and by newspapermen hungry for readership. Eventually the ideas became the stock and trade of academics, even of anthropologists who wrote of the "**primitive** societies" of Africa. These societies came to be known as the "**people without history**," as can be seen in the oft-quoted 1962 statement by the holder of the Chair of History at Oxford University, Professor Hugh Trevor Roper:

> perhaps in the future there will be some African history to teach. But at present there is none; there is only the history of Europeans in Africa. The rest is darkness...and darkness is not the subject of history.

This view of a backward African populace justified Europeans as they colonized, settled, civilized, missionized, and dominated the native peoples. Missionaries selected stories about **witchcraft**, headhunting and human sacrifice, even inventing them where necessary, to keep the donations flowing into their new ventures in "darkest Africa."

People ignorant of the importance of witchcraft in the history of Europe were willing to denigrate West Africans for the same beliefs. To believe in witches meant that Africans were not rational, but superstitious. Anthropologists have long since shown that a belief in witchcraft has a strong social control function for society, and can operate to reinforce the civic culture, more clearly demarcating the lines between morality and immorality. Furthermore, witchcraft still operates in Europe as I write these words, certainly in European villages where I have done fieldwork.

Such ideas about the inferiority of the peoples of Sub-Saharan Africa have been perpetuated by writers such as Margery Perham who wrote in July of 1951 that development in Africa was problematical since Africans lacked the wheel, stone houses, the plow, transport animals, any decent clothing except skins, writing and a history! Almost every claim is wrong or easily explained in ecological terms, but such ethnocentrism led to a great ignorance by Europeans of the great moral order that West Africans had created, of their true civilized nature. Whereas it was easy to see that West Africans did not live in stone houses or record their ideas in pen and ink—it was not so easy to see that for centuries they had developed strong ideas about truth, honesty and virtuous behavior. Note the statement by the 14th century world traveler in West Africa, Ibn Batuta regarding the Malian civilization of the Niger Bend (See Map 2.1):

> The Negroes possess some admirable qualities. They are seldom unjust, and have a greater abhorrence of injustice than any other people. There is complete security in their country. Neither traveler nor inhabitant in it has anything to fear from robbers or men of violence. They do not confiscate the property of any white man (Arab) who dies in their country, even it be uncounted wealth. On the contrary, they give it into the charge of some trustworthy person among the whites, until the rightful heir takes possession of it.

Europeans did not know much about the advancements made in West Africa before their arrival. The Ghanaian nationalist J. E. Casely-Hayford said:

> before even the British came into relations with our people, we were a developed people, having our own institutions, having our own ideas of government.

Judging everything in technological and ethnocentric terms, Europeans missed the moral and social sophistication of African civilization. One writer, perhaps struggling with a way to acknowledge Africans' accomplishments in a relative way, referred to them as a "primitive civilization." Even the French, often touted for their willingness to allow West Africans to assimilate, assumed that French culture was superior and that

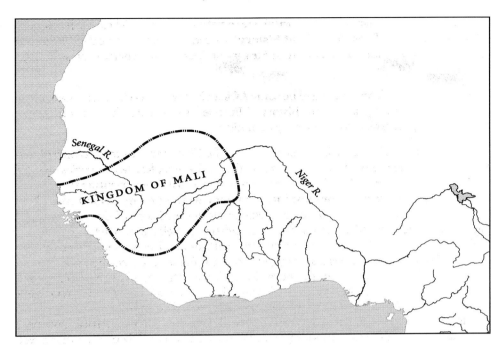

Map 2.1 Kingdom of Mali.

therefore, of course, backward peoples would want to improve themselves. Europeans, on the whole, could not conceive that civilization could be defined in any way other than technological measures. Yet when they found evidence in Africa of technological mastery at the great kilns and monuments of Zimbabwe and the beautifully crafted bronzes of the Nok culture, they resorted to the **Hamitic hypothesis** to try to explain it away—that somehow light-skinned Hamites had wandered into Sub-Saharan Africa to construct such wonders.

The Social Construction of Tradition—Some Theory

How and why did West Africans create their civilization? The answer is partly functional—that they did so in the same way and for the same reasons as humans everywhere—to survive in the physical world. Throughout this text I will take the **constructionist approach** to society and culture, that is, that both are fabrications in the sense that they are built up through human interaction over time.

Human beings are builders, and the people who first inhabited West Africa were no exception. They built houses and monuments and other material structures, but they also built up bodies of ideas which anthropologists call sociocultural formations. These are also called social structures, institutions, social formations and the like.

I prefer the terminology, **sociocultural formation** because it emphasizes the interactional nature of emergent groups of people and the process of the building up of ideas. Put simply, ideas accumulate as people interact in society, and those ideas form clumps or accretions that we call institutions. The clumping process is often carried out under the supervision of officeholders, who guard and dispense such information, filtering it for release to the public.

Once such rule-sets or sociocultural formations are in place, people inherit them, use them, alter them, and replace them in order to deal with perceived issues, opportunities, threats and problems in their lives. **Tradition**, then, is an ongoing experiment that can be used and molded to deal with new sociocultural or material realities that history and environment supply.

Such ideas and information are encoded in symbols. Symbols contain meanings that can be interpreted by people who know the code. I take a "social construction of reality" approach to sociocultural formation which is built on a dialectical epistemology. That is to say that I see all cultural and social formations as created ideas. There is a process of creation at work when human beings associate with one another. Based on perceived redundancy, people create patterns of behavior and even go beyond that to codify such patterns into rules and codes about how people *should* behave.

This **codification process** results in the slow distillation or accumulation of rules into rule-sets and institutions. Such institutions evolve out of the social interaction of interested parties. Historically, these interested parties were men who were concerned with political matters in the politico-jural domain, as Meyer Fortes called it. Operations in this domain had to do with two kinds of social control: internal and external. Men dealt with the need to control the behavior of others in their own society — with the exercise of power between factions, groups and individuals in society, and with matters in the external relations between societies. In other words, males came to deal with politics and war.

Anthropologists who view sociocultural formations as artifices see them as being built upon a foundation of assumptions or presuppositions. A **cultural presupposition** is an invisible and almost imperceptible assumption about the natural order of things, but the results of assumptions are seen in real outcomes. The Asante of Ghana assume that witches exist, then proceed to create witch-finding cults. The practitioners of these cults devise various strategies and techniques for identifying exactly which members of their society are witches. You can see the results of such witch hunts in special villages that are set aside for (primarily women) witches. Each village is presided over by a male "chief of the witches" who is charged with the responsibility to maintain order there. The material and social reality of these "witch villages" is based on the assumption that witchcraft is real.

All culture is composed of presuppositions and general ideas that are built on a bedrock of conjecture. A presupposition is nothing more than an idea that you or society take as a given. It is often presented to us as an incontestable idea: God exists; some men have the natural right to rule over others; witches exist. Thus, a given religion or political system or witch-finding cult is a structure of ideas built upon a foundation of presuppositions.

Such ideas are given palpable form as society's institutions. They were here before you were born, they exist now, and probably many of them will outlast you and me. While they may be artifices, they surely have lasting power to motivate behavior. These structures are made up of rules, bundles of which can be called offices, such as bishop, senator or shaman. The activities connected with such offices we call roles. Officeholders play official roles according to the rights and duties vested in their offices. Thus their behavior has some official, structural redundancy. These are official patterns of behavior or official roles.

An office/role complex is encountered by the new occupant/player as an *a priori* bundle of official rights and duties. Ideas about how an officeholder should act pre-date him or her. Anthropologists call this structure. In different kinds of structures, behavior varies. One should behave differently in church that on the floor of congress. Again, the behavior of Asante witch-finders in Ghana will be different from the actions of Buddhist monks in Tibet.

These structures—a church, a parliamentary system, a cult, a monastery—have an ongoing form to them. We can distinguish between behaviors in different formal realms. People in each realm feel compelled to act in disparate ways. Each has its routines.

In recognizing *a priori* forms, most members of society take them to be legitimate. People believe in God, therefore churches are accepted as normal and going to church is a normal behavior. Since the Asante believe in witches, it is a legitimate activity to be engaged in witch-finding. In fact, practitioners make a living at it, as do priests and bishops and other religious specialists in different social worlds. All these forms and behaviors are taken to be routine by true believers.

Power is inherent in such forms. That they exist has power over our minds. We take them as real because they were here before us and because others seem to take them as real. **Redundancy** enhances their apparent reality. Also, such structures have office-holders who wield power over others in their domains. The Pope tells Catholics what they can or cannot do. Politicians make rules about paying taxes or crossing a border. Monks chant. Witch doctors prescribe magical amulets to be worn to ward off witches.

In the human experience, as such concepts and structures became accepted as legit-imate, on-going aspects of society, each new generation of leaders inherited ready-made rule-bundles by which they could rule fellow group members, and influence re-lations between groups in the larger political sphere. This **influence**, over time, has become designated by society as **authority**, which was attained by socially accepted, privileged access to office. As such, authoritative rule-bundles were tools that could be used by corporate group officers to gain more access to property and power than non-officeholders.

Constructionalist-oriented social scientists are usually not enamored with the con-cept of **positivism**. Whereas positivists attempt to uncover truth, and see themselves as engaged in the discovery of facts, those with a dialectical or constructionist epistemol-ogy are more inclined to see the text of the "discoverer" as one more social construc-tion, merely another view of perceived reality. It is simply another discourse, a result of the dialectic between the mind of the observer and the behavior of people in the field-work setting. For example, I knew about the concept of **corporation** and that of **lin-eage** when I went to do fieldwork in Ghana. Later, in the journal *Africa*, I wrote about lineages among the Sisala of Northern Ghana. Would I have found corporate lineages and written about them if I had not had the concept beforehand? Do the Sisala really have lineages? Did I discover something real in Sisalaland? (See Tables 2.1 and 2.2).

Well, the answer to these questions is not simple. In fact, it is a "yes and no" answer. Yes, a social form that we call the lineage exists. The Sisala have a word *jachiking*, which I translate as lineage. So in a sense, armed with the concept of lineage I found real lineages. The "no" part applies when we move on to the epistemological status of the lineage. What is the real nature of a lineage—is it real like a rock is real? No, it is not. Rocks are not constructed by human beings, but lineages are. As they were con-structed, they could be dismantled or pass away. Does that mean that I dreamed up Sisala lineages? No, they existed before I went there to study them, they exist now and they will probably exist in a slightly altered form after I am dead.

Table 2.1 The Ideal Sisala Lineage Structure

Unit	Size in persons	Members	Descent principle	Joint activities	Land Tenure	Focal shrines
Lineage or *jachiking* 3 generations in depth	Average, 42	Extended or joint fraternal family	Agnatic descent	Farm, live together & perform rituals	Rights in usufruct over land	*LEIEE* and *virebaling*
Compound or *kaala* 2 generations in depth	10–20	Joint fraternal family*	Agnatic and/or uterine descent	Farm#, live together & perform rituals	Farm tenure, not land tenure	Personal shrines of members [*vuyaa*]
Small household or *diising* 1–2 generations in depth	4–10	Children of one mother*	Uterine and/or agnatic descent	Farm with agnates, but may farm separately	Farm tenure, not land tenure	Personal shrines of members [*vuyaa*]
Room or *dia* 1 generation in depth	1–3	Nuclear family	Marriage or descent	May farm alone or on a senior's farm	Farm tenure, not land tenure	Personal shrines of members [*vuyaa*]

* Normally
# Ideally, farm in addition to helping on the lineage farm

In short, although social forms are artificial constructions of human beings, they are existentially real over time and have real consequences in the here and now, and the consequences of past constructs carry over to influence the present and presumably continue into the future. All those women living in the witch villages of Ghana can attest to that. That is, once created, idea bundles have real consequences in the real world. They can even change nature. Remember that *real* rock? A human being can have a need to open a coconut, see a rock lying on the ground and so get an idea—"I can use the rock to break open the coconut." The broken coconut is the consequence of the idea.

Thus, anthropologists tend to see all tradition as created, being reworked from time to time according to the present political circumstances in society or the economic needs of the powerful. Tradition is the fixing of flux, the freezing of change into a momentary mold. The West Africanist Charles Piot makes the point that when anthropologists look at West African traditions, they have to realize that such mores have been influenced by the world system for some 500 years. West Africa has not existed in isolation from Europe, Asia or the world at large. Thus, her traditions can be seen as adaptations to new and changing circumstances—not as an eternal formation.

Terence Turner has pointed out that when colonials came to Africa they tended to value their own imaginations about the legitimacy of state institutions. Theirs was a history of hierarchy and monarchy. Thus, they tended to favor African states over acephalous peoples. They had no model of reference to understand acephaly—tribes without rulers. Since African kingdoms resembled European monarchies, Europeans assumed that their traditions were in tact. Acephalous societies, lacking visible leaders, were thought to have lost their hierarchical traditions. In fact, European administrators often sought to reinstate hierarchy and state institutions where they perceived their absence.

The Nigerian historian, Peter Ekeh, has shown that traditions such as corporate lineages and tribal unity most likely developed at the height of slaving as defense mechanisms against the violence perpetrated upon various West African peoples. My data (See *Continuity and Change in a West African Society*) on the rise of the *sipaalaaraa* or war chiefs among the Sisala support this thesis. Dr. Ekeh indicates that where the state could not defend, corporate kin ties and clientelist relations were strengthened to do so. Clientelism was on the rise as a way of pulling people together in defense of hearth and home. Among the Grunshi peoples of the **Voltaic Region** (See Map 1.11), like the Sisala, few if any state structures existed, so these peoples relied on strong community and kinship ties to hold off aggressors. Much like feudalism in Europe, **tribalism** and a strong sense of locality and ethnicity arose to fill a gap. Peter Ekeh continues, for:

> if in Europe the response to the failure of the state to provide security for the individual was the institution of feudalism, in Africa the response to the violation of the citizenry by the state, in its sponsorship of the slave trade, was the entrenchment of kinship corporations.

Tradition is something alive and dynamic. It is influenced by social change and by the forces of history. Tradition, then, serves purposes, depending on who is defining it, and who is using it in *political* ways.

Sociocultural formations have ecological functions. From this perspective, I see tradition as a body of fabricated ideas that enabled West Africans to adapt to their environment and to arrange themselves in ways that favored group survival as opposed to individual aggrandizement. Thus, the myths, institutions and cultural codes of West African society formed an adaptive civilization. Over time it evolved into a strong, relatively egalitarian and communalistic civic culture with effective checks and balances. This culture discouraged the rise of despots, it focused on family and community and it encouraged democratic input into decision-making—what political scientists like to call democracy.

Democracy comes from the Greek, *demos,* meaning "the people" and *kratein,* "to rule." The *Funk and Wagnall's Encyclopedia* defines it as a "political system in which the people of a country rule through any form of government they choose to establish." In West Africa the sociocultural formations of village life were built up over time, not by any despot, nor by any outside force, but by the people—hence democratically.

Furthermore, headmen came to rule by agreed upon procedures of succession to office, or by consensus among the elders as representatives of the people. Even chiefs and kings, where they arose, were not tyrants, and could not easily become so because they were under severe restrictions in the exercise of power. They were subject to the people directly, in many ways. They were also indirectly controlled by sacred communalistic ancestral sanctions. It was only with the introduction of slave trading and imported firearms that despotic tendencies began to emerge. This is an old story. New opportunities corrupted the leaders, but even then it was difficult for monarchs to overcome long-established restraints on their power (See Chapter 9).

In modern Western democracies, supreme authority is exercised for the most part by representatives elected by popular suffrage. This is not unlike what obtained in most West African civic cultures, where elders and chiefs acted as representatives of the people. Furthermore, the people could supplant such representatives, according to the legal procedures of recall and referendum and they were, at least in principle, responsible to the people. The people could bypass any man in line for office they deemed unsuitable, and they could throw out bad rulers.

West African **gerontocracies** and chiefdoms were not unlike republics where authority is delegated to representatives of the people. These officials were expected to act on their own best judgment concerning the needs and interests of the polity. But in most cases, these were tiny polities, not giant empires or nations. Even republican leaders were closely monitored by the youth, secret societies, voluntary associations, age-sets and other institutions in society, including the ancestor cult that was often in the hands of non-politicos.

Civic Culture: Cosmological Content

Much of West African's bedrock of social cohesion comes from the philosophical constructions anthropologists label as mythology. This term is not used by anthropologists in the popular sense as something false; it is exactly the opposite. Myth is a truth system. It is the repository of the fundamental assumptions of society. It is the set of ideas that underpins the civic culture, the moral order of a people giving their lives meaning and continuity from generation to generation.

The peoples who used to be called "primitive" come from historical circumstances that have placed Africans close to nature. Their culture is a thin buffer between people and their environment. Whereas Western culture tends to deny the human-nature connection, African society emphasizes it. The cultures of Africa recognize nature's power and omnipresence in people's lives, and nature is factored into the moral rules of society.

Anthropologists know that all peoples everywhere fabricate myths to support what they must do in the world. These are both rationalizations of existing actions and guides to future behavior. In West Africa, many of these cultural formations are in the hands of the elderly or specialists who can weave basic elements into complex mythologies. See, for example, the elaborate Dogon legends reported by Marcel Griaule in Box 2.1.

Box 2.1   Ogotemmêli's Mythology

The Dogon of Mali have an elaborate mythology. Here is an excerpt from Griaule's Conversations with a Dogon elder named Ogotemmêli.

Twenty-second day.

The Blood of Women

The European asked a question point blank, which seemed to have nothing to do with the subject of the conversation.

'Why,' he asked, 'do the eight families observe different prohibitions? Why all these animals?'

Ogotemmêli, who was never disconcerted, gave an answer which made his interlocutor smile with satisfaction.

'The prohibited animals,' he said, 'are different, because wombs may be of four different forms and the male sexual organ of three; the children produced by different combinations of these forms are therefore different. The animals, which are in a sense the twins of the different sorts of men, must therefore be different from one another.

At the beginning, he reminded them, the first created couple had eight children, of whom the four eldest were males and the four others females. The latter ranked fifth to eighth in the family; the wombs were assigned to them having the qualities associated with Nos. 5 and 8.

Form No. 5 is called *pobu* in allusion to the fruit of the tree of that name.

Ogotemmêli and Koguem both chuckled slyly at the word, which is one of the worst insults one can hurl at a woman.

The *pobu* form is egg-shaped, round below and somewhat pointed above. In the arrangement of the celestial granary it corresponds to compartment 5, that is, to the see of the bean, and is of the same oblong shape. It is ill-omened, and its offspring are malformed, because it is not deep enough and does not allow of normal development.

Its number is that of abortion and of sickly children.

Form 6 is called 'antelope's foot'. It is three-cornered, so that it has the shape of the male number 3, and should in theory give birth to male twins (2 x 3, twice the number of the male). It is propitious, as are the two following forms. It corresponds to the native sorrel.

Form 7, called 'split', is longer and thinner than form 5. It is split along its length like rice seed, to which it corresponds. It gives birth to twins of different sexes (4 + 3).

Form 8, called 'chest', is a trapezium upside down, like a man's chest. It has four sides (the female number), and produces female twins (2 x 4). It corresponds to the *Digitaria*.

No one knows how the different forms of the male organ were attributed to the first four ancestors, but the three forms are known as 'tick', 'lizard's head' and 'long'. The first of these, which is propitious is especially suited to the female forms 5 and 8. The second, which is spear-shaped, 'pricks'. It is unpropitious for all forms. Their third suits forms 6 and 7, but is unpropitious for the others.

These four female and three male forms are of course found in all the eight families. But at the dawn of humanity they were the origin of classifications.

Does this Dogon idea throw any light on what the linguists call nominal classes? The system is based on a classification of living creatures, objects, actions, and means of destruction of being, into categories. In those African languages which have been preserved, a distinct class of nouns, with special characteristics, appertains to each of these categories. The Dogon language, at first sight, does not seem to display this distinction; but on the other hand, it provides striking examples of categories of beings, objects, or abstractions, apparently disparate, but having names derived from the same root and, moreover, closely linked in the myths and in ritual as well as in the minds of those who participate in them. Thus the conversations with Ogotemmêli had brought to light the close connection, not merely verbal but also expressed in the objects and actions themselves, that linked cloth–clothing–speech–ornament–even–sun–cow–mother–lizzard (avatar of the prepuce)–four–granary–steal.

It would also be possible, though perhaps rather rash, to suggest a linguistic connection linking *Digitaria exilis*–menstruation, and voice–spiral–copper–rain, which are fundamental to the Dogon religious system.

But these ideas merely pass like a flash through the mind of the European, as he listened to the confidences uttered by Ogotemmêli in a low voice or a whisper according to the volume of noise from the street.

'After God made woman,' he was saying, 'he gave her bad blood, which has to flow every month.'

This tiresome affliction might be explained as a perpetual punishment for the primordial incest of the jackal's mating with his mother the earth. The jackal had laid hands on his mother's skirt, which Nummo [spirt twins associated with water] had plaited. Until then the fibres of this garment had been light-coloured: afterwards they were purple.

'The red colour of the fibres,' said the old man, 'is that of the menstrual blood which was thus introduced on the earth. But, as it is disrespectful to speak of the earth menstruating, I said that there had been a shower and that the fibres had got damp, and were now being put to dry in the sun.' The consequences of this exposure of blood will be referred to later.

The flow of menstrual blood is the result of the mating of son and mother, a thing forbidden.

In another connection Ogotemmêli compared this blood with that shed in circumcision which is regarded as the payment of a debt to the earth: woman, having been made of earth, owes the earth this debt. God imposed on her a debt of blood, and she has to pay it in the 'water of God's bosom'. Such was the name he gave to menstrual blood out of respect for women.

The earth remits payment of this obligation only during pregnancy and suckling, for the child itself counts as payment.

During these bad periods a woman has to be separated from the community. Contact with her would defile the men, and her presence in places where people live would weaken the altars [shrines]. She therefore lives on the edge of the village in a round house, symbol of the womb, and only leaves it at night to wash herself. She has to go by a prescribed path to the waters she is allowed to use, for if she goes anywhere else the area would be polluted, the pools would be troubled, and the headwaters of streams would boil.

'Woman is the Nummo's principal prohibition. He desires clean blood, and not this foul flow. He flies at the approach of a woman.'

And this is why the footsteps of a menstruating woman will drain all life away from places where she is forbidden to tread. She herself is, to a certain extent, the seat of disturbances comparable to thousand she would cause if she broke the rules. The flow from which she suffers is the excess blood ejected from within her by a superabundance of bile; and the bile is produced by the bad words which have entered into her.

'Not only do they unwind the fertilizing spiral of good words,' said Ogotemmêli, 'but they also accumulate in the gall-bladder and exert pressure on the blood.'

It is as if the Nummo, present in the liver and unable to leave without causing death, expelled from the body the unwanted blood, itself a symbol of the evil word.

'Pregnancy, on the other hand,' continued the old man, 'is the sign that good words have entered and have not been uncoiled from the womb. It is a sign that all is well.'

The ideologies of a people are dynamic. They are a collective system of thought that is adapted by sentient actors who adjust to new and changing circumstances. As the material world changes, ideologies also change to take these innovations into account.

A philosophy can be held by a small village or by a larger entity. The West African philosophy is community-focused: it sees the individual in a community context. This analysis could easily be extended to all of Sub-Saharan Africa. Some scholars, including **Léopold Sédar Senghor**, claimed that there is a concept of **Négritude**, a common "black metaphysic"—a common way of perceiving the world shared by all Africans. This may be going too far, but certainly the common material life experience in Africa has given peoples there a focus on the community, a centering on the importance of working collectively.

How did this communal ideology develop? First, it must be said that the typical community-based ethos is gods-oriented. It is founded on the assumption that nature and the supernatural impinge on the daily lives of human beings. This cosmology posits an eternal interactive exchange between society, nature and the **occult realm**.

Karin Barber says, "The idea that gods are made by men, not men made by gods, is a sociological truism." This may well be true, but contrary to the thesis of her fine article on the Yoruba, West African peoples would generally disagree. They believe that the high god has always existed and is a creator god. He may have created lesser gods, but man did not. Nevertheless, as Barber indicates, men in Yorubaland are responsible for maintaining their gods, which is also true in most West African societies. For example, among the Sisala the ancestors can move from the category living-dead to the dead-dead if living relatives do not periodically call out their names at sacrifices upon the ancestor shrines. The living-dead are dead people in the village of the ancestors who are ritually remembered by the living on earth. The dead-dead are those forgotten by their descendants. Thus, having eternal life, or *yiridindina*, is dependent on human action.

Barber's work on the Yoruba shows a similar process. They believe that their *òrìsà* gods are maintained and kept in existence by the attention of humans. Without this devotion, the *òrìsà* would be betrayed, exposed and reduced to nothingness. This is very West African. However Barber indicates that in Yoruba mythology, people make the *òrìsà*, which is not true in the West African perspective. There is a difference between initial creation and re-creation. Western sociologists believe in the former, West Africans in the latter.

Why do West Africans seem to have an interest in maintaining the personality and existence of their ancestors? Why do West African cosmologies typically posit an ongoing connection between the living and the living-dead? Perhaps the best explanation still lies with the father of sociocultural anthropology—Emile Durkheim. He says that men, in ritually maintaining gods, are really attempting to maintain the community. Worship of the gods, then, is worship of society. The relations between men in life are projected to a supernatural plane. What transpires in the occult world reinforces life on earth. Ideas about heaven are a reflection of social conditions in the living community.

Durkheim stressed the social aspect of ideas, but human relations in life have a material component too. They are part of a political economy and therefore deal with important material considerations. These include—the control of labor and people and their exchange between groups and succession to office and transmission of property between generations. These processes are often ritualized. Thus, having common rites indicates shared material interests and a common ethos. Barber puts it nicely when she says:

> I would like to suggest that if the Yoruba see the *òrìsà*'s power as being maintained and augmented by human attention, this is because they live in a kind of society where it is very clear that the *human* individual's power depends in the long run on the attention and acknowledgement of his fellow-men. (italics are hers).

Thus, ritual attention to spiritual beings is a way of paying attention to human relations and material concerns on earth. Cosmological ideas, as expressed in myth and ritual, are a reflection of the concerns of a living community.

When men (and occasionally women) become highly ranked, they are big because they have clients or followers. The same is true with gods. They retain their vitality by having devotees. A key question is: What is the source of an individual's power? In West Africa the answer is the same for both humans and gods—from the community, from fellows and followers.

In the group's consciousness, community based ritual gives humans, the living-dead and gods the power to thrive. But thriving, even surviving, is tenuous in West Africa. Both people and spirits can slip into insignificance. To maintain significance they must have followers who act on their behalf in life and remember them in ancestral sacrifices after they are dead. The ideal for a man is to leave behind a large family so that his name will be remembered at numerous sacrifices throughout the ages. The ideal for a woman is to have many children, especially sons, for the same reason. **Rituals of intensification** renew and maintain ties with the gods, and function to renew and maintain ties between people at the same time. They form a ritual bedrock for civic culture in West African society. Thus, the construction of life in the next world is an ideal representation of how people perceive their social and material world in this life.

In the context of West African cosmology, social ties are like a battery. Both need to be recharged periodically to maintain functionality. Blood sacrifice is thought to generate power, much like a battery does. Just as a battery cannot operate without electrical potency, the tie between a person and a god needs blood sacrifice. Likewise, a community needs to hold communal rites from time to time, ostensibly to regenerate its ties to the gods, but functionally to renew members' common commitment to each other.

The West African ethos says that individual choice is less reliable than group choice, that human collaboration is necessary for survival and success. The need for periodic sacrifice to the gods is a metaphor. It is a reminder of the need to regenerate the group's *communitas*—their sense of collective unity.

Kinship as a Model for Civic Life

No single concept is more important to the understanding of society in West Africa than **kinship** or **descent** (See Map 2.2). A **clan** is a descent group, the members of which claim descent from a distant ancestor. Descent is the foundation of social organization in West Africa, the basis of their civic culture. It is the model used by elders, wise men and women who want to influence young people. It is the paradigm that elders use to try to keep subordinates on the path of the ancestors.

A community paradigm can be both a model for and a model of behavior. It influences people to be moral. The idea of **consanguinity** serves to unite certain members of society that are said to have "one blood." Their connection may be real or fictive, bringing a set of people into a group as relatives with common interests, mutual rights and duties. As a "model of," kinship can explain relations that are said to exist between people in society. As a "model for," kinship can tell people how they should behave toward one another based on a shared ideology.

Consanguineal ties often create a corporate descent group. That group is set off from others in society. Its members share exclusive rights and duties. The group is a corporation sole, in that it existed before the life of any one member and outlives those of its current members. The descent group may enter into reciprocal relations with other groups, as mediated by representatives of each group.

In West Africa the individual is almost always genealogically connected to the group. S/he is a member of a generation-linked kin group that has a living membership on this earth and in the spirit realm. The timeless nature and importance of such consanguineal ties are presented to the West African in the fireside stories s/he hears in childhood, in ancestral myths passed down through the ages and in the rituals carried out at ancestor shrines. Collectively they say to the person, "You are part of something larger than yourself. You are never alone. No matter where you travel, to cities or across seas, you have kin and you are linked irrevocably to your progenitors."

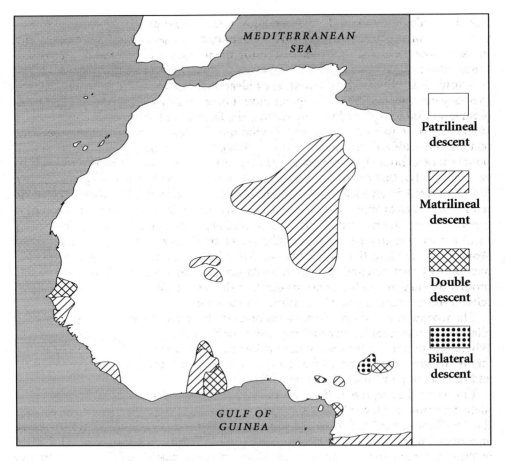

Map 2.2   Descent Patterns in West Africa.

Such an oral tradition tells the individual that s/he should maintain such kin ties; that linking with fellow kin in collective rites is crucial to personhood; and that de-linking is tantamount to a denial of one's fundamental identity as a kinsman, a fate reserved for slaves or witches.

Kinship is represented in myth, proverbs, stories, rites and in kinship terminology. **Kin terms** tell people who is a member of which kin group, and how they should behave toward each other.

All cultures make categories and divide the world into units. Classification systems commonly organize knowledge about time, colors, living things and social relations. A kin term is a completely arbitrary cultural imposition on biological reality. Calling one's male biological parent "father" "*nyimma*" or "*padre*" is arbitrary, just as there is no logic to why we call a tall, woody plant "tree," the Sisala call it "*tia*" and the Portuguese say "*árvore.*"

Kinship categories and terms for kin vary around the world and within West Africa. Some generalities can be made about West African kinship, however. Families tend to be large. Kin are highly valued and such groups may include thousands of persons, although functional groups of kin are much smaller. Kin and non-kin are grouped according to classificatory principles that include **filiation** or lineality—that kin can be linked genealogically through the generations; and by the principle of **generation**—that people in a given age cohort have some affinity in the way they are labeled, addressed, how people should behave towards them and how they should behave towards others.

Kinship is a collective representation or ideational model of and for social reality in everyday life. The principles of organization it uses are generation, filiation and **complementary filiation**. The first derives from the facts of biological aging and that individuals are born into cohorts of people who more or less share a common age and a relationship with adjacent generations. It is expected that members of such generational cohorts should have common interests and similar regards for those in abutting generations. For that reason kin terms sometimes reflect reciprocal roles, for example, in many West African societies all men in a generation address each other by a kinship term that means brother. They are addressed by the members of the first descending generation as fathers, and by the first ascending generation as sons. Likewise all women born into that generation will be sisters, mothers and daughters, respectively. Women married into that generation will be called by a term meaning wife by male members of that generation, and inheritance of such wives may pass from elder brother to younger brother upon the death of the senior. Thus, kin terminology often reflects and instructs the role to be played in the group.

The second way in which kin are terminologically and sociologically organized is by filiation. That is, people can be of one lineage or line of kin that extends through time. Whereas generation organizes kinsmen horizontally; filiation places people into a family tree on a lineal plane. Filiation can be matrilineal, coming from one's mother and her kin, or patrilineal, from one's father and his kin.

Kin terms that represent filial ties reflect hierarchy and authority between proximate generations. One calls one's own father and each person in his generation "father" or "little father," and should treat them with respect. Such relations are filled with an element of fear and tension. Likewise, moving down the line, one calls junior males in the first descending generation "sons" and can expect that they will be respectful in their behavior towards their "fathers."

Joking relations are common in West Africa. While tension exists between proximate generations, the relations between members of alternate generations is relaxed. For example, grandfathers will joke with their grandsons and vice versa. A grandson has great license in his grandfather's house, even to the point where he can steal things with impunity, or insult the elder. Great fun can be had between these males if they are adept at such repartée and the ensuing spoken exchanges can be the source of great entertainment to all those present.

A third way in which West African kinsmen are organized is that of complementary filiation. In a patrilineal society, this would be through the mother's side; in a matrilineal society it is through the father's line. This alternative way of organizing kin gives the child a second set of kinsmen with whom s/he has different obligations and rights. These alternative kin are called by different kin terms, and the behavior towards them is correspondingly different. For example, a man may have great oedipal tension with his own father, but may feel more free with the father of his mother, or the mother's brother (in a patrilineal society). In a matrilineal society, where the oedipal tension is between mother's brother and sister's son, the complementary relation will be with father and father's people.

Thus, kin terms and systems of classifying kin tell family members how to organize their perceptions of and behavior towards other relatives. The idea of consanguinity is symbolic of unity. The antithesis is **affinity**, or the relations between in-laws. Thus, members of clan A are consanguines to each other and take wives from clan B. The members of clan B are also consanguines to each other, but are collectively **affines** to those in clan A. **Marriage** is the relation between two groups of kin (commonly descent groups or clans). One can only marry non-kin, thus, clans exchange women to establish ties of affinity with one another. These affinal relations are an important source of labor and support in time of need when one's own kin cannot help.

Thus kinship is an ideational model that provides people with rules that guide their thought and behavior. Although kinship is very important to West Africans, they do not entirely conform to its norms. Some, perhaps most, behavior is adjusted to fit the rules, but there is deviance too. Sometimes the rules are bent or even broken to accommodate behavior that might not exactly coincide with the ideal model. A stranger may be incorporated into the descent group, for example, in spite of the fact that he is in reality a non-kinsman. Here, the tendency to fuse people into groups is greater than the need to be strict about kin group membership.

Kinship defines membership in a group and rights and duties in that group. These are supposed to be inalienable and automatic for those holding a genealogical position. However, one can lose one's kinship status in two ways—by becoming labeled as a witch, or by becoming a slave. Witches are seen as the antithesis of kinsmen and may never attain full consanguineal rights again. Similarly, a slave loses such rights upon enslavement, but may regain them at some future date.

On one hand the group can take away kinship status, but on the other hand, **fictive kinship** can be given to a complete stranger if certain institutionalized rites are performed. This can even happen for a slave, though not a witch. Thus, people adjust their behavior to their economic and political interests, too, and adjust the kinship model accordingly. This can be seen in the extreme case where a slave is afforded consanguineal status in the family if the family needs personnel. By definition s/he is a non-kinsman, a person without ancestors or the common funerary rights that transform a person into an ancestor.

In a patriarchal society like the Fra Fra, a son is supposed to obey his father's every command. Yet, sons waver, and even go against their father's wishes at times. The ideals of kinship are a guide, but not an absolute mandate to thought and behavior (See Nenkentie's Case in the Box 2.2).

Box 2.2   Nenkentie's Case: The Dutiful Son?

In Sisalaland, Northern Ghana in the 1970s, Nenkentie Badzongoly was the ideal son of his father, Kajia-Bein (See Photo 2.1). Before Nenkentie went off to Kumase to follow a university course, he was the most dutiful of sons. No father could wish for a better boy. Yet, when his father called him home to tell him to give up his studies, to get married and settle down to be a farmer alongside his father—Nenkentie Badzongoly refused, knowing full well that a secure future lay in wait if he could complete his accountancy course.

But the story does not end there. Nenkentie Badzongoly did complete his degree and took a fine job with an international firm in Kumase. Today he is the senior accountant at that firm. He also married an Asante girl and had children by her. Nevertheless, when his father again summoned him and told him to marry a handmaiden of family (the younger sister of a wife who had come to

Photo 2.1 Nenkentie Badzongoly.

help her), he obediently followed his father's wishes. As his economic status was such that he could afford a second wife, his behavior appeared to be dutiful; though when his economic concerns were incompatible with the ideals of kinship, an onlooker or his father could have labeled his behavior as disrespectful. In real life, kin relations involve much of both, a mix of personal and group interests.

Kin groups are those with a common consanguinity based on shared rights and duties in a conjoint patrimony. That is, they have a common interest in property and wealth, which in the West African context can mean people. Thus, a patrimony can include **jural relations** (involving rights and duties) *vis-à-vis* material goods, labor or ancestor shrines. Membership in a kin group gives one claims and responsibilities and places one in relation to other group members with regard to patrimonial value. This happens because people die and leave behind bundles of rights and duties—social roles. At funerals these roles are given to new players. Rights over, and responsibilities toward, people and property are rearranged to fill the void left by the departed family member.

Unilineal Descent

Unilineal descent is reckoning one's lineage either through one's father or one's mother. While there are other ways of reckoning descent in West Africa, by far the most common is patrilineality. This is often contrasted to the European way of calculating descent, which is called **cognatic (bilateral) descent** and involves tracing one's lineage through both mother and father. Nevertheless, in one of the most well known peoples, the Asante, descent is based on **matriliny**. Among many matrilineal societies postmarital residence is either **matrilocal** (living with mother) or **avunculocal** (living with mother's brother). In general, among Savannah peoples it is based on **patriliny**, and those West African peoples who reckon descent in the mother's line tend to be forest dwellers.

Using a sample of 797 farming societies, Michael Harner determined that a strong statistical association exists between an increased reliance on agriculture and the replacement of bilateral kin groups with unilineal ones (foraging is to bilateral kin groups as agriculture is to unilineal kin groups). Unilineal groups predominate in the world. In the ethnographic sample, farming village societies organized into unilineal descent groups outnumbered those organized cognatically 380 to 111 (77.4% to 22.6%). Population increase has been a fact in the history of humankind. It is likely that such a way of organizing inheritance and descent arises when there is population pressure on resources, and there is a need for men to organize around a common patrimony.

Of all unilineal descent groups in known societies, the vast majority are patrilineal. Seventy-one percent of 1179 societies in the HRAF (Human Relations Area Files) are either **patrilocal** (living with father after marriage) or **virilocal** (living with father's people), and patrilineal descent groups outnumber societies with matrilineal kin groups 588 to 164 (See also **neolocal residence** in glossary).

Unilineality involves passing inheritance of goods and succession to office through either the father's line or the mother's. Another variable involved is discipline of children, also a concomitant of inheritance and succession.

In other words, inheritance, succession and discipline all tend to pass in a unilineal manner. In a patrilineal society, property and social roles move from senior male to junior male, either from father to son or from elder brother to his younger male sibling.

In such a patriarchal society, women are under the control of men and are exchanged between male-centered groups (See Photo 2.2). They are exchanged as wives, and sometimes as foster children. **Fostering** is a common practice in West Africa. Labor is usually in short supply overall, but some families may have extra members who are "lent" to labor-short families. While a foster child retains kinship status in the giver-group, her or his labor is temporarily "loaned" to the taker-group.

When girls are exchanged as wives, typically men in the donor group receive **bridewealth** payments and **brideservice**. The former are customary goods exchanged for the rights over a woman's sexual, domestic and generative capacities. Brideservice is labor performed by the groom and his compatriots on the farm of the bride's father.

Among other things, such payments and customary labor establish the paternity of the children. In West African patriarchies, children most commonly reside patrilocally, that is with the father and his relatives. **Post-marital residence rules** are usually spelled out by custom.

In matrilineal societies, such as the Asante of the Ghanaian rain forest, all patrimony passes through females, but from man to man, normally from mother's brother

Photo 2.2 Woman Repairing Earth Floor Near Her Hearth.

to sister's son. Matriliny is not a mirror image of patriliny, in that in patriarchal societies men are in charge of the political economy, which is also the case in matrilineal ones. There is some indication that the status of women in such societies is slightly better, but the difference would be miniscule. Men rule in both.

Why matriliny? Patrilineal groups are associated with farming. Matriliny may develop when males must be away from home for extended periods of time in warfare or trade, and find it risky to leave the homestead in the hands of wives who are not experienced at cooperating with one another. As Marvin Harris says, "No one is home 'to mind the store,' so to speak." Patrilineal households involve adult females who are co-wives and who come from different natal homes. As strangers such co-wives are more prone to conflict than sisters. Matrilocality solves this problem because it creates a homestead centered on sisters who are accustomed to cooperating from birth onwards.

Furthermore, matrilineal societies contrast with patrilineal ones in that the former are bonded not by the exchange of women, but by the inmarrying of males from different descent groups. Scattering men into different households in various villages prevents the formation of competitive and disruptive fraternal interest groups.

Moreover, when women do the agricultural work, domestic chores and watch the household, men are freed up for warfare, and it has been noted that matrilineal societies are well suited for long-distance warfare, as seen among the Asante.

In a matrilineal society, a father is not a member in the same descent group as his children, nor does he take a strong hand in the discipline of his children. They reside with the mother who lives in close proximity to her brother who is in charge of the children's' upbringing. Upon the death of the mother's brother, his property, wives and offices will pass to the eldest son of his sister. Likewise, the children's father, upon his death, does not give them any significant patrimony, but instead passes it to his sister's son.

While in the patriarchal society a man holds both rights over the wife's sexual and domestic capacities (**rights in *uxorem***) and rights over her reproductive capacities (**rights in *genetricem***), in a matrilineal society the husband (or more correctly the corporate descent group of the husband) only hold's uxorial rights over the wife.

Double Descent

The Yakö of southeastern Nigeria, according the C. Daryll Forde, have a relatively unique variation on the principle of descent—a **double descent** system. They have both patriclans and matriclans. The patriclan is called the *yepun*. It is the dominant of the two clans, in that it is the basis for residence, production and the inheritance of fixed property (land). The *yepun* is also exogamous, daughters marrying into it in return for a payment of bridewealth to the *yepun* of the bride. All political offices pass in the patriline.

The *yajima* or matriclan is not exogamous, nor is it a territorially linked group, but mother's brother is an important figure in the life of sister's son. Upon the death of the former the latter will inherit from him all moveable property—yams, livestock, money, and any household goods that he might have, such as, weapons, skins, stools, and so on. Additionally, all ritual offices pass in the matriline.

Thus we see that descent involves marriage rules, residence, inheritance and succession to office. All West African societies have some sort of rules to govern these processes. Some emphasize the father's line (patrilineal or agnatic descent), others the mother's line (matrilineal or uterine descent) and still others, such as the Yakö, use one side for some purposes, and the other side for other purposes.

Marriage — Linking Two Descent Groups

In all West African societies, marriage occurs between those who are defined as non-kin. Marriage is usually a group affair between two descent groups, except for all but the most Europeanized of Africans. The traditional marriage bond links the two groups together, each having reciprocal rights and duties *vis-a-vis* the other.

As with most of the rest of the world, West African descent groups tend to be exogamous, that is, a person must marry outside his or her descent group, as defined by the cultural rules of that group. This is the rule of **exogamy**, which Levi-Strauss has hailed as the primary basis of kinship, even of society. This is because it causes men to prohibit sex and marriage with their own women, and requires them to give them to another group in exchange for goods or other women. Such groups are often hostile to each other, thus, the well-known African saying, "We marry our enemies." Such hostilities are mitigated by intermarriage, however, because eventually, if nature takes its course, the marriage will yield offspring that will be the kinsmen of men in both groups. As theory would have it, this lessens the chance that unilineal descent group A will attack unilineal descent group B since A has grandchildren in that affinal (in-law) descent group.

The above is the traditional perspective of marriage in the **emic** view of most West Africans. But anthropologists broaden the definition of marriage to include other arrangements besides that between a bride and groom or their kin groups. Kathleen Gough in an article in *Marriage, Family and Residence* states that marriage is a relationship established between a woman and one or more persons. Note that she does not say "a woman and one or more men." I will get to the reason for this when I discuss "female fathers" in Dahomey.

Anthropologists see marriage as a structure that functions to establish the legitimacy of the offspring of the union. The marriage relationship assures that a child born to the woman is given full birthright in some kin group. When marriage rites have been carried out between two persons in accordance with the norms of their society, the legality of the marriage makes the children legitimate in the eyes of society. They are rightful citizens and heirs in a community by virtue of their descent status.

As the anthropologist Bronislaw Malinowski put it, "Marriage is the licensing of parenthood." A legitimate marriage assigns birth status to the child. Also, it legally entitles the child and/or the mother to the husband's property upon his death, and sometimes a portion of it in case of divorce. Furthermore, marriage rites determine who is responsible for the child.

A common part of such rites in West Africa is the payment of bridewealth and the performance of brideservice by the groom and his descent group. Often this payment is in at least two parts. Among the Sisala of Northern Ghana, for example, the *haala-kiaa* (consumables) is initially paid to the bride's brother (who takes them on behalf of the bride's father). The groom will also perform three days of brideservice labor on the bride's father's farm. These goods and services are exchanged for the rights *in uxorem* — her sexual and domestic capacities — over the girl.

After the birth of a child, a second payment will be made called the *ha-jari-kiaa*. It is a cow. It is given for the rights *in genetricem*, or the rights to the children. Without its payment, the child is a bastard and all of her offspring would be bastards, since s/he would lack valid membership in a descent group.

Legitimate children have the right to affiliation with the father's kin group (or mother's brother in a matrilineal society) and to inherit his goods and succeed to his offices. Thus, from a materialist viewpoint, marriage rules are basically about the distribution of a patrimonial bundle of rights to property and offices. Certainly, as Jack Goody has pointed out in *Death, Property and Ancestors*, much of the content of West African funerals has to do with a reallocation of property rights and social roles.

Polygyny is the marriage of one man to more than one woman. It usually produces more children than any other marriage form. Marriages in West Africa are often polygynous, especially where labor is in short supply. Biologically, a man can impregnate many women, of course. His wives can be in various stages of reproduction, that is, his wives can have babies at different times. Some wives can be producing offspring while the others are prevented from doing so, due to pregnancy, extended lactation or other reasons. Such a marriage form produces large numbers of children, which is useful in a labor-short farming community.

However, polygyny is often an ideal that only big men can afford. In many polygynous societies in West Africa, most marriages are monogamous, since substantial resources are required for the bridewealth payments. Also, some men may not want multiple wives because of the conflict that usually develops between co-wives. The discord is not usually about sex, but about jealousy over children, the suspected mistreatment of children by a co-wife, the allocation of food and property to a favorite wife, and so forth.

Sometimes marriage and jealousy in West Africa *are* about sex, but not usually. Among West Africans who have not been exposed to foreign models of guilt, attitudes about sex are quite free and open. Often a first wife will push the husband to take a second wife, then the second one lobbies for a third, and so on. They are looking for

Photo 2.3   Child Labor in African Families Is Common.

help in the household. Sometimes this additional wife who comes is a sister to the previous wife (**sororal polygyny**), which gives her not only a helpmate, but a confidante in the household with whom she has a long-standing relationship based on kinship.

Children are an important focus of marriage—most West Africans would say *the* most important. Most men and women in West Africa want as many as they can have. That children are so highly cherished is a reflection of a larger joy West Africans seem to have in all human relationships. People are primary and material things are an important means of establishing and maintaining human relations, which, if you think about it, is the opposite of the Western approach where having commodities is given so much importance.

A woman who cannot have children is usually miserable. Some commit suicide, others leave their husbands, some migrate to the city to become prostitutes. Some of these unfortunate women fall prey to violence, illness or poverty, but some use their business acumen to become wealthy "big women." Such a **big woman** will gather around her a circle of young men and women to do her bidding.

Sometimes, as among the powerful women of Dahomean society, such big women pay the bridewealth for another woman and have her impregnated by a male retainer. However, in Dahomean society, the **female father** need not be divorced or separated from her husband. This gives the barren woman an out. She can remain married and produce offspring for herself through such fictional reproduction. Such women may foster other children or adopt them as well (See Photo 2.3).

On the male side, sometimes a Sisala man loses the ability to have children, or cannot produce them for biological reasons. In such a case, as the legal husband he may enter into a ritualized relationship with another man, a genitor, who has sex with the man's wife and begets children on behalf of the legal husband. Such a biological substitute (or cicisbeo) must be presented to the husband's ancestor for confirmation (a practice called **cicisbeism**). Once this is done, he comes and goes as a valued friend in the husband's home, having rights not unlike a favored son (for more details, see chapter 3 in *Continuity and Change in a West African Society*).

In the minds of many West Africans marriage is primarily about the production of legitimate children. But it also leads to the formation of a household. As children come along, or more wives are added, the household grows in size and eventually becomes three-generational in depth. At that point it may become a sub-segment of the **segmentary lineage system** discussed below. This is the ideal for the parents, who then preside over a large family. Leaving behind such a family at death gives an elder a much greater chance of achieving immortality in the world of the ancestors, as s/he has many living kin who will call out his or her name at ancestral rites. At the level of ideas, this highlights again the importance of kin relations, even with the dead members of the family.

The place of the ancestral spirits in West African traditional life cannot be overstated. This has led anthropologists to speak of the ancestor cult and ancestor worship, while these are best subsumed under the rubric of **ancestor veneration**. Ancestors form a focal point for community ritual and reverence. They remain an integral part of the extended family by afflicting living members when they deviate from customs. Thus, the dead members of the family become the guardians of the moral order. To alleviate misfortune, the living must placate the ancestors through blood sacrifice on ancestral shrines. As a subset of a larger belief in supernatural causation, ancestral affliction of family members forms the foundation of West African traditional religion (See Chapter 3). The path of the ancestors is a moral code that lays the groundwork for community life, spelling out what is right and wrong. By tying affliction to the idea of ancestral causation, West Africans have a built-in system of explanation for illness, accident and death.

Muslim ways have become common in some parts of the region, especially in the north and in the Savannah Zone (See Chapter 9). Under Islamic law, a man can have up to four legal wives and innumerable concubines. The later are not just sexual consorts to be discarded without recourse to Islamic law. They are legally connected to the male, but only receive a half share of a wife's inheritance. Few West African Muslims ever achieve the ideal of four wives outside of chiefs, kings and very wealthy big men.

Christian West Africans are limited to a single wife. This presents a problem if a polygynist is converted to Christianity. For example, it is ironic that the Mormon Church requires African polygynists to divest themselves of excess wives before becoming full members of the church, even though in Mormon doctrine, God is polygynous and all righteous male holders of the lay priesthood can eventually become polygynous in the next world.

Segmentary Lineage Systems

In West Africa, many of the kinship systems are of the segmentary type. As descent groups, clans are divided up into functional segments or sub-units that operate in different capacities. While the whole clan is usually descended from a common **apical ancestor**, all through the family tree there will be key men who form the apical focal point of sub-genealogies within the clan. The groups that descend from such men form the segments of the segmentary lineage system. That is, each of these segments has as their focus an ancestor that is common to them. Their unique genealogical linkage to this ancestor provides them with a common focus that sets them apart from

Table 2.2 The Segmentary Lineage System

GROUP SIZE	CONSTITUENT UNITS	UNIFYING PRINCIPLE	COMMON ACTIVITIES	LAND TENURE	SHRINES HELD
La Sisala (Tribe)					
59,000 (based on the 1960 census)	Unrelated clans of different origins	Chieftaincy established by the British and supported by the Ghanian government	None; treated as a unit by government	None	None
Viara (Clan)*					
1,500	Agnatically related jasing or villages in the southeastern part of Sisalaland	Agnatic descent from a common founding ancestor	Clan members do not meet, but elders do sacrifice on their behalf	Hold rights in usufruct over clan land	*Tingteeng, vene*
Jang (Village in Southeaatern Sisalaland)					
400	Two agnatically related maximal lineages	Agnatic descent	Common rituals; elders form village government	Elders allocate clan-owned land	*Tingteeng, vene*
Nyingniaa and Vaadongo (Maximal Lineage)					
One has 100, the other 300 persons	Patrilineages (*jachiking, jachikising*)	Agnatic descent	They sacrifice together and bury the dead of the other maximal lineage in their village	None	Some hold shrines; others do

Jachiking (Lineage)					
Average size is 42	Extended or joint fraternal families	Agnatic descent	Farm, live, and sacrifice together	While clan owns all land, lineages develop usufructory rights to plots, but land is freely given for the asking by the lineage head	LEIEE, most commonly approached ancestral shrine and *virebaling*, the lineage granary
Kaala (A Large Household)					
10 to 20 persons	Normally composed of children of one father	Agnatic and/or uterine descent	Live together within the lineage settlement and cultivate a farm in addition to the lineage farm	None; they can use any clan land	Only personal shrines of members (*vuyaa*)
Diising or Dia (A Small Household)					
4 to 10 persons	Normally composed of children of one mother	Agnatic and/or uterine descent	Normally farm with their lineage agnates, but they may decided to farm separately	None	Only personal shrines (*vuyaa*)
Dia (Room or Small Household)					
1 to 3 persons	Nuclear families	Marriage, agnatic, and/or uterine descent	Live together; may farm a separate plot	None	Only personal shrines (*vuyaa*)

*These data on the descent group are taken from the Crocodile clan of southwestern Sisalaland, near Bujan, for the year 1971.

other clan members. Kinsmen of the segment will honor their own ancestors in rituals that function to unite the members of that group around mutual respect for their forebears. Ancestral veneration provides group members with a joint set of religious ideas and ritual procedures that provides them meaning in life, as well as a unique sense of community.

Another way that families experience a sense of unity is by sharing a **totem**. **Totemism** sometimes occurs in conjunction with descent groups when the clan is united by a commonly revered totemic animal or **taboo**. Most of the time this is an animal, such as the crocodile or crow, but it can be a **taboo** of an inanimate object, such as a pot or rock. In tabooing the totem, group members cannot kill it or eat it (if it is a living thing) or use it (if it is an inanimate object). Usually there is some mythological explanation for the avoidance of the totem by members of the social group. For example, the small pot clan of Northern Ghana taboos using a specific kind of little clay vessel. This is because their clan myth of origin explains that their apical ancestor had bad luck after using this pot.

While a common apical ancestor and totem unite clansmen, each segment within may have more intense unity based on different functional foci. Their level of ritual participation may be greater, as is their overall social interaction. In fact, broader segments like clans may see only an infrequent gathering of its members, while lower-level segments such as households display daily interaction between members.

Unity has its uses. Segments are often functional units e.g., when the lineage acts as a farming community. But segments that do not conjoin on a daily basis, or even frequently, can be useful to each other in time of need. The segmentary system enables a given lineage segment to enlist the aid of progressively larger groups of related segments when its territory is threatened. Thus, there can be a defensive function to segmentation. The system also serves to regulate the relations between the various segments. If conflict arises within the clan, two clashing segments can appeal to the next higher order of segmentation to mediate the dispute.

But perhaps the most important function of segments is in relation to labor. The farm group is a key segment. Typically, farm group members will have a central granary in which the fruits of their labor are stored. Nevertheless, this group has the right to call on the labor of other segments when needed; and it must provide labor when asked. Reciprocal aid is part and parcel of West African community life.

Thus, clan segments have common interests of an economic, legal, political and religious nature. Functionally, at the most fundamental level, they are economic groups that harness and direct energy (labor) to perform production. In general, West African communities are labor short and land rich. Thus the clan segments serve to organize production, storage, distribution and consumption—the fundamental economic processes of human life.

To sum up, we can say that various segments within the overall family unit, the clan, serve to regulate marriage, land use, access to and use of labor, and provide mutual support in times of need.

Domestic Life in West African Kin Groups

In West Africa domestic activities are similar to those elsewhere in the world—they include preparation and consumption of food, child rearing, cleaning, grooming, education of children, sleeping and adult sexual intercourse. Household members organize and carry out a range of economic behaviors related to production, distribution, food storage and consumption. The domestic household usually maintains rules regarding these activities, as well as some pertaining to the discipline of children, inheritance and succession to household leadership positions.

Nevertheless, the household is a difficult concept to apply to real situations in the field. It is essentially an **etic** behavioral unit that is defined by researchers in terms of the activities of the domestic economy. For example, a Sisala clan is a large group of agnatic (patrilineal) kin who reckon decent from an apical male ancestor and who share a common totemic taboo. The clan is divided into sub-units. Members of these sub-groups live together, performing many of the functions listed for the household. Perhaps the most significant unit is the *jachiking* or lineage. It is a large household in that members live inside a single homestead, farm together, have a central granary and eat from that granary — the contents of which are meted out by a lineage headman.

Yet there are other households within the lineage. While the lineage may have about 40–50 persons within its walls, it is comprised of two or more *kaala* or smaller family units. A *kaala* has between ten and twenty persons who live together around a central yard. While the lineage family may be an **extended family** or **joint family** (in their case, fraternal) the *kaala* is usually occupied by the latter, as a sub-family to the larger lineage family.

Moreover, the *kaala* is sub-divided into two or more *diising* or smaller households of four to ten persons. This is usually composed of the children of one mother, a uterine domestic unit within the larger patrilineal *kaala*.

And again, the *diising* may be divided into different rooms or houses (*dia*) with one to three persons in each. Single individuals or nuclear families occupy such units. A **nuclear family** usually is made up of a man, his wife and their children.

One of the reasons that it is difficult to identify a household is that smaller units evolve into larger ones and larger ones may break apart into smaller ones. The developmental cycle of growth is driven by population growth; the devolution of a domestic unit may be due to a lack of growth or conflict between heads of units.

Again within matrilineal societies like the Asante, it is sometimes difficult for outsiders to understand the nature of the domestic unit or household. The husband lives in a household with his brothers as well as with his married and unmarried sisters and any children of his sisters' marriages. This household may be presided over by a mother or a set of sisters called mothers by the next descending generation. All children of his and his brothers' marriages live with their mothers, who in turn, live with their brothers, sisters and mothers.

Thus, the **matrifocal family** stays together, centered around a grandmother or a group of sisters and their offspring. Yet women still cook for their husbands. Thus, in the evening it is common to see small children carrying their father's dinner to him, walking (pot on head) from their mother's compound to their father's residence. Even though they do not share a common household, the husband has rights to his wife's domestic and sexual capacities. She will visit him from time to time for sex, or *vice versa*, depending on conditions, privacy and other situational factors.

Most West African households are comprised of extended families or joint families. There are large families living together composed of three generations — grandparents, parents and children, in the case of the extended family. The joint family often results when the grandparents die and leave behind parents and their children.

Photo 2.4 Women and Children Eating from a Common Bowl.

Such families commonly say, "we are one" and mean by this that they work, sleep and eat together. This can be emphasized by a phrase such as "we eat from the same bowl." (See Photo 2.4) Spatially or temporally, the individual is seldom alone in West Africa, nor does s/he want to be isolated. The family provides a sense of security—psychologically, socially, politically and economically. The metaphor of sharing food alludes to this commonality—mutual ancestors, a shared genealogy and common totemic avoidances.

Nuclear families in West Africa are more common in the urban areas, though as I have shown in *Continuity and Change in a West African Society,* some rural extended and joint families are breaking down into nuclear units under the impact of ideas of individualism and the appearance of economic opportunity. With global economic penetration into family life in farming communities, new opportunities allow the single person to pursue self-aggrandizement at the expense of traditional responsibilities to kin or community. Three "penetrators" are bringing such socioeconomic changes to rural West Africa: hi-tech inputs and consumer goods, cash-cropping and wage labor.

Since the West African family is often an economic unit in which production, distribution and consumption processes are carried out, changes in economic opportunities or the nature of work in the community will affect the structure of the household.

Nevertheless, even when West Africans live in cities and have a single male breadwinner, as in the case of Nenkentie Badzongoly (See Box 2.2), they tend to have large households if the economics permit it. For example, the 45-year old Nenkentie Badzongoly has two wives, five children and three distantly related kinsmen living in his urban household.

Although in everyday West African life it is very difficult to separate kinship behavior from ritual acts, in the next chapter I will turn to matters of a religious nature to illustrate how West Africans have constructed ideas about the moral order, proper civic responsibility and the relation of the individual and community to the supernatural. The reader should remember, however, that this largely takes place within the context of kinship groups or **sodalities** that are community-based.

Summary

This chapter has been a structural analysis of the ideal kinship model and civic culture of traditional society, primarily that of rural West Africa. I do not want to leave the reader with the impression that all was peace and harmony in the region before the coming of the White Man. It was not. The *jihad* wars of Islam had seriously disrupted and altered some communities. Even without this invasion of a foreign element, indigenes warred against each other, establishing overlordship and enslavement. But they also peaceably traded with each other, intermarried and participated in ritual exchanges. Sometimes conflicts were worked out through diplomacy and negotiation.

What I have tried to correct in this chapter is the common misperception that West Africans were devoid of civilization. In doing all the things that humans do everywhere, they sometimes fell into conflict and sometimes exploited their neighbors, but largely the civilization of West Africa was one of inclusion rather than exclusion, of peace rather than war.

Sometimes one tribe fought another, but there were few wars of annihilation till European-inspired slaving won the day. When one group conquered another, the vanquished were usually allowed to continue with life as usual, as long as they paid tribute to the subjugators. Often captives taken were assimilated into dominant societies after a period of domestic slavery.

In short, West Africans participated in age-old relations and exchanges that were not unlike those of Persia, Phoenicia, Greece or Rome, albeit with different weaponry and methods. They had well-developed ethics, political proceedings and diplomatic procedures designed to dominate people without destroying them or their lands. Those forced to pay tribute often kept their own political leaders and way of life. Those taken into slavery could eventually emancipate themselves or work into positions of power and authority among their conquerors. Even in warfare their civilized nature is apparent. That European traders and colonists overlooked or misunderstood this civilization does not mean it did not exist.

≈≈≈ CRITICAL THINKING QUESTIONS ≈≈≈

1. What is the popular concept of tradition (the unanimist position) and how do anthropologists view it differently these days? Phrase your answer in terms of the constructionist approach to sociocultural formations.
2. Discuss the basic assumptions of African and Western civilizations. Do they clash or mesh and why?
3. How does the author present democracy in the West African context?
4. Explain West African kinship in terms of how it might be perceived as a model for civic behavior.
5. Explain the principles of filiation and descent and how they are related.

6. Why are bridewealth and brideservice common forms of marital exchange in West Africa?

KEY CONCEPTS

Affines
Affinity
Ancestor veneration
Apical ancestor
Authority
Avunculocal residence
Big woman
Brideservice
Bridewealth
Cicisbeism
Civilization
Clan
Codification process
Cognatic (bilateral) descent
Communitas
Complementary filiation
Consanguinity
Constructionist approach
Corporation, the principle of
Cultural presupposition
Democracy
Descent
Double descent
Emic
Etic
Exogamy
Extended family
Eurasia
Female father
Fictive kinship
Filiation
Fostering
Generation
Gerontocracies (Sing. Gerontocracy)
Hamitic hypothesis
Influence
Jihad
Joint family
Joking relation
Jural relations
Kinship

Kin terms
Lineage
Marriage
Matrilocal
Matrifocal family
Matriliny
Mythology
Négritude
Neolocal residence
Nuclear family
Occult realm
Patriliny
Patrilocal residence
People without history
Polygyny
Positivism
Post-marital residence rules
Primitive
Primitive mentality
Redundancy
Rights *in genetricem*
Rights *in uxorem*
Rituals of intensification
Segmentary lineage system
Senghor, Léopold Sédar
Sociocultural formation
Sodalities
Sororal polygyny
Slippage
Taboo
Tendana
Totem
Totemism
Tradition
Tribalism
Unilineal descent
Virilocal residence
Voltaic Region
White Man's Burden
Witchcraft

≋ SOURCES & SUGGESTED READINGS ≋

Barber, Karin. 1997. How man makes god in West Africa: Yoruba attitudes towards the Òrìsà. In: Grinker, R. R. & C. B. Steiner (eds.). *Perspectives on Africa: A reader in culture, history, and representation.* London: Blackwell, 392–411.

Boahen, A. Adu. 1969. Asante and Fante A.D. 1000–1800. In: Ajayi, J. F. Ade and Ian Espie (eds.). *A thousand years of West African history.* Ibadan: Ibadan University Press, 165–190.

Davidson, Basil. 1992. *The black man's burden: Africa and the curse of the nation-state.* New York: Times Books.

Durkheim, Emile. 1965 [1915]. *The elementary forms of the religious life.* Translated from the French by Joseph Ward Swain. New York: Free Press.

Ekeh, Peter P. 1990. Social anthropology and two contrasting uses of tribalism in Africa. *Comparative studies in society and history* 32:4.

Forde, C. Daryll. 1941. *Marriage and the family among the Yakö in south-eastern Nigeria.* London: Publised for the London school of economics and political science by P. Lund, Humphries & Co. Ltd.

Fortes, Meyer. 1949. *The web of kinship among the Tallensi.* London:

Fortes, Meyer. 1969. *Kinship and the social order: the legacy of Lewis Henry Morgan.* Chicago: Aldine.

Goody, Jack. 1962. *Death, property and the Ancestors: A study of the mortuary customs of the LoDagaa of West Africa.* Stanford: University Press.

Griaule, Marcel. 1997. Conversations with Ogotemmêli. In: Grinker, R. R. & C. B. Steiner (eds.). *Perspectives on Africa: A reader in culture, history, and representation.* London: Blackwell, 366–378.

Harner, Michael. 1970. Population pressure and social evolution of agriculturalists. *Southwestern journal of anthropology* 26:67–86.

Harris, Marvin and Orna Johnson. 2000. *Cultural anthropology* (fifth ed.). Boston: Ally & Bacon.

Lance, James Merriman. 1995. *Seeking the political kingdom: British colonial impositions and African manipulations in the northern territories of the Gold Coast colony.* Ph.D. dissertation, Stanford University. Ann Arbor: University Microform (UMI) #9525856.

Mendonsa, Eugene L. 1976. Elders, Office-Holders and Ancestors among the Sisala of Northern Ghana. *Africa* 46:57–65.

Mendonsa, Eugene L. 1977. The Soul and Sacrifice among the Sisala. *Journal of Religion in Africa* 8:1–17.

Mendonsa, Eugene L. 1982. *The Politics of Divination.* Berkeley: University of California Press.

Mendonsa, Eugene L. 2001. *Continuity and Change in a West African Society: Globalization's Impact on the Sisala of Ghana.* Durham, NC: Carolina Academic Press.

Murdock, Geo. P. *Africa: Its peoples and their Culture History.* New York: McGraw-Hill Book Company.

Piot, Charles. 1999. *Remotely global: Village modernity in West Africa.* Chicago: University of Chicago Press.

Radcliffe-Brown, Alfred Reginald & C. Daryll Forde (eds.). 1950. *African systems of kinship and marriage.* London: Published for the International African Institute by the Oxford University Press.

Turner, Terence J. 1997. The invention of tradition in colonial Africa. In: Grinker, R. R. & C. B. Steiner (eds.). *Perspectives on Africa: A reader in culture, history and representation.* London: Blackwell, 597–612.

Winch, Peter. 1997. Understanding a primitive society. In: Grinker, R. R. & C. B. Steiner (eds.). *Perspectives on Africa: A reader in culture, history, and representation.* London: Blackwell, 312–326.

3 RELIGION IN WEST AFRICA

West Africans living under ancient and traditional conditions saw themselves as subject to the will of a variety of spirits. This human-spirit relation was codified in myth and acted out in ritual. The various forms of animistic religion that developed in the region set up a relation between civil society and the spirit world that governed how people should act.

That ancient system has been influenced by the intrusion of two World Religions—Islam and Christianity. This chapter shows this influence and how it has played out since contact.

If religion provides meaning in life, then the significance of life has become increasingly complex with the encroachment of two more and competing explanatory systems. West Africans have struggled with this ideational chaos by (1) sticking to their original religious ways (2) adopting one or other of the World Religions (3) creating a synthesis of the external ideology and the West African one.

West Africa today presents an interesting mix of religious fervor. So-called pagans or animists often keep to themselves, practicing age-old rites without the concept of proselytization inherent in Islam and Christianity. Muslims and Christians are often in conflict and each of them has splintered, to varying degrees. Fighting between such religions and factions has sometimes led to bloodshed.

Myth and Ancestors in West African Religion

West Africa's religious tradition is embedded in mythology, rites, songs, and epic poems like the **Bagre myth** of the Ghanaian Dagara peoples and other such oral traditions (See Box 3.1). These are sagas of legendary times when the earth was being formed, when God created humankind, when early men performed dauntless feats of heroic proportions. They relate the moral ways of the founding ancestors who had received the plan of life from God or his messengers. All traditional West African myth and ritual point back to such a morality.

Box 3.1 An Excerpt from The Black Version of the Bagre Myth

In the beginning there was god,
the god of the initiates,
and their gods,

---

the god who comes,
the god with the mark between the eyes,
the god with the white and black stripes,
the god with the white arse,
the thieving god,
the lying god,
the troubling god.
He was always troubling that one
in the big byre,
that man and the younger one.
Look at the younger one,
the thoughtful one.
He hurries out
of the big byre's door
and takes the path.
He sees something.
What is it?
It is Base,
against the wall.
So he greets it,
greets it softly,
and when he has done so,
he then sets off
on a meandering path.
He walks along
and quickly reaches
the river bank,
where he sees something.
It is a large canoe,
with a smaller one, which he greets softly.
when he has done so, he sees the reeds
which he also greets.
When he has done so,
he sees a person.
What sort of person?
It is a river person,
carrying a small quiver.
He sees a woman who is wearing leaves.
He greets them both,
greets them softly,
and they showed him something.
What sort of thing?
Do you see that stone
which he shows him?
When he has done so,
he shows him the canoe
which he begins to enter.
When he has done so,
the large canoe
begins to move.
Then fear
got hold of him.
. . . .

You know
the affairs of God
bring great suffering.
But I hold it,
keep it in my hand
and look after it.
I understand
in two days
we'll enter
the White Bagre room.
I understand
in three days' time
we'll enter
the White Bagre room.
I think that
on the third day
we'll enter
the White Bagre room.
When I go in it,
if a young lad
begins to speak
and does so well,
He's he's like an old guinea cock
which begins to peck,
pecks and leaves for others,
pecks briskly.
This is what
pleases me,
for the children
to know it.
We will greet
you, Bagre god;
we will greet
you, being's god;
we will greet
you, Bagre guardian;
we will greet
you, being's guardian.
And that is why
I say to you,
in this room,
it is a many-sided matter.
I cannot
teach you it all.
To show you
would take
three years
or even six.
That's why
they call it
the Black Bagre.
It is
a matter of childbirth.

> That's why
> they call it
> the Black Bagre.
> It is
> a matter of bows.
> That's why
> they call it
> the Black Bagre.
> It is
> a matter of farming.
> That's why
> they call it
> the Black Bagre.
> It is
> a matter of chicken-breeding.
> That's why
> they call it
> the Black Bagre.
> And now it is finished,
> I tell you.

The ancestors figure prominently in West Africans' ideas about what is moral behavior. Although each West African has many progenitors, only certain persons are remembered at the ancestral shrines. These are the founding ancestors and those who, in their lives, achieved some high status or apicality in their genealogical tree. An apical ancestor is one who heads a large segment of relatives.

This remembrance is crucial to West African religion because to be remembered in ritual is essential to the retention of life after death. African cosmology assumes that for a departed person to continue to live a life similar to that which s/he lived on earth, his or her descendants must regularly call the dead person's name at ancestral sacrifices. Without this the personality vanishes.

To have eternal life, it is best that a person leave behind a large family. This improves the chance that there will be frequent rites at which his or her name will come up. A person who dies without offspring has no chance of being a *yiridindina*, as it is called in one West African language, a "remembered ancestor with a long-lasting name." If a person does not make a name for herself or himself in this life, that person's name will fade from history. One makes a name by having many children, supporting them properly and being generous to kith and kin alike.

West Africans think that the key to civic life is contained in the words of their ancestors and are embedded in ritual institutions. While it is possible for a person to pray directly to God, this is not frequently done in traditional African religions. For example, in Sisala culture, direct prayer to God can be made by placing **cowry shells** on an anthill (See Box 3.2).

Box 3.2   Cowry Shells in West Africa

Cowries are tiny seashells that originated in the Maldive Islands off the coast of Africa in the Indian Ocean. Initially they were traded into East Africa and some made it into the trade routes that went to West Africa. The shells were used as money and are still used in West Africa today in ritual exchanges e.g.,

Photo 3.1 Cowrie Shells Embedded in a Modern Cement Grave.

the payment of bridewealth or to place on shrines or graves (See Photo 3.1). The majority of the cowries were picked up by the Portuguese and used as ballast on their return trips from India. They would drop them on the West African coast and take on other trade goods at that point.

See also: http://www.cowries.net/

Because they are continuously active, ants are associated with the Supreme Being who is always there as well. Human beings can also approach *Wia*, which means God, sun and sky, through **divination.** The two forms required for this are fairy calling and throwing cowries, both of which are common in West Africa. The **fairies** are "beings of the wild" called *jinn, kantome* and a variety of other names throughout West Africa. Also, through the auspices of Islam, a person can pray to God, as they can in Christianity.

In **animism**, which was practiced ubiquitously in West Africa before the introduction of **World Religions**, the ancestors are the central spirits to whom one "prays." God is still there, but He is a distant figure, an **otiose high god.** That is, He is a deity who has left His creation in the hands of other spiritual beings—the ancestors and lesser gods who may act as mediators between humans and the Creator.

At the earth's creation, God was thought to have given shrines to humans and instructed them to perform proper sacrifices to ward off misfortune and illness. Such shrines are often mud alters (See Photo 3.2), but they can be a grove of trees, a rock or any object that acts as a place where ancestral spirits can gather to receive the libations and hear the words of their descendants. By performing these ancient rites, it is believed that living human beings maintain the good will of their ancestors, who assure them good fortune.

Myths tell people how life should be lived. Hence, we can see myth as a charter for civic culture in the community context. Myth shows the way for human beings, giving them a path to follow. In Sisala culture this is called *wongbiing titi*, the "path of truth."

Photo 3.2 An Earthen Shrine.

West African religion is philosophically elegant. The concept of a correct path is common in World Religions and across Eurasia. Note the similarity, for example, between the "true path" metaphor above and the Mormon concept of "holding to the rod." Mormon scriptures tell of a prophet's dream by a prophet in which he sees an iron rod. People who hold fast to that rod are able to safely negotiate their way through life. Those who let go of the rod fall by the wayside and are lost. So too in Taoism, the Tao means "the way."

Morality in the West African context is treating your kith and kin well, much as you would like to be treated. It is being respectful to God and nature. It is concentrating on family and community matters, not on oneself.

It is important to realize that West Africans are dynamic and flexible. Their ideas are reformulated and adjusted from time to time to adapt to changing conditions in life. Among the Yoruba of the Southern Nigerian rain forest, high-*olodumare* is the Supreme Being or Sky God. In the most ancient oral traditions, he bequeathed power to *orishanla*, a lesser communicator spirit who created the earth and placed the chosen people from the realm of the Sky God on earth at Ife, the original site of the Yoruba nation. This mythical charter guided socioreligious thought for many generations until Islam came and a new god appeared in the mythology. The creator god *Oduduwa* was now said to be from the east (Arabia?).

It seems that West Africans, like people everywhere, like things neat and tidy. So those in charge of the oral traditions began to tinker with them, and they came up with an explanatory resolution to the apparent conflict between *orishanla* and *oduduwa*. It was explained that *oduduwa* became the creator of the earth through an accident. *Oduduwa* made the earth and peopled it but could not make it work correctly. The Supreme Being then had to send *orishanla* to make the earth function properly.

This spiritual clash at the level of myth reflected a real opposition between the pre-Islamic ways and the arrival of a new religious system. At a mythological level, but not sociologically, the conflict was resolved, perhaps proving that it is easier to adjust ideologies than people's actual behavior.

Another example comes from the Savannah regions of West Africa. Originally much of this land was inhabited by scattered settlements of people living under local headmen who were also religious functionaries. The religious leaders, called *tendanas* or *tenteing-tiinas* were considered to be "custodians of the Earth." They were usually the senior most men of the autochthonal (original) lineages of the aboriginal inhabitants.

Then mounted warriors arrived who conquered the landowners or sometimes peaceably settled among them with the result that communities became mixed. The Tallensi studied by Meyer Fortes were, at the time of his fieldwork in the 1930s, comprised of the *talis*, the original inhabitants and the "owners of the land" and the *namoos*, newcomers who had brought the concept of secular chiefship. Thus, such social groups came to have dual leadership—*tendanas* dealing with the ancestor cult[1] and rituals concerning the earth; and the **Na** or chief, the holder of a secular office, dealing with matters of political organization.

Twin governance is common in the Savannah region of West Africa. Accordingly, origin myths have often been adjusted to explain how dual governance is the primal way of the cultural heroes, the early forbears. New traditions become interwoven with aboriginal ones. At the level of ideas there is a blending between newcomers and **autochthons**. The new situation is re-legitimized or re-mythologized in new legends.

Myths also deal with such philosophical questions as: "What is truth?" or "What is the nature of the world and how does it work?" or: "What is moral behavior?" One answer given in African tradition is that an *élan vital* or life force flows through the cosmos—**occult power**. In Sisala culture this is called *dolung*. It can neither be created nor destroyed, but it can be harnessed, used or dissipated by misuse. *Dolung* can be concentrated in shrines and by the use of some set phrases, but mainly it is controlled through the performance of certain rites and blood sacrifices on appropriate altars or

---

1. A cult is a social group based on commonly held beliefs, but one usually conside~
mally organized than a church.

Photo 3.3 Child with Medicinal Talisman.

at sacred sites, much like the performance of the Catholic Mass is thought to transform the Eucharist, where the celebratory wine is turned into the blood of Christ.

Box 3.3 West African Cannibalism

Cannibalism (also called anthropophagy) was not widespread in West Africa, though its practice has been recorded. It is a widespread custom going back into early human history and it has been found among peoples on most continents. Some indications point to its practice as early as Neolithic times. The Greek historian Herodotus and other ancient writers described various cannibalistic peoples. Several motives have been proposed for cannibalism. In some cultures, it was believed that the person who ate the dead body of another would acquire the desired qualities of the person eaten, particularly of a brave enemy. Another belief was that the enemy's spirit would be annihilated or absorbed by the eater—his *élan vital* would be mixed with that of his killer. This eliminated any chance of vengeful ghosts.

Ritual provides a communications channel to the ancestors and an access to the life force of the universe. It is thought that when men use ritual frequently and properly, they make the ancestors happy, and the ancestors make supernatural power available to their living kin. Such concentrations of the life force in shrines, talismans, and sacred objects are necessary to protect the living against death, accident and illness and other misfortune (See Photo 3.3).

The life force is the greatest truth in the cosmos. The soul is a concentration of it. If the body loses the soul, it dies. If a community of kin loses the spiritual concentration of spiritual energy it has amassed to protect its members, it will begin to suffer ill fortune. When this happens, it is a sure sign that the ritual leaders need to reinvigorate

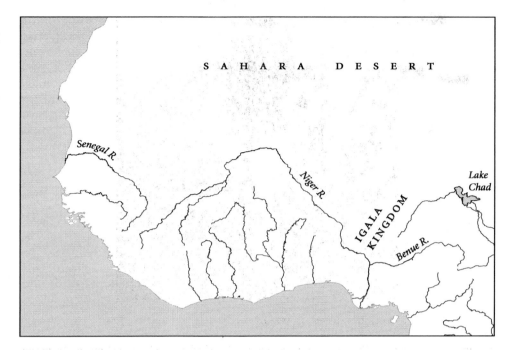

Map 3.1 Igala Kingdom.

the community's shrines and sacred places with a new infusion of mystical power. This is done through blood sacrifice.

Myth and the relation of the people to their ancestors is not a static ideology, but rather can be put to use, revised and applied in any political situation. To show this I will use the example from the Nigerian kingdom of Igala, which lies in a triangle at the confluence of the Benue and Niger Rivers, with its capital at Idah (See Map 3.1).

As in most West African societies, the past validates the present. The Igala give something credence by saying *abogujo igbili,* "it was known to the ancestors."

The Igala have two kinds of legends, *ohiala* and *ita. Ohiala* are fanciful fireside stories, fables and folk tales that are known to play with the facts. *Ita* are factual myths that function as a social charter. *Ita* portray history as it happened. Mostly *ita* are the histories of specific clans, but the myth of the royal clan is thought to depict the history of the entire Igala nation. It is seen as a dynastic record that uses the Igala king list to create a linear history of the entire kingdom. In other words, mythical validation proceeds logically rather than historically, reflecting the fact that subsequent keepers of the oral history have periodically adjusted the record. In fact, as J. S. Boston points out, *ita* are most likely creatively retold stories that reorganize the past to meet the political needs of the present. Professor Boston says:

> If the traditions are seen in their true perspective it at once appears that the mythological phase of the past is of paramount importance, and that historical function is correspondingly subordinate to the political function of the myths contained in these traditions.

By the "mythological phase" Boston is referring to the protodynastic period, an uncertain time when culture heroes lived. Protodynastic ancestors are represented in

contemporary kingship rites by a single symbolic cult object: the primal staff of the
Ata or king.

Though there were four known ancestors from this period, their individual names
are not recited. Also, these forebears are represented by only one grave in the royal
tomb. In this mythopoetic era, the specifics are less important than the collapse of history into a general "time before."

When the annual kinship rites are carried out, the primal staff representing these
early ancestors is offered the first libation, then the officiants proceed to pour libations
to each of the other twenty-two staffs at graveside.

The protodynastic period is the first phase in Igala mythology and is known as the
"age before Agagba" who was the first dynastic king in the royal genealogy. The mythology of this initial period establishes the relation between royals and commoners. It depicts the former as bearing hereditary kingship and the latter as the original owners of
the land, by virtue of the fact that their ancestors were the original inhabitants of the region. The mythical charter thus establishes and stresses the complementarity between
royals and non-royals, each having specific rights and duties *vis-à-vis* each other.

The second phase of lore in Igala society concerns the female *Ata*, Queen Ebele-
jonu. She became infatuated with a male Ibo slave and married him. She died childless, but her husband, a slave and a non-descendant, could not become king. Instead
the office went to the brother of the Queen.

Descent is an important principle in West Africa. In this legend, we see that descent
overrides achieved status. It reaffirms the primacy of kinship over non-kinship, claiming that opportunism is not the basis of rule, but that the monarchy is vested in royal
descent.

Yet the position of the immigrant king is also ambiguous. Unlike most West African
men, the Igala king wears earrings. This is inexplicable without reference to their
mythology, which describes the male *Ata* as the "wife" of the *Achadu*, the office held by
the man who represents commoner clans, who are the owners of the earth. As head of
the Igala Mela clan, he is head of the clan leaders who function as a council of kingmakers. Symbolically, the council represents the people. Thus royals are contrasted to
commoners. While royals are privileged, symbolically through myth and ritual the
male king is represented as a subordinate "wife" to the *Achadu*, and hence subservient
to the people. This is a classic case of a **rite of reversal**, wherein roles are symbolically
inverted. The supreme monarch is an inferior, while the *Achadu*, who represents the
subordinate commoners, is elevated to superior status. This principle is based on the
domestic model of superordination-subordination, the husband-wife relation from
the Igala household.

In an interesting installation rite for the new king, the *Achadu* participates in a ritual
"beating of his wife," then sends the king to the *Achadu*'s own senior wife to have his
ears pierced like a woman. As a "female," the *Ata* acts out his subordinate status to the
kingmakers. Through myth and ritual, the ambivalence of governance is expressed.

The third phase of Igala mythology, Agagba, is the beginning of history for the Igala.
The relative status of clans within the royal strata is measured by the closeness of their
genealogical connection to Agagba. In this historical phase, the war with the Jukun plays
a prominent role. Before Agagba, the Igala had paid tribute to the Jukun. The myth relates that Agagba was able to defeat the Jukun and stop payment of tribute by using cunning and **magic** (*juju*) to confuse his enemy, then destroying them militarily.

Such cunning and strategy are needed because, as another prominent theme in Igala
lore shows, the *Ata* frequently succeeded to office in a weakened position, and the king-

dom is often vulnerable in some way at the time of ascendancy. For the Igala this is a statement about the ambiguity inherent in the conflict between acephaly and kingship. Royal Igala myth is a symbolic statement about achievement and ascription. Even though the king has succeeded to office through descent (ascription), he still must earn prominence (achievement) as a king, carrying his kingdom to glory with him. According to Igala **ethos**, privileged office must be supplemented with hard work.

For example, in the myth about Agagba and the Jukun, the soon-to-be *Ata* used deception at the Jukun palace to confuse the foreign king. Then, upon his return home, Agagba found that his father had died, and that he had become the *Ata*. Shortly thereafter the Jukun attacked. Agagba was able to hold his own, but could not repel them. In Igala myth a new king is often portrayed as weak. Therefore, a neophyte king must prove himself. He did this by consulting the Ifa oracle of the Yoruba which told him to consult an Islamic priest in his court. He counseled with a Nupe *Mallam* in Idah, the capital of Igalaland. But the *Mallam* gave him some very disturbing news. To achieve victory over the Jukun, he had to sacrifice his favorite daughter to the earth in order to curry the favor of the Igala ancestors. He refused, but his daughter heard about the oracle's advice and voluntarily offered to sacrifice her life for the good of the kingdom. The king refused nine times, but finally the daughter was killed along with her slaves.

At that point, the *Mallam* gave some medicinal charms to Agagba, who was instructed to throw them into the river. The Jukun army was camped on the other side. When they ate the fish that had eaten the medicine, they died. Agagba then advanced on the weakened force and drove them from the kingdom. Thus, it is said that Agagba was the first to set the kingdom's boundaries.

Thus, the *Ata* was able to achieve victory through cunning and the use of magic. This myth also shows that the king has a ritual responsibility to the autochthonal ancestors (and hence commoners), and must maintain a proper relationship with the earth (which in West Africa is a metaphor for the progenitors of the living). The myth indicates that the king could not fulfill his mission to rule without honoring the ancestors and the earth and, by analogy, could not win without the people. The king is both dominant over the people and dependent upon them. The survival of the royal dynasty is dependent on proper maintenance of a ritual relation to the land, the ancestors and the common people.

Agagba is portrayed in most clan myths as the creator of the system of hereditary titles in the Igala political system. He is said to have given these titles, and their associated privileges, to clan heads that assisted in the Jukun war. As hereditary privileges, they structured the relations of royalty to commoners and of privileged commoners to less fortunate commoners. Today most clans, including newcomers, trace descent to Agagba to legitimate their claims to citizenship.

In order to renew the strength of the kingdom as a polity, annual ceremonies are held to regenerate the connection between the king's royal clan and the Igala Mela clan (kingmakers), who are a symbol of all commoners. The *Achadu*, as head of the Igala Mela, is the "husband" of the king, and dominates him, but is also dominated by him. The powerful *Ata* also has an ambivalent status. He is the supreme power in a secular sense, but is ritually and symbolically dependent on his "husband" the *Achadu* and the common people.

Myth in West African religion acts as a legendary injunction to establish and maintain the moral order. Rather than life adjusting to myth, it is often the other way round. Mythmakers and storytellers continually adapt myth to political and material realities in life, bringing the legends into balance with such lived experience. In the living reality of everyday life, as myth provides a guide to behavior, that very behavior is constantly altering the charter.

Religious Ideas and the Material World

Myths relate that in the dim past when West Africa was first being populated, nature was large and humans were small—nature was powerful and dangerous and the human community was feeble and tenuous by comparison.

Early settlements in the region were composed of small groups of relatives with just a handful of distant neighbors. The hamlets were separated from each other by large expanses of threatening bush. Thus, each settlement formed a psychological wall around itself, looking inward for safety and community. The members of a settlement had common interests, and they centered on production and reproduction, thus their religious ideas naturally reflect this twin focus.

In this context, a person without a family and community would be in serious trouble. In order to survive, the group had to stress cooperation. Just as with the Greek term *ekklêsia,* an African community was both a political assembly of citizens *and* a religious congregation. Basil Davidson, in *The African Genius* describes the African village in ancient times:

> This political unit was, even more, an economic one. Having made their homeland, the cluster of families had to survive in it. They could survive only by a process of trial and error as they grappled with its ecology; with its tsetse or floods of rain, its shallow soil or towering forest trees, its slides of hillside pasture or pockets of arable land amid lizard-gleaming humps of rock. This was the saving process of invention and adaptation that round out the group's charter and gave, to those who were fortunate, the sanction of success.

In other words, the culture that evolved emphasized the relation between humans and nature, between village and bush. This was not an easy place to live. To be successful required ingenuity, perseverance and a group of people willing to work together to overcome the vagaries of nature. They did this by creating a series of sociocultural formations that stressed the importance of the group over the individual. Africans did not survive as individuals, but as communities.

West African life is highly gendered, that is, men and women have different roles based on their biological inheritance. Reproduction of children and growing of crops, were female roles and were largely carried out inside the safety of the settlement, thus the village came to be seen as a female domain. Men hunted and dealt with intruders by venturing into the bush (See Photo 3.4). Not surprisingly then, the bush was defined as male. Further, the sky was male and the earth female, with the semen-like rain bringing life-giving fertility to Mother Earth.

Living in a high-risk environment breeds a conservative culture and West Africans accordingly developed a system that viewed any change as an injury to the protective social fabric. In this paradigm, ancestral rules were presented as ideal. The model postulated a perfect balance between society and nature, but only if humans would follow the rules.

When things go wrong it is because humans deviate from the rules. On the other hand, people have to experiment and innovate in order to survive. For example, the

Photo 3.4 A Hunter's Trophies.

intricate knowledge the West African farmer has about soils, climate and the stars—
all derive from eons of experimentation and accumulated knowledge that has built up
over time (See Box 3.4, Science on the Rooftop).

Box 3.4 Science on the Rooftop

While sitting on a rooftop with several villagers in 1970 one night in Sisalaland, Northern Ghana I remember being amazed by the use of the stars to guide
planting. We were drinking native beer (*pito*) and gazing at the stars. Noncha-
lantly one man turned to another and simply said, "I see that our planting star
has arrived. Tomorrow we must take the seeds to the farm." I looked at the sky
and saw nothing, certainly no obvious message about agriculture, but then I

lacked the accumulated experience of the thousands of West African farmers who sat observing the sky putting that information together with their experience about climate, soils, rainfall, etc to devise an adaptive system.

At that moment I came to realize that their science was in their heads, in the collective knowledge passed on from generation to generation. I looked to the fringes of our candlelight and saw the eager faces of children, little boys who always seemed to hang on the edge of adult groups, watching, listening and learning. Then I understood that education was an informal process, one in which science is absorbed by each new generation the members of which may add on small touches of their own as they put such knowledge to work making a living in that environment.

This presented a conflict for early leaders in West Africa: their religion said that truth was fixed and the social order was sacred and inviolate, yet they needed to be flexible enough to incorporate adaptive changes and innovations. They reconciled this contradiction through divination (See Box 3.5).

Box 3.5   Divination

Divination is a means of contacting the spirit world. There are two main forms—mechanical and by possession. In its mechanical form diviners use some physical means to ascertain messages from the occult realm. They throw lots, read the movement of animals in the sand or interpret sequences of code-objects. There are many ways diviners do this in West Africa, but the end result is the receipt of a message from the divine world to instruct the living how to act. Possession has the same end, but the method involves a spirit entering the body of the diviner. In a trance state, the diviner then communicates with living clients. Most diviners are paid for their services, just as **shamans** or local medical practitioners are paid.

In a possessed state, a diviner may tell people things that would otherwise be difficult, thereby injecting new ideas into society (See Photo 3.5). In mechanical divination, elders could manipulate the outcome of oracular sessions so that their innovations appeared to come from the ancestors. Using *vugung* divination among the Sisala, it became possible for an elder to present new ideas as sacred, as the pronouncements of the ancestral spirits. Speaking of African culture, Basil Davidson was aware of this when he said that "innovations, in order to become acceptable, had to be absorbed within an ancestral system which, by definition, was itself opposed to experiment or change."

The message here is that science has to be closeted within the armament of authoritative office. A woman or a junior male cannot openly appear to change the system. Only an elder can, through the unquestionable authority of divinatory pronouncements.

The West African concept of fate gives humans a paradigmatic safety value, a way out of the contradiction in their ideal order. For example, in the ideal paradigm of kinship amity and unity, the kin group should never split apart. Yet it frequently does because of a contradiction in the system itself as it articulates with the environment—the system is designed to generate food and as many children as possible. But the frag-

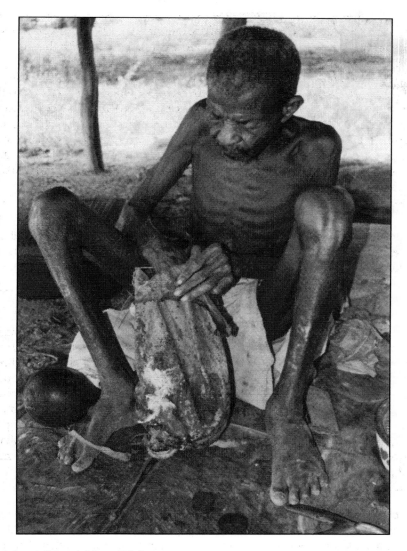

Photo 3.5   A West African Diviner.

ile ecosystem will not support high concentrations of people that stress the resources of the area. Those who wish to break out on their own are more likely to find better re-sources elsewhere—more access to water, land, firewood and so forth. Thus, the very reproductive success of lineage growth (coupled with bickering and interpersonal con-flicts) creates the tendency for group **fission**. The paradigm produces its own antithe-sis. The group should never splinter; but reproductive success (which is tied to pro-ductive success) causes it to do so.

The guarantee of survival in a dangerous material world called for strict adherence to specific and proven patterns of conduct. This is an etic view taken by ethnologists—ecology forms the structure of thought and sociocultural formations in society. West Africans take a different view. They see that their sociocultural formations are sacred trusts inherited from the kin group's forebears. The rules surrounding domestic, political and economic affairs are defined as immutable truth—"divinely unchangeable," so to speak.

An ecological anthropologist would say that politics, economics and religion in West Africa arose from the need to adapt to a harsh environment. Of course, it can be stated the other way round: that the ideas of the ancestor cult allowed continued life and adaptation in that dangerous world of the bush. Certainly, under such austere conditions with limited technology, sudden moves would have been risky, perhaps even disastrous and deadly. Common sense would have led one to conform to the norms, given the fact that isolated villagers had few alternatives.

Religion and Politics

Religious ideas can be useful to politicians. Most systems of social control and political power reinforce the mandates of political leaders with religious precepts. This is true of **acephalous peoples** whose gerontocratic headmen utilize the purported power of the ancestors to control their subordinates. It is also true of states. Among the Jukun of Nigeria, the *Aku* the Divine King had great powers of governance but he was subject to many ritual taboos that curtailed any tendency toward despotism. Jukun government was a theocracy in which the *Aku* represented Deity and constituted a link between the spiritual realm and his subjects. According to legend, the *Aku* was supreme, but in reality the customs and precepts of the Jukun government provided checks and balances (See Box 3.6, the Jukun *Aku*).

Box 3.6   The Jukun *Aku*

In the eyes of the people, the *Aku* was connected to economic success. Amongst this agricultural people, he was judged by the results of the harvest. Any breach of taboo and the harvest could be bad and the fortunes of the Jukun would decline. In fact, this is one of the functions of such a plethora of prohibitions. Any ill wind could be attributed to a breach of rule because there were so many, that no ruler could be considered entirely blameless.

Furthermore, the *Aku* had a council of advisors headed by the *Abu*, a kind of Prime Minister. His advisors could show disapproval of the *Aku* by boycotting his religious ceremonies, a procedure that could embarrass the king and undermine his authority and curb any dictatorial tendencies.

Additionally, there were many court priests. They were the guardians of the relics of previous *Akus*. As such, they could hold a headstrong king to ransom by threatening to expose these sacred objects to the public eye. Exposed sacredness becomes less sacred. Not only were the objects sacred and in need of sheltering, but the *Aku* himself was thought to be divine and could only be approached indirectly.

Thus, instead of ruling alone, problems and complaints for the king's advisement had to come through his counselors and priests. Thus, these advisors had a ready means of determining cases privately without the knowledge of the *Aku*, or of being a strong influence on his thinking.

We can see that sacredness puts a king on a pedestal, but from such a lofty and precarious perch it is difficult to reign without aids. The wise Divine King among the Jukun would in practice try not to alienate his counselors and priests. As representatives of the people of the Jukun State, these advisors, in effect, made the king beholden to the masses, as he was thought to be responsible to the gods.

In short, divine kingship in Africa often functions to limit the powers of the king through his mythical attachment to deity ensuring that the democracy so common in stateless communities would continue with the rise of hierarchical rule.

The Moral Order in Traditional Thought

The traditional moral order was "robustly collective" as one Africanist put it. Today, that ethos is under fire from modernism and the penetration of materialism from the West. However, when compared to more industrialized societies, those in West Africa still retain many precepts of collectivism, as Charles Piot has portrayed in his fine book, *Remotely Global*. In this work he shows that in spite of the rise of national politics, migration and advancing modernity in their lives, the Kabre of Northern Togo still possess a strong community spirit, still invest in social relationships, both for gain and because of their intrinsic value.

In societies like the Kabre, the Sisala and the Tallensi of West Africa, personal accumulation is downplayed, though respected in those who have become big men or wealthy women. This respect, however, is always tinged with a hint of envy. It is not that West Africans do not desire more things—they do. This can be seen among Awuna women who have recently got more money in their pockets through growing cash-crops. They invest much of it in their children and family members, but they also buy luxury items. This may be a certain highly prestigious cooking pot displayed proudly in the kitchen, but never used for cooking. It is a small ostentation, but ostentation nevertheless. However miniscule it whispers "look at me—I've made it."

As a rule, however, the good of the community is placed ahead of that of the individual. I do not wish to romanticize West African village life. It still remains a hard life for most. Many are leaving the countryside for cities. Rural life is often short and difficult, and the conservative community order does hold back innovation, creating material backwardness at times.

Some critics of Western society claim that it has become poverty stricken in the midst of plenty—an impoverishment of spirit and values. This cannot be said of West African culture. As it developed, it evolved into a strong civic culture, with a strong moral order governing its settlements. Many West Africans are poverty-stricken in material terms, but they are rich in human capital. If these societies lacked a certain dynamism, they excelled in subtler humanistic and civic ways.

West African moral codes contain principles of good and evil, but ones that differ from the morality of the industrialized world. Their morality is not connected to sex or poverty, as it is in the West. For example, Americans recently were in an uproar over President Clinton's alleged sexual indiscretions, a furor my West African informants found silly. Again, in the West we incarcerate or look down upon vagrants and those who have fallen on hard times. If they are not jailed, they certainly are shunned and ignored. My Ghanaian friends find such behavior out of kilter with their ideals. Do West Africans ever gossip about sexual indiscretions or ignore poor people? Yes, but, on the whole, morality is not about these matters, nor is it about shame of body, as in

Judeo-Christian values. Rather, the moral order of West Africans developed to enhance and extend human relations in life and into the next life as well.

This ethos developed in small isolated villages, but when these settlements grew in size or strangers moved into the area, new people were incorporated into the community, not always as kin, but in some way that established reciprocal rights and duties between parties. Their social contract both extended outward to others in society, and backwards and forwards in time, to include one's forbears who were thought to continue to live in the netherworld. This contract was a legendary constitution, an oral and ritual pact between the living and the dead.

I have tried to show that ecological success in the West African context required cooperation. Almost all West African societies utilize oracles and divination to reinforce the moral order. The West African moral order is all about incorporating people or labor into fixed relationships, ones that are both valued and useful.

Cosmology and Causation in West African Religion

The anthropologist A. F. C. Wallace defines religion as a set of rites, validated by myth, which mobilizes supernatural powers to achieve or prevent transformations of the ways things are with regard to people and nature. West African religion is not usually very far from the most worldly of actions—farming, going on a journey or building a house. It is part and parcel of everyday life. Yet, since these activities have always been important to survival, they are usually ritualized.

Europeans often divide the cosmos into a binary opposition between the natural world and the supernatural world. West Africans would understand this, but their tendency is to see more connections between the realms than differences. What is natural can be affected by forces from the unseen world, and sometimes the occult world shows itself to humans such as when bush fairies or gnomes reveal themselves to the living, or when the unborn or dead appear in dreams. In West African religion the dead do not return to a God in heaven, but live on spiritually in a world very similar to this one, but without its pain and tribulation—a paradise of sorts.

West African religion tends to lack the concept of salvation. Both the moral exemplar and the scoundrel will live on in the next life if they leave behind large families and their kin propitiate them at the ancestral shrines.

While Western scientists may see neutral forces at work in the universe and statisticians may account for events in terms of probability, West African village philosophers would see misfortune and causation differently. Causation in West Africa is personalized, that is, all events, good or bad, ultimately have some volition behind them, human or supernatural. Accidents don't just happen—they are willed by some sentient being, either of this world or the other world.

Take the case of snakebite. A man is walking home from his farm and a snake bites him. A scientist could figure out the statistical probability of the man being bitten by a snake, if he knew such variables as how many snakes there were in the area, how many times the man passed along the trail, and so on. West Africans are more interested to know what sentient being caused the snake to be there at that time and to bite that particular man.

When health workers explain the germ theory of illness to West Africans, they have no trouble with it. Yes, there are bad things in the world—wild animals, snakes, biting insects—why not germs too? The question the African asks is: "If I get sick from germs, who caused the germs to afflict me?" Germs and snakes are proximate causes, but the African searches his personalized universe more deeply to find the ultimate cause. This is where oracles and diviners fit into the picture—through their auspices an afflicted person or his relatives can discern the underlying causes of misfortune.

West African religion postulates that the cosmos is underpinned by a life force and sentient beings that use that force to affect the living. I will use the Sisala term, *dolung* in reference to this force. The early anthropologist R. R. Marret called this theory of universal power in nature, **animatism**. To West Africans such *dolung* causes all processes, gives animation to all living things, and is intimately tied up with the world of hyperphysicality. The nature of this *dolung* is that it can be harnessed or lost. The soul, for example, is a concentrated form of *dolung*. When the body loses it temporarily, the person goes into a coma or sleeps. Permanent loss leads to death.

When a shrine, medicine bundle or amulet is infused with *dolung* through ritual, it increases in sacredness and usefulness. It is a supercharged repository of *dolung*. That can have causal control over people or events. I have often heard villagers speak of their shrines as if they were sentient and willful beings. In fact, most shrines have names—for example, a mud altar may be called *Bosung* and the shrine-owner will invoke *Bosung* by name and ask him to do something on his behalf. Thus, when harnessed, *dolung* takes on consciousness and appears to be alive and capable of acting.

All societies have good and bad people. *Dolung*-infused objects or substances can be used both to protect and to harm. Those West Africans who keep shrines, use native medicines or wear amulets, do so for protection against malevolence. Yet, there are also thought to be aggressive and sinister people who use these powerful substances and objects to injure others or create havoc (See the discussion of witchcraft below). Of course, this is the very malevolence against which people use charms, shrines and **counter-magic**.

Sir Edward B. Tylor, another early anthropologist, developed the concept of animism to refer to primitive religions. To him, the most basic religion was based on a belief in spirit beings. When people saw unborn babies, themselves and the dead in dreams, they reasoned that souls must exist and be able to travel. Tylor wrote that early humans created a pantheon of souls, spirits, gods and all sorts of preternatural beings, based on dream visions. By this definition, certainly practitioners of traditional religion in West Africa could be called **animists**. In addition to the Supreme Creator, they believe in all sorts of spirits, gods and unseen forces.

As they learned about the African pantheon, early Christian missionaries accused Africans of being polytheistic. Of course, they are no more so than Christians who believe in angels, the devil, saints and have institutionalized exorcism rituals to expunge evil spirits who have infiltrated a possessed person's body. European missionaries also accused Africans of not believing in God. This is nonsense. Every African religion with which I am familiar has a concept of an otiose high god, usually associated with the sky and sun just as is the Christian deity who is associated with brilliant light and a heaven above. The African God is a creator god who, once his job was done, withdrew to his residence on high and left the running of life on earth to lesser spirit beings.

We can divide religious rites into two categories—rituals of intensification and those of passage. The former are usually performed at some crisis in life. Social scientists tell us that such rites have twin functions. First, they give psychological relief to the anxious individual by providing an action outlet and giving the individual the sense of *doing* something. It may not work, but it feels better than *not doing* anything. Secondly, ritual has a social function. It brings people together at a time of crisis. Collective performance of the rite binds people together and enhances communication to deal with the crisis.

For example, Jack Goody, in his book *Death, Property and Ancestors* showed that among the Dagara peoples of West Africa, funerary rituals function to administer the reallocation of the social roles of the departed. This is common throughout West Africa. Funerals act to redistribute a person's property, formal offices (such as a headmanship) or even informal roles such as that of a lover. Since death creates a void in the social fabric, ritual reweaves it, providing new actors in broken social relationships.

Rites of passage take place when a person vacates one status to take on another. West Africans normally mark such occasions symbols of separation such as shaving the head or discarding old clothes. Next comes a state of transition called **liminality**. At this stage of the ritual the transitional figure is "betwixt and between" social roles. This is a highly sacred and dangerous state and is often symbolized by painting the body white or wearing clothes that are turned inside out. The last part of the ritual involves incorporation into the new social role. This is often signified by donning new clothes or incising facial marks that indicate a new position in life.

An example of such a *rite de passage* in West Africa is that undergone by Mende (Sierra Leone) girls as they are incorporated into the Sande **secret society** (See Box 3.7). This is a type of **sodality** that is common in West Africa. It is secret in the sense that it has concealed knowledge, information divulged only to initiates.

Box 3.7   Mende Female Rites of Passage

Once Mende girls menstruate (separation between girl and woman), rituals are performed and the girls are removed from society and placed in seclusion for weeks or even months—a state of liminality. Upon leaving girlhood and entering the seclusion hut in the bush (a "not-village" state of liminality) the females remove their old clothes indicative of childhood. Their bodies are painted with white clay and they don brief skirts and many strands of beads.

Shortly afterwards they undergo a **clitoridectomy**, surgery that removes the girl's clitoris and part of the *labia minora*. In Mende society, it is thought that this genital mutilation enhances the girl's procreative potential. Sociologically, it is another transition symbol in the rite of passage. During the healing process and throughout their seclusion, the girls are instructed in how to be a woman. From Sande members, they receive instructions about sex, marriage, childbirth and the rearing of children.

Some in the West look on the mutilation of a girl's *genitalia* as cruel, and there are social movements against what they call **FGM** (female genital mutilation), but when viewed from the perspective of Mende culture, this is an important event in the life of a girl. She will never be considered a woman without it.

The period of separation is a time when the initiates bond, sing songs, dance and tell stories. They are thought to be under ritual protection from all malevolence while isolated. They are well fed, and find themselves the center of attention. Such initiates acquire a positive image of womanhood and a strong sense of sisterhood. It is very clear to them that they are soon to be women—officially.

At the end of their stay in the bush, the fledgling women emerge from the hut to be washed in a special medicinal concoction thought to be instrumental in removing the state of liminality, permitting them to leave the ritual protection of this transitional state and become full women. They are now marriageable and they know who they are—Mende women and members of the important Sande secret society (Mende men have a counterpart in the Poro secret society).

Sacrifice, Magic and Witchcraft in West Africa

Sacrifice, or the taking of animal life as part of ritual, is perhaps as old as humankind. Much has been written about why blood is shed in ritual. In general blood use is a human universal and functions as a symbol of social unity or kinship. Therefore, it is the perfect symbolic link between the living and the dead. Furthermore, when blood is drained onto a shrine, it is thought to infuse the shrine with power, making it more effective and enabling it to serve as a protector of the social group. If animal blood imparts power, human blood is considered even more potent.

Magic is a widespread concept that is equally at home in rural African villages or in American sports (also, note the magical properties claimed in dishwashing soap commercials!). But for most anthropologists, magic is the supposed use of supernatural power by a person to try to control human actions or natural events. In an illusory way, magic often seems to achieve results, but the results actually have other causes. There is some evidence to show, for example, that if a magician casts a mortal spell on a true believer, the victim will fall ill or even die due to **somatic compliance**, the shutting down of life systems due to severe depression.

Many anthropologists classify magic as homeopathic or contagious, according to its associative principle. The anthropologist Sir James G. Frazer first described these magical types in his book *The Golden Bough* (1890). **Homeopathic or imitative magic** is based on the belief that "like produces like." In this form of magic, shamans act out or imitate what they want to happen. They often use a likeness of whatever they want to influence. For example, a hunter may make a model of an antelope and pretend he is shooting it. He believes this magical imitation will assure him a successful hunt. Some West African peoples do not like their photographs taken for this reason—a practitioner of **sorcery** may work an evil spell on the photograph, which, as a good likeness, will cause harm to the person in the picture.

Contagious magic is based on the principle that once two things have had intimate contact, a magical spell on one will influence the other. Some West Africans are careful not to leave cuttings of their hair or fingernails lying around for fear that a witch may find them and work a spell over them.

Envoutement is when a magician sticks pins in a doll to harm someone. When the two forms are put together by making a doll in the likeness of a person, then dressing it in clothes made from cloth that had been in close contact with that person, it is thought to be very dangerous.

Many West Africans of a traditional stripe operate under a **personalistic theory of causation**. The flip side of highly concentrated congeries of kinsmen, affines and

Photo 3.6   A Leather War Smock with Talismans.

neighbors is the production of conflict, envy, and even hatred. These emotions are strongly suppressed—at least outwardly—by the norms of kinship amity. But they are sometimes expressed or thought to be expressed by means of black magic or **witchcraft**. An example of this occurred early in my fieldwork. A very big man in Tumu who had led an exemplary life came down with what I deemed to be cancer. He was robust man who literally withered away to a skeleton in a matter of weeks. However, he told me that it was witchcraft, that certain factions within his large and powerful extended family had resented his success and his desire to become a chief. In his estimation, they had employed sorcery to kill him. Shortly after he told me this, he did indeed die.

Magic can also involve spells that are thought to aid a person or social group. As possessors of the "word" (literacy) to early West Africans, the Muslims seemed to own strong magic and more than one ***Mallam*** made a living placing "special" words into an amulet worn about the neck, or sometimes sown onto the war garments of West African soldiers (See Photo 3.6).

A magician may employ a special object or **fetish** to do harm or to protect something valuable—the family or the farm, for example. Traditional part-time magicians may be called to be a member of a healing cult, or they may be entrepreneurial practitioners who strive to make a living at their craft.[2] Both men and women may be magicians or healers.

People tend to use good luck charms and magical spells as an edge in activities that cause high anxiety. For example, Sisala farmers place magical stones in their fields, painted with a special design made from a dark medicinal paint. It is thought to ward off witches who may come into the farm and suck the life force out of the crops. Since crops may fail or appear stunted in some fields and not in others, the theory is invoked

---

2. Such practitioners are usually paid in money or kind, but generally there is no fixed price.

to provide an explanation for this variation. Also, the use of protective magic explains success at farming.

People tend to forget magic's failures and are more impressed by its apparent successes. They may consider magic successful if it appears to work only ten per cent of the time, but no West African farmer or cattle herder is going to keep track of the percentage of successes or failures involved. Even when magic fails, people often explain away the failure without doubting the power of the magic. They may say that the magician made a mistake in reciting the spell or that another magician cast a more powerful spell against the magician.

West African culture developed under harsh living conditions. Many anthropologists postulate that people have faith in magic because they have a psychological need to believe in it. It is reassuring. People may turn to magic to reduce their fear and uncertainty if they feel they have no control over the outcome of a situation—and West Africa is full of situations in which humans have little control—bad weather, insects, wild animal attacks and the like.

Anxiety does not necessarily go away with the advance of education or science. The Ibibio of Nigeria have become increasingly exposed to modern scientific training and education, yet their reliance on witchcraft as an explanation for misfortune *has increased*. Ethnographic evidence shows that accusations of witchcraft rise in proportion to the amount of chaos or social disruption in an area. Among the Ibibio, life has involved just such a clash of traditional and European ways of life. In fact, it is the younger, more educated Ibibio who tend to make accusations of witchcraft against others, usually older, more traditional seniors in society. In this way, intergenerational tensions and hostility are expressed in their fast-changing society.

Similarly in Ibibio communities, if an enterprising young man cannot get a job or fails an exam, if a woman cannot control meddling in-laws, if someone loses their money on a fanciful scheme, if someone is struck by lightening, it can always be attributed to witchcraft. Indeed, virtually all misfortune can be seen as the result of the malevolent actions of sorcerers. Even though the Ibibio have alternative explanations of events through science or World Religions, they do not always see such explanations as opposed to the sorcery paradigm.

Who practices witchcraft? Ibibio witches are seen as persons of either gender who have within them a substance acquired from another witch. This acquired matter is comprised of red, white and black threads, needles and other nefarious ingredients that have been swallowed by the receiving witch. This magical substance holds a special power that enables the new witch to cause harm or death. This may come from conscious intent, or the witch may unknowingly cause harm to others. This is one of the reasons why people openly confess to being witches, claiming that they did not want to cause havoc, but have inadvertently been passed a sorcerer's concoction.

Witch power is thought to be purely psychic. Ibibio witches do not make use of evil medicines or perform rites to harm other (though some West African sorcerers do). The ingested matter gives them the ability to change into animals, to fly and to travel at the speed of light. Witches are thought to transfer the victim's soul or *élan vital* into an animal, and then the animal is devoured, killing the victim.

How can you spot an Ibibio witch? The Ibibio look for people who act deviantly in terms of the norms of their society like those who keep to themselves or enjoy flaunting deviant behavior or charge high prices for their market goods. Witches are apt to look and act mean. Witchcraft is the antithesis of appropriate behavior, but there are gradients of deviance. The Ibibio divide witches into categories of "black witches" who do absolutely evil things like eating children and committing incest and "white witches" who are mildly nonconforming, causing minor problems in society.[3]

Witchcraft is invoked as an explanation for social conflict throughout West Africa. For example, among the Grunshi peoples, who are farmers, the Fulani herders care for their cattle. Thus, the Grunshi trust the Fulani pastoralists with a lot of "hoof wealth." On the other hand, some Fulani are said to be thieves. It is said that they collaborate with brigands who come in and steal the cattle, take them to distant markets and sell them.

The Grunshi find themselves in a position where they have to trust people in which they have little faith. Consequently, they have ambivalent feelings toward the Fulani, and this conflict is manifest in the belief that Fulani can turn into monkeys and come into Grunshi houses, gnaw on food, cause yams to go bad in the fields and raise all sorts of mischief in Grunshi communities.

Islam in West Africa

While Christianity has only been around in a serious way in West Africa for about one hundred years, Islam has a thousand-year tradition in the region. Given this lengthy coexistence with animism, it is surprising that Islam has not made more inroads than it has.

Part of the reason could lie in the fact that Islam lacks a "Vatican." It is not bureaucratized and has no formal church. It is a lay religious movement in which missionary work is the responsibility of the individual. A good Muslim should proselytize his family, neighbors and acquaintances, but he is under no organizational mandate to do so.

Another part of the slow progression of Islam in West Africa is that to get deeply involved in the religion requires learning Arabic in order to read the *Qur'an*. Furthermore, there is little use for Arabic outside of the mosque or *Quranic* school, whereas a European language learned in a mission school doubles as a means of socioeconomic mobility in the modern sector. Islamists also practiced cultural imperialism in West African history, for example linguistically. Arabic was and is considered to be the language of Allah, the sacred language through which the *Qur'an* was revealed. The revered ideals of the *Qur'an* are thought to be intricately linked up with the language of Arabic. For this reason, the *Qur'an* is not translated into Anufo or Twi or other West African languages. Mosque Arabic, that used by **Marabouts** and *Mallams*, is an ideal language to strive for as one strives to understand Allah and his teachings.

A third reason for the slow but steady advance of Islam in West Africa is its autocratic approach and its inability to tolerate pagan ways. I must say that in my experience, Muslims are personally rather tolerant and accepting of animistic traditions — they both consult "pagan" institutions such as oracles, and they accept people as intimate friends who are non-Muslims; but "officially," in the minds of the devout and those who make a living off of Islam (the Marabouts and *Mallams*), a true believer should never tolerate fetishism.

A fourth reason is that Islam has been historically linked to military expansion and the concept of **jihad**, or Holy War. **Kaffirs** or non-believers were not merely looked

---

3. The white/black dichotomy has nothing to do with skin color, but refers to the universal concept of day/night being associated with good/bad.

down-upon, but they were sometimes conquered, enslaved, or killed by Muslim fanatics. This was political **imperialism** and some West Africans have not forgotten.

Historically Islam filtered into Africa along the trade routes. Slowly it was adopted by West African traders, the Djula for example, and eventually some kings of the Sudanic states. Today Islam is promoted by oil-rich states that send money to West Africa to build mosques and schools to teach the *Qur'an*. These schools are conducted in Arabic. Students learn important passages from the holy book based on rote memorization, often writing the Arabic script onto wooden tablets, which are washed off when the lesson is over. There is no scriptural translation into the tribal languages of West Africa, as the aim of Islam is displacement, not assimilation of pagan ways.

For the widespread network of Muslims, traders, clerics and common people, Islam does provide a common language, the same texts, a set of similar ideas that unites them across the boundaries of ethnicity, nation or occupation. As an autocratic and patriarchal theology, Islam does not disrupt the lives of West Africans when members of the community adopt it. They can keep their multiple wives, and some go on with their previous ritual activities. For example, the former Tumukuoro, (See **kuoro** in the glossary) the chief of the largest town in Sisalaland presides over many ancestral sacrifices. He used shrines such as the Tumuwiheye in the outyard of his palace to enforce the norms of society, requiring parties to disputes to swear oaths on it. The idea was that the ancestors connected to the shrine would kill or harm anyone who told lies in such an oath. Yet this same man was an *Al-hajj*, one who claimed to be a Muslim, indeed, one who fulfilled the five pillars of faith, something that most West African Muslims will never have the money to do.

This is at the behavioral level. At the level of ideas, Islam is against cultural pluralism. Muslim scholars promote universal adherence to the strict law of Islam, **Shar'ia Law**. They do this by invoking an ideal past that is associated with Arabia and the life of the prophet, Muhammad. Where Islam dominates the political structure, as in Northern Nigeria, politicians are pushing to make Islamic law the law of the land, an effort that has led to conflict and bloodshed as some intolerant Christians have taken to the streets to protest.

Today, most West Africans who become Muslims do so voluntarily. But some people are driven to accept the teachings of Mohammed when they find themselves facing a life crisis or dilemma. For example, among the Mossi of Burkina Faso, unbelieving barren women are sent to Muslim diviners. Their oracular findings sometimes show that the unborn children will not come to a *kaffir* woman. If the woman wants a child (which almost all West African women do) her obvious remedy is to convert to Islam.

In summary, we can say that Islam, following *Shari'a* Law, stresses orthodoxy, a revealed truth of a universal nature over the untruths of particularism. To disobey divine laws is a sin, a concept shared with Christianity. Islam is a sober approach to life that stresses adherence to a well-defined moral order. Many see politics as a means to insure morality. Some adherents do not see any need to separate church and state. This tendency for Islam to be associated with political orders and military campaigns is worrisome to many. It could become the basis for future disruptions in the peace of West African nations. For example, the imposition of *Shari'a* Law in Northern Nigeria has recently led to the death of hundreds of people. These are tendencies that need to be understood and addressed by those whose responsibility it is to govern in West Africa.

There is similarity between conversion to **Newbreed Churches** and to Islam. In Mali Islam advanced slowly until the colonial era, when conversions began to happen in the face of the confusion of the times. This wave of conversions can be seen, partially at least, as a reaction to French rule. However, since colonialism ended, Muslims have made an effort to reduce religious pluralism and stamp out non-Islamic practices—just as with the Christian zealots of the Newbreed Churches. Understandably, this has created conflict between Muslims and non-Muslims. However, it has also caused problems within the Islamic community, as I will describe below.

The world of Malian Islam is plagued with a concern about truth and right behavior. A central question is: What is proper and improper behavior for a Muslim? There are a number of practices in the West African Muslim community that many Muslims brand as heretical—as idolatry. The most ubiquitous is **spirit possession**. This only exists in Muslim communities, nevertheless many Muslims deny that it is compatible with the laws of Allah. Pious Muslims hurry past an area where a possession is going on, which can be identified by the drumming involved. Many do not even want to live next to a courtyard where such seances occur. An orthodox Muslim will not attend a spirit possession event, and if he did he would have to undergo spiritual cleansing for forty days and nights.

Yet spirit possession has a long history in the area. Europeans who traveled through the region before the French takeover noted its existence. Today it is regularly practiced in most Islamic communities in Mali.

In the Bamankan language common to Mali, spirit societies are called *jine-ton*. In Arabic *jinn* means spirit, and is a common usage in many languages of the Western Sudan. Mediums in these societies, who are almost always women, do the *jine-don*, "dance of spirits." The mediums are organized in a hierarchy of experience, with students at the bottom and adepts at the top. People consult *jine-don* mediums for the same reasons they go to any diviner in West Africa—for reasons of health, prosperity or simply to make sense of their world.

Many Muslims reject spirit possession, yet the *jine-don* mediums form an interstitial position with regard to the *doma*, or Bambara diviners of the non-Muslim domain and the pious Muslim community; but it is not for this contact that many Muslims deride their activities, even though *doma* divination is seen as un-Islamic, along with sacrifices of fetishes and the use of power objects (charms & talismans). Rather, it is because spirit possession is not *din*, a religion. *Din* praises Allah. The blood sacrifices associated with the seances are to the spirits, thereby denigrating God. Only Islamic prayer can be religion. As with Christianity's demand for the exclusivity of **Elohim**, Muslims require singular attention to Allah.

There may be an economic element to all of this. It must be said that both *doma* diviners and those who do the *jine-don* are a financial threat to the Muslim clerics who also perform healing and divinatory services for the faithful. Since there is no official church hierarchy to denounce *jine-ton* specialists, it is left to local *Mallams* and imams to do so.

Islamists are monotheists. Polytheism (Arabic, *shirk*) is evil. Polytheists are called *mushrikun*, idolaters. Making sacrifices at idols is doubly bad, because under Islamic law, no images should be made. In Islamic art, only geometric designs are permitted. Again, in the view of the true believers, any constructed image is demeaning to the Almighty. Secondly, since blood is spilt at sacrifices, there is always the chance that a Muslim in attendance would get some on his fingers, even inadvertently, and thereby possibly ingest it. This is strictly taboo in connection with any animal not sacrificed in strict accordance with the sacrificial codes laid down in the *Qur'an*.

The reality in Mali, as with much of West Africa, is that people from all walks of life mix the symbols of Islam with local ceremonies and oracular activities. It also common for Muslims to consult non-Islamic diviners and healers when pressed by events in their lives, and concomitantly, many non-believers will consult with Muslim clerics if they are faced with an intractable problem.

Throughout West Africa, Muslims and Christians face each other uneasily, while animists continue their age-old ways in spite of the fact that they are looked down upon by both World Religions.

Christianity in West Africa

Christianity came to West Africa with European contact, but was never accepted in a significant way by large numbers of people until the colonial era. Sociologists such as Robin Horton see conversion as associated with social upheaval and the substitution of one explanation of life's ills with another more "modern" explanation.

Christianity experienced an upsurge after the establishment of colonial domination in West Africa and into the early years of independence, but there is some indication, according to Jon Kirby that conversion to European churches is now falling off, that those already converted are leaving to join African churches based on Christian teachings. He also indicates that traditional African religions are making a comeback—though some would say that they never went anywhere, that many so-called converts to Christianity and Islam in West Africa have continued to believe in and be involved in traditional forms of ritual, divination and prayer.

People everywhere need a relatively stable social order to provide meaning in life and psychological security. They rarely abandon a stable system without good cause. It does seem that in West Africa, Christianity did not make significant inroads into the religious lives of the people until there was sufficient social upheaval to call for a new definition of the situation. As Robin Horton puts it, the acceptance of a universal explanation comes when microcosms (local rites and religions) start to unravel. When local cosmologies no longer seem to explain the world, new ones are accepted as whole cloth, or syntheses are made.

The data from the revivalist **Aladura Churches** of West Africa (so-called prayer churches) seem to bear this out. They and others like them are on the rise in West Africa today. They have arisen in times of extreme crisis: during and after the influenza pandemic of the early part of the colonial era, during outbreaks of bubonic plague, famines and economic depression. These disasters have led to a crisis in faith that has caused some people (primarily urban peoples and those living along the coast) to seek a new rationalization of changing times.

Characteristically these new syncretic interpretations of Christianity are "this-worldly" in orientation, very much like traditional African religions. It seems that many who find something attractive about Christianity reject the salvationist message about working hard in this life to achieve redemption in the next. West Africans seem to be more interested in healing and dealing with misfortune or uncertainty in the present.

I will give a West African example from Yorubaland in Nigeria—the Church of the Lord founded in the 1920s by Josiah Oshitelu. This was and is an *Aladura* Church in that his preaching stressed the doctrines and practices of faith, prayer, fasting and confession. He also emphasized the need to reject "**paganism**," traditional healers. Oshitelu called this "the gospel of joy."

Josiah Oshitelu had been educated at an Anglican mission in the early 1920s in Nigeria. He taught within this system for a number of years, but in 1925 he began to experience a series of terrifying visions. Using traditional logic based on West African causality, Oshitelu believed that witches caused these apparitions.

He was given a year off from his mission duties to pursue a cure, which he did through traditional West African healers, but he found no relief. Then he turned to an *aladura* leader named Brother Shomoye. The pastor took Oshitelu under his wing, teaching him a new way of thinking. Using European reasoning, Shomoye said that these visions were God's test of Oshitelu. The elder told the novitiate that he had an important mission ahead, that he had to abandon all thoughts of worshiping *olodumare*, the traditional God of the Yoruba. He must abandon the use of all pagan charms, medicines and forgo consulting traditional diviners and healers.

Instead, according to Shomoye, Oshitelu should put all of his faith in *Elohim*, the Hebrew god of the scriptures. Rather than use *Ifa*, the traditional oracle of the Yoruba, Oshitelu should use the power of prayer and fasting.

Josiah Oshitelu tried this and found some relief. The wild and dangerous beasts of his dreams were transformed into benign and kindly animals. In time, he began to hear heavenly voices calling him to a mission, as yet undefined. Feeling that he was finally on a firm path, Oshitelu began to write down the first of what would be thousands of revelations, for example, the divine voice that spoke saying:

> I will build a new Jerusalem in you. You are the one whom Jesus Christ has sent like the last Elijah to repair the Lord's road and make his way straight. I will give you the key to power like Moses, and will bless you like Job...I am the God of Kah...the God of Jah.

After being a member of Shomoye's church, and praying and fasting at times over a two-year period, Oshitelu received an order from heaven to found his own church, branching out on his own, establishing a "new" way to worship. Nevertheless, his fresh approach, like other syncretist sects, involved the piecing together of various threads from existing religions. He invented a "new" Arabic-like script for his church, "new" religious symbols, "new" taboos e.g., not eating pork, "new" secret "seal words," and he pontificated on the blunders made by other churches.

Nonetheless, in his discourse Oshitelu styled the Church of the Lord as a fresh start, assured that the God of Abraham would "spread his fame from Syria to the America." What was not new was human suffering, and it was intensifying at that time, along with the social disorganization brought about by colonialism. The bubonic plague followed on the heels of the worldwide spread of devastating influenza that decimated West Africa, as it did elsewhere. The urban areas of Nigeria especially were hard hit by an economic depression following these diseases, along with widespread famine. All in all, the church was begun in a whirlwind of turmoil.

The Church of the Lord was part of a broader reaction to the perceived chaos of the times. Religious revivals swept the Ijebu region where Oshitelu began his church, and he participated in that movement briefly, but he had a singular mission. He began to preach that the ills of the day—physical and social, were trials. He portrayed them as a result of God's judgement. He preached that both Christians and Muslims had strayed from God's teachings, and certainly pagans were simple idolaters and mistaken in their beliefs. Their practices were totally wrong and should be shunned, according to the evangelist.

Furthermore, Oshitelu predicted that more affliction was on the way unless people followed the Church of the Lord. He saw visions of locusts, famines, war (all of which happen from time to time in West Africa). He also predicted that eminently God would act to end it all. It was a typical "the kingdom of God is at hand" delivery.

If there were misfortunes amongst the people, Oshitelu had a solution. First of all, one must have faith, and then one must act on that faith. A church member was instructed to pray at least three hours a day, preferably at midnight and three am, which were seen as cardinal points in the day, those which would bring greater efficacy (he had a physical equivalent of this where people could stand at consecrated places to receive special blessings through prayer).

A church member was also advised to fast in association with prayer. This was said to bring greater spirituality and the possibility of visions of redemption. Along with faith, prayer and fasting, the member of the Church of the Lord had to reject completely and cleanly all pagan ideas and practices. Finally, confession was said to cleanse the soul.

Not only did the Church of the Lord arrive at a time of great socioeconomic turmoil, but also in the 1920s the Yoruba were going through an ideological crisis and wrenching acculturation. Traditional rites were seen as losing their efficacy, while Christianity was on the rise; paralleled, of course, by the decline of political power of West Africans and the increased domination by Europeans. From the sociological point of view, syncretistic churches were utilitarian attempts to deal with this chaos. J. D. Y. Peel puts it like this:

> Christianity was widely conceived of instrumentally, that is, it was believed to be efficacious in attaining this-worldly goals...Christians were in the habit of taking every other possible insurance and protection that they considered effective. When therefore, at a time of heavy religious change, the Yoruba were inflicted with a series of natural disasters — influenza, plagues, famines, and depression following the rapid growth of a monetary economy — these demanded a religious interpretation. Their unusually severe nature meant that the traditional religion, already fast declining was inadequate to explain or relieve them, and Christianity (which had every sign of permanence and was generally associated with what the young and ambitious felt desirable) was so used. The God whom the Christians preached had sent the disasters as a punishment, but the Christian religion provided a way out.

The logic went: if an omnipotent God caused the ills, no one but God could cure them. Oshitelu urged his followers to make a clean break with the past in order to have salvation, but not so much salvation in the coming world, but in this one. A cynic might say that the motto of such churches was and remains "follow me and pay me" for certainly men and women like Josiah Oshitelu have been making a nice living off such followers for quite some time.

Whatever the efficacy of such preaching and practices, they have been popular in West Africa since the early days of colonialism. By 1962 Oshitelu had 72 branches and ministers under his direction, with some in London to minister to the African diaspora there, and most spread throughout West Africa principally in Ghana, Liberia, and Sierra Leone.

In another commonly accepted revelation, Oshitelu was inspired to organize a pilgrimage called the Annual Festival of Mt. Taborar, a hill that he constructed and consecrated near his hometown of Ogere. It is held every August 22nd. Pilgrims bring gifts and offerings to the "Holy Mountain of Power." Such a trek is thought to bring forgiveness of sins and spiritual cleansing.

These are not really African ideas, unless we define them as problem solving, which I suspect is the way most West Africans see it. Traditional West Africans see themselves less as sinners than people afflicted by the trials and tribulations of life. Sin is not part of the African cosmological order. West Africans can anger spirits by ritual breaches, but sin in the Christian sense is absent from African philosophy.

From this sanctuary and the pulpit Josiah Oshitelu guides his followers and even provides "scripture." Take for example the following from Oshitelu's *The Book of Prayer with Uses and Power of Psalms*:

> For Psalm vii:
> If enemies rise against thee, recite this Psalm, standing facing the East in (sic) midnight with the Holy Name—ELL ELLIJJONI. You will be naked. And the enemy will be defeated at will (capital letters in original).

Such revivalists and preachers are syncretic organizers, those who can take the old and the new and come up with a plausible synthesis. If change is producing bad things, it also brings good too. Rather than centering on deferred salvation, the syncretist's message focuses on the here and now. Christ's word on the lips of preachers like Oshitelu is less about exhalation on high, than about attaining a better quality of life today—getting more goods, status, social mobility and things of this earth.

The "new" Christianity had and retains a distinctly West African flavor to it, in spite of its focus on material and social mobility in the imposed European order. It has not been a total intellectual revolution, however. It retains the structure of an old cosmology with age-old concerns—the desire for less illness, death and suffering, but new desires have crept into the prayers of *Aladura* Churches , for instance, Turner gives this example of an *aladura* prayer format for students:

> Make me holy for my blessing. Send me this moment Divine Helpers, Divine Intelligence, Divine Intermediaries and gracious look of Jesus Christ my Saviour...
> My examinations will come up (mention the time and place)...I call unto Thee for success...grant that I may study the right text and passage and subject...
> Jesus Christ let me feel Thy influence...Thy breath, and Thy assistance. Send to me most powerful angels, that these may fight out for me all dangers and evil besettings, that I may not be frightened, careless, nervous, and obsessed...

This is much like traditional West African religion, a means of achieving something good soon, or avoiding or removing something bad in the present, not in some future ethereal state. Many clerics in mainstream churches look upon these upstarts not as true churches, but as sects or cults—mere social movements that are not about worship so much as they are about the aggrandizement and egocentricity of their founders who prey on those who seek a solution to life's woes.

Thus independent churches, as these new approaches to Christianity are sometimes called, are an attempt to reorganize and synthesize African and Western ideas about religious matters. These new approaches shock many Westerners, especially the clergy sent out to convert West Africans.

However different these new churches are from modern Christianity (though they probably are not so different from early Christianity), they are focused on creating a new form of community similar to that of rural villages. In some ways these new

churches can be seen as urban villages within the context of the larger metropolitan scene.

The Catholic missionary and social anthropologist, Jon Kirby studied the Anufo of Northern Ghana. He is one of the few Christian missionaries seriously trying to tackle the problem of dual identities in West Africa, having founded the Tamale Institute for Cross-Cultural Studies in Ghana to train indigenous missionary students about the value of their own cultures and how to handle problems created by living in parallel cultures, African and Western.

The Anufo have a traditional animistic approach to solving life's problems using three kinds of shrines. The first are Earth shrines or those dealing with a territory or a social group occupying a certain piece of land. The second involve social shrines, those that deal more directly with the kin groups or territorially concentrated settlements. Finally, there are individual shrines used by people to protect themselves from real or imagined threats.

As has been described above, sacrifices occur on these shrines either by formal scheduling (**calendrical rites**) or spontaneously when a problem arises that must involve consultation with the ancestors, which palaver is always accompanied by libations and animal sacrifices to them. These are **piacular rites**.

Immediately after Ghanaian independence a European missionary came among the Anufo and had great success in "converting" thousands to the Presbyterian Church. This was a heady time when Ghanaians felt that they would make rapid moves toward modernization. It was not to be. When the good pastor left, his material contributions fell into misuse, and the Anufo made a mass apostasy. By the mid-1970s, most had left the church to become Muslims or they had "reverted" to their former animist ways.

It now seems clear that rather than spiritual conversion, the Anufo sought social and material progress—upward mobility and the acquisition of European skills and goods. While the well-meaning pastor was thinking of spiritual conversion to a distant reward, the Anufo were thinking of a better life in this world. This can be seen in a common Anufo verbalization. The Anufo called encounters with the missionary, *anyunu* ("to get your eyes opened,")—that is, to move into the White Man's world. The preacher was thinking about moving them into the White Man's heaven, not his worldly domain.

The missionary also had a pragmatic side to him. He helped the people by building a mission school, by setting up an agricultural program, creating local health services and running a literacy program. When these benefits were no longer available, the "converts" *unconverted* themselves. Such a mass apostasy opens the question of whether West Africans are converting to Christianity for spiritual or material reasons. It seems likely, in the Anufo case at least, that the local people saw Presbyterianism as an avenue to the affluent world of the European.

What the European evangelists did not understand was that African religion is practical. Evangelists saw no need to present Christianity as useful in the commonplace world. They did not realize that the Anufo and most other West African animists do approach their "gods" to solve such questions. Why did my crops fail this year? Will my journey be a safe one? Why did my elder brother die? Or, how can I deal with witches?

Not only did missionaries predominantly misread and reject African religion—they were there to *replace* it. Early missionaries (up to the 1960s) tended to regard African religion as wrong. Efforts to change such ethnocentrism, however minimal, are being made. Kirby reports that the Catholic Church in Ghana is now using some local songs, musical instruments, art works, artifacts and dance forms in their worship. Although the initial missionaries of European Imperialism desired to change

African ways; perhaps the tables have been turned. It seems that world churches are feeling the need to adapt to African ways. It remains to be seen the long-term significance of this slight shift.

Evangelical Fervor and Politics

There is a clear and present danger in the religious climate of West Africa. It concerns the "**otherizing process.**" Human beings everywhere seem quite capable of putting their fellow human beings into disparaged categories. Sometimes they take discriminatory and even violent action against those they have labeled. Unfortunately, this seems to be a human universal.

This is a common danger in West Africa today, especially with the rise of evangelical, Pentecostal and charismatic churches in the region—the so-called Newbreed Churches. The radicalism associated with religion has created a climate of intolerance and violence in some areas. The repeated religious turmoil and rioting in Nigeria since the 1980s is one example.

In some West African countries, such as Mali or Nigeria, Muslims have come to dominate in terms of population size. Muslims in Mali make up between 70 and 90 percent of the population, while in Nigeria the figure is near 60%. Ghana, on the other hand, has about 60% Christians, with the rest being divided between Muslims and animists. Whatever the actual figures, Muslims are clashing with Christians.

Since independence a general **conversionist ideology** has arisen in West Africa among both Muslims and Christians. Emotion runs high on both sides. While mainline Christian churches have tried to avoid confrontation with Islam for the most part, and have been able to live side by side with Muslims, the new churches stress evangelism, emotional commitment to proselytizing, ecstatic healing processes and prosperity through zealous action in the name of God.

More than mainstream Christian churches, the extremist members of Newbreed Churches, (the Evangelical Church of West Africa or the Church of Christ in Nigeria), are threats to the fragile peace in many West African countries. There is a long tradition of such evangelical fervor in the area, beginning with such churches as W. F. Kummanyi's Deeper Life Bible Church and the coming to Nigeria of the Apostolic Faith Mission in the 1930s and the scripture Union and Student Christian Movement in the 1940s. Such Newbreed Churches began the emphasis on personal salvation, strict Bible-centered morality and aggressive soul winning.

These forbears set the stage. Failed governments, unpopular military regimes, the hardships resulting from the **Structural Adjustment Programs (SAPs)** and the dashed socioeconomic expectations of post-colonial West Africans, have subsequently created a climate of frustration that has fanned the flames of evangelical intolerance. West Africans are frustrated with government and outside efforts to produce economic progress. With such a climate of chaos and despair, Newbreed Churches have become immensely popular, offering an otherworldly hope in the face of disintegration in the region—their belief is that "Only God can save us."

Sociocultural anthropologists would say that such piety and zealous action provide a frustrated population with catharsis, with a safety valve for their feelings of disappointment. Unfortunately, what might be release for them, is all too often directed in an aggressive way against others.

These Newbreed Churches take an unmerciful approach to animists or "pagans" as they call them, but their fervent ire is mainly directed towards what they call "Dead Christians" and Muslims. The former are Christians of mainline churches who are not "born again." As unenthusiastic followers of an outdated form of Christianity, they are defined by born again Christians as "unsaved." Thus, this newfound evangelical outlet has created a climate of exclusivism in these Newbreed Churches. According to their ideas, only those totally committed to the cause of Christianity will be saved in the coming millennial holocaust. This zeal sometimes spills over into the demonization of others.

West African radical religionists have had help from the outside as well. The German evangelist Reinhard Bonnke brought his Christ for All Nations Crusade to West Africa with a war cry of "Christianity from Cape to Cairo." This inflammatory rhetoric clearly frightened some Muslims and angered others. Rumors in the Muslim community were flying that the New Christians wanted to "replace the Crescent with the Cross." Arab states have also invested money in West Africa to build mosques and fund Quranic schools. Evangelicals on both sides have taken a proactive approach to proselytizing by targeting youth and schools, and by using a multimedia approach—radio, television, audiocassettes, loudspeaker vans, leaflets, magazines and personal confrontation of each person encountered by adherents to such missionary ardor. This fervor has placed them on a fast track collision course with the "enemy."

At present, this is primarily an urban problem, part of the modern sector of West African societies, but it is escalating because preachers are calling for immediate action with millenarian outcries. "The kingdom of God is at hand," they say. This leads converts to feel the need for urgency, for expeditious action against the archenemies of God.

Actions on the Islamic side have not helped either. For example in Nigeria, in 1979 there was an attempt to set up a *Shari'a* court of appeal in the national constitution. That was followed by Nigeria's President Babingida's government's intent to join the OIC (Organization of Islamic Conference) in 1986. *Shari'a* is an Islamic legal system and only an Islamic government can apply it. Nigeria is a sovereign state with a constitution and a President who is the commander-in-chief of the Armed Forces. The governor's actions are delegated by the constitution, which is supreme in Nigeria. If the constitution is superior to the *Shari'a*, then the Shari'a cannot work. Nevertheless, the *Shari'a* movement raised Christian fears that Nigeria was moving toward an Islamic state. Distrust heightened. Rumors flew that the government was spending tax money to build mosques. Christian extremists spoke out against the growing perceived threat. Headlines in the popular Christian magazine *Today's Challenge*[4] featured such warnings: "Fighting against the Forcible Islamisation of Nigeria," "Muslim Fanatics on the Rampage" and "Is Islam Lawlessness?" The then-editor of the magazine was fond of condemning the "satanic schemings...of the devil and his agents masquerading as Muslim fundamentalists."

Imprudent words came from the other side of the fence too. A respected Muslim leader claimed that 85% of Nigerians were Muslims. Later he changed the figure to 80%, and then had to reduce it to 70%. Christians were quite offended by the Nigerian Sheikh Gumi's 1987 claim that no Nigerian Muslim would ever accept a non-Muslim president. Such incautious verbiage had exacerbated the religious tensions in Nigeria.

---

4. Published by the Evangelical Church of West Africa in Nigeria.

Photo 3.7   Satellite Television is Now Available in West Africa.

More recently, the Muslim-controlled state governments of Northern Nigeria have instituted *Shari'a* Law in some places and apparently want to extend it to others, at least in the north. This led to riots and deaths in clashes between Christians and Muslims. There were rumors that Christians were being blocked from building churches in places like Kano, Kaduna and Zaria. It was alleged that government officials refused to allow land sales to Christians, or to give them building permits when they had land. Again, it was said that Muslims would erect a mosque next to every Christian church that was built in Muslim-dominated areas.

In this climate of religious bigotry, Christians used radio, loudspeakers and audio-cassettes to boast of how many *Al-hajis* (those devotees of Islam who have made a pilgrimage) they had recently converted. Some of these former Muslims even made such recordings and went on the air to further inflame their former compatriots. In Kumase, Ghana, for example, there is even a Converted Muslims Christian Ministry that has made a self-proclaimed crusade to Christianize the north, which is predominated by animists and Muslims, except among the heavily Christianized Dagara peoples of the northwest corner of the nation.

In this atmosphere of fear and suspicion, each side accuses the other of fanaticism. Zealots are spurred into action by inflammatory radio announcements of "a riot in progress" at such and such a location. On television Christians have imported Pat Robertson's conservative 700 Club program to run alongside their own extremist diatribes against nonbelievers (See Photo 3.7). Such madness continues as I write this. Furthermore, harsh punishments being handed out by northern Islamic courts make newspaper headlines in Southern Christian newspapers (See Box 3.8, Nigerian Amputee).

Box 3.8   Nigerian Amputee Gets 50,000 Naira in Remuneration

ThisdayOnLine.com reported that the government of Sokoto State has given Umaru Aliyu whose right wrist was amputated three weeks ago a cash gift of

N50,000 to resettle him. Umaru Aliyu, the first victim of the *Shari'a* legal system in the state, has been staying in a government hospital since the amputation took place July 6, 2001. The state Attorney-General and Commissioner of Justice, Barrister Aliyu Sayinna, over the weekend, handed Aliyu to the judge who convicted him. Barrister Aliyu said the N50,000 donation was in line with the state government's social security policy aimed at rehabilitating the needy. Such assistance, according to him, would go towards resettling the amputee, thereby making him more useful to the society. Responding, Umoru Aliyu stated that he was satisfied with the punishment meted out to him, stressing that he has nothing against anybody over the amputation. Asked why he did not file any appeal against the judgment, Aliyu said there was no way he could change his destiny adding that if the amputation did not happen through the court verdict, it would happen through another means (also see Chapter nine).

While most West African governments have followed a path of staying out of such matters, at least directly, for a brief time the Mormons and the Jehovah's Witnesses were banned from Ghana. Through negotiations the Mormons have been allowed back in and are even in the process of building a temple in Accra. About the same time as the government of **Jerry Rawlings** banned these Christians, he was welcoming the extremist Louis Farrakhan of the Nation of Islam—twice in the 1990s. Farrakhan, who is not known for tolerant or temperate speech, was given ample air time on Ghanaian television and radio and was accorded the status of a visiting diplomat.

In this milieu of extremism and anger, some are trying to take a more moderate road. The Christian evangelist James Wuye and Imam Muhammad Nurayn Ashafa jointly founded and coordinate the **Muslim/Christian Youth Dialogue Forum** in Kaduna, Northern Nigeria. Their organization holds forums and has published literature and books in an attempt to mediate the conflict between the two religious camps. They have toured several countries outside of West Africa to find ways to resolve such tensions and antagonisms. Their most well known work is *The Pastor and the Imam Responding to Conflict*. Unfortunately, their approach is not the mainstream one taken by most West African evangelicals and Muslim radicals.

Identity Issues and Religion in West Africa

Who am I? Where do I come from? Where am I going? These are fundamental questions that every religion tries to explicate. The coming of Europeans and their attempts to impose Christianity, as well as the spreading presence of Islam in West Africa, have made these questions less simple to answer for those practicing animism. The various particularisms of animist practice are now overlaid with the twin influences of Christianity and Islam.

In West Africa the search for identity goes on in a more complex ideological arena than ever before. Islam has been slow to make inroads in West Africa, given that it has been around so long. Christianity burst on the scene with great fanfare and the advantage of being associated with a promise of socioeconomic mobility and modernization, but increasingly West Africans seem to be turning to their own roots, looking for their cultural identity in traditional religion. Those who look at traditional society find that it has something of value. It contains a strong democratic civic culture, as well as a religious approach that some say more appropriately meets the needs of the West African than does Islam or Christianity.

The strong civic traditions of the African village stress a ritual link between the living and the dead. Some who have become dissatisfied with Islam or Christianity have gained a renewed interest in animism, the religion of their ancestors. These seekers do not see it as a second class system, though many acculturated West Africans have long seen it as such and many continue to denigrate traditional customs. It remains to be seen how strong this trend is.

As the Nigerian novelist Chinua Achebe tries to show in *No Longer at Ease*, many West Africans suffer from a dual identity, especially those in the modern sector—the urbanites. On one hand they have African ideas; on the other many envy "White" ways. This leads to a kind of **cultural schizophrenia**, a crisis of identity. The search for African roots is one way to handle this dilemma. So is total rejection of all things African. Yet another is some form of **syncretism**.

This perhaps explains the explosion of self-reliant Newbreed Churches in West Africa since independence. They come down hard on "paganism." They make life clear cut—Christianity is right; animism and other "fetish" behaviors are wrong. End of discussion. This provides the member of an Africanized Christian church with clear identity separation. The Newbreed ideology says that they have moved out of darkness into the light, leaving behind what was worthless for what is eternally valuable. Animism and fetishism are portrayed as ignoble, sinful and unenlightened.

But many modernized West Africans operate in an everyday world with parallel systems where in some contexts they would be required to act White; in others they would be expected to conform to traditional African norms.

Sometimes this duality would not emerge until a crisis point in their lives, such as the onset of a severe illness or the death of a loved one. While such people may adhere strongly to the Christian ideal, when faced with a turning point in their lives, they are forced to admit that they still "believe" in fetishes and traditional healing.

In many parts of West Africa being modern is seen as being "White" or being better than "pagans." Jon Kirby tells the story of being met upon his arrival at the mission in Ghana by an African man who warmly greeted him. The smiling man exclaimed his joy at the fact that his son had recently "become a White Man" (meaning he had been ordained a priest in the Catholic Church).

On the other hand, nowadays it is sometimes seen as wrong to be with Whites or to try to be "White" (See Box 3.9, The Fight over the White Man). Whereas in urban West Africa the old view was that European culture was superior (a view still held by some); today increasingly there is resentment against those who would try to be "White." This is understandable in that European technology and culture have mainly benefited a few metropolitan élites, and the average person has not seen better times yet.

Box 3.9   The Fight over the White Man

In 1998 I was in Kumase with the West African Nenkentie Badzongoly. He was helping me get my van repaired. In the course of his instructions to one of the fitters (mechanics), a passing Asante man got involved and made Nenkentie very angry, the only time I have seen him so. As with so many West Africans, he is by nature mild mannered. The passerby began to berate Nenkentie for "showing off" in front of a White Man. Of course, Nenkentie has known me for over thirty years and certainly does not need to show off, as he is very competent in most everything he does (driving my van is a possible exception). The argument became so heated that I had to step between them and send the Asante man on his way. As the crowd looked on with amazement, he left shouting the F-word in English, certainly not a very graceful exit, but then prejudice is never very pretty, is it?

After years of **cultural imperialism**, some West Africans are beginning to explore their roots, to search out truly African forms of organization and religion—and many never lost them. Even though metropolitan élites, the media, adverts and some black pastors of independent churches foster the view that European modernism is superior to antiquated traditions, fewer and fewer West Africans are buying the idea.

This "roots" phenomenon in West Africa today is affecting Christians. As Jon Kirby says, many "yearn for a return to their cultural roots and are fascinated by their traditional culture." Nevertheless, this would be truer of relatively acculturated and urbanized Africans rather than villagers, many of whom still hold idealized visions of the city and modern life.

Nor did I find it to be true among the youth of Sisalaland in Northern Ghana. Today, they largely see Islam as being modern, not Christianity which has been around for nearly 100 years, but has not made significant inroads there. Islam has exploded of late. In the 1960s Bruce Grindal found that only about eight percent of rural Sisala was Muslims, whereas by the end of the last millennium I found that figure to be about 78 percent, a fantastic increase in about forty years.

Granted, many of these "Muslims" are nominal converts—uninformed as to the tenets of their adopted religion. The point here is that this religion, and not the White Man's Christianity is now seen as modern in much of the north where Islam has been around for much longer. On the contrary, those in the south tend to see Christianity as the modern religion as contrasted with the animistic traditions of their forefathers.

In summary, we can say that there is some indication that West Africans are beginning to see the chimerical nature of modernization and the development ideologies associated with it (See Chapter 18). The people have been let down politically, economically and by the missionaries who present a religion that does not seem to meet the needs of everyday life.

This has led some to return to their roots, others to Africanize Christianity in the form of new churches. Certainly we can safely say that a synthesis of Western and African culture is in progress, and that a recombination of ideas from Africa and Christianity is part of that process. Sometimes new movements spring up based on indigenous ideas e.g., the *Tigare* **Cult**, a "witch-finding" movement of Ghana, which has spread throughout West Africa. With such movements, it is often difficult to distinguish between "traditional" beliefs and practices, and what is an indigenous church greatly influenced by African ideas, or again, what is a passing craze. The religious situation in West Africa today is very fluid.

Imperialistic Proselytizing

It would seem that the two World Religions that have most influenced West Africa, Islam and Christianity, both have been bent on **cultural monism**, as they each try to control the discourse of religiosity in the region. This is reflected in a recent New York Times article by Onishi, Norimitsu where he says:

> Almost all newspapers are based in Lagos, the New York City of Nigeria, and are owned and staffed by people from the largely Christian and relatively well-educated south. In the Muslim north, where illiteracy is widespread but where military power has long rested, the Lagos-based press is held in deep suspicion. And so while newspapers go unsold in northern cities, they are a vital part of the Lagos streetscape.

It would seem that if West Africans are beginning to engage in a search for their cultural identity, it will be those religions that help them find it that will prosper in West Africa, not those that stand in the way. Inflexible churches are likely to foster even further fragmentation of Christianity and spin-off theocracies.

Having said that, Islam seems to be growing in strength, at least in the north. While it is imperialistic in its attempt to stamp out pagan practices, it perhaps culturally fits better than Christianity with the lifestyle of most West Africans. Although there are Islamic ideological factions, there is no equivalent to formal Christian churches—no structured social factions since there is no organized all-encompassing church in Islam. While the gains of Christianity are being sapped by the growth in Newbreed Churches and magico-religious movements, such *Tigare*, when Islam fragments it splits into loose-knit ideological segments.

Conversion to both World Religions has been slow. It is of note that conversion to both Christianity and Islam only took off in West Africa when there was a period of severe disruption of the established sociocultural order. It seems that when there is cultural homogeneity and relative stasis, alternative forms of identity are not attractive; but when society becomes chaotic, not only do conversions to World Religions rise, but also offshoots and cult movements become attractive alternatives to traditional religion.

Anthropologists know that religion is sometimes about the creation of identity and difference. Metaphors and symbols of religious discourse often concern the establishment, mediation and transformation of power and a feeling of powerlessness.

West Africa is not in good economic and political shape. It is not surprising that her population is restless. Certainly, history has not dealt her a very playable hand. Post-independence high expectations have since plummeted. Structural Adjustment Programs (SAPs) have bitten deep into the lifestyle of many urbanites. Colonial missionary work devalued traditional West African religion. In this void, many have turned to emotionalist ideologies, and some are seeking out their traditional background. It is a time of religious flux.

On a positive side, there are more ideological choices open to West Africans today than before. Yet in spite of this plentitude of religious and conceptual options, more and more West Africans seem to be taking a polemical stance and this has led to an unfortunate state of intolerance, divisiveness and militant attitudes—a social climate conducive to violence.

Clearly what West Africa needs are more people like Imam Muhammad Nurayn Ashafa and Pastor James Wuye who have chosen a conciliatory path, using reason not emotion—their passion being directed toward the careful pursuit of peace. I cannot help thinking that this would be the path chosen by Christ and Muhammad, those great teachers from each tradition.

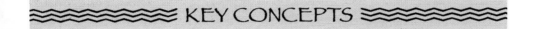

CRITICAL THINKING QUESTIONS

1. Why don't those following traditional religions in West Africa engage in missionary activity i.e., try to convert Christians and Muslims to their point of view?
2. Present evidence that traditional animistic religion can be considered to contain a moral order, that is, a model for right and proper behavior.
3. Explain the separation of powers or twin governance in West Africa that sometimes occurs and is symbolized in the Voltaic Region by the *Na–tendana* division. How does this relate to the Igala data from Nigeria? In what way is **sacralizing** involved? (See glossary).
4. What is the West African view of cosmic power?
5. West Africans often use the term *juju* to refer to things having to do with traditional religion and/or magic; but how do anthropologists separate the two realms of magic and religion and can this duality be accommodated under West African thinking about the cosmos?
6. What variant forms has Christianity taken in West Africa?
7. What seems to be the basis of religious conflict in West Africa today?
8. How does a personalistic theory of causation differ from science?

KEY CONCEPTS

Acephalous peoples
Aladura **Churches**
Animatism
Animism
Animists
Autochthons
Bagre myth
Calendrical rites
Cannibalism
Clitoridectomy
Contagious magic
Conversionist ideology
Counter-magic
Cowry shells or cowries
Cultural imperialism
Cultural monism
Cultural schizophrenia
Divination
Elohim
Envoutement
Ethos
Fairies
Fetish

FGM
Fission
Homeopathic or imitative magic
Imperialism
Imperialistic proselytizing
Juju
Kaffir
Kuoro
Liminality
Magic
Mallam
Marabout
Muslim/Christian Youth Dialogue Forum
Na
Newbreed Churches
Occult power
Otherizing process
Otiose high god
Paganism
Personalistic theory of causation
Piacular rites
Rawlings, Jerry
Rites of passage

Rites of reversal	Spirit possession
Ritual	SAPs
Sacrifice	Syncretism
Shamans	*Tigare* Cult
Shari'a Law	Twin governance
Somatic compliance	Unanimist fallacy
Sorcery	World Religions

≋ SOURCES & SUGGESTED READINGS ≋

Boston, J. S. 1968. *The Igala Kingdom.* Ibadan: Published for the Nigerian Institute of Social and Economic Research by Oxford University Press.

Cannibalism. 2001. Microsoft® Encarta® Online Encyclopedia. http:encarta.msn.com © 1997–2001 Microsoft Corporation.

Durkheim, Emile. 1995 [1915]. *The elementary forms of religious life.* Translated and with an introduction by Karen E. Fields. New York: Free Press.

Gennep, Arnold van. 1960. *The rites of passage.* Translated by Monika B. Vizedom and Gabrielle L. Caffe. Introduction by Solon T. Kimball. Chicago: University of Chicago Press.

Goody, Jack. 1962. *Death, property and the Ancestors: A study of the mortuary customs of the LoDagaa of West Africa.* Stanford: University Press.

Goody, Jack. 1972. *The myth of the Bagre.* Oxford: Clarendon Press.

Griaule, Marcel. 1965. *Conversations with Ogotemmêli: An introduction to Dogon religious ideas.* Oxford: Oxford University Press.

Griaule, Marcel. 1997. Conversations with Ogotemmêli. In: Grinker, R. R. & C. B. Steiner (eds.). *Perspectives on Africa: A reader in culture, history, and representation.* London: Blackwell, 366–378.

Grindal, Bruce T. 1973. Islamic affiliation and urban adaptation: The migrant in Accra, Ghana. *Africa* 63:333–46.

Hackett, R. I. J. 1999. Radical Christian revivalism in Nigeria and Ghana. In: An-Na'Islam, A. A. (ed.). *Proselytization and communal self-determination in Africa.* New York: Orbis Books, 246–267.

Horton, Robin. 1971. African conversion. *Africa* 41:2.

Kirby, Jon. 1986. *Gods, shrines and problem-solving among the Anufo of Northern Ghana.* Berlin: D. Reimer.

Kirby, Jon. 1994. Cultural change & religious conversion in West Africa. In: Blakeley, T. *et al* (eds). *Religion in Africa.* London: James Currey, 57–71.

Lévy-Bruhl, Lucien. 1985 [1926]. *How natives think.* Translation by Lilian A. Clare. Princeton, N.J.: Princeton University Press.

Mendonsa, Eugene L. 1975. The journey of the soul in Sisala cosmology. *Journal of religion in Africa* 7:1–9.

Mendonsa, Eugene L. 1982. *The politics of divination.* Berkeley: University of California Press.

Offiong, D. 1985. Witchcraft among the Ibibio of Nigeria. In: Lehmann, C. & J. E. Myers (eds.), *Magic, witchcraft and religion.* Palo Alto: Mayfield. 152–165.

Onishi, Norimitsu. 2001. Nigeria's Press Bounces Back From Military Rule. *New York Times,* February 21.

Peel, J.D.Y. 1969. *Aladura: A religious movement among the Yoruba.* London: Oxford University Press.

Piot, Charles. 1999. *Remotely global: Village modernity in West Africa.* Chicago: University of Chicago Press.

Popper, Karl. 1962. *Conjectures and refutations: the growth of scientific knowledge*. New York, Basic Books.

Ray, Benjamin. C. 1976. *African religions: Symbol, ritual and community*. Englewood Cliffs: Prentice-Hall.

Sanneh, Lamin. 1994. Translatability in Islam & in Christianity in Africa. In: Blakeley, T. *et al* (eds). *Religion in Africa*. London: James Currey, 23–45.

Soares, Benjamin F. 1999. Muslim proselytization as purification. In: An-Na'Islam, A. A. (ed.). *Proselytization and communal self-determination in Africa*. New York: Orbis Books, 228–245.

Tamuno, T. N. 1969. Peoples of the Niger-Benue confluence. In: Ajayi, J. F. Ade and Ian Espie (eds.). *A thousand years of West African history*. Ibadan: Ibadan University Press, 206–216.

Turner, H. 1967. *African independent church* (2 vols.). Oxford: The Clarendon Press.

Wallace, Anthony F. C. 1966. *Religion: An anthropological view*. New York: Random House.

Winch, Peter. 1997. Understanding a primitive society. In: Grinker, R. R. & C. B. Steiner (eds.). *Perspectives on Africa: A reader in culture, history, and representation*. London: Blackwell, 312–326.

4 ECONOMIC INSTITUTIONS

Early West Africans were hunters, gatherers and fishers, but today many rural peoples farm and/or herd cattle. This is still supplemented by foraging, fishing and the use of small domesticated animals and fowls. Wage labor is more common today and some urban people engage in penny capitalism or labor in the informal sector.

But West Africans are noted for their history of and acumen in local, regional commerce, and especially in long-distance trade with Asia and later Europe. While some West Africans are involved in small-scale manufacturing, this was never the region's forte, either historically or in the recent past. Furthermore, efforts to industrialize in the colonial and postcolonial eras have stalled. As in the past, trade with the outside has inhibited modernization. As in the past, West Africans largely trade minerals and agricultural exports for cheap imports from the world market. This chapter will show how trade developed through history and how some of the patterns that emerged in the region still plague the area today.

Introduction to West Africa Economics

What do we mean when we talk about economics? Since human beings are biological beings, but ones lacking much natural protection against the elements, we protect ourselves culturally—with clothes, shelter and food. This is the biological basis of economic behavior—food procurement or production plus activities directed toward constructing housing and fabricating the clothing and tools needed for life.

In the West African context this has traditionally been done through simple transformation of nature's products—using rocks and sticks for tools and later on hafted metal blades, once metallurgy was discovered. Clothes were made from animal skins, bark, cloth and even grass. Until the 1970s, for example, Kasena women wore leaves for garments. Houses or huts were constructed of **wattle and daub** or mud bricks and grass thatch (See Photo 4.1). The more ancient style is the round hut, but today most people who still live in mud houses make them square

Early West Africans were simple foragers, fishers and hunters. Today, although many rural people farm and/or herd cattle, they still use foraging, hunting and fishing to supplement their diets. Perhaps when desiccation of the environment in the north began to cause game to disappear, West Africans began to domesticate plants and animals, a process that has been called the **Neolithic Revolution**. At this time people became less mobile and settled in communities near water sources.

Photo 4.1   Man Thatching a Roof with Elephant Grass.

For the last four thousand years, most West Africans have been farmers living in rural villages. Some practiced **pastoralism**—herding cattle for a living, such as the Fulani (also called Fulbe or Peul). Still others practiced a variety of artisanal jobs such as blacksmithy, pottery production, weaving thread and cloth, dying cloth, soap making, divination, medicine production and curing, basketry and mat making.

West Africans are renowned as traders. From about the sixth century onwards, long-distance trade was in the hands of men who entered West Africa from across the great Sahara Desert. Gradually, however, locals such as the Dyula people began to specialize in trade. Over the centuries, and with impetus from the slave trade, many market towns and entrepôts sprang up throughout West Africa. Today this area has a reputation as being very commercially oriented, when compared to other regions of Africa.

Nowadays, many West Africans also work for wages, though in the past labor was based on **generalized reciprocity**. With the coming of colonialism, however, some young men were taken out of the village through forced labor while others left the countryside in search of wage employment. These were **formal sector** workers who helped build roads, canals, bridges or worked in mines and on plantations (See Photo 4.2). Some worked as day laborers and servants. Others became small business owners, setting up market stalls or small shops in town (See Photo 4.3).

Other West Africans entered the **informal sector**, selling trinkets and other objects on the street or cooking and selling food (See Photo 4.4). Others developed gardens on the edge of the city to sell various foodstuffs. In the past, as with today, some people engaged in unauthorized activities such as thievery or prostitution.

We tend to divide economic activities into separate categories—food procurement, trading, wage labor and so forth. West Africans would not describe their lives in these terms, however. In everyday life, economics, politics, kinship and religion are mixed

Photo 4.2 Bridge from the Colonial Era.

together. In fact, a useful way to view economics is as the bedrock of other kinds of activities—political, religious, recreational and kin-related.

Given this **embeddedness** of economic activities in social experience, it is sometimes difficult for the anthropologist to sort out what is going on in a West African context. If a man is seen giving a sheep to another, is it an economic exchange, or is

Photo 4.3 Street-Side Kiosks in a West African City.

Photo 4.4   Girl Working in the Informal Sector.

the sheep being handed over to be sacrificed on a family shrine? And if it is sacrificed, who gets the meat, and is the distribution of this food an economic exchange or part of a religious exchange? Since the people involved in the sacrifice are kinsmen, and each gets a specific part of the sheep, isn't this behavior better considered under the rubric of kinship? Well, you can see the problem for the ethnographer, but it is not a problem for the villagers—this behavior is called "life" and it is all interconnected, one part with another.

The Domestic Mode of Production

A **mode of production** is a patterned way of making a living. In West Africa families have farmed and/or herded animals since the Neolithic Revolution. The **domestic mode of production** has remained fairly constant, both in acephalous societies and under the domination of chiefs and kings. It even forms the basis of much agricultural production and pastoralism today, within the macro-context of nation-states in West Africa.

Much of farming in West Africa is horticultural rather than agricultural. **Horticulture** depends on nature for water, whereas **agriculture** uses artificial storage and distribution of water through irrigation. The rainy season in the Savannah is roughly from May to September. This is the only time when the peoples of the Savannah can farm, unless they have some stored source of water, or live near a river that runs year round. But dry season water is a problem. Most rivers evaporate or drain away to a trickle during the dry season. This makes any form of irrigation difficult. Natural lakes and ponds, as well as man-made reservoirs are scarce. The lack of water in the region is a severe limiting factor to farm production.

Aridity, plus the prevalence of tropical diseases have also kept the numbers of European-owned commercial farms low in the region, unlike their abundance in east and Southern Africa. Thus, farming and cattle ranching in West Africa have always primarily remained in the hands of Africans.

Other than the Fulani herders, most rural West Africans are farmers. Two types of farming are practiced, **extensive farming** and **intensive farming**, with the former method predominating. In the extensive method, people establish farm plots by burning the bush, cutting away as much of the wood and brush as possible, then cultivating the area for a number of years till the soil has been depleted. Farmers then repeat the process in anew area, leaving the original plot to fallow for a period of years.[1] This method is practiced in those areas of West Africa that have low population densities and high land availability. This type of farming, called **slash-and-burn** or **shifting cultivation,** was the most common throughout West Africa's history.

Why use such extensive farming methods in West Africa? The short answer is that they fit the environment. Since soils are not very fertile, farmers have had to devise shifting strategies to allow the fallow time that fields need to regenerate, as well as intricate intercropping methods to get maximum value from the fragile soils. In the weeks before the first rains begin to fall, the men and boys of the family clear a new plot of land by cutting brush and small trees. These are piled on the land and burned to provide a form of fertilizer. Large trees may be more difficult to cut down and may take more than one farming season to fell. The technique used is to burn the brush at their bases, then chop away at the charred trunk with machetes. Every time the family has some extra brush to burn, the process is repeated. Eventually the tree will die and topple. It can then be cut up and carried back to the village for firewood and beams for building houses.

Farms tend to be located either far from the village or right next to it. In extensive farming the bush farms are most often a few kilometers from the village in order to access ample land for rotation of fields. This also permits livestock to roam around the village. Sometimes the livestock problem is handled by making fenced "kitchen gardens attached to the house in the village. They keep out foraging livestock. Secondly, when land becomes scarce, that directly around the village may be farmed openly. In some villages the farms butt up against the farmers' houses. In this case goats and sheep are tethered and cattle herded to prevent them from entering the fields.

In extensive farming, men do the initial land clearing. In much of West Africa and elsewhere throughout the continent, women maintain and harvest the farms. When the first rains are due, the seed saved from the previous year is planted. All members of the family participate in this task. Depending on the intensity of the rains in the Savannah zone, two or three weedings will be required, as weeds grow rapidly and threaten to choke out the young seedlings. If weeding were not such an arduous task

---

1. In Northern Ghana where extensive farming is practiced, farms are usually cultivated for about seven years, then let alone for another fifteen to twenty years.

that requires large labor gangs, a person could work larger farms alone. The labor needs created by choking weeds means that a farmer needs family members to help. If the family is small the headman organizes work parties by calling on friends, in-laws and other members of the community.

As the crops begin to mature, small children scare birds and animals away, preventing them from decimating the ripening grains. Harvest is another time when communal labor is needed to pick and transport the crops back to the village to store them in family granaries.

Because there are two rainy seasons in the forest regions, more crops can be grown there than in the Savannah. Tubers are commonly grown in large numbers at the edge of the forest and deeper in the rain forest a variety of fruits are grown. Both extensive and intensive methods are used to farm forest plots.

Where West African populations became dense, farmers were forced to intensify their agricultural efforts. This method required much greater investment of time and labor. Farmers learned to use such methods as manuring, inter-cropping, terracing and irrigating to farm the land.

In general, both intensive and extensive farming were done with the hand held hoe, an ax (machete) to aid in clearing and a planting stick. For most of the history of West African farming, metallurgy has been known and farm implements have been made of iron blades with wooden handles. There were few other tools produced until the introduction of the plow in colonial times, which resulted in the cultivation of larger fields. Europeans also brought improved forms of metal, which are preferred today. Local blacksmiths now use industrially-hardened scrap metal to manufacture farming tools.

Some new farming approaches have been developed, but whether farmers work alone, form cooperatives or innovate with new types of work groups, the traditional method of farming still rests with the household, usually a three-generational extended family. This is called the lineage mode of production, a form of the domestic mode of production.

This type of farming is designed to support the whole family. The middle generation of strong adults constituted the core of the farm group, with the youngest generation helping with minor tasks such as fetching water and firewood, childcare and scaring birds. The older generation was often made up of retired farmers who reaped the social security benefits of communal production by eating from the product of the labor of their mature children. Every able-bodied person worked (or had worked) to contribute to a common pool of wealth. The collectivist approach has worked for centuries to provide an adaptive means of surviving in a harsh environment. It has also resulted in a strong community-based civic culture designed to redistribute the products of the labor of the strong members of society to those who cannot work—small children, the elderly and the infirm. The family farm still dominates West African agricultural.

Since a farm worker produces more than s/he can consume, there is a small surplus that can be used for next year's seed, to support non-farming members of the family and to act as an old-age pension system for the aged and infirm. Additionally, in the Savannah there is often a "starvation period" stretching sometimes weeks, or in drought years, even months. Commonly the few months prior to June can be difficult ones. The scarcity of farm produce requires careful planning so that they family can stretch the food out over this lean period.

As a corollary of this point, the more people working the farm, the greater the surplus. That is why adoption, fostering and natural childbirth are stressed in West Africa as ways of increasing the size of the family, and hence the labor force. Also, the more relations of affinity and friendship a group has, the more laborers they can call on to aid them in times of maximum need—weeding and harvesting. Not surprisingly, West African cosmologies stress communalism, kinship amity, sharing and cooperation.

Labor and land are exchanged between kin, friends, neighbors and in-laws. It is a common practice to lend land indefinitely to anyone, even strangers, who wish to settle in the community and farm. These settlers will usually offer a "first fruits" basket of grain to the headman of the group that owns the land. In fact, Charles Piot found that among the Kabre of Togo, a man will even exchange a good plot of ground for an inferior one, simply to have a relationship of friendship with another farmer. Such friendship has intrinsic value in human terms, but it can also be viewed as a form of "**social banking**." This means storing up good will that can be utilized later.

The concept of communalism is central to understanding West African economic behavior. It is at the basis of the **Wealth in People System** (**WIP**), where one invests in exchange relations needed for production. In West African canons it is important to meet the needs of others around you, by providing labor, giving them a daughter in marriage, "loaning" them a cow or giving up land to them. If their needs are met, you have "money in the bank," so to speak. That is, if you are ever in need, you have a friend to call on. This is called generalized reciprocity, where equivalencies are not calculated in exact terms, but neither are they forgotten.

West Africans, many of whom are excellent traders, are well aware of **specific reciprocity**, wherein one expects equivalent value for that given, but such tit-for-tat exchanges are not thought to be appropriate in close relationships and are usually reserved for the marketplace.

In general, West African farmers practice a **redistributive mode of production**. Farm produce is given to a headman, or in some cases a chief, who acts as a farm manager, allocating land, labor and inputs to produce a crop. He then directs the redistribution of the crop, most often storing a significant amount of it in a central granary, though he may allocate portions to lesser granaries of family heads beneath him in the genealogical framework. Storage is an extremely important art in West Africa because grain can be lost to water seepage, animals, insects or mold—as well as theft, though in West Africa stealing food is considered one of the most heinous of crimes and it is not common.

With a low level of surplus, this traditional redistributive system was incapable of producing inequalities, except for minor ones such as honorifically serving the headman first at a meal, or giving him the "first fruits" of a harvest on land he allocated to strangers or distant kinsmen. When I first went to West Africa in the early 1970s, family headmen definitely had minor advantages over subordinates. They were more likely to have a tin roof on their house, own a bicycle or have a shotgun, but for the most part, their lifestyle was similar to the other members of the family. By 1998, however, the surplus was notably greater, due to peasant production for urban markets and cash-cropping. Women and young men complained that senior men were abusing their traditional hold over them, keeping larger amounts of the income for their personal use.

At this time, the nature of farming began to change. First, women began to farm in 1978. They told me that they did this because of the poverty created by the Sahelian drought earlier in the 1970s, and because their husbands were not sharing much of the income from farming. Secondly, young men were striking out on their own, clearing separate farms and even building unattached houses of their own. Both of these developments were made possible in part by the use of tractors, petroleum, imported fertil-

Photo 4.5   Ghana Cotton Corporation (GCC) Plant.

izers, pesticides and loans from the **GCC**, the Ghana Cotton Corporation (See Photo 4.5). Such outside inputs, coupled with the chance of good profits from maize production, allowed subalterns to begin to farm apart from the lineage mode of production. The rising demand for maize comes from urban growth, so subordinates (young men and women) have a ready market for any maize they grow.

Under conditions lacking such inputs, it is much harder for subordinate males or females to farm separately, because of their inability to attract laborers to work their land at those times when large work parties are needed. So under ancient ecological conditions, unmarried boys and women were more dependent on the family farm.

The Economics of Polygyny in West Africa

Having several wives is an ideal in many non-Christian families in West Africa. Why? Plural marriage is about the political economy, that is, the control of women's labor in the context of ample land and limited workers.

Women are not see as oppressed by polygyny; some welcome one or more co-wives to share the burden of work in the household and farms. Also, when a woman is married patrilocally, bringing an additional wife from her own kin group provides her with a close companion and ally in an alien environment. Additional wives help the man economically, but they also reduce the labor burden on wives in the household.

Table 4.1 Percent Wealth Received by Yoruba Wives from Their Husbands	
Wife received from husband	Total
Nothing	19
Part of food	48
All food	28
All food, clothing & cash	5
Total	100

Boutillier reports that in the Ivory Coast, 85 percent of the women in an opinion survey preferred to live in polygynous marriages rather than monogamous ones.

But economics is central to the ideal of polygyny in West Africa. The UN Economic Commission for Africa (ECA) reports that "a man with several wives commands more land, can produce more food for his household and can achieve a high status due to the wealth which he can command." The greater the energy input into agriculture in West Africa, the greater the output.

The high value on polygyny evolved out of shifting cultivation societies where women have traditionally done most of the farming work. A single man, or a man with a single wife, has less help in cultivation, and will have less help in doing the heavy work of land preparation. The equation goes something like this: more wives (labor) = more children (labor) = more land cleared (production) = more prestige = more wealth = greater ability to get more wives. Thrown into the equation is also a supernatural factor. Men who preside over a large number of dependents (who become descendents when he dies) have a better chance of becoming an apical ancestor and attaining eternal life.

The value placed on polygynous marriage has continued into the 20th century. Galetti and others showed that Yoruba farmers in 1951 and 1952 believed that wives contributed more to the family income than the value of their keep. Furthermore, the increased progeny of polygynous households enhanced the dignity and standing of the family in the community. Yoruba husbands were clearly benefiting from the labor of their wives: five percent of the wives were totally supported by their husbands. It is normal in traditional African marriages for wives to support themselves and their children. When they cook for their husbands, all or part of the meal ingredients usually comes from their own labor. Percentages of household income going to women can be seen in Table 4.1.

More wives help a household in various ways. Among the cattle-herding Fulani, wives are expected to provide a large part of the cash expenses of the household out of their own earnings from the sale of milk products. If clothing or supplemental food is needed for the children, they buy it. Among the farming Sisala, where women only started to farm on their own in 1978, women have shown an increased contribution to the household's income. By paying school fees, buying clothing and providing additional food, women take some of the burden of provision off of their husbands.

Leisure is another factor in polygyny. To the extent that a man can marry several wives and produce multiple offspring, he will have more free time while young and active. Furthermore, he will more likely have a secure position in old age, having a large group to economically support him in his infirmity. Women with co-wives also have more leisure time.

It is likely that most West African men were never able to marry multiple wives. Polygyny was an ideal. While this remains the case, most West African men today still cannot acquire multiple wives due to economic limitations, and it is generally thought that polygyny is on the decline in West Africa. Boserup reports that most of the studies on polygyny in Africa show an average number of about 1.3 wives per married men, with only one-fifth of all married man having multiple wives at the time of inquiry. To some extent, the labor traditionally accessed by marriage can today be replaced by the use of hired labor.

Wage labor and polygyny may stand in an inverse relation. In his classic study of the Mende of Sierra Leone, Kenneth Little concludes that "a plurality of wives is an agricultural asset, since a large number of women makes it unnecessary to employ much wage labour."

In general, labor is in short supply in West Africa. There are three possible ways to develop agricultural production in West Africa: through the traditional polygynous household; by expanding the use of plow technology; or through the use of wage labor.

The introduction of certain labor-intensive cash-crops has increased the need for workers and made polygyny a viable economic strategy where it might otherwise have died out. Cotton, for example, is very labor intensive, especially in the plucking season, when the cotton balls must be removed by hand before they succumb to the weather or the many Savannah fires that occur in dry season.

In the main, West African cultures have formed in a crucible of adaptation to extensive agriculture. Thus, values and rules revolve around the control of labor in one form or another. Marriage rules give men access to the labor of women, as well as to their reproductive capacities, which in turn produces more laborers for the family. Some families seek foster children to shore up weak households. Other forms of controlling labor in West African history were slavery and pawning. Formal slavery has been outlawed, though it still exists *sub rosa*, but pawning of women and children to fulfill debts and obligations is another way of meeting economic needs in the West African context.

The well-known **Boserup Hypothesis** claims that shifting cultivation favors polygyny and that with the introduction of the plow and more intensive forms of agriculture the need for multiple marriage declines. My data on agriculture in Northern Ghana show the situation to be more complex. Polygyny is still the ideal. Men still need help in weeding and harvest activities, plus in economic activities adjunct to farming e.g., foraging, growing spices and vegetables, and domestic chores. Furthermore, the GCC is pushing cotton as a cash-crop and growing it requires more labor input than maize (See Photo 4.6).

Furthermore, women have started to farm on their own. They grow spices, vegetables, grain crops (mainly maize) and cotton. To do so they hire village boys to work their farms when the boys are free from other chores. Women also rely on tractors supplied by the Ghana Cotton Corporation to plow their lands. They also get supplies of imported fertilizer from the GCC to revive depleted soils so they don't have to clear new plots (See Photo 4.7). Because women now represent a new form of household wealth and security, they are even more valuable than in the past, or at least equally so. One would expect polygyny to remain strong under such conditions.

Exchange and Investment in Farming Societies

Rural farmers were predominantly subsistence farmers, exchanging goods and services in local daily and weekly markets. Subsistence farming means that what the fam-

Photo 4.6   Cotton Bales for the Global Economy.

ily produces, they consume everything, but it is not quite that simple. A headman may also give gifts of food to his friends, brothers, in-laws or even to strangers. Such gifts

Photo 4.7   A Cotton Processing Plant in West Africa.

are often given in return for a favor or to curry a relationship. Thus, if a lineage is the main focus of production, distribution, storage and consumption, it is not isolated from other such group. In fact, a successful farm unit will be tied to many others in relations of reciprocal assistance. A strategy to make a farm group vital and successful is to produce many children and to establish and maintain as many mutual relations with others as possible.

If the modern European world is based on market exchanges, the world of many rural West Africans is rooted in human exchanges, or in anthropological jargon, on generalized reciprocity. Much is given without any expectation if return is based on exact equivalence. Thus, to give or do something for somebody (*pa* in Isaalang) without any expectation of a specific return is highly valued. This is the basis of community life in rural West Africa and indeed in much of urban life as well.

Is this investment? Do West Africans give only in expectation of a return on their "investment?" I have called this "social banking," but the Sisala would say that relations between kin and friends should be based on the giving (*pa*) of gifts (*zilé*), not on selling (*yaling*) something in a market (*yøbø*). In a market exchange you can haggle or bargain (*barikE²*), you can even give a discount (*lo*). When you go to buy (*yøwE*) something you expect this type of haggling, but exchanges among kin and friends should not involve any calculation of value.

Hence, we can say that to a certain extent, the non-commercial exchanges within the civic culture of West African communities are incompatible with the market economy that penetrated West Africa with the modern era. It is not that such mercantile relations were not known in pre-contact times—they were, but they did not form the bedrock of village life. Markets were commonplace in West Africa long before the coming of Europeans, but buying and selling were seen as only one kind of exchange, and not the most fundamental one (See Box 4.1, The "Free" Mud Wall).

Box 4.1   The "Free" Mud Wall

One day in the village, I decided to build a mud brick wall to enclose my porch. I asked Bubachebe, my research assistant at the time, "Who can make the bricks and build the wall for me?" He brought several teenage boys to my house the next day. I inquired as to their rate of pay and was greeted with a stunned silence. After an uncomfortable moment or two, Bubachebe pulled me aside to tell me that they were doing it as a *zilé*, a gift. He went on to explain that since I was given fictive kin status and renamed **Salia Bujan** (See Photo 4.8), they were obligated to perform the labor for nothing. Apparently in the civic culture of West Africa, even fictive kin are not subjected to the market mentality.

The key to many exchanges in the civic life of West African villages is to enhance relationships, not to gain advantage in pecuniary terms. It is not that the teenagers in the story above never came to ask me for anything after building my wall. They did, and they felt that they had the right to do so because of my fictive kinship status and because they had done something for me. In the context of village life, generalized reci-

---

2. Borrowed from the Hausa.

Photo 4.8   Basi, Tiawan and Salia, 1970.

procity is the fuel that makes life work, or to use a slightly different metaphor, it is the glue that holds the community together.

To get the best of someone in a commercial exchange may adversely affect a social relationship. Paul Bohannan found this among the Tiv of Nigeria. In this society, in the past, the most apparent category of exchangeable items was foodstuffs (*yiagh*). For example, a common exchange would be to give pepper for locust-bean sauce. In such an exchange, quantities were never prescribed. If a woman needed locust-bean sauce and another needed pepper, the exchange would be mutually beneficial. Because both got what they wanted—it was said that the "market was good" and both went away happy.

More recently Charles Piot has noted the qualitative aspects of exchange among the Kabre of Togo. The Kabre say, "it is not good to die without having eaten off someone else's plate." In Kabre society "persons use things to gain access to persons rather than that they use persons to gain access to things." In Kabre interchange "all that matters is whether someone's immediate need/desire was fulfilled."

The Kabre are not unique in West Africa. They represent the normal way of thinking about a person, and about that person in exchange. Piot successfully shows that the self is contained in social relations in West Africa—it does not stand apart. The Sisala would agree. A person who is selfish (*siing* lit. "has greedy eyes") is horrific in Sisala culture. To "have too much desire" (*tuø-cheeng*) is not conducive to a civic culture. One of the interesting points made by Piot is that the coming of the market economy among the Kabre has not eroded such communalistic values, but has enhanced them. He says, speaking of the time before European contact:

> I am not suggesting that gift exchange did not also exist during this time period. But the evidence indicates that its sphere of operation was more restricted than it is today, and that it was only with the advent of colonialism and capitalist

wage relations in the south that it began to grow and came to occupy its current more dominant position.

According to Piot, the Kabre have not become more selfish as they have acquired more wealth in the market economy, rather "when money-making is put to use producing and enhancing social relations, it is regarded as something of great value." This seems to indicate that the basic civic culture of West Africans is much stronger than some have thought.

Yet West Africans have historically been profoundly impacted by outside market forces. Paul Bohannan shows that the Tiv distinguished between the subsistence-oriented category of *yiagh*, foodstuffs, and *shagba*, imported prestige items such as brass rods, *tugudo* cloths or iron bars and that one was not directly convertible into the other. However, Piot seems to be saying that the Kabre use money or prestige items, to enhance social relations, rather than to isolate themselves.

I must say that I have known both kinds of West Africans—those who are generous to a fault, and those who move far from their families so that they do not have to share their newfound wealth. But by far, the former predominate. While Bohannan seems somewhat pessimistic about the impact of the market economy on the Tiv, Piot reassures us that economic prosperity has not spoiled the Kabre. In my mind, the jury is still out on this one, but I hope Piot is right.

Subsistence, prestige and social relations are not unrelated. A wealthy entrepreneur who displays many prestige goods will be more likely to attract followers who can produce foodstuffs and other value for him or her. Building by giving is the key to West African economics and in this way any of the three values can be converted into any of the others or combinations thereof. "The giver attracts; the hoarder repels."

This again brings up the concept of investment. How is this done in a West African context? A person can invest in any of the three types of value mentioned above, but with the qualification that selfishness goes unrewarded. In the ancient moral order, only the wealthy person who shares his food will reap the reward. Likewise, the person who invests in multiple social relationships will have wealth and prestige. In the mix of the three variables, it is one's relations with others that are *the* most significant investment.

Paul Bohannan has shown that the Tiv traditionally had three chief categories of exchangeable items—foodstuffs (associated with kinship exchange), prestige items and market goods. They were arranged in a hierarchy on the basis of moral values. The most valued were kinship exchanges, which were those involving the creation and maintenance of relations with the living and the dead. Second came prestige exchanges, and lastly market exchanges. He says:

> The drive toward success leads most Tiv, to the greatest possible extent, to convert food into prestige items; to convert prestige items into dependents—wives and children.

In the traditional economy, the idea was to convert toward the highest and most valued—market to prestige to social relations. To convert subsistence wealth into prestige wealth and both into women or clients was the aim of the economic endeavor of the Tiv as well as most West Africans.

Bohannan goes on to show that this system resulted in two kinds of exchanges: exchanges of items within a single category, which he calls "conveyances" and those exchanges of items from one category to another, which he calls "conversions." Each is marked by separate and distinct moral attitudes. Conveyances were morally neutral; conversions had a strongly desirable quality in their rationalization. Note the following story from Tiv culture:

> When I was a very small child, my kinsmen gave me a baby chicken. I tended it carefully and when it grew up it laid eggs and hatched out more chickens; I exchanged these chickens for a young nanny goat, who bore kids, which I put out with various kinsmen until I could exchange them for a cow. The cow bore calves, and eventually I was able to sell the calves and procure a wife.

This story is illustrative. In a non-monetary economy, animals are used as a form of investment which naturally increases in value. A man should use this natural increase to get a wife, have children and in turn give each male child a chicken. Many other West African peoples have the same idea of investment—to expand wealth to expand the family, which in turn expands wealth. Women follow a similar path in life by having many children.

Likewise, a man who has much food, lots of prestige items and many social relations should share with others. In general, West Africans are very scornful of a man who is merely rich, with full granaries and plenty of cash. This is not morally worthy wealth. To make his riches worthy the man must convert them into social relationships, by sharing them, investing the wealth, so to speak, in the "social bank."

In Sisalaland, a greedy man is likened to a witch (*hila*). He has *siaa ba nEsE*, "four eyes." In one sense, he is respected because he has been able to amass material wealth. Some greedy men go so far as to have a sealed, windowless room (*dia bene*) which they fill with powerful shrines. Respect for him is tinged with fear because he does not use his wealth or power for social good. He is said to have a "strong chest" (*bøyE-dolung*). He is brave, but not morally upright. He is feared as a man of special but potentially evil talents. He is not a civic player.

Paul Bohannan did his work during the colonial era when the market economy was beginning to take hold in Tivland. Charles Piot and I have done our work at a later stage, after years of penetration by the global economy. Piot is the most optimistic of the triad. I am more inclined to agree with Bohannan and to see the market economy as eroding traditional ways. Professor Piot sees the Kabre adapting the market system to meet the higher need of enhancing social relationships. Bohannan says that the Tiv distrusted money and saw aggrandizement as a threat to the traditional moral economy of the day. Today the Sisala actively pursue money. Their lineage-based moral code is under fire because of rising individualism and the pernicious pursuit of the pecuniary. It remains to be seen which view of West Africa prevails.

The Coming of the Plow and Peasant Production

The energy source for farming in most West African cases was human labor. With the introduction of the plow, some West Africans learned to harness donkeys and cattle to plow their lands. Others got tractors and began to participate in what I have elsewhere called **petrofarming**. Today most West African farmers still rely on human energy for most of their farming tasks, but those peasants who produce cash-crops and food for cities are usually able to utilize modern transport. Such human-powered peasant production is still dependent on imported energy for the transport of the crops to distant markets.

While labor (energy) is a limiting factor in agricultural production, water is also restrictive. Most farmers practice rainfed horticulture, relying solely on nature for rain during the wet season. Since the Savannah dry season extends from October to May, farmers cannot farm during much of the year, even though crops would readily grow with irrigation.

Until late in the colonial period, most West African farmers were subsistence horticulturists, however as transportation and roads improved, connections to the metropole and global markets also got better. With the aid of colonial advisors and later **NGO** specialists in agricultural development, West African farmers began to produce for distant markets. Cash-crops such as rice, cotton and groundnuts were encouraged in the Savannah zones, while in the south cocoa, palm nuts, bananas, and other crops suited to the tropical rain forest were promoted.

The addition of cash-crops, and the expanding demand for food from the growing cities of West Africa, has created strong economic relations between villages and cities, between primary producers, middlemen and urban merchants.

Cash-crops in the Savannah mainly have been rice, cotton, and groundnuts; however with the rising demand for food from the cities, farmers are growing more and more maize as a cash-crop. In the south, cocoa is an important cash-crop. There are isolated pockets of specialized farming as well. For example, the Anlo of southeastern Ghana grow shallots in the sandy microniche of their land where poor soils form a narrow ridge between the ocean and the lagoon. This is a very arid area, but it has a high water table, so farmers are able to use water from shallow wells. Upkeep of these fragile beds is extremely labor-intensive and they frequently have to be rebuilt by carting in sand. The poor soils are combated with bat droppings (guano), cow dung, fish manure and chemical fertilizers.

Much of agriculture in West Africa today has become dependent on outside forces. This is a tenuous dependency. In 1980 I described the detrimental effects of tractor farming. The development policy of the 1970s was to stimulate large-scale commercial farming with mechanized systems. The Agricultural Development Bank was encouraged to advance loans to farmers to go into large-scale rice cultivation, using mainly tractors and high-yield rice seeds. Tractors were considered appropriate for modernizing Ghana's agriculture and several types were imported. At one point, as many as seventeen different makes were being used and spare parts obviously became a problem, especially in the remotest regions. The rising cost of tractors, parts, fuel, and lubricants discouraged the continued use of tractors, and many were ultimately abandoned. This affected agricultural production, making the "**green revolution**" policy unproductive.

By 1977 no farmers in my survey were using tractors or any kind of traction plowing. Even in 1974, the peak year of tractor use, only 48% of survey farmers used tractors (See Photo 4.9).

In 1998, when I returned to Sisalaland, I was shocked by the amount of change and especially by the fact that the tractors and petrofarming were back, albeit by a different avenue. A new infrastructure had developed based on private enterprise and development efforts by the Ghanaian government.

The village-city-global marketplace connection that began centuries ago in West Africa remains and will likely persist in some form in the future. The question really is

Photo 4.9 A Broken Tractor from the Green Revolution Effort of the 1970s.

what kind of productive technology the villagers will use to produce their subsistence crops and those shipped to urban areas. Elsewhere I have championed the use of animal traction technology over imported technology, because for the most part, it can be made locally, repaired by West African technicians and relies on a sustainable energy source—animal power.

Most West African rural people keep cows, donkeys, sheep, goats and a variety of fowls as a "bank account"—a reserve of protein. They use these in trade, to exchange with kin, friends and affines; as sacrificial offerings; and sometimes they are sold to get cash. These cattle and donkeys can be used as traction animals as well. One advantage of a traction animal over a tractor is that when the animal is too old to pull the plow, it can be eaten or sold. Mature bullocks (castrated bulls) in Northern Ghana bring much more in the market than those just beginning their careers as draft animals. Of course, the other advantage is that animals naturally reproduce at little cost to the owners, whereas imported tractors, petroleum and replacement parts are prohibitively costly for all but the wealthiest of West African farmers and they become more so with every passing season.

Land Tenure

While land is generally amply available in West Africa for farming, most land is owned in one way or another. Private ownership or long-term leasing, however, is a recent phenomenon, and is usually restricted to the larger towns and cities. More common is **communal land tenure**—property owned by families or larger kin units like the clan. Usually such ownership is tied to the mythology of the residents that describes the autochthony of their forbears. Descendants of those who came to the land first hold first rights to its use. Thus, land tenure in West Africa is intimately tied up with genealogies and one's relation to the ancestors. This ownership is most commonly demarcated though a ritual relationship to the ancestors at given groves of trees, ponds, rock outcrops or constructed shrines on the land. All kinsmen, who sacrifice upon these altars share a common patrimony in the land connected with them.

Individual farmers, operating under a communal WIP system, held **rights *in usufruct*** over land, not **rights *in rem***. The former refers to the fact that they could not sell the land, while the latter is a European concept giving the owner the title to the land and the right to sell it like any other commodity in the market.

Rules about land tenure or ownership were traditionally collectivist in nature, a fact that severely restricted development under colonialism. Europeans misunderstood the African land tenure system, denying a farmer bank credit because he could not put up private property as collateral. In later chapters we will see that colonials, in a further misunderstanding, declared eminent domain over "all unused lands," that is, if land appeared to be vacant, it belonged to the state. This caused many problems because in the West African land tenure system, especially where extensive farming was practiced, much of the land at any given time was left fallow. Furthermore, many sacred groves and other plots of land were thought to be intricately tied up with the ancestors and the supernatural. While to European eyes this land appeared to be unused, to the West African it had important ritual and moral value.

Today since farmers lack legal deeds to property, they have difficulty getting agricultural loans, as most West African governments have implemented European legal codes regarding collateral and property rights—ones that clash with traditional norms. Yet land remains a source of security for many, even those in urban areas, many of whom assiduously maintain their ties to rural kin groups and to a hoped for share of the patrimony of their forebears.

West African Trade

Trade arises when one community has something another community lacks and exchange is made possible. Geographical and environmental niche diversity almost always makes that possible—one has salt and fish, while the other has fruits and yams, for instance. Given the variety of eco-zones in West Africa, from seacoast to desert, trade was inevitable. But trade was also stimulated in West Africa by specialization. For example, in Northern Ghana different villages specialize in different crafts: Boti is known for its wooden chairs, Chinchan is known for charcoal-production. The Hausa city-state of Kano was famous for its dyed cloth and Bolgatanga in Northern Ghana

Photo 4.10   A Woman Weaving a Basket.

was famous for basketry and reed weaving (See Photo 4.10). Others made soap, had iron deposits or worked in leather.

Given the absence of money, simple barter was the first form of trade. Today, most West African villages have a daily market where women take their surplus edibles or manufactured goods. Markets occur in regular places at regular times which allows sellers and buyers to know with surety that goods and customers will be available.

The same regularity is assured for inter-community trade by the establishment of a weekly market. It is common for different major trade centers to rotate their market days, for instance in Sisalaland the market cycle is every six days, thus if the Tumu market is held this week on Thursday, next week it will be on Wednesday and the following week on Tuesday and so forth. On the other five days of the market week the fair will be held at different villages in a set rotation. Since people of a region know the schedule, they can be where they need to be at the appointed time.

Historically the sheer bulk of foodstuffs and the lack of an effective means of long-distance transport limited trade. Along the coast and throughout the rain forest zone, transport was by head bearer. Until the coming of the camel to the Sahara and lorries in the rain forest, long-distance trade tended to focus on lighter commodities of high value like ostrich feathers, precious stones, small amounts of gold and salt. Goods borne by human carriers through the forest would be loaded onto donkeys and horses at the edge of the Savannah.

The difficulty of portage in the rain forest was one reason why so many market towns were found along major rivers, such as the well-known markets of the Niger-Benue area—Raba, Egga and Funda. Not only could these **riverine** people transport goods by water, but they also were able to earn income ferrying caravan traders across the river.

Pack animals could be used within the Savannah and Sahelian zones, but heat and distance in trans-Saharan crossings kept that trade to a minimum until the introduction of the camel. Some scholars think that cattle were used initially to drag loads across the desert from one oasis to the next. Horses could not survive such arduous labor in the Sahara's heat and limited water. The use of the camel increased the freight loads that trading caravans could haul. Thus began the large-scale export of heavier items like gold and ivory.

Salt is in extremely limited supply in the non-coastal areas of West Africa and has always been a valuable trade item. Two main sources exist: Tagharza on the southern edge of the Maghrib and the seashore. A salt substitute called natron comes from Lake Chad but was used mainly by peoples living around that body of water. In the Saharan source at Tagharza (about 500 miles north of Timbuktu) salt was dug in slabs. It was so plentiful in that region that people there built their houses of salt blocks roofed with camel skins. Along the coast, people dug shallow ponds for seawater, allowed it to evaporate, then scrapped up the salty crust, cleaned it and packed it in baskets for transport to the interior. The 11th century Arab geographer, El Bekri, said that the Ferawi peoples who were mining gold for long-distance trade were so much in need of salt that they were willing to trade gold for an equal amount of salt!

Local crops, naturally occurring commodities and localized industries formed the basis of trade. Footpaths and minor roads linked different localities. Waterways were used where feasible. Where such natural and manmade arteries intersected, larger trade emporia grew such as Timbuktu connecting Gao with Jenné and Mopti, or Salaga, which developed as a major slave market. Such sites gave local political leaders a commanding middleman's position in commerce. Later states such as Asante and Dahomey grew because of their favored positioning relative to supply and demand.

For local or small regional markets, goods are usually carried and marketed by women. Long-distance trade called for specialized traders, most of which were men in ancient times, although today there are vast networks of Yoruba women and others who engaged in far-flung labyrinths of trade all over West Africa.

As trading centers grew, and the market became more complex, a need arose for market organization. Market officials, often under royal mandate, allotted pitches and market stalls, heard complaints, set times and prices and acted as market police to keep order. Such officials also taxed the traders, which provided wealth for the ruler.

At such intersectional markets, the opportunity for control of trade gave rise to political centralization. Chiefs became Kings as they were able to establish themselves at a fork of crosscutting routes or at a fortuitous point along a major route. The rise of states coincided with urban development brought on by long-distance trade. Central emporia such as Jenné, Timbuktu, Gao, Aïr and Sijilmasa developed large markets where traders of various backgrounds and nationalities could congregate to meet their customers. Whatever the nature of the commodities flowing through such entrepôts, kings established laws to get first rights to them.

The marketplace at all levels—village, regional and distant—functioned as more than a location for economic exchange. People went there to meet friends, hear news, have fun, encounter lovers, gossip and engage in political activity. Market day relieves tedium and boredom and usually brings one in contact with news from the wider world.

Gold discovered in the region stimulated long-distance trade and *vice versa*. As demand for gold rose, mining the ore became big business. According to Raymond Mauny, once this industry was fully organized, exports amounted to approximately nine tons of gold annually. This occurred without the advantages of modern machinery, engineering and sump pumps. From incoming gold at the terminus of the gold trade at Sijilmasa, in what is now Southern Morocco, the precious metal went to North African states where it was minted into gold coins. Gold was so common that sub-Saharan Africans bartered it away for superfluity—cheap textiles, leatherwork, cooking pots, beads, bracelets and mirrors. Just as with the later European trade, long-distance trade linking West Africa with the outside world centered on luxury items, not staple goods.

At first long-distance trade communication was a problem. The 10th century geographer Al-Masudi described how **silent barter** was used initially. Goods would be left in a designated spot, and then the trader would withdraw to await the coming of another trader. The second man would place the amount of exchangeable goods next to the first pile of goods. If the first trader accepted the amount offered, he would advance and take them, leaving his own goods behind for the second trader. If not, he would wait till the second trader added more or went away with his goods. This was an ancient custom. In the 4th century BC the Greek writer Herodotus described this practice for the northwest of Africa. Sometimes major emporia had resident bilinguals who acted as translators in commercial transactions. Eventually trading languages such as Arabic and Hausa developed to facilitate contact by foreign traders.

Some currency was used early on. This could be gold dust and coins from the Maghrib, iron coinage, cowries, cloth strips, metal bars and imported *manillas*, twisted metal bracelets from Europe. In the Niger-Benue confluence, a form of currency was used which resembled a small hoe. This hoe-money was known as far north as Katsina. The Idoma called it *akika*, the Tiv referred to it as *ibia* and the Hausa word was *agelema*.

So we can see that local spider webs of trade links united West Africa and eventually became intertwined with camel-stimulated trans-Saharan commerce and European trade before the Portuguese appeared in the 15th century. The whole of northwest Africa formed a vast commercial continuum, focused on great cities of the interior, kingdoms of the rain forest and coastal peoples. To an extent, this northwest trade corridor shifted east with the fall of Songhai after the 1591 invasion by the Moors, moving trade eastwards to Hausaland and Kanem-Bornu (See Chapter 9). Also, Sijilmasa was destroyed in the 16th century and never recovered at the northern terminus of trans-Saharan trade in the Western Sahara. But the north-south trade, by whatever avenue, was ongoing, as was internal commerce. Trans-Saharan trade did not end. It continued through Kano and the Lake Chad region on an important scale into the 20th century. Indeed there are still caravans that cross the vast expanse of desert and lorries carrying goods and migrants seeking a better life in Europe and the oil-rich countries of North Africa and the Middle East. Even slaves are still transported northwards across the sandy wastes of the Sahara (See Chapter 11).

Trade routes, local, regional and export crossed and re-crossed the region, linking West Africans with one another and with foreigners. Indeed, trade had established linkages between Europe and Black Africa long before Gil Eannes returned from Senegal to Lisbon in 1434 with a sprig of rosemary to show he had passed the barrenness of the Sahara Desert and found potential trading areas south of it.

In 1444 the Portuguese formed **The Lagos Company** and constructed a staging facility on Arguin Island. At that time there were two spheres of long-distance trade in West Africa. The older Muslim zone was in the north and the newer Christian orbit ran along the coast, linking up with suppliers and buyers in the coastal hinterlands.

Trading Organization and Credit

Trade requires finance. Traditionally, traders got credit from family backers, big men or royals. But the nature of finance changed with time, as did the form of trading groups. In the Niger Delta the trading unit was the "house," originally the extended family. With the rise of the **New Men**, the unit expanded to include all of a trader's associates, kin or otherwise. These units sometimes formed residential wards in urban areas.

Much business was done on credit, but a single individual found it hard to buy on credit, nor were sellers keen to sell to individuals who lacked a strong backer who would pay up in case of default. Buyers needed to have a social unit behind them. In the areas where Europeans lived, they fell under the protection of royal African landlords. Europeans felt confident in advancing trade goods to subjects backed by a king. This was European venture capital, which was given to African slavers who would then go inland, exchange the goods for slaves and return with the captives. If the slaver absconded with the goods or did not return or returned empty handed, the African landlord would be left with the debt, which he could recoup by selling the trader and his kin into slavery. Political power was an economic form of surety.

Trade was, then, very much under the control of wealthy men and occasionally women *senares* or *senhoras*. Europeans had to pay recognized trading dues, called **comey** in the Niger Delta. Additionally, dashes were expected: customary payments to begin business and a final gift at the conclusion of the transaction. (A **dash** is still considered part of many economic transactions in West Africa). Europeans were forever complaining about the need for such gratuities, yet, this was a well-organized trade system, carried on according to recognized commercial rules. It was a system based on mutual confidence and credit was backed by recognized social groups and powers.

The Impact of Foreign Trade

The rising commercialism of Europe would have a profound impact on West Africa. The arrival of European traders completely altered the economic map of the region. The coast, formerly the distant edge of the trade network was vaulted to center

Figure 4.1   *Imborivungwu* Smoking Pipe from the Cross River Hinterlands, Nigeria.

stage. Especially for those in the center of the trade web, it also meant an about-face. Whereas they had mainly looked north to the Saharan trade for centuries, they now began to receive manufactured goods from the coast and in much larger quantities — cooking pots, brass pans, metal bars, *manillas*, cowries, beads, cloth, firearms, powder, flints, shot, mirrors, distilled spirits and New World tobacco. (Tobacco was grown in West Africa, but American tobacco was still imported in large quantities, perhaps because of its prestige value as an import) (See Figure 4.1 of an ancient smoking pipe). Willem Bosman, a member of the West India Company operated by the Dutch, estimated that 150 different items were needed for trade on the Gold Coast.

As with the trans-Saharan trade, these goods were primarily luxuries rather than necessities, except for arms, which the Africans used as a means of procuring slaves and therefore could be considered a means of accumulating **capital**.

From the 16th century onward, the industrial economy of Europe was steadily increasing its output, and peripheral lands like West Africa not only were beginning to supply raw materials for the industrial behemoth, but they also served as markets for such merchandise. From this time forward, an immense demand for European goods developed, not only on the *Guiné* Coast, but also inland along well-established trade routes.

Between 1820 and 1850 trade between Europe and West Africa increased greatly. The nature of trade changed too, moving away from regional trade to an extractive **traffic economy**, a condition that continues into the present day. The export of slaves, ivory, beeswax, gum arabic, incense (sweet-smelling gums), and indigo declined, supplanted by oils needed in industrial manufacturing and the production of cooking oils, candles and soap for the increasingly wealthy working class in Europe (See Table 4.2). Also desired were hardwood timber, hides and rice. Europe exported to West Africa metals, hardware, liquor, salt, gunpowder, flints, munitions and cotton textiles.

As with most European goods, the latter were highly desired, but unlike most other manufactured goods, imported textiles were often of a quality inferior to some produced in West Africa itself. Despite this, the locals liked these imports.

Foreign-made goods did little to bolster local production. Christopher Fyfe writes about the impact of these imports on African's ability to accumulate capital:

> European trade discouraged industry. Hence, in a country where capital formation was in any case difficult... there was little incentive to improve production methods or to increase productivity.

In other words, it was much wiser to invest in trade goods to be resold than to try to compete with incoming manufactured goods. This is a five hundred-year-old pattern that continues today. All the CD players, automobiles, high-prestige imported gin and the immeasurable plethora of foreign goods are not made locally. Once they are consumed, they are gone forever. Present-day dependence has deep historical roots.

In ancient exchanges, as with today, these consumables were traded for raw materials that were not easily replaceable—timber, ore and ivory. Elephants were virtually wiped out by this demand. What was worse, for much of this early trading era, such trifles were exchanged for human beings. This imbalance in commerce continues today with **MNCs** extracting rare and valuable minerals and timber and utilizing cheap labor on their plantations to produce such excesses as cut flowers, pineapples, coffee and cocoa.

Slaving eventually ran its course. The move away from illegal trade caused some changes among the African élite class. The new élites switched to brokering the import-export business of West Africa. They surrounded themselves with servants, built miniature forts replete with cannons, and sent their children to school in Europe. They were to become the foundation of the metropolitan élites of today—the so-called **Mercedes Class**.

With new trade came new trade towns on the southern and northern edges of the forest zone and up into the drier grasslands. Local élites became traders and turned slaves into plantation workers producing for European markets. However, due to competition from Southeast Asia and the U.S. soybean industry, oil production in West Africa suffered.

Gradually, as Imperialism proceeded, European merchants began to take more interest in controlling the distribution of their imports and the extraction of West African's raw materials. Merchant houses were formed. Some producers switched to more profitable cocoa production; other local princes and merchant élites played a role in the administration of the colonies; yet others provided the vanguard for the nationalist movements that ended the colonial period.

Today contact with European society and the world economy has increased the linkage between villages, towns and cities in West Africa. There are few rural economies that are not in some way linked to distant demands for raw materials found in their region such as ore, timber or, more commonly, their agricultural produce.

Early writers, notably Fortes and Evans-Pritchard, emphasized the distinction between states and non-states in Africa. Catherine Coquery-Vidrovitch claims that the differences between stateless and state societies in Africa are overstated, at least with regard to economics. She says:

> No matter what society is examined, the permanence of trade transcends the traditional contrast between states and stateless societies.

Table 4.2 West African Trade Items by Zone

West Africa > Europe	Coast > North	Rain forest > South	Rain forest > North	Savannah > South	Savannah > North	Mediterranean/N. Africa > South
Gold	Salt	Kola nuts	Kola nuts	Salt	Gold	*Mfgd. goods*
Ivory	Fish	Slaves	Spices	Natron	Slaves	*Cloth*
Spices	*Guns*	Ivory	Slaves	Slaves	Gems	*Horses*
Slaves	*Munitions*	Gold	Gold			*Metal weapons*
Exotics*	*Mfgd. goods*		Cloth			Salt
			Gems			

Goods in italics are of European or foreign origin going to West Africa

Mfgd = manufactured

* For example, ostrich feathers, animal glands for perfume and gems.

To my way of thinking, this is an overstatement. Stateless societies tend to use the domestic mode of production and are *influenced* by trade; but African states allowed their people to carry on with the domestic mode of production while élites went about *controlling* trade and tribute. Just to say that all African societies have been affected in some way by trade is not the point. How much have they been influenced? In what ways? And what have been the results of that contact? If a small economy in the Savannah gets a few trinkets from the coast, that is one thing; but if the volume of trade increases to the point where aggrandizers gain control of it, that is another.

One can tentatively make the following hypothesis: the greater the volume of trade, the greater the centralization of society. State formation in West Africa has clearly been driven by opportunities opened up by trade, first internally, later with Europeans.

Before the rise of extensive trade routes, stateless peoples continued to farm using the domestic mode of production. Lacking political leaders above the family level, land was not appropriated by a chief or king. In fact, even when states arose, the African mode of production shows the absence of any significant private appropriation of land (but see the Dahomean case below). If trade influenced them, it had a minor effect.

State Economies

With states, however, it was a different matter. As aggrandizers, both upstarts and established monarchs, began to exact tolls and taxes from traders and demanded privileged rights to buy goods with "special" money or at reduced prices. For example, if a king ruled an area that produced a special cloth, he would declare a royal prerogative to trade in it and, furthermore, foreign goods could only be purchased with such cloth. Such ambitious monarchs tapped into the traditional mythology of West African society to justify their ascent to power. They did this by leaving the domestic mode of production in place, but appropriating the principle of lineality. Aggrandizers did not claim the right to rule as individuals, but as members of a royal descent group. Coquery-Vidrovitch says that "the masses were attached to patriarchal forms" so royals and bureaucrats kept these forms, honored local customs, expanding on the idea of generalized descent to included privileged descent—the right of royal lineages to dominate. This mythologizing of rule was true of both invading royals and chiefs who rose within autochthonal society.

Secondly, aggrandizing newcomers formed linkages with the autochthonal custodians of the land and their legends about the group's relation to the earth. In this way, they set themselves up in a franchised position to get at profits. They accomplished this in two ways: by extracting tolls from passing traders and/or reselling goods and by demanding tribute from family heads or neighbors that they came to dominate using armies supported from their trade profits.

Was this despotism, similar to the **Asiatic Mode of Production** made famous by Marx? No, but the result was similar, though less permanent, as control of trade is more fickle than domination over a peasantry tied to fixed fields. African monarchs tended not to be despots. Their power was more ephemeral and dependent on ongoing relations of generalized reciprocity with a large body of clients. When trade evaporated, their dynasties tended to disintegrate, as with the Sudanic kingdoms of the Niger Bend, or the Mandingo kingdoms of Sénégambia. In the latter case, when the ritual ties to the land began to weaken, they lost their power to command, and their control of trade slipped away.

It seems that the only time when African kings were able to move toward despotism was through contact with the capitalist mode of production, as in the case of Dahomey. Before extensive contact with Europeans the king of Dahomey lived on tribute from neighbors and wealth taken from descent groups in his own society, but this wealth was mostly redistributed at an annual potlatch-like ceremony. The king's aids would literally throw away goods, which the people could pick up. He also killed hundreds of slaves to show his invincibility.

This wealth was extracted, but given back. The king's main source of income, for the state and for himself, was derived from his privileged control of long-distance trade, which included slaving. Nevertheless, it is not so clear cut. The Dahomean king did require military service of his subjects, especially the special corps of **Amazon Women** he kept to work his fields and protect him.

When the slave trade slacked off and Europeans began to demand palm oil, the 19th century monarch, King Ghézo, made a move that was uncharacteristic of African kings—he declared certain lands to be eminent domain, lands of the state. These palm plantations were worked with slave labor. The plantations were also a source of personal income for King Ghézo and his family. Coquery-Vidrovitch points out that through a carefully maintained confusion between the "lands of the kingdom" and the "lands of the king," the monarch was able to privately appropriate the land and its product.

These holdings were clearly under the direct control of the state. The king had farm overseers who made sure the crops were tended correctly and that soil regeneration procedures followed. In addition to receiving 1/18th of the crop, he taxed all trade in palm products and all ships coming into his harbor. While contact by other kingdoms with Europeans tended to enhance their power over people, in Dahomey this was a unique move toward the Asiatic Mode of Production.

However, contact with European markets had an impact on polities elsewhere in West Africa. Francis Moore, an English trader in Wolof territory in The Gambia in the 18th century noted that the Wolof king of Saloum:

> was so absolute that he will not allow any of his people to advise with him, unless it be his Headman (and chief slave) called Ferbro (viz. Master of the Horse)...

Mahoney and Idowu comment that a Wolof chief appointed local overseers, often not of royal background, to manage groups of villages and farms. He gave them presents and wives, and in return they collected taxes for him. Proceeds were accepted in kind—cattle, grain and woven cotton cloth. They passed these on to the king after extracting their share. Thus, royal revenue was derived from recognized taxes on agriculturists, traders and Fulani nomads. Newly conquered peoples were required to pay tribute and become taxpayers. In return, the Wolof chief protected these subjects from raids by other kingdoms.

This is very close to feudalism, though Jack Goody makes a distinction between Eurasian feudalism and this sort of tax collecting, which worked only so long as the people were militarily circumscribed in some way. In Europe serfs were tied to the land in fixed ways, paying a portion of their crops to the feudal lord in return for protection, similar to the Wolof case, but the crucial difference is that Wolof subjects could leave the land and find alternative livelihood elsewhere if politico-military circumstances allowed.

More generally, under the African mode of production, there were two ways of accumulating a surplus by élites—war and control over long-distance trade. Coquery-Vidrovitch calls this "indirect domination," as opposed to a more explicit extraction of the **surplus value of labor** from the king's subjects. Nevertheless, it was still domination. Somebody in nearby weaker groups was losing out, both those who had to pay tribute and those enslaved to work the king's plantations.

In West Africa, ruling monarchs did not disrupt the practice of collective production in their communities. While they may have taken internal tribute, they were mainly concerned with control of long-distance trade and the extraction of wealth from tributary neighbors. This was done by (1) fabricating an ideology of protection—that the king was the paternalistic guardian of the people and (2) by stressing the linkage between the royal lineage and those in other lineages that controlled the ritual aspects of land. This fabrication of tradition allowed the states and aristocrats who buzzed around it to become entrepreneurial and pursue aggrandizement under the cloak of putative authority.

In Europe and Asia, monarchs often gained control over their subjects' labor value by claiming the need to invest in public works. Nevertheless, Godelier points out that in West Africa, state domination lacked monumental buildings and projects. That said, African rulers did maintain armies, build palisades and in some cases, erect town walls. Also, protection went beyond architectural structures. It was also ritual. The health of the monarch was a metaphor for the kingdom's health. Common people were often prevented from seeing the king perform any normal functions, for example, urinating or defecating, even standing up or sitting down were shielded from view. In some cases, when the king's health began to decline, he was killed and a new strong monarch was put in his place.

Writers have pointed out that in the Asiatic Mode of Production the state bureaucracy becomes quite developed and that bureaucrats get involved in the economy. Generally, the bureaucracy was minimal in West Africa. In some places it barely existed, as in the Mandingo kingdoms of Sénégambia. In others elaborate bureaucracies existed, as in Asanteland. But even there bureaucrats were less involved in the economic production of the people than in the great states of Eurasia. The efforts of states were aimed at control of trade and the market. Bureaucrats interfered only "indirectly" in the collective production by the families and communities of the realm. Rather, the bureaucracy acted in an entrepreneurial role, as an intermediary between the external market and the people. It was their move to control the opportunities generated by long-distance trade that enabled state building in West Africa.

Why didn't West African states rise without access to long-distance trade? In short, the domestic mode of production on poor soils with limited labor would not produce a sufficient surplus. Any attempt to extract that surplus would alienate the very labor pool needed to exploit the land. Exploited peoples could simply move away. There was no effective way to transform the domestic mode of production into anything else without using military force. West African leaders found it prudent to leave their own workers alone and dominate others militarily, creating lines of tribute or acquiring slaves that could be put to work or sold.

Thus, we can see that in West Africa there were several types of ascendancy by the ruling class that allowed them access to economic profits. Some evolved into parasitic military states, others focused on tribute and trade, and a few used slaves to produce food or exports. For non-royal élites, use of the slave mode of production occurred only in the 19th century when the demand for slaves by Europeans fell off, causing a concomitant drop in the price of slaves.

Wage Labor and the Informal Sector in Modern Cities

Modern cities are a magnet in West Africa. Many people are leaving rural areas to seek employment in the city. Keith Hart has shown for the Tallensi and other peoples of the northeast corner of Ghana, where land is in short supply, that emigration is necessary for many young people. But the pressure to move due to demographic pressure is only one variable in migration. Where this pressure is lacking others also choose to go to the cities in search of employment and a modern way of life. There are both push and pull factors drawing young people out of rural areas and attracting them to cities. Many simply want a "modern" way of life; others would like to escape their subservient status in their natal homes.

Hart notes that in 1960, international and long-distance migrants comprised 29 percent of Ghana's labor force, while inter-regional migrants accounted for a further 24 percent. Undoubtedly, these figures are low by present-day standards. I found that about 50 percent of the Sisala villagers of Bujan were away working in the city, in spite of the fact that there is ample land to farm and the peasant economy there is thriving.

Migrants are following in the footsteps of previous generations who loom as success stories in their minds, yet opportunities for wage employment in cities have been declining and many people return home empty handed, or live a *déclassé* existence in urban slums. Most who do go, move in with previous migrants while they seek some form of income. For example, as I write this, in the Kumase household of a successful migrant where I have stayed, there are three teenage boys from the north. One is an apprentice electrician, the other is learning to be a tailor and the newest arrival is working selling firewood.

Hart notes that many such migrants seek wage labor in cities, but only about half become formally employed (**proletarians**); the other half fall into a category he labels as sub-proletariat. He says:

> Price inflation, inadequate wages, and an increasing surplus to the requirements of the urban labour market have led to a high degree of informality in the income-generating activities of the sub-proletariat.

Half of the residents of Nima, a slum on the northern outskirts of Accra, are listed as self-employed, non-wage-earning, and un-employed, thus "a very large part of the urban labour force is not touched by wage employment."

Migrants often come from areas near the urban centers, but those that come from the far north suffer most, falling to the bottom of the wage scale. They employ several strategies to cope. They hold down more than one job at a time or double up on work shifts.

However, many cannot find jobs at all. They are forced to labor in the informal sector or as Sol Tax called it, engage in "**penny capitalism**." Some sell firewood collected in the bush, hawk other bush products or cheap imports purchased in bulk.

Some buy cartons of sugar, cigarettes, candles and the like and place a small table in front of their residence. It is a common sight to see such "entrepreneurs" sitting by their stands late into the night illuminated by the light of a kerosene lamp. Others walk the streets in search of customers. Crime is another option (See the Box 4.2 below).

Many of these bottom-end wage earners and informal workers live a hand-to-mouth existence, falling back from time to time on the generosity of kin, neighbors, or live on credit. Success for migrants is ephemeral. Hart says:

> The desire of migrants to improve their living standards, and to accumulate against retirement in the country, is not easily satisfied; as a result, most stay for a number of years, perhaps for all their working lives, in pursuit of a goal which for many is simply unrealizable.

In spite of the instability of the lives of many urban migrants, urbanization is on the increase in West Africa. If the opportunities for survival in the cities are fleeting, many believe their chances in urban areas are better than those in rural communities. These hopefuls have been all but ignored by development planners. Keith Hart has nicely categorized the income opportunities in West African cities:

Box 4.2   West African Urban Economic Sectors

Formal income opportunities
Public sector wages
Private sector wages
Transfer payments—pensions, unemployment benefits
Informal income opportunities: legitimate
Primary and secondary activities—farming, market gardening, building contractors and associated activities, self-employed artisans, shoemakers, tailors, manufacturers of beers and spirits.
Tertiary enterprise with relatively large capital inputs—housing, transport, utilities, commodity speculation, rentier activities.
Small-scale distribution—market operatives, petty traders, street hawkers, caterers in food and drink, bar attendants, carriers (*kayakaya*), commission agents, and dealers.
Other services—musicians, launderers, shoeshiners, barbers, night-soil removers, photographers, vehicle repair and other maintenance workers, brokerage and middlemanship (the *maigida* system in markets, law courts, etc), ritual services, magic and medicine.
Private transfer payments—gifts and similar flows of money and goods between persons; borrowing; begging.
Informal income opportunities: illegitimate
Services—hustlers and spivs in general; receivers of stolen goods; usury, and pawn-brokering (at illegal interest rates); drug-pushing, prostituting, poncing ("pilot boy"), smuggling, bribery, political corruption Tammany Hall-style, protection rackets.
Transfer—petty theft (e.g., pickpockets), larceny (e.g., burglary and armed robbery), speculation and embezzlement, confidence tricksters (e.g., money doublers), gambling.

Those denied success in the formal structure become the "reserve army of under-employed and unemployed" who seek alternative ways of making a living in the urban ghettos. Yet, there is an uneven distribution of economic opportunities between regional/ethnic groups in West Africa. In 1960, 21 percent of the Gã people of the Accra area held white-collar jobs, while only one percent of the northern Mole-Dagbani peoples of the north held such employment. When Keith Hart compared Frafra white-collar workers with those from the smaller Akwapims of Southern Ghana (with more contact with Europeans and more education), he found that the latter were 75 times more likely to have such jobs. In general, northerners tend to take jobs at the lower end of the scale and few will apply for an advertised job where they have no kin or tribal relationship. Nepotism is common in West Africa, so this is a realistic appraisal of their chances. Because of these nepotistic tendencies, migrants from one village or region tend to be clustered occupationally.

Thus, when people leave the village for the city, they often go to stay with a relative or friend and find employment in a sector known to employ people from their region or ethnic group. Such households rarely rely on one source of income, however. For example, in the Sisala household in Kumase referred to above, the household consisted of three teenage boys, five dependent children and three adults. The husband has a high-paying professional job, while each of his wives works—one makes **kenke** balls (cassava flour dough) to sell in the market, and the other works on an assembly line. Additionally, the husband runs a *tro-tro* (jitney) on the side, and maintains a kitchen garden and a farm some distance from his home in a Kumase suburb. Such diversity in income streams derives from the traditional risk-aversion of peasants under conditions of extreme poverty. It is less important to have one big income than to have many diverse flows.

The informal sector is a reality in West African cities, but scholars tend to view it from different perspectives. Some see it as a blessing, a sort of "bootstrap operation" while others see it as the result of capitalism's stranglehold on West Africa.

For those who decide to migrate to the cities, poverty is not far away. The informal sector does provide *some* means of making money while looking for a better income flow. In that sense, it may act as a buffer against pauperism. Nevertheless, in a region where food is being imported and rural food production has fallen behind demand, we have to ask ourselves this question: "Is a strong young man selling decals of Madonna in a West African city really the most productive use of his time?"

≋≋≋ CRITICAL THINKING QUESTIONS ≋≋≋

1. Explain the correlation between population growth, on the one hand; and the type of farming done in West Africa, on the other.
2. Explain the domestic mode of production in terms of the concept of corporation.
3. Explain the economics behind the institution of polygyny.
4. What are the implications of the West African traditional land tenure system for development?
5. Discuss the reasons why the informal sector is an important part of urban life in West Africa today.

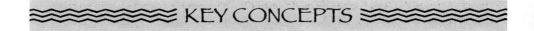

KEY CONCEPTS

Agriculture	Neolithic Revolution
Amazon Women	New Men
Asiatic Mode of Production	NGO
Boserup hypothesis	Pastoralism
Capital	Penny capitalism
Comey	Petrofarming
Communal land tenure	Proletarians
Dash	Resdistributive mode of production
Domestic mode of production	Rights *in rem*
Embeddedness	Rights *in usufruct*
Extensive farming	Riverine
Formal sector	Salia Bujan
GCC	*Senhoras*
Generalized reciprocity	Shifting cultivation
Green revolution	Silent barter
Horticulture	*Senares*
Informal sector	Slash-and-burn cultivation
Intensive farming	Social banking
Kenke	Specific reciprocity
Lagos Company, The	Surplus value of labor
Manillas	Traffic economy
Mercedes Class	Wattle and daub
MNC	Wealth in People System
Mode of production	WIP

SOURCES & SUGGESTED READINGS

Bekri, El. 1913. *Description de l'Afrique septentrionale* (Trans. de Slane). Algiers.

Bohannan, Paul. 1997. Some principles of exchange and investment among the Tiv. In: Grinker, R. R. & C. B. Steiner (eds.). *Perspectives on Africa*. Oxford: Blackwell, 119–128.

Boserup, E. 1965. *The conditions of economic growth*. Chicago: Aldine.

Boserup, Esther. 1997. The economics of polygamy. In: Grinker, R. R. & C. B. Steiner (eds.). *Perspectives on Africa*. Oxford: Blackwell, 506–517.

Bosman, Willem. 1967 [1705]. *A new and accurate description of the coast of Guinea, divided into the Gold, the Slave, and the Ivory Coasts*. New York: Barnes & Noble.

Boutillier, J. L. 1960. *Bongouanou Côte d'Ivoire*. Paris: *Presses universitaires de France*.

Coquery-Vidrovitch, Catherine. 1997. Research on an African Mode of Production. In: Grinker, R. R. & C. B. Steiner (eds.). *Perspectives on Africa*. Oxford: Blackwell, 129–141.

Fage, J. D. 1995. *A history of Africa*. (Third Edition). London: Routledge.

Fortes, M. & E. Evans-Pritchard. 1940. *African political systems*. London: Oxford University Press.

Fyfe, Christopher. 1969. West African Trade A.D. 1000–1800. In: Ajayi, J. F. Ade and Ian Espie (eds.). *A thousand years of West African history*. Ibadan: Ibadan University Press, 237–52.

Galletti, R., Baldwin, K. D. S., and Dina, I. O. 1956. *Nigerian Cocoa Farmers*. London: Oxford University Press.

Godelier, Maurice. 1963. *La notion de mode de production asiatique et les schemas marxistes d'évolution de sociétés*. Paris: C.F.R.M.

Goody, Jack. 1971. *Technology and the state in Africa*. London: Oxford University Press.

Hart, Keith. 1971. Migration and tribal identify among the Frafras of Ghana. *Journal of Asian and African studies* 6:26–35.

Hart, Keith. 1974. Migration and the opportunity structure: A Ghanaian case study. In: Amin, Samir (ed.). *Modern migrations in Africa*. London:Oxford University Press.

Hart, Keith. 1997. Informal income opportunities and urban employment in Ghana. In: Grinker, R. R. & C. B. Steiner (eds.). *Perspectives on Africa*. Oxford: Blackwell, 142–162.

Lance, James Merriman. 1995. *Seeking the political kingdom: British colonial impositions and African manipulations in the northern territories of the Gold Coast colony*. Ph.D. dissertation, Stanford University. Ann Arbor: University Microform (UMI) #9525856.

Little, K. L. 1948. The changing position of women in the Sierra Leone protectorate. *Africa* XVIII.

Mahoney, F. and H. O. Idowu. 1969. The peoples of Sénégambia. In: Ajayi, J. F. Ade and Ian Espie (eds.). *A thousand years of West African history*. Ibadan: Ibadan University Press, 132–148.

Mauny, Raymond. 1961. *Tableu géographic de l'Ouest Africain au Moyen Age*. Dakar: I.F.A.N.

Mendonsa, Eugene L. 1980. The failure of modern farming in Sisala-land, northern Ghana. *Human organization* 39:275–279.

Mendonsa, Eugene L. 1982. *The politics of divination*. Berkeley: University of California Press. See also the paperback reprint version, 2000 published Writers Club Press.

Mendonsa, Eugene L. 2001. *Continuity and Change in a West African Society: Globalization's impact on the Sisala of Ghana*. Durham: Carolina Academic Press.

Piot, Charles. 1999. *Remotely global: Village modernity in West Africa*. Chicago: University Press.

Riesman, Paul. 1974. *Freedom in Fulani social life: An introspective ethnography* (trans. Martha Fuller). Chicago: University Press.

Saul, Mahir. 1995. Economic life in African villages and towns. In: Martin, Phyllis M. & Patrick O'Meara (eds.). *Africa* (Third edition). Bloomington: Indiana University Press, 190–210.

Tamuno, T. N. 1969. Peoples of the Niger-Benue confluence. In: Ajayi, J. F. Ade and Ian Espie (eds.). *A thousand years of West African history*. Ibadan: Ibadan University Press, 206–216.

5 POLITICAL INSTITUTIONS

This chapter contrasts the democratically organized polities of pre-contact West Africa with those that emerged under European influence and Islam. It also discusses the concept of acephaly, which is the embeddedness of political functions in non-political institutions. West African political ways are described in their traditional forms and in their modern forms as these polities adapted to penetration of the region by two external forces—European culture and Islam.

Some Introductory Remarks

The developmental pattern from egalitarian to ranked polities was generally instigated by the production of surplus food and a growing population. **Storable surplus** was initially managed in the family, thus we get the development of **descent groups** and lineages to deal with the production, distribution and consumption of that surplus. Put simply, at this stage the **political economy** was family-bound. Headmen in lineages and other family groupings controlled agricultural products or family herds or both. There was no need for political leaders at a higher level because the problems and opportunities connected with production could be resolved at the family level.

Political **rank** was associated with the appearance of trade routes, discovery of gold, passing caravans and the resulting accumulation of wealth. Chiefs arose to handle these problems and opportunities that threatened or benefited larger congeries of family groups.

Today, family headmen usually do not exploit their kinsmen to any great extent. The intra-familial political economy is embedded in kinship and religious institutions that keep it contained. Family members have close access to such leaders and can exercise various means of control over them. But when tribal chiefs arise to deal with supra-familial problems, they may stand above such restraints. The opportunity for aggrandizement is greater where there is expansion of population, urbanization and the appearance of new threats or **poleconomic** opportunities. **States** are characterized by well-developed bureaucracies that supercede family or lineage organization. Such forms of government allow for the greatest extraction of value from the people, and the populace has less chance to interact with and influence politicos directly.

Below I present examples of pre-state political organization, seen in early **ranked societies** and **kingdoms.** Early forms of **communalism** at the village level were democratic although this decreased somewhat as states evolved. African kings generally could not be despotic since they often had reciprocal obligations to their subjects. Even though many achieved great wealth *vis-à-vis* their subjects, they also could be called on in times of need to supply assistance. This gave monarchs power over their dependents, but the general ethos of reciprocity and equality still prevented kings from blatant exploitation of the people.

The Pre-Political Phase

Early hunters and gatherers or **foragers** in West Africa did not have formal government. In these early **bands,** informal social pressure stressed cooperation among households that clustered in groups of about 50 or 100 individuals. Food production was managed in each household—the **household production system.** Legends, stories and verbal interaction in the band tended to stress **egalitarianism.** Gossip, ridicule and the very intimate nature of the band acted as a **leveling mechanism** in society.

Such small groups had a simple division of labor. Men hunted and women gathered wild edibles from the bush. In this form of economic organization individual accumulation was a liability. Because of their mobile lifestyle, households did not generate surplus goods or food that could be stored for long periods of time. This lack of a storable surplus is a crucial limiting factor in the development of wealth associated with a hierarchical political organization.

Social control among modern African foragers is usually informal and spontaneous. People who deviate from group norms are openly criticized, are shunned or become the subject of withering gossip. This is a common feature in bands everywhere. In pre-state Africa, the power of individuals was limited to **influence.** That is, no person had coercive power to force another individual to do something. In fact, it was not seen as good for any individual to rise above another, although some people had more influence than others by virtue of being superior hunters, storytellers, songsters, dancers, shamans or having greater all-around wisdom. Also, since all had equivalent **means of destruction**—spears, bows and arrows—no man or band of men had superior firepower. Conflicts between bands were limited to an occasional skirmish.

Stateless Peoples of West Africa

In the West African context we usually use the term stateless to refer to tribal peoples who had some developed political structures, unlike bands, but who had not yet developed formal **chiefdoms.** Many tribal peoples throughout West Africa are composed of congeries of families and clans that have no overseeing head. Their political processes tend to be embedded in other institutions such as descent groups, **age-sets,** secret societies or **voluntary associations** or other **sodalities.** These small groups of people are largely self-regulating.

A key feature of such stateless societies is the minimal use of hierarchy for organizational purposes, though they do recognize big men as having higher rank than non-big men. **Political power** is usually organized as a lateral distribution of authority or a

Photo 5.1　A West African Shaman.

heterarchy. A big man may exercise influence and a lineage elder may preside over his subalterns within the extended family, but beyond such basic exercise of power, authority is spread thinly over a wide variety of groups.

Tribal forms developed with the origins of agriculture and the domestication of animals.[1] These kinds of economies permitted the accumulation of small surpluses of wealth in the hands of family headmen. With incipient wealth, ideas about **bigness** and rank also began to coalesce as men acted to reglementate, or institutionalize, their access to the surplus labor of others. In short, the process of the formation of **privilege** had begun — power was being converted into **political authority**.

Once men had the opportunity to accumulate and store food-wealth (caloric energy) in granaries or herds, rules were necessary to govern production, distribution and consumption. Power no longer existed in nature alone. Power now came to be thought of as storable, much as grain in a bin. Men could collect power in two ways that came to be associated and connected more and more as time went by. First, shamans emerged that were thought capable of harnessing cosmic power in shrines and charms using secret knowledge (See Photo 5.1). Secondly, family headmen evolved who were thought to rule their lineages and clans by virtue of their genealogical position in the group's family tree. Such men were thought to hold office, and officeholding gave them certain rights and privileges of governance.

Legitimate coercion was now possible, even desirable, as a headman had to control the socioeconomic behavior of his subordinates in order to ensure the survival of the family. Cooperation was still the ethos of the group, but now reciprocity was sup-

---

1. In West Africa these were mainly cattle, goats, dogs, pigs, sheep, donkeys and a variety of fowls.

planted with the concept of redistribution—the idea that subordinates should give their product to the headman who would store it in a communal granary or herd (or both), and divvy it out as needed in a manner that would ensure group survival.

The power to control products and people's labor was vested in an authoritative office. An officeholder's authority was derived from seniority in the family genealogy and from the close connection of office to supernatural power. Only such senior men could exercise power embedded in ritual institutions. I will illustrate this with the example of the **virebaling** or lineage granary among the horticultural Sisala. When the grain crops were collected in this granary it was not seen simply as a utilitarian crib. It was considered a *vene*—a family shrine intimately connected with the ancestors and occult power. Anyone but the lineage headman caught putting a hand into the granary, or stealing food from it, would be subject to supernatural sanctions. It was thought that such a thief, when revealed by magical means, would be killed by the ancestors unless she or he confessed and made retribution for the crime, and showed contrition and submission to the authority of the headman.

If a headman discovered missing grains, or saw some on the ground near the granary, he would call his family members together and hold a **scorpion ordeal** or inquest. After finding a scorpion, which has a terribly painful sting, he would inform all that the scorpion (under the direction of the ancestors) was about to ferret out the thief. It was not uncommon for the deviant to step forward and confess at this point, thereby avoiding the pain of the sting and possible death. If not, the headman would place the bug on the arm of each family member until it stung someone.

It must be evident to the reader that political power and judicial inquiry are vested or embedded in the role of this family headman. As he acts as the head of the family, he is also judge and executioner in a political sense. He has the authority to make people do what they may not wish to do. He can legitimately coerce, using the force of his office and the occult power of the ancestral spirits. In a traditional acephalous society, this headman is the supreme authority—no chief or king stands above—only the ancestors, occult power and, very distantly, God.

It is important to note that this is the beginning of a marriage between earthly political power and that purported to exist in the extrahuman realm. It begins with headmen in descent groups, age-sets, voluntary associations, cults, and secret societies. As society becomes more complex, this affinity between mundane and supernatural power is extended to chiefs and kings.

Another significant idea is that of **heritability**—that (as with goods) the office of headman should be passed on to the next in line genealogically. Such orderly **succession to high office** is guaranteed by the creation of rules governing the reallocation of a man's offices and roles upon his death. Whereas a big man may rise through effort and skill to wield great influence in his lifetime, it passes away with him in death. With a formal headship the office is maintained as the new headman takes over.

This idea of the office being more than the man is amplified in the concept of **corporation sole**, where the group outlasts its members, and that such group officers hold rights to control people and products jointly owned by the group. Many of the funerary and sacrificial rites performed by West Africans have to do with the maintenance of such groups through time. The **fabrication of rules** surrounding the functions of group officers permits the group to survive by regulating economic processes within the corporation through time.

The mythology of the group stresses unity or brotherhood, obedience and succession to office through lineality—genealogically regulated transmission of political roles. The group's legends teach that elders as a cohort are superior to the next descending generation and that senior males rightfully hold authority over females as well as subordinate males.

Thus, we see that political functions and processes became embedded in kinship and other corporate groups after the Neolithic Revolution. In settings, where food production is marginal, it is necessary for someone to regulate food intake, so that no one uses too much food, threatening the survival of the whole group. Thus, in agricultural societies political office and its social control functions have an adaptive value. I will now turn to a description of how these processes develop among pastoralists.

Politics in Pastoral Society in West Africa

Pastoralism is cultural adaptation defined by a herding economy. It may have developed as an adaptive strategy to deal with marginal environments. This animal husbandry is thought to have arisen in the desiccating Sahara around pockets of water that attracted both animals and humans.

Pastoralists are usually strongly patrilineal, as control of wealth rests firmly with men, as does political control in camp and in larger settlements. While some sedentarism is part the pastoral way of life, camps frequently move to accommodate the feeding and drinking needs of herds. Some follow a pattern of transhumance, periodically searching for water and pasturage, while others practice nomadism, having no permanent camps. All herders symbiotically interact with settled peoples, forming an economy called mixed herding.

Herds are capital and are kept as storable wealth. Pastoralists drink their blood and milk, but rarely kill beasts to eat. Herds often become a focus of the culture. Some African herders develop elaborate songs and poetry about their cattle.

Some **Fulani** pastoralists focus on herding, while others have become part-time farmers. Both kinds of pastoralists are more or less dependent on nearby townsmen for manufactured products. The group I will describe has herds *and* they tend farms. They live in Northern Burkina Faso and Southern Mali in a region known as Jelgoji. They vary their activities by the seasons—moving their cattle to find good pasturage and planting their fields with the coming of the rains. Since the rains create pasturage for the cattle and regulate the farming season, the Jelgoji Fulani are tied to nature in an ecology that permeates their entire social system.

The traditional social organization is the segmentary lineage system (See glossary). Clans are internally comprised of various related lineages. All Fulani recognize the existence of a common culture but competition exists over land, cattle, political power and protection, as well as the control of skilled artisans and labor. As a consequence, clans are generally hostile to each other and the chief (*Kaananke*) must maintain peaceful relations between the competing clans.

Most Fulani live their lives within the context of the roaming *wuro*—the bush community formed by placing a brush fence around a small unit of huts. To them, this is domestic space, the domain of human life, as opposed to the *ladde* or bush, which is wild space, the domain of animals.

The ***Kaananke-Jooro* relationship** is important in this society. The "master of the *wuro*" is called the *Jom Muro* or *Jooro*. He is a "**little chief**" in that he holds power, but does not exercise it. As an authoritative headman, he has only the power of influence with the *wuro*. He is an arbiter, advisor and represents the community in dealings with outsiders. The *Jooro* cannot command or coerce, like a *Kaananke* chief, and unlike the latter, he does not take anything from his people.

Characteristic of many West African chiefs, the *Kaananke* is modeled on the father-son relationship. The chief is portrayed as a father to his subjects, but just as with the father-son relationship, the chief-subject relationship is sometimes ambiguous. Yet, no matter how much tension there is between a Fulani father and his son, that relationship has the advantage of filiation, the fact that the father sired the son. Lacking this filial bond, the chief must artificially create an acceptable power dependence relation. This is done through the fabrication of legends, the balladeering of the griots, the possession and display of emblems of office, and a standing army of slaves, among others. The result is legitimization that ends, most of the time, in the cooperation of the people with the wishes of the *Kaananke*.

Thus in both agricultural and pastoralist societies West Africans have created adaptive systems to deal with their environment. When society was demographically small and relatively uniform, small kin-based polities sufficed. When populations grew and/or outsiders moved in, a need arose for greater political organization, and chiefs emerged or were imposed to rule diverse congeries of peoples, as among the Jelgoji Fulani.

Little and Big Chiefs

Opportunity and need make big men and little chiefs. We have seen that in West Africa after the development of farming and herding the idea of rank emerged, with a positive valuation on "bigness." At first rank was limited to movement within family groups, lineages and clans. In time, this changed and leaders began to exercise authority over several congeries of family groups, uniting them in to a **tribe** or incipient chiefdom. These big men/little chiefs mediated between groups and oriented them toward solving certain common problems or exploiting economic opportunities that arose in their territory.

This happened in Sisalaland at the advent of the Atlantic Slave Trade. For the first time, their villages were heavily raided for slaves and the Sisala had to develop strategies to defend themselves. A big man was needed to negotiate with the slavers and to organize military defense of the village and sometimes confederations of villages (See Photo 5.2). Thus, attacks by slavers caused the rise of big men.

At the same time, more and more trade caravans were passing through Sisalaland. Big men and emerging war chiefs (**sipaalaaraa**) tended to rise in villages and towns located along trade routes. They achieved high rank by accumulating wealth. The same armies they raised and provisioned to defend their settlements could also be used aggressively to raid for slaves to sell to the passing traders, or to threaten the caravanners into paying tolls or "protection money" while in their territories.

The political economy expanded to include more than kinsmen under these dire, but opportunistic conditions. Alien clans that had warred with each other in the past were amalgamated under the leadership of one man, someone who transcended kinship and local ties. Little by little, such men created an aura of authoritative leadership that led to the acceptance of themselves and their offspring as hereditary chiefs.

The need to mediate the interactions between non-kin leads to the rise of mediating leaders or chiefs. This is the beginning of true political economy, wherein political

Photo 5.2 A West African Lancer in Quilted Armor Against Poisoned Arrows, 19th Century (from Denham, Clapperton & Oudney).

power gives the chief access to greater economic wealth. Likewise greater wealth gives men access to chiefly office, or positions within the chief's inner circle. Such poleconomic offices tend to rise with:

* the emergence of a storable and exploitable surplus
* increases in population density
* residential centralization
* the development of new opportunities to accumulate wealth
* increased inequality
* a rise of non-kinship relationships
* increased conflict

Since kinship was so important in the social organization of most West African peoples, chiefship was often built on kinship principles. The concept of a royal lineage and succession to high office meant that the role and authority of the chief passed to someone in the same or next descending generation upon his death.

Aggrandizers who sought to rule, or those who invaded from foreign lands, had to find ways to validate their exercise of power. They did this through the fabrication of rules and privileges and by representing themselves as saviors, protectors or fathers of the chiefdom. Kings merely expand on this formula to rule over larger populations, exercising control through a bureaucratic organization.

In the West African context, inauguration to high office gave the monarch privileged access to the:

* surplus produced by the labor of his subjects
* control over trade
* to the right to exploit passing caravans
* to the means of destruction

Accumulated wealth could be used to raise an army either to defend the chiefdom, or to raid others. Militaristic activities brought in booty and slaves. The latter could be used to produce more wealth either through farming or by acting as soldiers in warfare. Some slaves were castrated. These eunuchs were often installed as protectors of the monarch's harem. As palace guards they also functioned to coerce the populace and other soldiers who may have wanted to break away from the domination of the ruler.

Were such chiefs beneficial, providing advantages to their people? Or, were they merely using their advancement to benefit themselves and their families? Both altruism and aggrandizement played a part in the evolution of hierarchy in West Africa.

Scholars debate the effect of European trade demands and guns in West Africa. Most feel that contact accelerated the process of political **stratification** in West Africa. We know that when the historical and economic conditions are right, exploitative states emerge to dominate their citizenry. What we can say for West Africa is that such excesses sometimes happened, as I will show in the discussion of Mandingo kingdoms below, but exploitation did not usually happen without pressures from the world system.

The Mandingo Kingdoms of Sénégambia

Some kingdoms experienced great turmoil through their contact with Europeans—a rise in warfare, greater social mobility and increased stratification. Such turbulence affected the Mandingo kingdoms occupying the north and south banks of the River Gambia. They were among the first to be affected by the coming of Europeans along the north Guinea coast. Historical data below show that very few polities along the coast of West Africa were pristine after the coming of the Portuguese and that contact altered the forms of indigenous political systems.

Fifteen kingdoms ruled the banks of the River Gambia below Barrakunda Falls. Their power waxed and waned over the 500 years before independence.

These were commercial states before the arrival of the Portuguese in the 15th century—trading salt, beeswax, palm products and other local commodities. Indigenous traders got a huge boost when Europeans came looking for spices and slaves, bringing with them manufactured goods from industrial Europe that could be traded to the interior peoples of West Africa. During the slaving era these middlemen kingdoms thrived.

Relations between the various Mandingo kingdoms were tense at best, and often devolved into warfare, as the different kings and their advisors struggled to gain control of the lucrative trade in slaves and manufactured goods streaming through **Sénégambia**. Some kingdoms were subservient to others, but such power-dependence relations shifted over time, some kings rising to be kings over kings, others losing ground to aggrandizing men within their own realms. War became a constant in the region. Kings kept armies and hired foreign mercenaries to protect them and to raid others. Most were wars of domination in the early years, giving way to religious wars as the colonial era loomed.

Kings made their money in a variety of ways, many becoming fabulously wealthy, especially with increasing demand for slaves by Europeans. Kings traded in slaves and other goods, placed taxes on trade, exacted tolls from passing caravans, placed head taxes on their subjects, taxed their land and their produce. In fact, kings were quite creative in finding ways to accrue royal income—taxes were placed on wood, water, merchandise, boats, heads of locals, heads of passing caravanners, pack animals or cattle. Also, kings levied landing and docking fees along the river. Additionally, various ethnic and religious groups in the area paid certain customary fees, taxes and levies. Special wartime taxes were assessed to finance weapons, ammunition and horses.

The king, along with his council of big men, would act as judge and judiciary, hearing court cases. They received fines and taxed the sale of any slaves sent into bondage as a result of a court case. A rich man convicted of murder would have to pay an indemnity to the victimized family and one slave to the king. A poor murderer was enslaved by the offended family, which in turn paid three cattle to the king for receipt of the slave. By these means, kings, their families and the king's men became quite wealthy. Any association with high political office was clearly a means to accumulating riches.

The king also kept many diviners and priests who maintained mytho-ritual linkage with the earth and the ancestors, using traditional animist means of communicating with the spirit world. Such magico-religious activities gave supernatural backing and, therefore, legitimacy to the king's claims to rule. Mandingo kings were also fond of keeping Islamic clerics in court to tap what were thought to be supernatural powers that they materialized in the form of amulets and medicines. This was a common pattern in kingly courts throughout West Africa.

In the 17th century three kingdoms rose to be paramount over other Sénégambia kingdoms—Kantora, Salum and Wuli (See Map 5.1). Nevertheless, throughout most of the region's history, all of the Mandingo kings were equals, though some areas shared kingship on a rotating basis. Succession followed an elaborate system of rotation among several towns. The *Mansa* (King) was the senior man in the oldest lineage in the area. By virtue of his office, he had the right to allocate land to others, to receive tribute, to levy customs, tolls and taxes on those of his realm, or those passing through.

The explosion in commerce brought about by the European demand for slaves put a king in prime position to amass wealth beyond dreams. As time passed, competition for high office naturally increased.

This abnormal expansion of the trade in "**black gold**" allowed kings and members of their families and courtiers to live opulent and pleasurable lifestyles. They also adopted many European ways. Some of the royal daughters became *senares*, the wives or consorts of European slavers, learning their customs and languages. The daughter of an 18th century Niumi king was able to read and write in Portuguese, English and

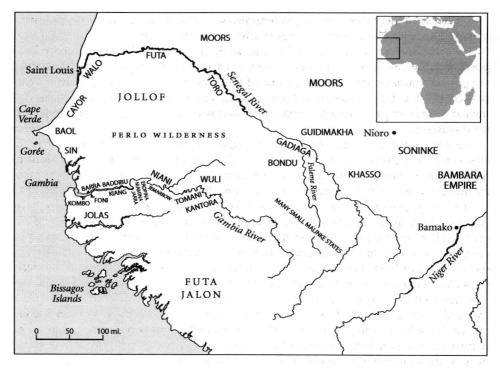

Map 5.1   Sénégambia, ca. 1735.

French. She acted for her father as broker with the Europeans in all trading transactions, amassing a fortune in the process. She lived a European lifestyle in a smart house in the Western style. This *senare* held lavish parties sporting imported linen, china, cutlery and other imported finery.

Contact with the world market increased social stratification in the Sénégambia area. The *Mansas* were becoming puffed up in their newly acquired wealth and power gained by trade and alliances with the powerful foreigners. European trade also reorganized the political power structure of the region. Although Mandingo kings were wealthy, they were not pure autocrats. The *Mansa* had to account for factions within the royal family, his councilors (the *beng*), lineage heads, wealthy and powerful men in the wider state and his own brokers and intermediaries. Men from any or all of these camps could rise in wealth and power to challenge the *Mansa*.

The *Mansa* had to follow the advice of the *beng* especially in matters of foreign policy and warfare. The king had to finance wars, but he could not lead them, in fact, the *beng* would select a *jawara* or general to lead the troops in battle. The *jawara* also became head of state for the duration of the war. Yet the *jawara's* position, powerful as it was, could not be passed on to anyone.

By the middle of the 19th century, social fragmentation and disintegration were rife. Non-royals and other segments of society began going it alone, leading to widespread turmoil and unrest along the River Gambia. Riches were proving to be the solvent of the region's kingdoms. Slave raiding and brigandry had become the order of the day, a milieu in which anyone holding sufficient wealth to hire mercenaries could further enrich himself and move up the political ladder. Mandingo kings were no longer able to prevent wayward towns from fortifying themselves. By then many provincial settlements had one and sometimes two walls, with ditches and lofty watch-towers to keep a sharp eye out for those wishing to make mischief.

This was also a time when wealth was becoming more diffused and centralized power was on the wane. Europeans encouraged this by plying the king's emissaries with direct gratuities and bequests. Some of these middlemen were actually in the employ of the king, but through secret deals, he was cut out of the loop. As the kings had turned away from protecting the interests of their people, the kings' men began to fend for themselves.

However, royals felt that they had a trump card and allied themselves more and more closely with the British against the rising dissidents of their kingdoms. They hoped to use European power to shore up their sagging authority. Nevertheless, another historical force was beginning to impinge on the region: the growing influence of Islam.

For many generations, Mandingo kings had resisted Islam, using *Mallams* only when it suited them. Slowly, however, Islamic Djula traders began to dominate commerce. After living alongside the animist rulers for centuries, Islamists were gaining an economic foothold and threatening to depose the Mandingo kings. This was part of a wider spread of Islam across West Africa in the 17th and 18th centuries and the riverine states were about to be engulfed in this movement.

In the 1840s this conflict came to a head in the Mandingo kingdom of Combo when war broke out between the Islamic Marabouts and the animist *Mansa*. By 1853 Combo was on the edge of collapse and the *Mansa* appealed to the British for support. The British had a special interest in Combo because it was closest to their colony of Bath-hurst at the mouth of the Gambia River. The British intervened, stopping the advance of the Islamic forces.

While the British were able to dominate militarily, they could not stamp out the spread of Islam. In 1875 the last *Mansa* converted. The increasing strength of their religion must have heartened the Marabouts as they again tried to invade the river states in 1894, but were again rebuffed by the British. Finally, the British decided to secure the political situation in the region and annexed it as the British colony of Gambia. Nevertheless, Islam was there to stay.

The history of the Mandingo Kingdoms exemplifies the internal and external forces that altered the nature of West African states over the course of the five hundred years leading up to colonialism in the region. Indigenous states were constantly bombarded by economic, political and religious forces from external sources—the Europeans' arrival, new trade items and magnified economic opportunities, the devastating impact of the rising demand for slaves, the influx of guns and manufactured goods from Europe, the displacement of native animist religion by Islam, and, in general, the penetrating influence of the world system.

Authentic and Imposed Political Systems

West African's ancient **political systems** ranged from expansive empires to local kin groups that regulated their own affairs. What each of these systems held in common was a process of organic evolution. Ancient systems developed differently as they adapted to changes in their physical and social environments. When Europeans arrived in West Africa they imposed their own systems such as the modern-day nation-state or its auxiliary, the Western bureaucracy. Today West Africans seek political au-

the members of which cultivated her farms and paid her tribute in kind. Along the coastal region of the empire, the *linger* also derived income from the salt industry.

Legal tribunals headed by women were set up to deal with female matters such as adultery. The *linger* oversaw these tribunals. Not only did selected women have judicial functions but in some Wolof states a woman could even succeed the king, taking the title of *Bur*. In fact, throughout West African history, there were several instances of women filling in on a temporary basis for an immature regent or in cases where a suitable male was unavailable.

Succession to ruling offices in the Wolof states was formerly transmitted matrilineally. At the time of European contact political form seems to have been in transition. European writers noted rivalry between sons and sisters' sons that often resulted in armed conflict. In Sine and Saloum, the king had to be of noble origin on his mother's side, and the status of his father did not matter. In Baol and Kayor, the candidates for high office had to belong to a noble matrilineage and be descended patrilineally from the first state ruler. Jolof was the only Wolof State in which succession was completely patrilineal.

Transformations Under Colonialism

Political domination began even before the official colonial era. Between 1892–1895 the French tried to establish a **protectorate** in the region. The Mossi kingdom was being surrounded. The French were pushing in from the east, the Germans from the southwest and the British from the south. As the French moved toward Ouagadougou they made treaties with local **tribes** that enveloped the Mossi. To firm up their southern border with the emerging colony of the Gold Coast in 1898 the French agreed on the 11° latitude as the border. In October 1902 they created a large military region called Sénégambia-Niger. In October 1904 it became an official colony, Haute-Sénégambia-Niger.

With their new colony in place, the French proceeded to create *cercles* (districts) within the artificial boundaries already established. As with the external colonial boundaries (See Map 5.2), these internal divisions took no account of indigenous ethnicity or true political borders.

The British also created specious borders in their colonies, but they tended to work through existing polities within the larger frame of the colony. Using the **Indirect Rule** approach, they wanted to rule through established chiefs and kings. The French wanted to weaken existing structures and did so by forming new administrative realities, replacing appointed indigenes who caused trouble, and by taking away the judicial powers of established chiefs.

The French encouraged both existing chiefs and those they created to extend their power to outlying villages, thereby expanding the size of their polities and creating an even greater resource base for exploitation. The French used chiefs to collect taxes and organize work gangs.

In Burkina Faso, as elsewhere in Haute-Sénégambia-Niger, the French experienced stiff resistance from some ethnic groups. Opposition flared up among the small groups such as the Bwa and some Mossi. The Imperialists could not tolerate this from peoples they considered to be primitive. They gave no measure, swooping down on villages and destroying them.

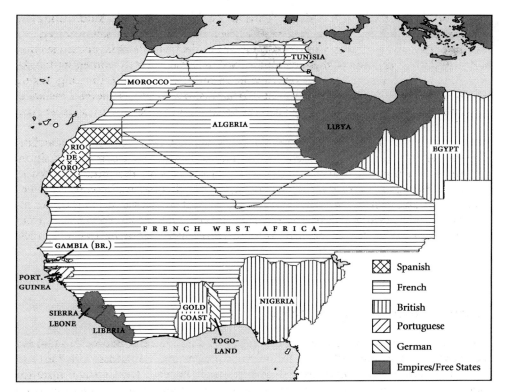

Map 5.2 Colonial Boundaries in 1914.

This severe repression shocked the people into temporary submission, but the area experienced sporadic uprisings again in 1915–1916. This time the French simply reinforced their military presence in the area and suppressed all resistance with force.

Traditional leaders were co-opted by colonial rule. Many collaborated with their oppressors. The *Mogoho Naba* himself recruited 2,000 laborers for the French work parties.

Other indigenous chiefs were kept happy and compliant with awards of medallions, a cut of the collected taxes, salaries and agricultural inputs. After the 1930 crash of the world markets and widespread drought and famine in *Haute Volta*, the French abandoned the colony. Still, the *Mogoho Naba* seemed to passively accept French rule, supporting the export of large numbers of his young men to aid in the development of *Cote d'Ivoire* (Ivory Coast) as well as the forced recruitment of soldiers for World War II. In fact, the *Mogoho Naba* led the way by enlisting two of his sons. About 10,000 Mossi enlisted in the *Tiralilleurs Sénégalais* (Senegalese Soldiers). It seems that both the chief and the people had come to accept the inevitability of a new political reality—colonial governance.

As the colonials had co-opted African political leaders with access to wealth, the process was being repeated with the new political leaders of independence in West Africa. Imposed and inappropriate political structures have from the very beginning of European domination, corrupted indigenous leaders. As colonialism gave way to independence, the pot got bigger and men continued to compete for the newly created wealth and power opportunities. The organic civic society of precolonial West Africa contrasted sharply with these overlying politics of exploitation. Whereas in the indigenous political orders the monarch was beholden to the people, in the newly imposed system, politicians were divorced from the people, and free to pursue any accumulation of wealth and power. There were no checks and balances in the new order. All over West Africa politicos took the money and rarely looked back.

Some Thoughts on West African Politics Through the Ages

Indigenous political systems of West Africa, as they were formed to adapt to the environment and history of the region, were significantly different from the forced political formations now in the region—modern nation-states and bureaucracies. The alien political forms of the modern world do not provide the people with access to, or control over, the political institutions that govern their lives. What we see, if we start with the relatively egalitarian groups who first inhabited West Africa, is a decline over time in the access of people to their political leaders and a reduction in their means of effectively influencing political outcomes.

As state-building grew in precolonial West Africa, chiefs and kings arose who were able to control trade and military forces. This created a political economy that allowed them to extract value from their followers to create and enhance royal lifestyles. Nonetheless, even in these early state systems, polities were mostly small, and the monarch was under social constraints of a civic nature. The ruler was never entirely free from community constraints. Where the polity was large, as with the Great Sudanic States (see Chapter 9), wealth extraction came from control over a cadre of traders, many of them foreigners.

This was not to last. As the **market economy** of Europe became more prominent in West Africa, native monarchs tapped into it and became more autocratic, more distanced from the masses of people in their domains. New wealth and European weapons allowed the development of large and militaristic kingdoms that raised havoc with less powerful peoples around them. Still, such large polities were characteristically African. Kings and their councilors were tied to the people through tradition and custom.

With the imposition of colonial forms of governance, these emerging state systems were strengthened and new chiefdoms were created where acephaly or benign governance had been the rule. A new and pernicious kind of government was introduced—the nation-state and its bureaucratic machinery. When, after three generations of colonial rule, this administrative armature was turned over to African élites they tried to employ traditional methods of governance. The result, which I deal with in more detail in chapter 16, has been less than effective. In short, patronage systems were adapted from organic governance, but they were particularistic. They fed a small portion of the populace. Whereas these new leaders were supposed to govern and help a nation, they governed the whole, but enriched only a few. This particularistic enrichment of family and friends was done at the expense of national development.

At the beginning of this chapter I posed the question with regard to West Africa: "Where has democracy gone?" It is still alive and well in the civic culture of small communities in West Africa. In many cases, however, it is being smothered by the forces of neocolonialism.

One of the truisms of West African history is that local polities were changed by contact with European societies. It is evident to many scholars of the region that European influence has not gone away. Rather it has been transformed into a new alliance between West African élites and Western economic interests to produce a form of governance that has been labeled **neocolonialism**. Underdevelopment and Dependency originated in the history of colonialism in the region. Overnight, polities great and small in West Africa lost their power, independence and identity as legitimate political bodies. Colonials imprisoned or exiled those leaders who would not cooperate and pampered those who would. When they could not find appropriate leaders, they created them. Colonials imposed foreign systems on the people with no regard for the psychological, social and political disorganization caused by such actions. Chiefs were forced on people accustomed to governing themselves democratically through public discussions.

The psychology of a people is hard to assess, but the loss of meaning connected with the restructuring of West African societies can be seen in the impoverishment of ritual traditions. The decline of secret societies and masked rites associated with them reflect this loss. Prior to the imposition of alien political controls, secret societies functioned to provide deep insight into the value of life as it had been constituted in West African cultures. With savage suddenness, Europeans intruded with Christianity and strange political forms that overwhelmed these civic institutions. Colonials in many cases set out to destroy what they thought was primitive or dangerous. Shrines were destroyed, dissenters imprisoned and royal art works taken away as "filthy idols."

All large polities in precolonial West Africa were multi-ethnic in nature. Integration and absorption were part of the organic process of empire building and the establishment of trade and diplomacy between peoples. There were wars, to be sure, but before the Atlantic Slave Trade and the availability of large numbers of firearms in West Africa, these conflicts were limited in nature. Colonialism interrupted the process of integrating disparate ethnicities, hardening the borders between them. To a large extent, ethnic conflicts that plague West Africa today are the creations of Imperialism in the region (See Chapter 15).

≋≋ CRITICAL THINKING QUESTIONS ≋≋

1. Since the pre-political phase of West African history was grounded in egalitarianism, demonstrate how that concept of equality was able to coexist with the concept of bigness or rank that arose in later West African societies.
2. What are the critical material changes that led to the rise of descent groups and sodalities and eventually to states in West Africa?
3. Explain what the author means by these three types of society: egalitarian, redistributive and extractive. What are the key differences between them?
4. What key variables began to cause the rise of chiefs in the Savannah zone, viz., the movement from acephaly to big men/little chiefs and on to formal chiefs?
5. Discuss the tension in the political economy of the Sénégambian kingdoms between royals and non-royal big men and how did this play out in their history?
6. What is the relation of the *Na* to the *Tendana* in the West African Savannah? Be able to discuss how this relation came about in history.

7. What happened to the office of king or *Mogoho Naba* among the Mossi through the ages, especially under the imposed suzerainty of the French?
8. What happened to the concept of democracy throughout West African history with regard to political evolution and the imposition of colonial hegemony?
9. Why didn't despotic kings rule in West Africa under a system of oriental despotism, as described by Karl Marx? Under what conditions did it begin to emerge in Dahomey?
10. Explain how the political economy is intimately tied up with West African religious concepts.

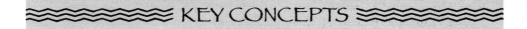

KEY CONCEPTS

Age-set
Aggrandizer
Band
Bigness
Black gold
Chiefdom
Communalism
Corporation sole
Descent group
Egalitarianism
Fabrication of rules
Foragers
Fulani
Heritability
Heterarchy
Household production system
Indirect Rule
Kaananke-Jooro relationship
Kingdom
Leveling mechanism
Little chief
Market economy
Means of destruction

Mogoho Naba
Political authority
Political power
Poleconomic
Political economy
Political systems
Privilege
Protectorate
Rank
Ranked societies
Redistributor ruler
Scorpion ordeal
Sénégambia
Sipaalaaraa
Social control
State
Storable surplus
Stratification
Succession to high office
Tirailleurs Sénégalais
Tribes
Virebaling

SOURCES & SUGGESTED READINGS

Balandier, Georges. 1970. *Political anthropology.* London: Allen Lane,The Penguin Press.
Denham, Dixon, Captain Clapperton & Major Oudney. 1828. *Narrative of travels and discoveries in Northern and Central Africa, in the years 1822, 1823, and 1824.* London: John Murray.
Fage, J. D. 1995. *A history of Africa.* (Third Edition). London: Routledge.
Fortes, M. & E. Evans-Pritchard. 1940. *African political systems.* London: Oxford University Press.

Godelier, Maurice. 1963. *La notion de mode de production asiatique et les schemas marxistes d'évolution de sociétés.* Paris: C.F.R.M.

Hiskett, Mervyn. 1984. *The development of Islam in West Africa.* London: Longman.

Lance, James Merriman. 1995. *Seeking the political kingdom: British colonial impositions and African manipulations in the northern territories of the Gold Coast colony.* Ph.D. dissertation, Stanford University. Ann Arbor: University Microform (UMI) #9525856.

Little, K. L. 1948. The changing position of women in the Sierra Leone protectorate. *Africa* XVIII.

Mendonsa, Eugene L. 1982. *The politics of divination.* Berkeley: University of California Press.

Mendonsa, Eugene L. 2001. *Continuity and Change in a West African Society: Sisala elders, youth and women.* Durham, NC: Carolina Academic Press.

Piot, Charles. 1999. *Remotely global: Village modernity in West Africa.* Chicago: University Press.

Quinn, Charlotte A. 1972. *Mandingo Kingdoms of the Sénégambia: Traditionalism, Islam and European Expansion.* Evanston: Northwestern University Press.

Riesman, Paul. 1974. *Freedom in Fulani social life: An introspective ethnography* (trans. Martha Fuller). Chicago: University Press.

Saul, Mahir. 1995. Economic life in African villages and towns. In: Martin, Phyllis M. & Patrick O'Meara (eds.). *Africa* (Third edition). Bloomington: Indiana University Press, 190–210.

6 ART IN WEST AFRICA

This chapter looks at art as it was created in the context of community life, an artistic form linked closely with spirituality. It also analyzes art subsidized by royals and describes how that art reflects a certain political economy. Art forms changed as states developed in West Africa, but it also changed with the arrival of Europeans. These changes are discussed as well as how African art has influenced European artists.

African Art—Then and Now

West Africa stands high in art production. Such European artists as Vlaminck, Braque, Derain, Picasso and Modigliani (See Figure 6.1) were influenced by African art forms, as anyone familiar with their works can see.

Since human beings make non-utilitarian things and perform music and dances that do not seem to produce an economic payoff, we might ask why. In West Africa, we cannot begin to answer this question without a knowledge of the social and religious context in which art was created, performed and displayed. West African artwork is usually a symbolic statement of social significance. It is often associated with secret societies. Many of their masks were used to instruct initiates and relate to various social responsibilities, such as fighting fires and making peace.

Much art is spiritual in nature. Many West African artists consciously depart from naturalistic images in their works. Others follow a more realistic path. Abstract pieces are an attempt to portray cosmic power through the intensification of natural features, searching for a way to convey the supernatural temper of spirits and supernatural beings (See Figure 6.2). Thus, artists use jagged lines, notches, rough edges, and bold curves to suggest dynamism and spiritual energy in their masks, statues and figurines. Those artists leading toward realism portray human and animal anatomy in organic forms, but tend to accentuate proportions to hint at an ethereal quality, an insinuation of occult qualities in addition to natural ones. In such pieces one finds an overemphasis of heads, eyes, hands and meticulously delineated eyebrows, lips, eyelids and cheeks. The intent is usually the conveyance of the omnipresence of cosmic power, the link between the spiritual world and the world of nature—that the supernatural is not separate from human and animal forms, but inherent in them.

The predominant art forms in West Africa were masks and figures that were generally used in religious ceremonies but they are also extraordinarily beautiful. Decorative

Figure 6.1
Statue by
Amedeo
Modigliani
Clearly In-
fluenced by
African Art.

Figure 6.2 *Sikilin* mask, Sisalaland,
Northern Ghana.

arts in textiles, wood, metals, leatherwork and tool ornamentation were vital in nearly all West African cultures. Art traditions are old, but exactly how old we do not know. Archaeological research has been minimal in West Africa, restricting our knowledge of the antiquity of African art. Compounding this problem is the fact that wood, leather and cloth decay in the tropical climate. Wood was one of the most frequently used materials—often embellished by clay, paint, shells, beads, ivory, metal, feathers, and shredded raffia.

In addition to woodwork and stone pieces, West African artists used many different media—cloth (See Figure 6.3), ivory, hair, beads, scrap iron, cement and paint. Even human bodies were decorated with tattoos and scarification. The masters of Dahomey produced appliquéd textiles, including banners using colorful materials that often depict historical events.

West African art ranges from the delightful primitiveness of the Fon of ancient Dahomey (modern-day Benin) to the sophisticated refinement of the Gouro of the Ivory Coast (See Figure 6.4). There are both abstract and naturalistic images. The artwork tends toward extreme simplification. The African artist seems to be searching for the essence of his craft, an effort to subtly convey what can only be achieved through great creative imagination. I cannot cover the wealth of West African art works in this general overview. The suggested readings at the end of this chapter offer further pursuit of the majesty of African art. There are several collections scattered around the world. In the United States, I would suggest the National Museum of African Art (Smithsonian Institution); the Michael C. Rockefeller wing of the Metropolitan Museum of Art, New York; the Field Museum and the Natural History Museum, Chicago; the Peabody Museum, Harvard; the University Museum at the University of Pennsylvania; and the Museum of Cultural History, Los Angeles. A web site displaying African art is: http://witcombe.sbc.edu/ARTHafrica.html. This comprehensive site covers the subject from Akan artwork to Zulu beadwork.

Figure 6.3 Insignia with European Head, Brocaded Cotton, Benin, Nigeria.

Figure 6.4 Ceremonial Mask, Gouro, Ivory Coast.

Introduction to West African Art in a Social Context

African civilization was firmly based in a community-centered ethos. Art can be about pride of place, ethnicity or polity, as we will see when looking at the art of the region and how peoples use their art to express their commonality.

The collectivist ethos of West African villages and towns was centered on the family as that form extended through time from ancestors to descendants. In West African culture there was a sharp division of labor between the sexes, indeed, men and women often functioned in two separate spheres of activity. These aspects of West African life emerge in their art forms, as does the power of the state, which supported many artists in precolonial times.

Art in West Africa fulfilled a multitude of functions. It could be thought to have communicative value, sending a message to the spirits. It could be a symbol of status and prestige to send a message to others in society. It could conceivably have had a political function, as a means to acquire and maintain political power. Artwork might be seen as utilitarian—as a stimulus to farming or trading. It is a common West African trait to depict gendered figures in art. It might be connected to a specific social form such as a secret society or a cult. Or, it might simply be designed for entertainment.

A small proportion of art was produced for art's sake—*l'art pour l'art*—that is, the artist was concerned to find a solution to certain artistic problems of style, form or the use of his medium. In modern times, the artist may be producing statues, paintings, clothwork, jewelry, and other artifacts for the tourist trade, or for secular plays that have replaced the sacred ceremonies of the past. Some West African artists produce for the global marketplace. Some contemporary West African artists have become well known around the world.

There has been a modification of traditional art production in West Africa over the past fifty to one hundred years, a change that reflects the impact of contact with the outside world. Just as art changed with the internal process of state formation—the artists becoming royal artisans producing for the state—artwork has more recently changed to reflect European influence. Since West African art was intimately tied up with culture, the rapid changes brought on by contact and colonialism have diminished artistic output.

Religion has influenced West African art. Neither Islam nor Christianity has seemed comfortable with idols and images as they were used in traditional West African culture. With the penetration of these world religions, the practice of indigenous rites has been touched by new influences. Some Muslims destroyed "pagan idols" and some Christianized West Africans avoided contact with African art used in animist rites.

In the coastal zone of West Africa tourism is more common than in the interior. There, artists may be diverted from careful production of magico-religious artifacts destined for serious use within the civic culture of the village. The demands of the market may lead an artist into mass production of trinkets, statues and the like for sightseers. This also occurs in the interior in large cities and in other places that have large universities or expatriate populations.

Today the market economy places new time demands on artists, but also on everyone in the village. The farmer and his family members no longer have time to attend lengthy rituals, some of which traditionally lasted for days, even weeks. Especially in the cities, people work long hours, leaving little time for long rites. As rituals have declined, so has the production of art for that purpose.

This is not to say that all traditional ritual had an artistic component. Not all peoples in West Africa seem to have an equal interest in aesthetics. The Sisala have almost no art in their social lives, while the Baule of the Ivory Coast seem to decorate the most utilitarian objects. Objects such as bobbins, spoons, combs, hairpins, combs, stools, doors and diviner's boxes are produced by Baule artists with a flair for elaboration. Some are beautiful in their simplicity of design e.g., the Boti chair from Sisalaland in Photo 6.1.

Artisanship is common in West Africa. It is sometimes, therefore, difficult to separate artisanal work by craftspersons and those works that emerge from the hands of "true" artists. In the past, artisans worked to produce raffia weavings for skirts and bags. They made mats of grass, baskets of reeds, fishing weirs, nets for fishing and hunting and clothing. They wove cotton cloth strips for smocks and other garments, worked in leather, carved calabashes (gourds), mined and worked ores to produce bronze and copper tools and pans, formed iron into farm implements and weapons and practiced gunsmithing once arms were introduced.

Today both artisanal production and artwork has been largely displaced by foreign objects. West African art is not dead but artists produce for different venues, some for posh art galleries in Cannes or New York. Others are still carving in secret, hiding their artwork for local rites. This art concerns family traditions, cultural identity and a personal quest to preserve what is meaningful and valuable to them, as it was to their forefathers.

Photo 6.1 Boti Chair.

Classical West African Art

Antiquities have been uncovered by archaeologists in formal digs, and also by workers at construction sites in West Africa. Unfortunately, much of this art languishes in European museums or private collections with little or no social description of the pieces. Some large stone statues and stelae still dot the forest regions of West Africa.

One art form remains on the rocks of West Africa—that is the glyphs of the early hunters and gatherers of the region. Foraging peoples once roamed all over the continent of Africa, but are now restricted to marginal areas like the Kalahari Desert of Southern Africa where the !Kung (also called the San or Ju/'hoansi) live, or the barren wastes of Tanzania inhabited by the Hadza. Mbuti pygmies live in the Ituri forest of Central Africa. These modern hunting and gathering peoples share a passion for animals with the ancient artists who left their drawings on the rocks of West Africa. Animals make up most of the subject matter of their art.

The main source of West African classics is the **Nok Culture** (ca. 900 BC–A.D. 200), in Northern Nigeria. Many terracotta statues, iron works and finely polished stone axes were accidentally uncovered in the process of tin mining (See Figure 6.5). This is the earliest known African sculptural tradition. It is likely that these terracotta statues reflected the refinement of an earlier tradition of wood carving, but we will probably never know for sure.

Although the Sao peoples lived on the periphery of West Africa, they represent another ancient style of the region. They lived in the Chari delta region, in present-day Chad and Northern Cameroon. Their descendants today are called the *Kotoko*. Their

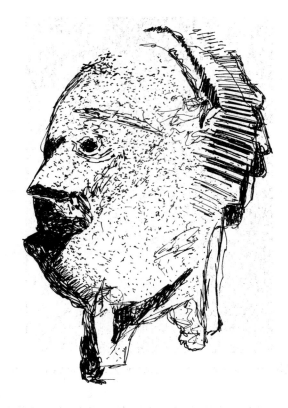

Figure 6.5   Nok Culture Terracotta Head (ca. 900BC–AD 200), Northern Nigeria.

culture grew in an area that was influenced by the various north-south and east-west trade routes crisscrossing the area. Their exact origin is unknown, but they were finally absorbed in the expansion of the Kanem-Bornu Empire in the 13th century. The Sao worked primarily in clay, making funerary urns, jewelry, stylized ancestor statues and even clay money. They also worked in bronze, though their metal work seemed to have a utilitarian bent. Archaeologists have uncovered bronze hoes (indicating agriculture) and many items used in hunting and fishing—harpoons fishhooks, knives and spearheads.

Since so little archaeology has been done in West Africa, we do not yet have a clear idea how these ancient traditions relate to more modern artistic fashions. However, it seems likely that there was a continuous (if changing) tradition in artistic production through the ages.

Art and Religion in West Africa

Religion is central to the art of West Africa, especially that produced in the media of wood and earth, two important elements connecting humans to the spiritual world. The artwork portrays ancestors, bush sprites, water spirits, and numerous supernatural beings that inhabit the West African pantheon of lesser gods. This art focuses on

Photo 6.2   Mud Shrine, Covered in Cement with a Design of a Winding Snake.

the creative power of the cosmos but none depicts the creator high god, reflecting his otiose and distant nature. Many are demi-gods of nature—thunder, rock outcrops and hills, rivers and lightening, for example. Others are the wandering ghosts of those who have not received proper funerals to incorporate them into the realm of the ancestors. Yet others are inexplicable phantoms.

West Africans have fabricated ideologies and artwork to link the social world of humans to this rarefied realm of spirits. African masks, figurines and fetishes are usually kept firmly in the hands of men, symbols of their control of the political economy. In most masquerades performed by male secret societies, women are not allowed to even see the masks or hear the songs. Women are marginal to the performance of most rituals in West African villages. In some areas, however, women have their own secret societies, although most do not have a masking tradition associated with these organizations.

Tutelary figures and masks are media for the concentration and expression of supernatural power and residences for spirits. They appear as anthropomorphic and zoomorphic figurines. Even when the material art form is not shaped as a person or animal, its resident power may be called by name and beseeched as a sentient being. Other such fetishes may have an outward representation of an animal. See the python shrine in Photo 6.2.

In the Western Sudan, religious carvings have mainly to do with the ancestor cult and farm fertility. Masks, sculptures and utilitarian objects are made of wood, some of which have artistic designs carved into them. The humanistic door locks done by Bambara carver-blacksmiths are one example. Smith-carvers also make ancestor figurines, fertility statues, twin dolls and masks for the various secret societies. Most of these societies are involved in bringing fertility and rain to the farms and their artwork

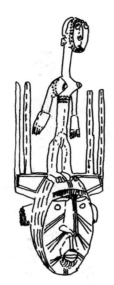

Figure 6.6
Tyi Wara Mask,
Bambara, Mali.

Figure 6.7 *Tellem*
Ancestral Figurine
(Likely of Dogon
Origin).

is linked to the mythical charters they maintain in their oral histories. For example, among the Bambara, the wife of the high god is thought to have mated with a snake, producing **tyi wara**, a half man/half snake figure that taught humankind the art of horticulture. The *tyi wara* masks are stylized depictions of an antelope venerated in honor of the legendary culture hero (See Figure 6.6). Thus, it is important to understand that when West Africans utilize art in connection with their religion, it is not an idle linkage—it usually recalls something of their mythology and oral history. It also relates to their moral order. When, for example, the Dogon carve statues of their ancestors and place them on the roofs of their houses, they are giving the ancestral soul a place of residence when traveling from *manga*, the village of the dead. The Dogon believe that ancestors come and go, visiting the living, then returning to *manga*. Such statues are not just representations—the Dogon believe that the ancestral spirit can enter and reside in the statue. When they place food before it, they are feeding the spiritual power that has come to inhabit it. Such feedings are a form of prayer, an expression of reverence for the linkage between the extended family and the cosmic order. Apparently this Dogon carving tradition is quite old, as *Tellem* ancestral figures have been unearthed in Dogonland and are thought to be remains from ancient precursors to the Dogon (See Figure 6.7).

As with most secret societies in the Western Sudan, the *awa* society of the Dogon deals mainly with ancestor veneration. When circumcised Dogon males become members of the *awa* secret society. At the core of their religious beliefs is that the soul of their first ancestor inhabits the great *imina na* mask. Since this sacred relic decays within a century or so, it is re-carved at an important festival (*sigui*) held every sixty years. The *imina na* mask is kept in a special shrine house but is brought out on the death of an important member of the community (See Figure 6.8). It is placed in his funeral hut for the duration of the funeral then returned to its proper abode. Such an act links the just-departed and the living with the first Dogon to have died. In West African cosmologies, such linkages form a circle, creating a holistic image of the connectedness of past with present, the nether world with this one, and art functions to help establish that ring of life.

Figure 6.9
Female Figurine,
Bijogo, Guinea-
Bissau.

Figure 6.8   Dogon Mask, Mali.

Dogon carvers may use a combination of human and animal traits in carving their masks. The *kanaga* mask, for example, is an anthropomorphized crocodile. This symbolizes their belief in the unity of nature and cultured human beings.

To the southwest of Dogon country is a zone of peoples who have an art style focusing on masks. This zone stretches from the Bissagos Islands to the Ivory Coast. Along the coast the land is swampy, while in the north the terrain is Savannah, but a masking tradition has likely diffused into both topographies. Most of the art of this zone is concerned with cultic activities, perhaps the most famous of which are the male Poro and the female Sande secret societies.

Dan-Kran art, from Sierra Leone and Ivory Coast, is linked to their mythology. As with all West African peoples, they believe in an otiose, anthropomorhous, omnipotent high god (*Zlan* in Dan) who created everything, including masks. He cannot be approached directly, only through the authority of the ancestors, but even they can only be communicated with through the agency of masks, those sacred carvings of the **Go** cult. This cult is headed by an important and powerful priest who functions as a political authority and social control agent to young men and women.

Only men can have and wear masks, and the *Go* priest controls all sacred masks, telling men when they can carve a new one, or when they can wear an existing mask and for what purpose. Only the *Go* priest can use masks to communicate with the ancestors on behalf of the community. He is in charge of the sacred *Go* hut where the *Go* fetish is kept, as well as the masks of all culture heroes and big men of the past. When the ancestors come to visit, they stay in or near this fetish hut, which is the power center of society, both in a supernatural sense and a political one.

A man receives a mask in one of two ways. He can carve a new one if the *Go* priest directs him to do so, or he can inherit one from his father. Inherited masks that have passed through several generations are thought to possess the spiritual power and au-

Photo 6.3   Shrine to Guard the Farm Against Evildoers.

thority of all men who owned the mask. As such, they are much more sacred and more potent than newly carved ones. Each owner adds his power to the mask as it passes through the generations. It can be seen that the hut of the *Go* cult, having many masks owned by the culture heroes of the village, is a place of intense power and sanctimony.

There is hardly any social or ritual activity in which masks do not play a central role. Their power stems from the habitation of the masks by the spirits of the ancestors who previously owned them. Secondly, blood sacrifice increases the likelihood that cosmic power will reside in the masks. The people believe that the ancestors come to "feed" at the blood sacrifice. Masks are fed blood, meat and especially the liver.

Control of these masks gives initiated men and the *Go* priest great political and judicial power in society. The masks are thought to "judge the people," as interpreted by the *Go* priest. Masks are also worn to educate initiates, pass laws, judge wrongdoers, carry important messages, cure others, wage war, clown around and entertain others. Also, some lesser masks are carved to represent individual personalities.

Many carved figures represent ancestors who are honored artistically in order to ensure continued protection of villagers and to thwart any aggression by angry ancestors. Figurines and other forms of art sometimes have to do with one's soul, personal destiny or guardian spirits.

Most West African artists were men and most figures depicted artistically were male. Female figures in art often have to do with fertility and fecundity (See Figure 6.9). They are depicted with children or performing domestic tasks indicative of female roles in the sociocultural formation. They often accompany a male figure, showing the importance of the sexual division of labor in West Africa. The pairing of gendered art figures is a metaphor for **gendered dualistic complementarity** in society at large. The complementarity of the two constitute society, the full unity. Art is a microcosm of the whole.

Some artwork, shrines and charms are used by West Africans to ward off evil perpetrated by living people. See Photo 6.3, showing a Sisala farmer's black cross medicine fetish. This is thought to ward off witches and thieves from his fields. If magical power can be used aggressively by malevolent people and spirits, it can also be countered by certain material objects, some of which can be considered artwork. However, the popular image of the voodoo doll with pins sticking in it is an oversimplification. In Benin, the temple of the high priest and **Vodoun** practitioners is filled with artistic representations of the various spiritual manifestations of the high god, *Mawu — Gu, Legba, Damballa* and *Hevioso*. But this is just one of many native religions that honors different demi-gods as exemplars of cosmic power. Such organizations are civic entities, promoting moral good, not the malevolence that is the stuff of popular fiction and cinema.

Anthropologists are not saying that West African art is concerned only with supernatural explanations. West Africans also experiment in everyday life. Most of their activities, such as farm work or building a house, rely on practical knowledge handed down through the generations, but these actions are also often ritualized, and sometimes the process of sacramentalizing activities is represented artistically. Sometimes inter-village competitions were held to see which community could produce the best art, houses or masquerades. Dr. G. I. Jones puts it like this:

> It was this sphere of 'experimental' and fashionable religion and magic that was most subject to change and variation; it also offered the most scope for artistic expression. Fashion was associated with social competition. People who could afford to have the right kind of cults and masquerades liked to demonstrate this fact by having superior and more impressive cult objects, and one of the commonest ways of achieving this was through sculpture. In the same way competing villages vied at producing bigger and better masquerades.

Since no one knows exactly what bush spirits or water spirits look like, the artist experiments with various forms of human and animal characteristics. For example, the Cross River war drums are thought to hold the male spirits of the sky, as well as the female essences of the earth, thus the artist has carved male figures on one drum and female characters on the other. Such gender complementarity in West African art is quite common.

Religion was, and is, a major stimulus to artistic production. The other catalysts have been state support, and demand by Europeans, first by colonials and today by tourists. Not all West African art is necessarily serious, however. Some is simply produced by both adults and children for their enjoyment. Photo 6.4 shows a lorry made out of tin cans, a common street toy of budding artists in West Africa. Photo 6.5 shows a phallic bottle opener used in Kumase beer bars. It could be shaped differently and still remove the bottle caps — but it seems that the phallic form is more fun — more likely to create hilarity.

Art and Secret Societies in West Africa

Carved masks are especially associated with secret societies in West Africa (See Figure 6.10). For example, in the Delta area of Nigeria the *'emo* masks are formed out of mangrove wood from the swamps. Their very duality — being part cultural fabrica-

Photo 6.4 Metal Toy Car Made by a Ghanian Child from Tin Cans (Body), Flip-Flop (Tires) and Bic Pen Shafts (Axles). 1998. Collection of Eugene Mendonsa.

tion and part natural—makes them ambiguous figures, and ones that symbolically link the life of villagers to their wild surroundings.

Photo 6.5 Phallic Bottle Opener Purchased from a Waitress Using It in a Kumase Beer Bar, Ghana, 1998. Hardwood and Two Screws. Collection of Eugene Mendonsa.

Figure 6.10   Mask of the *Ekpo* Secret Society, Region of Benin, Nigeria.

Some masquerades of secret societies are kept absolutely secret, while others are open to be viewed by non-members in the community, although all contain some hidden elements. These, to varying degrees, make the masquerade a unique situation. When hidden things are brought out in the open, everyone present is impressed by the import of the moment, the abnormality of the act. This is accentuated by the hidden identity of the maskers, their extraordinary movements, animalistic sounds emanating from behind the masks or from the nearby bush—all lend a feeling of the strange, amazing and exotic. Furthermore, it is thought that the mask becomes a repository of the spirit associated with the carving, and in some cases the man wearing the mask himself is possessed, his own personality being replaced by that of the mask's specter.

G. I. Jones sees three broad categories of secret society in Eastern Nigeria, where such societies abound. The first is the ghost society where members venerate the deceased spirit of a culture hero or prominent man of the past. These are usually benevolent spirits. The ghost societies can be seen as an extension of the ancestor cult.

In the *ovia* ceremony of the Edo people, each *ovia* member masquerades as his father, or another member of his descent group if his father is still living. Such ghost-oriented secret societies emphasize the connection between the living and the dead, and the continued role of the latter in the lives of the former.

The second type of secret society is that of the water spirits. They fit more closely with our model of a secret society, with a clubhouse, regular meetings and broader functions in the community than ghost societies.

One such sodality is the **Ekine society** of the Kalabari Ijo in Nigeria. Since most adult males belong to the *Ekine* society, the sodality forms an important part of the civic organization of the village, as well as putting on an annual festival that provides an opportunity for much gaiety and enjoyment.

The *Ekine* society is an age-graded sodality given to men by the goddess *Ekine*. This is a common theme in West Africa: what females originated, men have come to domi-

Figure 6.11   Kalabari Water-Spirit Mask in the Form of a Crocodile Along with the Customary Long Robe that Covers the Masker.

nate. As initiates move through the various grades of the sodality, they are increasingly exposed to information about mask care, mimes, songs, music and lore of the secret society.

The society's masks, worn by men only, are a combination of anthropomorphic and zoomorphic carvings, which represent natural forces, human beings of the past, animals, pythons, fish and crocodiles (See Figure 6.11). Along with shrines bordering the creeks and those in the village, the masks are representational loci of the water spirits thought to protect the village.

The *Ekine* festival covers several days of music, dancing, miming, masquerading, and the singing of honorific songs about the power of the water spirits. The secret society members do this to ensure that the spirits will extend their protection over the activities of the villagers in the coming year. In preparation, members take out the masks, strip them of old paint, wash and repaint them. This is symbolic of the regeneration of the power of the water spirits. Then the *Ekine* priest dons a mask and calls on the spirits to "come and eat." Animals are sacrificed on the village shrine and some of the blood is smeared on each mask. Villagers pass by the shrine throwing coins on the fetish and seeking help in their lives.

At this point, the priest begins to dance and goes into a state of possession. It is thought that the mask and the dancer are infused with the cosmic power of the spiritual entity taking over his thoughts, speech and actions. During the festival, many different dancers will follow suit to honor the specific spirit of their masks.

The rite called the "filling of the canoe of the water people" marks the end of the festival. The masked *Ekine* men row back to the sacred beach, symbolizing the return of the water people to their place of abode. No women are allowed to go along. At the creek's edge, the men remove their masks and dip them in the water. This is thought to "release" the spirit of the mask to return home. With the completion of this ritual, the village is safe for another year.

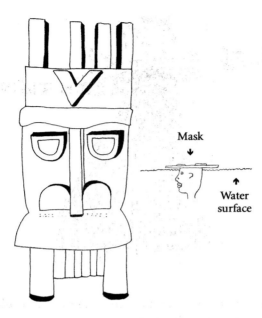

Mask

Water
surface

Figure 6.12   Kalabari *Otobo* (Hippo) Mask of the *Ekine* Secret Society. The Hippopotamus Mask is Worn Flat on the Head. When the Masker Wades Through the Water, the Hippo Appears to Glide Across the Surface.

Villagers hold other rituals to honor their culture heroes. For the "swimming festival," villagers prepare a large canoe. When ready, a masker is seated in the vessel and it is pulled toward the "resting place of the spirits" by swimmers. On the trip, however, there is a planned hitch. An ugly and angry masker stops the canoe. This fierce spirit demands to be placated, which the villagers do with prepared stashes of gin. Satisfied, the ugly masker allows the canoe to pass, and the villagers proceed to the sacred beach of the water spirits to offer libations to them.

The symbolism here is clear and conforms to a general pattern in West Africa. The village is seen as the locus of human creativity. The rite symbolizes the fact that no matter what humans do, they are still dependent on nature—the fish, the creeks and the water spirits who live in this wild domain.

The ugly spirit demands that humans recognize their dependence on him, as a representative of nature as a whole. To continue with their plans, the bearers of culture must pay their respects through sacrifices and by offering libations.

This interdependence between man and nature is depicted in the artistic construction of masks. They tend to be carved as half animal/half human. The *otobo* masker wades out into the swampy waters up to his chin. The horizontal head mask appears to move across the water with the same motion of a hippopotamus (See Figure 6.12). Remember, in the belief system of the villagers, the spirit of *otobo* enters the mask and makes it move, not the person wearing the mask. This water play dramatically confirms that nature is the prime mover, not humankind.

The third type of secret society is that revolving around the veneration of forest demons or sprites, common in unfarmed bush of the Cross River Area. Forest demon cults are ultra secret societies. Members stress the danger to young initiates and the uninitiated members of the community who may inadvertently come upon some of the society's secrets. They have a clubhouse and hold frequent meetings, but their "demons" are never seen, their voices being produced by bullroarers and friction drums manned by society members away from the main ceremony.

For artwork to flourish within a society, it must be connected to a mythical charter. It needs be conjoined with ongoing cultic activity supported by the society's power élite. Furthermore, we note that young people need to be involved in ritual life in order to be socialized into the idea base that underpins art production and use. We also see that an art tradition can die out if the younger generation is not socialized to its significance.

Art and Politics in West Africa

In the village context, politics are often embedded in kinship institutions and sodalities; thus we find art pieces reflecting those spheres of life, rather than an overtly political domain. However, when large chiefdoms or kingdoms arise, there is usually a great enough surplus to support specialists, including artists, and kings use art to justify and support their claims to sovereignty.

The art of kingdoms is centered more on political power and the regalia of the kingdom. Royals tend to support art that depicts their omnipotence through insignias, accomplishments in war, plaques, lavish ornamentation, scepters, palace walls, doors, umbrellas, thrones and royal stools.

Whereas village artists work in wood, bone, mud and other inexpensive materials, artists with the support of royalty tend to produce artwork in gold, ivory, precious stones and bronze. When stone is used, the monuments tend to be large and/or numerous. Many of the works by the artists of the highborn tend to cast depictions of the king, queen or queen mother, as well as courtiers who carry out the functions of the state. A common theme in such royal art is war and power, the latter being frequently symbolized by fierce animals, subtly linking supernatural power of the bush to the king and his activities. This link to the occult is also seen in the choice of materials. For example, ivory (from an animal) symbolized kingly power. Ivory, gold, coral and other precious materials were most often used in élite art.

It is often the goal of the artist to link the rulers and the polity to a larger cosmic order. For example, among the Asante of Ghana, the famous **golden stool** (*sike gwa*) of the *Asantehene* is not only a symbol of the power of the sovereign, but is thought to be the very repository of the nation's soul. It is so sacred that even the king does not sit on it. Akan art is tied to their cosmological ideas. The origin legend for the *sike gwa* tells of a time in the reign of Osei Tutu when there was a great storm, with much thunder and lightening. At one point the skies opened and the sacred stool descended to earth and landed in the lap of the *Asantehene*. Of course, this is a dramatic representation of the legitimate right of the *Asantehene* to rule the nation. Note again, the connection in such myths between the sky, sun and earth—giving life a mythological wholeness, a unity between male and female, the forces of the sky and those of the earth. Though the stool is rarely seen, it is a fine work of art, having attached to it many gold bells, masks and portraits of vanquished enemies.

While the stool is the central symbol of Asante unity and royal sovereignty, animals are also used to represent the power of kings—especially the elephant, lion and the leopard. The king of Benin wore a scorpion pendant on his back to indicate that he too had "a sting."

The Fon king's palace was at Abomey, his kingdom being known as Dahomey. It was adorned with wood and metal bas-reliefs, as were most palaces of West African kings. This 17th century kingdom supported many artists who produced innumerable wall panels depicting the panther, the primary royal beast, as well as representations of other royal creatures like the shark and the lion. These works of art were designed to glorify the sovereigns, their exploits and egos. Scenes would represent battles, the war god named *Gu* and the king dressed in his royal finery, accompanied by coats of arms and emblems of power. Some palace panels also contained sayings. The motto of the Ghezo kings of Abomey was: "All beasts touch the ground, but the elephant (king) tramples it." Other symbols of office—the parasol, the stool or a *recade*—were also portrayed in royal artwork.

Yoruba art has become some of the most famous in the world, especially the Ife bronzes. They show a sophistication of craftsmanship that belies a long tradition leading up to them, but we know little of that history. They were found by Fronbenius in 1910. He developed **Fronbenius' Theory of Mediterranean Origin** concerning them. Another twenty heads were discovered in 1938. Contrary to Fronbenius' ethnocentric evaluation of their origin, it is now clear that these busts represent a long tradition of royal support of artists in this Sub-Saharan kingdom.

Ife and Benin have also given us some superb bronze and wood plaques in which battles are memorialized, and the feats of kings chronicled. The characteristic naturalistic heads of the Yoruba artists clearly depict specific kings and members of royalty. The sculptors were not trying to alter features to depict a connection to the supernatural realm in these works; they are attempts at showing a royal patron in his true form, surrounded by his symbols of power.

Unlike the rural-based animistic art, royal art production was most often an urban phenomenon. Artists, traders and craftsmen were supported by kings, organized in guilds embedded in corporate lineages and occupied named wards of the city. Allowed to devote their energies to full-time art production, these artists achieved incredible heights in developing beauty in pliant form.

Art and Gender in West Africa

While some women in present-day West Africa have become artists and even teach art at major universities, traditionally art production was in the hands of men. When ancestor figures are carved and used in rituals, they often appear in pairs—one male, the other female. In most art forms, women are depicted as supporting men. Nevertheless, women are also shown alone performing female tasks such as pounding food or caring for children. Sometimes, the roles of women in funerary rites are pictured. Both rituals and art often idealize women's roles through behavioral and artistic forms.

Women are also intimately connected to fertility in West African thought. This can be seen in the large-headed *akua'ba* (fertility) dolls of the Asante (See Figure 6.13). They are carved for a woman when she becomes pregnant, and she will keep the doll with her throughout her pregnancy.

Another set of carved figurines common in West Africa are the ***Ibeji* dolls**. When a woman gives birth to twins and loses one, an artist will carve her an *Ibeji* doll. As her

Figure 6.13 *Akua'ba*
(Fertility) Doll of the
Asante, Ghana.

remaining twin grows up, she does everything for the doll that she does for the live twin—feeds, washes and clothes it. When the surviving twin is grown, s/he will continue the care of the *Ibeji* doll. Female ancestor figurines are also common.

The complimentary role of women portrayed in West African religious art is carried on in the art produced under royal patronage. The king is usually male, with supporting players such as the queen mother, the queen, a harem—even female warriors and palace guards in the Dahomean case.

Just as a complementarity is artistically posited between culture and nature (village and bush), West African artists declare the importance of gender balance in the division of labor. Art, as well as ideology in many West African societies, plays down the asymmetry in power and economic status between men and women in wider society, rather stressing their co-equal need for each other to achieve full adulthood and fulfillment in life. Art may be part of the need for West African males to downplay male dominance in the political economy. It may also be seen as a representation of the deeper dependence of men on women, a depiction of the complementary nature of gender in West Africa.

Non-Wood Media in West African Art

Whereas wood is a widely used medium for artistic expression in West Africa, earthen forms and figures are also prevalent.

Wood signifies the wild bush—a male realm of un-domestication and tutelary spirits. Earthen figures conjure up images of a connection with the earth, ancestors and fertility and fecundity, both associated with femininity. Pottery making is usually a feminine activity, whereas carvers are men. Women work clay into various cultural forms (See Photo 6.6). In making pots or terracotta statues, the artist combines two elements vital to life—water and earth. These objects are then subjected to another im-

Village	Earth	Bush
Female realm	Female realm	Male realm
Culture	Mediating Rules	Wildness
Human Behavior	Ancestors	Animalistic Behavior
Human life	Ancestral life dominated by men	Life of wild animals & dangerous spirits
Earthen art & pottery making	Linkage ↔	Wood

portant force—fire. The combination of earth, water and fire resulted in the fabrication of a cultural artifact.

Mud is commonly used to make shrines. The ordinary form of such a fetish is a conical projection of the earth itself. It is a literal and figurative extension of the earth, and connotes the power of the ancestors who dwell therein. Such shrines are located in the village or at its edge, metaphorically linking village to bush.

The most elaborate and developed form of mud sculpture in West Africa can be seen in the *Oratta Mbari* works. These are kept in a central **Mbari House** constructed under the direction of professional artists. This construction usually takes six to nine months. During this period the community keeps the workers—the youth of the village—in ritual seclusion. At the completion celebration, the youth are ritually brought forth from their seclusion and given great honor in the village. Once this dedication is

Photo 6.6   A Large Water Pot in an Abandoned Village Site.

Photo 6.7   Cowries in Use on Modern Cement Graves.

performed, no one can ever touch any part of the *Mbari* House without necessitating elaborate cleansing rites. As a sacred spot in which much civic effort has been invested, it remains taboo, or set apart, a focal point of community pride and interest.

Villages compete against each other as to who can model the best *Mbari* House. When construction is complete, other communities are invited to attend a dedication ceremony. All remains of the food provided for the cloistered youth are left in a large heap near the *Mbari* House to show how much support the village gave to its workers during their sequestration. In addition to anthropomorphic mud statuary, the walls of the *Mbari* House are elaborately painted with bright geometric designs.

With the coming of cement after European contact, some artists have begun to use this medium to make artwork, especially in the construction of graves. Note the use of cowries in Photos 6.7 above and 3.1 on page 75 to spell out words and praises to the departed on this shrine, as well as the inclusion of animal horns to indicate high status. Modern cement sculptures are also being produced.

In some parts of West Africa, especially among the Efik and the people of the Cross Rivers area, cement is used to make funerary statues and commemorative monuments in the European style. Note the grave in Photo 3.1 that is constructed in the European style, this one being placed alongside the *Mbari* House.

Some large royally-supported stonework was done in hard stone, but smaller pieces were often done in soapstone or **steatite**, a soft metamorphic rock composed mostly of the mineral talc. This has been a favorite medium for carvers throughout West African history. Examples exist from Sherbro Island off the coast of Sierra Leone to Kissi country in Guinea.

Some of the most interesting statues are the Cross River *akwanshi* **phallic statues** that are found in the forest region of southeastern Nigeria, an area today inhabited by the Ekoi peoples. These tall phallic symbols are found scattered throughout the rain

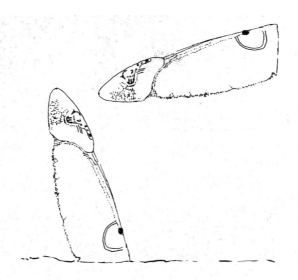

Figure 6.14   Cross River *Akwanshi* Phallic Statues Found in the Forest Region of Southeastern Nigeria.

forest in 29 groupings and 11 isolated specimens, all in abandoned or in present-day villages, some 300 statues in all. They are mostly carved in basalt rock. All are phallic in nature, but they range in a general progression from pure phalluses to humanoid phalluses, those that have facial features, breasts, and protuberant navels with decorations.

The most prolific area in West Africa for ancient stone art seems to have been Nigeria. Indeed while I was living there, I happened to be in a small village near Ife. Coming through a grove of dense trees in this heavily forested area, I emerged into a small clearing. I found myself staring at a twenty-foot tall granite phallus, the head of the stone penis expertly carved to leave no doubt as to the intent of the ancient sculptor (See Figure 6.14). Such art is "just there" the locals told me. They don't know who made it, or why. Some Nigerians say that the gods created these artworks in the timeless past.

The largest group of stone carvings is the *Esie* **sculptures**. There are about 800 of them, ranging from 20 centimeters high to a full meter. The majority of the figures are sitting on stools. These soapstone carvings show that the stool was the most common form of seating throughout West African history, as well as giving us a glimpse into the kinds of headdresses and hairdos that were in fashion at the time (some of which are still in fashion, see Photo 6.8).

Another well-known medium for carvers in West Africa was ivory. Africa became famous very early as a source of ivory that could be worked into *objects d'art* and utilitarian items such as spoons, weaving spools (See Figure 6.15), salt cellars (See Figure 6.16) and the like. The ivory trade from Nubia to Egypt was known to have existed as far back as the second millennium BC, and along with gold, was transported frequently along the caravan routes across the Sahara.

West African carvers also utilized animal bone and the teeth of warthogs and hippopotami. The range of colors in some ivory pieces stems from the fact that they are from one source or another, or because dyes or whiteners have been applied. For ex-

Photo 6.8   Hair Doing.

ample, some ivories can appear to be a warm blond color, while others are pure white, an effect achieved in Benin by applying citrus juice or sometimes an application of chalk. Baule women attain a fine white color by rubbing the ivory with sand.

To achieve a colored effect, dyes, palm oil and/or camwood powder were used. Artists could also change the color by exposing ivory to smoke or rubbing it with iron-rich earth.

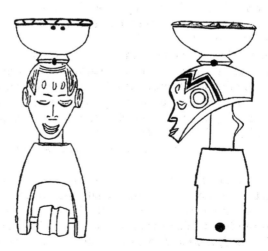

Figure 6.15   Carved Wooden Weaving Spool. Gouro, Ivory Coast.

Figure 6.16 Detail
of Portuguese Soldier
Taken from a 16th
Century Ivory Saltceller.

To carve the ivories, artists used the same tools applied to woodcarving—the adze
and the knife. The areas of West Africa most known for ivory carving were the coastal
regions of Sierra Leone and the Yoruba kingdoms, especially Benin. The arrival of the
Portuguese stimulated the production of artistically worked ivories called **Afro-Portuguese Ivories**. Their arrival began a tradition of producing pieces elaborately carved
with scenes taken from European life such as boar and stag hunts. Another common
theme was European heraldry and emblems such as the Beja Cross of the Military
Order of Christ, a Portuguese crusader group that had been given a grant to govern
the Crown's territories in the 15th century.

Portuguese traders commissioned these ivories and took them to Europe where
they became well known fixtures in the curio cabinets of the wealthy, although in
those days they were thought *not* to have come from Africa. Racist ideas led traders
and buyers to perpetrate the fraud that they were of European or Asian origin. Some
of these pieces were carved as horns patterned after European end-blown horns (West
African horns are usually side-blown).

Gold was another medium used by artists. Asante goldsmiths used (and still use)
the *cire perdue* (lost wax) method to produce delicate gold weights that have developed a worldwide reputation for their dainty ethereality (See Figure 6.17). Briefly, the
cire perdue method involves making a wax image, then coating it with clay. A hole is
left at the bottom of the clay covering, and when the clay is fired, the heated wax runs
out leaving the mold hollow. The artist then fills the mold with liquid metal, allows it
to dry, then cracks open the pottery mold to reveal a metal figure in the image of the
original wax model.

Working in gold was a high status occupation supported by the *Asantehene*, who
had a monopoly on the trade in the precious metal. Apprentices leaned from their fathers or some other skilled member of the family. The status of goldsmiths was quite
high, as these artists produced objects of great value for political officials.

While working in wood, mud and soft stone was practiced by independent artists,
working in hard stone, metals and ivory was more often supported by royal patronage.
Wood, mud and soft stone, therefore, were more likely to be found in connection with

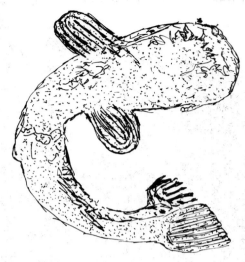

Figure 6.17   Asante Gold Weight.

religious and fertility art, while large statues in hard stone, ivories and metal work in bronze and gold was associated with state polities.

In contemporary urban West Africa one sees a variety of art forms on the streets. Some art is designed to sell a product or service (See Photo 6.9). Some are simply children's toys. Others decorate hotels and restaurants to attract tourists (See Photo 6.10). And, of course, some artists produce modern works for the world market such as the

Photo 6.9   Urban Commercial Art.

Photo 6.10   An Urban Hotel in West Africa.

well-known Senegalese artist, More Faye, Moustapha Dimé or the Nigerian artist, Princess Elizabeth Olowo.

The Art of Contact

As Europeans appeared in West Africa and began to interact with the locals, their presence began to influence the art of the region. Some art historians feel that the arrival of Europeans destroyed African art, but others see artists as innovating to incorporate new images into their work. Rather than being destroyed by contact, African art was transformed by the introduction of new representations. The decline of the slave trade impoverished some royals and support of art production fell off, but instead of being put out of work entirely African artists began to produce a different kind of art, sometimes for a different audience and sometimes with new materials. After the kings, came the Europeans, and finally tourists from all over the world who visit West Africa today. Artistic changes seem to follow historical ones.

African art in European thought came into its own in the first decade of the 20th century. Fauves and cubists sought in "primitive" art an argument for their flight from convention. When artists like Modigliani and Picasso saw African art for the first time, they were greatly impressed, and their subsequent efforts reflected the profoundness of that impression. In 1908, Henri Matisse had over twenty African statues in his private collection. In 1915, Carl Einstein wrote the first work on African sculpture, **Negerplastik**.

Certainly African art was making an imprint on European artists, but the influx of Europeans was also coming to be reflected in West African art. Four new figures emerge in the contact period, with the bulk of them appearing from the 1880s on-

Figure 6.18   Wood Figurine of a
White Woman by a Dahomean Artist.

ward—the soldier, the white trader, the missionary and finally the colonial administrator. White women were rare in West Africa and are rarely portrayed in the art of the
region (See Figure 6.18)

As the historical context of art changed, some traditional forms continued, but new
ones were added. Sherbro and Benin artists, for example, began to produce spoons
and salt cellars.

As funding and forms changed, so did the media used. Large stone figures gave way
to smaller wood pieces and bronzes. Ivories were European favorites. Also, artists
began to use new items of European origin such as beads from India and Europe,
cowries (brought by ship from the Maldive isles), nails, *manillas*, chains, bells, cheap
mirrors and the like. Today, artists incorporate modern European materials into their
masterpieces. A ceremonial costume of the *Arishola* secret society in Freetown uses
Christmas tree ornaments, tinsel, plastic beads, and European yarn to construct a
modern-day version of an old form.

But it is in the area of content where we see the biggest shift. Christianity starts to
emerge in artistic renditions—the cross, saints, the Madonna and missionaries in their
frocks. Artists also incorporated many symbols of secular power and foreign intrusive-
ness as well—bottles, newspapers and letters, clothes, umbrellas, keys, helmets, guns,
cameras, walking sticks, pipes and cigarettes, beards and side whiskers and sailing
ships.

Christianity also led to a decline in participation in secret societies and masquerades in that its churches provided similar functions. If secret societies granted a non-
kinship mode of association, so did the church. If the former gave men a means of
achievement, so did the church. As contact enhanced the presence of Christianity in
the coastal zone of West Africa, men sought out mission schools and prayer meetings,
rather than the activities of *"juju"* cults.

African Art — Summary

The art of West Africa is part of a larger corpus of works from the part of the African continent called Sub-Saharan Africa. While there is great diversity in this art, there is also a continuity of genius and sensibility.

Not surprisingly, some common themes can be found in African art — the most prominent is the importance of community, its extension through time and across the boundary between this world and the occult.

A second theme stands out: the might of the king and the right of big men to rule. African art shows kings at lofty heights, but they are always represented as being linked to nature and to the people.

A third theme that emerges strongly from African art is the ecology of life, that human cultural activities do not take place in isolation. Humankind is portrayed as linked to animal life and the bush. Like African ritual, the art of Sub-Saharan Africa stresses continuity and connectedness with all facets of the natural world. It says, loud and clear, "the place of humankind is in nature, not above it."

Finally, within African art, we see incredible beauty and artistic genius.

≋≋ CRITICAL THINKING QUESTIONS ≋≋

1. In what ways did African art influence European artists?
2. Why is some socially functioning African art disappearing from Africa?
3. What are the main social functions of non-royal art production in West Africa?
4. Given the information you have about West African cosmological ideas about the wilds, explain why many carvers and artists working in wood are also blacksmiths.
5. With the rise of West African states, how did art change?
6. In what ways did the coming of the Europeans influence African art?
7. What was the impact of Christianity on masquerades, secret societies and *juju* cults in general?

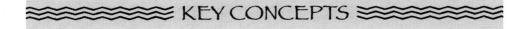 KEY CONCEPTS ≋≋

Afro-Portuguese Ivories
Akwanshi **phallic statues**
Artisanship
Dogon
Ekine **society**
Esie statues
Fronbenius' Theory of Mediterranean Origin
Gendered dualistic complementarity
Go **cult**

Golden stool
Ibeji **dolls**
Mbari **House**
Negerplastik
Nok Culture
Steatite
Tutelary figures
Tyi wara
Vodoun

≋ SOURCES & SUGGESTED READINGS ≋

Adams, Monni. 1982. *Designs for living: symbolic communication in African art.* Cambridge, MA: Carpenter Center for the Visual Arts, in cooperation with the Peabody Museum of Archaeology and Ethnology, Harvard University.

African art. 1999. *The Columbia Encyclopedia.* Fifth Edition. Infonautics Corporation.

Bascom, Wm. & Paul Gebauer. 1953. *Handbook of West African Art.* Assembled and edited by Robert E. Ritzenhaler. Milwaukee: Bruce Publishing Co.

Bodrogi, Tibor. 1968. *Art in Africa.* New York: McGraw-Hill.

Brain, Robert. 1980. *Art and society in Africa.* London: Longman.

Ezra, Kate. 1984. *African Ivories.* New York: Metropolitan Museum of Art.

Ezra, Kate. 1992. *Royal art of Benin: the Perls collection in the Metropolitan Museum of Art.* New York: Metropolitan Museum of Art.

French, Howard. W. 1996 (March 10). Voodoo Lives on in West Africa. *New York Times.*

Leuzinger, Elsy. 1960. (Trans. A. E. Keep). *Africa: The art of the negro peoples.* New York: Crown.

Leuzinger, Elsy. 1976. *The art of Black Africa.* Photographs by isabelle Wettstein & Brigitte Kauf. New York: Rizzoli.

No Author. 1965. *Picasso: Fifty-five years of his graphic work.* New York: Harry N. Abrams, Inc.

Nunley, John W. 1987. *Moving with the face of the devil : art and politics in urban West Africa.* Urbana: University of Illinois Press.

Nunley, John W. 1999. *Masks: faces of culture.* New York: Abrams.

Roy, Claude. 1985. *Modigliani.* New York: Rizzoli.

Vogel, Susan. 1991. *Africa explores : 20th century African art* (Assisted by Ima Ebong; contributions by Walter E.A. van Beek (et al.). New York : Center for African Art.

Warren, Fred. 1970. *The music of Africa: An introduction.* Englewood Cliffs: Prentice-Hall.

7 MUSIC & SOCIETY IN WEST AFRICA

> Music is a social marker for gender, ethnicity, cult membership and nationality in West Africa. It can even be emblematic of "being modern" as with young people who eschew traditional music for more modern forms such as High Life, Reggae, Rock or Hip Hop.
>
> Traditional music is integral to ritual life in West Africa but it also is frequently integrated into the daily work activities of people. Most events and work were traditionally accompanied by music, as were many rites, ceremonies, masquerades and other socio-ritual events. Of course, music is also an integral part of dances held on ceremonial occasions or spontaneous events held for entertainment.
>
> Musicians may play for their own enjoyment but are frequently part of musical cults. When music is embedded in cults, it is tied to mystical concepts of control over supernatural power and the relation between its concentration in medicines and artisanal ability. *Griots* or praise singers also are organized and their abilities are ritualized and tied to magical properties, shrines and cult membership. Singers may praise political leaders and be charged with remembering complicated oral histories. This chapter details the *gØgØ* musicians' cult among the Sisala of Northern Ghana. It also notes the common musical styles and instruments used in West African music.

Music in West Africa

Indigenous sub-Saharan African musical and dance expressions are maintained by oral tradition. They are stylistically distinct from the music and dance of both the Arabic cultures of North Africa and the Western settler populations of eastern and Southern Africa. Like the plastic arts discussed above, song and dance function to integrate the individual into the social group. Much African art, especially in mask form, is involved in masquerades, dances and musical events in the community, making an interwoven connection between art forms.

Music in West Africa is not static. In the precolonial period, trade, wars, migrations, and religion stimulated interaction among sub-Saharan societies, encouraging them to borrow musical resources from one another, including some Arabic instruments and techniques.

The area's music, as with that distributed more broadly throughout Africa, tends to be polyrhythmic. While European music specializes in polytonality, the musicians playing several tones as once, African music is composed of complex combinations of different rhythms, all played at once. While this elaborate musical form is found throughout West Africa, some smaller culture areas show specialized styles, for example, in the Savannah belt musicians show great virtuosic instrumental styles and public music is often performed or accompanied by a class of professional praise singers, or **griots**.

In West Africa, as elsewhere on the continent, music is usually a social event. Though I have seen musicians playing by themselves for their own enjoyment, the music usually attracts a crowd fairly quickly. I realized this one afternoon when I absentmindedly turned on my tape recorder in the village. The tape played out xylophone music I had recorded some days before. As I worked over my field notes with the music playing in the background, I became aware that a crowd was gathering outside my hut. Soon we had a full-fledged dance going, many people dropping whatever it was they were doing to join in. Dancing to music seems the natural thing to do in the African context, given that it is largely **polyrhythmic music**. Bohannan and Curtin say:

> African dancing follows those polyrhythms. Different parts of the body take up one of the different rhythms in the orchestra. The polyrhythms in the orchestra are thus duplicated by the dancer's body. The head moves to one rhythm, the shoulders in another, and the feet in still another. A viewer who has learned to see and feel the polyrhythms in the dance as it reflects the music can appreciate that African dancing both demands great precision and allows great freedom of expression to the dancers.

African musical traditions also greatly emphasize dance, for movement is regarded as an important mode of communication. The dance utilizes symbolic gestures, mime, props, masks, costumes, body painting and other visual devices. The basic movements may be simple, emphasizing the upper body, torso, or feet; or they may be complex, involving coordination of different body parts and intricate actions such as fast rotation, ripples of the body, and contraction and release, as well as variations in dynamics and use of space.

When the community holds festivals, rituals or has collective tasks to perform, music is usually an accompaniment. I first experienced this one day in a Sisala village when a group of women were repairing a flat roof to a woman's house (See Photo 7.1). One woman stood tall singing out a female song called *tingtElE*, and those women who bent to the task of pounding fresh earth into the mud roof were responding in unison with the chorus. Men weeding in the fields did the same thing. Such songs are thought to make the work more enjoyable and uniform.

Yet ritual and music seem to be undergoing a transition in West Africa, especially in the north where the influence of Islam is growing. Islamic rites are replacing animistic ones to some extent. The decline in traditional ritual has affected the production and maintenance of musical instruments normally played at such ceremonies. In 1998 I was present when an animist funeral was to be held in a village, but had to be postponed because there were no functioning xylophones left in the community. The artists who carved them and kept them in tune had either migrated or died out. Today few young people know how to play traditional instruments, and I have attended more than one "dance" where young boys simply pounded out a beat on tin cans and aluminum bowls. For one funeral, modern snare drums were brought from town (See Photo 7.2).

Photo 7.1   Three Roof Styles—Female House (with Nuts), Male Thatched and Male Tin.

Village youth are more aware of music played on Ghanaian television. Boom boxes and radios are ubiquitous, even in rural areas. Young people can listen to American rock and pop tunes and many identify more with such "modern" ways than with the music of their forefathers.

Photo 7.2   Muslim Funeral with Modern Drums.

Traditional music does seem to be surviving where it is embedded in cult structures. Music is sometimes part of the traditions owned by corporate groups who hold in common certain beliefs and values. Musical traditions may be shared widely by a community of ethnically and linguistically homogenous persons, or they might be attached to smaller corporate sodalities within the community, such as secret societies, voluntary associations or age-sets.

Participating in commonly understood songs and dances gives members a sense of unity and oneness so important to social solidarity. Music reinforces common convictions and valuations, and it encourages involvement in collective behavior, strengthening social bonds. In short, it inspires corporate life; it is a tangible expression of group sentiments, a focal symbol of oneness. Collective life of the group comes alive in the shared performance of music, song and dance. It is the sensate expression of group life.

Throughout this text I have tried to show that the communalistic nature of West African sociocultural formations has evolved out of a need to work together. Music expresses that need, but it can also be played spontaneously by the musician for his own enjoyment.[1] The spontaneous expression of music might start out as an individual endeavor, and evolve into a group session. I witnessed this among some village children after a rain. The tension of being cooped up inside broke out into rhythms beat out on a tin drum and a discarded metal pan. It began with a small group of boys, and quickly grew into a full-blown songfest with dancing. Women passing through the village on their way to another stopped and joined in. People from distant homesteads heard the music and came. In a way, music is like a magnet in Africa.

Almost all events are, or can be, "musicalized"—there are cradle songs, grinding songs, songs to pound millet by and songs to sing while weeding the crops. When I announced one day that I would be giving out bottles of gin in thanks, people came with drums and xylophones and we had a dance. This is the **musicalization of social events** so common in West Africa.

Not all music is played for social events. Individuals may play alone for their own pleasure, but even then there may be a spiritual being involved, as when a Konkomba lute player performs for himself when he wants to commune with a tutelary spirit. Also music can be performed to while away the hours—for example, when cowherds are tending cattle in the bush, they might play a *mbira* hand piano or make reed flutes to divert themselves.

Musical Cults and Musicians

A young man who wishes to pursue music will often attach himself to the head musician of a cult. He will be given training and allowed to play at some affairs along with a more trained guide. Throughout West Africa there are wandering drummers and musicians who make a living by playing for wealthy men in this town or that. However, most musicians of a cult are tied to a community and play music that reflects that community's civic pride. Most are part-time players who make some money from

---

1. Musicians are largely males, though women will join in spontaneously by clapping hands, making noise or keeping rhythm by hitting a piece of metal against another or by singing or dancing. Female work groups also sing songs, sometimes to the accompaniment of clapping or rhythmic sounds produced by one or all of the women.

their playing, but they are principally farmers or have some other occupation besides playing music.

In addition to these semi-pros, most people sing and some women may accompany the musicians by shaking a rattle, or even just beating on a tin can with a spoon. All West African traditions emphasize singing, because song is used as an avenue of communication, as is dance. Both say something about the singer, dancer and the community.

Because many African languages are tonal languages in which pitch level determines meaning, the melodies and rhythms of songs generally follow the intonation contour and rhythms of the song texts. Melodies are usually organized within a scale of four, five, six or seven tones. In group singing, some societies sing in unison or in parallel octaves with sporadic fourths or fifths; others sing in two or three parts, using parallel thirds or fourths. Songs generally are in **call-response form.**

Most social occasions — funerals, weddings or festivals bring the skilled musician and the commoner together to make a musical event. The skilled musicians form the core, while a variety of people dance, sing or keep time on minor instruments such as rattles, tambourine or even by merely clapping their hands.

Musical Instruments and Structure

The music of the African continent shares many similarities, perhaps pointing toward a past of sharing and migration. Dr. Nketia says that the music of Africa is composed of "a network of overlapping styles, which share common features of structure, basic procedures and similar contextual relations."

The kinds of instruments used in West African music are partially determined by the environment in which the music was formulated. Traditionally, the surrounding bush yielded wood, leather, reeds, gourds, bone, ivory and seeds to make rattles. Cowries imported from the Maldive Isles added another dimension to idiophones. When metalwork became widespread, blacksmiths could make percussion instruments, giving yet a new sound to the music. With the arrival of European manufactured goods, West African musicians had even more with which to work.

I once attended a fairy-calling séance in Burkina Faso, in which the musical prelude was performed on drums and fiddles made of Mobil Oil cans. I can attest to the fact that after several hours of listening to this band in a closed room, I was ready to see fairies or almost anything else!

Materials and instrument styles no doubt have long diffused across the region. Traditional instruments include: xylophones, drums, idiophones, rattles, sistrums, castanets or finger symbols, the hand piano, membraphones, flutes, fiddles, trumpets, reed pipes, zithers, chordophones, lutes, harps and bells (See Photo 7.3). The total corpus of instruments is still expanding, with electric guitars, keyboards and the like being used in West African cities.

In addition to music produced with these instruments, West Africans often sing along, dance with complex movements, or accompany the music with hand clapping, chest thumping, feet stamping, spoken lyrics or even vocal grunts. Professor Nketia says of the music of his home:

> The structure used in African music represents usages which are learned
> through participation in musical events, passed on aurally from generation to

Photo 7.3   Xylophones, Which Are Usually Played as a Pair.

generation, and applied, modified, and expanded by succeeding generations. They include melodic and rhythmic elements, both linear and multilinear, which permit limited improvisations to be made where appropriate.

Music may be played individually, but it is usually performed in a social context. It may be presented alone or accompanied by singing and/or dancing. The singing can be solo, performed by groups or a family in a call-response pattern. Some music is freely open to the public, while other music may be reserved for members of secret societies. Music is often performed by secret societies for the general public in dance dramas in which the dancer/musician uses elaborate costumes and masks to hide his identity.

Music is a shared tradition, an important marker of ethnic identity. As with myths, proverbs, dance styles, clothing patterns, house design and other cultural identifiers, music performed in social settings binds people together and links them to their cultural heritage and those members of the society who previously played and enjoyed the music.

Ranking high among the most important aspects of social life, music is an essential part of almost every facet of daily life in West Africa. Dr. Fred Warren says that "Music follows the African through his entire day from early in the morning till late at night, and through all the changes of his life, from the time he came into this world until after he has left it." I find this a bit of an overstatement, having lived a number of years in Africa myself, I would say that much gets done without a musical accompaniment, but important matters are often musicalized, especially rites of passage and collective work parties. Above all, African music is social, mostly played collectively for groups and it supplements a civic culture that is designed to bind people together through enjoyment of shared meanings.

Music is part of almost every walk of life in West Africa. Since movement to and from the urban areas is so common these days, young people encounter new styles of music just waling down the street in a modern city like Kumase or Dakar. Most young people who can afford a portable stereo have them. Inexpensive cassettes are to be had everywhere, many of them pirated. CDs were still a bit pricey the last time I was there, but they are becoming more and more popular as the days go by.

One of the most common forms of urban music in West Africa is called **High Life**, originating in the streets of Ghanaian cities. Its bands play a brand of joyous music that has a folk tinge to it, not unlike peasant music from other parts of the world. Many stores in the West African cities play this music for people passing by on the street. The boulevards and avenues are usually alive with music and it is not uncommon to see people dancing in the street or on the sidewalk.

Today in many West African towns and cities, revivalist churches flourish. On Sunday their music is heard everywhere: in the churches themselves, on street corners where music is interspersed with sermons, wafting down the avenues and alleyways of the big cities. As many social events are in traditional society, Christian church services are musicalized. This pattern of musicalization also has been continued among those of African descent in the Diaspora.

With urbanization and the impact of Western culture, traditional forms of music and dance have decreased. New idioms have emerged, however, that combine African and Western elements. Lagos and New York musicians play back up for each other. New musical forms have been emerging from this interaction including West African High Life, which shows certain Caribbean traits. I even have a CD called African Salsa!

The Music of the Sisala of Northern Ghana

The music of the Sisala has been studied and preserved in archival form by Dr. Marry Seavoy, working at UCLA. Sisala musicians mainly use percussion instruments. In fact, the general term for musical instrument is *ku-duulung*, "a struck thing." Instruments such as the drums (*dunung*) or xylophone (*jengsing*) are struck with a mallet or—*dunnlo* (See Photo 7.4).

The drum is the single most widely used musical instrument in West Africa. The Sisala use the hourglass-shaped *singsenge*, a drum with two laced heads, the pitch of

Photo 7.4 Talking Drums.

which can be changed by squeezing the thongs connecting the twin heads between the arm and body. The Sisala also have the *goriku* drum which is very similar to the twin *tEngpEnning*, or talking drums—those that are drummed at the chief's compound and which are used to call people from the farms (See Photo 7.5). However, the *goriku* or *kurungbanga* is a drum with a single, pegged head over an open conical shell.

A common pattern of **genderization of musical instruments** occurs among the Sisala as with many other West African societies. The two *tEngpEnning* drums are gendered, the larger of the two (the *tEngpEng-niing*) is placed at the drummers left. Its deeper tone carries a female association, while the higher-toned *tEngpEng-bele*, the smaller of the two, is placed on the drummer's right and is thought to be male. As with African statuary, these drums represent the complementarity of male and female in the world. These are called the "talking drums" because their tone can be changed to imitate speech. Everyone has a drum name, and most people can recognize when the drums are calling them. Children while away the hours at the farm playing the *vakuonung*, a children's *tEngpEnning* drum. On this they practice the speech and rhythms of the talking drums.

The drummer of the *tEngpEnning* drums is called the *tEngpEng-duuro*, but the player of the talking drums at the palace of the Sisala chief of Tumu is referred to by

Photo 7.4   Head Drummer, Chief's Compound, Tumu, Ghana.

the Asante term, *akarima*.[2] While the Sisala reside some 300 miles north of the Asante, this shows that they have had contact over the years and have incorporated some Akan terms into their vocabulary.

The Sisala also have a *gugo-bele*, a small wooden hand-held drum played at festivals, and the smaller *pendere*, which is made out of a skin stretched over the hole of a large gourd. This latter drum is played in the women's songs or *ha-gØgung* and *tingtElE*, but is most commonly used as the third instrument accompanying two xylophones played at funerals. The *ha-gØgung* are the women's funeral songs which can be used for praise, gossip, slander, allusion and coercion. The *tingtElE* is a dance for women, appropriate for funerals and other celebrations, accompanied by handclapping and the *pendere* drum.

While drums are important, the musical instrument I most associate with the Sisala is the xylophone, the *jengsing*. It is played at almost every social occasion in conjunction with drums and other instruments. This is a single instrument, referred to in the plural of *jengsi*, which means to lift something up together or to work cooperatively. Here we can see the African emphasis on collectivity expressed in their musical terminology. Just as a group of men might *jengsi* the center beam of a house in unison, the collection of several keys of the *jengsing* play as one. Harmony and unity in music are equated with the same in social life.

The Sisala xylophone is a gourd-resonated instrument with 17 wooden keys suspended over an open frame. It is played with a pair of rubber-knobbed mallets. *Jengsing* are almost always played in pairs and are often combined with the *pendere* drum to form the classical ensemble of the Sisala funeral.

---

2. This term is a form of the Twi word *ØkyerEma*, meaning drummer, but in the Sisala context *akarima* would have the connotation of "official drummer."

The cult of the xylophone players (*jeng-duuroo*) is led by a senior man, called the *jeng-duuri-hiang*, the headman of the musician's cult. It will have regular members and *gØgØ-biising*, or apprentice musicians. As with most West African cults, a xylophone-playing shrine (*jeng-lurung*) is assocated with the players. It is a medicine shrine of the class of non-ancestral shrines called *tØmung*. These are personal or cult shrines associated with individual or artisanal activities such as blacksmithing, carving or hunting. Of course, it is not difficult to understand the magical quality of music as it emerges from a collection of wood, leather and gourds. As with carvers and medicine men, the musicians make their instruments out of bush products, and hence understand the magicoreligious connection between the supernatural powers of the wilds and the fabricated cultural modes of music produced by the *jeng-du-uroo*.

The Sisala have other, less socially-important musical instruments like the *cheng* or reed zither. This is my personal favorite. It is an ideochordic raft zither composed of eleven single and double courses of split reeds (*chengfulaa*). It is hand held and played with the thumbs. It is usually played by individuals for mere enjoyment, but it can also accompany praise singing at funerals. Players also attach small metal discs called *cheng-chiiming* to the zither. As the player moves the instrument in playing, these discs provided added musicality.

The Sisala also have bells and rattles. It is common for non-musicians at a songfest to join in with words or to snap their fingers rhythmically, clap their hands or use some minor instruments like a brass finger bell (*piisa*). A *piisa* is a globular bell suspended from the dancer's finger and struck with an iron thumb ring. Like other aspects of life, music is also gendered and only men play the *piisa* to male songs.

The praise singers, or *griots*, accompany their songs with music from the *gØgØ-pire*, or musician's hoe. This is similar to a regular farmer's hoe. It is struck with a pair of *nenii-piring*, or iron finger rings used by the male praise singer for beating out rhythmic patterns on his hoe.

Sisala musicians sometimes play a double bell of forged iron that is struck with an animal horn. Iron ankle rattles are sometimes worn by dancers. They are divided into male and female rattlers, with the lower-pitched rattle placed on the right foot. Likewise the xylophone players sometimes attach *jengchika* or iron rattles to their wrists. These add rhythm to the music as the player strikes the keys with mallets.

Sisala musicians also use wind instruments. The *nyile* is a side-blown animal horn. The *sekele nyile* is also a side-blown instrument, a "stalk horn." After the harvest, children make these from left-over corn stalks and practice their *nyile-yiilaa* or "horn songs." Children also make a short wooden end-blown flute called *ngmulung*.

Music accompanies many social affairs in Sisalaland. Roughly, songs and dances are divided into male and female categories. *Bayiililaa* (s. *bayiiling*) are men's songs that most frequently accompany a dance performed at the funeral of an elderly male, as processional music for the entrance of the mock-body or *gungung*. This is a substitute for the dead body, which used to be part of the ceremony, until the British banned the practice. In songs, associated with hunting and war, men often fire off muskets and carry *saachØnung* axes (human headed) which are placed beside the substitute body. In this music, Sisala men extol all things they consider to be masculine.

Women have their own funeral music called the *naasaring*. During this dance they wear leaves over their waist cloths to indicate their ancestral dress. Symbolic of their role as women, they carry firewood and sing and dance in a circular pattern around the musical ensemble.

Music is an integral part of Sisala funerals of which there are two kinds: **hot funerals** and **cool funerals**. A "hot" funeral is a sad one because the departed was young, so the music and duration of the funeral will be curtailed. A "cool" funeral is that of an elderly person and will last longer[3] with more merriment and music. Generally, the funeral starts off with a dirge, *hangyie* music. This is a slow wailing accompanied by soft drumming. As the funeral proceeds, the music becomes more up-tempo and in a "cool" funeral it become downright raucous near the end.

There are a variety of dances performed by different groups of people, including the *chingcheng*—a dance for women performed at the funeral of an old man to celebrate the lover (*hiila*) relationship. This is done by women who carry sticks of wood in their hands or on their heads, dancing sideways around the centralized pair of xylophones and a gourd drum. They may sing about the loves of the departed.

By far the most common dance is *jeng-yiiling*, the xylophone dance. It is danced at night by young people at a cool funeral. It involves a long (conga-like) line of dancers moving slowly and in close formation around the musical instruments at the center of the funeral grounds. Another favorite female dance is the *jangnga* dance. It is an energetic dance in which the dancers alternate in pairs and conclude their short sequence in a center dance ring by knocking their buttocks together. This brings squeals of delight from the dancers and onlookers alike.

Other dances and songs such as hunters' songs (*nangkpaana*), depict various aspects of life and social groupings or artisanal endeavors in Sisalaland. Perhaps the most important dance at the funeral of an old man is the final *kuorung*, or the dance of the big man. Each male in-law dances in turn, joined by friends and family. This marks the culmination of the official activities and responsibilities of the attendees. If, indeed, the departed was a big man, the family will display many articles to indicate his high status, and it is expected that the dancers will be adorned in their finest clothing for this dance.

Like most Savannah-dwellers, the Sisala kept their traditions orally. Praise singers (male, *gØgØ-dingdEnnE;* female, *ha-gØgØ*) were the historians of their society. The female praise singers have their own cult, with a female head, the *ha-gØgØ-hiang*. At funerals and other special occasions, these *gØgØ* sing out the feats of the departed, his family tree, the exploits of his lineage and clan. Every person has a praise-name, as well as families, some animals, gods and other significant entities in the cosmology of the Sisala. Praises are sung by one who is skilled and experienced in the spontaneous delivery of texts that incorporate historical references, metaphors and allusions to the strength and well-being of the family.

The type of music selected for a funeral often says something about the departed or his or her family. For example, *gØgØ-yiilaa* (musicians' songs) are only sung at the funeral of a musician, or someone very close to a prominent musician. *Nangbagili-yiilaa* are hunters' songs performed with the appropriate dance at the funeral of a hunter. This may involve the performance of a pantomime and drama portraying the feats of the dead hunter. Praises to a great farmer (*paare-dEnnE*) are actually shouted from the rooftops, the *griot* standing atop a woman's flat-roofed dwelling to do so. Diviners also have their own cult dances and music (*vugira-guala*).

---

3. As a general rule, African music and dance last much longer than most uninitiated Europeans expect. I have been at African parties where a single dance with accompanying music has lasted a half hour. Even those West Africans making records and CDs today include cuts of twenty to thirty minutes. In the West this is uncommon because of the dictates of radio stations that want two to three minute songs.

In short, Sisala music, song and dance is fundamentally social, highlighting social groups, occupations, genders and the accomplishments of big men and valued wives, even their infidelities, as in the *chingcheng* dance for lovers mentioned above. The funeral is less a sad affair, than a celebration of life. I know of many Sisala living in the south who travel hundreds of miles to attend a funeral, to pay their respects to the departed, but also to hear and participate in their own music, something that symbolizes the essence of being Sisala.

CRITICAL THINKING QUESTIONS

1. Discuss the importance of music among the Sisala as a social identifier and ethnic marker and as a mark of one's membership in a specialized craft.
2. What is meant by the musicalization of social events and what functions are associated with it e.g., why do people use music with work, for example?
3. In musical cults, why is medicine and/or magic involved and how does that relate to other artisanal endeavors? Relate this to the West African concept of cosmic power and how that works in artisan activities.

KEY CONCEPTS

Call-response form
Cool funeral
Genderization of musical instruments
Griots
High life

Hot funeral
Mbira
Musicalization of social events
Polyrhythmic music

SOURCES & SUGGESTED READINGS

Blass, Regina (ed). 1975. *Sisaala — English, English — Sisaala Dictionary.* Kumase, Ghana: Institute of Linguistics.

Bohannan, Paul and Phillip Curtin. 1995. *Africa and Africans* (Fourth Ed.). Prospect Heights, IL: Waveland Press.

Mendonsa, Eugene L. 1982. *The politics of divination.* Berkeley: University of California Press.

Nketia, J. H. Kwabena. 1974. *The music of Africa.* New York: W. W. Norton & Co.

Seavoy, Mary H. 1982. *The Sisaala Xylophone Tradition.* Ph.D dissertation. UCLA.

Warren, Fred. 1970. *The music of Africa: An introduction.* Englewood Cliffs: Prentice-Hall.

8 THE EARLY HISTORY OF WEST AFRICA

> This chapter looks at the prehistory of West Africa compared to other parts of the continent and Eurasia. It discusses developments from the Stone Age through the Iron Age and the growth of indigenous civilization in villages and cities. West Africans employed various tools and technologies to adapt to different ecological zones. They also developed different economic modes of production to survive in the region—foraging, farming, herding, trade and metallurgy. Along with the emergence of city life came the rise of kingdoms, the development of which was influenced by trade opportunities and geographical location.

Prehistory

Africa has a long history that is increasingly being revealed through the efforts of archaeologists, paleontologists, historians and anthropologists. Research into Africa's civilization began belatedly, as the European view generally held that nothing of scientific value existed in Africa. Africans were thought to lack history and certainly anything like the monumental material finds archaeologists had uncovered in Eurasia or Central America. When archaeologists did find evidence of complex societies, in Nok for example, early interpreters explained them away as intrusions from elsewhere. They assumed that fine art and delicate metalwork could not possibly have been made by the backward tribes of *Guiné*.

Much of the prehistory of West Africa still remains to be written. This area of the world contains many unexplored archaeological sites waiting for research and excavation. Also, since most African archaeology has been done in other parts of the continent, we have a very poor understanding of the prehistoric relations between Eastern, Southern Africa and West Africa. West Africans' relations with peoples of the north—in Mediterranean, Northern Africa and the Near East—are also unclear.

The African continent has a long tradition of migration and mixing of various populations. West Africa has no natural barriers to movement by land—no high mountain ranges or inhospitable lands south of the forbidding wastes of the Sahara—and even that sandy wilderness could not deter the human lust for exploration, contact and trade. In time West Africa became a meeting point of various overland commercial routes along which flowed goods, people and information (See Map 1.4). Archaeologists tell us that interregional, subcontinental and intercontinental connections have conditioned life in West Africa for more than a thousand years. However, two factors make the prehistory of West Africa somewhat vague. The first is the lack of archaeological work in the area. The second, somewhat linked to the first, is the lack of material remains to be found due to the harsh tropical climate, and to the perishability of many of the materials used by early inhabitants of the region. Wood, leather, adobe, grass—all tend to quickly deteriorate in the tropics. We are usually left with stone and metal and sometimes bone.

Nevertheless, based on linguistic studies, and scant archaeological work, we know that a **Bantu migration** from an area near the Nigeria-Cameroon border likely occurred before 7,000 BP. These peoples eventually mingled with others who moved ahead of the desiccating Sahara between 7,000 and 5,000 BP (See Table 8.1 below). As these early West Africans spread over much of Sub-Saharan Africa, they may have been enabled by the metal technology they carried with them—the iron spear, hoe, machete and axe.

Some groups stayed in the rain forest while others inhabited the **Sudanic Zone** north of the heavily forested belt near the equator (See Map 1.2). These Savannah-dwellers are of special interest because their descendants eventually formed the great Sudanic Kingdoms of Tekrur, Kanem-Bornu, Ghana, Mali and Songhai. Later the forest-dwellers created the great states of **Asante**, Dahomey, **Ife**, Benin, Oyo and other kingdoms, as well as a number of smaller chiefdoms (See Maps 8.1 & 9.6).

Early humans in West Africa existed in a long Stone Age of about two million years, eventually developing metallurgy to improve their tool kit in the Iron Age. Of all the metals, it seems that iron was worked first. Thus, unlike in Eurasia, Africans skipped the Bronze Age. Ancient Egypt was a Bronze Age civilization, but Sub-Saharan Africa went directly from using stone to the use of iron, though copper and brass were imported from the Mediterranean.

A find in nearby Chad, indicates that *Homo erectus* lived there as far back as the Middle Pleistocene (900,000 to 127,000 BP). These remains have been found in association with **Acheullean tools** (See Figure 8.1). Remains of *Homo erectus* in other parts of Africa are found from about 500,000 BP, so it is likely that there is some connection between these finds in Chad and other *Home erectus* sites on the continent. Acheullean tools are common to West Africa, being found widely from Mauritania and Senegal on the West to Nigeria on the East. They show a progression of skill from early tools that are crude and unpolished to later tools with fine flaking that are polished.

The many stone tools recovered in this region—hand axes, adzes, picks and scrapers—along with seeds of wild grains, fruits and oil palms indicate that hunting and gathering were common. Not only did these early West Africans use tools of stone, but also constructed others made of bone, horn and wood. Eventually hand held tools gave way to hafted ones, bringing in the age of the handled hand axe. Archaeologists have found polished stone axes, flaked arrowheads, bone harpoons and some pottery remnants dating from 12,000 to 4,000 BP—evidence of increased technological sophistication.

Though early West Africans were foragers, excavations at Daima in present-day Northern Nigeria, have revealed evidence of a pastoral society in which the people seemed to have been involved in some food production as well. These people may have come from the north about 7,000 BP looking for pasturage and water. This would fit with present-day oral traditions that depict ancient migrations from the north and northeast. Ceramic art from the site shows humans and many animals, especially cows. These are contemporary with Nok finds, but they are distinct in style, simpler, with far less detail (See Nok Culture below).

	Table 8.1 Dates in West African History
BP Dates	**West African Events**
900,000–127,000	Middle Pleistocene/Acheullean toolkit
500,000 >	*Homo erectus* found in Africa
12,000 >	Polished stone axes/advance in toolkit
12,000–8,000	Lakeside incipient pastoralism and foraging in Sahara
12,000	Iwo Eleru skeleton in rock shelter
11,000	Near Eastern Neolithic Revolution
10,000	Evidence of ingressed copper and brass objects in West Africa
8,000	Evidence for cattle & goat domestication, Nigeria
7,000	Neolithic Revolution spreads to Nile Valley
< 7,000	Bantu migration
7,000	Northern pastoralists begin move south looking for pasturage
7,000–5,000 >	Desiccation of the Sahara
5,000 >	Iron-working in Taruga, Nigeria
4,000	Evidence of pastoralism from Gao
4,000–2,800	Tichitt-Oualata State, Mauritania
3,500	Stone Bowl agricultural Culture, East Africa
3,200	Bulrush millet cultivated in Mauritania
3,000	First evidence of Saharan pastoralists domesticating plants
3,000	Begho iron-age agricultural urban settlement
3,000	Camel comes to West Africa
2,900 or 2,500–1,800	Nok Culture
2,250–600	Jenné-Jeno
1,200	Evidence of lost-wax method from Igbo-Ukwu
1,900	Domesticated rice at Jenné-Jeno
1,600	Jenné-Jeno expands long-distance trade
1,400	Jenné-Jeno an 82-acre urban center
1,400	Rise of Kingdom of Ghana
1,300	Iron-working introduced to the western areas of Guinea, Sierra Leone and Liberia.
1,250	Islamic peoples begin to enter West Africa
1,200	Earliest known African use of the lost-wax method at Igbo-Ukwu in modern-day Nigeria.

Stone-Age Foragers in Africa

The archaeological evidence from the African continent points to a shift from Stone Age hunting and gathering to Iron Age farming and animal husbandry about 4,000 or 5,000 BP. Early hunters and gatherers had a fairly simple division of labor — men hunted and women foraged for fruits, leaves and tubers. We have little archaeological

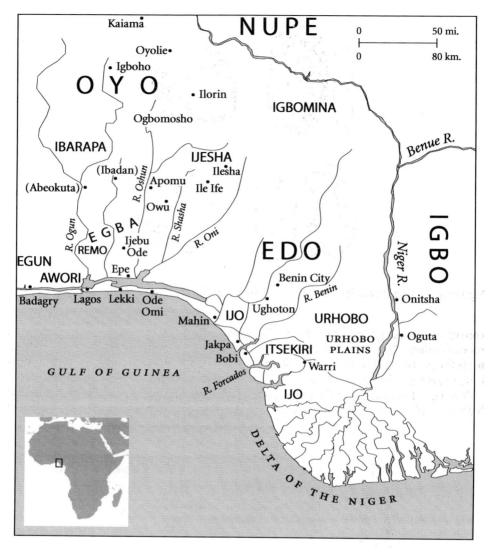

Map 8.1   Oyo, Nupe, Benin & Igbo of Western & Midwestern Nigeria.

evidence of cultural details, but based on our ethnographic and archaeological knowledge from other parts of Africa, we can assume that early West African foragers had an egalitarian culture. This would have entailed simple distinctions between male and female tasks, and some age grading.

The archaeological evidence shows three main trends. First, West Africans employed a strategy based on extensive exploitation of resources, relying on different food sources and moving from one ecological niche to another. Secondly, during the long Stone Age there was an increasing sophistication of the tool kit. One such improvement was the invention of the bow and arrow. Another was the appearance of **microliths** (See Figure 8.2), or tiny stone chips that were often embedded in bone or wood to make **composite tools** (See Figure 8.3). These miniature stone tools appeared in Southern Africa before they show up in the West African record. They may have

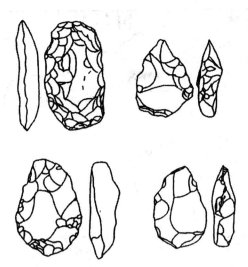

Figure 8.1 Late Acheullean & Middle Stone Age Tools.

spread into West Africa from there. The third trend was the progressive increase in specialization. This is indicated by the production of a greater range of standardized tools for particular purposes. Steadily there was a more economical use of carefully selected raw materials for tool making.

The age of microliths in the latter part of the Stone Age reveals an innovation on the hafting tradition already in use—attaching a wood handle to a stone head by means of

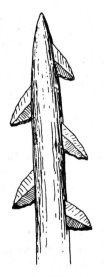

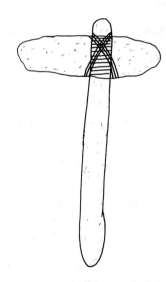

Figure 8.2 An Example of a Microlithic Tool, Stone Set in Wood or Bone.

Figure 8.3 An Example of a Composite Tool, an Ax of Stone Hafted to Wood or Bone.

Photo 8.1   Woman Grinding with a Stone.

thongs and/or pitch. This marked the appearance of composite tools. By inserting flaking residue into wood, bone and antler, late Stone Age Man was not only showing technological sophistication, but also parsimony. He was utilizing the tiny remains of grosser work to create more complex tools, the precursor of which may have been the bola. The pace of technological change was quickening. This likely led to a growing population as well.

As the ancestors of modern-day West Africans were working out the science of survival in an ecological sense, they were also developing ways of cooperating to cope better. What emerged was a set of kinship and religious institutions that stressed a communalistic way of life in which the strong took care of the weak, the aged and infants.

The residence pattern was dispersed, shifting and flexible. Foragers may have made temporary huts of brush and mud, but we do not find any such remains. Researchers have found the material works of early humans in caves and rock shelters, and also a few skeletal remains. Many rock shelter and cave finds indicate that early humans used such sites as temporary homes, perhaps when passing through an area—the shelters acting as a sort of early Holiday Inn. Indeed, the successive layers at **Iwo Eleru** unveil a long history of residence.

Other shelters have been found in Guinea, Sierra Leone, Burkina Faso and Liberia. Those from Guinea have microliths, ground stone axes, grinding stones, pottery and a kind of flat pick that some have interpreted as a stone hoe (See Photo 8.1). This assemblage would indicate the possibility of agriculture, or perhaps these tools were used in foraging. The rock shelters in southeast Guinea, at Blandè, have ground stone axes and pottery, but no microliths, which are also lacking in caves farther south. This could reflect a lack of appropriate stone to produce microliths, or that the tradition was intrusive into the more northern areas, but did not reach to the south. At Bosumpra Cave in Ghana evidence of habitation has been found in polished stone tools, microliths, composite tools, rasps and pottery. This find indicates a series of occupations over long periods linking Stone Age hunters with later peoples capable of making pottery.

Early people also made mud, stick and grass shelters, which have long since returned to nature. In Ghana, however, some rock houses have been excavated in the area where ample stone was available for use in construction.

As these early *Homo sapiens* became more adaptable, they were able to respond more readily to changing environmental opportunities. This was important because as the last ice age of the Pleistocene waned there were worldwide adjustments in sea level and climate. The once arid Sahara became a more lush and a habitable environment with many lakes, rivers and forested areas. We know this from the rock art in the region and the remains found at lakeside habitats, from about 12,000 to 8,000 BP. It seems that the foragers who moved into this verdant Sahara region fed on fish and game. David Phillipson says:

> Beside these waters, previously nomadic groups established semipermanent habitations that were supported by the rich year-round supplies of fish that the lakes provided, supplemented by hunting for meat and by collecting wild vegetable foods. Sites of these settled peoples are characterized by the barbed-bone heads of the harpoons with which they fished and by the pottery of which their settled lifestyle enabled them to make use.

Microlithic tools and grinding stones used to process wild grains were also found in these lakeside settlements. This shows early **sedentism** that gave rise to a flowering of culture. These early Africans domesticated the indigenous, humpless, wild ox (*Bos primigenius*), sheep and goats, the latter being imports from the Near East *via* Egypt or from more complex societies in North Africa. Again, this would show a sedentary lifestyle—domestication of animals and grinding stones usually accompany incipient domestication.

It is likely that through incipient herding early residents of the Sahara experimented with controlling animal populations. Conceivably *Bos primigenius* was loosely herded first in the wild where they would have were kept close to water and in close association with humans. Animals were systematically culled for features desired by the emerging herdsmen. This close association between humans and feral cattle eventually led to the appearance of genetically altered domesticated cattle (*Bos taurus*). Rock paintings from as far south as Northern Nigeria show humpless cattle, but they are difficult to date.

This period of Saharan luxuriance did not last, however. Between 7,000 and 5,00 BP the climate of the Sahara once again began to deteriorate. These pastoralist/foragers again had to adapt by moving. Sources of fish became depleted, many wild animal herds moved south to better-watered regions and plant foods became less reliable.

As Africans moved into the Sahel, their cattle encountered the tsetse fly[1] (the carrier of trypanosomiasis or bovine sleeping sickness). This pest has long since moved into the rain forest, but then it existed in the more luxuriant Sahel. Given the difficulty of finding water, pasturage and having to cope with trypanosomiasis in their herds, these Africans began to innovate—to come up with adaptive responses to their changing circumstances. It was around 3,000 BP that we find the first evidence of attempts to control plants—steps that led in due course to the development of farming.

---

1. The tsetse has been steadily moving south with the drying out of the Sahara.

These early Africans were keen ecologists and sociologists. They understood the importance of maintaining their ecological balance with nature and their social relations with each other. Their closeness to nature would have been paralleled by the need to develop close bonds between members of roving bands and members of smaller constituent households. It is probable that small bands of family groups wandered in seasonal migration cycles. Some had cattle, some were simply foragers. Others may have experimented with growing crops and settling down. The extended period of hunting and gathering in West Africa would have developed a strong communal ethos among the people, an institutionalization of the realized fact that to survive in the African bush, they must work together. This legacy remains strong throughout West African history.

The Move to Farming and Herding

About four thousand years ago we begin to see evidence of domestication of animals and plants—the great Neolithic Revolution was underway in West Africa. At this time in the archaeological record bones of domesticated sheep, cattle and goats become commonplace.[2] Also, seeds and agricultural implements are increasingly found in association with skeletal remains. It is unknown how domestication began in West Africa. It might have diffused across a more luxuriant Sahara, but it could have occurred as independent invention as well. It is possible that both happened. Of the continent's important domestic animals, goats and sheep are not known to have occurred wild in Africa but humpless cattle were common in the luxuriant period of the Sahara. Archaeological sites from Libya, Algeria, Niger and the Sudan contain bones of wild cattle. These are dated mostly from the seventh or sixth millennia BP. Apparently early Africans domesticated these beasts, which seems to indicate both local invention and diffusion from elsewhere.

It seems that in West Africa, at least, animals were brought under human control first, then plant life. It also appears that this happened first in the lush Saharan zone, but that may be a reflection of the fact that the deposits there have been better preserved by the desert climate.

Again it looks as if a broad swath of cultures dominated by animal husbandry spread across the Sahel in the fifth millennium BP, from the modern state of Sudan to Mauritania. They left behind small stone and earthen tumuli (graves or interments), which attest to a degree of social ranking probably based on the possession of livestock and widely traded polished stone objects.

Generally, the Neolithic Revolution is believed to have occurred about eight to twelve thousand years ago in the Near East, but in West Africa evidence giving us a firm time sequence is fragmented. In Nigeria, near Bornu, there is archaeological evidence of domesticated goats and cattle as far back as 8,000 BP. In Gao, we have strong evidence of pastoralism from 4,000 BP. Domesticated African rice (*oryza glaberrima*) is found from sites dating as late as 1,000 BP, but much earlier sites at Kintampo in Ghana show the use of cowpeas, hackberry and oil palm from about 4,000 BP (See below). Unfortunately, archaeologists sometimes find it difficult to know whether

---

2. Archeologists are able to distinguish the bones of animals raised by humans from those in the wild.

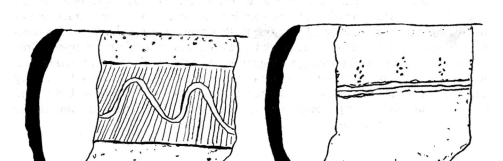

Figure 8.4   Kintampo Potsherd (left) & a Contemporary One from Sisalaland, Ghana.

such finds are evidence of farming or merely the result of gathering activities by foragers.

The transition to farming was slow. It is likely that people used their extensive
knowledge of nature to begin to "nudge" natural processes by weeding around grain-
bearing plants they wished to harvest at a later date, or by clearing brush from around
desirable fruit trees to prevent the fruits from being burned by bush fires. Such incipient horticulture may have eventually led people to settle down and farm if they found
good spots with sufficient quantities of land, water and wood, the three essentials for
sedentism in West Africa. Once people had these essentials and the ability to store
grains, village life became possible and the modern pattern of habitation began—the
village-field complex, or what some have called the tribal way of life.

Using a combination of herding, foraging and rainfed horticulture, these early inhabitants of the Savannah zone adopted a way of life that still exists in many parts of
the region today. Many wandered the area in search of food, but eventually most people settled in villages and towns. A small percentage remained pastoralists, herding
cattle, goats and sheep. The only major pastoral group in West Africa today is the Fulani. There are no extant groups of foragers left in West Africa, as there are in other
parts of the continent.

The tools used in early farming were made of wood, bone and stone. Wood decays
easily in the tropics, but we find remains of stone hoe blades, long hoe-like stones
wielded with two hands and numerous arrowheads and lance heads indicating that
hunting and gathering continued alongside of farming practices, as they do today.

In the well-known **Kintampo Culture** sites in Ghana, stone tools are found in conjunction with clay works—pottery (See Figure 8.4), figurines and the famous and
mysterious terracotta "cigars" (See Figure 8.5). These may have been rasps, but their
exact function is still unknown. Additionally, there were arm rings, beads and arrowheads. At Ntereso, just west of Tamale in Northern Ghana, a site has been found with
Saharan Neolithic arrowheads, bone fishhooks and harpoons.

Dating agriculture's appearance in West Africa is fraught with problems. Indirect
evidence of farming comes from the discovery of heavily used grinding stones in sixth
millennia BP sites in the Sudanese Nile Valley. By 3,200 BP in Mauritania we find firm

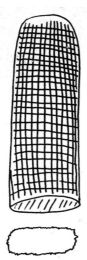

Figure 8.5 Kintampo "Cigar" Rasp.

evidence of the use of bulrush millet being intensively cultivated. Tools alone can be misleading, however. Some, such as the flat pick and grinding stone were also suitable for use by foragers to dig wild tubers and to grind undomesticated grain seeds.

In Dhar Tichitt in modern day Mauritania (See Map 8.2) environmental and social factors apparently crystallized these mobile societies into more sedentary and complex polities (this also happened at Kerma, to the east, which was likely the first Nubian State). At Dhar Tichitt and again at Dhar Oualata nearby the first substantial masonry structures in Africa outside the Nile Valley were built. There, a pristine chiefdom ruled from about 4,000 to about 2,800 BP. This early state might have survived longer, but its environmental base steadily deteriorated over time. Today, Mauritania claims little or no arable land and increasingly cities fill as modern-day pastoralists leave the skimpy pastures of rural areas for a new life as urbanites. The environmental deterioration that began to affect the Tichitt-Oualata society three or four thousand years ago continues today.

No one knows for sure how the **Tichitt-Oualata State** evolved or if it ingressed from elsewhere. Researchers have revealed a four-tier settlement hierarchy, with the largest regional centers exceeding 220 acres. From the granaries and stonewalled kraals we know that this was a mixed economy. Domestic millet, cattle, sheep and goats are evidenced in the ruins. The same inorganic wealth as found elsewhere across the Sahelian zone is found in Dhar Tichitt: carnelian and amazonite beads, polished bracelets of siltstone and a plethora of small stone axes. The wide distribution of these prestige goods indicates travel, contact and trade across the breadth of the African Savannah. Such contact and trade were important. These were the same processes that would lead to later state building in the region.

Early Trade and Its Impact

Control of trade gave West African élites the surplus to build state apparatuses. Success at gold mining and the advent of metallurgy (See more below) gave rise to even

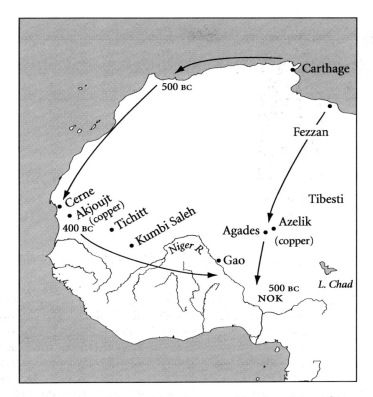

Map 8.2   Possible Routes of the Spread of Ironworking into West Africa.

further **long-distance trade** and to the rise of complex societies. In addition to ivory and other exotica from the forests, precious metals, ore, jewelry and fine metalwork were to figure prominently in international trade. About 1,400 years ago, the ancient **Empire of Ghana** began to emerge. Initially, the economic base of the state was regional trade. When, after 1,250 BP, Islamic peoples began to pour into the Niger Bend area and develop the trans-Saharan trade, Ghanaian monarchs befriended them, taxed them and regulated their trading activities. However, archaeological evidence of trade predates the coming of the Arabs. Long-distance trade was added to an already existing regional commerce.

Because of free access by the general public (non-élites) to ample land in West Africa, ambitious men could not easily control a population of farmers to extract surplus value from them. Trade was easier to control. For the first time this dominance led to the rise of a privileged class in West Africa. By imposing tolls and tariffs on trade, especially long-distance trade, élites were able to grow wealthy while commoners pursued low-yield agriculture relatively independently. In West Africa, it was the control of merchants and the flow of merchandise, not farmers, that led to political power.

Those societies that were fortuitously situated between the north and south grew as a result. For example, the excavations at **Jenné-Jeno** (which means "old Jenné) show a trading town that began about 2,250 BP and lasted over 1,600 years (See Map 8.3). It reached its height about 1,200 years ago and began to decline around 350 years later to be abandoned by 600 BP. In evidence at this tell-site are signs of trade with adjoining lands. The vast inland area in which Jenné-Jeno is situated, the **Middle Niger Zone,**

Map 8.3   Some Important West African Archaeological Sites.

was filled with swamps and standing water. This made it remarkably fertile, but it lacked stone (for querns and smithing tools), copper or iron ore. The area did produce ample crops and had an abundance of fish. Jenné-Jeno's strategic location along a navigable river in a productive floodplain lacking raw materials stimulated exchange. Trade networks developed that allowed the people of Jenné-Jeno to market their produce and exchange it for ore and stone from up to 30 miles away.

Long-distance trade across the Sahara followed the domestication of the camel, which first occurred in Arabia. Camel caravans diffused to the Sahara in the third millennium BP. The arrival of the camel had an important effect on the economy by providing a means of regular long-distance transport across the desert. With the development of long-distance trade, villages such as Jenné-Jeno developed into important entrepôts or emporia in the Middle Niger River floodplain. The development of the trans-Saharan trading enterprise allowed Jenné-Jeno to expand its trading network about 1,600 BP to include copper, Mediterranean trade items and salt from the Sahara. Between 1,400 and 1,200 BP head-bearers began to bring gold and forest products from the south. Well situated in the crucible of trade, Jenné-Jeno and other cities such as Gao and Timbuktu were able to thrive on such commerce.

The dig at Jenné-Jeno has revealed an interesting function for ceramic jars: they were used as burial urns. The deceased were placed in the bottom of jars and were then interred in crowded urban cemeteries. Along with ceramic burial urns, many well-manufactured fired pots decorated with twine impressions were unearthed. Commodities such as copper, iron and sandstone are in evidence in Jenné-Jeno by more than two centuries before the arrival of Arab traders. Furthermore, by 1,600 BP local craft specialization and a regional hierarchy were centered at Jenné-Jeno, indicating a fully urban status for the site.

The archaeological excavations at Jenné-Jeno have also revealed the first evidence in West Africa of the use of domesticated African rice (*Oryza glaberrima*). It dates to *circa* 1,900 BP. It was found in association with wild foods, fish, reedbuck (African antelope) and domestic cattle. Elsewhere the seeds of *Digitaria* or fonio also indicate its early use in West Africa.

Over two millennia ago West Africans began to smelt iron, as archaeologists can tell from the iron slag and manufacturing technology preserved at Jenné-Jeno. Since there are thousands of unexcavated sites along the middle course of the Niger River, iron working may have been widespread in the region. From Jenné-Jeno, furnace debris and stone crucibles suggest that, even in the absence of local ore, smelting ore was well developed in the Niger Bend region. As larger and more complex polities grew, this and other artisanal activities were likely brought under the control of urban royalty.

The use of fire by **blacksmiths** and potters must have facilitated the creation of non-utilitarian objects as well. Artwork found in Jenné-Jeno includes sculptures of humans and animals in several styles. Human figurines predominate—several showing signs of disease, others covered with snakes. The majority depicts persons in iconic poses or in various lifelike positions. The skill evidenced in this art indicates the existence of a professional rank of artists.

Jenné-Jeno shows evidence of material development. The urban area started out as a collection of simple circular huts made of brush, grass and mud. Later residents lived in square mud brick dwellings, forming a prosperous farming and fishing community increasingly involved in trade. There is also evidence of warfare. Once Jenné-Jeno and other communities began to prosper, fortifications were necessary. By the time of the rise of the kingdom of Ghana (See Map 8.4), about 1,400 BP, Jenné-Jeno was an urban center covering about 82 acres and boasting of a mud wall 1.2 miles in circumference and about 12 feet thick. Also as part of the trans-Saharan trade, swords entered into the arsenal of weapons of the region's powerful men. Warfare and defense had clearly become part of West African life.

The Advent of Metallurgy: Tools and Art

The origins of metallurgy in Africa are still unclear, but generally speaking, the continent lacked a Bronze Age as found in Europe (See Map 8.2). However, there is some disputed evidence from Mauritania and Niger for the use of copper tools during the middle centuries of the third millennium BP. During the third quarter of the third millennium BP, evidence of iron making is found just to the south in the Jos Plateau area of modern-day Nigeria. In all likelihood, the ancient inhabitants of this area were

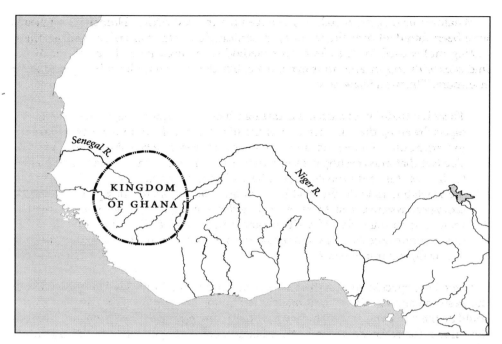

Map 8.4   The Kingdom of Ghana.

the first manufacturers of iron in West Africa. Archaeologists have found furnaces in Nigeria at Taruga that have been dated to around 5,000 BP. Iron tools were used alongside stone tools in this part of West Africa, showing a gradual transition from the Stone Age to the Iron Age. This advance in tool production gave West Africans more control over their environment.

There are four theories about the origins of metallurgy in West Africa. First, some scholars think it diffused into the area from the Carthaginian colonies of western Mediterranean Africa. Secondly, it is said to have originated in Egypt. Thirdly, some scholars think it came in along the trade routes linking West Africa with the eastern part of the continent, where discoveries have revealed an ancient tradition of metalworking in old Zimbabwe and presumably elsewhere along the east coast of Africa. The fourth hypothesis is that metallurgy was independently invented in West Africa. Dating problems have prevented the emergence of any firm conclusion.

What is acknowledged is that once the techniques of smelting and working in iron were known, it spread like wildfire. From the sixth century onwards, Sudanic kings of Ghana, Mali and Songhai supported smithies. By the time of the coming of the Portuguese in the 15th century almost every village had at least one resident blacksmith and usually more. Also, to the south, iron axes and adzes improved the efficiency of forest clearance and agriculture.

The theory of diffusion from Carthage gets some support by the discovery of rock engravings from the Western Sahara showing wheeled horse-drawn vehicles and a map that seems to parallel the Atlantic seaboard in a north-south route connecting the Maghrib with the Middle Niger Bend (See Figure 1.1). It is also known that the Carthaginians engaged in a brisk trade with the Berbers of the western desert, who also traded with the Negroid peoples of the south.

Whatever its origins, metallurgy changed life in West Africa. Numerous slagheaps have been found all over the territory in conjunction with charcoal, as well as brass-casting molds used for the *cire perdue* method (lost-wax). As early as 10,000 BP we find sites with copper and brass ornaments, but they may have been brought in from elsewhere. Thurston Shaw says:

> There is a tradition of such brass-casting which runs right through West Africa, especially along the northern part of the high forest belt, from the Ivory Coast to Cameroun—Baoule, Ashanti, Dahomey, Ife, Benin, Igbo-Ukwu, Bamenda. The fact that brass casting runs especially through this particular belt of country in West Africa is probably not to be explained so much in direct relation to the vegetation as to the fact that it was in this zone, at the meeting point of two ecological systems, that there were provided the requisite conditions for the growth of centralisation of political power and commercial wealth or both. In this situation objects of brass were luxury goods, only produced for royal courts or socially important people.

Some have speculated that the lost-wax method began in the gold-bearing areas of the western parts of this belt and that the technique was applied to brass work later. It could be the other way round, however, with the *cire perdue* method being used first in the eastern forest for brass work, then being applied to gold work, especially in the Akan region.

This technique likely spread into West Africa from the Near East, as suggested by the fact that archaeologists have discovered copies in brass of Byzantine lamps of the fifth and seventh century style in Ghana. The oldest known use of the lost-wax method comes from the excavations at **Igbo-Ukwu** in Nigeria and are dated at about 1,200 BP (See below).

The earliest brass and terracotta art works in Africa have been recovered from the ancient Nok Culture, named after the village by that name in Nigeria. The Nok culture was an ancient Iron Age civilization that existed on the Benue Plateau of Nigeria between about 2,900–1,800 BP.[3] Many Stone Age and Iron Age artifacts have been recovered from Nok sites including small arrowheads, flat stone hoes, facial plugs for lips, ears and noses, small ground axes, hammer stones, pottery furnace parts, tuyères (furnace stokers) and smelting slags.

Although the culture died out around 1,800 BP, this artwork continued to influence other West African cultures and art traditions. The Nok people left behind a legacy of fine art and metal working that speaks of a high civilization. Their primary metallurgy was in iron obtained locally, but the fine art in bronze was done with imported metals.

Artifacts of similar features were found near Nok over an area that stretched about 300 miles east to west and 200 miles north to south. A 2,000-year-old terracotta head was discovered at Jemaa in Kaduna State of Northern Nigeria in 1944. To date, over a hundred ceramic heads, life-size and smaller, one miniature full figurine, body fragments and several sculptures of animals have been uncovered. Most of these finds are now housed in the museum at Jos in North-Central Nigeria.

The one excavated site at Taruga indicates that makers of most sculptures were agriculturists and ironworkers, as evidenced by furnace slag and tuyères. Ceramics from

---

3. Some scholars would put this last date at ca. 2,500 BP.

Yelwa, some 200 miles northwest of Nok date from the same era and may be distantly related. The technology was conceivably more widespread than indicated by isolated discoveries.

The Rise of the Forest Kingdoms

The West African rain forest stretches in a narrow swath along the coast between Sierra Leone in the west and Cameroon to the east. To the north this jungle is bordered by transitional forest and orchard bush of the Savannah. This terrain is more open than the rain forest. It extends southward to the coast between Ghana and Nigeria, separating the forest into eastern and western segments (See Map 1.2).

We are beginning to understand the early history of the rain forest better. About a thousand years ago, during Jenné-Jeno's floruit (period of excellence) to the north, a forest kingdom was developing in the southern forests of present-day Nigeria. The archaeological excavations at Igbo-Ukwu, a site that was accidentally discovered in 1939 have revealed beautiful artifacts that demonstrate that this little known kingdom was rich and artistically expressive. Because the Nri Igbo once occupied these sites, scholars associate the ancient culture with that of this Igbo branch.

This was an important discovery. Together with other early city-based kingdoms, Igbo-Ukwu demonstrates the first evidence of urbanization in the forest area. Here, the ancestors of the modern Igbo (See Map 8.1) had, as early as the 9th century, settlements showing elaborate storehouses and élite burial chambers filled with an impressive array of prestige items, elephant tusks and ornate pottery. One site revealed an elaborate burial of an official or wealthy titled Nri man wearing copper alloy regalia, superb brass castings and over 150,000 imported glass beads, indicating that this forest kingdom was in contact with trans-Saharan traders or their Sudanic intermediaries. The digging at this site indicates a well-organized system of trade controlled by a wealthy élite, which supported craft specialization and the production of artwork.

Another forest nation of this area, which emerged about 1,100 years ago, is Ife. It is one of the larger centers and probably the oldest town of the Yoruba people. Considered by the Yoruba to be a holy city and the legendary birthplace of humankind, it is held to have been founded by a son of the god *Oduduwa*. Probably named for *Ifa*, the god of divination, Ife was the capital of a well-established kingdom by the early 11th century. By the late 12th or early 13th century, its artisans were producing the naturalistic terracotta heads and bronze pieces made by the lost-wax process for which the Ife kingdom is now well known.

That this was a wealthy kingdom is evidenced by the capital city's defensive wall, many elaborate shrines, and the city's most unique feature—elaborate paved streets made of pottery remnants or potsherds. The city was rich in sculpture and other forms of art in brass and terracotta. In the sculptures, élite personages are depicted richly adorned in ceremonial regalia, which correspond to the sumptuous nature of their royal burials. Since Ife shrines contain artwork depicting highborn leaders, it is highly likely that this points to the historical development of a form of divine kingship in the region.

To support this large élite and artisanal population, Ife's subsistence base appears to have been founded on farming and small livestock. Royals and their priests must have extracted some service and tithe/taxes from the people and controlled the comings and goings of traders.

Ife had great political and cultural influence over the Edo kingdom of Benin to the southeast, until about five hundred years ago when the city began to decline. The region's power center shifted to Benin and Old Oyo (Katunga), which became the seats of more important kingdoms. Nevertheless, Ile-Ife remained the chief religious center for the Yoruba. Ritual power was its defense against the mightier Yoruba kingdoms nearby. For example, in return for the *ida oranyan* ("sword of state," symbolizing spiritual authority) given to an *Alafin* ("king") of Oyo upon his coronation, the *Alafin* had to promise not to attack Ife. When the Oyo monarch, *Alafin* Awole, tried to raid Ife territory for slaves in 1793, this desecrating attack brought strong internal resistance and a series of wars that destroyed the **Oyo Empire**.

Benin City was another massive Yoruba settlement in the rain forest (See Map 8.1). It began about a thousand years ago and reached its greatest extent in the 15th century when European seafarers reached the city. It was the center of a divine kingship ruled by the *Oba*, the principle political and religious leader of the nation. The size and grandeur of this civilization is remarkable, especially given its location in the dense forest, which makes expansion and construction especially arduous. Yet these early Yoruba flourished. Archaeological research has revealed a vast complex of walls and ditches spanning some 9,900 miles in total length and covering some 2,500 square miles! Apparently, Benin employed its extensive army to expand its frontiers and to subjugate provincial populations, demanding tribute from them. The earthworks surrounding the city indicate conflict with neighbors and the likelihood that royals were maintaining such battlements to defend their wealth.

Benin, as with the other forest kingdoms, was trading with the north. This is clear from the large amount of European trade beads and other foreign objects found in the sites, but long-distance trade is also apparent from the extensive use of brass and bronze in casting their exquisite artwork. The ore for these alloys is not found in the rain forest. Royals traded to acquire substantial accumulations of this luxury material.

Farther to the west, people of the Savannah zone and those of the forest have long been in association. At the edge of the rain forest at **Begho**, in the Akan region of modern-day Ghana, more evidence has been uncovered of settled urban civilization, founded by Iron-Age agriculturists in the third millennium BP. These early West Africans occupied the site continuously until about nine hundred years ago.

Begho emerged as a trading center near the forest margin, a point that may have allowed the residents of the town to capture the flow of trade goods moving back and forth between the northern Savannah and the rain forest and coast to the south—all distinct environmental zones with different goods to offer. That Begho was in contact with the north is clear from the dual nature of the town. In addition to the main part of the settlement, there was a special quarter set aside for Muslims, presumably merchants from the north. This **dual urban residential pattern** is a common archetype in West African cities of the past, remnants of which, called *zongos* or strangers' quarters, are still seen in cities of the region today. Kwame Arhin says of the *zongo*:

> It was an enclave, the land equivalent of the port of trade, making possible an agglomeration of various races [sic] who were then permitted to evolve a political order consistent with the conduct of a 'free' market. That freedom required that marketers and the market be conceptually and, indeed, substantially removed from the detailed supervision of the neighbouring power-holders. The

Photo 8.2   A Modern-Day Urban Market.

establishment of a market settlement of the kind could be made possible by a
dominant power such as Asante...[at Kintampo, for example. Brackets are
mine].

Most of these early states, as well as the Sudanic states of Tekrur, Ghana, Mali and
Songhai were involved in long-distance trade and had the *zongo*.

Recent thinking suggests that the origins of the small, competitive city-states of the
eastern Niger delta south of Igboland, with which Europeans were to develop flour-
ishing commerce from the 17th century may well be associated with earlier, purely indigenous trading activities of which very little is at present known. The Igbo-Ukwu
State, Begho, Ife and others are thought to have come to prominence through the
control of local products such as ivory, gold, peppers and kola nuts. These early markets were probably local and regional, given the lack of non-human portage in the
rain forest (Photo 8.2 shows a modern market). By coordinated and centralized effort,
goods were traded northwards linking up with long-distance trade networks. Human
porters carried the goods northwards to the boundary of the tsetse/trypanosomiasis

zone at the forest's edge, where they were loaded onto donkeys and horses for the continuing journey, sometimes to be further reloaded onto camels at the edge of the desert.

Farther west still, in the rain forests of Sierra Leone, Liberia and Guinea, evidence of rising political complexity and urban life is more limited. Iron smelting was introduced into this region by about 1,300 BP but there are no indications of large urban groupings or political stratification. Perhaps ancient civilizations existed there and are merely lost in the dense jungle, as has so often been the case in Latin America and even in the eastern rain forests of West Africa. For the western zone, this hypothesis is supported by the fact that when the Portuguese arrived at the beginning of the 15th century they reported many large settlements in the region. Additionally, archaeologists have identified numerous fortified towns and hilltop locations ideal for holding off invaders. Such defensive structures are usually associated with conflict between wealthy societies and those seeking wealth. Furthermore, oral histories and documentary evidence indicate that these settlements often remained autonomous or loosely united under a prominent war chief. It is likely that great civilizations existed in the region, as they did elsewhere in West Africa, and that they await the archeologist's trowel.

The Stone Circles of the Upper Windward Coast[4]

The Upper Windward Coast is a territory that today lies within the states of Senegal, The Gambia and Guinea-Bissau along the Atlantic Coast and Mali in the interior. It is also known as Sénégambia. Unlike the Lower Windward Coast, the Sénégambia region has no high mountain ranges to separate coast from interior. The vicinity is generally low-lying, well-watered by creeks and navigable rivers that facilitated trade and migration. Behind the mangrove marshlands of the lower river banks lay rich alluvial lands that people used for rice and some millet cultivation.

In ancient times, inhabitants of this region fashioned large stone circles, which can still be seen today. Like Stonehenge, these grouped stone monuments have puzzled the few travelers who have examined them. The Sénégambia has one of the largest concentrations of such stone circles in the world, though similar formations are found in Britain, mainland Europe and the Near East.

It is fair to assume that the presence of such a large number of monuments of this type in a relatively localized setting implies the presence of a well established, dynamic culture that existed before the oral traditions of local people. Who were these people? No one is quite sure.

There are hundreds of circles containing many curious features and in particular the unique Lyre stones. The most common shape is round like a pillar with a flat top. Others are square, some taper upwards. There are small stones with a cup-shaped hollow on top. Others have a ball cut in the round top of the stone. Also, there is a type of reclining stone shaped like a pillow.

The circles are composed of standing stones between ten and twenty four in any particular formation. One of the striking features is that almost all the stones making up a particular circle are of the same height and size.

---

4. See http://home3.inet.tele.dk/mcamara/stones.html

The largest stones, which are at N'jai Kunda weigh about ten tons each, according to Momodou Camera, an expert in such stone rings. It is likely that they were brought down a steep hillside by rollers or on hammocks. This transport must have presented formidable difficulties and have required a considerable labor force and political organization.

As a result of laboratory tests at the University of Dakar, the date of the sample from a site at Wassu was found to be from 750 A.D. plus or minus 110 years. The stones were cut out of laterite that occurs in large outcrops in this region. It is a feature of this stone that it hardens upon exposure to the air, and that prior to such exposure it is relatively easy to quarry.

Many hypotheses have been given about the Sénégambia Stone Circles. Some local Islamic clerics have said that the shape of the stone indicates different burial or ritual practices. Also, oral tradition has it that the circles were built around mounds of kings and chiefs, in the same way that royal persons were buried in the ancient empire of Ghana. Even though no one knows exactly why they were built, through the ages their presence has invited locals to use them for ritual purposes. Area residents leave offerings on the monoliths, or sacrifice animals to their gods there. Some people place small stones and vegetables like tomatoes on the monoliths. Local lore says that some of these stones shine brightly at night.

That local people use them for ritual purposes supports the theory that their original purpose was religious, but that is still conjecture. Baumann and Westermann suggest that before the penetration of Islam, a "paleonigritic divinity," perhaps the Earth, was worshipped at these sites. It seems conceivable that during the past these stone circles were ritual sites for celebration of the Cult of the Earth, which is certainly a common cultural trait running across all of West Africa.

The Development of Cities, Trade and Stratification

About 3,000 BP there appear to have been two main groups of people inhabiting the Savannah zone: The Kanuric-speakers of the area between Lake Chad and Northern Nigeria, and the Mande-speakers of the zone around the upper Niger River. It is probable that peoples from these two groups spread out through the region, and were supplemented by newcomers from both the north and south. As population densities were low, new lands were open for settlement and travelers must have been able to move slowly, living off their herds and the land as they went, since in those days the wild animal populations of the region were much higher.

West Africa developed urban centers and state structures of governance just as occurred in Eurasia, but with a twist. In Europe and Asia the heavy soils welcomed the invention of the plow pulled by animals. In West Africa, bovines were restricted to the Savannah zone by the presence of the tsetse fly in the forest regions, and everywhere the soils were (and remain) delicate, thin and prone to erosion if turned rudely. Human labor and the hand-held hoe were more adaptive to the African environment and this led to extensive methods of farming, not intensive ones as in Eurasia. Whereas Eurasian monarchs could control rich land and therefore people, in Africa it was the control of people to work the less productive land that mattered (as well as control of trade). The Asiatic Mode of Production, as the Eurasian system of state-controlled agriculture was called, never fully developed in West Africa, though certainly in many areas men had structural or socially legitimated control over the labor of women, children and young male subordinates.

City-states did arise, but through control by royals of three forces: imagined realities or religion; the means of destruction or the military; and trade or commerce. As they did in Eurasia, state supported priests developed cosmologies and rites to bolster the power of rulers in the eyes of the people. These ideational forms became part of the structure of domination. Ritual centers, such as Ile-Ife in Yorubaland, became focal points of ethnic unity and housed a priesthood charged with the role of creating and maintaining social cohesion through a shared theology.

Monarchs also supported production of weapons and armies to defend the state, to extend its hegemony and to retain dominance over its outlying districts. This development coincided with the growth of the division of labor, with the state funding the work of blacksmiths, weapons-makers, priests and other artisans and artists. This social differentiation eventually developed into social stratification. Highborn was distinguished from lowly, urbanites were seen as different from rural peoples and all were held together in a complex symbolic system supporting the collection of taxes and tribute, as well as the legitimacy of highborns controlling the profits from trade.

Trade was important in the area because the different zones from the Mediterranean to the shores of the Guinea Coast—seashore, forest, Savannah and the Sahara—provided a naturally interactive zone for commerce. Salt and fish were traded up from the coast, forest products such as kola were added to the trade routes by forest dwellers, as were exotica such as ostrich feathers and ivory. Agricultural products were combined at every stop. Gold was a precious trade commodity coming from West Africa's rich fields. From the Mediterranean came manufactured goods, spices from Asia, cloth, sumptuaries and other articles of trade not available in West Africa. By befriending long-distance traders and providing them with safe passage, albeit for a fee, West African kings were able to control exchange and extract a profit from it. This was the main stimulus to state formation in those areas that fortuitously sat on major trade routes that crisscrossed the region.

But this was not a static culture. Urbanization brought change to the relatively egalitarian lifestyle of villagers. The people in the towns began to have a life that differed from those who remained in the villages and the herders and hunters who roamed the countryside. Eventually townsfolk became more cosmopolitan, influenced by the comings and goings of traders from faraway lands. Ultimately, many adopted Islam and some became literate. Urban-based rulers arose to lead the emerging states and to attempt to establish rule over surrounding peoples.

The villagers remained more isolated from the cosmopolitan ideas of the cities, and tended to keep to their ancestral and animistic religions and follow their time-honored customs. Their lives centered on the family, the village and the clan. For the most part, they were acephalous peoples, meaning "without a head." They lacked extra-familial chiefs. Political functions tended to be embedded in their kinship order, the rules of proper behavior being enforced by family headmen and purportedly by the ancestors through such auspices as shamans and diviners.

In spite of a prevalent egalitarian ethos in rural community life, chiefs and kings were able to emerge to form **centralized polities**, a rise facilitated by the widespread and pre-state concept of the **big man**. Bigness, ranking or high rank was possible, even respected, in those men who were able to amass more wives, granaries, cattle, children and general control over people. Societies formed around these concepts are called ranked societies. The rise of chiefs and kings, once they had their hands on sufficient sources of wealth, was merely a playing out of the concept of bigness. Thus, as the material conditions changed with the coming of new technologies and trade contacts with other civilizations, big men took advantage of the opportunities these changes engendered, elevating themselves into formal offices, surrounded by *viziers* (advisors), sycophants, courtiers and followers. When such a ranked political economy allows élites privileged access to wealth, anthropologists call this a stratified society.

Architecture also changed with urbanization. While early on bush houses were constructed as circular dwellings, urban architecture shows a rectangular structure. This pattern, which seems to have come from the north, was facilitated by the development of sun-dried rectangular bricks, a style that ultimately filtered out into the villages. Some early urban architecture also shows clay roof pipes to aid in the draining of the flat-roofed houses. In addition to single story modest houses, in these early cities, we also encounter the first **"storyed" houses**—edifices with multiple levels, indicating differences in rank.

The urban-rural dichotomy was beginning to be a significant difference between peoples in the region. Natural increase in population due to an improved tool kit was likely augmented by people arriving from the north, which was drying out, and perhaps further migrations of forest peoples in search of new lands. These peoples brought with them new ideas e.g., the knowledge of iron working may have come with those who left metallurgical centers such as Nok.

Technological innovations fed population growth, urban life and political centralization. Society flourished and the division of labor broadened to include blacksmiths, carvers, potters and basket makers, farmers, hunters and herders. Male work and female work were still sharply differentiated, as it still is so today in West Africa, but this burgeoning civilization was beginning to lay the foundation for a more complex society.

Summary

The prehistory of West Africa, compared to other parts of the continent and Eurasia, shows that West Africans went through stages of development that were influenced by the ecological relations between populations and their environment.

From the Stone Age through the Iron Age early West Africans developed an indigenous civilization, both in villages and cities, that was communalistic. That is, it was designed to help the group survive and emphasized the responsibilities of the individual to community life.

That is not to say that West Africans did not develop stratified societies where élites were able to lead privileged lives, but the effects of the community-based ethos held exploitation to a minimum in the years before the region's people were subject to contact with Europeans. Clearly, like people everywhere, Africans developed ranked and stratified institutions that could be manipulated by some to be exploitative of society at large and the less-privileged more specifically. But they did this within the context of a generalized system based on communal help, altruism and a deep respect for traditions stressing the importance of the community and ascribed status.

In adapting to the various zones of the regions, West Africans became hunters and gatherers then domesticated animals and plants to evolve into agricultural societies and some based on herding, or pastoralism. With the advent of metallurgy, technology flourished, as did forms of art that still astonish scholars for their beauty and craftsmanship. Such kingdoms tended to develop where geography and economic opportunity allowed for their fluorescence.

We have seen that geography and environment have been important in the development of political and economic life in West Africa, as was the emergence of metalworking and long-distance trade, facilitated by the outgrowth of mining technology and the introduction of the camel to traverse a desiccated Sahara. Increasingly mastery of the environment through improved tool kits allowed the development of more complex forms of sociopolitical organization and urbanization.

≋≋ CRITICAL THINKING QUESTIONS ≋≋

1. Why is little known of the prehistory of West Africa compared to some other parts of the world?
2. How did geography affect trade?
3. Describe the similarities and differences between the Savannah states and those of the rain forest.
4. What in the physical record uncovered by archaeologists in West Africa gives an indication of an evolution from acephaly to stratified societies?
5. Why did many ancient urban areas have a dual residential pattern and what is the relation between that and long-distance trade?

≋≋ KEY CONCEPTS ≋≋

Acheullean tools
Asante
Bantu migration
Begho
Benin City
Big man
Blacksmiths
Centralized polities
Composite tools
Dual urban residential pattern
Ghana, Empire of
Ife
Igbo-Ukwu

Iwo Eleru
Jenné-Jeno
Kintampo Culture
Long-distance trade
Microliths
Middle Niger Zone
Oyo Empire
Sedentism
Storyed houses
Sudanic Zone
Tichitt-Oualata State
Zongo or pl. *zongos*

≋≋ SOURCES & SUGGESTED READINGS ≋≋

Afolayan, Funso. 2000. Kingdoms of West Africa: Benin, Oyo, and Asante. In: Falola, Tony (ed.). *Africa: African history before 1885* (Volume 1). Durham, NC: Carolina Academic Press, 161–189.

Arhin, Kwame. 1979. *West African traders in Ghana in the nineteenth and twentieth centuries.* London: Longmans.

Baumann, H. & D. Westerman. 1957. *Les peuples et les civilisations de L'Afrique.* Translated from the German by L. Homburger. Paris: Payot.

Boyd, Robert & Joan Silk. 2000. *How Humans Evolved.* (Second Edition). Berkeley: University of California Press.

Cole, Herbert M. 1996. West African sculpture. In: Brian M. Fagan, (ed.). *The Oxford Companion to Archaeology.* Oxford: Oxford University Press, 751–753.

Connah, Graham. 1996. Benin. In: Brian M. Fagan, (ed.). *The Oxford Companion to Archaeology.* Oxford: Oxford University Press, 751.

de Barros, Philip. 2000. Learning from negative evidence. *Backdirt* fall/winter, www.sscnet.ucla.edu/ioa/pubs/backdirt/Fallwinter00/oti.html

DeCorse, Christopher R. 1996. West African forest kingdoms. In: Brian M. Fagan, (ed.). *The Oxford Companion to Archaeology.* Oxford: Oxford University Press, 747–748.

Fagan, Brian M. 2001. *People of the earth* (Tenth Edition). Upper Saddle River, NJ: Prentice-Hall.

Fage, J. D. 1995. *A history of Africa.* London: Routledge. Chapter. 13

Ifemesia, C. C. 1969. The peoples of West Africa around A. D. 1000. In: Ajayi, J. F. Ade and Ian Espie (eds.). *A thousand years of West African history.* Ibadan: Ibadan University Press, 39–54.

Johanson, Donald & Blake Edgar. 1996. *From Lucy to Language.* New York: Simon & Schuster.

Kasule, Samuel. 1998. *The history atlas of Africa.* New York: Macmillan.

McDonald, Kevin. 1996. The rise of kingdoms and states in Africa. In: Brian M. Fagan, (ed.). *The Oxford Companion to Archaeology.* Oxford: Oxford University Press, 15–16.

McIntosh, Susan K. & Roderick J. McIntosh. 1996. West African Savanna kingdoms. In: Brian M. Fagan, (ed.). *The Oxford Companion to Archaeology.* Oxford: Oxford University Press. 748–750.

Mahoney, F. and H. O. Idowu. 1969. The peoples of Sénégambia. In: Ajayi, J. F. Ade and Ian Espie (eds.). *A thousand years of West African history.* Ibadan: Ibadan University Press, 132–148.

Phillipson, David W. 1996. Prehistory of Africa. In: Brian M. Fagan, (ed.). *The Oxford Companion to Archaeology.* Oxford: Oxford University Press, 12–14.

Price, T. D. & G. M. Feinman. 2001. *Images of the past* (Third Edition). Mountain View, CA: Mayfield.

Robinson, Rowan. 1996. *The great book of hemp.* Rochester, VT: Park Street Press.

Shaw, Thurstan. 1971. The prehistory of Africa. In: Ajayi, J. F. A. & M. Crowder (eds.). *History of West Africa.* New York: Columbia University Press, 33–77.

9 WEST AFRICA'S GREAT STATES & ISLAM

> The Niger Bend Region of the Savannah zone in West Africa saw the rise of three major kingdoms—Ghana, Mali and Songhai. Each of these exhibited the following processes: urbanization, state-building and conquest of neighbors. There were many other states like Tekrur and Kanem-Bornu that manifested the same processes. They did so by capturing a monopoly on trade goods. Traveling merchants from the north brought more than goods—they also brought Islam to West Africa. Islam started as a religion of traders, passed to royalty and eventually to the common people.
>
> Islam is a proselytizing religion. Its precepts indicate that a Muslim has the obligation to spread the gospel of Islam and to resist all forms of blasphemy. Consequently, over time, Islam grew to be a powerful force in the region. Since the religion also has a political component, based on *Shari'a* Law, and further holds that a Holy War is at times justified to bring nonbelievers into the fold, Islam was spread aggressively by *jihadist* reformers across the Savannah zone, and by later reform movements right up to the European conquest.
>
> Europeans brought Christianity into the area and today these two foreign ideologies stand in opposition to each other. Not only was there a clash between Islam and traditional African religions, but today Muslims and Christians are locked in an ideological battle, which unfortunately has spilled into the streets, resulting in violence and death.

Introduction: Some Thoughts on West African History

All societies evolve as they adapt to new circumstances but they do so at different rates and not always in a linear "forward" movement. Societies rise and fall. Some extend over thousands of years, such as China; others are new and quickly powerful such as the United States.

When Europeans came into contact with West Africans they assumed that while Westerners had been changing over the ages, Africans had been mired in savagery. Europeans looked at the simple technology in West Africa and assumed that the ideas and social structures of the people must be equally backward.

But when Anglo Saxon tribes were just settling England and Viking tribes were moving into Scotland and Holland, the great African cities of Timbuktu, Jenné and Gao were forming the urban basis for the rise of the Kingdom of Ghana (See Table 9.1 &

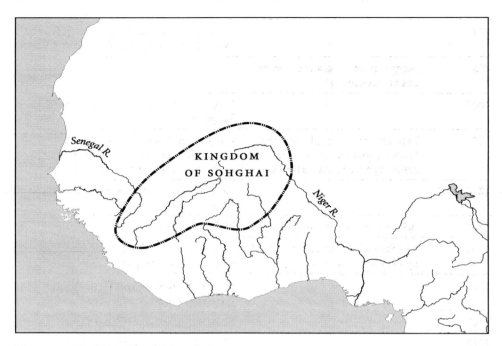

Map 9.1   The Kingdom of Songhai.

Map 8.4). In some ways, this kingdom and the later empires of Mali (See Map 2.1) and
Songhai (See Map 9.1) were more sophisticated than those in Europe. As we saw in the
last chapter, the magnificent artwork found in association with the ancient Iron Age
Nok people dates from around five hundred years before Christ. West Africans have
had a long history of material growth, artistic development and cultural elaboration.

Below I will delve into the growth and nature of the great civilizations of the Niger
Bend—Ghana (See Map 8.4), Mali (See Map 2.1) and Songhai (See Map 9.1), as well as
the diffusion of Islam across the vast expanse of the Sahara Desert and its impact on the
history of West Africa (See Map 1.9). We will see that before Charlemagne mounted his
throne, there were mighty kings and traders in the region the Portuguese called *Guiné*.

Table 9.1 Dates in West African and Western History		
AD DATES	**THE WEST**	**AFRICA**
1–200	Tribal life in much of Europe	Nok culture on the decline in West Africa after about 1100 years of high civilization; beginning of the Tekrur kingdom on the Senegal River.
600	Anglo Saxon tribes settle England & Viking tribes settle Scotland & Holland; eventually conquest and war leads to state formation.	Rise of cities such as Timbuktu, Jenné and Gao & the beginning of the formation of the Kingdom of Ghana
700	English epic Beowulf composed	Rise of the state of Ife in West Africa
768	Charlemagne becomes king over the feudal Frankish estates	

774		Al-Fazari makes the first written reference to Al-Ghana, "the land of Gold"
895	Magyar tribes attack the Eastern Franks (Germany)	
1000		Zimbabwe created by people of the Shona Kingdom
1200	Manorial enclosures by wealthy landowners that caused great suffering among the peasants	Kingdom of Ghana breaks apart into competing mini-states, which again begin to coalesce into the state of Mali
1240–1255		Sundiata Keita becomes the first king of Mali
1268	British common law formalized.	Mali Empire expands
1300	The Spanish monarchy is formed by the Mendoça family	Peak of Mali Empire, a federation with semi-autonomous provinces
1300		Bronze art flourishes in West Africa; metalworking widespread.
1300		Kingdom of Kongo; Kanem-Bornu
1312		*Mansa* Musa becomes king of Mali
1324		*Mansa* Musa takes pilgrimage & founds the University of Sankore at Timbuktu.
1381	A peasant revolt is violently quashed by Richard II	
1400		Roswi Empire at Great Zimbabwe, Mali begins to decline
1415	Portugal invades Cueta in the Maghrib	
1418		Kingdom of Benin
1434	Portugal rounds Cape Bojador	
1441	Portuguese return with first slaves	
1444	Portuguese discover Cape Verde Islands & establish The Lagos Company which profits in slaves and gold	
1450		Kingdom of Songhai
1458	Portugal promises not to enslave coastal peoples if coastal kings will sell slaves to them	
1460	Portuguese go to Sierra Leone, establishment of the Brotherhood of the Virgin of the Rosary, a specifically black community in Lisbon.	

1462	Portuguese land in the Gold Coast.	
1475	Portugal and Spain at war	
1479	Treaty of Alcaçovas ends Spanish-Portuguese war. Portuguese consolidate "monopoly" in Guinea.	
1480	Spanish Inquisition kills thousands of Jews.	
1481	*Casa dos Escravos* (House of Slaves) is established in Lisbon to regulate the slave trade	
1482	Portuguese establish *Castelo São Jorge da Mina* in present day Ghana	
1492	Columbus discovers America	The death of Sunni Ali Ber, King of Songhai, *Askia* Muhammad begins his reign and enlarges the Empire of Songhai
1498	Portuguese reach India	Kingdom of Bornu
1515	First shipment of sugar leaves the Americas for Europe.	
1518	First slaves shipped directly from West Africa to the West Indies.	
1528		End of *Askia* Muhammad's reign; Songhai goes into decline
1536		1st slave revolt against Portuguese planters on São Tomé
1558		Angry British traders burn the town of Samma when natives refuse to trade
1578	Portuguese King killed in battle in North Africa and Portugal begins to decline. Spain annexes Portugal 2 years later.	
1590		Moroccan King Al Mansur moves against Songhai
1608	Dutch buy *Castelo São Jorge da Mina* from the Portuguese.	
1618		Morocco withdraws from conflict with Songhai; Asante King Osei Tutu wages war against the Denkyira.
1625	Plantation system gets underway in the New World.	Rise of Dahomey Kingdom
1637	Dutch East India Company takes over *Castelo São Jorge da Mina*.	
1660		Denkyira Kingdom trades with Europeans & begins expansion along the Mina Coast.

1688		Beginning of Muslim *Jihads; Bondo* Kingdom.
1693		Gā attack Danish Christianborg Castle in Accra holding inhabitants for ransom.
1700		Rise of Asante Kingdom
1702		Denkyira controlled much of the coast as far as Whydah.
1725		Futa Jalon Kingdom
1737	Monrovian Brethren first major organization of missionaries to arrive in West Africa.	
1750		Kingdom of Massina; Osei Tutu dies.
1756		European fort at Accra destroyed by the Gā
1772	**Mansfield Decision** in Britain frees all slaves who set foot on the Island.	
1776		Futa Toro Kingdom
1788	British form African Association to explore Africa.	
1789	Olaudah Equiano writes his autobiography.	
1792	British establish Freetown, Sierra Leone.	
1794	African Association sends Mungo Park to explore the Niger River.	*Al-Hajj* Umar born to become jihadist.
1802	*Société de l Afrique intérieure et de Découvertes* formed in France.	
1804	Christian Missionary Society formed in Sierra Leone.	Sokoto Empire of Usman dan Fodio.
1805	Mungo Park returns to West Africa.	
1806		Asante wage two-year war against Fante.
1807	Britain outlaws British involvement in slaving; British make a treaty with the Asante.	
1811	Wesleyan Missionaries arrive.	
1821	Hugh Clapperton and Richard Lander leave Tripoli to explore the source of the Niger.	Ex-slave King Jaja born in Igboland.
1822	American Colonization Society establishes Liberia.	
1824	Gov. MacCarthy invades Asante and is killed, as his troops are defeated.	Asante defeat the British invaders.

1827	Clapperton dies at Sokoto; organized missionary activity begins along the Mina Coast; George Maclean (the headof the Merchants Association) is given political control in *Mina*.	
1830	The Lander brothers explore the Niger River.	
1831	African Association folded into the Geographical Society.	Maclean signs peace treaty for Britain with the Asante.
1833	Britain outlaws slavery in its outlying territories & orders all slaves freed.	
1837		British install King Pepple of Bonny as a puppet ruler.
1839		First Christian missionary visits Kumase.
1843	Parliament takes back control in West Africa from the Merchants Association.	
1846	Britain repeals its Corn Laws, opening its market to foreign im-ports and setting up the wide-spread trade of its manufactured goods for raw materials and agricultural products.	*Saro* missionaries from Sierra Leone to Yorubaland.
1847	Alexander Bryson notices the benefits of quinine; residents of Liberia apply for international recognition as a nation.	
1849	Dr. Henry Barth leaves Tripoli to explore the interior of West Africa.	
1852		*Al-hajj* Umar receives vision to lead a *jihad* against the Bambara.
1854	Dr. William Balfour Baikie is given credit for applying quinine successfully.	King Pepple is deported for insubordina-tion.
1861	End of British Anti-Slavery Naval Squadron patrols along the Guinea Coast; Lagos made a colony.	Tukolor Empire takes over Ségou. British reinstate King Pepple.
1863	Emancipation Proclamation in USA; Richard Burton to Dahomey.	
1864	Henry Townsend, pioneer mis-sioary in West Africa, opposes the appointment of Samuel Adjai Crowther, a West African, as bishop in the church.	*Al-Hajj* Umar is killed in battle.

1867		British defeated by Asante leading to two years of war.
1868	Catholic White Fathers organize in West Africa.	
1869		King Jaja founded the coastal trading state of Opobo.
1870	France defeated by Prussia; France extends limited citizenship rights to 4 communes in West Africa establishing the policy of assimilation.	Samori Touré begins his empire quest
1874	British invade Asante; Gold Coast becomes a British colony.	Kofi Kakari (King Coffee), the *Asantehene*, abdicates to be replaced by his brother, Mensa Bonsu.
1879	French move into Umar's Kingdom	
1882	British buy *Castelo São Jorge da Mina* from the Dutch who exit after 274 continuous years of occupation.	
1883	French Protectorate established over Porto Novo.	
1884–85	Berlin Conference partitions Africa.	
1886	British Royal Niger Company chartered. Boundaries of southern Sierra Leone established.	
1888	The Frenchman, Louis Binger visits Ouagadougou in the Mossi Kingdom.	Asante queen mother installs her 15-year old son, Agyemon Prempeh, on the Golden Stool.
1889	Anglo-French Agreement signed.	
1892	Sierra Leonean *Krios* ask for a protectorate. French occupy Dahomey; King Behanzin goes to Algeria, where he died in 1906	*Oba* of Benin signs a treaty with the British.
1893	British found Niger Coast Protectorate.	Benin sacked by British.
1894	Frederick Lugard heads Goldie's company military force in Nigeria; French take Timbuktu.	Agyemon Prempeh formally installed.*
1895	Joseph Chamberlain made Colonial Secretary; Frontier Force, made up of West African soldiers, formed by the British; Yorubaland conquered.	Traders in State of Brass revolt against tax imposed by Royal Niger Company.
1896	Sierra Leone Protectorate established.	British imperialists Scott and Maxwell humiliate *Asantehene* and demand the Golden Stool.

1897	Frederick Lugard given command of Colonial Office military forces in Nigeria; Benin conquered.	
1898	Ashanti Goldfields Corporation makes first dig.	Samori Touré captured by French.
1899	Captain Armitage searches for the Golden Stool; Royal Niger Company charter revoked.	
1900	Nigeria declared a British Protectorate of Southern Nigeria with Frederick Lugard as High Commissioner.	First Pan-African Congress held in London.
1901		British destroy the Arochukwu shrine in Igboland.
1906	In December British troops march into Tumu in Sisalaland Northern Ghana.	
1910	Ivory Coast under French rule.	
1912	British complete rail service between the coast and Kano.	
1914	World War I begins.	Widespread famine in West Africa.
1918	World War I ends; Portuguese begin an Apartheid-like system in Guinea-Bissau.	Beginning of two-year pandemic of Spanish Influenza.
1919	Sir Gordon Guggisburg becomes governor of Gold Coast.	
1923	Sekondi-Kumase railway completed.	
1924		King Prempeh returns from exile.
1927	Sir Gordon Guggisburg retires as governor of Gold Coast.	
1929	British pass the Colonial Development Act and vow to put more money into developing West Africa: this was never fulfilled.	
1931		Prempeh dies leading to a four-year interregnum.
1933	French in Mauritania still suffering regular rebel attacks.	
1935		Nana Osei Agyeman Prempeh II enstooled.
1939	One hundred and ninety-one British colonial administrators rule four million people in Gold Coast; World War II begins.	Cocoa Holdup, farmers withhold crops in protest of exploitation by **Marketing Boards**.

1944	Bretton Woods Conference leads to the development of IFIs and SAPS.	Pan African Federation formed in London.
1945	World War II ends.	Sixth Pan-African Congress in Manchester attended by many future African leaders e.g., Kwame Nkrumah.
1946	West Africans from French West Africa given second-class citizenship.	Félix Houphouët-Boigny forms the *Rassemblement Démocratique Africain* or RDA
1948		Gold Coasters attack European trading companies and shops.
1951		J. B. Danquah, a prominent Gold Coast lawyer, drafted a new constitution super vised closely by the British. However, Kwame Nkrumah's CPP party wins elections while he is in jail.
1956		Houphouët-Boigny and the RDA were able to secure the passage of the *loi-cadre*, the "outline law." Under this statute, each colony in French West Africa was to have a separate locally elected assembly with real powers to control policy and finance. Amílcar Cabral returns to Portuguese *Guiné*.
1957		Ghana first Sub-Saharan African country to receive independence from colonial overlord.
1958	Last rebel stronghold put down in Mauritania; Charles DeGaulle returned to power in the Fifth Republic; advocates a French West African *Communité* similar to the British Commonwealth.	Guinea becomes independent under Sékou Touré who is the only African leader in French West Africa to refuse membership in the *Communité*.
1959		First PAIGC demonstration—the Seaman's Strike in Bissau fails; Amílcar Cabral goes into a contemplative seclusion.
1960		Nigeria becomes independent.
1961		Sierra Leone becomes independent; Amílcar Cabral emerges from seclusion committed to violent revolution.
1962		First violence by PAIGC.
1963		String of military takeovers begin. PAIGC attacks Portuguese barracks; OAU formed.
1965		The Gambia becomes independent.
1966		Kwame Nkrumah deposed.
1967		Gnassingbe Eyadéma comes to power in Togo in a military coup.

1972		PAIGC granted observer status at UN.
1973	OPEC price hike.	Guinea-Bissau declares independence from Portugal forming the People's National Assembly (ANP)
1974	Red Carnation revolution in Lisbon.	Official independence of Guinea-Bissau.
1975		Tractor farming has failed in Northern Ghana.
1977	US Congress passes the Foreign Corrupt Practices Act (FCPA)	
1978		Sisala women begin to farm.
1981	World Bank critical of African governments and blames leadership for lack of development; IFIs begin to link access to foreign aid and loans to economic liberalization.	Léopold Senghor steps down in Senegal.
1984		Guinea-Bissau constitution further centralizes power in the presidency.
1990		Benin Conference drafted a new democratic constitution. Dictator Mathieu Kérékou was defeated in the subsequent presidential election.
1991		One-party rule ended in Guinea-Bissau.
1992	World Bank supports SAPs.	
1994		ANC takes power in South Africa
1999		Otumfuo Osei Tutu II enstooled.
2001	World Bank claims not to support SAPs and embraces a Poverty Reduction Development Program (PRDP).	

* This was delayed because the Asante had not paid reparations to Britain due to their impoverishment.

The Great Sudanic States — Ghana

The **Soninke** people (also called Sarakole, Seraculeh, or Serahuli) were a millet-growing people located in present-day Senegal near Bakel on the Senegal River. The Bakel Soninke, by first controlling local trade then the trans-Saharan trade flowing through the area, became the founders of the great Soninke Empire of Ghana (1400 to 600 BP). With a Soninke base at Awkar serving as a nucleus, Ghana had expanded to embrace a large territory in the western Sudan (See Map 8.4) by the 10th century.

Map 9.2   The Western & Central Sudan, ca. 8th to 17th Centuries.

In the course of imperial expansion Sudanic Kingdoms found it increasingly important to bring trade under control by dominating the prosperous trading centers of the region—Walata (Oualâta, Mauritania), Gao, Jenné and Timbuktu (See Map 9.2). When they gained control of these towns, Sudanic monarchs could fully reap the advantages of the trans-Saharan trade.

Strategically positioned, Ghana was able to control two main Trans-Saharan trade routes that stretched north to Morocco and Libya and west to the Bornu region near Lake Chad, where it connected with the Nile Valley trade. The potentates levied caravanners and provided them protection and established special enclaves in which they could rest and regroup in safety. Undoubtedly, Ghanaian kings also benefited more directly from trading, having privileged access to goods coming from the south and from the north.

In the late eighth century AD an Arab geographer living in Baghdad mentioned Ghana, "land of gold." In 872, another Arab, Al-Ya'qubi placed the urban states of Ghana and Gao among the greatest of the Sub-Saharan kingdoms. Both arose on the southern margin of the Sahara, the Sahel, in the second half of the third millennium BP when the climate was significantly wetter than at present. Gao converted to Islam in the 11th century, the religion providing a common language and legal system for trade, although the Ghanaian kings held out several decades longer. Gao was later absorbed into Ghana.

The first sector in the kingdom was a walled city called Al Ghana. The word Ghana means "the capital", "the king" or "the whole state". Al Ghana was the residence of the King and his courtiers, family members and followers. When the king gave audience to his people, to listen to their complaints and adjudicate disputes, he sat in a pavilion around which stood ten pages holding shields and gold-mounted swords. Only the king and crown prince could wear sewn clothes. Commoners had to prostrate themselves before the monarch, placing dust on their heads as a sign of submission. On the king's right hand were the sons of princes (often his grandsons), splendidly clad, with gold plaited into their hair. The governor of the city sat on the ground in front of the king and all around him were his advisers. The gate of the chamber was guarded by dogs that never left the king's seat. The royal pedigreed guard dogs wore collars of gold and silver, as did the king's horses. The beginning of a royal audience was announced by the beating of a drum that they called *deba*, made of a long piece of hollowed wood. The people gathered when they heard this drum.

Through control of gold, Ghana became very powerful and wealthy. Gold was both a commodity and a symbol of sovereignty. Control of gold brought Ghanaians to the attention of the powerful states to the north and the Berbers who controlled the trans-Saharan trade in the western Sudan. These Berber notables were centered at the important commercial hub of Awdaghast to the north of Ghana. In an effort to keep trade flowing, the Ghanaian king established diplomatic relations with the Awdaghast rulers, but in 922 it was decided to take Awdaghast by force. Thereafter, Ghana was in control of the southern section of the western trans-Saharan trade route.

The second sector of the kingdom was six miles from the King's palace—the Muslim quarter, which had twelve mosques and centers of Islamic learning. There was also a mosque in Al Ghana where Muslims could pray when they came on diplomatic missions to the king. Even though the early Ghanaian kings remained pagans, Muslims acted as interpreters, advisors, scribes and treasurers in court. At this time the king also employed non-Islamic "priest-magicians" and together with them practiced their traditional religion. These court propagandists were charged with the task of spinning legends to support state rule. At this time, Islam was an adjunct to a pagan court and the creative imaginings of court-based canonists called *griots*. It was their business to act as the kingdom's collective memory and hand down from generation to generation the history of the people and, of course, the glories of the king, his family and the state apparatus. Lacking writing, kings found such methods essential and *griots* or praise-singers can still be found in almost every traditional court in modern-day West Africa.

In spite of the nonbeliever status of early Ghanaian kings, their use of Muslims in government and the overall spread of Islam tended to undermine the power of the monarchy as the number of Muslim *viziers* grew to dominate the court. By the time Ghana reached its apex of power, most of the king's ministers and treasurers had become Muslim. Later kings simply adopted Islam as a state religion.

The control of trade allowed the Sudanic kings of Ghana and later empires to develop the means of destruction that also brought in revenue through the capture of booty and slaves and the payment of tribute from outlying areas. Even though the kings had mighty armies and controlled the great north-south trade routes, the Ghanaian monarchy had a fundamental source of weakness—the kingdom was not a tightly knit entity. Its military expansion would often outstrip the administrative ability of the monarchy to govern outlying regions. The monarchy was constantly trying to deal with internal strife, provincial troubles and raids from foreign enemies. There were issues of ethnicity as well. Imperial expansion was often accomplished by force under the direction of a supreme leader of the imperium of a particular ethnic group. This dominant group would use fear and persuasion to establish control over the countryside. Not only were provincials subalterns, but they often spoke a different language from their oppressors, had different customs and resented imperial governance by a foreign element.

Another weakness of Ghana and most other Sudanic Kingdoms was the lack of a fixed law of succession to high office. Upon the death of the king, the court would be wracked with palace intrigues and succession disputes. This sometimes led to open warfare. An interregnum often meant a time of weakness and chaos.

Any sign of weakness caused the state two problems. First, it was a signal to peripheral dependencies to revolt. Second, it often led external enemies to mount an attack. A constant threat to the empire was found in the militaristic nomadic hoards beyond its northern boundaries—the Tuaregs to the northeast and the Berbers to the northwest. They carried on a continuous succession of hit-and-run raids against the empires of the Sudan, and when they perceived problems within the monarchy, they mounted more sustained sieges.

Ghana entered a period of decline about the 11th century AD. In 1076 a Berber army from Morocco led by religious reformers called **Almoravids** attacked Ghana, and plunged it into a period of disorganization. These religious zealots were descendants of the same desert Berbers who had been attacked at Awdaghast by the Ghanaians. They had two main motives—to erase Ghana's persistent heresy and to regain control of the north-south trade route. In 1055 they recaptured Awdaghast; in 1061 they attacked northward to take Sijilmasa.

With the core of Ghana under attack from the Berbers and internal strife in the capital, subalterns in the provinces now took advantage of the chaos to rebel. Anabara, a tributary west of Al-Ghana, was the first to revolt. The Susu of Kaniaga to the south followed suit. With pressure from outside and from within, Ghana collapsed and many Soninke were massacred; others were forced to adopt Islam.

The Almoravid Berbers established their capital at Marrakech in 1062. Their leader, Yusuf, assumed the title of *amir al-muslimin* (Commander of the Faithful), but still paid homage to the 'Abbasid *caliph* (*amir al-mu'minin*, Commander of the Faithful) in Baghdad. Yusuf entered Spain, eventually taking much of that land. When Almoravid's interest turned toward Europe, the surviving Soninke remnant regained their independence and began a comeback. Their freedom, however, was short-lived. In 1203, one of the provincial lords in Susuland, Sumaguru Kante, succeeded in conquering the remaining fragment of the once-powerful Ghana. This was the final blow to the great state.

Ghana was followed by a series of smaller states. The merchant families who had made Ghana an economic powerhouse moved their base first to Walata in 1224 and later set up shop in the town of Jenné in 1250.

The Great Sudanic States—Mali

The Mandinka **Empire of Mali** rose to power at a time when Islam was filtering into the area. **Sundiata Keita** was the first king of Mali, ruling the empire from about 1240 until his death in AD 1255. During his reign he established the territorial base of the empire and laid the foundations for its future prosperity and political solidarity. Sundiata was a Mandingo from the small kingdom of Kangaba, near the present Mali-Guinea border. Little is known about his early life. Oral traditions indicate that he was one of twelve royal brothers who were heirs to the throne of Kangaba. When Sumanguru, potentate of the neighbouring state of Kaniaga, overran Kangaba at the beginning of the 13th century, he murdered all of Sundiata's brothers.

According to tradition, Sundiata was spared because he was a sickly boy who already appeared to be near death. A true aggrandizer, he grew strong, organized a private army and consolidated his position among his own people before challenging the power of Sumanguru and the neighbouring Susu people. He defeated Sumanguru decisively in the Battle of Kirina about 1235 and succeeded in forcing the former tributary states of Kaniaga to recognize his suzerainty. In 1240 Sundiata razed Kumbi, the former capital of Soninke Ghana, and by this act succeeded in obliterating the last symbol of Ghana's past imperial glory.

After 1240 Sundiata apparently led no further conquests but he consolidated his hold on the states already under his control. Nonetheless, his generals continued to extend Mali's boundaries to include areas as far north as the southern fringes of the Sahara (including the important trade center of Walata) and east to the Niger River Bend. They also moved south to the goldfields of Wangara (the exact location is still unknown to scholars) and west to the Senegal River.

Soon after 1240 Sundiata moved the seat of his empire from Jeriba to Niani (also called Mali), near the confluence of the Niger and Sankarani rivers. Merchants were attracted to Mali because of its domination of the gold fields and the relative tranquility forged under Sundiata's rule. During his rule King Sundiata developed Mali in three ways: he promoted agriculture over war; he took control of trans-Saharan trade; and he mined gold.

Niani soon became a key commercial center in the Sudan. Although the new king was nominally a Muslim and therefore acceptable to the predominantly Muslim merchant class, he managed to retain his support among the non-Muslim population. He did so by fulfilling many of the traditional religious functions expected of rulers in the West African societies whose political leaders were viewed as religious figures with quasi-divine powers.

Little is known about the actual administration of Mali during Sundiata's time. The imperial system he established, however, survived the years of internecine conflicts after his death. King Uli (1255–70) who moved the kingdom toward Islam followed Sundiata. After Uli's rule there was a period of chaos and degeneracy. In 1274 King Khalifa took office only to be deposed the next year by one of the court officials, Abu Bakr (1275–85), who brought a decade of stability. Upon his death a court official and a freed slave named Sakura took the reigns. He consolidated the power of the monarchy and expanded the state, calling himself Mansa or Emperor.

Perhaps the most well known ruler of Mali was the pious **Mansa Musa** (AD 1307–1332) who made a famous *hajj* (pilgrimage) to Mecca in AD 1324. He was a great favorite of the *'ulama*, the learned men of Islam who wrote its history. Under *Mansa* Musa's control, militarism once again became a driving force for imperial expansion and the state doubled in size through conquest. He also fostered Islamization of the empire.

To Europeans, *Mansa* Musa is best known for his gifts of gold while on his journey to Mecca. It was this pilgrimage that awakened the world to the stupendous wealth of Mali, spreading rumors of a kingdom of gold throughout the Mediterranean world. Slightly over a century later, in 1415, **Prince Henry the Navigator** of Portugal (See

Chapter 10) became so intrigued by such tales that he began his quest to navigate along the coast of *Guiné*. He wanted not only to find a route to Asia's spices, but also to find the famous king who was surrounded by gold.

Cairo and Mecca received *Mansa* Musa whose glittering procession, in the superlatives employed by Arab chroniclers, almost "put Africa's sun to shame." He went from Niani to Walata and on to Tuat (now in Algeria). Then he made his way to Cairo accompanied by a caravan of 60,000 men, including a personal retinue of 12,000 slaves, all clad in brocade and Persian silk. The emperor himself rode on horseback and was directly preceded by 500 slaves, each carrying a gold-adorned staff. In addition, *Mansa* Musa had a baggage train of 90 camels, each carrying 300 pounds of gold. His prodigious generosity and piety, as well as the fine clothes and exemplary comportment of his followers did not fail to create a most favorable impression. The historian al-'Umari, who visited Cairo twelve years after the emperor's visit, found the inhabitants of this city, with a population estimated at one million, still singing the praises of *Mansa* Musa. So lavish was the emperor in his spending that he flooded the Cairo market with gold, causing such a decline in its value that even at the time of al-'Umari's visit, the market had still not fully recovered.

Rulers of West African states had made pilgrimages to Mecca before *Mansa* Musa. Nonetheless, the effect of his flamboyant journey was to advertise Black Africa and to stimulate a desire among the Muslim kingdoms of North Africa, and among many of European nations as well, to reach the source of this incredible wealth.

Almost all of the great kingdoms in West African history used their military might (control over the means of destruction) to expand their boundaries and subjugate neighboring peoples, seeking obedience, tribute and corvée labor. But there is an inherent problem with such provinces. First, they are often far away. Second, they almost always contain local élites who remain a threat to the central ruler. Third, the king wants them to thrive enough to be able to supply laborers and revenue to the central coffers, but not so much that they become a threat. *Mansa* Musa handled these issues by appointing a provincial resident called the *Fari-ba* or *Faren*. This provincial governor was to keep an eye on local élites and ensure that tribute was collected and transported back to Mali.

Songhai and Mali were rivals, but at the time of Musa's pilgrimage, Mali was on the ascendancy. Even in his absence, the king's men were expanding the Empire, in spite of the fact that Mali was already one of the largest in the world at that time. One of his generals, Sagmandia, captured the Songhai capital of Gao in 1325. Even before that, it was said that it would take a year to travel from one end of the Mali Empire to the other (perhaps an exaggeration). The 14th century traveler **Ibn Battuta** noted that it took about four months to travel from Mali's northern borders to Niani in the south.

Musa wanted to Islamize his empire as well as expand it. He was so overjoyed by the acquisition of Gao that he decided to delay his return to Niani and to visit Gao instead to receive the personal submission of the Songhai king and take the king's two sons as hostages. He also commissioned the construction of mosques at both Gao and Timbuktu, another Songhai city almost rivaling Gao in importance.

The Gao mosque, built of burnt bricks, a novelty in West Africa at the time, was still being admired as late as the 17th century. Under *Mansa* Musa, Timbuktu grew to be a very important commercial city having caravan connections with Egypt and all other important trade centers in North Africa. *Mansa* Musa also fostered literacy. On his return from Mecca, he brought back scholars who were mainly interested in history, Quranic theology and law. They were to make the mosque of Sankore in Timbuktu a teaching center, which laid the foundations of the **University of Sankore**. Professors and students from all over the Muslim world were attracted to this center of higher education.

With the close of the 14th century, Mali's epoch had passed. About 1400 the Mossi, Mali's neighbors to the south, attacked the empire and sacked Timbuktu. Mali recaptured it, but soon after lost it and Walata to Berber and Tuareg raiders from the north. Mali declined, while Songhai was on the rise. The final blow came when **Sunni Ali Ber** (d. 1492) the monarch of the **Empire of Songhai** captured Jenné and Timbuktu in 1468.

The Great Sudanic States—Songhai

Songhai began to emerge from Mali's vassal state of Gao, which became the capital of the *Dia* kings. Although the Songhai people are said to have established themselves in the city about AD 800, they did not regard it as their capital until the beginning of the 11th century during the reign of *Dia* (king) Kossoi, a Songhai convert to Islam. In about 1335 the Dia lineage of rulers gave way to Sulaiman-Mar, who won back Gao's independence. In 1468, Sunni Ali Ber repulsed a Mossi attack on Timbuktu and defeated the Dogon and Fulani in the hills of Bandiagara, clearing the empire of any immediate danger. He later evicted the Tuareg from Timbuktu, took Jenné in 1473 and had subjugated the lakes region of the middle Niger to the west of Timbuktu by 1476.

An uncompromising warrior-king, Ali Ber extended the Songhai empire by controlling the Niger River with a navy of war vessels. The civil policy of Ali Ber, who was a non-Muslim, was to conciliate the interests of his pagan pastoralist subjects with those of the Muslim city-dwellers, on whose wealth and scholarship the Songhai Empire depended.

Conflicts between urban and rural interests and between Muslims and pagans seeped into the court. Ali Ber's son Sunni Baru (reigned 1493), who sided with the pagan pastoralists, was deposed by *Askia* **Muhammad**[1] (reigned 1493–1528). He welded the central region of the western Sudan into a single Islamic empire, relying on military prowess, evidenced by his title of *Askia*, which means General.

By this time the conflict between Muslims and animists, added to lust for wealth and power, had led to an era of widespread warfare. *Askia* Muhammad, too, fought the Mossi of Yatenga, tackled **Kanem-Bornu** (sometimes Borgnu or Bornu), in what is now northwestern Nigeria (See Map 9.3) and mounted campaigns against the Diara, against the kingdom of Futa Toro in Senegal, and against the Hausa (See Map 9.4) states of modern-day Northern Nigeria.

During his reign, *Askia* **Muhammad** made Songhai the largest empire in the history of West Africa. He restored the tradition of Islamic learning to the University of Sankore, made Islam the court religion and made his own spectacular *hajj* to Mecca where he was appointed as *Caliph* of western Sudan by the ruler of all Islam. Throughout the uncertainty of successive reigns (*Askia* Musa, 1528–31, *Askia* Muhammad II, 1531–37, *Askia* Ismail, 1537–39, *Askia* Issihak I, 1539–49), urbanized Muslims continued to act as middlemen in the profitable gold trade with the states of Akan in central Guinea.

---

1. Also known as Muhammad Touré or *Askia* the Great.

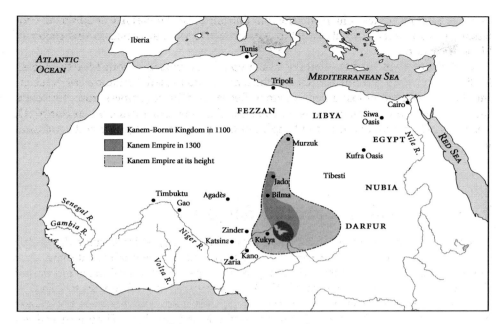

Map 9.3 The Expansion of the Kanem-Bornu Empire.

The temporary peace and prosperity of *Askia* Dawud's reign (1549–82) was followed by a raid initiated by Sultan Ahmad al-Mansur of Morocco on the salt deposits of **Tagharza**. Tensions with the north continued to worsen under Muhammad Bani

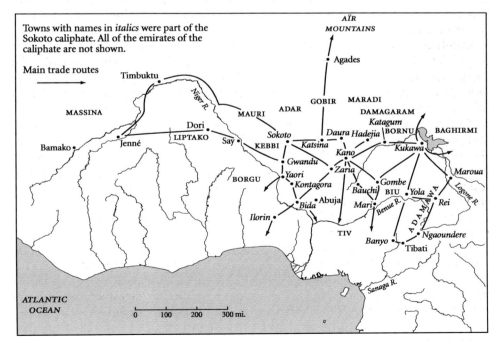

Map 9.4 The Sokoto Caliphate & Bornu.

(1586–88). The conflict ended disastrously for Songhai under Issihak II (1588–91) when Moroccan forces, using firearms, advanced into the Songhai Empire to rout Issihak's troops at Tondibi, Timbuktu and Gao. Retaliatory guerrilla action of the pastoral Songhai failed to restore the state, the economic and administrative centers of which remained in Moroccan hands. The Moroccans never conquered the empire, but warfare resulted in the political disintegration of Songhai, and an assimilation of the Moroccans into the populace.

A Moorish Pashalic was established over the old Songhai area. Many Moorish soldiers settled in this part of the Sudan, married local girls, and their descendants now constitute a distinct social group known as the **arma**. Morocco turned its attention to conflicts with Europe and left the region in the hands of Moorish Pashas assisted by financial and military officials. The southeastern part of the Dendi region was left to the old inhabitants of the Empire of Songhai.

The Early Hausa States

The Hausa inhabit the northwestern and north central parts of modern-day Nigeria, and spread farther west and north in the Republic of Niger up to the edges of the Sahara desert. In fact, as with Swahili in East Africa, the Hausa language is a major trade language all over West Africa and Hausa traders live in various places throughout the region.

Those ancients who came to be known as Hausa were of mixed ethnic backgrounds, fed by migrations and invasions through the ages. The autochthons are usually referred to as the Habe. Though some early kings likely emerged among the Habe, there were also invasions by powerful élites into Hausaland e.g., the Kwarau dynasty. The early Hausa kings were pagans, practicing animism and using magic, medicines and divination in court to support their rule. During this era the ruling *Sarki* was not allowed to die of natural causes, an indication of the common practice in Africa of associating the health of the king with that of the kingdom's prosperity. Within the Hausa royal household was an officer called the *Kariagiwa* who was responsible for killing the sovereign if he became old or incapacitated. A new king was selected through divinatory auspices thought to bring messages from the ancestors.

Box 9.1   Hausa Kingly Offices

Kano — *Sarakunan Baba* — chief of the indigo dyers
Rano — *Sarakunan Baba* — chief of the indigo dyers
Zaria — *Sarkin Bayi* — chief of slave and procurer of labor
Daura — *Sarakunan Kasuwa* — chief of the market and
    Sarkin Noma — chief of agriculture
Katsina — *Sarakunan Kasuwa* — chief of the market
Biram — reputedly the original seat of government was left out
Gobir — *Sarkin* Yaki — war leader and commander-in-chief

Early Hausaland was dotted with various city-states that were sometimes hostile to each other and at other times entering into alliances. The built environment of the region with its many fortified city walls indicates the extent to which raiding and warfare dominated the lives of early inhabitants. Hausaland was raided from as far away as Timbuktu. *Askia* the Great (Muhammad Touré) of Songhai undertook a military campaign against Hausaland in the second decade of the 16th century. He defeated and sacked the Hausa States of Gobir, Katsina, Kano, Zamfara and Zaria between 1512–13. Had the Hausa States not been so hostile to each other, they could have united and easily repulsed the invaders. Although there was no long-term occupation of Hausaland, some states were forced to pay tribute to Songhai and were required to accept resident Songhai agents in their midst. The aggression of Songhai may have helped to forge a greater sense of Hausa identity among the previously hostile states. Also, contact with the learned men of Timbuktu helped stimulate literacy and the dissemination of Islamic culture in Hausaland.

The *birni* or stockaded town was different from the *gari*, the village or hamlet. The *birni* wall enclosed an urban community of residents and provided protection for surrounding villagers should an attack occur. This was usually an encircled self-sufficient community that was unified by trade, industry and had within its walls a large area with wells and farmland. Thus, the inhabitants could withstand a long siege.

The incessant bloodshed in the region explains why Hausa kings could impose taxes on farmers. They were partly dependent on the towns and their governments for protection in such an unstable world. The first king in Hausa history to go on record as having imposed such tax was *Sarki* Naguji, who exacted one-eighth of the crop from all farmers.

Some Hausa were able to exact revenge on Songhai. *Sarki* Kotal Kanta, the monarch of Kebbi, defeated the Songhai army at a place called Tara. Kotal Kanta had been in the service of *Askia* Muhammad in his campaign against Aïr, but subsequently quarreled over the booty. In 1516 he rebelled and successfully founded the independent state of Kebbi. After routing the Songhai, he turned his attention against various states in the region.

He brought Aïr to heel and forced the Asbenawa to pay him tribute. Then he overran Gobir, Katsina, Kano, Daura and Zaria, even penetrating Nupe to the south, establishing a sub-kingdom called Gabi at Mokwa. From these peoples he exacted tribute and used forced labor gangs to build the town of Gungu. This is merely a short story in the long saga of conflict, fission and military ascendancy by a rebel force and their establishment of a new polity.

Kings of early Hausaland not only needed revenue, but also legitimacy. They achieved that, as other monarchs did before and have done since, through manipulation of symbols of authority. One of the greatest of these early *Sarki* was Muhammad Rimfa (1463–99) who is remembered as the greatest Kano king before the Fulani *jihad*. He extended the city walls and fortifications, constructed the great Kurmi Market and made tactical innovations in warfare. To glorify his monarchy, he introduced special royal clothing and accouterments such as the *figinni* or ostrich-feather fan and special sandals that could only be worn by royalty. He also built a magnificent palace, the *Darkin Rimfa* or Rimfa's Palace, to demonstrate to the world how powerful he was.

In the realm of government, Muhammad Rimfa established the *Tara-ta-Kano*, a nine-man council of state, two of which were of servile origin and one of them, the *Sarkin Bai*, a eunuch. King Rimfa was the first to appoint eunuchs to important state offices. They came to be in charge of the treasury, the town, palace guards, communication between king and freeborn officeholders and control of the king's household. This latter responsibility was especially suited to eunuchs as Muhammad Rimfa had instituted the principle of **Purdah** (Hausa *kulle*) or wife-seclusion and the eunuchs watched over these women.

In an important symbolic act, Muhammad Rimfa cut down the sacred tree of Kano (*ardëb*) that represented the state's reliance on the ancestor cult and built a mosque on the site—a powerful symbolic statement. Moreover, he inaugurated the public celebration of *'Id al-Fitr*, the feast following the fast of Ramadan.

Queen Amina of Zaria

It would seem that under the sociopolitical conditions that existed before the rise of states in Northern Nigeria and the coming of Islam that the status of women was higher, indeed there is some evidence that earlier societies were matrilineal. In spite of the resultant patriarchies in the region, the retention of the importance of queens, queen mothers and sisters and their strong role as government advisors seems to point in that direction.

One of the most dominant women in Hausa history is *Sarauniya* (Queen) Amina of Zaria (Zakzak or Zazzau). The walled city, which is now the site of Ahmadu Bello University, was founded in 1536–37 by *Sarkin* Bawa Turunku, who is thought to have been a woman. The first of Turunku's daughters was Amina who reigned later in the 16th century. She made war on surrounding peoples and expanded the territory of Zakzak. The Kano Chronicle, an anonymous late 19th century compilation based on oral traditions, expresses the achievements of Queen Amina in emphatic terms:

> At this time Zaria, under Queen Amina, conquered all the towns as far as Kwararafa and Nupe. Every town paid tribute to her. The *Sarkin* Nupe sent forty eunuchs and ten thousand kolas to her. She first had eunuchs and kolas in Hausaland. Her conquest extended over thirty-four years. In her time the whole of the products of the west (from Zaria) were brought to Hausaland.

Queen Amina was especially known for building fortifications and walls. In fact, such walls all over Hausaland today are known as *ganuwar* Amina or Amina's walls. There is also a well known proverb in Hausa, *ya dade kamar ganuwar Amina*, "it has lasted as long as Queen Amina's walls."

Not only was this female monarch as bloodthirsty in warfare as her male counterparts, but as the promoter of such fortified towns she had to have exploited slave and corvée labor.

The Nature and History of Islam

Islam, like the other world religions born in what is known as the Middle East today—Christianity and Judaism—is based on monotheism, a belief in a single deity. To Muslims, there is but one God, Allah. Today one in three Africans is said to be a Muslim, even though Islam is not an indigenous African religion. And Islam seems to be on the up swing among rural peoples, even though it began as a cult movement in the non-African country of Arabia.

Islam originated in Arabia in the 7th century AD. *'Arab* means desert or desert people. These nomads were also called Bedouins. The **Bedouin** were organized into many tribes, each with its own gods and spirits. An otiose high god named Allah was known, but like the Sky God in many African religions, he was an original creator and not concerned in the everyday affairs of human beings.

The Bedouin survived by foraging, herding and raiding the trade routes that bisected the Arabian Peninsula and the Fertile Crescent where they settled. While there they learned an alphabet which would become the basis of their own written language.

Islam's founder was Muhammad, who claimed to have revelations from Allah. These revelations were recorded in the Islamic holy book, the *Qur'an*. Muhammad was born in AD 570 in the Arabian city of Mecca, which was the site of a local shrine called the *ka'ba*. This shrine has since become the center of worship for the Islamic World. In AD 610 the Prophet Muhammad claims to have heard the Archangel Gabriel speak to him saying, "There is no God but Allah, Muhammad is the messenger of God."

The *Qur'an* was committed to memory by Muhammad's followers after his death in 632. It was written down on scraps of parchment and bones initially, but eventually it became a bound volume held by Muslims to be the very word of God. It is a brief book—slightly shorter than the New Testament. Since there is no formal Islamic church, the *Qur'an* holds a unique position of authority in the religion. The *Qur'an* has two foci: (1) it is a volume of scripture dealing with the attributes of Allah and his essence and the relation of human beings to God. (2) it is also a book containing legal prescriptions and proscriptions about the governance of society. This is one of the reasons that Islam sometimes comes into conflict with secular laws and governments. This conflict has come out in West African history in the *jihads,* and more recently in modern-day Northern Nigeria where Islamic law has clashed with state law.

Unlike most traditional African religions, Islam is a literate religion, based on a book of formal codes and values. **'Ulama** are learned scholars of the *Qur'an*. The laws of the Holy Book are referred to as **Shari'a Law**, a form of Canon Law that lays out the **Sunna,** or path to righteousness, the established practice of the Prophet. While there are four distinct schools of Islamic law, in West Africa the Maliki Law School predominates. The Maliki School was founded by Imam Malik who made a series of deductions from selected passages in the *Qur'an*. It appears that there are more than five hundred fundamental principles in the Maliki School, but since other scholars have also made different conclusions, there is more than one set of precepts in the whole of Islam. This has led to factionalism, especially given the absence of a Pope-like figure or a centralized body of canonists.

Islamic fundamentalists, like proselytizers in Christianity, have been known to try to push *Shari'a* Law onto nonbelievers. That was part of the reason why Bai Bureh went to war again Bokari in Temneland in 1865. Bokari had alienated his sub-chiefs when he developed a policy of imposing correct law from the *Qur'an* on his followers and they enlisted the war master Bai Bureh to aid them in their struggle to free themselves. The ensuing 20-year *jihad* ended with Bokari's death in battle in 1885.

The Coming of Islam to Hausaland

These early states were loose congeries of people formed around a central government in a large urban area. To a degree a linguistic and cultural homogeneity was forming, but the states fought amongst themselves and did not always unite against outside enemies. When Islam came to the ruling classes in the 15th century it was a unifying factor, although it was not well received at first. Thousands opposing the penetration of alien elements defiled mosques and spoke out against alien ideas. Muslim scribes recorded that Allah appropriately punished such resisters by causing them to go blind, a commentary on scribal piety if not historical accuracy.

Islam did provide the Hausa with a common framework for intellectual development. It brought writing, law, precepts of administration and new concepts of morality. Under Islamic influence, the *Sarki* acquired more and more political authority, but not unlike other African kingdoms, the actual implementation of authority was checked by the king's council, which was composed of the chief ministers and territorial officials who were powerful *viziers*. With the force of time and tradition behind them, these men could exert great pressure on the king and those who influenced him.

With the adoption of Islam, an elaborate system of taxes developed, partly based on ancient local custom, but with a more organized and extractive nature. The *Qur'an* authorizes a *zakat*, a tax on available income, to be used for charitable purposes. The idea is that the richer members of society have some social obligation to the poorer members. On livestock, a Muslim was to pay the *jangali* tax and on land, a *kharaj* tax. Special taxes were placed on luxury crops—tobacco, onions and sugar cane. Since trade was a major source of revenue in the region, tolls were collected on passing caravans. On conquered peoples, there was a head tax (*jizya*), usually paid in slaves. All men visiting the king brought *Gaisua* (tribute). There were also taxes placed on certain professions such as craftsmen, butchers, prostitutes, dyers and dancing girls.

Collection was left in the hands of court favorites. These were influential men and fief-holders who resided in the capital or functioned as courtiers, but who delegated their duties to minor officials in the outlying districts. While this system of taxation allowed the collection of state revenues, it also afforded many opportunities for corruption and abuse by officials and their field lieutenants or tax collectors. Moreover, there are indications that some noblemen refused to pay, leaving the bulk of taxation on those who could not exert power to avoid payment. In a system of graft, field representatives of the state sometimes used arbitrary assessment methods and collecting processes that amounted to extortion. Since field collectors and court officials were taking a cut of such revenues, only a portion of the taxes collected ever reached the central authority.

The coming of the Fulani from the west during the reign of the Kano *Sarki* Yaqub (1452–63) was a far more powerful Islamic influence on Hausaland than that of earlier missionaries. The ruling élite embraced Islam, though the masses at this time did not even adopt a veneer of the religion. In the early days, before it became so entrenched in West Africa, Islam may have been perceived as just one of many cults that spread through the area, coming into prominence, then fading away. At this stage, any deep knowledge of Islam was probably lacking. It may be that monarchs merely saw it as a new, but useful tool to add to their existing persuasions.

Islam as an Overlay to West African Religions

Much of Islam's infiltration into the region was non-violent. The carriers of Islam were traders and itinerant clerics or *Mallams*. It became a binding force between rulers, traders and the Islamic clerics who often accompanied traders to the Savannah zone. It gave them a common set of ideas and principles upon which to build alliances.

The *Mallams* were devout men who desired to share their valued perspective with others, but Islam also functioned as social glue in trading relations. It gave traders and local merchants a common bond; a way of creating the trust needed to carry on long-distance trade and commerce.

The masses of people continued to follow their own local religions, but as the ruling élite interacted frequently with Islamic traders and clerics, politicos and wealthy families at first tolerated, then joined them in the worship of Allah.

At first Islam was an overlay on traditional authority structures in the Sudan. While Muslims were kept at court, the real power rested with the pagan kings and kinship still held sway over monotheism. Such kings and their priests were seen as middlemen who could effectively communicate with the supernatural and whose well being intimately affected that of the community. The kings often maintained pagan officials to deal with the local people, and learned Muslims to instruct and advise those courtiers who chose Islam. The rulers of the Savannah Kingdoms gave safe passage to the Islamic northerners and built enclosures where they could reside and worship at mosques.

Thus, Islam was an overlay and supplement to the spiritual needs of the people of early West Africa, acting as social glue for traders in the Sudan. It remained marginal till the Moorish invasion that opened the door to Islam wider than ever before.

Islam and the Windward Coast

The Windward Coast was geographically cut off from the state-building process of the Western Sudan to the north. It did not experience a major impact from the Great Sudanic Kingdoms of Ghana, Mali and Songhai. Nonetheless, wandering Muslim traders were most assuredly trekking through the smaller communities of the Windward Coast by the early 17th century and likely before that. Since most long-distance traders in West Africa are Muslims, and since most Muslims take proselytizing seriously, they were undoubtedly spreading the word with their commercial activity. This was a disjointed effort until about 1725 when Muslims in the **Futa Jalon** joined together to wage a *jihad*. Ibrahima Suri led them in a long and bitter war against their animist overlords. The inhabitants of the Futa Jalon were forced to adopt Islam or be driven away. Futa Jalon became a Muslim State.

The peoples of the Windward Coast to the south of this Islamic State were affected directly by the Holy War. Many Susu refused to adopt Islam and moved south where they dominated other Windward Coast peoples. Thus the *jihad* to the north contributed to the development of states in the south and west. Some of these conquerors were Muslims who established themselves as rulers; some were even asked in by communities who wanted the protection and prestige afforded by a Muslim State. Other Windward Coast peoples, although ruled by Muslims, retained their animist religions. Although Islam spread widely through the region in the 18th century, it did not penetrate deeply.

The Fulani and Mande Migrations

The development of such major Savannah kingdoms as **Tekrur** (See Map 9.2), Ghana, Mali, Songhai, the Hausa states, and Kanem-Bornu had a number of important

coming of the Kunta Arabs from the north, the spread of Islaminized Fulani across the region and the commercial activities of Dyula traders. First, Kunta Arabs[2] drifted down through modern-day Mauritania, then turned east along the northern bank of the River Niger towards the Zinder area of present-day Niger. On this journey, some splinter groups stopped where they found good pasturage for their herds. Others moved on, spreading their religion and culture across the land. The first in a long string of Kunta Arab clerics was Shaikh Sidi Ahmad al-Bakka'i (d. 1504). He inspired the Kunta to become more active proselytizers in the religion, to be what one observer has described as a "clerical tribe." We can see that influence as late as the beginning of the 19th century in the missionary work of Kunta-based **Sidi Mukhtar al-Kunti** (1729–1811) who created a widespread spiritual alliance that spread across the Western Sahelian zone. He also made treaties and alliances with the militant Tuareg, acting as a mediator in disputes. He was a builder rather than a destroyer. He was also a scholar, authoring over 300 treatises on Islam.

Secondly, Islam was spread in the turbulence of the *jihad* movements of the Fulani diaspora as they moved out of their homeland in the Futa Toro, beginning around the 13th century. This journey carried the Fulani as far east as Kanem-Bornu.

Thirdly, Dyula traders are said to have introduced Islam wherever they did business, most notably in Hausaland in the second half of the 14th century. Wherever trade went, so did scholars. Almost every caravan had an *imam* along. Some found communities to their liking and were given wives, settling down to minister to a community of the faithful. In this way, literate scholars who also possessed some political force by virtue of their piety and learnedness spread the word of Allah.

Islam was moving away from being just a private religion of the merchant class. It was spreading out and moving down the socioeconomic ladder to encompass the common people. Learning centers were established, mosques were built and missionaries preached the word of Allah to all who would listen.

Yet, not all peoples in West Africa accepted Islam. Some resisted. The Mossi and Akan were exposed to Islam but only used Muslims in their courts and made accommodations for traveling Muslims in their territories. They did not adopt the religion on a wholesale basis. Even the Mamprusi, who are largely Islmanized today, experienced early conflicts of interest between members of the traditional royal household and Muslims.

In contrast, the nearby Gonja used the religion as a basis for their state formation. For them, Islam could be used to challenge the legitimacy of tribal political structures, and the rituals on which they were based.

In general, Islam became a way for the dispossessed and dominated to rise up against the hegemons, using the universal principles of brotherhood against such perceived tyrants. Religious texts and interpretations by the learned clerics of the day were used to build up a set of ideas that defined non-Muslim communities (*dar al-harb*) in a negative light, and Muslim society (*dar al-Islam*) as the "abode of God" and therefore the only just society. It was a society based on *Shari'a* Law, a militant code of fundamentalist thinking and adherence to a single way.

Such writings and interpretations led to much conflict and turmoil in the centuries before colonial domination in West Africa. In many cases, this led to the invocation of *jihad* as we will highlight in the next section, and it continues to be a source of friction and factionalism in the artificially imposed nation-states of West Africa today.

---

2. They originally came from the area of Tuwat in southern Algeria in the 12th or 13th century.

The Jihadist Movements

From about 1688 the Muslims began to wage *jihads* to overthrow animist states. In the far west, Bondu had been created through a *jihad* as early as 1688, but most holy wars took place in the following two centuries. The early western state of Futa Jalon was established in 1725, then Futa Toro in 1776, followed by the great Sokoto Empire in 1804–1817 among the Hausa peoples, a movement that spilled over into neighboring areas (See Map 9.4). The Fulani jihadist, **Usman dan Fodio** (1754–1802), led this last massive *jihad*.

One West African people particularly associated with the Holy Wars was the Fulani. They have been the herdsmen of the western and central Sudan for centuries. They called themselves, *boroje*, and were originally pagans or polytheists. They lived in a symbiotic relationship with sedentary farmers, herding their cattle on the farmers' land, exchanging dairy products and services for grain and support. Eventually, some Fulani settled in towns, but were considered second class citizens and had no ritual protection. Thus, they tended to convert to Islam to acquire such protection and a sense of brotherhood.

In time, a class of urban-based, literate clerics (*torodbe*) arose. These learned reformists began to argue that the Muslims and Fulani should have more rights. Such a revolution could come by peaceful means, but violence was justified in the effort to impose *Shari'a* Law on idolaters. *Jihad* was a natural principle supported by Holy Scripture. Such scriptural interpretations took place in the context of growing populations of Fulani who were increasingly coming into conflict with sedentary peoples over land, water and other material resources. Conflicts and tensions resulted first in resentment, then war.

The first eruptions took place in Bondu and the Futa Jalon of the far west, south of the middle Senegal River. The idea was to bring about a unified state based on Quranic principles. This can be seen in the efforts of the *torodbe*, Malik Si (d. 1699?). He organized the Fulani into a new political unit called the *eliman* or *al-imam*, "of the cleric."

From about 1725 onwards the Muslim Fulani challenged the right of the local peoples to tax and dominate them, especially the privilege of locals to control the process of land allocation and herding rights. This occurred under increasing demographic pressure by the burgeoning Fulani presence in the Futa Jalon region. By 1750, the sociopolitical balance was reversed, and the local Jalonke peoples were paying tribute to the Fulani. Alfa Ibrahim (also known as Karamoko Alfa) who had spearheaded the movement became the Commander of the Faithful, the *amir al-mu'minin*. This honor was alternatively held by Ibrahima Suri who had helped or replaced Alfa Ibrahim and deserving members of both families.

Still, these movements fell short of establishing a theocratic hegemony in the area. Factionalism and competition for power and resources were common. The main conflict, internally, was between the Muslim clerics and the military men of Fulani society. Also, the leading families of the Fulani movement competed for the spoils of success and, of course, tension remained between the dominant Fulani and the dispossessed Jalonke.

Not surprisingly, the friction between the learned men and those in the military was settled in favor of those with the guns. A new leader arose, one Ibrahim Sori. He was installed as the *almamy*, the supreme head over both religion and the military. He moved to organize society and consolidate Fulani solidarity, attempting to control the

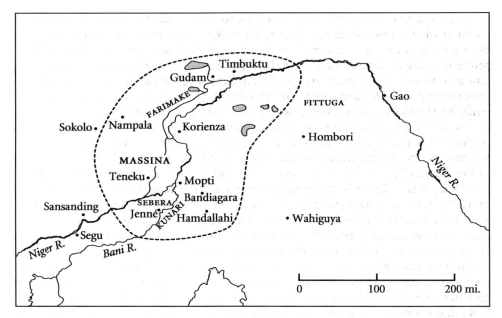

Map 9.5   The State of Massina.

region's trade routes. These trade arteries had become very lucrative with the addition of the demand for slaves on top of that for gold, and of course, European manufactured goods were in great demand everywhere. In spite of his efforts, he was never totally successful in bringing about a unified state.

Massina, near Timbuktu, also saw a dramatic influx of Fulani into the region. A dual mandate resulted in Timbuktu and Jenné between the *arma*, or Mande and Songhai kings, and the *ardo*, the Fulani chiefs, with the *arma* being dominant. This was a conflictual arrangement, which persisted through the 17th century into the 18th when control was centralized in Ségou, which housed the Bambara kings. In a fashion now familiar to us, the *torodbe* clerics preached against the abuses of the system. The man who rose to the fore in this reformation was Ahamadu ibn Hammadi (c. 1745–1844). He was a **Qadi** (religious judge) who united the Fulani then led a successful holy war to establish the 50,000 square mile state of Massina (See Map 9.5). Ahamadu ibn Hammadi established his capital at Hamdallahi (Praise be to God) near Jenné. But after his death in 1844, there was much dissention in the state. Other ardent Muslims were aghast at the disorder and moved in a second *jihad* led by **Al-Hajj Umar** (c. 1794–1864), a **Tukolor** cleric-warrior from Futa Toro. As a member of the **Tijaniyya** order, he was a fundamentalist who believed in using any means to establish a just theocracy. He had not only a solid spiritual background, but guns as well. His initial thrust was north through the Bambuk and Boure gold fields. In 1854 the fighting led to the death of the Bambara king of Kaarta and Ahamadu ibn Hammadi entered and occupied his capital of Nyoro.

Between 1857 and 1859 Hammadi was harassed by the French, but in 1861 he conquered Ségou on the upper Niger River. This angered some Muslims of Massina who claimed that this attack on Ségou was illegal by Quranic law. Hammadi turned on Massina and, even though they were fellow Muslims, sacked the capital of Hamdallahi. In 1863 he took Timbuktu. But as with the other western theocracies, there was much infighting, factionalism and brigandry in the area.

These western *jihads* pale in comparison to that of *Shehu* (*Shaykh*) Usman dan Fodio in what is now Northern Nigeria. There the Hausa states were engulfed in war during most of the 18th century. The tiny state of Katsina contested control of trade routes with the larger and more powerful state of Kano and was in turn challenged by Zamfara. Gobir, on the desert fringe of Hausaland, took advantage of the situation to seize fertile grazing land on the Savannah from Zamfara. It was a time of widespread strife. All the Hausa states suffered as a result of this incessant warfare.

The turmoil in Hausaland was symptomatic of the decline that had begun among traditional states across the western Sudan. Since coming into Hausaland in the sixteenth century, the urbanized Fulani had been the watchdogs of Islamic orthodoxy in the Hausa cities. In the latter part of the century they had precipitated religious revolts against religiously negligent rulers who were accused of offending public morality. One such insurrection was launched in 1804 by Usman dan Fodio, a widely traveled Fulani *Mallam* (teacher), against the Hausa *sarkin* (king) of Gobir. Usman dan Fodio had been born in Gobir, a frontier state that suffered frequent Tuareg raids. It was a lightly populated state with much rangeland, so the Fulani population there was greater than it was in other Hausa states of the area. Most of these Fulani were pagan. However, there was a small urban cohort of *torodbe*, or learned men in Gobir. *Shehu* Usman came from one such family. With this background, and as a religious judge, he knew the literature and history of Islam. Thus, he was prepared to launch a justifiable holy war to institute a just government under *Shari'a* Law.

From his base at Dengel near the Gobir capital, he began to gather the necessary men around him to make his move on the Gobir monarch. At first, Usman tried peaceful means to infiltrate the Gobir government and reform from within. As he was working toward this end, the Gobir *sarkin* tried to assassinate Usman, then attacked Dengel. As Usman was aware of the principle of *jihad*, he was equally aware of another doctrine of the prophet Muhammad, that of *hegira*—strategic retreat. He moved his community west near Kebbi in 1805.

According to the practiced formula for a return to purity, Usman proclaimed a *jihad* against Gobir. By 1810 he had made the most of Hausa disunity, deposing their kings. In their place he imposed Fulani hegemony in Gobir, and ultimately throughout Hausaland. Usman and his followers established the Fulani capital at Gwandu.

Usman's militantism inspired many other uprisings in the area. Within in a ten-year span, all of the Hausa states fell: Daura, Zaria, Kano, Katsina and Gobir. Usman's influence took the movement outside of Hausaland, as well. Spin off *jihads* took place in at least 15 other states in the surrounding areas.

Back in Hausaland, Fulani leaders assumed the offices of power in the Hausa states, although the structure of government did not change significantly. Islam became an overlay uniting the emirates, preventing internecine aggression and conflicts. In what came to be known as the Sokoto Caliphate, Usman, his brothers and followers were able to build a state that had greater security and efficiency than was normal in West Africa at that time.

Usman was recognized as *caliph* (religious leader) and *sultan* (political autocrat) in the empire, taking the title *emir al mu'minin* (Commander of the Faithful). Although, strictly speaking, religious *qadis* should dominate any polity since a theocracy is the ideal in Islamic culture, the political realities were such that secular power and religious power often existed side by side.

Usman made gifts of conquered cities as emirates to loyal followers among the Fulani aristocracy, reserving for himself the Sokoto Sultantate as supreme among them.

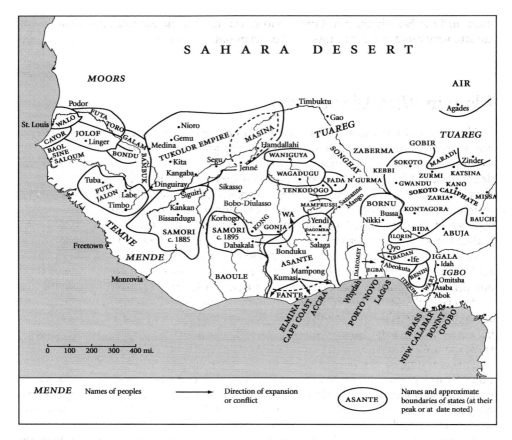

Map 9.6   States of West Africa.

Although the other emirs owed personal allegiance to him and his successors at Sokoto, the emirates were otherwise regarded as independent states, with Kano the second in importance.

The Sultantate of Sokoto was enormous, covering some 180,000 square miles and involved perhaps ten million people. By horse, it took four months to ride from the western to the eastern border, and two months to ride north to south.

Elsewhere in West Africa, similar movements were afoot on the eve of colonial domination by the European nations. Shortly afterwards the imanate of Massina was formed (1810) near Timbuktu, and **Samori Touré** was making his scorched-earth sweep out of the west until he was stopped short and arrested by the French (See Map 9.6).

All these revolutions brought a world religion into the centers of power in these areas, eventually leading to widespread adoption of the religion by the common people, rulers and élites. The entry of Islam into West Africa also stimulated the spread of a form of literacy.

When threatened by the British the emirs did not put up resistance. This may have been due to the fact that the leaders were secure in knowing that the theocracy would last in spite of this conquest by the British. The firm belief in *Shari'a* Law gave the emirs the confidence to work with the British colonialists, and not against them. Perhaps this is hindsight reasoning, but in any case, the Fulani-Hausa emirates are still there and the British are not. Furthermore, we see that the emirates and *Shari'a* Law are still very much a force in modern Nigerian politics (See below).

Islam in West Africa Today

Since the AD 639 move into Egypt, Islam has come to influence the lives of about one in every three Africans, and its influence is growing. Traditionally, Islam spread along trade routes and was more popular with urbanized Africans than with rural residents. Today, it is spreading to the smallest villages in the remotest regions of the continent. It seems that this is, in part, due to a growing awareness of a need to move away from animism and local beliefs, and to search for more universal protection from the vagaries of life. In short, Islam is thought to provide protection to the individual no matter where he or she may be, in the village, in town, traveling or in a large city.

Also today oil rich countries of the Middle East are pouring in funds to foster the faith. Their monies go to employ *Mallams*, build mosques, support Arabic schools and generally to further the spread of the religion of Islam.

Additionally, the efforts of governments in heavily Islamized regions of West Africa serve to foster the spread of this religious way of life. For example, *Shari'a* Law recently became the law of the land in certain regions of Northern Nigeria, and as I write this, there are calls for the spread of this law to the south.

This is a struggle between two imposed systems of law, one from Arabia, and the other from Britain. Throughout most of Nigeria, English common law serves as the basis for court decisions. Prior to 1966, before the military became involved in Nigerian politics there was an embodied Islamic Personal Law in the Penal Code to accommodate those in that camp. After 1977 the opposition between Christian views on law and those of the followers of Allah flared into a war of words in the Nigerian press and in the legislative halls.

The main opposition in Nigerian politics today is between the north and south, with the former being primarily Islamic and Hausa, the latter being primarily Christian and Yoruba, with a strong Ibo contingent that has not always been unified with the Yoruba. Of late, there has been pressure to extend the rule of *Shari'a* Law to all of Nigeria, a move most southerners would resist. In 1991 the flames of this fear were fanned when Nigeria joined the OIC, Organization of Islamic Conference.

Some Nigerians have voiced the fear that "maybe the *jihad* started by Usman dan Fodio is not over." It could spread to unify all of Nigeria, or it could break apart the fragile structure of federalism that has held the country together so far. To paraphrase Dr. Femi Ajayi "Is a religious war between the Christians and the Muslims looming over the cloudy Nigerian political process with the trade of words between Christians and Muslims?"

Conclusions

West Africa has seen the rise of major kingdoms that have impacted less developed peoples through conquest, trade and culture contact. They mostly centralized by establishing a monopoly on trade goods. Connected with centralization of polities, conquest and trade was the spread of Islam into the region from North Africa. Arab merchants brought more goods and they brought a foreign religion. Starting as a religion of traders, Islam passed to royalty and eventually to the common people.

Islam has had both organizing and disorganizing effects in the region. It is a prose-lytizing religion. Its precepts indicate that a Muslim has the obligation to spread the gospel of Islam and to resist all forms of blasphemy. This missionary spirit has led to the spread of the religion, but one that has come into conflict with traditional ways at times and another imposed theology—Christianity. Furthermore, Islamic principles contain ideas about political governance. The religion has a political component, based on *Shari'a* Law. It holds that a Holy War is sometimes justified to bring nonbe-lievers into the fold. Consequently, Islam has come into conflict with secular forms of rule and was spread aggressively by *Jihadist* reformers across the region by zealous re-formers up to the European conquest.

Europeans brought Christianity into the area and today these two foreign ideologies stand in opposition to each other. Not only was there a clash between Islam and tradi-tional African religions, but today Muslims and Christians are locked in an ideological battle, which unfortunately has spilled into the streets, resulting in violence and death. Islam also threatens secular law in some places such as Northern Nigeria where Mus-lims dominate regional government. As local and regional leaders attempt to impose *Shari'a* Law on all residents, animist and Christians included with Muslims, conflict and violence has resulted, calling into question the sovereignty of the nation-state.

As we will see in later chapters, another foreign ideology has swept into West Africa—neoliberalist ideas of the importance of parliamentary democracy and **free trade**. Along with this come other Western ideas about political organization, freedom and the treatment of women that pose potential conflicts with Islamic principles, a microcosm of a culture clash being played out on a larger stage today.

CRITICAL THINKING QUESTIONS

1. Social historians tell us that most states arise when an élite group gains control of something. In the Great Sudanic States of the Niger Bend region, what did royals con-trol to give them power? In what ways did this vary from Ghana to Mali to Songhai?
2. Describe the origin and rise of Islam and how it spread into West Africa.
3. If we depict traditional African religions as non-missionary oriented, not involved in proselytizing, what evidence in history shows Islam to be interested in convert-ing others?
4 What foreign ideologies have influenced West Africa? How are they similar or dif-ferent?
5. Discuss the relation between these themes discussed in this chapter: political cen-tralization, trade, religion and military conquest.

KEY CONCEPTS

Al-Hajj Umar
Almoravids

Arma
Askia **Muhammad**

Bedouin
Communité
Free trade
Futa Jalon
Ibn Battuta
Kanem-Bornu
Keita, Sundiata
Mali, Empire of
Mansa Musa
Mansfield Decision
Marketing Boards
Neoliberalism
Prince Henry the Navigator
Purdah

Samori Touré
Sidi Mukhtar al-Kunti
Songhai, Empire of
Soninke
Sundiata Keita
Sunni Ali Ber
Tagharza
Tekrur
Tijaniyya
Tukolor (Empire)
'Ulama
University of Sankore
Usman dan Fodio

≋ SOURCES & SUGGESTED READINGS ≋

Adekunle, J. O. 2000. The jihads of West Africa. In: Falola, Tony (ed.). *Africa: African history before 1885* (Volume 1). Durham, NC: Carolina Academic Press, 299–319.

Awe, Bolanle. 1965. Empires of the Western Sudan: Ghana, Mali, Songhai. In: Ajayi, J. F. Ade and Ian Espie (eds.). *A thousand years of West African history*. Ibadan: Ibadan University Press, 55–70.

Bravmann, René A. 1983. *African Islam*. London: Ethnographica.

Brenner, Louis (ed.). 1993. *Muslim identity and social change in Sub-Saharan Africa*. Bloomington: Indiana University Press.

Cohen, Ronald. 1967. *The Kanuri of Bornu*. New York: Holt, Rinehart and Winston.

Dibua, J. I. 2000. Sudanese kingdoms of West Africa. In: Falola, Tony (ed.). *Africa: African history before 1885* (Volume 1). Durham, NC: Carolina Academic Press, 137–159.

Drucker-Brown, Susan. 1975. *Ritual aspects of the Mamprusi kingdom*. Leiden: Afrika-Studiencentrum.

Fage, J. D. 1995. *A history of Africa*. London: Routledge. Chapter. 13

Falola, Tony & Steven J. Salm. 2000. Islam. In: Falola, Tony (ed.). *Africa: African Cultures and Societies before 1885* (Volume 2). Durham, NC: Carolina Academic Press, 107–128.

Fyfe, Christopher. 1969. Peoples of the Windward Coast. In: Ajayi, J. F. Ade and Ian Espie (eds.). *A thousand years of West African history*. Ibadan: Ibadan University Press, 149–164.

Grindal, Bruce. 1973. Islamic affiliation and urban adaptation: The migrant in Accra, Ghana. *Africa* 63:333–46.

Hanson, John. H. 1995. Islam and African societies. In: Martin, Phyllis M. & Patrick O'Meara (eds.). *Africa* (Third edition). Bloomington: Indiana University Press, 97–114.

Hunwick, J.O. 1969. Islam in West Africa A.D. 1000–1800. In: Ajayi, J. F. Ade and Ian Espie (eds.). *A thousand years of West African history*. Ibadan: Ibadan University Press, 113–131.

Ifemesia, C. C. 1969. States of the Central Sudan. In: Ajayi, J. F. Ade and Ian Espie (eds.). *A thousand years of West African history*. Ibadan: Ibadan University Press, 72–112.

Kasule, Samuel. 1998. *The history atlas of Africa*. New York: Macmillan.

Levtzion, N. 1968. *Muslims and chiefs in West Africa: A study of Islam in the Middle Volta Basin in the pre-colonial period*. Oxford: Oxford University Press.

Mahoney, F. and H. O. Idowu. 1969. The peoples of Sénégambia. In: Ajayi, J. F. Ade and Ian Espie
    (eds.). *A thousand years of West African history*. Ibadan: Ibadan University Press, 132–148.
Mendonsa, Eugene L. 2001. *Continuity and Change in a West African Society: Globalization's
    impact on the Sisala of Ghana*. Durham: Carolina Academic Press.

10 FIRST CONTACT: THE EUROPEANS ARRIVE

> This chapter covers the arrival of the Portuguese in West Africa. They were interested in trade, but were forced to remain on the coast, dealing with interior suppliers through middlemen. Their demand for slaves started a process of dehumanization and social disorganization from which West Africa has never entirely recovered. While the Portuguese professed an interest in proselytizing in *Guiné*, they were largely interested in commerce and increasingly became involved in slaving. In fact they attempted to monopolize the region's commerce, but other European nations recognized the economic potential there and began to compete for access to suppliers and profits. The Portuguese lost out, for the most part, in this competition, being replaced by the British, French and Dutch. One effect of this European competition was social disruption of traditional society in West Africa and the stratification of society.

Portugal in West African History

The leading national actor in the push into **Guinea (*Guiné*)** was the tiny Iberian kingdom of Portugal. In 1415 Portugal invaded Cueta in Morocco, then proceeded to look southwards, to the unknown regions "beyond the sand." The roots of the Portuguese adventure in *Guiné* lay in the great expansion of mercantile enterprise that transformed Europe in the later Middle Ages. Swelling towns, expanding wealth and growing populations hastened the pace of international commerce.

Portugal was well placed to start the navigational revolution along the African coast. As a fishing nation, it was well acquainted with the sea and maritime technology. Being isolated from the rest of Europe, it escaped the ravages of the Hundred Years War. In relative isolation the country began to urbanize and seek riches through commerce.

Prince Henry the Navigator was the third son of King John I of Portugal. When the Portuguese took control of Cueta, Henry became the first governor of the territory. While there, he began to hear tales from Arab traders of *Bilad Ghana*, a kingdom near a great river, governed by a mighty king who had access to large quantities of gold. This country was called Melli (Mali) and the king was Mandimansa (*Mansa* Musa). There were stories of a "gold mart" at a place called Timbuktu. Henry became determined to find the source of this gold.

Prince Henry helped to unlock the secrets of Africa by setting up a school for sailors and innovating with new navigational technology. He also paid for many sailing expeditions. Furthermore, he employed cartographers to create the most sophisticated maps of their time, which were jealously guarded over the next century in an attempt to keep other Europeans from tapping into the riches if West Africa.

Henry the Navigator, in the very beginning of Portuguese expansion into Africa, had stressed that in addition to trade, peace and evangelism were values to be fostered. This has come to be known as the **Henrician tradition**, but it pretty much ended with Henry.[1] The desire for gold and other trade goods came to dominate the quest for discovery and spreading the Christian gospel was subordinate.

Around 1419 Henry became fascinated with the possibility of making sea voyages south and west of Europe. To this end, he established himself in Sagres in the Algarve, on the southern most tip of Portugal and began investigating new ship designs and sailing methods that could carry his crews south to *Bilad Ghana* or perhaps to the East Indies. Asia was a prized destination because spices and other luxury items such as sugar flowed from there, through Egypt, to Venice, but the Venetians had a virtual monopoly on the small quantities of such items that managed to reach Europe, and the prices were high.

In an economic atmosphere where European demand was growing and supplies were limited, merchants knew that if they could find a sea route to the East Indies, they would have a gold mine. It had long been believed that a sea route to India was possible by either sailing south or west, as **Christopher Columbus** did, but limited technology and maps were a hindrance.

In 1418 Henry's sailors discovered the Island of Madeira (Map 1.5). The following year he retired from the court and became governor of the Algarve. There, on the rocky promontory of Sagres, he founded a small court of his own, to which he attracted seamen, cartographers, astronomers, shipbuilders, and instrument makers. In 1420, at the age of 26, he was made grand master of the Order of Christ, the supreme order sponsored by the Pope, which had replaced the crusading order of the Templars in Portugal. The funds made available through the order largely financed his great enterprise of discovery. A secondary goal was the conversion of the pagans to Christianity. For this reason, all of Henry's ships bore a red cross on their sails. With this endowment Henry began to dispatch his ships along the North African coast.

In 1434, Henry's captain, Gil Eannes, accomplished the first and most difficult leg of the journey around Africa. He rounded **Cape Bojador** (See Map 1.5). Only seven years later, on the maiden voyage of the innovative **caravel** sailing ship, **Antam Gonçalves** returned from the Guinea Coast with the first cargo of slaves and gold. Gonçalves' maiden voyage opened up a flow of trade between West Africa and Portugal. Soon Lisbon merchants were trading in ostrich feathers and eggs, amber, gum Arabic, goats, gems, peppers, dried fish, wax, hides, ivory, elephant teeth, leopard pelts and civet cat glands used in making perfume.

Other islands were discovered as well: the Azores in 1439 and the Cape Verde Islands in 1444. In that same year, Portuguese ships sailed up the Rio de Oro south of Cape Bojador in modern-day Western Sahara. They called the narrow strait of the Atlantic Ocean at present-day Dakhla the "River of Gold" because the local inhabitants along this inlet traded the gold dust of the interior. Over the next decade these adventurers discovered many parts of *Guiné*, reaching Sierra Leone in 1460. Every time these buccaneers came upon a river, they sailed inland hoping to find the fabled Kingdom of Gold.

---

1. Part of this tradition was the search for **Prestor John** (See glossary).

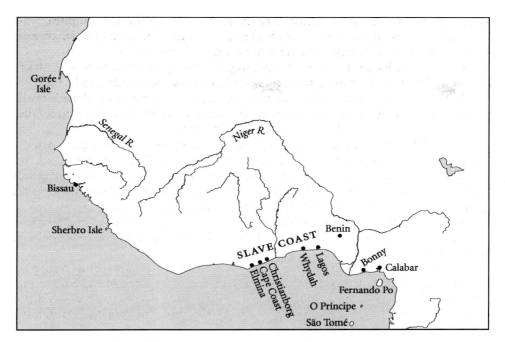

Map 10.1 Slave Harbors of 19th Century West Africa.

Each trip that Henry's navigators made, they recorded the hydrography, geography, astronomy, and even the customs and economy of the peoples they encountered. Each subsequent journey built on the previously acquired knowledge in a scientific manner.

The Portuguese took an authoritarian approach to Africans. They made demands or threats and backed these up with force when deemed necessary. West Africans feared the Portuguese who developed a reputation for repression. However, most of the time they merely used intimidation or bribery to accomplish their ends. Additionally, the Portuguese traders developed some tricks. They learned that chiefs, kings and potentates all over Guinea valued alcohol, so spirits were given as gifts and bribes. The Europeans also became involved in local politics, playing one local group or faction against another. This began a long history of interference in West African affairs, with various European interests trying to turn the locals against their commercial rivals in West Africa.

In general, coastal peoples interested in trade tolerated the coming of the Europeans, giving them just enough land or help or water to keep them coming back with their goods. There were occasional minor skirmishes and sometimes outright clashes. At Accra, the natives tricked the Portuguese into opening the front gate of their fort, then swept inside and massacred all occupants.

About the end of the 15th century, direct transport of slaves from the mainland to São Tomé (See Map 10.1) began with the idea of creating **sugar plantations**. Although the plantations eventually declined, slaves continued to be warehoused there in transit to the Spanish West Indies. In 1530 the Lisbon-based *Casa da Mina de Guiné* contracted to deliver slaves in the island to merchants representing the government of Castile.

In addition to sugar cane, the Portuguese introduced many fruits and vegetables into islands along the Guinea Coast. This was to provide food for settlers and provi-

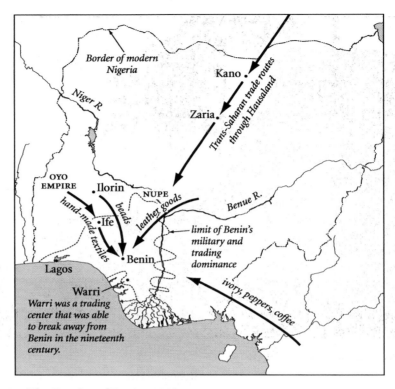

Border of modern Nigeria

Kano

Niger R.

Zaria

Trans-Saharan trade routes through Hausaland

OYO EMPIRE

Ilorin

NUPE

Benue R.

hand-made textiles

beads

leather goods

•Ife

limit of Benin's military and trading dominance

•Benin

Lagos

Warri

Warri was a trading center that was able to break away from Benin in the nineteenth century.

ivory, peppers, coffee

Map 10.2   The Empire of Benin, 1800.

sions for ships plying the waters. These plants later spread to the mainland and became major food crops — maize, pineapples, pawpaws, guavas and sweet potatoes. Cassava was brought from the Americas at the beginning of the 17th century. The coconut and Asiatic yam came from the east, oranges, melons, lemons and some other fruits from Portugal.

Along the Guinea Coast, the Portuguese used strongarm tactics to get locals not to trade with their rivals, to restrict their business to Portuguese traders. Local traders often disobeyed these strictures, and were generally antagonized by slave raids.

In some places, indigenes benefited from European contact. Benin, for example, was remarkably accessible from the coast that led to its minimal but perceptible "Portuguesization" (See Map 10.2). When the English trader Capt. Thomas Wyndham visited Benin in 1553, he found that the king there spoke Portuguese and had adopted other European habits. Wyndham noted that there was no servitude there, but rather the Portuguese had to clear their activities with the king. Indeed, the Portuguese had an unfortified trading post there from about 1486 to 1506. It yielded a supply of slaves, who were bartered for gold at ***Castelo São Jorge da Mina*** or *Mina*, as it became known (now Elmina, See Photo 10.1).

In 1485, when Benin was a well-established empire, the Portuguese came in search of trade and in the wake of these traders came missionaries, anxious to found churches. Here, as elsewhere in West Africa, was a familiar pattern that disrupted life in such places — first a seemingly peaceful appearance of traders and their religious counterparts followed by guns and a demand for slaves.

Photo 10.1   Elmina Castle, Ghana.

The Coastalization of the Europeans

As a rule, the peoples of the interior had less experience with Europeans. Those few Westerners who ventured inland usually did so with native guides and clearances from West African rulers along the way. It was said by some that at *Dois Partes,* no resident of *Castelo São Jorge da Mina* dared go a mile inland without the permission and protection of the local chiefs.

The Portuguese could not reach many of the interior kingdoms for trade, having instead to deal through middlemen most of the time. West Africans were content to have the Europeans on the coast as trading partners, but when they tried to penetrate the interior they met with armed resistance in many cases.

As the interest of the Portuguese was drawn down the coast toward *Mina,* supervision of the Portuguese citizenry settling in Upper *Guiné* was relaxed. This encouraged the growth of a settler population there, made up of adventurers and runaways. At the river mouths and along the waterways of Sénégambia, some local women married Portuguese men and became known as *senhoras* (Fr. *senares or sinares*), using their connections to become wealthy and powerful traders in the area. A sizeable half-caste or mulatto community developed, and from there many **lançados** launched commercial enterprises that upset the Portuguese monarch. In 1518 this led to a royal decree mandating the death penalty for all who did not immediately leave Africa. It was universally ignored. In fact, after Mandinka, the *lingua franca* of Sénégambia, Portuguese Creole was the most important language. These multilingual and multicultural traders provided a point of contact for their African and European counterparts along the rich riverine valleys of Sénégambia.

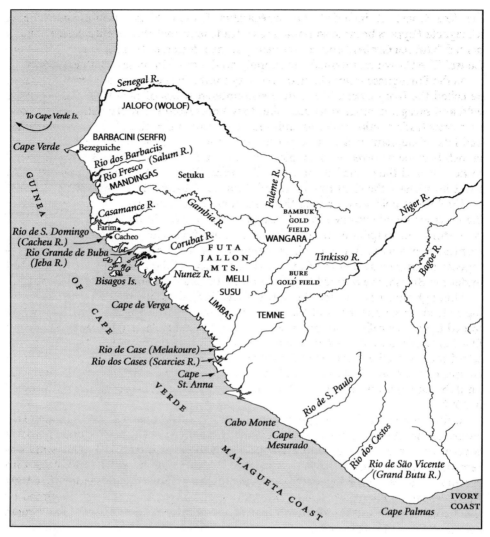

Map 10.3   *Guiné* and the Malagueta Coast.

These *lançados* left their mark on the region. As shrewd men and women of business, boat experts, skilled mechanics, translators, and contractors, they helped build the extractive economy of the European world system along the Atlantic Coast. Mulattos influenced indigenous architecture by juxtaposing their solid and spacious dwellings with the less durable round mud huts of their Mandinka neighbors. These European-style houses were rectangular and contained several rooms. They were raised two or three feet above the ground with a central courtyard being a distinguishing feature. In their gardens, they planted ornamental trees for shade and fruit trees for food. Before long, the royals and big men along the coast began to imitate this architectural elegance.

Slowly, the Portuguese navigators worked their way along the coast of Africa, working off the African islands at first, then learning to navigate to the **Malagueta Coast**, which they named after the peppers they found there (See Map 10.3). Also known as the Kru Coast, it included the Sénégambia Region, Sierra Leone and Liberia. Malagueta Peppers became so popular as a trade item that they eventually were nicknamed "**Guinea Grains**," and consequently some referred to that region as the "**Grain Coast**." The Crown maintained a monopoly on the trade in these valuable peppers.

As the Portuguese sailors inched their way south, they came to the area that was to be called the Ivory Coast. There they encountered tribes of people who they saw as wild and savage, compared to the tribes they knew from the Malagueta Coast. However, once trade relations were established, it was found that these "barbarous peoples" had lots of elephant tusks and teeth to sell, hence the name Ivory Coast. When the French became involved in the region, great quantities of elephant teeth were traded to Europe and they called it the *Coste de Dents*, "the Tooth Coast." Apparently that name didn't have the right ring to it, and it was eventually called *Côte d'Ivoire*.

The lure of gold was drawing the Portuguese ever southwards. They noticed that the precious metal became more common as they moved in that direction, and there were stories of kingdoms of gold that must have filled the gossip of the day. Their eventual goal was to find the mines where such gold was produced. When the Portuguese eventually settled in what was later to become the colony of the Gold Coast under the British, the referred to the region as the *Costa da Mina*, the Mine Coast.

Although they never found the mines, they did find coastal peoples who were willing to trade large quantities of the metal in exchange for European goods. They first traded in an area called Samma or Shama, then moved eastward to the present site of El Mina Castle in modern-day Ghana. In 1482, at a village they called *Dois Partes*, they established a fortified settlement, *Castelo São Jorge da Mina*, The Castle of Saint George of the Mine. Gold was clearly on their minds. The Portuguese held the castle until the Dutch captured it in 1637. A subsidiary trading fort at Axim was constructed in 1502.

In that same year the Portuguese built the *Casa da Mina de Guiné* in Lisboa. This House of the Mine of Guinea combined the functions of a merchant company with a government office to oversee events in the newly discovered lands. *Casa da Mina* was receiving between 2,000 and 5,000 pounds of gold annually around the end of the 15th century. Venture capital profits were about 500 %. At the time, it seemed that West Africa was to be Portugal's vein of gold, though its importance was soon eclipsed by the discoveries in the New World ten years later and the founding of the Portuguese colony at Goa in India in 1498.

In *Mina* they encountered coastal tribes who fished the sea using canoes, and whom the Portuguese deemed to be "astute traders." The Portuguese did not venture inland, being content to deal with the gold brokers on the coast.

Climate and terrain also kept the Portuguese on the coast. Native peoples were not helpful to any Europeans who wanted to go inland, as this would deprive them of their broker status and a newfound source of livelihood. Even if the Portuguese had tried to venture inland, they would have had a difficult time finding appropriate guides to help them.

Then there was the matter of time. By trial and error Portuguese navigators had learned that they could only sail to West Africa during what they called the "**Guinea Season**," which we now call the dry season. During the rains of June-September, Europeans found the climate insufferable and there were adverse currents and winds to confound the sailors. Through experience, they determined that the proper trading season was October to May. By leaving in the European autumn, they could usually make the Lisbon to *El Mina* journey in two months or less. However, time was of the

Photo 10.2   A Villager Wearing a Second-Hand Mechanic's Suit and Ski Cap.

essence while in the region, because the return journey took more time, and the longer they waited, the more dangerous it became. Given the prevailing currents and winds in the late Guinea Season, a ship that tarried too long could find itself becalmed, and more than one crew died at sea of thirst or starvation going to their deaths on a ship loaded with gold, ivory and other trade goods from the Guinea Coast.

The Portuguese Crown had supported and profited from the West African adventure. In 1444, they sanctioned the formation of The Lagos Company, which constructed a staging facility on Arguin Island just south of Cape Blanco.[2] The founding entrepreneurs of the company made huge profits in slaves and gold, ranging between 50 and 800 %. The Crown usually took a fifth of the profits, so it had both a civil and pecuniary interest in protecting Portuguese hegemony in West Africa. In addition to **"Black Ivory"** (slaves) and gold, many other items were on the trade lists bound for Europe: ostrich eggs, goats, dried fish, gum, amber, wax, hides, musk, ivory and elephant teeth. Interestingly, at this pre-industrial point in history, palm oil was a very small part of the export pattern, but one that would become enormously important later. The Portuguese learned that West Africans would trade these highly desirables for mere trifles like basins, brass rings, beads, even used clothing from Europe (hence the beginning of a used clothes industry that continues today in West Africa, 500 years later—See Photo 10.2).

Even though the Portuguese Crown did everything in its power to keep the trade in Guinea a secret, the Andalusians of Castile and Cadiz heard the stories of gold and great profits, and sent an expedition to the region around 1454. The Portuguese at-

---

2. The Lagos Company is named after a southern Portuguese city, not the former capital of modern-day Nigeria.

tacked the fleet and captured one ship, taking it and the crew back to Lisbon for trial. Diplomatic protests were made to the Andalusians and the Pope. The Portuguese Crown made threats of war towards the Spanish, primarily King John II of Castile. As the Roman Papacy often acted as an arbiter in such disputes in Christendom, the Portuguese Crown made a strong case with the Pope that Portugal "owned" Guinea by right of first discovery. From an African point of view this was a ludicrous claim, since the native peoples of West Africa had their own systems of land tenure and political organization.

Rome sided with the Portuguese, but the Andalusians kept trying between 1454 and 1475, sending voyages to the Guinea Coast. However when King John II died, the effort fizzled, and the Portuguese efforts through The Lagos Company continued unabated. King Alfonso V of Portugal granted **Fernão Gomes**, a wealthy Lisbon merchant, a charter to explore the coast of Guinea beyond Sierra Leone, which was to prove very profitable for both Gomes and the government of Portugal as this led to the discovery of the Gold Coast. As part of the agreement, Gomes has to explore 100 leagues (about 400 miles) of coastline every year. In total, Gomes' people explored some 2000 miles of coastline, though he never went there himself. It is interesting to note that after a lifetime of exploitation of the riches of West Africa, Gomes was awarded a knighthood by the Crown. On his coat of arms he had a silver shield embossed with the figure of three Negro chiefs wearing gold rings and gold collars. Through exploitation of West Africa this Portuguese investor was able to become rich beyond dreams, and was given his country's highest honors.

Trying to keep the lid on their exploitation of the region, the Portuguese Crown forbade discussion of their trips with foreigners. They also enjoined the sale of arms, sailing technology or iron to the natives of Guinea. But making rules and enforcing them were two different things in the newly discovered and dangerous waters of the Guinea Coast. Interlopers from Europe began to make a "mini-scramble" for Africa. The Portuguese Regent tried in vain to keep out such intruders, requiring all ships trading in African waters to register with the government. Nevertheless, four types of fleets continued working the Guinea Coast: Crown-sponsored ships, those of merchants registered with the Portuguese State, foreign trespassers and pirates.

The essential conflict in the 1400s was one that has a modern resonance to it: **Free Trade versus Government Regulation.** The Portuguese Crown wanted to control trade in Guinea and its islands. Merchants and entrepreneurs from Portugal and other European sovereignties wanted free access to this new source of wealth, especially after Fernão Gomes discovered the Gold Coast and began to haul back shiploads of gold dust. Historians consider this discovery one of the most important in the exploitative history of the European penetration of West Africa.

However, the success of Fernão Gomes was Portugal's predicament. If it had been difficult to keep the lid on their secret "*Mina*" before that, it now became virtually impossible. Other Europeans felt that this was too much wealth to be ignored or left to a tiny kingdom like Portugal. In 1475, Spain declared war on Portugal. For the next few years Castile would harass the Portuguese efforts in Guinea, the war eventually being settled by the **Treaty of Alcaçovas** in 1479.

While Portugal "won" the war and its right by first discovery was upheld by the Papacy and European opinion, Castile did not do badly, as it won the right to govern the Canary Islands. Nevertheless, Portugal retained the lucrative **Mina Coast** and the rest of Guinea. Between 1479 and 1530 the Portuguese spent their time consolidating their monopoly over the region and extracting monstrous profits from Guinea. The Crown of Portugal, backed by the Pope, renewed its interest in regulating trade in Guinea. It built the coastal forts along the Gold Coast and outfitted armadas to patrol the waters of Guinea.

But alas, the word was out. The English and Flemish made expeditions to the region and the rush was on. Portugal could handle the occasional Spanish galleon, but when the rest of Europe began to invade the African coast, there was no efficient way to police them. Between 1480 and 1578, the Portuguese pursued a policy of entrenchment, building more and more fortresses along the Guinea Coast and using such bases to secure a hold on the key points of extraction.

Gold came from mines in the interior by four main routes to the sea: at Samma, *Dois Partes* (Two Parts—both near Elmina, See Map 10.1), Axim and Accra (See Christianborg, Map 10.1). The first two were serviced by Akan-speakers, the latter two by Gã-speaking peoples.

The Portuguese also followed a settlement approach, at least in Cape Verde, Fernando Po, São Tomé and Príncipe (See Map 10.1). Settlers established a sugar industry on these islands. Many island settlers began to trade with the mainland. These were called *lançados*, trader-settlers. They became favored trading partners to Europeans. In 1466 the inhabitants of the Cape Verde Isles were granted a privilege giving them the right to trade with the *Guiné* coast between the Senegal River and Sierra Leone, although they had to pay trade dues to the Crown. A similar grant was made to the first settlers of São Tomé in 1485 that allowed them to trade from the Niger Delta southwards.

The two main foci of Portuguese extraction were Samma near Cape Three Points, and the village of *Dois Partes*, where the largest fort was built, *Castelo São Jorge da Mina*. Apparently this native settlement contained two ethnic groups, the Fetu and Comani, hence the name Two Parts. This was the most important Portuguese fortification along the Mina Coast, which stretched from Samma to *Cabo das Redes*.

While Portugal was trying to maintain its right to exploit Guinea, other world forces were at work against them. First, there were conflicts and diplomatic squabbles within Europe that occupied the time and energies of the Crown. Secondly, the East and West Indies had been opened up and Guinea's importance diminished considerably. Portuguese trade in West Africa in the 16th century amounted to only 14% of the trade she did in the East Indies. The growing significance of her colony in Brazil reduced this even further.

The Lusitanian Crown negotiated with King Caramansa at *Dois Partes* village for permission to build the castle, about the amount of the rents paid to him and to get Caramansa to supply laborers and supplies. Once these negotiations were complete, the Portuguese government sent Diogo d'Azambuja to Mina with 600 men, three women, ten ships and two barges. With a large crew of masons and laborers, they had completed a chapel, central watchtower, a spacious warehouse and an encircling wall in just a few weeks.

At this point, most Europeans returned to Portugal, leaving d'Azambuja behind with 60 men and three women. By 1486, *Castelo São Jorge da Mina* had been awarded the status and privileges of a *cidade*, a city in Portuguese legal statues. On the same date, King João II assumed the pretentious title of Lord of Guinea.

Once *Castelo São Jorge* was completed, the Portuguese set about to dot the Mina Coast with other fortifications, including one at Accra, which was later to become the capital of the colony of the Gold Coast, and remains the capital of modern-day Ghana. The Gã king destroyed the original fort at Accra in 1756. Relations between the whites and the blacks seemed to wax and wane. The Portuguese had to take punitive expeditions into the Benin River area between 1487–1507; then in 1514 we find the king of Benin sending emissaries to Portugal to invite Christian missionaries into his realm! It seems he was maneuvering to try to get firearms from the Portuguese. He also complained about slaving and plantations on the islands of São Tomé and Príncipe. He wanted the Europeans to stop raiding his people to supply these enterprises. The Portuguese Crown denied his request. Eventually the difficulties between these two kingdoms led to Benin closing its doors to European slaving.

The only fort built in Sénégambia was at Byhurt at the mouth of the Senegal River, but it was soon abandoned. Another settlement was attempted at Cacheo on the banks of the *Rio de São Domingo*, but it too collapsed. Fort St. Martha was built and successfully manned on the Cape Verde island of Santiago, and another at Sierra Leone, but like Byhurt, it was abandoned after a short while. Europeans found it difficult to live permanently in Guinea.

In the beginning, working class Portuguese did not want to settle too far from home, so São Tomé and Príncipe had to be settled with convicts, undesirables and Jews. People from these marginal categories established plantations using sugar cane imported from Madeira and the Canary Islands, and slaves from Benin and the Congo. Things did not go smoothly at these plantations, however. The climate was unhealthy for Europeans, and slave revolts led to a decline in the **plantation system**. Eventually, São Tomé and Príncipe became slave entrepôts.

Around 1530 things began to heat up in the waters of Guinea. While diplomatic pressures worked to some extent on overtly national voyages, many of the fleets going to Guinea were privateers and even pirates. But, even the private entrepreneurs got royal backing. For example, the French King issued a writ to French merchants giving them the right to recoup any losses at the hands of the Portuguese by retaliation against the Portuguese navy. In some ways, there was an informal state of war in Guinean waters between France and Portugal, while at the formal level, diplomats scurried to and fro.

The issue then, as it is now in much of the world, the conflict between the principle of Free Trade or Open Waters (**mare abertum**) and that of Closed Waters (**mare clausum**) or monopoly of certain seas by a given nation. And it was not a simple matter of the French blatantly intruding on a closed zone of trade, as they needed Portugal as an ally in the shifting sands of European politics. Nevertheless, the French penetration continued, as did the retaliations and the diplomatic protests.

The Portuguese-French conflict was made ever more complex by the entrance of the British on this stage, widening the breach of Portuguese monopoly. Later other European nations entered the fray as well.

The Portuguese were burdened by their expansionist efforts in Brazil, East Indies and Guinea. In West Africa their fortifications were poor, the climate inhospitable and there was a general shortage of potable water. For all intents and purposes, the Portuguese Crown conceded their monopoly in Guinea by about the middle of the 16th century. Ships began to leave the British Isles bound for West Africa around 1540. Not only were the Portuguese unhappy with this development, but the French and British were bitter rivals on other battlefields, and they could not have been happy to see British traders sailing the Guinean seas.

Many West Africans got caught between **European rivalries**. At Samma, for example, the Portuguese prevented the natives from trading with either the British or the French. In 1558, when the British traders went ashore with their goods, they were rebuffed. This angered the British, so they burnt the town to the ground.

Portugal's involvement in West Africa showed that Africa could not compete with the East Indies or the Americas in supplying legal goods. Eventually, the trade relations between Europe and Guinea were dominated by the slave trade, moving "black ivory" to Europe initially, then to the Americas once the plantation system was firmly established there.

Early Christian Missionaries

Early Christians in West Africa were there primarily to minister to Europeans in forts and those passing through on ships. Little organized effort was made at proselytizing among the natives. But the zeal to convert was never wholly absent from Portuguese efforts in *Guiné*.

Priests regarded the local people as benign pagans, and Muslims as the enemy. They courted the former and attacked the latter whenever the opportunity presented itself. This casual missionary effort, however, scored few successes on either front. In 1456 a Gambian chief converted but in general, the Christian message did not travel far beyond the walls of the fortified European settlements.

The most thriving community of Christian converts was in Warri, where a veneer of Christianity existed for more than 200 years, but few of these early conversions were sincere or seriously affected daily life in the communities.

Sometimes a sympathetic slave trader would take an African customer or his child to Europe. Some African children were sent to European schools where they came in contact with Christianity. In the 1780s there were said to be more than fifty such children in English schools. On their return these educated children normally used their linguistic skills in trade rather than proselytizing.

Portugal's Decline and Social Upheaval

After 1530 the fortunes of Portugal in West Africa began to decline. In the middle of the 16th century the Portuguese tried to reinforce its naval patrols along the Guinea Coast, but the balance of naval power was shifting toward the British. Furthermore, with the annexation of Portugal to Spain in 1580 and the subsequent domination by Spain for the next 60 years, the Portuguese heyday came to an end.

Somewhat later, in 1596, the Dutch mounted an attack on *Castelo São Jorge da Mina* intending to drive out the Portuguese. They were unsuccessful, though they would capture the castle some 40 years later in 1637. The Dutch aggression was an earnest indication of their growing power in the region. Rather than leave the area, they ingratiated themselves with the king of Saboe, neighbors to the Fante on the Mina coast. The Dutch later supported the Saboe sovereign against the Fante. In 1612 they built a fort at Mouree under the very noses of the Portuguese. In 1617 they constructed two more forts at Gorée Island (See Map 1.7), securing their rising hold on the slave trade. Decades after their intercession into the *Guiné* trade, the Dutch were probably doing more commerce than all other European nations combined. Under Spanish hegemony, Portugal could do little to stop Dutch expansion.

This was the age of the chartered company. After an early abortive start, Dutch businessmen created the West India Company in 1621. It was established by a charter that gave it a 24-year monopoly on all Holland's trade with the Americas and West Africa from the Tropic of Cancer to the Cape of Good Hope. In 1630 the company launched its career of New World conquest in Brazil. The company trafficked in slaves and secured a large quantity of gold from *Mina*. But it had competition from others within Holland, for example, the more successful *Vereenigde Oost-indische Compagnie*, or United East India Company. Some Dutch entrepreneurs also sailed under Danish or Brandenburg (Eastern Germany) flags. Another interloper was the Middelburg Commercial Company, which did a thriving business in slaving beginning in 1732. While eventually out-competed, the West India Company remained in existence till 1794.

Competition in the region was picking up. These European rivals attacked their competitors and urged their indigenous allies to wage war on other coastal kings who stood in their way. Such rivalry was straining coastal alliances and stability. As Europeans competed for the control or favor of indigenous states, they disorganized the peoples of the coastal zone. In 1694, for example, the Dutch instigated an attack by the Ahanta peoples of the eastern Mina coast on the English fort at Sekondi. For their part, the British incited war by the Commany people against the Dutch.

It is important for the reader to know that the social disruption caused by Europeans was profound. Europeans tended to exacerbate pre-existing tensions between African groups and fed fuel into the flames of their conflicts. For example, in the mid-16th century invaders from inland attacked peoples of the Windward Coast. These aggressors, called "Manes" by the Portuguese, had a reputation as ferocious combatants who were said to eat their prisoners. These attackers descended either the Mano or Moa rivers to the sea then turned northward up the coast sacking villages. Because the Portuguese profited from the carnage, they aided the Mane invaders. In fact, Portuguese ships followed them watching for burning huts in Bulom and Temne towns, to pick up the fugitives as slaves.

The Portuguese, and later other Europeans, were more than willing to profit from any conflict they encountered, even to promote it if it worked to their advantage. But what was good for foreign trade was often disruptive to the local economy. At times, the presence of the Europeans stimulated changes that seemed innocuous, but which drastically altered the lives of groups. The rough geography of the Windward Coast gave European mariners difficulty as they tried to negotiate the rough seas in small landing craft. The Kru peoples were at home in and on the tempestuous waters, were expert fishermen, swimmers and canoeists. Consequently they were hired aboard foreign bound ships as "Krumen." The Krus could easily perform such tricky work as bringing a canoe loaded with slaves through heavy surf to a waiting slave ship. They also worked on naval ships and were soon regarded as essential members of the European enterprise along the Guinea Coast. Sometimes they went to distant places to perform land-based tasks. By the end of the 18th century wherever Europeans set up shop, Kru workers were to be found.

Though some never returned home, most Krus practiced circular migration, a pattern that remains in West Africa today. A Kru would leave home as a boy and work with a gang of his people, giving his wages to an older master and protector. When he grew older he kept the wages and had apprentices working under his tutelage. Every few months he would return home with the wealth he had accumulated, build a house, take a new wife and generally prepare his place of retirement. After a number of years, he would settle down in the community with his wives and children.

On the surface, this seems benign. But in the long run, its effects were far reaching. Some men adopted European clothes. African monarchs and big men used imported chairs and tables. Some adopted the use of China and forks and knives for eating. Henry Tucker, a successful Creole (Krio) trader in Sherbroland in the mid-18th century kept a sideboard in his house with silver plate displayed in an obvious imitation of European fashion.

This influence came first from the Portuguese, but their day eventually came to an end, to be replaced by others from Europe. But the Portuguese had begun what could not be stopped—a process of acculturation that continues today. The Portuguese involved Africans in external trade linkages that set in motion unequal exchanges—raw materials from Africa for European manufactured goods—an exploitative process that also continues in present-day West Africa. The Portuguese also began the introduction of West Africans to a materialistic way of life, one where economics dominates social relations, where individual advancement is defined by possession, not by generosity. This was to have profound effects in the formation of a dual pattern to life in West Africa for the next 500 years: coastal/ urban modernity and rural/inland parochialism. The Portuguese also set in motion the tinkering Europeans would do pitting one ethnic group in the region against another. In addition to providing a new source of wealth in slaves and new means of political domination in modern firearms, the Portuguese supported the rise of some West Africans to the demise of others. Most significant of all, the Portuguese established the first contact between West Africans and the world economy, articulating them to a growing industrial leviathan. It is a connection from which West Africans have yet to recover. With the Portuguese these were nascent processes, ones to be enhanced by other Europeans to follower their lead.

CRITICAL THINKING QUESTIONS

1. Why was Portugal well positioned and suited for the exploration of the West African coast, as opposed to other European nations?
2. What was Portugal's contribution to West Africa?
3. What was the issue between the principles of *mare abertum* and that of *mare clausum* with regard to West Africa?
4. What was the effect of European rivalries on West Africa?
5. What was the impact of sugar on West Africa?
6. What was the impact of Christianity on West Africans under the Portuguese?

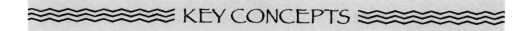

KEY CONCEPTS

Antam Gonçalves
Black Ivory
Cape Bojador
Caravel
Castelo São Jorge da Mina
Columbus, Christopher

Coste de dentes
European rivalries
Fernão Gomes
Guinea (*Guiné*)
Guinea grains
Guinea season

Grain Coast
Henrician tradition
Lançados
Malagueta Coast
Mare abertum
Mare clausum

Mina Coast
Plantation system
Prestor John
Sugar plantations
Treaty of Alcaçovas

≈ SOURCES & SUGGESTED READINGS ≈

Fage, J. D. 1995. *A history of Africa*. London: Routledge.

Funk & Wagnalls Standard encyclopedic college dictionary. 1968. New York: Funk & Wagnalls.

Fyfe, Christopher. 1969. Peoples of the Windward Coast. In: Ajayi, J. F. Ade and Ian Espie (eds.). *A thousand years of West African history*. Ibadan: Ibadan University Press, 149–164.

Kasule, Samuel. 1998. *The history atlas of Africa*. New York: Macmillan.

Mahoney, F. and H. O. Idowu. 1969. The peoples of Sénégambia. In: Ajayi, J. F. Ade and Ian Espie (eds.). *A thousand years of West African history*. Ibadan: Ibadan University Press, 132–148.

Oliveira Martins, J. P. 1914. *The golden age of Prince Henry the Navigator*. Trans. with additions and annotations, by Jas. Johnston Abraham and Wm. Edward Reynolds. London: Chapman and Hall, Ltd.

Ryder, A. F. C. 1965. Portuguese and Dutch in West Africa before 1800. In: Ajayi, J. F. Ade and Ian Espie (eds.). *A thousand years of West African history*. Ibadan: Ibadan University Press, 217–236.

Saul, Mahir. 1995. In: Martin, Phyllis M. & Patrick O'Meara (eds.). *Africa* (Third edition). Bloomington: Indiana University Press, 190–210.

Sanceau, Elaine. 1944. *The land of Prester John, a chronicle of Portuguese exploration*. New York: Knopf.

Wilks, Ivor. 1982. Wangara, Akan and Portuguese in fifteenth and sixteenth centuries. I. The Matter of Bitu. *Journal of African history* 23:333–49.

Zurara, Gomes Eanes de. 1963. *The chronicle of the discovery and conquest of Guinea*. Trans. Charles Raymond Beazley and Edgar Prestage. New York: B. Franklin.

11 SLAVERY IN WEST AFRICA

"I herded them as if they had been cattle towards the boats."

Diogo Gomes
c. 1460
On the river Gambia, West Africa

> This chapter focuses on the crimes against humanity perpetrated by Europeans who formulated the triangular system of Atlantic Slave Trade exchanging manufactured goods for human beings in order to produce crops on New World plantations. Slaving was not direct, but required the participation of Africans who did most of the raiding, then traded their captives to Europeans who transported the enslaved unfortunates to the Americas on ships—the infamous "middle passage." This chattel slavery contrasted with domestic slavery as practiced traditionally in Africa and with the Trans-Saharan slave trade, if only in magnitude. Many Africans on the coast raided less powerful peoples of the interior using firearms purchased from Europeans. Those set upon by slavers fled or resisted and the result was many decades of bloodshed, warfare and chaos (See Photo 11.1). This turbulent period of West African history is one of social disruption based on an intrusive political economy of extraction that eventually led to anti-slavery movements both in West Africa and Europe. In spite of this, both the political economy of extraction and slavery continue today in the region and many of the problems of governance and lack of development in West Africa can be linked to the social disturbances resulting from this criminal period in her history.

Why Did West Africans Go Along with the Slave Trade?

Today the commonly held view of slaving in Africa is that Europeans with guns swept into the innards of the continent and physically captured people, chained them together and marched them to the coast, loaded them on ships and sailed for the Americas.

This direct procurement of slaves was tried, but given up after the first years of contact for the easier method of bartering with coastal peoples for slaves. Thus, West

Photo 11.1 Nineteenth Century Drawing of Slavers (from Denham, Clapperton & Oudney).

Africans were instrumental in the slave trade. Why would they do this? Why would they sell their own?

The answer is that "their own" as perceived by Europeans and "their own" as perceived by West Africans were two different things. **Domestic slavery** was a common practice long before Europeans arrived. Kings, chiefs and big men had long held slaves, even selling them into the **Trans-Saharan Slave Trade** along which they were taken to the Mediterranean and Middle East (See Maps 1.4 & 9.2).

It was common to hold, sell or barter slaves as any other commodity. They could be given as gifts, as one would give a field of yams, or a bushel of millet. Indeed, when the Europeans first arrived in West Africa, they were often given slaves as gifts, and also bartered for them. When the English captain John Hawkins helped a Sierra Leonean king in battle, he was given war prisoners as slaves.

People who could not pay their debts were sold into slavery till the debt was paid off. Among the Yoruba these indentured servants or pawns were referred to as *Iwofa*, and among the Asante they were called *Awowa*. Such people sometimes became absorbed into the families to which they were attached, or their children might become free. Criminals, witches and people who were generally not liked for one reason or another, the undesirables, were enslaved.

Slaves in West Africa were not without rights, though they did lack certain ritual rights that set them apart from freeborn people. Slaves could bring evidence in court against a master, change masters if they could prove need, or sometimes they could even inherit the property of a childless man.

Indeed a slave with initiative could rise out of servitude to lead nations, as was the case with several famous slaves who became wealthy traders and even kings.

The slave in West Africa had two main deficiencies that prevented him or her from becoming a full person. First, s/he was not free to come and go at will. S/he could be bought, sold, traded, lent and in some states, such as Asante, killed in rituals or for large national celebrations. Some slaves of wealthy men were killed upon his death to accompany him to the next life and serve him there.

Secondly, and more importantly from a West African perspective, the slave lacked the full rights of a person because s/he could not sacrifice to his or her ancestors, and upon death, the slave was usually not given a normal funeral. Sometimes their bodies were merely thrown on the trash heap, at other times they were discarded in a river. Early European visitors to **Kumase** reported that executed slaves were unceremoniously dumped in a heap, which set up a malodorous stench.

What were lacking at the death of a slave were the ceremonies where the living soul is transformed into an ancestral spirit. Then and only then could the person have a chance to achieve eternal life. With this ritual performance, a freeborn West African could life forever if his or her descendants called out his or her name at periodic ancestral sacrifices. A slave lacked this capacity.

Domestic slaves sometimes ran away, but life without any connection to a home village or ancestral shrines was usually less attractive than staying with a master. The British were always astonished when freed Asante slaves returned voluntarily to their masters.

Domestic slaves had substantial latitude within the framework of their status. For example, a villager in Ghana once told me that when he was a boy his father owned a slave. The slave would take all the young boys of the family to the farm, and acted as the straw boss over them. They didn't like the man because he was cruel to them, even taking a cane to them at times.

Muslims justified taking pagan or infidel slaves in a holy war (*jihad*) if the intent was to eventually teach them the ways of Allah. Sometimes this became a blanket justification for wars of conquest. Nevertheless, for devout Muslims, **manumission** of slaves was seen as a duty, one thought to bring special rewards in paradise.

Slaves were an integral part of the political economy of the great forest states of Oyo, Dahomey and Asante. King Glele of Dahomey put the people of Ketu to work on his plantations. In Asante the ***Asantehene***, royals and most big men held slaves who worked to clear the forest, farm, mine gold and to perform domestic labor.

With the arrival of the Europeans, the practice of slavery was fundamentally changed. **Chattel slavery** became the order of the day. Furthermore, the demand for slaves skyrocketed. West African big men, chiefs and kings were under pressure to sell slaves because Europeans wanted them, and were willing to pay. Furthermore, the Europeans would withhold their desired manufactured goods till they got what they wanted in return. Increasingly this was slave.

Firearms and Slave Raiding

Trade increasingly involved a "slaves for guns swap." The first kingdoms to get guns were on the coast or in the immediate hinterland. Having greater firepower, they could then subdue nearby groups, taking slaves in war or setting tribute demands in slaves.

This monopoly on **firearms** was short-lived, however. Eventually every group acquired guns.

This new and enormous demand for slaves began to damage democratic institutions in West Africa. The "guns for slaves" swaps corrupted African institutions converting some states into pariahs. The disease of materialism had come to the region.

Along with the slave trade came the importation of firearms. West Africans could not manufacture muskets. To get guns West Africans had to trade with the Europeans and the latter wanted slaves in return.

While the Portuguese had initially and cautiously tried to keep guns from West Africans, the competition between Europeans for the region's trade led to a breakdown in this rule. Once one kingdom had them, others had to procure guns as well, and the arms race was on. In fact, the means of destruction was also a means of production, because guns could be used to capture people who provided labor, which has always been in short supply in West Africa. Furthermore, such captives could be traded to the Europeans for other manufactured goods such as iron bars which blacksmiths made into hoes to be used in farming.

Firearms also spurred the rise of militarism in West Africa, or at least changed its face. By the 18th century about 200,000 muskets a year were pouring into the region—so many that small tribes in the extreme hinterlands of the Asante were said to be able to get thousands, limited only by the expense involved. The region was awash in guns.

Given the fact that royalty could afford and access arms easier than commoners, and that they had the economic wherewithal to maintain them, train musketeers, supply them with shot and powder—the introduction of these firearms enhanced the power of state leaders. In fact, like horses, they became a symbol of manhood and political power.

For the Europeans guns were a good news/bad news item. On the one hand, they helped the West African kings to get the slaves they needed to trade for other manufactured goods; on the other hand, guns gave Africans the power to resist European domination, as seen with the defeat of the British by the Asante armies. Because the Europeans competed with another they could not agree on an arms sales moratorium. If one country held back, the West Africans could always buy them from a European rival.

Slavery Methods in West Africa

On their first visits to *Guiné* **direct capture** of slaves did not work well because the Europeans could not penetrate very far inland. They were limited at first to extracting slaves from the coastal region, thereby alienating the very people they depended on for other trade goods. In time they resorted to a system of barter with these same coastal traders who began to supply them with unfortunates from their own societies, and captives taken from the hinterland.

One common trick used by early European slave traders was to make friends with a chief and eventually invite him and his "brothers" on board for a feast. When all had been ferried out to the ship, they were seized, placed in the hold, and the ship sailed back to Europe. Of course this only worked once or twice in a given port. (Sometimes the tables were turned. In 1475 a Spanish vessel sailed to *Guiné*. When they tried to take slaves, the West Africans turned on them and the whites were captured and eaten, according to Spanish reports.)

In 1458 the Portuguese Crown sent Diogo Gomes to West Africa to assure the Guinea kings that henceforth this practice would stop, and that they would instead barter for slaves. Presumably Gomes delivered the Crown's message, but he was out of his sovereign's sight, as he noted in his journal:

> ... twenty-two people who were sleeping, I herded them as if they had been cat-
> tle towards the boats. And we all did the same, and we captured on that day...
> nearly 650 people, and we went back to Portugal...

This was a time for freebooting and brigandry. The sovereign tried to keep control of the burgeoning trade in *Guiné*, but what transpired far from Lisbon was either not known, or uncontrollable. Nonetheless, the Crown was now buying slaves from coastal peoples in increasing numbers. Haphazard slave raiding gave way to systematic development of the trade. The purchased slaves were transported to Arguin Island then on to Iberia. By 1455, it is estimated that about a thousand a year passed through that island depot.

West Africans, royals and New Men, or entrepreneurs,[1] quickly realized that in addition to ostrich feathers and peppers, these white men wanted laborers, too. The kings established royal license control on the trade; the New Men of the **Slave Coast** and **Niger Delta** (See Map 9.6 & 10.1) formed trade associations to set the regulations.

At first the Portuguese used slaves in their own country, but soon they were selling them in Spain as well. There was some public sentiment against selling slaves to foreigners. Blacks had been put to work draining swamps in Portugal, thus making more productive land available to rich landowners. They were also working on the Island sugar plantations of the coast of Upper Guinea. But since the Crown was making huge profits, sales continued. In 1466, a traveler to the region noted that the Portuguese king was making more money by selling slaves to foreigners "than from all the taxes levied on the entire kingdom."

By 1473 a law was passed in Lisbon that all slaves had to be brought first to that city. After 1481, all ships setting off for West Africa were required to register with the *Casa dos Escravos*, the House of Slaves in the Portuguese capital. A royal official was named the "receiver of all Moors and Mooresses and whatever other things which, God willing, may come to us from our trade in Guinea."

At various times West Africans resisted the intrusion of Europeans in their world, but no matter what they did, the white men kept coming. At first these foreigners traded from their ships or came ashore for brief bartering sessions. Eventually, however, they built 41 trading castles (See Map 10.1). By the 17th century they had firmly established a strong presence along the coast of Upper and Lower Guinea, and expanded this even further in the 18th century.

One of the driving forces in the slave trade was the Dutch entry into the commercial mix. The **Dutch East India Company** occupied the forts of Elmina (*Castelo São Jorge da Mina*), Gold Coast Castle, Axim, Samma and others. From Senegal to the Congo, the Dutch (and others) traded in human beings from the mid-17th century through

---

1. Some of these New Men or entrepreneurs were so-called **Brasileiros** or slaves captured at sea or returned from the New World to Africa.

the middle of the 19th. During this time there was a ten-fold increase in slave trafficking and the Europeans scurried to secure a foothold in this lucrative commerce.

In general, the Portuguese controlled the trade south of the equator, while the Dutch held the forts on the Guinea coast to the north. But this did not last long. Dutch success attracted competitors. Seeing the lucrative nature of the slave trade in areas they had been expelled from, the Portuguese again began to sail the waters off the Mina and Slave Coasts. In so doing they not only had to compete with the well-entrenched Dutch, but with France, Britain, Sweden, Denmark and Brandenburg (Prussia), as well.

In the beginning this competition existed all up and down the coast, but its focus was on *Mina*, which had the advantage of having quantities of both slaves and gold. Nevertheless, as the New World demand for slaves increased dramatically by the mid-17th century, Europeans turned their attention to the Slave Coast from Accra to Lagos (See Map 10.1). This was a sandy area, often filled with mangrove swamps, so it was difficult for European power to build forts. This made diplomacy all the more important in dealing with the indigenous middlemen.

Most of the bartering was done from the hulks or from temporarily moored ships, though some Europeans did establish inland bases. Some West Africans were wary of these bases. The Aja kings, for example, required that such edifices be built directly next to their palaces so that they could keep an eye on the wily white men. Because Europeans could trade only with the blessing of the West African kings, they were forced to recognize African sovereignty in all transactions. They had to pay rent and customs duties to the royals.

Slaving and the States of the Niger Delta

The Delta States grew prosperous from the Atlantic Slave Trade because of their strategic geographical positioning at the mouth of the rivers connecting the coast with a densely populated hinterland. It was a perfect setting for the sea-states—the Europeans were increasingly demanding slaves, and the Igbo (formerly Ibo) were in between the white traders and what they wanted—weaker people of the hinterlands.

Wisely, coastal kings established firm rules which prevented the Europeans from coming ashore on a permanent basis. They also prevented the sea captains from sailing up the rivers in an effort to cut out the middlemen.

This well organized system of raiding and trading had regulations enforced by commercial associations such as the **Ekpe Trading Association**. If the Europeans misbehaved, the Ekpe would close the river mouths and refuse to do business till the disorderly conduct ceased.

The Ekpe was not the only innovation in the coastal zone. As there was much competition for the European trade, descent groups tended to give way to wards, each with a New Man at the head, and each competing with the other wards. Such a new system replaced traditional status with position based on achievement. Social mobility became the order of the day.

In this highly volatile ambiance, even some slaves rose to great heights. **Jaja** was an Igbo slave in Bonny (See Map 10.1) who rose to the headmanship of a ward. When he ran afoul of others, he established a similar organization as the Delta State of Opobo and took away much of Bonny's trade. Such was the free-for-all frontier attitude of the

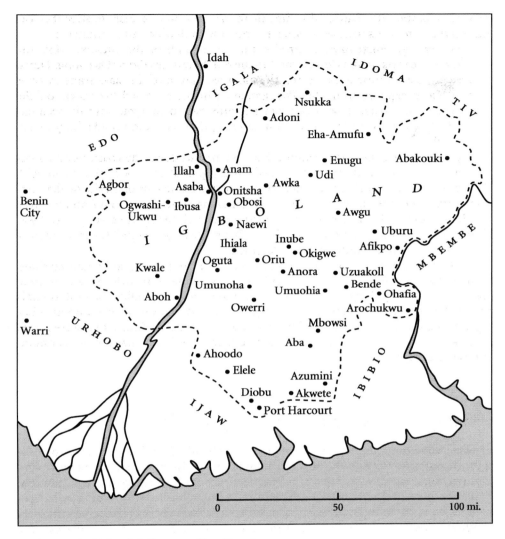

Map 11.1   Igboland & Surrounding Peoples.

times where yams or people were traded with equal avarice based on individual effort and competitive acumen in the art of commerce.

These Niger Delta states had trading relations with another Igbo people who called themselves Aro (by other Igbo they were known as *Umu-Chuku*, "children of God"). They had established a powerful oracle in their main town of Arochukwu. Partially because of the supposed power of this oracle, they were able to recruit mercenaries and penetrate the rest of Igboland, and to establish outposts and trading networks that enabled them to extract many Igbo slaves. They sold them to the coastal states, which in turn sold them to the traders (See Map 11.1).

The largest Delta State was Bonny where 20,000 slaves a year passed on their fateful journey to the New World. Davidson estimates that 16,000 of those were Igbos, so it can easily be computed that very many African-Americans and residents of Brazil and the Caribbean can trace their ancestry back to Eastern Nigeria.

Slaving and the Interior States

Just as the demand for slaves had a stimulating effect on the rise of states along the coast, it generated or magnified some of those in the interior, especially by increasing opportunity for wealth accumulation and access to guns.

About 1660 the **Denkyira** people established a political hegemony by engaging in trade with Europeans through coastal brokers. At first they expanded northwards along the old trade routes to Banda and Bono, then they turned south and tried to establish direct contact with Europeans, thereby bypassing the southerly neighbors. By 1700 they controlled all of the Western Gold Coast.

Theirs was a lucrative trade. They brought slaves, gold and other forest products from the north and exchanged them for guns, manufactured goods and salt. But they were not alone. A splinter group of Akan had established themselves about 40 miles north of Accra and established the kingdom of Akwamu. They also traveled to the coast to deal directly with the European traders. In 1681 they conquered Accra and began to expand eastwards. By 1702 they controlled the whole eastern seaboard to Whydah (See Map 9.6).

The aggressive expansion southwards of the kingdoms of Denkyira and Akwamu were the direct result of the influence of the world system[2] on the Guinea coast. Expanding trade opportunities spurred Akan aggrandizers to seek more gold, slaves and trade goods and to do so through military means.

Conflict continued between Denkyira and Akwamu. This gave rise to another splinter group that moved north in the 17th century to form small states on the northerly edge of the great rain forest that stretches across the hinterland of the coastal plain of West Africa. These people followed another of the ancient north-south trade routes, expanding trade as they went. They built alliances with the northern traders to the north, and with the Denkyira to the south, paying tribute to the latter.

Under increasing stimulation of raiding and trading, these northerly states began to centralize around the *Kumasehene*, the King of Kumase. Eventually this office evolved into the *Asantehene*, the King of the Asante. The Asante became the most powerful Empire in West Africa: at its height in the 19th century, it ruled over 3 million subjects. By the time they were conquered by the British, the *Asantehene* could expect tributary payments from 40 neighboring kingdoms, and the Europeans had to pay him rent and customs duties to live and trade along the coast to the south of the Asante heartland.

Expansion of the Atlantic Slave Trade

Slaving in Guinea had started slowly, with a relatively small number of ships taking slaves back to Iberia or Madeira and the Canary Islands. Some ships bought slaves in one area of Guinea and traded them in another.

Slaves were also kept on board and at the forts and castles that were eventually built along the Mina Coast (See Map 10.1), working blacksmitheries, carpenters' shops, and kitchens. Some were simply placed in the brig to await further consignment. But all

---

2. There are historians and theorists who note that after 1500 out of Europe there developed a relatively unified world wide economic system that began to penetrate every corner of the earth.

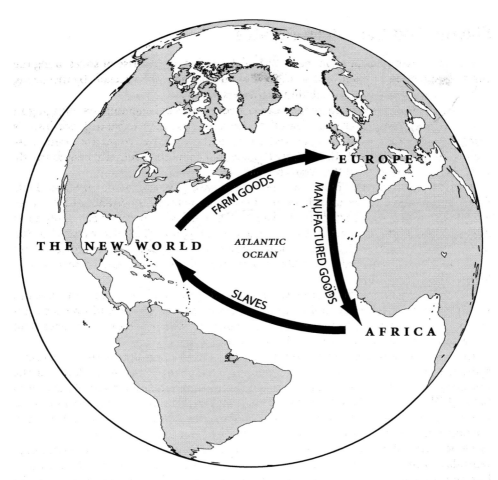

Map 11.2   The Atlantic or Triangular Slave Trade.

told, the impact of slaving remained quite small till Christopher Columbus made his historic voyages, and set in motion a new dynamic in the world system.

As settler demand for cheap labor in the New World rose with the inability to use local Amerindians as workers because of their susceptibility to European diseases, entrepreneurs turned to Africa for black slaves. Such were thought to be adapted to the tropical climate of Brazil and the West Indies.

In 1515 the first shipment of sugar left the Americas for Europe. It was, in hindsight, an ominous beginning of a sad chapter in European exploitation. In 1518 the first slaves were shipped directly from West Africa to the West Indies, launching the **Triangular Slave Trade** (See Map 11.2). This was a circular system of shipping and trade. Ships would leave Europe laden with manufactured goods and other items desired by West Africans such as spirits and iron bars. Upon arriving in West Africa, the sea captains would bargain away such items in return for slaves, which were carried to the Americas. There, after offloading the slaves, they would take on sugar, coffee, molasses, tobacco and other such goods and then would return to Europe to begin the cycle again. After this beginning, there was nothing but growth in the slave trade. The rapid increase in the Triangular Trade helped build the industrial and technical progress of Western Europe in the 18th and 19th centuries, with Britain and France benefiting most.

How many slaves were forced to go to the Americas? Scholars are still debating this, but the figure seems to be somewhere between ten and 15 million. These figures, however, refer to those who actually landed in the New World. Many more died *en route*, others were killed at the point of attack, or died in chains while being brought from their homes to the coast, or in the cells and stockades of the European forts while waiting passage to their new fate.

Of course, slavery had been common in the trans-Saharan trade, the Nile River network and the maritime commerce in the Indian Ocean. But the total number of slaves extracted from the African continent by such avenues was relatively small when compared to the massive relocation forced in the Atlantic Slave Trade. Scholars have estimated that only about a 1,000 slaves a year were sent across the Sahara from West Africa, while at the height of the Atlantic Slave Trade, 20,000 slaves a year passed through the Coastal State of Bonny alone.

Resistance to the Slave Trade

Though West Africans were used to domestic slavery and had sold slaves to Mediterranean bound caravans, and though slaves were taken in war and sold at will, there was resistance by some to the excessive slaving of the last three centuries before the colonial era. Some kings wrote letters to European monarchs protesting the practice. The *Almany* (King) of Futa Toro in Senegal not only would not permit slaving in his land, he issued an edict prohibiting slave caravans passing through his territory.

The French were used to sailing up the Senegal River to get such slaves. They tried giving the *Almany* gifts, which he promptly returned. They tried negotiating with him, but he refused to listen. To him slaving was wrong, and that was that. Finally the French had to send word to the hinterland slavers to meet them at a different spot, and the evil trade bypassed the land of the high-minded King of Futa Toro.

Not only did some West Africa kings object to slaving, but also local people resisted slavers with all their might. In Northern Ghana they fought back with bows and poison-tipped arrows, they built walls around their towns, and some took to the hills to build forts from which to fight the slavers. In West African cities such as Kano in Northern Nigeria, elaborate precautions were taken. This important city had a mud wall 50 feet high and 40 feet thick, with two defensive ditches as well, enclosing an urban area half the size of Manhattan.

Even in the Forts the Europeans were not safe from the anger of West Africans. For example, in 1693 the Danish Christianborg Castle in Accra was seized and held till the Danes paid a large ransom in gold to the King of Akwamu to get the captives released.

Once captured, many slaves tried to escape, hence the need for chains and shackles (See Photo 11.2). Even on board, slave revolts were not unheard of, the most famous success being the revolt aboard the Amistad. Even after being put to work on the plantations, slaves had to be constantly watched, and European settlers took special pains to prevent them from communicating in ways that might lead to revolt.

Some were able to escape and formed free communities in the New World, some even made it back to Africa.

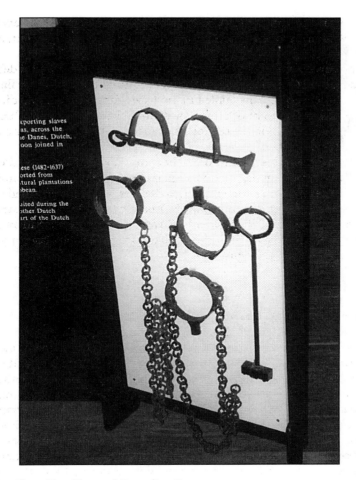

Photo 11.2 Slave Shackles and Branding Iron.

Such isolated resistance was futile, after all. The world system depended on slaving at that time, and if slaving was to stop, the system that generated it would have to change; plus, there were a few West African élites who were getting very wealthy off the trade themselves. But that change was to come later, after millions of people were captured and ripped out of their normal lives.

There were slave revolts against both European masters, as on the Portuguese plantations of São Tomé and Príncipe; or against West African masters e.g., the Koranko slave revolt in 1838 against the Susu of Sierra Leone spearheaded by Bilale. The Koranko even built a fortified town where ex-slaves could find sanctuary.

Sometimes the "revolt" was milder e.g., when in Calabar (See Map 10.1) the slaves united in an association called the **Blood Men**, and forced the freeborn to respect their human rights. Even once captured and taken to Europe, slaves resisted and revolted, but they also organized themselves e.g., there was the **Brotherhood of the Virgin of the Rosary**, a specifically black community that existed in Lisbon by 1460.

However, not all the activities of those early slaves in Portugal were so integrated with the Portuguese mores. For instance, in 1461, the parliamentary representatives from the city of Santarém in the *Cortes* (the Portuguese parliament) complained that,

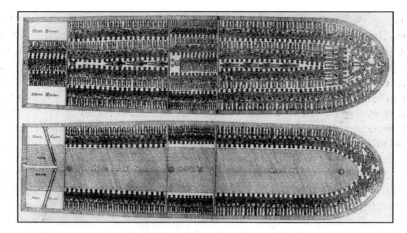

Figure 11.1   Slaves Packed in Ship's Hold for the Terrible Middle Passage.

to serve the feasts that the slaves of Santarém organized, some chickens, ducks and even lambs had been stolen. It was also indicated that these slaves used the cover of such "religious" festivals, celebrating Sunday or saints, to hatch escape plans. So the *Cortes* forbade the West Africans to hold such parties.

The Consequences of the Slave Trade in West Africa

The consequences of this Triangular Slave Trade for Europe were great. This trade went a long way towards securing its wealth and dominant position in the world system. For West Africa it was disastrous. Only a few West Africans benefited, mainly those at the top of the political structure and wealthy traders.

The triangular system stimulated the formation of social classes in West Africa. By trafficking in slaves, the powerful got more powerful and the wealthy got even richer. The weak, poor, defenseless, those without guns, armies or states to defend themselves suffered unspeakable horrors. Those who were enslaved were beaten, chained together, shackled, whipped, branded, stripped naked, pushed into airless under-decks and crushed together in the most inhuman conditions.

It is estimated that one of every six slaves died on the infamous "**middle passage**" to the Americas. Between 10 and 15 million arrived in the New World, though many more were killed in battles and died in the voyage over (See Figure 11.1).

Such decimation of the population of West Africa, especially since it was the strong men and women being taken away, drained off labor, and severely crippled the economy of the region. The labor of the slaves made the European plantation owners wealthy, while West African wealth was depleted.

By retarding West Africa and advancing Europe, slaving created a situation where West Africans became economic subalterns and Europeans could eventually become their colonial masters. The superior-inferior relation created by unequal trade paved the way for imperialism at a later stage.

But not all of West Africa was retarded by the slave trade. From the Gold Coast to the Niger Delta the coast became dotted with small city-states, and even interior peoples like the Fon were energized by the expansion of trade and the slave raids on their people. Further centralization was an effort to defend themselves. Those who lived along the coast were in what Basil Davidson called the "frontier of opportunity." These peoples were situated to benefit from the comings and goings of European ships. They had first chance at the incoming goods at the best prices and they could profit by selling those goods in the interior. This was the zone of the "New Men" who became fabulously wealthy, some even controlling the traditional rulers with their wealth and power.

Around 1650, the best known of these seaside states were Whydah (Ouidah or Fida), Jakin, Grand Popo and Great Ardrah (Allada) (See Maps 9.6 & 10.1). Later versions of such city-states were Badagry and Ajase (Porto Novo). The political patrimonies of such states grew large because of their middleman status and the increased volume of goods, especially slaves, flowing through their territories.

Whydah kings had royal agents who were instructed to bargain with the white seamerchants when they arrived. They also made the Europeans pay taxes and customs fees. Furthermore, they made profits by selling food and water to provision the ships for the next leg of their journey. They even had to take steps to prevent bickering and fighting between European rivals, dealing with each separately.

This was not an insignificant trade in human beings. French, British, Portuguese and Dutch ships arrived at Whydah alone in numbers between 40–50 ships per year. As the volume of slaving grew, and as more guns poured into the region, the violence between such states grew concomitantly. Strong states raided weaker ones, often demanding tribute from them in slaves.

Both Whydah and Ardrah raided weaker peoples in the hinterland. One such group was the Fon. As they lived in open country, they were especially susceptible to cavalry attacks. This slave raiding and warfare led them to centralize around a supreme king, and to organize both male and female military regiments. These "Amazons," as the Europeans dubbed them, caught the imagination of the Victorian World. They were portrayed as especially fierce in battle and adept at hand-to-hand combat. Later in West African history, more than one French soldier had his nose bitten off while trying to kill his female opponent.

The **Fon Kingdom** eventually became known as Dahomey. Dire times in their kingdom called for autocratic rule. About 1650 King Wegbaja became elevated to a high office thought to be the very soul of his people. King Akaba followed him in 1685, then by the strong King Agaja who ruled from 1708–1740.

Although the Fon still paid tribute to Oyo, they organized and moved southwards conquering the coastal states. King Agaja wanted to end their slave raids in his land, but he also wanted to cut out the middlemen in the lucrative commerce of the day. Furthermore, Agaja wanted more and cheaper guns, shot and powder. This was to expand his power, defend himself against Oyo and other enemies; but he also had to pay annual tribute in guns to the Emperor of Oyo.

Dahomey continued to grow in strength, sacking and conquering Great Ardrah in 1725, Savi and Whydah in 1728 and Jakin in 1732. Whydah was a popular trading depot for Europeans and they helped the Whydah fight back, but Dahomey prevailed and came to control the entire coast by 1740. Whydah became a colony with a resident governor from Dahomey called the *yevogan*, who did all the dealing with seatraders.

There followed a series of kings between 1740 and 1797 when rivalries within Dahomey led to civil war. Finally King Gezo (ruled 1818–1858) regained control and took Grand Popo and Little Popo to extend Dahomean hegemony.

Although slaving affected different parts of West Africa in various ways, J. D. Fage makes three generalizations about its impact on the region. First, was a constraint on population growth. Second, it was through the enormous trade in slaves and the goods paid for them that most West Africans gained contact with the rapid changes occurring in the industrialized world at that time.

Third, slaving was a major force for change in African society. It created new polities on the coast, changed the face of whole political systems in the interior, expanded and entrenched a broad network of trade routes inter-linking the region and it introduced the gun to the region.

On the coast entrepreneurs flourished in the wake of European demand for goods and slaves. As the volume of trade increased over time, these merchant princes increased their power and became stratified into a class of urban élites. They did not use European guns to extract wealth from their people, they used commercial acumen. From atop the newly created class structure these "New Men" accumulated a spectacular political patrimony.

While the traders, royals and entrepreneurs of these coastal states benefited economically from the trade in human beings, the less organized people of the interior suffered greatly. For example, Samori Touré obtained his human capital by raiding over a vast area, capturing villages and towns and slaughtering old people and babies. As Freestone has chronicled, when the Europeans followed in his wake, this is an example of what they encountered:

> Ellis took his column over the narrow Woa river and, seven miles from Kommendi, marched into a nightmare: the ruins of Tekwiama.
>
> This had once been a fairly big town of between three and four thousand people. Ellis and his men found it a stinking horror.
>
> Human remains were lying about on all sides and the stench was intolerable. In one place they counted forty headless corpses with hands and feet tied together showing they had been bound prisoners when they had been slaughtered. 'I saw a great number of bodies of little babies and children too young to walk and who were of no use to the *Sofas* to sell as slaves,' Ellis wrote.
>
> (The European) Gwynn was sickened. 'The place was a veritable city of the dead. Not a house possessed a roof, and the only living creatures were the birds which were hovering over their carrion.'....

There was nothing they could do to help, and so they moved on, deeper into the festering belt of slaving induced misery, a swathe of desolation thirty-one miles wide. The British thought they were hardened to the cruelty of the slavers, but they found how wrong they were at Kayima. Ellis, in his report wrote:

> Here a spectacle met the eyes of which exceeded anything yet seen. On the left-hand side entering the gate in the stockade was a pile of corpses from seven to eight feet high. Lower ones were probably some weeks old but those on top were quite recent. In an examination, necessarily brief because of the horrible effluvium, I counted on the surface of the heap of bodies of twenty-seven women, children and infants, and the heap itself must have contained at least one hundred corpses.

One of the guides informed me that these were Mende and Kono captives whom the *Sofas* had slain, and that he had been present there a short time before when one of his father's wives had been slaughtered with her two children. At the exit of the camp more corpses were met with.

The stench of decomposition was something awful,' he said. 'The vicinity of the camp was strewn with headless corpses, chiefly those of women and children and young people, although the bodies of some men were seen with their hands still tied behind their backs.' With a terrible sense of despair, the column marched on.

We must never forget that however great was the misery aboard ship for captured slaves, and no matter what degradations were endured by the slaves who reached the new world, terrible atrocities lay behind their capture. They reached the coastal slave ships along a trail of blood.

This can be considered a form of internal imperialism. As Lance has pointed out, African responses to what he called "internal colonialism" were very much like those of the European brand. Some fought back, others joined in, yet others tried to negotiate their way through the morass. Both kinds of imperialism represented massive destruction to the autonomy and peace of African communities. And both also presented aggrandizing Africans with poleconomic opportunities unheard of before the advent of modern large-scale warfare.

Not only was there terrible destruction of village life, but slaves were mistreated in the market. In Northern Ghana, Benedict Der reports about the slave entrepôt **Salaga** (See Map 9.6):

Visitors to Salaga gave horrifying accounts of the treatment of slaves. The slaves were sold in the open in the slave section of the market. They were usually chained together in groups of ten to fifteen by the neck, and exposed the whole day from morning till evening in the burning sun. They were left hungry and thirsty, naked, ailing, often sick and weak and were kept standing in that condition till one after the other had been sold. The slaves were obviously poorly fed. Mothers were torn from their children and sold. Young children were likewise taken from their mothers and sold to different buyers. The old, weak and sick had much to endure, since it took some time before they were sold. This meant enduring hardships such as beating, whipping or other ill-treatment. The worst part of it all was that they had no idea of what their fate would be: whether they would fall into more cruel hands, or whether they would be sold again and again until they fell into the hands of benign buyers.

As the slaves were too closely chained together, exposed to the piercing sun, poorly fed or otherwise neglected, many naturally died under this cruel treatment. Some succumbed to sickness and other diseases. After their sale, the slaves were made to trek the long distances to Asanteland and in the eighteenth and early nineteenth centuries finally to the European forts and castles for export to the New World. In the long marches to the coast, the sick were unchained from their companions, mercilessly thrown aside and left to fend for themselves until they either recovered or died.

The Abolition of the Slave Trade

The abolition of the slave trade was one of the three major events affecting West African society in the 19th century, the other two being the Islamic revolutions of the Western Sudan and the partitioning of Africa by the Europeans.

No one can deny that the slave trade was driven by a powerful political economy in the world system. That had begun when the Portuguese Crown became involved in the procurement and processing of slaves, the royals taking their cut in return for the issuance of charters and monopolistic rights to certain individuals and companies. Other countries entered this political economy at various times, and likewise, they exited from the system at different times, depending on their economic needs and how those needs were played out in their national politics.

While some Scandinavian countries had moved to abolish the slave trade earlier, it was not until Britain abolished such trafficking in Britain in 1807, and in its outlying territories in 1833, that slaving in West Africa came under intense international scrutiny.

The world system of capitalism at the time was being driven by the industrialization of Britain and the trading done by the industrializing countries. Much of this involved the triangular Atlantic Slave Trade, moving slaves, sugar, tobacco and other items between Europe, Africa and the New World. Sugar and slave barons who obviously wanted it to continue drove this trade by the decisions they made and their influence on the political decision-making process.

But times were changing. In the last quarter of the 18th century several events transpired to affect the thinking about enslavement of human beings. A new concern arose for the welfare of humankind, a new spirit of humanism. There was also a revival of evangelical concern with the consequences of slavery associated with Methodism in the Christian church. "**Otherizing**" (See conclusion below) was coming into question by both atheists and religionists.

In addition, the French and American revolutions had created a new air of liberalism, espousing the principles of equality, liberty and the brotherhood of humankind.

There arose in the United Kingdom a group known as the Abolitionists. In 1772 Granville Sharp obtained a writ in the courts making slavery in England illegal. He won the case, establishing the principle that any slave would become free upon reaching British soil.

Five years later, he and others formed The Society for the Abolition of the Slave Trade with William Wilberforce. While Thomas Clarkson gathered the facts and stories of brutality to arouse public opposition, persistent campaigning by abolitionists through clergymen's sermons, newspapers, pamphlets, and books, led to an Act of Parliament 1807 making it illegal for British ships to carry slaves or for the British colonies to import them. Finally the Abolition Act 1833 provided for the freeing of all slaves in British colonies and for their owners to be compensated.

Nevertheless, the evil commerce continued, other nations rushing in to fill the void left by Britain's departure, including the United States, the last country to stop slaving.

Between 1833 and 1861 a British Anti-Slavery Naval Squadron was stationed in the waters off West Africa. Their charge was to stop all slave ships, seize their cargoes and release the slaves in Sierra Leone. A bevy of missionaries were stationed there to introduce these newcomers to the ideas of Christianity.

At the level of ideology, Christians claimed to be doing this for the good of humankind. There were other motives, however, behind Britain's moral stance. At that time, she was a century ahead of France and the United States, being the only truly industrialized nation at that time. She needed three things from West Africa—palm oil to lessen her dependence on the United States where she was getting her industrial lubricants; land to grow cotton for her textile mills; and a market for her cheap manufactured goods.

The French, Americans and Portuguese did not need palm oil or cotton, and had fewer goods to sell in West Africa. They were making their profits on the Triangular Trade. They loudly accused the British of hypocrisy in furthering their economic interests under the mask of humanitarianism.

Indeed, the British hoped that the missionaries in Sierra Leone could produce a generation of educated entrepreneurs that would take up cotton production. Although the West African kings had adequately organized the palm oil trade, they had not taken to cotton production. The idea was that the Christianized West Africans would become commercial partners with the British. They hoped that the educated and religious West Africans would run British operations in the region, supervising the growing, collecting and preparation of raw cotton for the British mills back home.

The French, Americans and Portuguese continued to traffic in slaves, while the British tried bullying and bribery to stop them. The United States and France consented on paper, but in practice went right on with the slaving. After taking bribes, the Portuguese and Spanish Crowns allowed the British to search their ships, but they failed to stop slave running.

One disadvantage for the West Africans taken aboard ship as slaves was the habit of the captains of such ships to throw their human cargoes overboard if a British Naval Vessel approached. This led to the passage of the "**equipment clause,**" which stated that if the British boarded a ship that had slave-carrying equipment, they had the right to seize the vessel.

The United States was not easily bullied away from slaving, so Britain used their strongarm tactics on the weaker Spanish and Portuguese nations. British squadrons began seizing their ships illegally, compelling the two countries to sign treaties in the 1840s.

Again, these were paper agreements. What actually happened was that many non-American crews began to sail slave ships registered in Brazil or the United States. This led the British to bully the coastal kings of West Africa. Many were made to agree to give Britain the right to blockade the major slave ports along the coast. However, it could never block them all, especially those along the estuaries of the Niger Delta such as Kalabari, Nembe or Whydah. These were located on a maze of creeks and mangrove swamps that allowed the slavers to come and go in relative safety.

Lieutenant Forbes, of the Royal Navy's blockade effort, noted that it was not very effective. According to his calculations during a twenty-six year period, 103,000 slaves were taken from the high seas and liberated, but during that same time frame 1,795,000 slaves were actually landed in the Americas. When we take into account that one in seven slaves died in passage, then something on the order of 20 slaves made it through the British blockade for every one captured and repatriated.

In Bonny, King Pepple was put on the throne with British help (1837). He remained their puppet because his palace was exposed to bombardment from British gun ships. The British negotiated several treaties with him and kept none of them. When he objected in 1854, they deported him, although in 1861 they had to reinstate him because they could not find another suitable yes-man. Thus, Pepple's support of abolition was "induced."[3]

In response both the United States and the French sent bogus "anti-slavery" squadrons to West Africa, but their actual responsibilities were to protect their own economic interests. The Americans wanted to protect their own palm-oil industries by suppressing British trade with West African producers. They also used their might to force West African kings and traders to pay their debts. One of the American squadron's first acts in West Africa was to kill a coastal king and burn four of his villages for allegedly mistreating an American merchant.

Brazil and the United States, the two nations with the most land and greatest need of labor, were the last importers to stop trafficking in slaves.

With much hypocrisy, the slave trade continued until the Civil War broke out in America in 1861. In 1863 Abraham Lincoln signed the Emancipation Proclamation, and in that same year the first American was hanged for trading in slaves. Almost immediately the Atlantic Slave Trade came to a halt.

West African political economies of large states had come to depend on raiding and trading of slaves. When the Europeans finally found a conscience with regard to the Atlantic Slave Trade, West Africans had to switch to other products, such as palm oil exported to world markets, or internally as with the Asante kola trade northwards.

Many West African states on the coast were forced to stop slaving as well. Those who could produce palm oil had an advantage, but there were limited environments in West Africa where the palm trees would grow. And where they did, being so labor intensive, palm oil production actually increased slavery internal to those zones.

Some West Africans opposed abolition, while others supported it, just as in the West. Before abolition, when the British were trying to stimulate the production of palm oil in West Africa, the Efik of Calabar moved quickly to make **palm oil plantations**. The Efik found that the slave trade was a hindrance to their legal commercial interests. They became rabid abolitionists. They acted as informers to the British navy by reporting on the movement of slave ships. Even though the French threatened to bombard Calabar if they didn't supply them with slaves, the Efik leadership persisted and the French were rebuffed.

Thus, in both the West and in West Africa the degree to which the political economy of nations was dependent on the trade in slaves was an extremely important factor in their attitude toward abolition.

The British had always used their naval squadrons to protect and enhance their economic interests along the West African coast. They bullied nations like Dahomey and Bonny. Other West African states helped slavers (the United States and Brazil, for example) to continue their slaving activities just to spite the British.

Some West Africans seemed to be driven by sincere morality. For example, **Olaudah Equiano**, an Igbo who escaped from slavery in the Americas in 1789, wrote an autobiography in which he counseled to treat West Africans as customers, not as merchandise. Another was Ottobah Cugoano, a Fante man who had been enslaved. In his *Thoughts and Sentiments on the Evil of Slavery* (1787) he called upon the British to blockade the waters of West Africa to stop the inhuman trade in people.

---

3. He should have paid attention to what happened in Lagos where the king entered into early agreement with the British, only to be the first on the coast to lose his independence. As Webster & Boahen nicely put it, "a British treaty was the first step to subjugation."

In Sierra Leone a Muslim Mandinka scholar named Momodu Yeli was a sharp opponent of slavery among Muslims and Christians. At around the same time, Sidi Muhammad al-Sanusi, founder of the Sanusiyya Brotherhood, started a program of buying and freeing slaves from the Trans-Saharan caravans.

Unfortunately, the efforts of such moral crusaders have not been able to eradicate this scourge from the world. Slavery is still widespread in Africa and other parts of our planet. See: http://www.antislavery.org/ and http://www.state.gov/www/global/human _rights/1999_hrp_report/cotedivo.html.

The Making of the "Other"

How could these terrible crimes against humanity have happened? What processes lead people to bind fellow humans to a life of degradation? Enslavement is not possible unless you make a human being into the "other" — that is, not like you. This is a cognitive process. It seems that noticing differences is easier that observing similarities. Human beings seem intent on defining someone with an obvious difference, skin color or hair type for example, as "other." I call this the process of "otherizing."

There may be something in the psyche of humans that requires an "other" in social life, someone to dominate or exclude. I will leave that issue for psychologists and sociologists to sort out, but in the history of West Africa, we can clearly see that in the very beginning, with the Portuguese explorations, black Africans were taken back to Iberia as slaves and were quickly defined as inferior.

For example, in 1575 the Portuguese priest of the Holy Roman Church wrote home to say that the Africans would have to be conquered by force because "the conversion of these barbarians will not be attained by love."

Back home the good father Martín Alfonso de Córdoba in 1460 wrote a guide for young ladies of high station, a collection of pious precepts commissioned by Queen Isabella, the Portuguese queen of Spain. Like others of his time, Fray Alfonso was starting the "otherizing" of blacks being brought back from West Africa, a prelude to the establishment of a firm justification for the barbarity of European slaving. In *A Garden of Noble Maidens* he wrote:

> ...the barbarians are those who live without the law; the Latins, those who have law; for it is the law of nations that men who live and ruled by law shall be lords of those who have none. Wherefore they may seize and enslave them, because they are by nature the slaves of the wise.

No better example exists of the subtle concepts that enabled the Iberians to begin to justify their exploitation of human beings from faraway lands. Latins have law, presumably Canon Law scripted by the Vatican. Therefore they are wise and they are the natural masters of blacks who lack law, and being unwise, are the natural servants of the wise law-holders.

Prejudice and discrimination, even abominable acts of terrorism, flow from just such assumptions. Chattel slavery was one such terrorist act perpetrated by the Europeans on West Africans.

Chattel, cognate with the word cattle, refers to moveable capital. The Portuguese brought back mainly consumables from West Africa e.g., peppers, ivory and the like.

They returned with ships laden with such items to be sold and dissipated. The only capital goods they brought back were enslaved human beings who, like cattle, can produce something and who also reproduce.

The journals, ships' logs and letters of the Europeans involved in the exploration and exploitation of West Africa show clearly that they perceived blacks to be "different" and in some cases "inferior," at least in manufacturing capacity. The odd man out would praise their commercial sense, their military tactics or their skill as bargainers, but on the whole they were seen and portrayed as "less than," as subalterns to be. The cobblestones were being laid in the path to dominance.

Such racism persisted through time. In a letter he wrote to his wife, the new governor of the Gold Coast, while still in Sierra Leone, General Sir Garnet Wolseley, said in 1873 that "The Negroes are like so many monkeys; they are a lazy, good-for-nothing race." His disposition toward West Africans did not improve upon arrival at Cape Coast Castle (See Map 10.1). There he declared that "the African" is an "objectionable animal" who is intended to be "the White Man's servant." Such was the "otherizing" that led up to the colonial era in West Africa.

Such racist ideas developed out of the intellectual climate of the day that began to use pseudoscience to fabricate ideas that justified their Imperialistic desires toward peripheral areas of the world and their eventual colonial domination of such peoples (See Box 11.1, 19th Century Racism Masquerades as Science).

Box 11.1   19th Century Racism Masquerades as Science

Until the mid-19th century, two general views dominated thinking about the origins and development of humankind: **monogenism** and **polygenism**. Monogenists believed that all humans were descended from a single creation event or a single origin; that human groups had degenerated since the original event, which accounted for differences between groups and resulted in the existence of different races of humankind; and, finally, that some races had degenerated more—fallen further from grace—than others, which explained the natural superiority or inferiority of various peoples. A driving question for scientists at that time was how to define and classify racial variation. Linnaeus (1758) described four races: *Americanus, Europaeus, Asiaticus* and *Afer*. Although his definitions were purportedly based on biological characteristics, note the subjective contrasts between the following:

Homo sapiens europaeus: White, serious, strong. Hair blond, flowing. Eyes blue. Active, very smart, inventive. Covered by tight clothing. Ruled by laws.

Homo sapiens afer: Black, impassive, lazy. Hair kinked. Skin silky. Nose flat. Lips thick. Crafty, slow, foolish. Anoints himself with grease. Ruled by caprice.

Buffon, a contemporary of Linnaeus, was less interested in classification than understanding the conditions creating diversity. Although he, too, was a product of his social class, Buffon was adamantly opposed to slavery. Writing about African groups in *Varieties of the Human Species* (1749), he includes a philosophical digression:

They are therefore endowed...with excellent heart and possess the seeds of every virtue. I cannot write their history without addressing their state...Is it necessary to degrade them, beat them, and to treat them as animals?... They are forced to labor, and yet commonly are not even adequately nourished. It is said that they tolerate hunger easily, that they can live for three days on a portion of a European meal; that however little they eat or sleep, they are always equally tough, equally strong, and equally fit for labor. How can men in whom there rests any feeling of humanity adopt such views? How do they presume to legitimize by such reasoning those excesses which originate solely from their thirst for gold?

Buffon's work was influential in the scientific community of his time, but it was Linnaeus' classificatory biology that held sway—and the quest to divide humans into discrete categories based on physical types continued through the 20th century.

Polygenists claim that different races are the result of separate creation events or separate evolutionary trajectories and, hence, there is no biological connection from one race to another. This view was less popular than monogeny but was supported by some well-respected and well-known individuals. The philosopher David Hume was profoundly influenced by his observations as Steward of the English Colonial Office in 1766:

I am apt to suspect the negroes and in general all the other species of men (for there are four or five different kinds) to be naturally inferior to the whites. There never was a civilized nation of any other complexion than white, nor even any individual eminent either in action or speculation. No ingenious manufacturers amongst them, no arts, no sciences... Such a uniform and constant difference could not happen in so many countries and ages, if nature had not made an original distinction betwixt these breeds of men.

The assumptions voiced by Hume may seem appalling from our point of view in the 21st century. But it was this kind of view that people in Europe and the United States were exposed to in the 1700's and 1800's. Scientists, philosophers, statesmen and politicians struggled with issues of social ranking, subjugation of one people by another, economic disparity and political exploitation that emanated from perceptions of difference named as race and used to justify privilege.

Anthropologists today explain that there is no biological basis for race; genetically, we are all one species. The term "race" is still common in our culture, but it is recognized now as only a social category. Unfortunately, the same issues named above still plague us. Hopefully, as we continue to be more critical in assessing the implications of public policy and more self-conscious in our social actions, we can move closer to attaining a condition of equality for all peoples.

When the discovery of the New World and the development of the plantation system stimulated the need for a large quantity of slaves, Europeans already had 200 years experience at taking black people as captives, and they had well trodden trade routes in West Africa where large numbers of human beings could be enslaved.

The Atlantic Slave Trade was a continuation of the racist policies of earlier Europeans who took black people out of their homeland and forced them into servitude in Europe. Unfortunately, it was a virtual explosion of that practice, one in which other

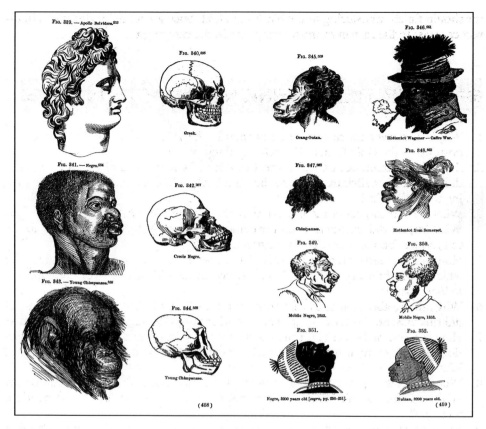

Figure 11.2   Apes, Negroes and Apollo.

black people, primarily élites, participated. They did so by defining certain of their fellow West Africans as "other," labeling them as felons, witches, pagans, or just powerless
people who are "less than."

Both whites and blacks in West African history were guilty of enormous cruelty. For
example, early in the 19th century an Asante general named Apokoo would, when he
captured the enemy, cut off their arms and then informed them that they were now
free to go.

What both the Europeans and West African élites seem to have been incapable of
seeing was the common humanity shared by all involved in this terrible period of our
human history. One only has to read the newspapers coming out of West Africa today
(or Northern Ireland or Bosnia or Central Africa or Northern Spain, *ad infinitum, ad
nauseum*) to see that we still have not learned this lesson.

Humanity is still in its infancy, and that was even more the case in the early history
of West Africa. Nevertheless individuals were and are capable of recognizing our common humanity, despite apparent differences of skin color or culture. During the
Wolseley campaign against the Asante, a young white officer was wounded and carried
to the infirmary to be patched up by the doctors. When he arrived, the only available
doctor was treating a West African soldier. When he stopped administering to the
African and began to treat the British soldier, the latter protested saying that the doc-

tor should finish ministering to the black man first. Such an act of kindness was in direct contrast to the racism of most Europeans in the campaign.

≈≈≈ CRITICAL THINKING QUESTIONS ≈≈≈

1. Why was slavery considered to be normal in the 15th century, and what was the position of the Holy Roman Church on taking slaves?
2. Explain the difference between direct capture of slaves and indirect capture. Why did Europeans switch from one to the other? Who did the bulk of actual slave raiding in West Africa?
3. What was the impact of the importation of guns into West Africa?
4. What impact did slaving have on the demographics of West Africa and their ability to produce food and develop the region?
5. How was the slave trade gendered, that is, which sex of slave was preferred for which type of slavery and why? What consequences did this have for development in West Africa?
6. Why did the abolition of slavery come about in the 19th century and what impact did this have on West African kingdoms and the great city-states of the Slave Coast?
7. How can you make a case for the point of view, which says that, the industrialization and enrichment of Europe to a large extent was based on the exploitation of West Africa?
8. Who were the opponents in the anti-slavery blockade of 19th century West Africa? Who opposed the continuation of slavery and who was in favor of its continuation, and why?
9. Has slavery completely disappeared by the present day? If not, why do you think it persists?

≈≈≈ KEY CONCEPTS ≈≈≈

Asantehene
Blood Men
Brotherhood of the Virgin of the Rosary
Chattel slavery
Dahomey
Denkyira
Direct capture
Domestic slavery
Dutch East India Company
Ekpe Trading Association
Equipment clause
Firearms

Fon Kingdom
Kumase
Manumission
Middle passage
Niger Delta
Olaudah Equiano
Otherizing
Palm oil plantations
Salaga
Slave Coast
Trans-Saharan Slave Trade

≈≈ SOURCES & SUGGESTED READINGS ≈≈

Aderibigbe, A. A. B. 1965. Empires of the Western Sudan: Ghana, Mali, Songhai. In: Ajayi, J.
   F. Ade and Ian Espie (eds.). *A thousand years of West African history.* Ibadan: Ibadan University Press, 191–205.

Blake, John W. 1977. *West Africa: Quest for God and Gold 1454–1578.* London: Curzon Press.

Davidson, Basil. 1992. *The black man's burden: Africa and the curse of the nation-state.* New
   York: Times Books.

Davidson, Basil. 1998. *West Africa before the Colonial Era: A history to 1850.* London: Longman.

Der, Benedict G. 1998. *The slave trade in Northern Ghana.* Acra: Woeli Publishing Services.

Edgerton, Robert B. 1995. *The Fall of the Asante Empire: The Hundred-Year War for Africa's
   Gold Coast.* New York: The Free Press.

Forbes, Lt. Patrick E. 1969. [London, 1849]. *Six Months' Service in the African Blockade* . London: Dawsons.

Fage, J. D. 1995. *A history of Africa.* (Third Edition). London: Routledge.

Fage, J. D. 1966. *A history of West Africa.* Cambridge: Cambridge University Press.

Gould, Stephen J. 1981. *The mismeasure of Man.* New York: W.W. Norton & Co.

Holden, Jeff. 1970. The Samorian impact upon Buna: An essay in methodology. In: Allen, C.
   & R. W. Johnson (eds.). *African perspectives.* Cambridge: Cambridge University Press.

Howe, Russell W. 1969. *Black Africa: Africa south of the Sahara from pre-history to independence.* New York: Walker and Company.

Lance, James Merriman. 1995. *Seeking the political kingdom: British colonial impositions and
   African manipulations in the northern territories of the Gold Coast colony.* Ph.D. dissertation,
   Stanford University. Ann Arbor: University Microform (UMI) #9525856.

Lloyd, Christopher. 1973. *The search for the Niger.* London: Collins.

Lovejoy, Paul. 1983. *Transformations in slavery: A history of slavery in Africa.* Cambridge: Cambridge University Press.

Marks, Jonathan. 1995. *Human biodiversity: Genes, race and history.* New York: Aldine De
   Gruyter.

Nott, J. C. and G. R. Gliddon. 1854. *Types of mankind.* Philadelphia: Lippincott, Grambo & Co.

Thomas, Hugh. 1997. *The slave trade: The story of the Atlantic Slave Trade: 1440–1870.* New
   York: Simon & Schuster.

Webster, J. B. & A. A. Boahen, with a contribution by H. O. Idowu. 1967. *History of West
   Africa: The Revolutionary Years— 1815 to Independence.* New York: Praeger.

12 WAR & RESISTANCE AGAINST EUROPE

> Whether Muslim or animist, Africans did not always passively accept European imperialism. This chapter chronicles just two of many resistance movements in West Africa—that of the Asante against the British and that of *Al-Hajj* Umar against the French. Their eventual defeat was not due to a lack of bravery, military acumen or effort. It was due to the overwhelming firepower of the invaders.

Penetration of and Reaction to Imperialism

Nowhere in Africa did Europeans penetrate the interior of Africa very successfully, and West Africa was especially forbidding. Europeans often referred to this disease-ridden area as the "White Man's Grave." During the slaving era, about half of the Europeans on the coast died along with a fifth of the European crewmembers of slaving ships.

After initial contact and settlement, most Europeans stayed on the coast in forts, castles or barricaded settlements. The interior of Africa was a great unknown, mysterious and titillating to the European imagination, though few wanted to go there. Eventually the general public became fascinated with Africa and the exploration of her enigmatic interior. Popular magazines of the Victorian Era regularly ran articles about adventures in Africa, the most famous being the loss of Dr. Livingston and Henry Morton Stanley's attempts to locate him. Africa's interior also stimulated Joseph Conrad to write the famous novel, *Heart of Darkness*, which perhaps tells us more about Europeans than it does about Africa herself.

In the 15th century there were few medicines to counteract malaria, dengue fever, cerebral-spinal meningitis, yellow fever and the myriad of other diseases that could strike down a European traveler who lacked the natural immunities of the native population. Plus, Africa was unknown territory, with no maps. Europeans did not know the routes, and even most coastal Africans did not know exactly how to reach some of the internal kingdoms like Mossi, Mamprusi, Kanem-Bornu.

Travel was arduous in the heat and humidity of the rain forest with insects, lack of potable water and the difficulty of transporting goods. Everything had to be carried by Head-bearers, and not all of them wanted to venture into unknown territory. Once cowry shells became the accepted currency in West Africa, Europeans struggled with the huge quantities of shells they needed just to pay their porters, let alone to purchase supplies along the way, give as gifts and hire other services in the interior. It was simply a physical impossibility to carry enough cowry shells to do this.

In summary, we can say that Europeans went to Africa with commercial reasons in mind. They stayed on the coast, for the most part and engaged in trade with coastal peoples who acted as middlemen in dealing with tribes in the hinterlands. The intent of these European traders was extraction, the taking of raw materials in exchange for manufactured goods that could not be had in Africa at the time.

Contact with Europe over time has enhanced class formation and stratification in West Africa. It has enriched a few and impoverished many. It has made trading the route to wealth, at the expense of production and manufacturing. Little is produced in West Africa that can be sold, either internally or exported. It is the precious raw materials that West Africans have been exporting to get enough hard currency to buy all the consumer items on the world market—the television sets, boom boxes, fashionable clothes, jewelry, and so forth. Some of the beads and baubles have changed, but the pattern has not (See Photo 12.1).

At first, West Africans and Europeans interacted more or less as equals. Europeans were kept on the coast and often had to bend their will to fit the dictates of West African monarchs and traders. In the beginning European influence was limited, but as time went by and the lure of profits drew more and more to Africa, Europeans became increasingly imperialistic.

Some coastal peoples, like the Fante, cooperated with the Europeans against their traditional enemies. Others simply wanted to make money by trading with the newcomers. But, it is a fallacy that West Africans passively accepted European domination. The greater part of West Africa was occupied by force of arms. Those chiefs that meekly gave in often did so after learning of the firepower and destruction wrought by the European troops in neighboring areas, and their decisions were more wise than based on timidity or lack of fighting spirit. According to the eminent West African historian, Michael Crowder, "at least two-thirds of the peoples of West Africa have a history of overt resistance to colonial penetration."

Clearly those coastal kings who were benefiting from the European trade tried to accommodate the foreigners. Other peoples shunned the Europeans and some fought back directly—Dahomey, Asante, Tukolor, Fulani Empire, Bornu under Rabeh, most of the hill tribes of the Nigerian Plateau, Abuja and many others. Still others like the Yoruba and Volta Basin Grunshi expressed thanks for the arrival of European forces who brought an end to war, raiding and chaos in their lands. But overall, once the people understood the exploitative nature of the European presence in their land, they began to resist. As James Lance has said, "Africans found ways to insinuate themselves within the various matrices of colonial rule, influencing its contours and their development." Far from the European stereotypes of childlike docility or barbaric savagery, Africans came to comprehend the nature of the colonial project in social engineering and acted in ways to control it as best they could.

I will present one extended analysis of the British-Asante interactions to show how the Asante resisted British incursions and the British attitude toward their opponents. Although ultimately the Asante were to lose their homeland, they held up well and fought bravely against the Europeans, with their superior firepower.

A Note on State-Building Processes

In this text I am saying that the arrival of Europeans led to culture change and social disorganization in West Africa. When I say "disorganization" I do not mean a con-

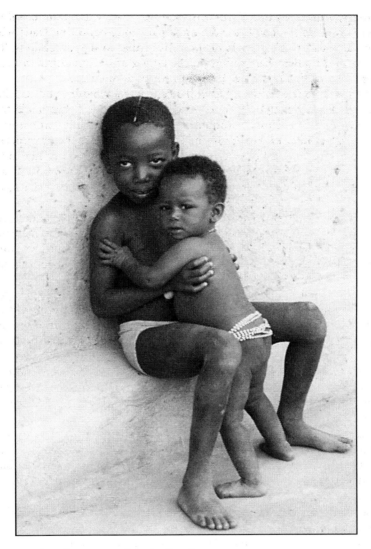

Photo 12.1   Girl with Imported Waist Beads.

dition of total chaos, but a reformulation of previously existing sociopolitical forms. In 1629 there were many different tribes and small states (See Map 9.6). Within a hundred years, larger polities began to dominate the region such as the Denkyira, Akyem and Akwamu and more importantly to European dealings, the Asante and Fante (See Map 9.6).

Wars, conquests and empire-building were not unknown prior to the coming of the Europeans. However, they were greatly stimulated by alliances with the new arrivals, the introduction of firearms and the European desire to trade for gold and their willingness to buy slaves.

This stimulation from the world economy radically restructured the political face of West Africa. As A. A. Boahen says:

A political revolution had obviously taken place in the Gold Coast during the relatively short period between 1680 and 1750, which resulted in the partition of the Gold Coast among the two leading Akan peoples, the Fante and the Asante...

Asante was on the rise as the Denkyira had problems maintaining their unity. Small groups of Denkyira broke off and moved north to the region of modern-day Kumase. In a normal process of state conflict, Denkyira tried to conquer these small states, which gave them the impetus to coalesce around a central leader of the Oyoko clan. This leader was the Kumasehene (who eventually became the *Asantehene*). Both the Denkyira and the Asante were responding to outside influences that were stimulating war, conquest and eventually a large-scale trade in human flesh. Until late in the 19th century the Asante tried to gain direct access to the coast through Lomé in Togo by skirting around the newly-established Gold Coast Colony. The great empire of Asante could not have arisen so fast and extended so far without the impetus of European trade, especially the proliferation of guns.

Aggrandizers respond to danger, but also to opportunities. The arrival of the Europeans provided opportunities for trade and the first *Asantehenes* responded with ambition, martial fervor, sagacity and statesmanship. They broke free of Denkyira and began to expand themselves, trading in gold, guns and slaves. Political savvy was evident in the very first leader in Kumase, its founder Obiri Yeboa. Through diplomacy and warfare, he enlarged the Oyoko clan to about ten families by incorporating the ruling families of most of the states and city-states in the immediate vicinity. This secured the central position of his leadership and that of his clan. His keen leadership was continued by his successor, Osei Tutu (See below) who, by adding a ritual element through the auspices of the Golden Stool, was able to bring together a number of disparate peoples.

The Formation and Structure of Asante

Asante had all the attributes of a nation — a set territory with known boundaries, a centralized government with a police force and army, an encompassing language, widely accepted law, a king's council and a means of channeling input from the people to the monarch, the queen mother and their councilmen (See Map 9.6).

The Asante had seventy-seven laws which, as noted by Naomi Chazan, "set out the structure of the government [and] the divisions of labour, and the main elements of early Asante political culture." The Asante ultimately became the most powerful empire in West Africa ruling over 3 million subjects, at its height in the 19th century. By the time the Asante were conquered by the British, the *Asantehene* could expect tributary payments from 40 neighboring kingdoms, and the Europeans had to pay him rent and customs duties to live and trade along the coast to the south of the Asante heartland.

This centralization of political economy can be seen in the fact that whereas in the late 1500s **Akan** country contained at least 38 small states, by the mid-1600s it had only a handful, and by 1700 only one state, the kingdom of gold, Asante.

T. E. Bowdich, who was one of the first European visitors to Kumase, claimed that at any one time the *Asantehene* could call up an army of 200,000 (the Asante never had a standing army). By the time the Asante ran into the technological strength of the British, they ruled 500 miles of the Mina Coast.

Various segments of the broader Akan-speaking world had embraced the mythical charter of the Golden Stool. As the oral history tells it, the King's priest, Anokye, called the Golden Stool down from the heavens to rest on the lap of the *Asantehene*, Osei Tutu. Anokye explained that the stool contained the very soul of the Akan people. Even today, it is thought to be so sacred that even the *Asantehene* does not actually sit on it. Note the symbolism in the sacred legend that the stool chose the *Asantehene* by settling on his lap. In other words, the soul of the people chose the king and in a sense is superior to the king, a very democratic principle. The stool is the symbol of political authority in the forest kingdoms. When Osei Tutu assumed rule, he required that all subaltern political leaders bury their stools. No better example exists of the symbolic connection of a ruler with the divine. This stool, which was later to be coveted by the British, became the symbol of the new nation of Asante, and the priests of court maintained that it contained the very soul and substance of the Asante Union.

Osei Tutu (*fl. ca.* 1680–?1717) is credited with directing a war of liberation against the Denkyira, with some military backing from Akwamu, where he had been a prince in residence for a number of years. Minor battles had shown the Denkyira king that the Asante would move on them sooner or later so he tried to forced a premature attack in order to take them at less than full strength. In 1698, while the favorite wife of the *Asantehene* was on a state visit to the Denkyira court, the king raped her and sent her home in tears to tell her husband. True to form, the Asante moved against the Denkyira. Within three years, Asante attained supremacy over Denkyira.

While the war engine drove them to prominence, it was diplomacy and a well-organized system of governance that kept the Asante there. Contrary to the slanderous portrayals of them by the British, the Asante were especially keen on solving problems with neighbors by negotiation and compromise rather than war. For example, while the Fante sometimes killed Asante diplomats, hanging their bodies in public for all to see— the *Asantehene* would not retaliate immediately, preferring to try more diplomacy first.

By about 1730, Asante seemed to be looking to northern lands, where there was more gold and slaves. By conquering Bono, Gonja and Dagomba they annexed states that paid them tribute. The Dagomba alone had to supply a thousand slaves a year.

Those provincial kingdoms that had gold paid in that medium. The 50-mile circle around Kumase was rich in gold, but that ore seemed to be prevalent in an alluvial band leading northwards through Bono to the Lobi gold fields. It has been estimated that between 1400–1900, about seven thousand tons of gold had been extracted from around 40,000 different mines in this field. Gold mining remains one of Ghana's main sources of foreign exchange today. Modern Ghana mines located in Asanteland have made that West African nation the 13th largest producer of gold in the world, producing one percent of the world's gold, 17.3 tons per year.

Europeans were astounded at the amount of gold the *Asantehene* and his court displayed just in jewelry. Some of the wrist ornaments were so heavy that there were special "arm bearers" to hold up the laden limbs of the *Asantehene* and his wealthy court companions. His courtiers were called **sikapo** (also *asikafo*), which means "people of wealth" in the Twi language. The *Asantehene* had a state treasury with untold millions in gold, and some *sikapo* also could amass great amounts of gold. These élites must have lived better lives nutritionally as well. European visitors noted that they were taller that the lower members of society, or **ahiato**. This **sikapo-ahiato ranking** shows that Asante was clearly a stratified society.

One Asante merchant died leaving US$500,000 in gold dust. The *Asantehene* and his men feared the rise of a merchant class and passed laws limiting how much wealth they could have in their lifetimes. Also, upon the death of a wealthy Asante man, only a small portion of his amassed riches could be passed on to his kin, the bulk reverting to the king's coffers.

While the Asante were busy annexing these northern areas, they made sufficient raids to the south to cause the formation of a **Fante Federation of States**, an organizational framework designed to deal with Asante aggression and secure the "slaves for goods" trade routes to the north. From historical records and local traditions, it appears that Fante was fundamentally a city-state until the 1650s. This was divided into sections, each with its own ruler or *Braffo*. They were under the suzerainty of a Supreme "*Braffo* of Fantyn," according to the Dutch factor in 1653, although his position was likely "first among equals." As with other African monarchs, he had to act in consultation with his advisors, the *Braffos* and elders.

Like other states, Fante had fissiparous tendencies and various groups began to move out of the coastal capital to found new colonies and states, culminating in 19 different states. Population pressure and the desire to find new locations to cash in on the growing wealth brought by trade stimulated this expansion. Slaving played a large part, too. In the words of Boahen, we can discern how world affairs were influencing people in West Africa:

> the Atlantic trade became increasingly voluminous and prosperous, particularly following the introduction of sugar plantations in the West Indies after 1640 with consequent phenomenal rise in the demand for slaves. The Fante presumably felt the need to occupy the surrounding areas more effectively so as to be able to control the routes leading into the interior. Finally, political rivalry among the various quarters may also have been an important factor.

By 1750 the Fante on the coast and the Asante in the interior had emerged as the dominant peoples of *Mina*. The following years saw countless conflicts and alliances between these two giants, as they fought each other or joined together to war on their neighbors.

The presence of Europeans was an important factor in this mix. Both the Asante and Fante had favorite European trading partners. The Fante of the east dealt primarily with the British; the westerly Asante trafficked with the Dutch, who had by this time occupied *Castelo São Jorge da Mina* or *Al Mina* (later Elmina). From 1765 till the end of the century, the British adopted a strategy of dissuading the Asante from harassing the Fante. It appears that during the reign of **Osei Kwadro**, who perhaps did not want to alienate the British, the Asante abstained from attacking the Fante. However, British policy ultimately failed. Seeking more options in trade, the Asante overran the Fante in the war of 1806–1807. This brought the Asante fatefully into contact with the British who would become their archenemies over the next 100 years.

The powerful nation-state of Asante secured effective control over the whole of what was to be, two centuries later, the republic of modern Ghana. In effect, Asante had now become an empire. But expansion also brought problems of succession that were common to many kingdoms that had grown rapidly with the increase in economic and military opportunities spurred by the presence of world trade. Like so many West African kings, the *Kumasehene* ruled as the head of a royal descent group. Therefore, his kin had deep and natural ties of attachment to him; but those that he conquered did not have such intimate bonds (provincial Akan-speakers, and to an extent the non-Asante states of the north). His problem, then, was to maintain allegiance of tributaries and sub-kingdoms with whom he had shallower unions.

While this problem had arisen before in West Africa, it was exacerbated at this time by the fact that now economic opportunities were plentiful and any prince or *sikapo* could get muskets and men, start slaving and become relatively wealthy overnight, which represented a significant challenge to the authority of the *Asantehene.*

Osei Tutu was succeeded by Opoku Ware, who increased Asante's gold trade, tried to reduce dependence on European imports by establishing local distilling and weaving industries, and greatly increased the size of Asante. At his death in 1750, his realm stretched from the immediate hinterland of the Gold Coast to the Savannah of present-day northern Ghana. By this time Asante controlled an area of about 100,000 square miles and a population of two to three million.

The next *Asantehene* of note, Osei Kwadro (1764–1777), and his successors achieved an ingenious solution to the problem of governing a diverse set of Akan-speakers from Kumase. They created a professional bureaucracy of administrators, police, soldiers and traders who were unconnected to the traditional power structures of Asante and owed their positions to the *Asantehene* alone. They were career bureaucrats who were well taken care of by their patron, as long as they efficiently carried out their respective roles within the political framework that had been worked out. Many of these government functionaries led lives of splendor and power, owing their élite lifestyle to the king himself.

Since these career bureaucrats came from disparate parts of the realm, they supported the concept of national unity framed under a dome of universal laws, with non-Akan speaking provinces, like Gonja and Dagomba, being able to maintain their own local charters of identity.

The only major problem came at the interregnum period. Again an adroit solution was found. When the *Asantehene* died it was (and still is) kept a secret. With time to deliberate, these advisors selected an appropriate replacement, enstooled him (the equivalent of enthroning) and announced that although the king was dead, the king lived on.

Many such institutions developed over time to support the supreme rule of the *Asantehene*, and the Asante kings and councilors were especially adept at governance. They relied on more than ritual beliefs to preserve power. They maintained a far-flung network of spies in all provinces and tributaries, rather than formal provincial governors. They allowed local chiefs to continue to rule in their own chiefdoms as long as they paid tribute to the *Asantehene*, and showed him proper respect. Sometimes the *Asantehene* would actually return the tribute in a gracious gesture, at times even adding special gifts for chiefs who were in favor, or who needed pacification.

All kingdoms use ceremony to instill a sense of union in their people. In Kumase, one such ceremony was the annual yam festival. Each provincial ruler had to attend and sacrifice slaves, the blood of which was placed in the holes where the yams had been extracted. This act was thought to ensure renewal of this vital crop. But slaves were not the only ones to die at such festivals. Sometimes, when spies had revealed treasonous behavior on the part of a chief, he would be seized by surprise attack at the festival, tortured and killed. The common method was to slice and hack his body with knives, then pour in *piri piri* or hot pepper powder. Toward the end, the executioners would cut off his ears and nose, then decapitate him. However, should a provincial chief not attend, it was considered an act of war. The heads of such traitors were paraded throughout the festival for all to see, especially the visiting chiefs, then their skulls used by the royal entertainers as drums, tapping on them ominously with knives proclaiming a musical message about treason.

Asante bureaucrats (**amradofo** or "those responsible for maintaining law") were part of an elaborate royal system that even included royal pickpockets. These boys would infiltrate the daily market in Kumase. If a pickpocket was caught, the offended person could beat him, but their skills were such that this was an uncommon event. Each night the little thieves would return to the palace to display their spoils. Eventually, most of this wealth made its way into the already bursting royal treasury. Perhaps there has never been a more blatant but trivial example of a **kleptocracy**.

Below was the Asante **Kotoko**, or Inner Council of 18 elders who held wide-ranging powers and privileges. Most came from the royal clan of the metropolitan area. The *Asantehene* was not an autocrat, having to deal with both the powers of the *Kotoko* and the 200-man National Council just below the *Kotoko* in rank. The National Council was comprised of the *amanhene* who were great men and representatives from all the provinces within the Asante Union. Thus, with a typical African distrust of power, the Asante nation-state was constituted of a series of checks and balances not unlike the principles enshrined in the U.S. constitution. In both, the constitutional checks and balances tended to prevent abuses of power. Some Asante kings were more despotic than others, but they were dealt with, some even dethroned, by other members of the ruling élite. Between the Asante State and the Akan people there was an acknowledged recognition of ties of mutual obligation and respect. As with America, the Asante nation-state had its ups and downs, and Davidson, in *The Black Man's Burden*, says that the:

> system had to absorb repeated and sometime abrasive adjustments to ambitions, corruptions, careers, and circumstances that threatened uproar and upset, and not seldom produced disgraceful setbacks to law and order [but] the polity had found the means and ability to weather such storms...the system proved self-adjusting [brackets added].

The annual yam festival was also an occasion for the *Asantehene* and his councilors to join in a meeting called the *Asantemanhyiamu* to discuss the state of the nation. The *Asantehene* was a centralizing figure, a symbol of the unity of the nation-state, but he and his inner circle had to depend on a system of participation that could only work if they were seen to be responding to the will of the people. This was the basis of much of the pomp and ceremony of the yam festival, as well as the political deliberations at this time.

Slaves were owned by prominent men in the Asante union and were in such great demand at one point that the Portuguese actually imported slaves from Angola for the Asante to use on their farms, in mining and in infrastructural construction and repair. The Portuguese supplied perhaps 12,000 slaves to Akan country between 1500 and 1535, and continued selling slaves from São Tomé and Nigeria to the Gold Coast throughout the 16th century.

The labor of these slaves enabled the Akan to expand gold production by developing deep-level mining in addition to panning in alluvial soils. Even more importantly, slave labor enabled the Akan to undertake the immensely laborious task of clearing the dense forests of Southern Ghana for farming. The most prominent historian of Asante, Ivor Wilks, suggests that while some farming had been practiced on a very limited scale in the *Mina* forests for millennia, only when the Akan began importing slaves in the 15th and 16th centuries were they able to shift from an economy that relied primarily on hunting and gathering to one which became primarily agricultural. Farming led to rapid increase of population in the forest region.

It is easy to see how the Asante were able to adapt their political economy to the increase in demand for slaves when the Atlantic Slave Trade began to escalate. Mercantilism was a way of life, and slaves were already part of the mix. The Asante were business-oriented and well aware of the connection between their commercial acumen and the political order. This can be seen in this proverb: "you should sell your mother for power, because when powerful there are many avenues to make money, and when wealthy you can always buy her back."

The Asante Wars with the British

Some of the bloodiest wars in West African history were fought between the British and the Asante. The Asante were able to inflict great damage to the British armies by their courage, moral strength as a nation and brilliance in tactical warfare. They were greatly outgunned, having mostly shoddily made muskets that were difficult to maintain. Some of these guns were left over from previous wars in Europe and others were manufactured for export to the colonies. In 1829 alone, British merchants sold more the 52,000 pistols and muskets and two million pounds of gunpowder in West Africa. The Asante armed themselves with these less reliable guns, but were only able to get their hands on a few breachloaders later in their battles with the British. Around 1853 the British had breachloading Enfield rifles and later the .577-caliber Snider rifles which were even more efficient. Later still, the Sniders were replaced with more efficient Martini-Henry repeating rifles. They also had big guns, rapid-firing 75-mm artillery; and machine guns, first the Gattling Gun, replaced by the Maxim Gun.

While the British had been in contact with the Fante and other coastal peoples for a long time, they had not been in direct contact with the Asante until the official named T. E. Bowdich traveled there in 1817 with the new British governor of the African Company of Merchants at Cape Coast, John Hope Smith. At this time the merchants were the political power, not the official British government. Smith was alarmed the year before when a Dutch envoy named J. P. T. Huydecoper visited Kumase. He hurried north to secure access to the rich gold fields of Asanteland.

Bowdich and Smith negotiated a mild treaty of good will with the *Asantehene*, but the king did not want a resident merchant in the capital, nor would he consider the presence of Christian missionaries.

The Europeans found Kumase to be a thriving city with élites decked in gold and finery, many slaves, huge festivals and a court to rival any in medieval Europe. Bowdich was fascinated by the place and wrote an account of his visit that is still consulted by historians today. Clearly, he admired the Asante, but most British officials did not.

In 1822 Gov. Smith was replaced by Sir Charles MacCarthy, former governor of Sierra Leone. He and his men did nothing but antagonize the *Asantehene* and minor military scuffles broke out between the two nations. True to their habit, the *Asantehene* tried diplomacy to solve the conflict. MacCarthy, like many of the British officials sent to the Gold Coast, saw the West African indigenes as stupid, lazy savages. Being made "the other" they needed conquering, and war was the means to accomplish this.

MacCarthy set about to buttress the fort at Cape Coast and put together an army in anticipation of attacking Kumase. The Asante were aware of these preparations and when diplomacy failed they resorted to war. In June 1823, their army began the journey south to meet the British at Cape Coast. MacCarthy went out to meet them, was killed and his army summarily routed. This was a blow to the British ego and their view of themselves as more advanced than mere "natives."

About the same time the *Asantehene* Osei Bonsu died. He was replaced by the more aggressive **Osei Yaw**, the only *Asantehene* that really could be considered as belligerent toward the British.

Thinking to quickly follow up on one victory in hopes of a total triumph, Osei Yaw sent an army of 30,000 Asante warriors to Cape Coast, but the fort held. Stymied in this effort, the Asante army turned on the Fante countryside and ravaged the villages and towns of that coastal kingdom, finally withdrawing to Kumase. In January 1826, the Asante troops again moved south, but this time to attack Accra. For seven months they raged through the south sacking everything in sight.

The feckless Fante were no match for the disciplined warriors from Asante. Also the British were slow to prepare, partly because the majority of the white men were sick or died shortly after arriving in West Africa. But when they did move against the Asante troops they were armed with Congreve rockets. Western technology began to assert itself. In the battle at Katamanso the Asante had the upper hand until the British commander set off the rockets. They made orange smoke streams before hitting their target; the explosions left massive devastation. The Asante army turned and fled.

Osei Yaw quarreled with a member of his Inner Council, Kwadwo Adusei, over dealings with the British. The *Asantehene* became so enraged that he had Adusei seized and pounded to death in a mortar by an elephant tusk pestle, as women pound yams for food, a humiliating death for an élite Asante. This impetuous act turned the council against the venomous *Asantehene*, forcing him to make an offer of peace to the British. In 1829 a joint agreement was worked out between Asante dignitaries and British officials, but it was never signed because the British officials pulled out of the Gold Coast and turned governance back over to the **Merchant Council**.

A president of the Merchant Council was installed, but failed to move ahead. In short order, **George Maclean**, a Captain in the Royal Colonial Corps, replaced him. Stationed at Cape Coast, he immediately opened negotiations with the Asante, and a treaty was signed in 1831. This ushered in 16 years of peace and open trade, largely due to Maclean's skill in diplomacy, and his genuine respect for West Africans. The locals reciprocated that esteem. It is a great tribute to Maclean that the Asante referred to him as "The White Man in whose time all slept soundly." Unfortunately for West Africa, as we shall see, the Europeans had few administrators like Maclean.

In 1834 Osei Yaw died and was succeeded by Kwaku Dua I. Maclean died in 1847 and things began to slide downhill again. In 1839 the first European missionary had visited Kumase. The Reverend Thomas B. Freeman had established a mission station there. Kwaku Dua was wise and prudent as a ruler, but he was not in favor of having a mission in Kumase. He told this to the new governor posted at Cape Coast, Sir William Winniet. Kwaka Dua was piqued by the fact that the British press was painting him and the Asante people as "bloodthirsty savages." Winniet lacked Maclean's diplomatic skills, and a rift began to develop between the two men, as well as between their respective nations.

Winniet was replaced by a new governor, Richard Pine, who found himself in hot water with the Asante almost immediately. A disagreement had developed between the

Asantehene and some distant members of his nation. Fearing for their safety, they fled to Cape Coast and sought refuge in the British castle. When Kwaku Dua demanded their release into his custody, Pine refused.

The *Asantehene* mobilized an army 60,000 strong and headed for the coast, but bad weather slowed their progress. Gov. Pine went north to meet the force in April 1867, only to be defeated by the Asante. About that time Kwaku Dua died in his sleep. In the mourning ceremonies that followed, many of his slaves were killed to accompany their master to the next life. Such exotic customs shocked the Victorian World and were used as grist for the racist mill.

Kwaku Dua I was succeeded by Kofi Kakari, whom the British called "**King Coffee.**" At 30 years of age, he had no military experience and was unduly influenced by the court Muslims, diviners and priests. An intemperate man, he was given to sexual extravagance and debauchery, which further clashed with the spirit of the Victorian Age. Having the unfortunate habit of lavishing gold on his paramours, he was known by several unflattering nicknames, one of which was *osape*, "one who scatters gold." In his scattering Kofi Kakari managed to mightily deplete the royal treasury.

The next crisis came when the Fante decided to blockade the Dutch castle of Elmina. As the Asante were not effectively trading with the British, this cut off a vital source of European goods, especially guns and powder. This action precipitated a two-year war (1868–1869) that resulted in the Asante taking some European hostages to Kumase.

Kofi Kakari tried to use these captives as leverage against the British, but he did not realize that they were not British subjects. Furthermore, at that same time, the Dutch decided to get out of the Gold Coast and offered Elmina Castle to the British. Kofi Kakari objected, saying that he was the owner and the Dutch were mere renters. The Bowdich/Smith treaty of 1807 confirmed this assertion.

The soon-to-be colonials, however, wanted it their way. When Asante dignitaries pleaded their case, the British allowed them to be roughed up by their guards and sent packing. The *Asantehene* was fuming mad. He was about to get madder. In a concocted story that defies belief, the Dutch told the British that the *Asantehene* was their employee, and that the money paid had been wages! What was also incredible in this sordid affair was that the British accepted this barefaced lie and bought Elmina in 1882. To make matters even worse, a forged document emerged that indicated that the *Asantehene* had renounced all his rights to Elmina.

After 274 years of continuous occupation, the Dutch exited the West African scene, leaving the British to face the Asante. Needless to say, the *Asantehene* was furious. He assembled an army of 80,000 men and marched southwards, camping about five miles above the coast. For some reason there was no major attack, just small forays and skirmishes between the Asante and the Fante/British alliance. In time the unsanitary conditions in the Asante war camp produced disease. They had also depleted the food in the countryside and were forced to return to Kumase.

This ignoble campaign did not sit well with the inner circle and court nobles, giving way to dissention in Kumase. While the Asante fought amongst themselves, the British government was preparing for war. They sent out a sternly efficient officer to be the new governor and commanding officer. General Sir **Garnet Wolseley** was a racist, intent on destroying the Asante nation by violent means.

Wolseley didn't like Africans and his disposition was not improved when he learned that the Asante had been killing Europeans in small-scale skirmishes. Rather than attacking the Castle where Wolseley had taken up residence, the Asante generals decided to move on Elmina with ladders to try to scale the walls. The savage firepower of the

British troops inside cut down about 1,000 Asante warriors in their attempt to storm the castle.

Wolseley heard of the attack and sent a small force along the beach to attack the weakened enemy, but this only resulted in small-scale encounters with few casualties. Again the Asante troops around Elmina ran out of food, and when disease began to plague them, they returned to Kumase. Their campaign had been a disappointment.

Immediately Wolseley sent to London for more troops. He had assessed the fighting ability of the Fante and other blacks as nil, and wanted white men in his army. He was not alone in this. Captain Maurice who served under Wolseley referred to the African troops under his command as "a nigger company." (His views were compatible with Wolseley's.) As a racist of extraordinary proportions, even for his Victorian Era, Wolseley made this astonishing declaration to his troops at Cape Coast: "It must never be forgotten by our soldiers that Providence has implanted in the heart of every native of Africa a superstitious awe and dread of the white man that prevents the negro from daring to meet us face to face in combat." He would soon find out how very wrong he was in that regard.

Before the arrival of the anticipated troops from Britain, Wolseley began building a 12-foot wide road to Kumase. He also built eight camps along the way on the southern side of the Pra River where he was able to store provisions and provide amenities for his soldiers. His problem was on the other side of the river, where Fante head-bearers did not like to venture.

In a classic case of cultural misunderstanding, the British consistently had trouble with carriers. West African men simply did not see carrying loads as real work because this task was performed by women in most West African societies. Restricted by their own cultural mores, the British did not like seeing women subjected to enemy fire, and their presence created the potential for sexual tensions and conflicts in camp.

The British had about 6,000 head-bearers. Colonel Colley was put in charge of the carriers, of whom 1,600 were women. Colley, a subordinate to Wolseley, was an organized man. When he took over the responsibility for transport, he inherited only 201 carriers, the rest having run off. By the time Wolseley was ready to move northwards, Colley had assembled the 6,000 already mentioned. He succeeded in this by less than honorable means, however, beginning the British practice of **forced labor** in West Africa. Colley attacked and burned the villages of any carriers who deserted him. Although he paid them, they were essentially enslaved, having guards to watch them at all times.

Wolseley's total force came to 3,520 combat troops, of which 2,500 were white. By the time they were ready to move, Colley had upped the carrier corps to 8,000.

Meanwhile, as Wolseley prepared for his assault on Kumase, there was dissention in the capital. Kofi Kakari was pushing to take the war to Wolseley because he did not want Kumase invaded. The elders of the inner circle, however, had become informed about the weaponry held by the British. They felt that since half of their army had recently been killed at Elmina, perhaps diplomacy was a better course of action.

The queen mother, who along with other prominent women was expected to speak out at times of national peril, counseled peace. To achieve this she recommended that they release the white prisoners and pay any indemnity. Not surprisingly, the generals wanted war.

In the mean time, Wolseley sent a message to Kumase demanding that they pay the indemnification of 50,000 ounces of gold (ca. US$6 million), an enormous sum in 1873, plus submit to an unconditional surrender. But the British underestimated the national honor at stake. Many of the older men of the inner circle felt that they could not submit, as it would violate their sacred honor and besmirch their ancestors. In fact, Wolseley had painted them into a corner, giving them no alternative but to plan for war. Carnage was now assured as the Asante prepared to defend their capital city and their national pride.

It is part of the culture of many West African societies to look for omens when undertaking a serious task. On the day that the Inner Council decided on war a terrible windstorm blew over the sacred tree in Kumase that symbolized Asante nationhood. To see if this was truly a bad omen, the diviners tied two men in the bush with knives stuck through their cheeks to prevent them from uttering foul epithets against the *Asantehene*. These priests said that if the men died quickly the windstorm would be innocuous, but if they lingered, the downing of the tree should be taken as an ill omen. One man lived 5 days, the other 9 days. An upsetting harbinger, to be sure.

The *Asantehene* decided to release one of the white hostages, the German Johannes Kühne. The King instructed him to tell Wolseley "I want peace." Kühne did just the opposite. He told the governor that the Asante army was weak, that there was much dissention in the land, and that victory was assured if he attacked.

King Coffee's spies returned to say that the British were continuing with their war preparations. The *Asantehene* paid huge sums of money to the resident Muslims to conjure up magical means to repel the invaders. Many Muslims in Kumase and elsewhere in West Africa made a living making magical charms, amulets and potions to help people in their endeavors. They were thought to have special supernatural powers.

Meanwhile, outside the palace, the people were busy making shot to go in the muskets. Proper shot was always in short supply, so the Asante improvised by cutting up iron bars and using anything that would do damage to their enemy. The generals were especially worried about this war because they were very short of shot and powder.

On January 21, 1873 the *Asantehene* released the Swiss Missionary Friedrich Ramseyer, his wife and two children, as well as the French merchant, Marie-Joseph Bonnat. He hoped that this gesture would soften Wolseley's attitude toward the Asante. "Tell them we want peace," he told the hostages.

When Wolseley received this message he decided to make a show of meeting with the *Asantehene*, even though it was clear to all in his camp that he desperately wanted to attack. That is borne out by what he told the *Asantehene*. Wolseley did not negotiate. He simply made these demands: (1) immediate full payment of the US$6 million in gold; (2) the imprisonment of the queen mother and six royals as hostages.

Wolseley knew that the *Asantehene* could not secure the full indemnity payment on short notice. War was now assured.

After Wolseley returned to his war camp, the generals began to move their troops south to Amoafo. A few days later the battle commenced when Wolseley attacked the Asante line there. The fighting was vicious and King Coffee, who had boasted of his bravery, and who had come to the front to see the fighting first hand, fled unceremoniously.

Wolseley's forces and weaponry overpowered the Asante army and Wolseley marched into Kumase. Almost immediately the town burst into flames as the British forces looted and burned the city's houses. When one looter was caught, Wolseley ordered a public hanging to deter others. While the British press and most white men in the region considered the Asante to be barbarians, the hanging showed that no people has a corner on barbarity. When the man was hung, he did not die and flopped around at the end of the rope, gagging and struggling for the breath of life. The rope was retied, this time passing through his mouth, and when he was hung the second time it took several minutes for him to expire in terrible agony. The on-looking Asante were aghast at this display. They were about to have even more shocks.

The *Asantehene* was in hiding outside the city. Wolseley sent word to him to come and sign the documents of surrender. In the meantime his men looted the palace, then exploded charges around it to destroy it. The remaining buildings were then torched throughout the city.

Then King Coffee did the unspeakable. As the British troops were beginning their march south, the *Asantehene* sent a messenger with some gold, saying that he agreed to the signing. The people of Kumase had seen their army defeated, their city sacked, the palace destroyed, and now they had to witness their *Asantehene* rifling the graves of his ancestors to get enough gold to pay the British. Most royals were buried with copious amounts of gold jewelry, and it was these jewels that King Coffee wanted to retrieve to pay off the British.

The Inner Council and the people in general were so shocked by this defilement of the ancestors that there were widespread calls for the destoolment of the king. On October 21, 1874, in the same year that the Gold Coast became an official colony of Britain, the *Asantehene* abdicated. His younger brother, Mensa Bonsu, replaced him.

The new king brought a breath of fresh air to the Asante leadership. He appealed to the British to maintain peace in the land, open the roads and support trade to allow the people to reestablish their lives. However, the British feared the *Asantehene's* powers and wanted to break up the Asante Union. Instead of backing the *Asantehene*, they supported a rival, the king of Dwaben named Asafo Agyei.

Immediately the Dwaben king not only declared independence from Kumase, but also claimed supremacy over the *Asantehene*. What is more, he took steps to block the *Asantehene's* trade routes to the north.

With the decline of large-scale demand for slaves by Europeans, the trade in kola nuts with northerners had become all the more important. This interference with commerce was too much for Mensa Bonsu. In August 1875 his troops invaded Dwaben, routing their king. The Asante armies killed all they could catch and the rest fled into the bush for their lives. The British did not come to the aid of the Dwaben monarch, but they did continue to support various chiefs and kings throughout Asanteland in an effort to weaken the authority of the Kumasehene. Incited by this meddling, some states seceded from the Asante Empire.

Throughout Asanteland there was confusion. With the authority of the *Asantehene* in shambles, the Asante police force was replaced on the roads by brigands and bandits. Life was very insecure and famine ravaged the land. The impact of colonial disruption was growing.

Under the influence of his European-educated brother, Prince John Owusu Ansa, the *Asantehene* tried to institute democratic reforms to bring Asante more in line with the British way of doing things. He even went so far as to replace some Asante civil servants with Europeans, but since there was a lack of skilled Europeans in West Africa at that time, this did not work out well. Furthermore, many whites in the region were scoundrels, not given to sound administrative dealings. These radical changes threatened the traditional power structure of the councils and civil servants, and there were calls for the destoolment of Mensa Bonsu. However, the king remained in office.

In 1879 a cult arose in the land that called for a return to traditional Asante values and the ways of the ancestors. Mensa Bonsu was pressured to discard his innovations, but he refused to do so. After more than one *coup d'état* attempt in 1883, the king and his palace sentinels retaliated, spreading a reign of terror throughout his domain. His palace guards had managed to get breechloading repeating riffles, with which they began indiscriminately killing people.

Apparently all this was a bit much for Mensa Bonsu, who retreated into a drunken stupor and debauchery of unparalleled proportions. As people fled the city for their lives, Kumase was left a ghost town.

As the councilors of the land were pushing for Mensa Bonsu's removal, his brother, general Owusu Koko, succeeded and sent the *Asantehene* into exile, but the councilors could not agree on a successor.

At this time civil war erupted in the Asante Union, state turning against state, king against king. The chaos raged for two years, during which time warlords and private armies joined the fray. It is estimated that half the Asante population died or fled the country.

By 1885 all former tributary states to Kumase had become independent and Kumase was a ruined city. The palace was no longer an elegant stone structure, but merely a simple bamboo thatched hut. It sat idle.

In 1888 a royal faction led by Yaa Akyaa put her 15-year old son, **Agyemon Prempeh**, on the Golden Stool. This new administration was so strapped for money that they actually asked the British for the cash for the enstoolment ceremony, but declined this help when the British attached too many stipulations. It was not until 1894 that Prempeh was ceremonially enstooled.

The skillful diplomacy of the queen mother, Yaa Akyaa, and the admirable character of her son attracted good councilors to the seat of power. Slowly they were able to renew the Asante Empire, reestablishing a rule of law throughout the land to the point where gold production was regenerated, along with the new products of rubber and cocoa.

Despite these improvements, the British were still depicting the Asante as bloodthirsty primitives, and the *Asantehene* as an uncontrollable despot. They called for the destruction of this dangerous empire.

At this time in Britain, there was a growing move toward reinforcing colonial control of the distant parts of their empire. The apologist for imperial expansion, Joseph Chamberlain, was the new secretary of state with responsibility for the colonies. He and Africa-watchers feared that the French were trying to get control of more land in West Africa, which they were.

As the British were trying to extend their dominion over the Asante hinterlands to thwart the French advance, pundits in Britain called the Asante a "nuisance." As some of the Asante were now literate, they were well aware of their bad press in Britain. The *Asantehene* sent a six-man delegation to London to sue for peace and set the record straight about **human sacrifice**. Ritual carnage seemed to be the main cause of the calls for their destruction, though in reality the British wanted their gold, their land and to position themselves in the north to prevent an Asante/French alliance.

The delegates had a hard time meeting with Chamberlain, hiring barristers to plead their case before the government. In these appeals the Asante said that they were willing to grant preferred business concessions to the British, to allow the presence of a European resident governor in Kumase, to submit to the authority of the British Crown, and to guarantee the end to human sacrifice, which had in fact already been abolished.

Chamberlain went ahead with plans to invade Asanteland anyway. There was such a distrust of the French motives in West Africa that Chamberlain wanted to control a buffer zone between French West Africa and the lucrative Gold Coast Colony. When the Asante delegates left the United Kingdom, some actually sailed back to the Gold Coast on ships carrying war munitions to be used against the Asante.

In Kumase, preparations for war had begun. The *Asantehene* hid the Golden Stool and other valuables to prevent looting by the British. He also made one more effort for a peaceful settlement, sending Asante diplomats to the Cape Coast Castle, but the governor rebuffed them.

Governor Maxwell appointed Colonel Sir Francis Scott to lead a war party against Kumase. While this time the Asante still had their rickety Dane guns (muskets), the British had even better weaponry than during the last war. Martini-Henry repeating rifles had replaced the Sniders. Also they still used the Maxim Gun, 75-mm cannons and the very effective bayonets. The latter were potent weapons close in because the Asante warriors did not use swords or knives in hand to hand combat. Colonel Scott knew this and he knew the Asante had a penchant for shooting high, hence most British riflemen fired from the prone position. The British not only had better weapons they now had experience fighting against the Asante.

As Scott's men moved north and crossed the Pra River, there was no sign of the Asante armies, and indeed, they had not yet been mobilized. On January 16, 1896 as the column neared Kumase, Scott was met by high-ranking members of the inner circle who pleaded for peace. They were roughed up by Hausa guards and sent back to Kumase.

The next day Colonel Scott marched into Kumase unopposed. He was a man not unlike Wolseley in his triumph and in his racism. When some Asante captives of the king pleaded to be released, Scott replied that he would not bother because "black people did not mind or care much about their fate."

In a short time Governor Maxwell joined Scott, and the Asante people were subjected to still further humiliations. The *Asantehene* and the queen mother were made to bow down to the two men and hug their boots. The governor also demanded that all the indemnity monies be paid immediately, but the *Asantehene* pleaded for payment in installments.

After this shocking display of obeisance by the West Africans and arrogance by the Europeans, Maxwell said that the *Asantehene*, the queen mother and certain Asante officials were to become hostages and taken to Elmina Castle. The *Asantehene* was stripped of all symbols of office (although he had cleverly hidden the most important one, the famous Golden Stool).

British soldiers smashed open the door of the palace looking for loot. Upon finding that the place had been sanitized against just such despoilment, they seized more royal Asantes to be taken into exile. Widespread looting and burning in the city, including the wanton destruction of the people's ancestor shrines, followed this.

On January 22 the Europeans left Kumase to imprison the royals at Elmina Castle. The prisoners remained there about one year and were then moved to Sierra Leone. However, they had to be moved again because so many Asante royals and councilors were willing to make the trip to that neighboring state to visit and cheer up the hostages. Eventually they were exiled from West Africa to the Seychelles, islands in the Indian Ocean.

Prempeh lived in exile there till 1924. He and his people suffered this ignominy because of the long history of rivalry between Britain, France and Germany. The British feared that the Asante would link up with one or both of these nations. That the British were willing to break so many rules of international law and etiquette to bring down a nation which had so long wanted peace and trade led Robert Edgerton to entitle a chapter on this sad history as "Britannia waives the rules," reversing the lines in the famous song. It was another example of growing imperial arrogance.

During the next few years Opoku Mensa ruled in Kumase for the *Asantehene, in absentia,* watched closely by a British resident and his Hausa guards. Despite the efforts of the Europeans to break up the Asante nation, it continued to operate even without its formal leader.

Maxwell had permitted the opening of the country to trade, building up the infrastructure there with forced labor. By the end of 1899, 25 commercial licenses had been issued to British companies to mine gold, cut timber and export rubber. This was the financial payoff for years of violent efforts to invade and dominate Asanteland.[1]

The British objected loudly to human sacrifice and wanted to Christianize the Asante, but the real reason they sought domination had more to do the political economy of extraction. Christian missionaries had been operating in greater Asanteland, but were not allowed into metropolitan Kumase, even by Prempeh, who ironically converted to Christianity while in exile. At the time, however, these missionaries were spreading lurid tales in the provinces about the savagery of the Asante and acted as spies for the British. In more open support, they supplied head-bearers for the military columns of the British. As a reward, after Prempeh was sent away, the missionaries were allowed into Kumase.

The one failure of Scott's campaign against Prempeh was the failure to find the Golden Stool. They did not understand the complete meaning of the stool to the Asante, or they would not have wanted to take it from them. Had they succeeded in doing so, it seems a surety that the Asante nation would have risen up in war once again. The British merely thought that it was a symbol of power, much like the crown of a European king. They reasoned that by taking the Golden Stool, they would be depriving the Asante of a mere symbol around which to rally.

Of course, in the Asante belief system, the Golden Stool was a symbol of power, but it was much more. It was the substantive repository of the soul of the nation. The fate of the Golden Stool was the fate of the people. The well-being of the people depended on the preservation of the stool. To them, it was intricately tied up with their ancestors, the most sacred aspect of their cosmology. To allow anyone to take the stool would be tantamount to saying that the Asante, past, present and future, were no more.

The resident British administrator in Kumase was Captain W. B. Davidson-Houston. Anthropology was just a fledgling science in his day, and he certainly did not understand the depth of feeling the Asante people had for the Golden Stool. Part of his job was to track down rumors as to its whereabouts.

In December 1899 an Asante boy came to his residence and said that he knew where the Golden Stool was buried. Governor Sir Frederick Hodgson dispatched Captain C. H. Armitage to get it. They searched for it in vain, as the boy seemed to have been lying, but their very public search made everyone aware of the fact that they wanted the Golden Stool.

Hodgson aggravated matters further when he visited Kumase and again demanded that the 50,000 ounces of gold must be paid forthwith, but now with interest! He then went on to list each chief, king and élite who needed to contribute gold to the indemnity, and the amounts owed by each. This was astonishing to the Asante, but the *caus*

---

1. Over the years, 25 million ounces of gold have derived from its efforts—$10 billion dollars' worth if it were all valued at today's price. (To know more about gold mining today in Asanteland, see http://www.ashantigold.com/, and for the history see http://www.ashantigold.com/agc-hist.htm.)

belli (cause of conflict) was about to fall off Governor Hodgson's lips. He demanded that the Asante hand over their Golden Stool, and then uttered the fateful words: "Why am I not sitting on the Golden Stool at this moment?" The Asante had heard some pretty insane utterances from Europeans, but this topped the list. The crowd was stunned.

The Golden Stool was so sacred that only the *Asantehene* could sit on it, and then only rarely, on ceremonial occasions that called for such a consecrated act. For this haughty European to suggest that he wanted to sit on the stool was an affront of unparalleled proportions to the Asante nation. War was a certainty now.

This verbal slap in the face was accompanied by the British takeover of Asante lands and gold, and British use of free Asante men in forced labor to farm, mine, log and build the infrastructure of colonial domination. Freeborn Asante men were even required to be carriers for the Europeans, and if they refused, they were whipped by Hausa guards.

It is ironic that the nation that was so moralistic about the abolition of the slave trade was content to use forced labor to build the underpinnings of imperialism.

To illustrate the difference between this form of slavery, where men have to be whipped into shape, and the domestic slavery practiced by the Asante, one only has to remember that when the British imperiously freed Asante slaves, they refused to leave their masters. If the British took them away, they went back.

Furthermore, the Asante resented the imposition of the alien Christian dogma on their children, and the irritating paternalism and incessant racism of the Europeans.

Thus, there were many reasons for the great chiefs and nobles, male and female, to meet in secret to decide on a course of action. All along they had been secretly stockpiling guns under the nose of the resident, Captain W. B. Davidson-Houston. As the queen mother was in exile with Prempeh, another prominent woman rose to speak. She hated the British for exiling Prempeh and her son as well. Her name was Yaa Asantewaa, the queen mother of Edweso, the very place where the Golden Stool had been hidden. Yaa Asantewaa was adamant in saying that she would not pay a farthing to the British. When some nobleman suggested that they could not defeat the superior weapons of the British, she ridiculed his manhood by suggesting that he needed to wear a woman's undergarments. In a heated moment she grabbed a gun from a man and fired it off in bravado, demanding war of her men. This woman wore a sword in her belt as a symbol of insurgence and defiance, though there is no indication that she, or other Asante women, ever fought in battle.

In the end the chiefs swore an oath of national liberation, but they were betrayed, the results of their meeting being conveyed to the British governor. Several of the men at the meeting were arrested and deported. What the British didn't count on was the fact that these men were merely replaced by others, and they continued to prepare for war.

Again the same Asante boy showed up at the residents quarters saying that he had discovered the whereabouts of the Golden Stool. This was another wild goose chase, but more. The boy led the Europeans into an ambush. The boy had taken the Europeans into a densely forested area and when they emerged into a clearing they found themselves staring into the faces of a regiment of Asante warriors, all with their guns aimed at the handful of British soldiers. In what has to be a singularly British response, the officers pulled out the folding table that was always carried on which to prepare tea. While the incredulous Asante soldiers looked on, they set up the table. Calmly they set out the teapot, the cups and laid out the makings of tea. Then they quietly sat down to afternoon tea.

However much the Asante generals may have respected the coolness of these British officers, they fired anyway, sending the contents of the table flying in every direction. The British officers received minor wounds and together with their Hausa guard fought their way back to Kumase to report the attack.

While the British did not understand the depth of feeling about the Golden Stool; the Asante did not comprehend that when Brits are having their tea, you do not interrupt, and you certainly don't fire upon them.

The whites had made it to the British fort in Kumase, but they were now prisoners along with men, women, children and the Hausa guards. The missionaries also took refuge behind the fort's stout walls. When the hostilities broke out they rushed to the fort along with their black converts, but in what should have been a clear message about how whites felt about West Africans, only the whites were allowed to enter into safety. The Asante Christians were left to fend for themselves against their fellows, who saw them as traitors. Apparently the Sermon on the Mount did not apply to black faces.

Preparations for war continued. The political leader of the Asante became Opoku Mensa, and the general in charge was Kofi Kofia. They had learned about stockades that had been built in other West African areas, and reasoned that if they could block all roads in and out of metropolitan Asante they could hold out against the superior firepower of the British. It was a massive engineering feat to build these stockades, some of which were as long as 400 yards. Most were six feet high and six feet thick. They were constructed of huge logs cut by hand from the rain forest, and lashed together with the telegraph wire the British had strung linking the fort in Kumase with Cape Coast Castle. They were so strong that they could resist a direct hit from the British canons.

The Asante built war camps behind each barrier that gave their soldiers all the comforts of home, including a market where they could buy food, tobacco and gin.

The British at Cape Coast Castle had also been preparing for war, recruiting West Africans to help them fight against the Asante, as well as troops from as far away as Zanzibar and Mombassa. Captain Aplin with an all too small force pushed toward Kumase, but his column was shredded along the way by Asante fire. Those who were not killed made it to the fort in Kumase, but now they were prisoners as well. What was worse, having brought few provisions, they were an additional burden on the rapidly diminishing stocks of food.

Several relief columns tried to reach the hostages, but were turned back by heavy fire at the barricades. Now the people in the fort were starving, with a death rate of 30–40 per day. It was decided that some should make an escape effort. In the cover of night they slipped away and made it to safety. Eventually, too, the British broke through the Asante defenses and retook the fort and metropolitan Asante, which was left in ruins once more. This was to be the last in a string of senseless wars between Britain and Asante.

After the British victory, the colonials seemed intent on building rather than destroying, although their construction was mainly oriented toward economic annihilation, rather than creating better living conditions for the people. For example, in 1903 the Secondi to Kumase railway was opened. Although people needed health clinics, potable water facilities and education, the railway would get the timber, rubber, gold and cocoa to the coast, while returning with Britain's manufactured goods to sell in Asanteland. Nevertheless, relative prosperity began to spread through the land.

Another tense moment arose in 1921 when a road construction project was about to pave over the site where the Golden Stool was buried. It was removed in time, but some angry Asante were again calling for war. Fortunately by this time the British had been educated by the government anthropologist Robert S. Rattray about the true nature of the Golden Stool and its sacred importance to the Asante.

Another event involving the Golden Stool also helped Asante-British relations. While the stool was being moved from its threatened hiding place, thieves stole parts of the treasure, which were noticed for sale in the Kumase market. The Inner Council appealed to the British to arrest the perpetrators and bring them to trial. The British did and publicly announced that the Asante nation could keep the Golden Stool forever.

In November 1924 King Prempeh returned to head up his nation once more, ruling till his death in 1931. After a long interregnum in 1935, Nana Osei Agyeman Prempeh II was enstooled and the Golden Stool put on display at this happy celebration.

Asante kingship and a proud people have continued to the present day. But while the Akan people had legitimated the holder of the Golden Stool, they were alienated by the imposition of a nation-state by the British, and this resentment continued into the postcolonial period, as can be seen by the fact that the *Asantehene* was not present at the celebrations in Accra in 1957, when Ghana came under what some Asante perceived as a new form of absentee and illegitimate governance.

More recently Asante, the kingdom of gold, celebrated a new ruler when, on April 26, 1999, the Otumfuo Osei Tutu II was enstooled as the new *Asantehene*.[2]

The Islamic Reaction to European Imperialism

Islam was a counterforce to European penetration of the region. Whereas many peoples defended their territorial integrity against these foreigners, men like *Al-Hajj* Umar had another issue—to defend the sacred faith against the infidel.

Umar had been born Umar Said Tall in 1794 in Futa Toro. He was raised a scholar and converted to the *Tijaniyya* order, which had been founded by Ahmad al-Tijani, who claimed to have had direct communication with the Prophet Muhammad. More egalitarian than its rival order in the Western Sudan, the Qadariyya, Tijaniism promised spiritual enlightenment and possible sainthood to all who joined. Any member could access its leadership directly, but also anyone leaving the order would be considered a *kaffir*, an infidel. The combination of egalitarianism and tight-knit brotherhood of the *Tijaniyya* movement seemed to have an appeal in the chaotic times leading up to the colonial era.

While no Europeans understood this at the time, Islam had suffered a great fall in the Western Sudan. Once it was the religion of powerful kings, but after the fall of Songhai in 1600, a watershed event in the history of Islam in West Africa, the political fortunes of Islam suffered. Muslims see the next centuries as an Islamic Dark Age. The *Tarikh-es-Sudan*, written from an Islamic point of view, records that as a result of the fall of Songhai:

> Security gave way to danger, wealth to poverty, distress and calamities and violence succeeded tranquility; in every place there was plundering...Disorder was general and spread everywhere, rising to the highest degree of intensity.

---

2. (for a photo of Otumfuo Osei Tutu II see: http://www.ashantigold.com/news2.htm).

Clearly Muslims felt insecure and marginalized in the land. In Islam, there is no separation of church and state — rule should be uniformly according to the dictates of the teachings of the *Qur'an*. Subjugation to non-Muslim rule was seen as degrading. Muslim clerics were kept at court, but only to supply additional magical power to pagan shrines and medicines.

During this Dark Age, Muslims kept in touch informally throughout the Western Sudan. There were rumors and prophecies of the coming of a great **mujaddid (pl. mujihaddin)** or reformer. He would lead a *jihad* and become the *Caliph* of the Western Sudan.

The opposition of *Al-Hajj* Umar and other Muslims to French rule has to be seen in light of this background. Islamic reformers were trying to establish a theocratic state and, clearly, the imperialist dreams of the Europeans did not fit into that plan.

Some saw *Al-Hajj* Umar as the reformer. Indeed, though it is unlikely, he claimed to have been made *Caliph* of the Western Sudan while undertaking his pilgrimage to Mecca. Certainly he was in touch with the other major Islamic thinkers of the day. He married a daughter of the *Shehu* of Bornu on his way back from Mecca. From there he went to nearby Sokoto and married a daughter of Sultan Bello. He lived there five years and participated in the revolutionary fervor of the times. Eventually he returned to the Futa Jallon region to prepare his own *jihad*.

Al-Hajj Umar settled at Diagaakou with the agreement of the Almany of the area around 1840. However, at his *Tijaniyya* colony, his reformist teachings alarmed the king, and he was asked to leave. From there he established a base at Dinguiray, where he began to teach his gospel and train men in the art of war. On September 6, 1852 he claims to have had a divine revelation from Allah in which he was instructed to lead a *jihad*.

At first he did not move against his home area, but attacked the Bambara kingdom of Kaarta, defeating it in 1854. Umar had been in communication with the French, even assuring them that he had no aggressive intent against them, while trying to buy arms from them. They refused, and Umar increased his rhetoric against these foreigners. In 1855 in a letter to the Muslim community of St. Louis he wrote:

> From now on I will make use of force and I will not cease until peace is demanded from me by your tyrant [the French Governor].

Umar saw the French as the enemy of Islam, and Governor Faidherrbe likewise saw the *Al-Haji* as a threat to his expansionist vision. Faidherrbe was right to think this. *Al-Hajj* Umar was manufacturing his own guns and trading with Europeans, requiring them to pay the traditional *jizya* or tribute levied against non-Muslims under Islamic rule.

As the French tried to get a foothold in Sénégambia, the two expansionist movements came to loggerheads — the Christian French against the defenders of Islam. Faidherrbe built a fort at Medina in 1855 and two years later the first open clash came when the *Tijaniyya* reformer attacked the French and sustained a long siege against their fort, though he eventually withdrew. His primary aim was to reestablish Islamic control over his homeland, the Senegalese Futa, so he turned his attention away from the French. Although he again attacked them briefly at Matam, he was content to allow a stalemate that was to last two decades.

Umar had been successful in slowing the French advance along the River Senegal. He was mainly interested in expanding his empire and, after settling at Guémou, he conquered more territory to the east and continued his anti-Christian propaganda, making small-scale attacks on the French from time to time. In October 1855 the French moved on Guémou, destroying it.

Umar retreated to the east, but continued to harass the French, even stopping caravans bound for the French outposts carrying supplies. By 1863 Al-Hajj Umar had created a vast empire stretching from the French outpost of Medina to Timbuktu, an area almost as large as the Kingdom of Songhai (See Map 9.1). Without the presence of the French imperialists, Umar undoubtedly would have built an even larger empire.

Governor Faidherrbe tried to negotiate a line of demarcation between French territory and that of Umar's domain, but Umar was killed in battle in 1864 while talks were proceeding between the emissaries of the two polities. After Umar's death, the French did not push into his territory, holding the unconfirmed line till 1879 when they finally moved along the Niger River from the west. Ultimately they destroyed the *Tijaniyya* Tukolor Empire.

In sum, whether pagan or Muslim, Africans did not always passively accept European imperialism. Their eventual defeat was not due to a lack of bravery, military acumen or effort. It was due to the overwhelming firepower of the invaders.

CRITICAL THINKING QUESTIONS

1. Why did the Asante buy slaves from the Europeans?
2. In spite of the fact that most of the kings of Asante tried to sue for peace with the British, why did the British go to war against them?
3. In their dealings with the Asante, the British acted in ways that led Robert Edgerton to entitle a chapter in his book on the Asante as "Britannia waves the rules," reversing the lines in the famous song. What did he mean by this?
4. How did the Asante view the Golden Stool and why was it so important for them to hide it and keep the British from taking it? And why did they find Governor Hodgson's statement so outrageous when he said: "Why am I not sitting on the Golden Stool at this moment?"
5. From what you have read, what is the role of women in Asante politics?
6. Using the story of the Asante firing on the British while they were having their afternoon tea, what evidence can you present that both the Asante and British did not understand each other's cultures?

KEY CONCEPTS

Agyemon Prempeh
Ahiato
Akan
Amradofo
George Maclean (Captain)
Fante Federation of States
Forced labor

Jizya
King Coffee
Kleptocracy
Kotoko
Human sacrifice
Merchant Council
Mujaddid (pl. *mujihaddin*)

Osei Kwadro   *Sikapo*
Osei Tutu   *Sikapo-ahiato* ranking
Osei Yaw   Garnet Wolseley

≋ SOURCES & SUGGESTED READINGS ≋

Boahen, A. Adu. 1969. Asante and Fante A.D. 1000–1800. In: Ajayi, J. F. Ade and Ian Espie (eds.). *A thousand years of West African history*. Ibadan: Ibadan University Press, 165–190.

Bosman, Willem. 1967 [1705]. *A new and accurate description of the coast of Guinea, divided into the Gold, the Slave, and the Ivory Coasts*. New York: Barnes & Noble.

Bovill, E.W. 1958. *The Golden Trade of the Moors*. London: Oxford University Press.

Blake, John W. 1977. *West Africa: Quest for God and Gold 1454–1578*. London: Curzon Press.

Chazan, Naomi. 1988. The Asante Case. In: S. N. Eisenstadt (ed.). *The early state in African perspective*. Leiden: Brill.

Crowder, Michael. 1968. *West Africa under Colonial Rule*. Evanston: Northwestern University Press.

Davidson, Basil. 1992. *The black man's burden: Africa and the curse of the nation-state*. New York: Times Books.

Davidson, Basil. 1998. *West Africa before the Colonial Era: A history to 1850*. London: Longman.

Edgerton, Robert B. 1995. *The fall of the Asante Empire: The Hundred-Year War for Africa's Gold Coast*. New York: The Free Press.

Fage, J. D. 1969. *A history of West Africa*. Cambridge: Cambridge University Press.

Fage, J. D. 1995. *A history of Africa*. (Third Edition). London: Routledge.

Hogendorn, Jan & Marion Johnson. 1986. *The shell money of the slave trade*. Cambridge:Cambridge University Press.

Klein, Curtis. 1995. Africa and Europe before 1900. In: Martin, Phyllis M. & Patrick O'Meara [eds.]. *Africa* [Third edition]. Bloomington: Indiana University Press, 115–134.

Lance, James Merriman. 1995. *Seeking the political kingdom: British colonial impositions and African manipulations in the northern territories of the Gold Coast colony*. Ph.D. dissertation, Stanford University. Ann Arbor: University Microform (UMI) #9525856.

Lloyd, Christopher. 1973. *The search for the Niger*. London: Collins.

Lovejoy, Paul. 1983. *Transformations in slavery: A history of slavery in Africa*. Cambridge: Cambridge University Press.

Thomas, Hugh. 1997. *The slave trade: The story of the Atlantic Slave Trade: 1440–1870*. New York: Simon & Schuster.

13 TOWARD COLONIALISM

> Little by little competition between European nations led them to contemplate formal administration of these distant territories. This chapter details the events and circumstances of this transition. The historian, Michael Crowder had left us a periodization for colonial rule in West Africa:
> 1) 1880–1885: Proto-Colonial Period
> 2) 1885–1960: Colonial Period. This period of formal administration was divided as follows:
>   a) 1885–1900 = Period of Conquest & Occupation
>   b) 1900–1919 = Period of pacification & elaboration of systems of administration
>   c) 1919–1939 = Period of Colonial Rule Proper
>   d) 1939–1945 = The Watershed between Colonial Rule and Decolonization
>   e) 1945–1960 = Decolonization

The Push to the Interior

During the Proto-Colonial Period (1880–1885) some adventurers and exploration clubs were pushing for more knowledge of Africa's geography. Once they knew the boundaries, the peoples and the political leaders they had to deal with, Europeans sent their emissaries into the interior to get them to sign treaties and pledge allegiance to their country to the exclusion of other European countries. These newcomers wanted exclusive trade rights and political treaties were seen as a way of claiming this right. Although the French were ultimately more successful in penetrating the interior, they were slower to move toward control of their West African territories than the British. One reason was that the British were more industrialized and had a greater commercial interest in the region. Another reason was that the French had had some initial problems with their attempts at settlement. After the Treaty of Paris finalized the end of the Napoleonic wars, they tried to establish a colony on the Cape Verde peninsula, but failed. They then turned their efforts to their ancient base at the head of the Senegal River, St. Louis. France again tried to establish agricultural settlements, and again her efforts misfired. Ultimately, France simply maintained St. Louis as a trading base for the gum trade on the river and as a garrison town.

In 1802, largely out of scientific interest in exploration, French adventurers formed the *Société de l Afrique intérieure et de Découvertes*. However, their movements into the hinterlands were tentative at first. They did establish some alliances for trading purposes with chiefs on the Ivory Coast, and they opened the old French post at Ouidah in Dahomey but, all in all, their efforts in the first fifty years of the 19th century were feeble compared to those of the British. That would change with the appointment of **Governor Faidherrbe** in Senegal, who was to lead the French on their adventures into the interior. This soldier-governor challenged the forces of militant Islam and laid down the basis of France's empire in West Africa.

Before the military became involved, European adventurers wanted to map the course of the Niger River and explore the Guinea hinterlands out of scientific interest. The search for the Nile had caught the Victorian Imagination through adventure stories published in newspapers, popular books and even dramatic appearances of travelers before the Royal Geographical Society. In 1788, British politicians, philanthropists, clergymen, military men, and members of the nobility founded the **African Association** (later, the Geographical Society) that was to employ explorers to find the full course of the Niger. The first attempts came from the north, across the Sahara. This was dangerous because of the heat and arduous travel, but also because many Muslim rulers did not take kindly to infidels in their country. For this reason most who attempted this crossing went disguised in the ample garments of desert dwellers. However, many of these early trips ended in failure.

It was decided to attempt exploration of the Niger from Sénégambia. Major Daniel Houghton tried this route in "Moorish dress," but was presumably murdered along the way. Though he never returned, Houghton did send back glowing reports, mostly overstated, of untold riches in the interior. European capitalists were already accustomed to profits as high as 800% by simply trading from the coast—the possibility of cutting out the middlemen by actually reaching interior sources of goods was very attractive to these entrepreneurs.

In 1794, the African Association chose the 23-year old **Mungo Park** as a "geographical missionary" to follow in Houghton's footsteps. Park, a Scot, arrived at the mouth of the Gambia River in June 1795 and immediately went to the Association's outpost at Pisania upriver. Within a month he was struck down with fever. After his recovery, Park left for the interior on what was to be a harrowing journey, the first of two.

During the trip, Mungo Park was robbed repeatedly, suffered thirst and hunger, fainted several times from exhaustion, but with the kindness of several indigenous women along the way and an occasional ruler, Park was able to reach the Niger near Ségou in modern-day Mali. He wanted to push on to the mysterious Timbuktu, but was forced to turn back for lack of supplies and extreme exhaustion.

On his return trip he hooked up with a slave caravan taking captives to the coast. He noted that the slaves were treated very badly, being driven by whips, to the point that Park witnessed the suicides of two women who preferred death to captivity. The slaves, Park said, "are commonly secured by putting the right leg of one and the left of another into the same pair of fetters. By supporting the fetters with a string, they can walk, though slowly. Every four slaves are likewise fastened together by the necks with a strong rope of twisted thongs; and in the night an additional pair of fetters is put on their hands, and sometimes a light iron chair passed round their necks."

While the slaves suffered untold misery at the hands of their captors, they nursed the ill Park, giving him water and making a bed of leaves for him each night. By making about 20 to 30 miles a day, they reached Pisania on June 11, 1797 and Park was back in the United Kingdom by Christmas of that year.

Mungo Park, partially because of his odd name, became an overnight hero in the popular media. In 1799 he published a book about his journey then took up a post as the resident doctor in a small town in Northern Britain. However, he grew restless and took the chance to return to West Africa when offered a position by the Association.

On January 31, 1805 he landed again in Sénégambia. On this trip he had more supplies, personnel and indigenous helpers. He reached the Niger again, taking a more southerly route to avoid the dangers of the Islamic north. He purchased a boat and proceeded down the Niger to chart its course, but he was ambushed along the way and drowned while trying to swim to safety.

After the loss of Mungo Park, the African Association again tried the northern approach across the Sahara, but these attempts, too, ended in failure. Other explorers like Gordon Laing and Huge Clapperton made the journey to trace the Niger but were murdered or died from illness. **Richard Lander**, Clapperton's young servant, eventually would be credited with the discovery of the complete route of the Niger. Lander made his way south after his master died in 1827, hooked up with a European ship and returned to the United Kingdom. In 1830, he and his younger brother John sailed from England to Cape Coast Castle, then to Accra and on to Badagry. From there they went overland to Bussa, where Mungo Park had been killed, and sailed back down the Niger to the coast, showing that the great river did indeed, as Park had forecast, flow into the ocean. The Lander brothers published a book on their feat in 1832 entitled: A *Journal of an Expedition to Explore the Course and Termination of the Niger.*

Even though the Niger had been explored, there seemed to be some romanticism in crossing the Sahara in disguise. It was done again by Dr. **Henry Barth,** one of the last explorers to be sponsored by British interests. His travels in West Africa came at the end of the era of adventures, however, and his published account did not come by the attention that others before had received. But Barth's account is full of interesting detail. The doctor, explored West Africa in the Victorian Era, and was a German gentleman of means. As such, he exemplified form and manners. In spite of the fact that he traveled wearing long robes, his skin darkened with henna to give him an Arab appearance, he was thoroughly European. After some weeks in Timbuktu he was ready to leave. The night before his departure he was asked by the local ruler to dress once for him in European clothing as a parting gesture. Dr. Barth showed up at court in a black tuxedo, replete with full tails. With henna-stained skin, that must have been a sight. In retrospect, it also appears a sad, if humorous, comment on the inappropriateness of Victorian values in West Africa.

The last adventurer of note was Dr. **William Balfour Baikie** who is given credit for having proved the prophylactic powers of quinine in 1854.[1] This medical breakthrough opened up West Africa more than steamships up the Niger, more than adventuresome explorations across the Sahara. It gave the average trader and colonial administrator the medical technology to stay the course in the "White Man's Grave." It allowed such men to live in West Africa long enough to begin to build the infrastructure of extraction and exploitation.

Once the general geography of the region was known, the politicians of Europe began to covet it. The French, Germans and British especially began to move troops

---

1. In 1847, Alexander Bryson first noticed the beneficial effects of using quinine to combat fevers.

into the area to secure portions of the land for themselves. They tried to get kings and chiefs to sign treaties of alliance. These efforts were to come to a head at the end of the 19th century when the boundaries of Europe's colonies began to take shape.

The Proto-Colonial Period to the Berlin Conference

Despite these adventurous journeys by a few bold men, the interior of West Africa remained a challenge for those wishing to extend colonial control and trade. The years from 1880–1885 were crucial in our understanding of the intense rivalry between various European nations over the lands of West Africa both on the coast and in the interior.

Portugal was not expansive in West Africa. It still held a tiny fort called *São João Batista da Ajuda* at Ouidah on the Slave Coast. More importantly for their continued presence in the region, they held forts at Cacheu and Bissau in what was to be Portuguese Guine. Britain and France turned from a casual interest to an outright, scrambling competition with each other. In the words of Lord Salisbury:

> When I left the Foreign Office in 1880 nobody thought about Africa. When I returned to it in 1885 the nations of Europe were almost quarreling with each other as to the various portions of Africa they could obtain.

The British Colonial Office turned English traders loose in the interior. Their watchword of the day was that if high risks brought high profits, then commercialists could foot their own bills. On the part of the traders, this was not considered a bad deal, as they liked not having to pay taxes, although they called for the gunboat in the name of nationalism whenever they felt the need. Missionaries, too, were independent-minded, preferring their own administration to that of the government. Their idea was to help Africans help themselves through the light of Christ and the establishment of small Christian communities that would be self-governing.

In London the politicians had bigger fish to fry than West Africa, as Britain was the dominant player on the world stage of the day. So they let traders and missionaries slowly expand European influence over parts of the hinterland. While traders came first in the Niger Delta and missionaries followed, the reverse was true in the chaotic and war-torn area to the north of Lagos. There, missionaries established strong centers at Abeokuta and Ibadan, encouraged trade, and then the merchants arrived. In this zone of strife, people were receptive to the orderliness promised by mission settlements and hoped that eventually the flag would follow, which it did. In the Niger Delta region the Anglican Church had founded a diocese of the Niger under the care of the West African **Bishop Samuel Ajayi Crowther**. Thus, British colonial hegemony was spreading slowly behind the impetus of commerce and mission work in most cases.

The situation was different in the Francophone areas. In the early 1880s French military forces were aggressively pushing into the heart of the Western Sudan. To an extent this was driven by French traders who needed replacement products for the human cargo they had been trading, but there was more to it than that. The French military was smarting from defeats by the British and Prussians and so turned to Africa in their quest for empire. In addition, the economy of France was different from that of Britain. France had industrialized late, in the 1840s, and her economy was self-sufficient with no strong need for external markets. As the slave trade wound down, French traders in the Sénégambia area were left with a desultory trade in gum. It was hoped that by expanding into the interior and securing rights to the hinterlands, the French could pull an end run on the British

In both British and French territories, traders acted similarly. They wanted a hand free of government and taxation, but pressured the government when they thought it was in their interest to do so. When French traders wanted to expand French influence, they complained to the government about British excesses, and the British traders used French expansion in the same way, as a political lever in the halls of power in London. By the 1870s, French traders began to try to break the hold of the British in the Niger Delta and along the Niger River. Additionally, they had more manufactured goods by that time that they hoped to sell in West Africa. As Michael Crowder put it, "the French traders saw the Niger as a highway to commerce with the interior."

We are left with the question of why Europeans moved to colonialism at all, since they already had the ability to extract whatever they wanted from West Africa. Trade had been the driving force in expansion, but trade in West Africa was changing. It could not continue without transformations in the political arena. In the Niger Delta, competition was making commerce more and more difficult. Not only were there more traders and companies coming out from Britain, but the French and Germans were now very much interested in finding a way to the anticipated riches of the hinterlands. The coast had already been tapped for resources; now traders were looking northward for further opportunities. It was these traders, missionaries and in-country administrators who were most pressing their home governments to commit to colonial overlordship.

In general, home governments were reluctant to get more deeply involved, but some politicos were better able to see the economic writing on the wall than others. Jules Ferry rhetorically asked, while speaking before the French Chamber of Deputies on 12 November 1884:

> Is it not clear that, for all the great powers of modern Europe, since their industrial power commenced, there is posed an immense and difficult problem, which is the basis of industrial life, the very condition of existence *the question of "markets"*? Have you not seen the great industrial nations one by one arrive at a colonial policy? And can we say that this colonial policy is a lunacy for modern nations? Not at all, *Messieurs*, this policy is, for all of us, a necessity like the "market" itself.

It was the commercial class, then, that drove colonialism, through spokesmen such as Ferry. They wanted markets and feared protectionism—the threat that other European powers might set up trade barriers to their commercial ventures in West Africa. This mutual suspicion drove them to greater efforts to dominate their respective "zones" in the region. The Berlin Conference of 1884–85 was an attempt to bring some discipline to the imperialist process. In actuality, it was nothing more than a formal but *post facto* recognition of what had long been taking place in Africa.

At the Berlin Conference, the major European powers summarily divided up the continent by drawing arbitrary lines on a map according to each nation's claims. There were two keys to laying a valid claim to African lands: documentary evidence and occupation. At the conference, signatories agreed to notify each other of any claim to territory by supplying proof of occupation and any treaties with local African monarchs.

These rules were designed to bring some degree of uniformity to the scramble that was already in progress. The decisions made there laid the foundation for the modern map of Africa. Though in West Africa there have been minor name changes: Upper Volta to Burkina Faso and Dahomey to Benin, actual boundary changes have been few, the main one being the readjustment of the border between Nigeria and Cameroon. Most significant was the absence of African representation at the conference. Europeans, in their ignorance of African cultural identity, created artificial borders that cut through the lands of various peoples and clumped together other ethnic groups in alien ways. The modern-day state of Nigeria, for example, has some 434 different ethnic groups, some of which have historically been enemies to each other.

It is somewhat ironic that just as political rule was becoming more liberal in Europe, the politicos of that area were establishing dictatorial regimes in the colonies. **Authoritarian rule** became the order of the day in West Africa. Since the indigenes were seen as "child-like," paternalism formed the core of despotic rule and was used as one justification for absolutism. The need to spread Christianity as the one true religion was another.

Of course, at the basis of this rule was a strong current of racism. Colonialists viewed West Africans as technologically backward; therefore, they *had to be* mentally inferior. Why else would they not have achieved all the material developments that Europeans associated with "civilization"? **European materialism** seemed to indicate superiority. Since West Africans lacked many material achievements, they were defined as subordinate.

Furthermore, Europeans had been slaving heavily for centuries. Negroes were brought to Europe in chains. Black skin was equated with servitude and degradation. Missionaries saw tribals as heathens in need of rectification and salvation. In short, Europeans sat high on their throne of materialism and looked down on the indigenes of West Africa. In retrospect, given the social climate of Europe in the 19th century, colonial domination seems to have been inevitable.

When the map of West Africa was finally drawn to the satisfaction of the Europeans, France and Britain were the big winners, with Germany and Portugal receiving small slices of the pie. France got most of the territory with a large area called French West Africa that eventually evolved into the countries of Mali, Burkina Faso, Ivory Coast, Senegal, French Cameroon, Niger and Chad. England got the Gold Coast (Ghana), Nigeria and Sierra Leone, where it had offloaded many slaves captured by raiding slave ships on the high seas. Germany received tiny Togo and Cameroon, and Portugal got Guinea-Bissau. The United States had created Liberia in 1822 as a depository for freed slaves.

Toward an Informal Empire:
Conquest & Occupation

Whether the interior came to be controlled by the French, Germans or British, what happened at this time was a dramatic shift in West African history. Whereas previously, interior trade had been in the hands of Africans, now it was taken over by Europeans. Also, the West African peoples of the interior had ruled themselves throughout the 400 years of contact with Europe; now they came under Western domination. In the thirty years leading up to the 20th century, they lost more sovereignty than in all the previous contact period.

This was a contest between two civilizations—one that had concentrated on developing social relationships and one that had focused on technology. It was the superior technology of the steamship, the rail line, the gattling gun and quinine that allowed Europeans to prevail in their quest for empire. It was also the compliance and cooperation of some West Africans who came to see benefit in such collaboration. This included chiefs and emirs who operated under Indirect Rule, but also the **Frontier Force**, formed in 1895, made up of African soldiers and commanded by a small cadre of British officers. It also included the big men who were able to make the transition from slave trading to some form of legitimate trade or plantation farming for export.

Not only did the Europeans have the advantage of technology, but their schemes and commercial enterprises were backed by the sophisticated banking system of Europe, allowing them access to credit. Mining and other large businesses like trucking companies and plantations required capital. An infrastructure was needed for extraction—roads, rail lines, bridges and the like. European finance made these large-scale projects possible. In contrast, West African traders and farmers had to rely on limited funds from savings, family and friends.

African traders and entrepreneurs were reduced to a subordinate status. Some benefited, though, especially men who had been installed as chiefs. They were able to parlay their newfound offices into riches. They did this by using the labor of their new subjects, demanding bribes and having access to government information that allowed their projects to thrive, and their family members to pluck the prime administrative positions in the new empire. But, while some royal families did very well, most West Africans became subalterns.

This was not yet a colonial hegemony, but an **informal empire**. What is more, Europeans began to claim natural supremacy over West Africans, seen in the writings of many early adventurers, missionaries and colonists. For example, the famous explorer and consul Richard Burton said of his mission to Dahomey in 1863 that "the Negro, in mass, will not improve beyond a certain point, and that not respectable." Louis Binger, on a visit to the Mossi kingdom of Wagadugu in 1888, said: "If the European should ever come here, he should come as master." This assumption of European cultural and biological superiority was common; even men of the cloth were prone to see Europeans as natural masters. Henry Townsend, a pioneer missionary, opposed the appointment of West African Samuel Adjai Crowther, as bishop in the church in 1864. Crowther had been captured and sold as a slave, then dramatically rescued. He became a Christian, founded many mission stations and translated the Bible into Yoruba. Townsend's reasoning was that even most Africans themselves recognized that Europeans had been entrusted with a *special talent* to be used to help the more childlike Africans. No better example of paternalism do we find. Europeans began to portray Africans as simple savages, as children in need of fatherly care. This attitude of paternalism and superiority permeated European activities in establishing hegemonic controls over trade and, eventually, politics.

In 1886 **George Goldie's** consortium was chartered by the British government as the **Royal Niger Company**, and granted broad concessionary powers in "all the territory of the basin of the Niger." He entered a rough and ready area, a frontier with virtually no rules. The legitimate trade in commodities attracted a number of roughneck merchants. The trading companies that opened depots along the coast were often ruthlessly competitive, frequently using force to compel African suppliers to meet their demands. It was a chaotic situation that begged for order.

In turning to the Royal Niger Company, the British were trying to stop other Europeans from entering the area, establish some semblance of free trade within their own limits, and prevent outlandish violence to local customs "except so far as may be necessary in the interests of humanity." Goldie was also charged with the responsibility of ending slaving practices in the region.

The Royal Niger Company had established its headquarters far inland at Lokoja and assumed responsibility for the administration of areas along the Niger and Benue rivers where it operated depots. It was from this initial base that Goldie extended the company's jurisdiction to include territories acquired by treaty. Once a treaty was in hand, Goldie would install company administrators and a British-led indigenous constabulary that kept order and protected trade routes. Through clever diplomacy, Goldie was able to get treaties with Sokoto, Kano, Bornu, and Nupe, guaranteeing the company exclusive access to trade in those areas in return for the payment of an annual tribute. Though he may not have known it at the time, George Goldie was creating what was to become Nigeria.

At the end of the Berlin Conference in 1885, the British government held only Lagos and a small strip of land adjacent to the city (See Map 10.2). Goldie's company, with tepid backing by the nascent colonial administration, held lands from Minna in the north to Onitsha in the south; and from Ilorin on the west to Lafia on the east.

In time, the British established the Oil Rivers Protectorate and its Consul worked with Goldie to secure treaties from local chiefs. Trade led the way backed by the gunboat when needed. But the hold of the company was still nominal in some areas, and the British held an even looser hegemony in areas outside the Lagos Protectorate.

Their strategy at this time was exclusionary: simply to back the Royal Niger Company and keep competitors, both national and entrepreneurial, out. This was seen as a cost-effective way to control the land with few personnel and little investment. Although it was illegal under the laws of the Berlin Conference, Goldie had a *de facto* monopoly over the region. The company set up a string of trading posts along the Niger River linked with their headquarters at Asaba near Onitsha in the south. There, they established a High Court and a small garrison of 150 African troops led by three European officers.

One of the functions of the constabulary was to extract dues or levies from other traders who entered the lands controlled by the Royal Niger Company. This practice angered the Liverpool traders, who protested to London. But the biggest brouhaha developed when the German trader, Jacob Hoenigsberg, informed the emir of Nupe that Goldie was exacting levies in his kingdom, and also that the British considered his lands to be theirs. This angered the emir and caused the British to scurry to Nupe's overlord, Gwandu, with whom the British had a treaty. They were able to settle the matter and threw Hoenigsberg out of the territory. London didn't mind a little chicanery by the autocratic Goldie, but they were embarrassed when it made the international gossip columns.

This created a diplomatic mess, leading to formal protests flying back and forth from Foreign Office to Foreign Office. It was a clash between *de facto* and *de jure* control. Officially, by the standards of the Berlin Conference, the British could not claim suzerainty based on "a clerk and a warehouse." Other Europeans argued that legal occupation could not be claimed just because Goldie's company traded in the region. Since this almost brought England and France to war, Britain took formal control in 1899 of the lands held by the Royal Niger Company. In 1900 the territories of the Royal Niger Company south of Idah were integrated into the Niger Coast Protectorate to become the Protectorate of Southern Nigeria.

Nascent Administration

By 1902, Europe "owned" most of Sub-Saharan Africa, only Liberia had never been subjugated to formal colonial rule. Such "ownership" and colonial governance was seen as a Christian/European privilege. But Europeans did not understand West Africa, with its varied social forms and different environment. Communication and transport problems were formidable. Governance of the hinterlands presented early administrators located on the coast with ongoing headaches. There was little money to build an **extractive infrastructure**, little idea of how to manage the enormous task of governing such a vast and misunderstood area of the world. Furthermore, the men who were sent to do the job were given little support from home. They often had to rely on the Europeans who were already in Africa, the traders, missionaries and ruffians. Their initial approach was military and authoritarian.

Frederick Lugard (later Lord) went out to East Africa at the age of 30 in 1888, then headed Sir George Goldie's military force for the Royal Niger Company in 1894. When the Colonial Office divested Goldie of the responsibility of governance in 1897, Lugard was given command. In 1900 he became the High Commissioner (Governor) of the new colony of Nigeria. There, in trying to determine how to rule vast numbers of people and territory with a handful of Europeans, he devised his famous concept of Indirect Rule. This meant that a few White administrators were able to govern vast populations of West Africans through co-opted rulers.

In a general sense, the establishment and spread of European hegemony began to degrade the economic and political activities of some West Africans, while elevating others to positions of newly created power. Indirect Rule formalized the power of the Fulani emirs, for example, but in areas where chiefs of this magnitude did not exist, Lugard's administrators had to create them. The chiefs of the Grunshi peoples of Northern Ghana, avaricious and quick-handed, were able to gain enormous power overnight.

While many big men and chiefs landed on their feet, the average person now had to pay a head tax or hut tax in colonial currency. For most, the only way to earn such currency was to seek wage labor in the more developed parts of the colonies. Sometimes colonists forced men to work on road construction crews, but taxation drove many others to seek such employment. In addition, chiefs sometimes abused their newfound power and demanded that common farmers work their farms. Thus, the average person was probably worse off under colonial rule than before.

It is one of the ironies of West African history, however, that the tiny cadre of colonial administrators could not have created the institutions of domination without West African compliance. The building and continuance of the imperial structure needed the active participation of African brokers, clerks, *Tirailleurs*, messengers, cooks, maids, servants, policemen, porters, artisans and *aides de camp*. Perhaps at the time such West Africans did not see that they were contributing to their own political demise, seeing only the possibilities of individual advancement. While they did not see the newly created colonies as legitimate formations, they did accommodate themselves to the newly imposed conditions to make the best of it.

In this way, colonialism was done "on the cheap." Domination advanced with few European overseers, little money and no real urgency to develop the region beyond the immediate needs of extraction. Those in the private sector looked to government and those governing were expecting entrepreneurs and concessionary companies to do the lion's share of creating the physical infrastructure of roads, communications and the like. However, West Africa did not attract large numbers of European settlers. Those who did venture there in search of profits wanted to extract high value items such as minerals, rubber, timber and ivory—without maintaining a long-term presence.

In the hinterland provinces, concessionary companies really functioned as small polities. Many made their own laws, and ignored others that did not suit them. Some had their own police force, and all had considerable powers of administration in their local areas. Some went so far as to enter into international relations with foreign governments. Such extensions of power led to conflicts that finally induced their home governments to step in. For example, one of the most aggressive and powerful companies, The Royal Niger Company, had their charter terminated in 1899.

For all its timber, minerals and other products, West Africa was not the tropical treasure chest waiting to be opened by colonials. In fact, without slaving factored in, profits from the region were low. Part of the reason lay in the fact that governments were small and faced monumental tasks. However much they might have wanted to help develop the region, colonial administrators had little money and few personnel with which to work. In 1939, for example, there were only 191 European officials governing four million people in the Gold Coast.

At first, colonies were not paying for themselves and required government subsidies. Some in the Colonial Office saw West Africa as a drain on their funds. Others saw the need for government grants to bridge the gap between income from the region and the cost of the colonial administration. And these were not development grants, but were just to operate the imperial regimes that had been set up, however minimal they were. Such endowments continued into the second decade of the 20th century.

Most coastal colonies, standing alone, could have supported themselves. The hinterlands, however, were less developed, had sparse populations and were rarely self-supporting. As a rule, the coastals were financing the peoples of the interior, although most of the benefits of modernity lay near the coast as well.

Europeans were also frustrated by what they perceived as a lack of agricultural development. Their Christian heritage, in part, taught that good stewards of the land brought it "under the plow," as productive farms. Europeans blamed the lack of development on the laziness of the indigenes. They came to West Africa and saw vast stretches of unexploited land, and couldn't figure out why it wasn't being used. They did not realize that the delicate nature of African soils and the lack of good sources of irrigation water make intensive farming nearly impossible. A more rational approach, developed by indigenous farmers, is to farm extensively, using slash-and-burn techniques, moving from plot to plot and investing labor when the rains come.

During the dry season, tasks are varied, and more difficult for strangers to understand—repairing a roof, hunting, setting traps in the bush, foraging for bush products or weaving rope. What appears as laziness and inefficiency to an outsider, is part of a long tradition of knowledge about the environment—how to survive in the most effective way, given the climate, tools and materials with which the people have to work. In actual fact, it has been shown empirically that Africans are very efficient—producing more with less. For example, African farmers produce as many calories with 1,000 hours of work as Asian farmers produce with ten times that amount of labor.

There were too few Europeans to build colonies by themselves, so strong young men were forced or lured into labor, often far from their homes. They were needed as head-bearers, soldiers, workers on road gangs, policemen, miners, and servants and for a plethora of tasks in the colonial service. Those left back home suffered, as the youth taken from them had been their old age security. The lack of strong young men to carry on the tradition of the family farm meant that many old men had to struggle on in the fields with infirmities. Under precolonial conditions, they would have been able to retire and live off the efforts of their sons.

For most West Africans, then, colonialism was destructive. The European extractive economy meant loss of land, timber and mineral wealth. Colonial governance also meant new taxes, new forms of arduous labor, disruption of their normal lifecycles, a loss of labor on the farms and an erosion of the familial security net for the elderly.

Conflict in the Niger Delta

An ex-slave of Igbo origin named Jaja (1821–1891), had broken away from the ancient trading state of Bonny to found his own state in 1869 at Opobo. Jaja wanted to modernize his state to be independent of the Europeans. He established control over the palm oil trade in the region, brought in the latest technology and equipped his army with modern weaponry. Jaja was a man of high skill in trade and organization, but did manage to make a fatal mistake—he alienated the British Consul, missionaries and traders in the area. While Jaja was willing to adopt European technology, he was adamant about keeping out Christianity. His authority rested partly on animistic magico-religious practices and Christian teachings were potentially undermining.

The Opobo trading area soon attracted Europeans who sought to capture this trading route. Jaja put up fierce resistance to this outside intervention. He was successful for many years.

From the traders' perspective, Jaja's control over the river was too tight. They were miffed by his practice of imposing levies, even though, under the details of Jaja's treaty with the British, this was an acceptable and legal practice. Jaja had the power to back up his demands for payment—he simply closed down the river to all travel.

Under pressure from merchants in the region, Consul Johnston, who neither liked Jaja personally nor respected the rights of African monarchs, told Jaja to stop placing levies and closing the river lanes. Jaja defied him. The Consul sailed by gunboat to Opobo and lured Jaja aboard with a promise of safe passage. When on board, Jaja was told he could leave and war would start, or he could submit to a trial in Accra on his "illegal" closure of river traffic. He was sent to Accra for trial, an act that even Lord Salisbury called a "kidnapping."

The interference with Jaja's efforts to establish a modern trading kingdom was cut short by the meddling of Consul Johnston, but this was just one example of his unofficial bullying in the region. He did not want to deal with local chiefs and kings as equals, so he set up Governing Councils of African leaders with himself at the head. They never functioned well, but Consul Johnston's administration of the area drew some attention in London. In 1889, the British government sent out a Special Commissioner: Major Claude Macdonald. After an investigation, he filed a report recommending that the Johnston should pay more heed to African needs and wishes, but the report was never published.

Two years later London officials upgraded the position of Consul to Commissioner and installed Macdonald as the first to hold that office. In 1893, the name of the Protectorate was changed to that of Niger Coast. All this indicated a closer involvement by the Foreign Office in the affairs of the Niger Delta. Macdonald was true to his word and pursued peaceful relations with African leaders but, when he was on leave, his

Deputy, Ralph Moor pursued a different agenda. He began to move against King Nana, who was very much like Jaja in his progressiveness and skill at commerce. King Nana controlled the trade along the Benin River and its tributaries. From time to time he would blockade the river and demand tribute from passing traders. This angered his neighbors, as well as the Europeans.

Acting Commissioner Moor, under pressure from European traders, moved against King Nana on trumped-up charges that he was using slave labor. Most of the people of the area considered Nana to be the legitimate ruler, but as Moor stated, it "had become necessary to convince them to the contrary." Moor then provoked a fight with the king and attacked his capital. Apparently the king had been expecting trouble with the British, because the Europeans found a moat under construction along with other fortifications, 106 cannon, 445 blunderbusses, 640 Dane guns, ten revolvers, 1,640 kegs of gunpowder and 2,500 rounds of machine gun ammunition. King Nana was tried on the trumped up charges and exiled.

Africans like Jaja and King Nana tried to manage trade and modernize their own countries but were overrun by European interests. It is not that the British or other Europeans were anti-development, but they wanted to ensure that their own interests were promoted and felt their hegemonic policies were natural, given the role of paternalism they had assumed.

Some African monarchs were not aggressive and preferred to have as little contact as possible with Europeans. The *Oba* of Benin had signed a treaty of protection with the British in 1892, but following that, they had had little contact with outsiders. Unfortunately, stories of human sacrifice filtered out of the kingdom, and this was too much for the straight-laced British. Acting Consul-General Phillips was sent to dress down the *Oba*. However, in typical disregard for African ways, Phillips sent the *Oba* a message that he was coming but departed for Benin without waiting for a reply. As it turned out, an important festival was in progress, during which time the *Oba* could not interact with strangers.

When the king was informed that a party of white men was headed toward the capital, he sent out a party to intercept them and ask them to turn back. Apparently there was a dispute of some sort, and Phillips and all his men were killed on the spot.

Britain had its excuse to move against Benin. A punitive expedition was immediately formed, comprising 1,500 troops. They sacked the Benin capital and looted as much as they could carry, including some of the famous Benin art treasures. The conquest of Benin gave the British suzerainty over the entire coast, although the hinterlands did not come under their domination until after World War I.

Yorubaland was a prize that both the British and French wanted, but it was in a constant state of civil war in the 19th century. The British had established a strong presence there with trading posts and missions and wanted to keep the French out.

The Oyo kingdom had been dominant, but was losing power and the Yoruba were in the process of breaking into smaller polities (Abeokuta, Ibadan and Ijebu). As the Oyo hegemony disintegrated, European missionaries and administrators used trade goods and technology to play one faction against another. This led to even more disruption. Yoruba leaders feared that Britain was going to take over their lands. Many saw missionary work as an advance of political domination. For this reason, Abeokuta threw out all European missionaries in 1867.

When the British took over Lagos in 1861, Yoruba sovereigns became increasingly suspicious of European intentions. As the wars continued and the French lurked, the British tried to bring about some unity to the area. There were many European missionaries there, as well as the so-called *Saro* missionaries, who were ex-slaves from Sierra Leone. Through their influence, the area was experiencing a relatively high degree of acculturation. By the time of the Berlin Conference, missions had produced a substantial, educated élite with modernizing tendencies.

There was, however, some degree of conflict between various denominations and even missions from the same faith, as well as differences with the Lagos government. By the 1880s, the British administrators in Lagos and London saw the need for intervention. Conflicts were disrupting trade, merchants were losing money; and Lagos administrators were losing taxes. First they tried to negotiate a peace between the warring factions through the good faith efforts of two Christian Africans, the Reverend Samuel Johnson, a noted author, and the Reverend G. Phillips. When these talks stalled in 1893, Governor Carter took his troops into Yorubaland and, because of the disorder there, rather easily established British domination.

Only Ibadan objected strenuously to the stationing of a British Resident in their midst, though they acquiesced after receiving assurances from the Governor that he would not interfere with their internal affairs. Once pacification came to the area, many Yoruba were pleased with the prospect of peace and prosperity.

States like Asante and Benin were actually easier to subdue and govern than decentralized peoples like the Igbo. In moving eastward, the British encountered a land with no one ruler they could dethrone. Each settlement seemed a polity unto itself. When military skirmishes broke out, the enemy was elusive, fighting stealthily from the bushes. Because of the guerilla tactics of these independent-minded Africans, the British were not able to effectively subdue the Igbo without a great many punitive expeditions that continued into the second decade of the 20th century.

The British were also beginning to encounter institutions they did not entirely understand, but which they feared. One of these was the Arochukwu oracle held by the Aro Igbo. This segment of the Igbo people had long dominated the area's trade in slaves and legitimate goods. They could do so partly because of the their possession of the highly authoritative revelatory shrine.

The supernatural powers of this fetish protected the movements of Aro traders in most of Igboland. The supernatural reputation of the oracle allowed the Aro to trade with the coast and in lands that otherwise might have been hostile. The great profits they made off the slave trade also enabled them to build a significant military force. Needless to say, the Aro were strongly opposed to British rule. After many conflicts, the British attacked the site of the oracle on Christmas Eve, 1901. They hanged the chiefs and destroyed the oracle. Their suzerainty in the south was assured, although they had to deal with guerilla fighters for more than a decade longer.

The Move into the North

George Goldie knew that he could not easily subdue the powerful emirates of the north without British aid. Since the French were pressing in on the area, it was not difficult to convince London to back aggressive moves in that direction.

On the northern edge of the British Protectorate, the Nupe and Ilorin were especially troublesome, both to the Royal Niger Company and the British government. Had there been more unity among the British in Nigeria Goldie could have moved more quickly, but the various "protecting agencies" of the region were often in competition with each other as to who could secure a prized territory first. Not only was there an international scramble going on, but an internal scramble for West African land as well.

The continued raiding of Ilorin warriors into the Lagos Protectorate provided Goldie and Governor Carter with the justification they needed to attack. They were successful; the British installed a puppet emir and ceded Southern Nupe to the Royal Niger Company.

As Crowder put it, "Once Nupe and Ilorin, marcher emirates of the Sokoto **Caliphate,** had been conquered the stage was set for the eventual occupation of the rest of Northern Nigeria." Britain began to look northward and shift their administration from using the Royal Niger Company to formal rule. At the century's end the company's administrative duties were dissolved and on the first day of the 20th century the Colonial Office appointed Frederick Lugard as High Commissioner of the Protectorate of Northern Nigeria, installing him as ruler over lands that neither he, nor any other European had yet seen.

With little Colonial Office backing and a small budget, Lugard faced the vast Sokoto Caliphate. He knew that the area probably would not be taken easily or peacefully, as the emirs were very hostile to foreign rule in their domains. Lugard succeeded in his offensive and the great Sokoto Caliphate fell quite easily. Crowder explains:

> the Caliphate fell to Lugard's tiny forces because it never succeeded in co-ordinating the resistance of its constituent emirates nor in adapting its traditional military strategies to those of the invader. Nupe and Ilorin fought Goldie separately as did the emirates Lugard. Each victory for Lugard was a tragic 'Charge of the Light Brigade' for the Fulani. The will to resist was there, the military acumen lacking.

The deposed Sultan of Sokoto called on those faithful to Islam to follow him eastwards. While on this trek, the British caught up with him at Burmi and he was killed along with many others, though a group of 25,000 continued on to eventually settle on the Blue Nile near the Ethiopian border.

Even in defeat, the emirs remained powerful, a potent force with which Lugard had to reckon. For example, they demanded that Lugard prevent the coming of Christian missionaries, and although at first he favored their entry into the north, he agreed to the wishes of the emirs. The ruling structure was still in place. In fact, some have noted that British occupation and Indirect Rule probably froze the archaic structure of the political system, preventing movement toward modernization.

With the conquest of the north of Nigeria the British were nearing the end of their expansion in West Africa. Two more areas to be pacified were the hinterland of Sierra Leone and the Gambia.

The port of Freetown in Sierra Leone and its environs had been established by the abolitionist **Granville Sharpe** as a repository for freed slaves, but it was not a fertile spot. The rains are exceedingly heavy in the area and the soils poor for farming.

By 1886, the boundaries of the southern part of Sierra Leone had been established. Freetown's economy depended mainly on trade. The Sierra Leonean governors were not allowed to extend their lands to the north, but did sign treaties with local chiefs and held an informal interest in the area. British influence was minimal however, and in some towns, nothing more than "a police sergeant and the flag" represented British hegemony.

Creoles, many of whom were the result of a mixture of white settlers and freed slaves, controlled trade in Sierra Leone. They were getting rich, and consequently were able to lobby London for favors and to influence the choice of Governor in the area. When hinterland chiefs tried to bypass these middlemen, the Creoles fought back in what was known as the Trade Wars. They pushed the Colonial Office to annex the north and send punitive raids against disruptive chiefs.

Yet pressure from Freetown traders was only one factor in the decision to annex the north; the other was the fear of French occupation and the loss of the vital port at Freetown. In spite of their rivalry with the French, the British were hesitant to formalize their control of the Sierra Leone hinterland. They decided to do what they were already doing in the Asante hinterland: send treaty-makers around to various chiefs. In 1890 commissioners Garrett and Alldridge went about asking chiefs to sign these treaties of "friendship," not to sign any treaties with any other European powers and to accept a small contingent of Frontier Police in their areas. The British assured the chiefs that such police were there only to keep the peace and would not interfere with their rule.

In 1892 the Creole population drafted a proposal to London to set up a Protectorate with them in charge. This was denied and, instead, Governor Cardew was appointed in 1894, stressing the British philosophy that only white men should administer Africans, not Creoles.

When the British established a formal Protectorate in 1896 and Cardew imposed a ten shillings hut tax, the Mende in the south reacted with some violence. The Temne chief, Bai Bureh of Kasseh, in the north led a nine-month revolt against British expansion. The British reacted savagely, hanging the leaders of the revolt and killing many others. Although Cardew was criticized in an official report, the British imposed their dominion on both the Creole population and the indigenous peoples of Sierra Leone.

French Expansionism in West Africa

France and Britain were the major post-Berlin Conference players in the **scramble for Africa**. Portugal and Germany were bit players, with the latter eventually losing her territories after World War I.

The French thrust to the interior of the Western Sudan was essentially a military one, with the Marine as the driving force. But, not all military men felt that expansion was worthwhile for the nation. General Mangin said of the Western Sudan that it was a desert "where nothing can be grown except the decorations that flourish on the uniforms of officers impatient for promotion...." This aggrandizing spirit drove the flag to preceed the trader in the interior, while on the coast French traders went first, then governance followed. By 1895 the French had conquered over half of the total territories they would hold as colonies.

The push for territory in the Western Sudan by the French was driven by self-aggrandizement and the autonomy of command held by military men. They were better trained to make war than to sue for peace, and they tended to think in conquest terms. Michael Crowder says:

> The soldiers, with autonomy of command on the Upper Niger, for the most part determined what should be acquired for France and were more disposed to conquest than treaty-making even if possibilities of promotion were not at stake. Furthermore, they tended to think in terms of square *kilométrege* of land acquired rather than its quality as a sign of success.

Many British colonials laughed at the French "Empire of Sand" and the large military expenditures and sacrifices made to acquire it. Four-fifths of the French colonial budget was military, and they ultimately acquired 1,800,000 square miles of sub-optimal land with fewer than 11 million people.

Though soldiers were the driving force in French expansion, businessmen were not far behind. Greater distances and larger territories meant longer rail lines, more roads and bridges, great stretches to be covered by telegraph lines, many more administrative buildings and more troops to be supplied. Colonial ministers tended to support these commercial interests. Take for example the statement by Eugène Étienne, the minister for the colonies, speaking of Francophone West Africa:

> We have there a vast and immense domain which is ours to colonise and to make fruitful; and I think that, at this time, taking into account the world-wide movement of expansion, at the same time as foreign markets are closing against us, and we ourselves are thinking of our own market. I repeat, that it is wise to look to the future and reserve to French commerce and industry those outlets which are opened to her in the colonies and by the colonies.

Civil administration was less organized than either the traders or the military, however. Between 1882 and 1899 the Paris-based head of colonial operations in West Africa changed a total of twenty-one times! Nevertheless, there were two goals driving French expansion to the east. (1) France wanted an empire that would stretch from the Atlantic coast of Africa to the Indian Ocean. (2) They wanted to gain control of a navigable stretch of the Niger River, and as much of it as possible to halt the progress of Goldie's Royal Niger Company.

In pursuit of these goals, the French parliament authorized the expenditure of funds in 1880 to begin to build the Senegal-Niger Railway. This was not a simple engineering project or a casual business venture. It was to go through the Tukolor Empire and ultimately would enter country claimed by *Almamy* (king) Samori Touré. Before they could move east, French forces had to secure the area surrounding the Niger River and deal with a number of dissidents in the area. In addition, Lat Dior, the *Damel* (king) of Cayor, opposed the coming of the railway to his kingdom. He took up arms against the French and they retaliated, driving him from his capital. In his place they put a puppet ruler, but Lat Dior continued raids against the French until his defeat in 1886.

There were many such shifting alliances as local rulers came to observe the aggressive tactics of the French. Chiefs who had signed treaties with them, turned against them. One of the biggest thorns in the side of the French was Mahamadou Lamine. He was a Muslim Marabout and self-proclaimed **Mahdi**. He wanted to reestablish a great Sarakole Empire in the Western Sudan. In 1886 he attacked the French fort at Bakel, but after a prolonged siege, was beaten back. He then invaded the kingdom of Bondou and killed its ruler. Next he attacked the French at Sénédoubou, but the African lieutenant in charge repelled that attack. He continued to harass the French until his defeat and death in December 1887 at Tambacounda in Upper Gambia. The French officer in charge, Gallieni, had Lamine's wives distributed amongst his African soldiers and shot his 18-year old son.

Lamine's death meant that France's hold over her Senegalese base was now secure. Her problems lay to the east, in the Tukolor Empire and with Samori Touré east of the Niger River. This was a difficult time for France, as she was becoming embroiled in many imperialist adventures from Indo-China to North Africa to the Congo. As a result, she moved cautiously toward the Western Sudan. This gave the son of *Al-Hajj* Umar, Ahmadou Sékou, a chance to secure his position as successor to his *jihadist* father. From his capital at Ségou, he ruled an empire stretching from Bamako to Timbuktu. Many of his relatives ruled provinces and provincial towns, though his control over them was not absolute. In spite of his ephemeral power, in 1874 he declared himself Commander of the Faithful.

In 1880 Gallieni arrived in Ségou to make a treaty with Ahmadou Sékou concerning the building of the railway and the establishment of a French protectorate over Tukolor. The monarch stalled the French for ten months and then refused to allow a protectorate. In the Treaty of Niango, he did agree to give France favored nation status in trade in return for the French promise not to invade any Tukolor lands. The French Governor of Senegal never signed the document, though he changed it to give the French the right to establish a protectorate.

To build their railway, the French wanted complete security in the region. With imported Chinese and Moroccan workers, they started construction in 1881. They then encountered trouble with Samori Touré. In 1881, 1883 and 1885 Samori Touré's *sofa army* attacked the French, but each time the *sofas* were forced to retreat back across the Niger River to the east and south. In 1885 Samori was able to drive the French from their post at Nafadié, then met them and signed a treaty, sending his son Karamoko to Paris as a hostage.

Both the French and British wanted the land controlled by Samori Touré. While the French were advancing in his direction, the traders of Sierra Leone were urging the British government to establish a protectorate in the hinterlands. Indeed, Samori contemplated going along in order to get British protection against the military aggression of the French. In the end, he decided to fight both European powers to the bitter end.

On another front, the newly installed French commandant, Archinard wanted to make a name for himself through conquest in Haute Fleuve and he began to move on Ahmadou Sékou's Tukolor Empire. In 1890 he moved on Ségou, though Ahmadou had fled before the invasion. As Archinard marched toward Nioro, he encountered fierce resistance. In the end the chief of the town, Bandiougou Diara blew himself up in the powder room rather than submit to defeat at the hands of Archinard.

In January 1891 the French took Nioro, but again Ahmadou, following the Muslim principle of *hijra*, had strategically retreated to Massina. During his stay there, Ahmadou Sékou tried to link up with Samori Touré, but the alliance never materialized. Ahmadou moved to Dounge, where he ruled for three years. When he sensed that the French were moving in on him, he tried to link up with the Sultan of Sokoto, but he died along the way. He did not live to see the French victory over the Western Sudan.

Before that victory could be completed, however, the French had to deal with the man Marie Péroz called the "Bonaparte of the Soudan," Samori Touré. In the end Samori took on the French alone, although it would have perhaps been a different story if the three main empires in the north—Sokoto, Tukolor and Samori's *sofas*— had been able to form an alliance against the infidel invaders. In a letter to Ahmadou Sékou, Samori Touré wrote:

> If you continue to make war on your own, the whites will have no trouble in defeating you. I have already undergone the experience in trying my strength against them. Let us therefore unite. You will hit the French from the North, I will harass them in the south, and we will certainly manage to get rid of them.

But Samori also had been negotiating with the British and had treaties with the French. In 1891 a seven-year war broke out between the latter and the *Almamy*. Each accused the other of breaking the Treaty of Bissandougou and a long engagement began involving 13 major battles. Eventually Samori was forced six hundred kilometers to the east before he was captured and exiled.

Samori Touré proved a flexible and brilliant military strategist and administrator of a vast empire. He was always aware of the need to keep his supply lines open, and indeed, even after the fall of Sikasso in 1898, he was captured while bargaining for more supplies to fight back. Not only was Samori a good military strategist and planner, he also organized a vast agricultural empire with thousands of workers. He also established arms factories with more than three hundred specialists making and repairing guns.

What the French wanted was an empire linking Guinea and Senegal on the West with their lands in the Ivory Coast and Dahomey. The Mossi kingdom was the prize coveted by the French because their lands would give the French a bridge to Dahomey and much needed labor to exploit the rich Ivory Coast. Another area where the scramble was even more intensive was the Slave Coast, that stretch of shoreline between Accra and Lagos. Several countries had a foothold there, but the French and British were the major contestants. The former thought that the British wanted take the Slave Coast to link up Accra and Lagos; and the British were worried about French activity in Porto Novo and Cotonou, as well as their "meddling" in the Niger Delta.

In 1851 Bouët-Willaumez signed a treaty of commerce with King Ghezo of Dahomey. This began a series of treaties and failed **protectorates** in the region. In 1868, the successor to Ghezo, King Glele, entered into a trade agreement with the French over Cotonou. In a typical misunderstanding, the French thought they were getting full rights to the port, while the Dahomeans saw it as theirs, since France was paying them tribute. Of course, the French just saw the payments as a courtesy. Nevertheless, the French sought to enhance their treaty regarding Cotonou and did so with the King's agent (*yevogan*) in Cotonou in 1878, bringing in a French resident the following year. The French saw him as a governor, while King Glele and his men saw the Frenchman as a trade facilitator and nothing more.

The French set up a protectorate over Porto Novo in 1883 at the behest of its monarch. This set off a series of protectorates in Grand Popo, Agoué, Petite Popo and Porto Seguro which alarmed the British. Furthermore, in 1889 the French lieutenant Mizon sailed up the Niger and Benue Rivers to sign treaties. Under the auspices of the Berlin Conference he had the right to do so, but this further frightened the British. They stepped up their own treaty-making trips *contra* the French efforts.

When King Glele died, he was succeeded by King Behanzin who began to reassert his suzerainty over the ports of the Slave Coast. This was worrisome to the French, as was the fact that they knew he was buying arms from the Germans and was still raiding for slaves. But it was not until he took French hostages that they decided to engage the king in combat. In the battle of Cotonou, there were heavy losses on both sides and a peaceful settlement appeared to be agreeable. However, by 1892 the French made up their minds to occupy Dahomey once and for all.

The French general, Dodds, took on the Dahomean army in five major battles, eventually winning the day and exiling King Behanzin to Algeria where he died in 1906. His brother was made a puppet king within the French Protectorate.

With this success in securing Dahomey, the French began to look north for more territory and a way to control a navigable section of the Niger River. The most likely stretch was below the Bussa Rapids, in the kingdom of Bornu. There was some dispute about the suzerainty of the king of Bornu, the monarch of Nikki claiming hegemony over Bornu. Both the French and the British decided to scurry to Nikki to get a signed treaty. Captain Decoeur left Marseilles and proceeded overland to Nikki. Lugard knew of Decoeur's efforts and left London for Akassa, the headquarters of the Royal Niger Company where he continued by river steamer, beating Decoeur by five days. Though the king signed Lugard's treaty, he also signed one with Decoeur. The Europeans finally settled the matter, the British taking Bussa and the French getting Nikki.

As the scramble was accelerating, France moved to secure as much Sudanic territory in the Sudan as possible. In February 1894 the French took Timbuktu. In 1897 they moved toward Lake Chad, taking the town of Say the next year. The French then turned their attention to the desert terrain north of Senegal. It was not that they wanted more "sand," but the Moors there continuously raided across the border into French territory. They sent a Monsieur Coppolani, an Arabic-speaking Corsican, to negotiate with the Moors. At first, in 1902, he succeeded in securing Trarza, and the French made him Commissioner of the new civil territory of Mauritania. But while trying to extend French hegemony northeast to Tagânt and Adrar, the Sultan of Trarza conspired to have him killed, then he attacked the French with full force. At this point, the Moroccans entered the fray, laying siege to the city of Tidjika in the Tagânt. The French were able to drive them out but this was a difficult task, as the desert and mountainous terrain gave guerilla fighters good cover. The French suffered regular attacks until 1933, and while they had some control over Mauritania throughout the first half of the 20th century, it was tenuous.

The last area in Francophone West Africa to be pacified was the interior of the *Côte d'Ivoire*. It came under French rule in 1910 under the aggressive leadership of Governor Gabriel Angoulvant.

Few saw the commercial potential of the Ivory Coast, which at that time exported just a little coffee and other sundry items, but Angoulvant saw its potential. He advocated using military force to bring more natives under taxation and to stimulate export production. In 1909 Governor-General William Ponty agreed to Angoulvant's plan and moved his troops into the hinterlands. Speaking to his *Commandants de Cercle*, (District Commissioners), Angoulvant said:

It is necessary to establish a permanent contact between us and the native and to make him appreciate by example and with advice that we are inspired by the principles of humanity from which he had been chosen to be the first to derive both moral and material benefit. The fact that his character is indifferent to our good works must not discourage us; whether he likes it or not, the influence of our efforts and of our action is being exerted... If we should seem not to be taking into account from the very first the desires of the native, it is important that we follow without weakness the only way susceptible of bringing us to our goal. One must make no mistake about it: the desires of these natives are essentially unproductive, and opposed to all progress....

That some natives should be killed in the struggle is inevitable, and even desirable, otherwise the victor would be of no consequence in the future because the battle will have been fought without peril... to destroy a village is of no significance, so quickly are these agglomerations rebuilt... but the destruction of materials, when they are inevitable, should only be visited on annual crops, and never at all on trees of slow growth...

Governor Angoulvant pursued military action until World War I. The conquest of Francophone West Africa was accomplished with much violence on the part of the French and at great cost in African lives.

Culture Change in West Africa

In West Africa, contact with Europeans brought change, but there was a great deal of variance in that change, in the way it impacted different peoples in different ways at different times. Nor has the rate of change been equal.

With regard to West Africa, we can say that there has been a long period of infiltration by European culture; the appearance of the Portuguese ships and slavers was a dramatic event in some places, with early consequences. In other parts of the region, the impact of the White Man was not felt till centuries later.

In general, the coastal societies felt the impact first and most viciously. But over the next 500 years, there was a ripple effect from the coast to the interior. That rippling occurred primarily in the form of trading and raiding for slaves. The impact of European influence waxed and waned from contact to the end of the 19th century. After the Berlin Conference, the speed of change accelerated, as did its scope. Whereas the Europeans had previously remained marginalized in their offshore trading hulks or castles on the coast, they now ventured inland to claim political hegemony. The sent emissaries into the interior to strike treaties with the kings and chiefs of those faraway polities, and those early diplomats were soon followed by colonial officers and troops.

This was a time of rapid penetration — from the1880s to the first decade of the 20th century. This acceleration of change continued throughout the colonial era and into the early postcolonial period. The African people were bombarded with new religions, new political forms and new technologies.

To some, colonialism brought opportunities for education and travel abroad to attend universities; to others it meant the need to scratch the earth a little harder to get the money to pay the government's head tax.

The arrival of Europeans affected the civic culture of West Africans. However, some elements of change were incorporated without weakening the civic culture. For example, West Africans readily accepted cassava, tobacco, maize and yams from the New World. But European interference did influence culture change, as when Europeans stymied Jaja's development efforts.

The unevenness of diffusion and acceptance of new ideas and artifacts is based on a number of factors affecting the adoption of innovation. These include the duration of contact, its intensity, variance in colonial policies, the differing reaction by various West African groups (ranging from exuberant acceptance to armed resistance) and selectivity — that is, not all innovations are equally accepted. For example, government-provided health care may be universally accepted, while monogamy may not.

Igbo Receptivity to Change

After the end of slaving, between 1860 and 1915, hundreds of thousands of Igbo migrated to large cities in colonial Nigeria. The anthropologist Simon Ottenberg says that the Igbo found urban life "stimulating and rewarding." The Igbo saw education as a means of achievement in the new colonial structure and, using it, they acquired top jobs in the bureaucracy or took other urban jobs. They also excelled in trade, commerce and politics. The Igbo, although staunchly anti-colonial, were ready to seek Westernization, seeing education, acquisition of bureaucracy and political posts as a way to undermine British rule. They firmly believed that Westernization would proceed faster once the British had been pushed out.

Contact with British culture changed Igbo structures somewhat. Unilineal descent groups became less important and smaller household groups became more prominent. The ancestor cult was nudged aside to make room for Christianity. And Indirect Rule weakened the traditional authority structure, allowing the rise of educated and acculturated young men to council with traditional elders.

The Igbo experienced a long history of slaving and the opportunities for advancement and wealth accumulation it brought to a few aggrandizers. When slaving ended, farming and trading in palm products took its place. Western buyers were in constant contact with small producers through an elaborate system of trade networks.

This new trade gave the Igbo a continued contact with the West and a sufficient surplus to acquire new manufactured goods for prestige and to educate children who would then bring their supporters more prestige and wealth.

The Arochukwu Igbo (See Map 11.1) who moved to the coast and who were heavily involved in the trade in humans were highly acculturated and powerful during the 300 years of slave trading. When that ended, palm production was not easily dominated by the coastal Igbo who lost power to a more diffuse network of merchants and producers in the interior. With the commercial monopoly broken, trade became anybody's business.

In Igboland, mission work flourished and was seen as a means of acquiring education and modernization. Many Igbos readily converted to the new religion, although not all forsook their other deities.

Ottenberg notes that Igbo culture is highly individualistic, but assertiveness in a group setting is valued. The kin group is also important, but a man must prove himself and make his own way in the world, even if he inherits a position of authority or wealth. Achievement is equally important along with ascription. The Igbo value aggressiveness, skill in oratory and knowledge of their ancestral lore. Igbo men had many non-descent related organizations through which to express their individuality and assertiveness—title societies, voluntary associations, secret societies, and a variety of other cults and sodalities. Aggrandizers needed wealth to join title societies and other sodalities, thus much cultural emphasis was placed on developing wide-flung networks of kin, non-kin and persons of influence who could make loans and provide support to an up-and-coming young man. Contacts were very important.

But this was not a restrictive society favoring only the wealthy. High status was open to anyone of non-slave origin. Positions of prestige, authority and leadership were largely achieved, based on assertiveness and will.

The Igbo did not want the British presence, but they wanted the education they provided, largely through mission schools. They saw education as the way to take over the bureaucracy organized under colonial rule. If aggrandizement was always a part of Igbo culture, at least during the contact phase, then colonialism merely provided more opportunities for advancement. It provided access to government posts, positions as priests or assistants in missions, new trade opportunities, wage labor—all sorts of new prospects for advancement.

In Igbo culture both individuals and groups are competitive. Villages compete with each other for prestige. Kin groups try to outdo each other. Sodalities go to great expense and effort to put on masquerades and festivals that outdo neighboring sodalities. Relative status is very important in Igbo culture. In the Igbo system, both people and groups can slide up and down a scale of prestige, being continually judged by their actions.

European society merely gave the Igbo new life chances. It gave rivalries between individuals and groups new dimensions of expression. Ottenberg says:

> Villages compete to build the first or the best school, village groups to improve their markets. Many social groups strive to push some of their "sons" ahead in schooling and to obtain scholarships in competition with other groups. Individuals who acquire schooling, wealth or political influence are expected to use their new social standing to benefit the groups with which they are associated.

Igboland had many sodalities and had adopted many new ways from migrants, other than Europeans, even from groups that moved in and adopted the Igbo language. Population increase also led to out-migration and the need to adapt to new and changing conditions. Spatial and social mobility became an accepted part of Igbo culture.

Given the multitude of opportunities, Igbo culture adapted by developing a cultural penchant toward egalitarianism and flexibility. It is perhaps not surprising, then, that it was the Igbo who first resisted the shackles of the federal Nigerian government and attempted to break away to form their own state of Biafra in the 1960s. Unused to overrule and driven by cultural principles of freedom and achievement, they sought to find their own way outside the framework imposed on them by the British.

Culture Change in Fante Cults

The Fante live in Southern Ghana. With the coming of the Portuguese in 1462, they were some of the first peoples along the Gold Coast to have intense contact with Europeans. Eventually they became instrumental in helping the British overcome the powerful kingdom of Asante in the interior.

The Fante had ancestor cults that underpinned the authority of the leaders of matrilineal clans. In certain ways the authority of chiefs was tied to spirits and the rites associated with them. The Fante also believe in a variety of deities that can become tutelary spirits to a priest by possessing him.

A **possession** may occur in private or as part of a public ceremony. A person who first becomes possessed by walking alone in the bush may choose to become an apprentice to the priesthood. If initiates wish to learn the secrets associated with possession they serve a five-year apprenticeship, during which time they learn the songs and drum patterns used to call the spirits, as well as herbs, talismans and techniques associated with the calling.

The object of possession is divination. A client wants to know the source of a misfortune and the priest contacts the supernatural world to find out the cause. Usually some deviant act on the part of the living is deemed to be the cause of the illness or misfortune.

That is the traditional etiology. However with the coming of the confusion brought by the White Man, accusations and fears of witchcraft rose significantly. Thus, priests also came to find *asuman* or charms commonly buried on the beach in the sand. It was

Photo 13.1   An Ancestral Sacrifice.

thought that witches buried these to cause harm. The witch might include some of the victim's hair, nail clippings, a piece of clothing worn by them or some mud containing the victim's urine. It is for this reason that the Fante are careful to collect such paraphernalia or to urinate in secret. If a possessed priest uncovers a charm, throwing it away in a latrine or burning it can neutralize its power.

These Fante beliefs have changed somewhat due to their long contact with Europeans. The Fante had interacted with Europeans in political and economic transactions since 1482. However, their acculturation accelerated in 1827 when organized missionary activity began. Today the Fante are among some of the most acculturated peoples in West Africa and much of the mission work is in their hands.

Contact with Europeans and Christianity has weakened some structures of Fante society, although Western values and ethics have only been partially accepted. From the very beginning, Christian missionaries denounced "fetishism" among the Fante. This included the worship of idols and other rituals involving blood sacrifice and veneration of any deity other than the Christian god (See Photo 13.1). Since many of these rites underpinned clan and political structures, these structures were weakened. Many calendrical rites supported the power of chiefs and the councils of elders, and their influence diminished in the eyes of converts.

Furthermore, the matrilineal ideas of the Fante were in conflict with the patriarchy of Christianity. Western attitudes about sex were contrary to those of the Fante. But the overall individualism of Christianity and its accompanying economic system were destabilizing, because they ran counter to the corporate responsibility of the clan. These foreign ideas increased atomization in Fante culture. Parliamentary forms of government supported by the Europeans were incompatible with traditional geronto-cratic ones. European education also undermined traditional ideas.

Fantes have a difficult time reconciling some Christian stances—monotheism, for example, does not fit well in their polytheistic world. Certainly it is hard to see why one god pushes out others. Many Fante are inclined to practice Christianity in an additive way. Some rarely go to church, but carry on with their ancestral rites, others attend church and conceal the sacred marks on their bodies or charms they wear as magical protection—all considered "fetishism" to the Christian priests and pastors. It is difficult for people in rapid change to understand similarities and differences, and some of them may even seem silly. For example, polygyny occurs in the Bible yet it is forbidden in Christian practice. And sometimes life interferes with ideals. One **komfo** priestess said that her first spirit possession took place while sitting in a Methodist meeting.

Devout Christians exist in Fanteland, but many are able to compartmentalize their lives sufficiently to attend Christian meetings and still support the rites of their families and chiefs. Sometimes the religious contradiction is resolved through compromise. Traditionally, Friday was a day of rest for farmers. This was the sacred day of *Asaare Efua*, the Earth Goddess. The fisherman had another Sabbath day—Tuesday, the day of rest from fishing in honor of *Bosompo*, the God of the Sea. The Fante now have a five-day workweek with Christian fishermen resting on Tuesday and Sunday and farmers on Sunday and Friday.

The syncretism we find in West Africa is not unlike the New World pattern where Catholic saints were combined with African deities. The difference is that among the Fante, the imports are from Europe. For example, at Esiam the people worship a bell left behind by the Portuguese. At Elmina, a statue of São Antonio was associated with a local deity, *Ntona*. The worshipers of these sacralized objects are called the adherents of *Santa Mariafo*, *-fo* meaning people in Fante—thus, the followers of St. Mary.

The Fante have another class of priests called the *osofo*. These are celebrants who attend to prominent deities in Fante mythology. They are never associated with magic or the use of medicines. Today, the same term is used to apply to all Christian leaders.

There has been a general decline in traditional religion and a rise in new cults and modified versions of Christianity. Fishing communities (See Photo 13.2) have retained more rites from the past, while farming communities have retained very few. Overall, the Fante appear to be more insecure, more anxious about life conditions and their requests to shrines and attendant priests have changed.

Supplication is a common pattern throughout West Africa. The supplicant makes a small offering to a shrine and promises a greater contribution if his or her request is granted. That pattern is followed with the new shrines, many of which are imported from Northern Ghana. Mendicants often seek aid or information. Today that may include an entrance examination or an application for a job. Lorry drivers seek safety charms, and medicine to ensure good fares. Defendants in a court case procure medi-

Photo 13.2   Fishing Boats on the West African Coast.

cine to "lock up the tongue" of witnesses (medicine applied to a store-bought lock). Students want to pass exams. Fans request medicine to cause opposing football teams to stumble. Applicants want supernatural help in getting a job. Farmers would like assurance that the world price of cocoa will remain high, or that their crops will be bypassed by the dreaded cocoa shoot disease. Even criminals seek medicine to make them invisible to the police.

Ideas about the supernatural have not diminished in modern times, but they have shifted. Many Africans believed that the success of Kwame Nkrumah and the CPP party during his imprisonment by the British was due to the fact that he had powerful medicine that allowed him to fly out of jail at night to visit his trusted advisors—an application of old ideas to new situations. Priests of old and new cults regularly make sacrifices for overall government success in delivering promises and social services.

But new cults are different from old ones. First of all, fees have become pecuniary rather than in kind, and they have become inflated. Whereas in the old days a supplicant may have paid a few kola nuts, made his request and paid a chicken or a goat upon receipt of his request, these days a "sacrifice" means an agreed upon sum of money.

Rising anxieties in modern life have produced greater activity by witches, or in Fante culture, *anyen*, the worker of evil magic. These are not sorcerers who use medicine to harm, but ordinary people who have the capacity to project their ill will on others. They have all the traditional characteristics of witches—they fly at night, are invisible and suck people's blood. They are an explanation for evil and misfortune in life. They kill, make people sterile and cause general chaos in society.

Witchcraft was a widespread belief in Africa, but the new form of this phenomenon is different. In traditional Fante culture witches were confined to the members of the matriclan of the afflicted person, those with whom the victim was most likely to have real conflicts or grudges. In the modern version of witchcraft, witches are everywhere, coming from any social group.

The British tried to stamp out anti-witch activity, but failed. In the traditional setting, witches were identified at the funeral. Carried on family members' heads, the body would point out a witch who had killed him, and then the accused would be required to drink poison. If he survived, he was innocent. The British banned this practice early in their rule, but by the 1930s it had been replaced by new witch-finding cults.

The new witch finding cults, such as *Tigare* (Tiger, though none exist in Africa), are often a combination of African, Muslim and Christian elements. Characteristic of other similar cults, adherents of the *Tigare* sect pay a fee for lifelong membership. Normally they submit to the power of a medicine that will kill them if they break the rules of the cult. It is thought that the medicine will kill any follower who deviates from the code. Such cults function to create order in society in the face of apparent confusion.

There are material signs of syncretism as well. The *Tigare* priest dresses in Muslim-style robes, uses some Muslim ritual and often gives out talismans with writings from the *Qur'an*. But whereas Muslims prohibit spirit possession, *Tigare* priests divine by going into a trance. Old-style Fante priests were the only ones who could go into a trance in a public festival, but modern cults allow anyone to be so overcome. Cynical Fante accuse *Tigare* priests of making a living on people's fears, and they might be right. The normal pattern is for a solicitor to pay a couple of shillings, eat a "sacralized" kola nut, make promises of future sacrifice if his wish is granted and wait for the outcome. The priest pockets the shillings and receives further payment, as agreed, if the supplicant is happy.

Admission to the priesthood works somewhat like a pyramid scheme. An "ordained" priest sponsors a novice by paying his initiation fees and leads him through his apprenticeship. When the novitiate begins to earn money, he pays the sponsor back with interest.

Can we say that colonialism and the false promise of modernization have produced some kind of mass neurosis among the Fante and others in West Africa? Perhaps that is too strong, but certainly the failure of modern life to live up to expectations has heightened insecurity and uncertainty among acculturated peoples in the region. Cults like *Tigare* are an attempt to explain and ameliorate the malaise of modernity.

Conclusions

In their efforts to trade in West Africa, Europeans started by dealing with coastal brokers, but eventually decided to penetrate deeper into the interior to try to cut out the middlemen in their commercial transactions. Sometimes trading companies made treaties with locals, at other times it was through government backing. In either case, this was a prelude to European domination in the area. Inevitably, this led to the establishment of protectorates, and in due time, colonies.

Even though Africans had prevented a takeover by Europeans for centuries and had dealt with these foreigners as equals throughout that time, the racism of Whites ultimately led them to define Blacks as the "other." Even Creoles were placed in this category. As such, they were in need of a paternalistic imperial regime to care for their needs.

While there were pockets of military and guerilla resistance to European penetration, West Africa's submission to colonial rule was relatively quiet compared to other parts of Africa. Coastals found dealing with Europeans profitable, and those in the interior simply did not have the military hardware or the battle tactics to resist the cannons and machine guns of the intruders.

After a period of pacification and elaboration of the systems of colonial administration in West Africa, roughly in the first two decades of the 20th century, the period of colonial rule officially began. It lasted until 1939. World War II was a watershed event that produced forces that accelerated the dismantling of colonial rule.

≋≋ CRITICAL THINKING QUESTIONS ≋≋

1. Why didn't the Europeans move directly into the interior and why did they begin to do so when they did decide to penetrate the hinterlands?
2. In what ways did technology, not just in the military form, enable Europeans to penetrate the West African hinterlands?
3. Discuss the concept of an Informal Empire and the concessionary powers given to trading companies and their period of rule in West Africa. Relate this to the concept of political economy.
4. How did paternalism and racism enter into the way Europeans dealt with Creoles and indigenous peoples in West Africa?
5. Why did European troops have a relatively easy time in battles against West Africans, even great empires such as Sokoto?
6. In what ways could the actions of the Europeans be seen as a damper on West African development?
7. Does all culture change occur as part of a passive process of simple encounters between traits? In what way are agency and an aggressive desire to change other cultures involved? Give examples from West Africa.

≋≋ KEY CONCEPTS ≋≋

African Association
Authoritarian rule
Bishop Samuel Ajayi Crowther
Caliphate
European materialism
Extractive infrastructure
Faidherrbe, Governor
Francophone
Frontier Force
George Goldie (Sir)
Granville Sharpe
Henry Barth
Hijra

Informal empire
Jaja
Komfo
Mahdi
Mungo Park
Possession
Protectorates
Richard Lander
Royal Niger Company
Saro
Scramble for Africa
Sofa army
William Balfour Baikie

≋ SOURCES & SUGGESTED READINGS ≋

Angoulvant, Gabriel. 1916. *La Pacification de la Côte d'Ivoire 1908–1915: Méthodes et Résultats*. Paris.

Crowder, Michael. 1968. *West Africa under Colonial Rule*. Evanston: Northwestern University Press.

Fage, J. D. 1995. *A history of Africa*. London: Routledge. Chapter. 13

Hobson, John Atkinson. 1948. *Imperialism*. London: G. Allen & Unwin Ltd.

Lenin, Vladimir Ilich. 1933. *Imperialism, the highest stage of capitalism: A popular outline*. New York: International Publishers.

Lloyd, Christopher. 1973. *The search for the Niger*. London: Collins.

Nwaubani, Ebere. 2000. Acephalous societies. In: Falola, Tony (ed.). *Africa: African history before 1885* (Volume 1). Durham, NC: Carolina Academic Press, 275–294.

Ottenberg, Simon. 1959. Ibo receptivity to change. In W. R. Bascom and M. J. Herskovits (eds.), *Continuity and Change in African cultures*. Chicago: University of Chicago Press, 130–143.

Roberts, Stephen H. 1963. *The history of French colonial policy, 1870–1925* (second edition). London: Cass.

Skinner, Elliot P. 1964. *The Mossi of the Upper Volta; the political development of a Sudanese people*. Stanford, California: Stanford University Press.

Smith, Mary. 1964. *Baba of Karo: A woman of the Moslem Hausa*. With an introduction and notes by M.G. Smith. Preface by C. Daryll Forde. New York, Praeger.

Toutée, Major. *Dahomé-Niger-Toureg*. Paris.

14 COLONIALISM IN ACTION

Generally, colonialism is thought to have been detrimental to the organic development of African society. During its day, however, proponents of colonialism said it would bring progress. Yet, Europeans misunderstood African political structures and imposed their own ruling frameworks, which further complicated social life in colonies that already had artificial borders and ignored ethnic sensibilities. Nevertheless, because of a lack of a large European settler population and land grabs that occurred elsewhere in Africa, most West Africans tried to accommodate themselves to the colonial situation and some thought it an improvement and that it would led to further betterment. Sadly, this was not to be the case. Colonialism was grounded in commercialism, a system to extract raw materials and create markets for European manufactures. Its developmental foundations were laid upon the sands of exploitation. Colonial apologists noted that they had brought Christianity to a pagan land, but the unfolding of religious conflict in the region between Christians, Muslims and traditionalists has proved that advent to be less than fortuitous. There were variations in colonial rule by different European imperialists, but the end result was the same: Africans were dominated, given little chance of improvement and eventually had to throw off the mantle of colonialism through freedom struggles of various sorts. Unfortunately, the young educated men who took power in the postcolonial era embraced the artificial boundaries of colonialists and their national framework of regulation. African ways were replaced by European governance that has proved divisive and less than functional.

The Benefits of Colonialism?

In this text I am critical of colonialism and see its effects on West Africa in rather a trenchant light. Others may say that colonialism brought progress to an unenlightened land. For example, H. E. Egerton, the professor of colonial history at Oxford University in 1922 said of colonized Africa that what was happening there was "the introduction of order into blank, uninteresting, brutal barbarism." Such a statement could be seen as ethnocentric at best and racist in a more veridical reading, but in spite of this, let us briefly look at this point of view as it appears in a more modern form.

As to the advances brought by colonialism, European administrators pointed out that slaving had been put to bed. They said that colonial rule brought relative peace in the land. They pointed to new roads, wells, schools, health clinics and churches.

In the case of the French, people could become citizens with rights equal to the residents of Paris or Toulouse.

At least at the ideal level, the French espoused a **policy of assimilation**. This policy had begun in 1870 when France extended such rights to residents of the four *communes* of Senegal: Gorée, St. Louis, Rufisque and Dakar.

As for the British, their loss of the American colonies showed them that they needed to have some local representation along with taxation and colonial domination. The 1880s established Legislative Councils in Lagos, the Gold Coast, Sierra Leone and the Gambia. Each had some elected West African members, but the British were less inclined toward assimilation, relying more heavily on the concept of Indirect Rule, while leaving local political structures in place. The French, on the other hand, essentially dismantled local structures.

Whereas the British subtly worked through indigenous institutions to get West Africans to follow the British way, the French created new political structures to force indigenes to comply with the French way. This was done through an authoritarian system, which had a well-defined chain of command, starting with the Colonial Ministry in Paris, through the governor-general in Dakar, who sent commands on to individual colony governors. These men, in turn, sent commands to provincial commissioners, and they to officers in charge of districts called *Commandants de Cercle*, the equivalent of the District Commissioners in the British system.

While the British clearly saw Africans as subaltern auxiliaries, they did give them a greater degree of political autonomy than the French did. The latter, espoused the principle of assimilation, but proceeded in a strict, authoritarian fashion, justifying their imperial domination with the idea that French citizenship was the prize at the end of the gauntlet. Nonetheless, this was an ideal that remained unrealized for most West Africans under Francophone control. To gain citizenship, one had to attain formal education in a French school, be fluent in the language, know the culture, perform military service, have a minimum amount of employment in the French system, remain a monogamist, and forego traditional animistic religions and Islam.

The statistics on assimilation in the four *communes* of Senegal exemplify these difficulties. By 1939, of the 15 million West Africans under French rule, only 2, 500 had acquired citizenship: only 0.0002% of the population! Another 0.005% had been given citizenship by birth to French parents. Furthermore, when these criteria were granted to the rest of West Africans, the percentages became absurdly diluted.

There was some social mobility under British colonialism. West Africans even became District Commissioners and functioned as judges, medical officers, diplomats and emissaries to foreign lands. In the 1880s, however, only one-fourth of the British establishment in West Africa was Black. This proportion did not change until West Africans were able to wrest back their independence from Britain, in the mid-20th century.

British District Commissioners were residents in the courts of the emirs and other local rulers, not autocratic overlords. This was, when compared to the other European colonial systems, "subtle superiority." Indirect Rule in Northern Nigeria was so successful that it became the model for the rest of British West Africa. Lugard's "**Dual Mandate**" worked best in already established kingdoms and chiefdoms; it was less effective in acephalous segmentary societies that lay at the edges of the great kingdoms of West Africa. Indirect Rule also faltered in those West African polities that had been severely disrupted by the European presence such as the Yoruba kingdoms.

Apologists for colonialism claim that its institutions linked West Africa to the modern world in a positive way, that however brief, colonialism was a time of tutelage. I would have to agree with Michael Crowder and other critics of the colonial endeavor in seeing the administrative system of colonialism as having retarded and misdirected development.

Governance in West Africa

West Africa never had a large settler population. While other parts of Africa like Kenya, Zimbabwe and South Africa have a history of land grabbing and social disruption, in West Africa, Europeans were merely trying to keep the peace so that they could extract raw materials and carry on trade. They had very few administrators and militia to accomplish this. Thus, Lord Lugard devised his famous policy of Indirect Rule whereby a tiny White minority used existing chiefs, kings and emirs to rule for them. The Europeans co-opted leaders by giving them privileges and backing their rule. This policy worked well with the hierarchical Hausa emirates of Northern Nigeria, but it did not effectively translate to smaller, acephalous groups.

Let's look first at how the British dealt with the acephalous Grunshi. In these groups, polities were organized along kinship lines, with political functions embedded in descent groups and powers of governance vested in family headmen. When colonial administrators encountered the Grunshi, they imposed their own pecking-order ideas of governance.

When looking for chiefs in chiefless societies, administrators were baffled. The leaders presented to them did not conform to European stereotypes of what a chief should be like. This can be seen in the following reference in the *Official Diary of the Tumu District* on 1 January 1914 by Dr. William Ryan, the District Commissioner (1913–1914). His reference is to the headman of the Sisala village of Sekai:

> Sekai is an old man clad in a short shirt which is filthy dirty. He has absolutely no attributes of a chief: No appearance: Dirty: No wives: No personal possessions: No authority...

The colonials wanted chiefs who looked the part, and they either ferreted them out or set them up. Lots of ambitious men rose to power and wealth under the tutelage of the colonial administrations who just wanted law and order and who did not have much time, money or men to bring this about. Even former slaves rose to assume chiefly office either by their own cunning or when presented as "chiefs" as a means of protecting the true leaders from detection. After all, how could powerful men know what these white men really wanted with them?

The second kind of polity in the Northern Territories was more easily discerned by the British. C. H. Armitage, Chief Commissioner of the Northern Territories, wrote guidelines for local administrators: where the "right" type of chiefs existed, they were to be encouraged to continue to rule and those chiefs who resisted British rule were to be dismissed from office. The British wanted to establish an administrative framework based on traditional authority, but only if the chiefs were docile.

Another aspect of political rule in traditional society escaped the British. That was the sharing of power between those holding *Naam*, or political authority and those holding *Teng*, or ritual authority. The British consistently conflated the two. For example, among the Mamprusi, the king did stand for the ultimate symbol of political authority, but local officials and members of the kin groups holding *Teng* carried out much of the day-to-day governance. Effective political rule rested firmly within a localized context of kinship affiliations. The British wanted absolute rulers and worked to transform the more democratic forms they encountered into autocratic ones. The British were baffled by the underlying democratic nature of African states. For example, Major A. Festing, Provincial Commissioner of the North-eastern Province, summarized the situation:

> ...the chiefs live in *uninteresting equality* with one another. This roughly sums up the general state of things throughout the Province. Mamprusi, although he does his best, has little power over the minor chiefs, who, except for acknowledging him as their titular head, practically ignore him [italics are mine].

Apparently, in Festig's mind, as with other officials as well, chiefs should be absolutely obeyed (as dictated by the European sense of tradition.) Armitage remained steadfast in his desire to "rehabilitate the lost prestige" of the kings and chiefs. In a letter to the Colonial Secretary in Accra, he explained:

> ...it is impossible to introduce the "Pax Britannica" into a comparatively thickly-populated country, when each little village Headman remains a law unto himself and his immediate following...

To Armitage and others in the field, such independence was anarchy, an anathema to "true" governance. Major Festing expressed his reservations about Armitage's policy:

> My experience in working amongst pagan communities such as we have to deal with in this Province is that one had to be guided to a considerable extent by the feelings of the people and that it is very difficult to force a chief upon them. Around Navarro [Navrongo] there are I believe so-called Grunshis who have never accepted Mamprusi. Also in Kanjarga [Builsa] I gather Mamprusi influence is small. We shall also have to think seriously therefore as to whether we can force them to acknowledge Mamprusi or failing this whether there is anyone amongst them who can take the lead [brackets in original].

The British thought that Mamprusi's hegemony was much wider than it was and that the recalcitrance of rural Grunshi to the idea of Mamprusi rule was stubborn resistance to a traditionally rightful ruler.

Armitage was aware of the difficulties his field commanders were having enforcing hierarchical rule on people who were more comfortable with democracy, but he was having none of it. He wrote back to Festing:

> ...from what I have seen in the North-eastern Province, I feel convinced that we shall have little or no difficulty in *reasserting the authority of the Chiefs*, when once the people are made to understand how very much to their advantage the new system will prove... [emphasis mine].

Armitage imagined that the Mamprusi king had traditional authority over a wide range of independent peoples. In spite of their reservations the local DCs proceeded with his instructions. They began to install a whole new set of chiefs where there were none, and to solidify the power of existing kings and chiefs. For example, Armitage presented this letter to a new Mamprusi chief upon his "appointment:"

Cecil Hamilton Armitage, a Captain in the Reserve of Officers and Chief Commissioner of the Northern Territories hereby appoints Mahama, chief of Nalerigu, styled *Na* of Mamprusi, Paramount Chief of all lands within the boundaries of the North-eastern Province of the Northern Territories. (See **paramountcy** in the glossary)

This effectively extended the Mamprusi chief's rule over stateless peoples who had been democratically ruling themselves prior to the arrival of the colonial overlords.

Of course the chiefs who received such backing thought it was great, as they could now use their offices to collect taxes and exert corvée labor rules on their people. Many saw the colonial structure as a means to enrich themselves and their families. But among the people, there was a conspicuous antipathy to the administrative policies of Armitage. One incorrectly optimistic provincial governor wrote of the 1913 visit of the *Nayiri* to Navrongo:

> If his welcome was less than warm in Grunshi, it was due to the avaricious temperament of the chief of [that town], who has never been known to give anything away, rather than to the fact that the Grunshis are less proud than the others of being including in the Mamprusi race [brackets mine].

People who resisted or chiefs who were less than cooperative were fined by the colonial regime. If they were especially rebellious, they were sent off on forced labor gangs or incarcerated. Among the Tallensi to the east and among the Sisala to the west, the installation of chiefs severely interfered with traditional patterns of authority and leadership through the patriclan, lineages and *Teng* or ritual authority. Where chiefs did exist, the British sometimes elevated the wrong ones, placing them above others who had been their superiors. In short, in ignorance of the real political landscape, the British created an artifical system of governance and imposed it on the people.

Yet it seems that the British DCs were surprised when the people disrespected these incorrectly appointed chiefs. The DC reported: Concerning the British-backed chief of the Tallensi:

> ...his influence is anything but on the increase. It was only last week that he came to ask me to request his chiefs to supply him with guinea corn and other foodstuffs, and also with labour to build his house. The Tallensi chiefs in general don't visit him for the purpose of settling affairs and generally he is not regarded by them as their head...My hands are really quite full trying to foster the idea that the various tribal groups should follow one paramount chief.

The DC's hands were "quite full" because, in part, there were inherent contradictions in Armitage's proposals. They used the concept of "election" but without knowing from which units of society to draw their electors. For example, Captain G.A.E. Poole, the third administrator in Sisalaland wrote in 1914:

> A matter which has been engaging my attention since I took over here, and which strikes me as so peculiar in the Tumu District, consisting as it does of the country occupied by the Issala Race, is the absence of any paramount Chief, and there being thirteen so-called Head-Chiefs. This is, no doubt due to the inter-tribal factions of the past times. The day for this state of affairs has passed, and it is my hope gradually to create an inter-relationship between these vari-

ous petty Chiefs, finally establishing one elected man from among them to lead
the Race.

The so-called Head-Chiefs that Poole found were probably the creations of the two
British administrators who preceded him between 1912 and 1913, and that of the
colonial administrators who tried to bring some sort of order to the area after the defeat of the slave raiders. This DC was not satisfied with "this state of affairs," and
wanted a paramount chief to govern all Sisala. In this way the British authorities set
out systematically to create a political structure consistent with their own hierarchical
ideas and their previous experience with formalized state systems.

The biggest contradiction was between the European conception of rule and that of
the native population. The kind of leader the Europeans wanted had to look the part.
They should have been cleaner than the average, better dressed, possess many wives
and exhibit obvious signs of authority like palaces, fine robes, umbrellas, a court, an
interpreter, a staff and talking drums. The indigenous view was not connected with
such material symbols. To West Africans authority comes from genealogical position
and possession of appropriate ancestral shrines.

After a while the DCs figured out that mistakes had been made and tried desperately to cope with the contradictions of Armitage's reforms. In Sisalaland he called the
family heads together pleading with them to support the new chiefs, especially the Tumukuoro, the new installed Paramount Chief. As late as 1931, the DC had to meet
with local leaders on this matter:

> Col. P. F. Whittall D.S.O. held a meeting at Kwouchoggo of all the Issalla chiefs
> with a view to finding out whether there was any real hereditary chief of the
> Issallas. All chiefs gave the same statement:- viz. that before the white man came
> there were no Issalla chiefs.

They then voted to continue their support of Kanton I as the paramount chief (See
Kanton Family in glossary & See Photo 14.1). It was the backing of the colonial rulers
that gave these men their power. When rumors flew that the Europeans were getting
ready to pull up stakes, the chiefs became apprehensive. One chief came to the DC
Nash in 1911 telling him that his subjects had advised him "to follow the whiteman
out of the country or else he would be killed." Again, the chief of Zuarungu stated:
"Before I was made chief, the people around here used to say—'When the whiteman
goes away we will teach you chiefs some sense."

Of course, the "whiteman" didn't leave for decades, by which time the position of
chief or elevated monarch had become entrenched. The Europeans did leave periodically. In August of 1914, after the outbreak of World War I, the company of the Gold
Coast Regiment stationed at Zuarungu and Navrongo left to fight the Germans in
Togo. A week after their departure, the DC began receiving complaints from the
chiefs that the people were refusing to obey their orders. In a fit of paternalism the
DC noted:

> ...no doubt some of these childish people living in remote parts jump to a wrong
> conclusion. Like children they must have ocular demonstration of their mistake.

Indeed, in spite of any "ocular demonstration" of the presence or absence of the Constabulary, this was merely one of many outbreaks of rebellion by peoples in the region.

Photo 14.1   A Christmas Card Received by the Author.

This perturbed the colonial administrators. They could not seem to understand that their heavy-handed tactics alienated the people who were accustomed to self-governance. For example in 1910, Armitage ordered the destruction of the Tenzugu shrine of the Tallensi in the Tong Hills. The protest that followed was merely one of many that broke out during these early years. The British would douse the flames of protest with force, but they would flare up again somewhere else. From time to time a constable would lose his life and the British would sack the village involved claiming the inhabitants to be a "wild and ignorant people." When one DC felt especially threatened by the uprisings in Bongo and Bawku, he wrote to Armitage asking for a Maxim gun. Armitage obliged, sending one with 40 constables to quell the riots raised by these "truculent children." The DC and his soldiers swept through the area encountering little armed resistance. Nonetheless, the European field commander gave his men orders to fire indiscriminately into all the homesteads. At day's end, the constabulary had no casualties and 59 locals from various villages lay dead, scores of compounds were on fire and the colonials had made off with a sizeable quantity of cattle. Two days later, the constables shot dead 25 more resisters and chased countless others across the border into French West Africa.

Armitage was befuddled by such resistance, perhaps blinded by his surety of the correctness of his policies and the paternalistic calling he had received. Characteristically he wrote of the uprisings:

> It makes me sick at heart to think that these savages who poured from their compounds and followed me for miles like a crowd of merry children when I travelled without escort through their country in 1915, should have retrograded to the extent of resisting our authority.

Armitage had mistaken curiosity for compliance.

There was a fundamental misreading of native law and patterns of governance by the Europeans. They thought that before their arrival, anarchy had prevailed in the land—that "every man was a law unto himself." Again and again, they railed against the refusal of these "children" to obey "proper" authority. Armitage and others in the colonial service believed that the West Africans in their charge were in need of civilizing and developing, a process that continues today under the SAP programs of the **World Bank** and **IMF** (See chapter 18). As Lance nicely summarized it:

> Development is a key word here, for colonial inference with the indigenous centralized polities in the region was part of a self-conscious British project of "advancing" African societies under their tutelage toward "civilization" and "modernity."...Africans resisted colonial tampering with indigenous political processes. The British fundamentally misunderstood the nature of this resistance, regarding it as an atavistic and anti-progressive reaction against the enlightened political and social development that British rule offered. But African resistance was not directed against the concept of change or against novel ideas. Nor was it directed explicitly against a colonial presence in the region. It was primarily directed against colonially instigated transgressions of clearly and cogently defined demarcations between the ritual and religious aspects of authority and its secular and political parameters.

Europeans also believed that the West African people were too backward to govern themselves. Note the passage from the 1922 *Record Book for the North Mamprusi District* that depicts Africans as both childlike and dangerous:

> Our work is to educate the chiefs to govern and the people to obey...I wish throughout to demonstrate by 'repetition oft repeated' Lord Crower's great axiom on administration of savage people: 'Remember they are but children, wayward, obstinate children; but remember too they are children with adult passions.'

Colonial administrators were also critical of the conduct of African women. Officers proposed that education was the best way to diminish the "sexual licentiousness" they thought afflicted the constitutions of African females. In a 1926 memo, Mr. Wellman, Secretary for Native Affairs in the Gold Coast said:

> The education of the women and especially the training of their characters and the development of a higher sense of responsibility as mothers, founded on definite instruction as to the danger of loose living, is a very urgent need. The most dangerous thing in the country at the present time and the most fatal to social improvement is the appallingly easy accessibility of the women. Until women can be trained to be more self-respecting, and capable of keeping men at a respectful distance, very little progress will be made.

Thus, Africans could not develop themselves, but had to be developed by outsiders. As the colonials saw it, the trajectory of advancement would naturally follow a path laid down by Europeans. Not only would such a civilizing course be set for Africans by the colonials, but it might be necessary from time to time to "fine tune" their traditional ways of doing things in order to propagate modernization. It is a shame that much of this thinking still pervades development policy fostered today by the **IFIs** and the forces of "development" at work in modern-day West Africa.

West African Reaction to Colonialism

For the most part, the people of West Africa accepted the coming of the Europeans, though some resisted at different times over different issues. In parts of West Africa, colonists were seen as saviors who ended the slave wars; in others they were barely tolerated; in yet others, they were actively resisted. Villagers, and the majority of West Africans, ignored colonial rule as much as possible where they saw it as contrary to their interests. They also used colonials when it profited them in getting jobs in the city, for example, or a well for the village. Some attached themselves to Europeans as servants, domestic or civil, or as business partners with *assimilados* in Portuguese territories.

Some locals actively resisted colonial rule. Railway workers in West Africa were among the first to organize a labor union: a fact that is made ironic by the dilapidated state of the railroads in West Africa today. A protest called the **Cocoa Holdup** occurred in 1939 when cocoa farmers tried to exert their power against the force of their exploiters. From time to time, female traders staged protests, using the fact that they controlled the flow of many goods through the marketplace as leverage in talks with colonists.

For some West Africans, colonialism was a positive force. Europeans were seen as saviors who put an end to the slave wars, as harbingers of progress, Christianity and the chance for modern education.

Others sought to rise through **"evangelical mobility"** — alignment with missionaries, education in mission schools, or entering convents or the priesthood.

Another reaction, after about 1920, was to accept colonialism but to operate within its framework. Lance showed that "Instead of violently resisting the impositions above the ground as before, African actors now sought to burrow like moles in the earth, within the developing structure of indirect rule." For the common man, this was not manipulation to change the system so much as to get something out of it, although some intellectuals were clearly trying to change the colonial frame itself.

The Political Economy of Colonialism

Political economy is that complex of institutions and relations involving political powers and related economic endeavors. In most behavioral arenas, politics and economics go hand in glove. Politicians work with wealthy patrons, each influencing the other. More and more social scientists are realizing the fundamental importance of this complex as a driving force behind behaviors that heretofore were spoken of as separately — political or economic, not both in combination.

Europeans exerted political power over West Africans in order to nurture a robust economy at home, to extract raw materials with as little investment as possible. Their strategies to maintain the flow of goods changed over time. Slaving gave way to "legitimate trade." Corporations replaced "wildcat entrepreneurs" and "gunboat politics was transposed to colonialism.

For better or worse, colonialism continued to link village and city, bringing previously isolated people into contact with the metropole and market through new development projects, technology, transportation, cash-crops and consumerism. This brought some improvements to water quality and health care in remote villages, and made travel safer and more convenient with the advent of better roads and motor transport.

As I have said, the presence of Europeans in West Africa began with commerce, and that did not change in the colonial era. Extraction of local products and raw materials was the order of the day, and European nations involved in the colonization of Africa found a ready market for all sorts of very basic manufactured goods, since Africa lacked a manufacturing base of any consequence. While the village population got some improvements under colonial rule, the main benefits went to metropolitan élites and the Europeans who were trading, proselytizing and running the institutions of colonialism.

Colonial policy involved land expropriation, forced labor, gangs and camps of paid workers forced to live far away from their families. Labor barracks for mine workers brought men together under new circumstances that must have favored prostitution, drinking and other vices to compensate for their long absences from home. Colonial labor requirements tended to stimulate male out-migration, drain labor away from family farms, undermine the authority of village elders and place a strain on family relations.

This **urban development bias**, resulting from the power base of colonial bureaucracies in the cities, survives today. The labor barracks are still there in some cases, but most migrants live in strangers' quarters or squatter settlements and find work selling charcoal, firewood or cheap imports on the street. This growing informal sector in today's West African cities has a linkage with the colonial need for servants and laborers in the urban areas of the colonies. Just as urban élites had benefited under trade, both legal and illegal, with Europe, and just as they continued to disproportionately gain during the colonial era, metropolitan élites today concentrate on the development of the urban infrastructure. They also run the businesses that exchange West Africa's valuable raw materials for consumer items being sold in *their* stores and small shops, and by millions of semi-employed street peddlers to whom they distribute. Many of the urban poor are forced to live under appalling living conditions, e.g., the slums of Accra that lack sewers and running water and where it is difficult to walk the narrow alleys between homes without encountering human feces and an overwhelming malodor.

While the Portuguese had a short-lived monopoly in West Africa, other European nations soon began to compete with each other to trade in the region. By the last quarter of the 19th century that competition had reached a fever pitch. Why? There are several reasons. First, European nations like Britain, France and Germany were competitors in other arenas, and those rivalries spilled over onto the Guinean scene.

Secondly, Britain had led the way in showing the world that a "true" imperial power was one with overseas possessions, and to some extent, other powers in Europe were emulating the empire upon which the sun never set.

Thirdly, as J. A. Hobson's *Imperialism* (1902) pointed out, for capitalism to continue to operate, it needs new markets for its manufactured goods and new sources of raw materials. To an extent, the scramble for Africa was about saving capitalism, a way of extending the industrial revolution. The historian of Africa, J. D. Fage, tries to counter Hobson's points in the African context, saying that the total extracted profits were low when compared to other colonies and territories held by the European powers. He cites the fact that in 1913 only 4 percent of the total foreign investment was in Africa; and by 1929 this had only risen to 7 percent, with most of that investment being in the atypical South Africa.

However Fage misses the point. That was the beauty of imperial extraction from Africa—*it took very little investment in infrastructure to get the goods out*. This pattern was established right at the beginning with the coastal barter system, where Europeans stayed on the coast and let the Africans do the mining or farming or harvesting and transport of the goods to the coast. Once the transactions were completed, the Europeans hauled the goods off to Europe. That pattern continued throughout the colonial period and is a large part of why the Europeans left West Africa with so little infrastructure when they packed their bags.

European powers were not in West Africa to build roads, railways, bridges, educational systems, social services and the like—they were there to take raw materials, and take they did. They took hardwood trees, minerals and agricultural products that oiled the industrial machines in Europe. They took what luxury items like ivory and civet cat extract they could get their hands on, without going to any manufacturing or much procurement trouble. This was the beauty of the West African economy right from the start: European imperialists could extract great value with little investment in infrastructure. The value was not so much, as Fage would have it, with investment or even with total valuation in monetary terms; the value was in the type of materials being taken—ones that were difficult to find elsewhere: gold, lubricants, bauxite, hardwoods. The industrial revolution would not have ground to a halt if all West African sources of these goods disappeared overnight. It must be said that once buyers had suppliers and pipelines to sources, and had invested something in maintaining those sources, they were likely to want to continue extracting value. As long as the value was to be had, they persisted. This was more the case since so little investment was needed to maintain valuable sources of supply.

For centuries, Europeans had been able to extricate the raw materials of West Africa by staying on the coast. It seems, however, that in the late 19th century there was a greater desire to make the operations more efficient, faster and less costly—to optimize the profits of the extractive processes. To do this, European capitalists figured that they needed to get direct contact with the sources of their supplies, to cut out the African middlemen. If the mines and forests and farms were in the interior of West Africa, then that's where the European traders had to go. In bypassing the brokers, costs would be cut and efficiencies established according to European, not African standards. In general, West Africans resisted this move to the interior.

But alas, European powers had the gadgets—the gattling guns, the surveying instruments, the steel girders for the bridges, the technology to pave roads. They had a new and powerful technology and the moral certainty that they were destined to spread this to the underdeveloped parts of the world. In short, industrialization changed the mix in European-West African relations. The balance of power swung in Europe's direction, and colonialism seemed more attainable, a more reasonable way to extract raw materials and create markets for Europe's cheap manufactured goods— e.g., enamel pans, knives, trinkets, cloth, etc. As befitting the force of Western materialism, technology changed the mix in Guinea.

So if we take it that Europe had other interests in the world, other areas where it was extracting raw materials and creating markets for its goods, and that West Africa was a small part of that mix — it was still a part, and not a completely insignificant one. The history of the late 19th century and the first sixty years of the last century evidence this. Europe wanted West Africa. Europe moved in to stay, but eventually it could not, and history took it in a different direction.

The two main powers that seemed to want to stay the course in West Africa were France and Britain, the two nations that eventually got most of the colonial territory there. In 1879 French troops began to move out of Sénégambia across from the valley of the upper Senegal River into that of the upper Niger; and around the same time British merchants and humanitarians were taking the first tentative steps toward true colonial occupation of West African territory. British sea power had largely destroyed the French West African trading empire between 1793–1815. Nevertheless French entrepreneurs were interested in rebuilding what they had before, and in starting new ventures, and they got some official backing from the French government which did not want the British to have exclusive access to West Africa.

Both countries and West Africans had to deal with the specter of slaving. In the late 17th century slaving was a major source of income for both the Europeans and indigenous slave traders, many of whom were monarchs or members of royal families. To develop export staples to replace slaves was not an easy process. It proceeded gradually, and was quite disruptive in places, for example, among the competing Yoruba kingdoms, who fought over access to palm oil delivery routes to the Europeans on the coast.

Some Europeans withdrew or curtailed their activities in West Africa as soon as slaving began to fade from the scene. The Danes in 1850 and the Dutch in 1872 exited for the most part. The Portuguese were left with small territories and settlements in West Africa, although they still had a presence in Angola and Moçambique elsewhere on the continent.

However it was Britain that had been most involved in the slave trade, and they became the primary force in policing the area for slavers after they found a conscience. They were the first to make formal moves toward colonial control. In the quarter century before the end of slaving in 1807, British ships carried some two-thirds of the slaves taken from West Africa, and nearly half of those taken to the Americas.

Furthermore, unlike the French who depended little on foreign economics, both West Africans and the British had a major economic stake in finding a solution to the replacement problem. Britain already saw West Africa as a major market for British manufactured goods. Economics would be the dog that would shake the tail of colonial involvement in West Africa.

If the British were somewhat economically dependent on West Africa, its traders were even more deeply involved in supplying Europeans with West Africa products and ferrying their manufactured goods into the market networks that spread like spider webs throughout the region. These traders had less economic latitude than the European traders, and therefore a harder time adapting to the loss of slave revenues.

Slaving had helped to stimulate the rise of monarchs and royal families involved in slaving. These politicos had created violent slave-producing machines, and such polities found adapting to the loss of demand for Black Ivory difficult.

Since the price of slaves dropped dramatically at this time, some tried putting slaves to work on plantations to produce for Western markets, but many were saddled with cumbersome state bureaucracies that made such a transition difficult. Their whole orientation was to maintain and extend their hegemony over as many people as possible, which was an axiom of West African political domination. In short, in West Africa politics, defined as the control of labor, was economics. One rarely existed without the other.

Revenue from selling slaves had fueled the solidification and expansion of political power and such polities were ill adapted to the replacement of slaves with crops such as palm oil and kernels, groundnuts and later coffee and cocoa. These crops favored small farmers or independent plantation owners, or New Men who were not encumbered by a state bureaucracy, and who could adapt quickly to the changing economic scene.

Small producers, humble collectors and traders began to channel such replacement products to European traders on the coast, as did some politicos who were able to change with the times. However, most political economies of kingdoms began to suffer at the loss of slave revenues, and Europeans began to wonder if they might not be better served by taking over political control of those areas of West Africa that advanced their profits.

Philosophy, Christianity & Acculturation

In the 1800s, Christian missionaries began to have success converting coastal peoples who had, to some extent, been dislodged from their traditional beliefs by the presence of the Europeans. They had acculturated to Western ways and looked to Europe for moral guidance. These acculturated coastals became a West African vanguard in helping Europeans to gain a colonial foothold. They were agents in the process of drawing Europe into closer involvement in West Africa. Philip Quaque, a native of the Gold Coast, was sent to England at the age of 13. He was educated there by the Society for the Propagation of the Gospel in Foreign Parts (S.P.G.). Eventually, he was ordained a priest in the Anglican Church. In 1766, the Reverend Philip Quaque returned to the Gold Coast as a missionary to his own people.

The famous broker of Cape Coast, Cudjo Caboceer, was a man in both worlds— European and West African. Employed by the Royal African Company during the 1720s, he still worked for the successor company at the time of this death in 1776. He was a linguist and go-between, linking the Europeans of the Castle with neighboring people. He functioned in a semi-diplomatic way to smooth over the relations between Whites and Blacks.

It is not surprising that some West Africans were coming to view colonialism as a way forward. Acculturation to European habits and ideas had been in progress for centuries among the coastal peoples. Throughout West Africa, it was becoming common for southerners to see themselves as modern, and those of the northern hinterland as backward, even savage. This is a situation that still exists today in Ghana and Togo, to name only two examples. From the 18th century onwards, Christian missionaries had promoted European ideas of "civilization"—the so-called **Civilizing Mission** of the West. In the 19th century, many more missionaries flooded into West Africa, coupling education with their message of faith. Missions also became more organized: the Christian Missionary Society, the Wesleyan Missionaries and the White Fathers established operations in West Africa that still remain today.

This deluge of missionaries in West Africa was the result of an evangelical revolution in Europe in the 18th century. Crusaders and humanitarians had taken up the anti-slavery cause and coupled it with their mission of "civilizing" the people of West Africa. A nascent philosophy fostered by evangelicals and administrators and accepted by some locals was that European culture was better than West African culture. This mentality is depicted in the novel, *No Longer at Ease*, by Chinua Achebe. The protagonist, Obi Okonkwo, is a young Igbo educated in Britain, but caught between two worlds. When Obi's parents become too frail to support themselves, Obi faces the dual responsibilities of a man with a foot in two cultures:

> Obi did not sleep for a long time after he had lain down. He thought about his responsibilities. It was clear that his parents could no longer stand on their own. They had never relied on his father's meagre pension. He planted yams and his wife planted cassava and coco yams. She also made soap from leachings of palm ash and oil and sold it to the villagers for a little profit. But now they were too old for these things.
>
> "I must give them a monthly allowance from my salary." How much? Could he afford ten pounds? If only he did not have to pay back twenty pounds a month to the Umuofia Progressive Union. Then there was John's school fees.
>
> "We'll manage somehow," he said aloud to himself. "One cannot have it both ways. There are many young men in this country today who would sacrifice themselves to get the opportunity I have had."
>
> Outside a strong wind had suddenly arisen and the disturbed trees became noisy. Flashes of lightning showed through the jalousie. It was going to rain.

Although some West Africans embraced this "civilization," many did not. In fact, the majority of West Africans had no contact with Europeans. Most African peoples rejected Christianity and the European way of life because they were antithetical to their own moral systems.

The acculturation of coastal élites was fostered by the development of a Creole community in Sierra Leone, many of whom had been exposed to Christianity as part of their captivity. They also received better education in mission schools. Creoles from Sierra Leone became successful traders, clerks, artisans, teachers, priests, doctors, lawyers and administrators. They fanned out along the coast, becoming models for other West Africans with new aspirations. They moved eastwards along the Gold Coast and into Southern Yorubaland, which had been disrupted by incessant rivalries and war in the demise of the Oyo Empire. In such social vacuums as Freetown and Lagos, the Creoles and other acculturated coastal élites found an open society with opportunities for social mobility. It was an ideal environment for West African entrepreneurs, an urbane world with new rules fostered by economic drives, and a new political order that nurtured them. Some Yoruba New Men, those with initiative, became wealthy enough in this atmosphere to buy their own ships to transport palm oil and other products.

The activity of the Europeans on the coast created two kinds of West Africans: acculturated coastal élites and the people of the hinterlands. The urbanized élites of the coast did not completely understand the peoples of the backcountry. Some took on the European idea that such societies were uncivilized and backward. Coastal élites saw themselves as aiding in the process of bringing a better way of life to West Africa.

World Changes and Colonialism

The firming up of colonial rule in West Africa was taking place at a time when Europe was in the throes of war and rapid change. The First World War caused Germany to lose her holdings in Togo and Cameroon. But, the war was less an influence in the region than the ideological changes that had resulted in the establishment of the League of Nations and President Wilson's 14 points. These articles affirmed the right of self-determination for colonial peoples and limitations on the use of forced labor and appropriation of autochthonal lands. In general, the old orders and strict orthodoxies of past European societies were rapidly changing in the face of a new global order, boisterous industrialization and a general liberalization of thought.

One of the changes on the world scene that came to influence colonial administrations was the emerging idea that government should be more involved in creating social progress. The socialist revolution in Russia and Roosevelt's New Deal are two examples.

This opening of European social thinking influenced West Africans educated between the two world wars. For example, Lamine Gueye founded a Socialist Party in Senegal, affiliated with the parent organization in France. Casely Hayford, a barrister in the Gold Coast, formed the National Congress of British West Africa. Many educated West Africans who were active in political circles and Legislative Councils were elected to parliament, opening the way for eventually regaining independence.

The Second World War weakened Europe's self-confidence in its own unified superiority and undermined its imperial agenda. In contrast to the totalitarian ideas of the Germans and the Japanese, the democratic ideals of the United States and liberal European nations rose to the fore. Liberal ideas were everywhere, some of them revolutionary. Rights of indigenous peoples were discussed at the same time as indigenous rule, even independence. While colonists were acting out a 19th century scenario in West Africa, the world was changing around them. Universal rights of humankind were emerging as a global topic of discussion.

Few colonial administrators had a coherent plan of action in West Africa, and this led to little social progress for the autochthonous population by the end of W.W.II. An exception was Sir **Gordon Guggisburg** in the Gold Coast who governed from 1919–1927. He was unique in his concern for husbanding the human and natural resources of the colony. He wanted to build railways, roads, schools and colleges and a new economic force fortuitously provided some financial backing—the advent of cocoa production as a staple export crop. This gave the colonial government a new and steady income for the first time. After his retirement, the Gold Coast was administered by less able men and the colony again stumbled.

In 1929, Britain passed the Colonial Development Act, vowing to be more involved in supplying grants-in-aid for development purposes. One million pounds sterling were awarded to the entire British Empire, a mere pittance. Even by 1946, this allowance had reached only 12 million pounds.

With the approach of W.W.II the raw materials of West African colonies became strategically important. Colonial administrations were drawn into the drama of the European conflict by having to increase security over their exports. When Germany invaded France, French West Africa supported the Vichy regime (that was pro-German), but as the war proceeded and the tide turned against the Germans, they came to embrace the DeGaulle government in exile.

The Portuguese in Guinea-Bissau

The Portuguese presence in West Africa was fueled by commercialism, like all European interests there. But Portugal was different from France or the United Kingdom.

While other European nations were industrializing and growing in stature, Portugal was in decline. Marginalized in the European political economy and with the loss of Brazil, they desperately tried to hold on to their African territories—*Cabo Verde*, Guinea-Bissau, Angola and Moçambique. The 1900 laws created a new imperialism—forced labor replaced slavery, but the relation of exploitation was the same. In 1901 the colonial state appropriated all lands not in private control, revised the banking system to favor the mercantile bourgeoisie and created new import taxes. In precolonial Guinea-Bissau, traders had predominated; now Portugal reinforced its civil service and military and began to create other forms of extraction beyond commercialism, such as institutional formations that allowed Portuguese companies to exploit the resources of Africans.

The people of Portuguese Guinea resisted these imperialistic moves, but along with administrators came soldiers who backed up the dictatorial rule of colonial administrators. For example, the infamous Teixeira Pinto led government troops in a pillaging rampage across Portuguese *Guiné*. He was told by Lisbon to pacify the natives without much in the way of financial backing. He was forced live off the spoils of his ravage. For his savage efforts the Portuguese State awarded him the *Cavaleiro da Ordem da Torre e Espada* (Noble of the Order of the Bull and Sword), Portugal's highest military honor.

In 1918 under the tutelage of José Ferreira Diniz, the colony moved toward a system not unlike Apartheid as it was constituted in South Africa. In justifying a policy of separation Diniz said:

> Native policy that encourages the native to collaborate with the European [can] achieve what neither of them can do on his own, since what the European lacks—physical resistance—is almost the only thing the native can provide.... native policy of associating the brain of the European who thinks, with the hand of the native who executes, and one that will supply the European with the necessary ingredient to understand the native's childlike spirit and to impose authority on him, by kindness, without despising him or making the mistake of identifying with him.

From the 1920s on, colonials systematically formulated laws preventing native participation in the political economy. The 1930 Colonial Act placed the investment needs of the *grande bourgeoisie* above the needs of the people, with an eye toward achieving an industrial take-off in Africa. Industrialists, traders, plantation owners and shipping tycoons were thriving, protected by isolationist tariffs. Cash-cropping of groundnuts was pushed heavily by this time. But, because Portugal was isolated from European expansion, she tied herself increasingly to colonial markets. The system of exchange extracted raw materials, sent them to the home country to be manufactured, then returned them to the colonies for sale at high profits. Africans were seen as obliging buyers. In the words of Armindo Monteiro, the African "is the great strength of production, the abundant and docile consumer element..." Yet the African was not so docile as the Portuguese would have liked. There was widespread resistance to cash-cropping and public works projects. Armando Castro was moved to remark that "the population resists recruitment and will work only under coercion..."

One aspect of coercion used by the colonial state was what Sally Falk Moore called the "reglementation process"—the art of making rules, that in this case favored European capitalists. A good example can be seen in the displacement of the traditional rice-hulling method, performed by locals by hand. This method, which produced "pestle rice," came into competition with four hulling plants built with Portuguese investment in 1953. The colonial rule-makers simply made "pestle rice" illegal and gave all the business to the Lisbon investors. What had been a simple way of making a living now became illegal.

With such abuses and the changing mood in world politics, conflicts were developing between two societies in Guinea-Bissau: colonialist and liberationist. Intellectuals both in Portugal and in the colonies began to question whether a viable society could be founded on imperialism.

Although perhaps an extreme case, the undevelopment of Guinea-Bissau proceeded along the same lines as elsewhere in Francophone or Anglophone Africa. Portuguese investment in infrastructural development was kept to a minimum, however. By 1953, after hundreds of years of Portuguese presence in the region and fifty years of formal colonial hegemony, there were only ten kilometers of paved roads, two sawmills constituted the country's total industry, and one hospital in the capital served the entire country. The Portuguese had built two quays to get the goods in and out of the colony, however.

Chiefs and the Bugbear of Tribalism

Once independence was a reality in West Africa, two sets of privileges clashed—those of the traditional chiefs and those of the educated élites. The latter were the new Black nationalists who had been influenced by Western education. Some chiefs and many colonial administrators saw these young men as upstarts, mere "verandah boys." Some chiefs were educated, but their duties at home prevented them from active participation in nationalist politics, at least with the degree of freedom enjoyed by the younger set. These "upstarts," on the other hand, wanted to move Africa ahead and thought the only way to do this was to continue the colonial framework as nation-states. In this view the older traditional chiefs and those who presented themselves as speaking for the past opposed them. To nationalists, these chiefs represented the specter of tribalism, a word synonymous with anarchy in the "learned" circles of the day.

History seemed to be clothing these youthful urbanites with the raiment of power. Some were installed in legislative councils in British West Africa, or were taken into the halls of governance in France; others took to the streets to rally the populace to the cause of nationalism.

While the young lions embraced the concept of the nation-state, other West African intellectuals agreed with the chiefs that there were neocolonial dangers in nation-statism. Some tried to find something African upon which to base the move forward, even if they eschewed the traditionalism of the chiefs. Others played with concepts such as African socialism, trying to incorporate the communal nature of village life. Yet others went into the ethereal realms of philosophy developing the idea of *négritude*, a nice sounding word with a hollow ring to those bent on *realpolitik*.

The West African masses surged into politics through associations such as the Igbo National Union and the Yoruba-based Egbe Omo Oduduwa, both of which evolved into political parties vying for power. This competition for rule within the new arena of the nation-state stimulated rivalry between ethnic groups as rarely experienced before in West Africa.

Both the European colonials and the new breed of nationalists feared chiefly power and the particularism of tribal affiliation. Their interests were aligned and both had their sights set on an orderly transfer of power to the nation-state. Some intellectuals supported federalism, a system where power would be shared by regions or ethnic factions, rather than centralized in the hands of a few young men ensconced in the capital city. Federalists were sidelined, if listened to at all.[1]

Colonial disregard for ethnic sensibilities and traditional forms of political organization created problems for African leaders, ones that have yet to be seriously solved. As both European and West African nationalists planned the future, the borders laid down in the Berlin Conference of 1884–85 became even more sacrosanct, a hoped for assurance against chiefly particularism and ethnic conflict. No one wanted to raise the fear that perhaps the nation-statist project might fail. No one wanted to utter the T-word — *tribalism*. It became treasonous to question the validity of nationalism. Anything smacking of a threat to the anti-colonial struggle was quickly marginalized by the neophytes of nationalism.

Conclusions

Generally, colonialism has been injurious to the natural evolvement of African society. During its day, however, proponents of a paternalistic approach to governance in the region said it would bring progress, civilization and development. Yet, Europeans misunderstood African political structures and imposed their own rule, which further complicated life in colonies that already had artificial borders and ignored ethnic histories and relations. Nevertheless, because of a lack of a large European settler population and appropriation of prime land that occurred elsewhere in Africa, most West Africans tried to adapt to the colonial situation and some actually thought it would usher in a better day. Unhappily, this was not to be. Colonialism was grounded in a commercial system designed to extract raw materials and create outlets for European manufactured goods. Its developmental footing was grounded in exploitation. Colonial apologists noted that they had brought Christianity to a backward land, but the fact that the region has experienced a great deal of religious conflict between Christians, Muslims and traditionalists has called into question this claim.

There were divergences in forms of colonial governance, but the final result was the same: under a paternalistic and autocratic colonial framework, Africans were given little opportunity for improvement and ultimately had to throw off the cloak of colonialism through various forms of resistance. Woefully, the young lions who took power in the postcolonial era adopted the counterfeit borders of colonialists and their national framework of rule. European-style governance has proved divisive and dysfunctional in West African politics, a condition of instability exacerbated by the creation of large military regiments, ethnic unrest, religious conflict and ongoing meddling in regional affairs by international organizations.

---

1. In chapter fifteen I noted that Nigeria has gone to a federalist system (See glossary). This system is being tried because of the extraordinary ethnic diversity of the former British colony. Nevertheless, Nigeria remains a place plagued with ethnic and religious violence as well as massive corruption at the national level, conditions frequent military takeovers have not solved.

CRITICAL THINKING QUESTIONS

1. What were the benefits of colonialism and what were its negative aspects?
2. What were Lord Lugard's ideas about a Dual Mandate and Indirect Rule? Did these ideas work for West Africans as he had envisioned?
3. Which kinds of West Africans benefited from colonialism and how?
4. Discuss the racist ideas of the colonialists and missionaries in light of the commonly held evolutionary views of the day.
5. Discuss the relationship between coinage, the market system and taxation in colonial West Africa. What were the effects of the interplay of these forces?
6. Discuss how the Christian missions and European traders on the coast led to a split in West African peoples. What was the nature of the split and what was its geographical nature?
7. What impact did the ideas surrounding WWI and WWII have on West Africa?
8. Why did Portugal try to hold on to Guinea-Bissau and her other African colonies longer than the other European powers in the region?

KEY CONCEPTS

Assimilados	IFIs
Civilizing Mission	IMF
Cocoa Holdup	Legislative Councils
Dual Mandate	Paramountcy
Evangelical mobility	Policy of assimilation
Gordon Guggisburg, Sir	Urban development bias
Kanton Family	World Bank

SOURCES & SUGGESTED READINGS

Annual Report N.T. 1912. PRO C.O. 98/21. Quoted in Lance.
Armitage to Colonial Secretary, 11 September 1911. NAG ADM 56/1/68 file #361/78/1911. Quoted in Lance.
Armitage to Festing, 22 July 1911. NAG ADM 56/1/121. Quoted in Lance.
Circular to District Commissioners, North-eastern Province (N.E.P), 20 July 1911. NAG ADM 56/1/61. Quoted in Lance.
Colonial Report—Annual. No. 807 (1914). PRO Accounts and Papers. Quoted in Lance.
Crowder, Michael. 1968. *West Africa under Colonial Rule*. Evanston: Northwestern University Press.
Diniz, José Ferreira. 1946. A politica indígena na Guiné Portuguese. *Congresso Comemorativo do Quinto Centenário do Descobrimento da Guiné*. London: Routledge. 2 vols. Lisbon.
Egerton, H. E. 1922. *British colonial political in the XXth century*. Oxford: Oxford University Press.
Fage, J. D. 1995. *A history of Africa*. London: Routledge. Chapter. 13
Festing, Handing Over Notes, 9 December 1909. NAG ADM 56/1/137. Quoted in Lance.

Gellar, Sheldon. 1995. The Colonial Era. In: Martin, Phyllis M. & Patrick O'Meara (eds.). *Africa* (Third edition). Bloomington: Indiana University Press, 135–155.

Informal Diaries, Zuarungu, 15 October 1913. NAG ADM 68/5/1. Quoted in Lance, 1995.

Jones, W. J. A. 1936. Minutes of the Dagomba Conference Held at Yendi in March 1936. RAT 2/29. Quoted in Lance.

Kimble, David. 1972. *A political history of Ghana: The rise of Gold Coast nationalism, 1850–1928*. Oxford: Oxford University Press.

Lance, James Merriman. 1995. *Seeking the political kingdom: British colonial impositions and African manipulations in the northern territories of the Gold Coast colony*. Ph.D. dissertation, Stanford University. Ann Arbor: University Microform (UMI) #9525856.

Lopes, Carlos. 1987. *Guinea-Bissau: From liberation struggle to independent statehood*. Trans. Michael Wolfers. Boulder: Westview Press.

Mendonsa, Eugene L. 2001. *Continuity and Change in a West African Society: Globalization's impact on the Sisala of Ghana*. Durham: Carolina Academic Press.

Monthly Reports, North Eastern Province. 1910. NAG ADM 56/1/441. Quoted in Lance, 1995.

Nash to Commissioner, North-eastern Province, 23 December 1911. NAG ADM 56/1/137. Quoted in Lance, 1995.

Proclamation found in NAG ADM 56/1/121. Quoted in Lance.

Rattray, R. 1932. *The tribes of the Ashanti hinterland*. London: Oxford University Press. Two Vols.

Record Book for the North Mamprusi District. 1922. NAG ADM 68/4/3. Quoted in Lance.

Roberts, Stephen H. 1963. *The history of French colonial policy, 1870–1925* (second edition). London: Cass.

Watherston, H. E. 1906 (6 June). NAG ADM 56/1/46. Quoted in Lance.

Wellman, Secretary for Native Affairs. 1926 (1 March). PRO CO 96/663. Quoted in Lance.

15 THE MOVE TO FREEDOM & THE TRIUMPH OF PREBENDALISM

While some West Africans quietly accepted European imperialism and colonization, others resisted and became freedom fighters. Yet others worked within the colonial system to replace it. As Africans eventually succeeded in taking positions in post-colonial administrations, they were often caught up in naïve development efforts and bureaucrat orders that have been dubbed kleptocracies. As kleptocrats, many of these new politicians facilitated relations of dependency that have enmeshed West Africa in a neocolonial web.

Move Toward Independence

After W.W. II the push for development and independence became stronger. Colonial governments began to formulate ten-year plans as stepping-stones to their exodus. West African élites began to return from abroad to agitate for political reform and independence. West Africa was becoming integrated into the mainstream of liberal ideas in the world, and by the mid-1950s, became involved in the global economy as never before. Productivity was rising, making traders wealthier, but since populations were also rising, most West Africans remained poor. In fact, in some areas, like Nigeria, population growth may have actually outstripped economic growth, causing greater poverty than before the colonial era.

Certainly it can be said that social progress and economic development were very uneven in West Africa. J. D. Fage, the well-known historian of Africa, thinks that Indirect Rule may have restricted education in British colonies. While that may be the case, it was only one cause. The overall record of all European nations on providing education, social services and avenues for advancement was dismal under colonial rule.

Nevertheless, throwing off the shackles of colonialism was just a matter of time because, as professor Fage so beautifully put it, "colonialism carried its own solvent" — the very process of colonizing West Africans acculturated them and therefore élite black traders had frequent contact with the white man, beginning with the early Portuguese traders. This interaction taught them how to operate in the world of global trade. Later, under the system of Indirect Rule, chiefs and kings gained intimate knowledge of the workings of European political rule. Those who attended mission schools were learning more than the Bible in the process. The soldiers who fought be-

side white men in the foxholes of W.W.II came to be educated about their human frail-
ties and observed that some black men were braver, stronger and had more character
than some white men did. They also saw white men bleed to death before their eyes.
Being dragged into forced labor teams far from home was also educational. Entering
the labor market made people more urbane and changed their perspective of the
world.

Thus, in building the colonial edifice, colonists unknowingly were doing what they
said they intended to do—educate the indigenes. The problem was that, like students
everywhere, the indigenes were learning some things that were not intended. Nationalism and the desire for self-determination were embedded in the very processes of
colonial domination. Even though Europeans wanted to hold their colonies, colonialism in West Africa lasted only three generations, and by the 1960s was in full retreat.
Four unstoppable forces seemed to be driving its demise: *Négritude*, **Pan-Africanism**,
Islamic fundamentalist movements and changes in colonial policy itself. These forces
were grounded in the effects of two world wars, a global depression and a loss of European faith in its *mission civilisatrice*.

Intellectuals and administrators alike began to ask, "Who is civilized?" In other
words, Europeans began to question their assumed superiority over West Africans.
The emirs of Islamic states felt that their systems were more civilized than those of the
infidels.

In *Continuity and Change in a West African Society*, I have challenged the assumption that Western culture is superior, and put forth the hypothesis that its emphasis on
materialism may actually erode the civilizing effects of traditional society. If to be civil
is to have non-exploitative relations with one's fellows, then many precolonial West
African societies were far more civilized than the interlopers from Europe.

Eventually those in the Colonial Office and area administrators began to see that it
was not in their self-interests to continue with tight political control of West Africans.
If those interests were essentially economic and extractive, they could continue to be
met without the cost of maintaining colonies. If the political superstructure was
handed over to West African élites, the need for European expertise would not evaporate overnight. The extractive economy was in place. It would stay in place, perhaps
even grow. Of course, this is what happened under conditions that came to be known
as **neocolonialism**.

Furthermore, some reasoned that any attempt to maintain colonial hegemony
would undoubtedly lead to conflicts and the use of force. This would have been disruptive to economic activities for both West African and European companies, a "lose-
lose" situation. Since people in West Africa were far more involved in world trade than
those in east, central or Southern Africa, a non-violent move toward self-determination
had the potential to be a "win-win situation," and by and large, that is what happened.

And education was a big factor. In 1960 in the Belgian Congo, only 50 Africans
graduated from college, whereas in Senegal the number was 1,000, and in the Gold
Coast and Nigeria, 5,000 students graduated each year. Thus, West Africans tended to
be more modernized, especially in the coastal urban centers. Consequently they were
demanding to be partners in progress, rather than servants and subalterns.

Nor did West Africans wait for action by colonists. They set about to use European
forms of organization against their oppressors. They organized social clubs, chambers
of commerce, professional associations, trade unions, churches and eventually political parties. However closed the British Polo Club was to indigenous residents of West
Africa, the latter were creating their own modern society alongside.

While communist and socialist literature was often banned, the flow of these ideas could not be stopped. Many educated West Africans were studying for higher degrees abroad and were involved with the movements of *Négritude* and Pan-Africanism in the communities of the African diaspora. The ideas of Marcus Garvey and **W. E. B. DuBois** were influential in West Africa. Residence in universities in Europe and the United States, and contact with those in the African diaspora proved effective training grounds for African nationalism. From 1900 onwards, West African élites had been going to the **Pan-African Congresses** held in major cities around the world. The first congress was convened in London in 1900, followed by others in Paris (1919), London and Brussels (1921), London and Lisbon (1923), and New York City (1927). At first these congresses were attended by the black intelligentsia of the African diaspora, and did not propose immediate African independence. Rather, they favored gradual self-government and interracialism. In 1944, several African organizations in London joined to form the Pan-African Federation, which for the first time demanded African autonomy. The Federation convened the Sixth Pan-African Congress (1945) in Manchester, which included such future political figures as Jomo Kenyatta from Kenya, **Kwame Nkrumah** from the Gold Coast, S. L. Akintola from Nigeria, Wallace Johnson from Sierra Leone, and Ralph Armattoe from Togo. When these educated men returned home, they used these newly acquired ideas to push for freedom.

French West Africans were influenced by their counterparts in the French West Indies, such as **Aimé Césaire**, who had developed the doctrine of *Négritude*. Fage nicely sums up the message delivered by this and Pan-Africanist philosophies:

> The Black Man need not be an inferior replica of the White; he had his own distinctive culture and history behind him. If he and his kind could unite, and absorb what they needed from White culture and let it absorb them, the African nation would be reborn and could equal or excel anything the Whites could do.

By the 1940s, men bearing this gospel were returning in numbers to West Africa. While those in French West Africa had a less educated populace, those returning to Nigeria and the Gold Coast found fertile ground in a large number of people who had at least a primary school education. Furthermore, in these countries there were many who were highly trained professionals, in addition to clerks, farmers and servicemen returning from W.W.II. The latter had fought and won against tyranny and oppression, only to return home to a land under domination.

And there had been promises. In French West Africa, indigenes had been given assurances that they would receive equality in the 1946 constitution. When the French voted, however, French West Africans got only second-class status, it taking ten votes by Africans to equal one vote by a full French citizen in Paris or Marseilles.

Ambitious development plans raised the expectations of West Africans everywhere. Change was in the air, but West Africans were to be disappointed. The development plans went ahead, but to the benefit of Europeans, not West Africans. European companies who profited from the construction of the roads, bridges and buildings brought materials from Europe. Few West Africans were employed, as skilled workers and even laborers were also brought in from Europe. It was a continuation of the same old story begun by the Portuguese—European profits at the expense of West Africans.

With its literate population and high degree of acculturation, the Gold Coast had the highest expectations, and it is not surprising then that the first violence broke out there in February of 1948. Rioters attacked and looted the stores of the major European trading companies. The dead numbered 29, with 297 injured. While the British had experienced far greater violence in their other colonies, this was a shock in this model colony. British policy-makers were stunned and quickly set up a commission of inquiry.

The commission recommended a new constitution that was to be framed by West Africans. This was seen as the first stage in a gradual move toward self-government. As political activity in the Gold Coast was already quite advanced, there were many well-qualified men to draft the constitution. The Colonial Office carefully chose those who would have the opportunity to write the future. One was J. B. Danquah, a prominent lawyer, who had founded the **United Gold Coast Convention (UGCC)**. This political association was filled with prosperous urbanites who were likely to be sympathetic to British interests. The one member of the UGCC not invited to frame the new constitution was the fiery Kwame Nkrumah. Without the future leader of the new nation of Ghana, Danquah and associates drafted a constitution that was almost entirely accepted by the colonial powers and became law in 1951.

The younger, more radical Kwame Nkrumah was educated in America and Europe. Also, he had been a major figure in the Pan-Africanist Congress in 1945. He saw Danquah and his affluent supporters as being co-opted by the British.

Following the nonviolent or "positive action" tactics of Ghandi, Kwame Nkrumah turned to the masses. He founded a rival party, the **Convention Peoples Party (CPP)** with the revolutionary slogan of "self-government now!" Nkrumah organized boycotts that earned him and some of his associates a place in the stockade. Of course, being jailed made him all the more popular in the press and with the people.

When elections were held in 1951, Nkrumah's CPP won almost all the seats open to direct election to the new Legislative Assembly. Nkrumah and his political associates were invited to take most of the ministerial seats in the executive council. Dr. Nkrumah proved not only to be an effective grass-roots organizer, but was also able to work effectively with the Gold Coast Governor, Sir Charles Arden-Clarke, to form the structural basis of the new nation of Ghana, which became independent in 1957.

Ghana's emergence as a member of the United Nations, the first Sub-Saharan African independent nation-state, was to open the floodgates. In the next decade most African colonies followed in her footsteps to independence.

Nigeria was the next logical candidate for independence in West Africa, but it had much more ethnic and regional diversity with which to cope. As perhaps the worst example of map-making in West Africa, Nigeria had been created out of many unrelated tribes, religions and peoples—each with various levels of acculturation to Western ways. From the traditional-minded Fulani emirates of the north, to the more acculturated Christians of the south, diversity clogged the machinery of Nigerian unity (as it does today).

Since the Hausa, the Igbo and the Yoruba had fundamentally hostile relations in the past, it is not surprising that parties formed along ethnic or tribal lines in the colony that was to become Nigeria. The Igbo of the east had The National Council of Nigeria and Cameroon, or NCNC. Nnamdi Azikiwe, who had worked for a time with Kwame Nkrumah, formed this party. The Yoruba of the west formed an opposition party simply called The Action Group. The Northerners had the Northern Peoples' Congress, or NPC. The battle lines were drawn.

Faced with this ethnic rivalry, British administrators hit on the idea of a **Nigerian Federal System**, with each region having a certain amount of autonomy. That was all well and good, but to whom should they give control? When the NCNC formed an alliance with the NPC against the Yoruba, in spite of the ongoing ethnic tensions and the well-known corruption within the coalition, Britain beat a hasty retreat, granting independence to Nigeria in 1960. Sierra Leone followed in 1961, and The Gambia in 1965.

French West Africa was different. To a large extent, it had been governed as a block from Dakar with more or less uniform policies. French West African intellectuals were divided as to whether independence was to create a unified entity, or was to be achieved as separate colonies negotiating their own independence.

Félix Houphouët-Boigny who was to become president of *Côte d'Ivoire* for 33 years (1960–1993), was a wealthy man of colonial politics in the Ivory Coast. About 1946 he formed the **Rassemblement Démocratique Africain** or **RDA**, which was aligned with the French Communist Party. Not surprisingly, the conservative colonial administrators of French West Africa suppressed the RDA, but Houphouët-Boigny outmaneuvered them. He offered the votes of his party's legislative representatives to the many coalitions in France trying to form a government. Given the unstable political conditions in post-war France, any coalition hoping to gain power needed French West African support. French West Africans were then rewarded with ministerial posts in the French government.

In 1956, Houphouët-Boigny and the RDA were able to secure the passage of the *loi-cadre*, the "outline law." Under this statute, each colony in French West Africa was to have a separate, locally elected assembly with real powers to control policy and finance.

Opposing this view, Léopold Senghor, the principle apostle of *Négritude* in French West Africa, said that *loi-cadre* threatened to break up the combined power of Black people in French West Africa—that individual colonies were too poor and had too few people to effectively deal with the political clout of France. It is probably also significant that Senegal (which Senghor eventually became president of) was the basis of, and had greatly benefited from, the government administration based in the capital of Dakar.

In French Guinea, **Sékou Touré** who was a trade unionist organizer and member of the *Rassemblement Démocratique Africain* also opposed its breakup. Under Touré's leadership, Guinea became the only colony to vote against the constitution of the French Community in 1958 and to opt for complete independence, which was achieved on October 2 of that year. France retaliated by severing relations and withdrawing all financial and technical aid. Guinea cultivated close relations with the Soviet Union but expelled the Soviet ambassador in 1961 for alleged interference in the country's internal affairs.

Sékou Touré also advocated African unity and steered Guinea into a union (largely symbolic) with Nkrumah's Ghana in 1958, then Mali joined in 1961. In the late 1960s, Guinea sought improved relations with the West, although its basic international posture was one of nonalignment. Touré fostered Pan-Africanism, and in 1966, when Ghana's President Kwame Nkrumah was deposed, Touré welcomed him to Guinea as joint president. Sékou Touré held the presidency of Guinea from the date of independence until his death in 1984. Under his rule the country was a one-party Marxist-socialist republic.

In 1958 Charles DeGaulle returned to power in the Fifth Republic. The French constitution held the concept of **Communité**, similar to that of the British Commonwealth. Each colony in French West Africa was to be given the choice of joining or refusing membership in the elections held in September, 1958. Only Guinea under Sékou Touré refused membership, preferring pure independence outside of the *Communité*. Touré was closely aligned at the time with Kwame Nkrumah who offered support. Other backing eventually came from communist countries.

Eventually, leaders of the French West African colonies realized that DeGaulle's *Communité* was "an unnecessary piece of Gallic embroidery" and they moved toward dealing more directly with their former colonial overlords.

Some West African leaders, upon taking power from the colonialists, felt the need to establish one-party states. The feeling here was that true democracy, with various parties competing for elected positions in the government, would be divisive, given the artificial nature of some of the national boundaries and the ensuing ethnic conflicts. In the beginning, at least, it was argued that such developing nations needed stability more than pluralism, a strong leader with a strong party. Democratic elections were workable for more developed countries in Europe and America, but not in West Africa.

In some ways, this reinforced the West African tradition of being led by a king or patriarchs who acted as fathers of the nation, paternalistically handing down all things good to their people. It was thought that a leader for life at the head of a vibrant party could mobilize the nation to develop and industrialize. Like divine monarchs, such men led their people confidently into the future. They did this without the encumbrances of elections and representative government, but this raised other problems. Whereas in traditional monarchies there was a strong connection between political actors and civil society, in the new polities of West Africa there was no such affinity. It did not seem to matter whether the politicians held elections or not. The modern nation-state, as imposed by Europe, didn't seem to work well in West Africa.

Between 1963 and 1987, there were over 60 military takeovers in Africa, giving the continent a somewhat distorted image of political instability. As an aggregate, it was probably no more or less stable than post-war France or Italy, or, more recently, the Balkans. Violence always seemed to make the news headlines, but the majority of African nations went on struggling quietly against overwhelming odds—poverty, rising populations, disease, lack of infrastructure upon which to develop, debt, and also incompetence and corruption.

Such struggles led some in the military to conclude that they could do it better. They had the guns; politicians did not. They reasoned that the unassailable force of military might would provide the needed stability for governance. Some took over and held power. Others promised to return to civilian rule when the time was right. Some military men created structures of co-governance with civilians. In the case of Jerry Rawlings in Ghana, a military man pulled off a *coup d'etat*, ruled, returned the government to civilians, then took it back again when they did not perform as he saw fit.

What is fairly easy to see, in hindsight, is that while leaders at the top were changed, the middle and lower level administrators, magistrates, police chiefs and others who ran the bureaucracy on a day-to-day basis remained the same. The fraternity of men that could be drawn upon to fill these posts was limited. Things stayed pretty much the same in the bureaucracy, and the problems of poverty, disease, poor infrastructure, neocolonialism and rising debt did not disappear.

As Léopold Senghor predicted, some countries in West Africa were simply too poor and weak to modernize and meet their citizens' expectations—countries such as Upper Volta (Later Burkina Faso), Mali and Niger fell into this category. These former French colonies were land-locked, had few resources, small populations and lacked the deep cadre of educated élites who could manage affairs of state.

Both the Francophone and Anglophone West African countries have found themselves saddled with residual structures of colonialism, the effects of acculturation to European way and a **bourgeois mentality** among their ruling élites—all of which

Table 15.1 ECOWAS Counties & Their Colonial Overlords	
West African Country	**Colonial Masters**
Benin	France
Burkina Faso	France
Cape Verde	Portugal
Gambia, The	United Kingdom
Ghana	United Kingdom
Guinea	France
Guinea-Bissau	Portugal
Ivory Coast	France
Liberia	USA
Mali	France
Mauritania	France
Niger	France
Nigeria	United Kingdom
Senegal	France
Sierra Leone	United Kingdom
Togo	France/Germany

have contributed to a state of continued dependency on their former colonial masters, and more generally on the core industrial countries of the **G-7**.

While some freedom fighters had radical ideas and were anti-capitalists, most were not. Others set aside such ideas fairly quickly to tap into the resources that they saw flowing into the **periphery** (**South**) from **international capital**. In the next section I will present the case of the freedom movement in Portuguese *Guiné*, which was clearly a Marxist-Leninist movement, but which stumbled in the postcolonial period, finding itself in very much the same state of dependency presently experienced by other ECOWAS countries.

The Freedom Movement in Portuguese *Guiné*

In Portuguese *Guiné* the left-wing liberation struggle of the ***Union of the Peoples of Guiné and Cape Verde*** (**PAIGC**) had successes in war and in winning the hearts of the people, but it eventually failed as an instrument of a just, collectivist society. It could not overcome the bourgeois mentality of many of its leaders, or the linkages of its resources with international capital. The power of neocolonialism has brought all West African states to more or less the same place, that is, to a state of dependency on international capital. **Dependency theory** states that the peripheral states in the underdeveloped world only have symbolic freedom. In the periphery, there is really a severe condition of reliance on international capital; or put another way, the core controls the periphery poleconomically.

I offer the case of Portuguese *Guiné* as a prime example of the power of neocolonialism because, unlike some right-leaning leaders in West Africa who openly called for greater involvement in the global economy, the PAIGC leaders operated under a Marxist-Leninist umbrella and had high hopes for the creation of a more egalitarian society. Their failure informs us of the extreme difficulty of achieving this in the context of the penetration of the global market in West Africa.

In general the liberation movements against colonial oppression were peaceful and pulled off by intellectuals such as Felix Houphouet-Boigny, **Ahmed Sékou Touré** and Kwame Nkrumah through use of the legal processes of the state or through mobilization of popular interest. When compared with the strife and bloodshed of similar movements elsewhere in Africa, West Africa experienced the transition from colonialism to nationhood in relative peace.

However, this was not true everywhere. The freedom movement to liberate the people from Portuguese oppression was, like most others in West Africa, begun by a small group of intellectuals in Lisbon, one of whom was **Amílcar Cabral.** Independence was in the air elsewhere in Africa, but the Portuguese were adamant about keeping their colonies. Cabral and his compatriots were involved in a number of left wing organizations, but they increasingly felt the need for an African solution to the problem of colonialism. In that year they founded the Centre for African Studies (CEA) in Lisbon. Initially the center was designed to deal with cultural concerns about identity and nationalism, but increasingly members came to confront political issues regarding colonial hegemony and the need for independence from Portugal.

In 1956 Cabral returned to Portuguese *Guiné.* There in the capital of Bissau, he founded the liberation movement, the *Union of the Peoples of Guiné and Cape Verde.* It was designed to redress the humiliation and degradation suffered under colonial slavery. One of the first tasks was to raise the consciousness of the masses. The PAIGC faced two problems in this regard: the lack of a unified national consciousness felt by different ethnic groups and the general reluctance of rural farmers to embrace change.

The first step to a solution was the creation of a training school in Bissau to educate cadres who would go among the people and preach the gospel of national liberation through an underground network. Cabral espoused Marxist-Leninist tactics. He also knew what Mao had done in China and what was happening in the Angolan liberation struggle. He set up a "party-like" structure to push for a peaceful and nonviolent resolution. On 3 August 1959 the PAIGC staged its first organized demonstration and received its first lesson in Portuguese entrenchment and power. In the **Bissau Seaman's Strike,** the Portuguese police attacked and killed 50 people, and wounded over 100.

After this, Cabral went into a period of reflection, to rethink his commitment to nonviolence, emerging in 1961 with a resolution to move forward through armed struggle. He came to see that it was too dangerous to make the initial moves in cities, because that was where the Portuguese arms were, and failures there could create a spirit of futility among the cadres. In that year he sent an open letter to the Portuguese government stating his intentions to move his freedom fight into the countryside if the Portuguese did not concede. They did not.

In 1962 the PAIGC sabotaged Portuguese installations near the capital city. This resulted in a backlash that ended with 2,000 arrests of both freedom fighters and villagers and many deaths. Seeking input from world leaders, Cabral went before the UN to speak of the evils of Portuguese domination in his country. Still the Portuguese resisted. In January 1963, PAIGC troops attacked a Portuguese army barracks. The *luta* (struggle) continued.

As the armed struggle spread, some field commanders began to alienate the people. Cabral realized that the struggle needed to be a mass movement to succeed. To rein in the brigands, he called a Congress at Cassaça in the deep bush. There he disarmed the offenders and reiterated the need for a popular-based movement in the guerilla war against tyranny. The cadres emerged from the Congress with a renewed sense of commitment and the slogan, *Tudo para a volta*, "Everything for the revolution!" However, in hindsight, we can see that self interest among Cabral's cadre reflected bourgeois elements that would emerge again after victory to undermine the struggle for a just society.

One of the bases of the revolution was the establishment of a **parallel economy** for those supporting the liberation struggle. The PAIGC created people's stores and market depots to provide villagers with goods on a barter basis, to bypass the use of colonial coinage and to stop the penetration of the market economy in the countryside. People began to see the PAIGC's commitment to them, and there was a growing sense of a return to self-sufficiency. The PAIGC also built over 150 schools. Through the extension of political, economic and military hegemony, the PAIGC was able to win over numerous villages in the countryside and the hearts of many urbanites. As the international community became aware of the liberation struggle, it lent its further legitimacy. On 22 November 1972 the PAIGC was granted observer status at the United Nations. On 24 September 1973 the *independistas* proclaimed the **People's National Assembly (ANP)** in the hills of Boé. Elections were held and the assembly was filled with some of those who had fought for this freedom. The Republic of Guinea-Bissau was on its way. The European power tenaciously held on in spite of the fact that Portugal lost well over 8,000 soldiers and in spite of their technological superiority and untold wealth, they had achieved no victory.

But alas, they were not allowed to fight to the bitter end. Events in Portugal overcame those in the newly proclaimed Guinea-Bissau. On the 25th of April 1974 the **Red Carnation Revolution** erupted in Portugal. As tanks rolled into Lisbon under the direction of the young officers of the Armed Forces Movement (AFM), hundreds of thousands of workers crowded the streets to celebrate the overthrow of the hated regime, some placing long-stemmed red carnations down the gun barrels of the left-leaning soldiers. Portugal had suffered decades of injustice under the fascist dictator Salazar. In 1974 these army units were disillusioned with the carnage and injustice of the wars in Africa, as well as the fascism of the Portuguese autocrat, Caetano, who had followed in the footsteps of the dictator Salazar.

To the AFM, the African wars were a crippling cancer on society, both at home and in Africa. After 13 years it was clear that these wars were unwinnable, a determination made by soldiers who had fought there. Before the coup, General Spinola, the former commander of Portugal's armed forces in Africa, had written a book calling for the end of the wars. In an interesting turn for military men, they had been revolutionized by the role they were called upon to play in the oppression and exploitation of Africans. Now the AFM acknowledged that PAIGC was the legitimate power of Guinea-Bissau, although liberation wars dragged on elsewhere.

The main aim of Portuguese colonialism, as with the French and British versions, was the perpetuation of a political economy of exploitation. Consequently the colonial state that had been constructed by the extractors was fit for that purpose, but little else. It was not designed to provide good governance or the provision of social services to the people. The writer Carlos Lopes noted of the colonial structure of Portuguese *Guiné*, "The state's visible administration and institutional characteristics were hardly suitably fashioned for a newly independent state."

Not only had the Portuguese not formulated a just system of governance, and not only had they failed to train sufficient Africans to take over what state structures existed, but the liberators who fought in the bush to win power were themselves more attuned to military maneuvers than to governing a nation-state. Mário Cabral, another revolutionary leader in *Guiné,* said:

> There was no preparation for the takeover of power and even after the formal proclamation of the State at Boé, there was still argument over how the various Commissariats (ministries) should be organized. There was not the slightest awareness of what was implied in the mass of bureaucratic work that would be necessary to do away with.

As with most of the other leaders of liberation movements in Francophone and Anglophone West Africa, Amílcar Cabral and other cadres in Portuguese *Guiné* were intellectuals and freedom fighters, but they had little or no experience running a state. Of course, the events of the 25th of April revolution in Lisbon thrust governance on them in an unexpected way, making the transition from the colonial state to an independent Guinea-Bissau even more difficult. Leaders had to move from being actively involved in guerilla warfare to dealing with an inefficient and understaffed bureaucracy, and they had to do this with essentially untrained personnel.

And what kind of a bureaucracy was it? In general, throughout West Africa, colonials had imposed **antiquated bureaucracies**. Administrative structures that were put in place were (and largely remain) grounded more in the 19th century than in modern times. They were cumbersome and composed of such arcane and complex rule sets that efficiency was virtually impossible.[1] Writing in 1987 Professor Lopes noted that "Laws which were obsolete in Portugal at the time of Guinean independence are still being enforced in Guinea-Bissau of today." I cannot speak for that country, but in Ghana and Nigeria I have personally experienced the convoluted and inexpert nature of the bureaucracy wherein one is saddled with the need for excessive paperwork, signatures and authorizations in quantities that surpass belief. To simply pay my bill at the University rest house at Legon I had to spend 45 minutes, go to three offices and I wound up with a fistful of elaborately scripted receipts.

Furthermore, and this is an important point, little within the political economy of extraction changed with the replacement of Portuguese governors. The long established pattern of dependence on a distant **metropole** was still in place, and it did not allow for the formation of indigenous capital and expertise. Investment and profits were by and for the Portuguese. There were no African factories, trading companies, entrepreneurs or firms to carry on the economic processes needed to earn revenues to run the new Guinea-Bissau State. Colonial administrators may have stepped aside, but the Portuguese traders, entrepreneurs and firms did not.

A good example of the corrosive result of the lack of development can be seen in the move to replace the Portuguese Escudo. The **shift to the Guinea-Bissau Peso** is a classic case of postcolonial dependency. There was no expertise to design, produce or distribute such currency within the new nation, moving the administration to look outside for help. Eventually Algeria became the supplier of the Peso currency. Dependency is still dependency. Guinea-Bissau had simply substituted its reliance on Portugal with a new supplier. In this way peripheral nations participate in the modern world without having the capacity to produce many of the essentials of modernity.

As with their Francophone and Anglophone counterparts, the new leaders of Guinea-Bissau were faced with a neocolonial state of affairs before the ashes of colo-

---

1. As of this writing, this situation largely remains in modern-day Guinea-Bissau.

nialism were cool. In 1975–1976, there was some recognition of the strong mental or **acculturative impact of European culture** on the residents of Bissau. To correct this, the party organized a series of urban-based committees, cells and discussion groups. The best and the brightest of the cadres were taken out of the provinces to come to Bissau. The idea was to revolutionize the city, but the effect was the demobilization of rural efforts.

In the revolutionary fervor of the early days, the top men of the party headed these newly formed groups. Within five years, however, no top men could take the time for such trivial matters, being drawn instead into the affairs of state. The organization atrophied. As Carlos Lopes put it, "Bissau was thus the main instrument in demobilizing the PAIGC." The revolutionary party was accommodating itself to urbanism, power, high finance and playing on the world stage.

After the exhilarating confusion of takeover and transition, stagnation soon settled in. This allowed the forces of underdevelopment to continue. The ideology of populism was stopped in its tracks, usurped by the needs of governance. It was not as if the revolutionaries could start afresh. They had to pick up the reigns of the state and govern in the residue of colonialism. Carlos Lopes put it like this:

> Little by little the seeds left by the colonist sprouted. Soon they covered all the ground. Through laissez-faire policy, and through increasing demobilization of the national liberation movement, the colonial civil servants won the vacant ground and reintroduced their logic. How was this possible?

The answer lies with two tendencies of the **petty bourgeoisie** (middle class, also called petite bourgeoisie) that came together to create a new and indirect dependence on distant capital. Petty bourgeoisie are privileged members of society. In West Africa they are usually those who have succeeded within the educational frame to take up the major posts in government, the bureaucracy and civic positions throughout society. With such privileged access comes a certain way of thinking, one that is anything but revolutionary. Of the commercial petty bourgeoisie, the Guinea-Bissauean Lopes says:

> [They] have always sought the protection of the colonizing metropole. Its tastes, training and life style are inanely copied from the West. Its selfish individualism leads it to dreams of power, of social climbing.

What we realize now, but could not see in those heady days of African liberation, is that the market had penetrated well into the interior of West Africa. The configuration of extraction and domination would not just magically disappear once black men sat in parliament.

For example, export crops had been introduced, primarily oilseed production, and this was always under the monopolistic control of a marketing structure, the *Companhia União Fabril* (CUF). This is a good example of how such foreign interests were able to exploit the West African people, and at the same time destroy local habitat. The CUF continually increased groundnut production, not by improving productivity, or by developing an industrial base, but simply by utilizing cheap labor and expanding the exploited territory. Ultimately, this resulted in severe environmental damage.

These were the entrenched relations of domination that the PAIGC faced upon taking up the mantle of governance. Moreover, the focus on groundnuts as a profit-making enterprise for Lisbon capitalists cut into the labor time of peasants. As they increased export crop production, they had to decrease rice production, which had been the traditional crop of the region. As a result, Portuguese *Guiné* began to import rice. Portuguese *Guiné* was made dependent on foreign capital for its food, while producing oil for Core consumption. This can be seen as forced commercialization under a **traffic economy**, a condition that continues into the present day.

The revolutionary government continued to rely on peasant production of export crops to earn foreign currency. In colonial times peasants were forced to produce, while under the new government they were enticed, but the result was the same—commercialization of agriculture demanded by the national government wherein the peasant produced what he could not consume.

The penetration of the market economy is a mental process as well as an economic one. As farmers were drawn into production for distant markets, they became accustomed to having cash earnings to buy European manufactured goods. This extractive system functioned because it required little investment of capital to make high profits off the labor of West African farmers. Once they were habituated to the cash economy and imports, the system was self-perpetuating. The result, as Amílcar Cabral noted, was stagnation of productive forces—profits without development. This is the torpid traffic economy inherited by the revolutionaries.

The new state also needed revenue. One way to get it was to keep such structures as the CUF in place but to filter the proceeds of extraction through the state. By linking the state to development and growth, it took on a prebendal nature (See **prebendalism** in the glossary). This furthered the needs of the Lisbon **bourgeoisie** and the emerging metropolitan élites of the PAIGC. It must be remembered that not all members of their leadership were of one mind. Middle-class thinking was pervasive; it is therefore not surprising that once in power, these centrist tendencies surfaced and some became aggrandizers using state structures to exploit the people as their Portuguese predecessors had done.

Endless debates exist as to whether the African bourgeoisie is a class in the Marxist sense. Szentes Entralgo says no, since they do not control the means of production. This is an outdated view. If you control wealth and power you control a means of increasing both, which is precisely what state administrators had and did through the prebendal state. By controlling the structures through which capital flows, opportunists can siphon off wealth for the use of the state, and divert into their own particular ventures or bank accounts. Shivji rejects the idea that a class needs to have direct control over the means of production. He says of the **prebendal class**:

> It does have an economic base, but the base itself is that of *underdeveloped* capitalism as part of international capitalism (italics in original).

He goes on to note that the prebendal class of urban élites only lack the ultimate control of the means of production, but that as a class of operators they do benefit from a limited form of international capitalism—underdeveloped capitalism—even though the primary controllers and beneficiaries live in distant lands.

The necessary adjustments made during the postcolonial period created a circumstance wherein aggrandizers thrived. Mismanagement, waste and corruption flourished. This stagnant condition, with no real movement toward true development, permitted profit-taking to proceed as usual. Toward the end of colonialism, the Portuguese capitalists had allowed more and more *assimilados* (mulattos) to participate in the exploitation of the people, brown faces replacing tan ones. With the emergence of a new state, black faces could be seen at the "feeding trough" too.

Two structures were very difficult to overcome even by a revolutionary consciousness. First was the widespread cash economy of the market system. Second was unwieldy bureaucracy. The latter set the rules of the game and imparted one of the most devastating legacies of the colonial era—the "civil service mentality." In this perspective, the bureaucracy is the arbiter of all political and economic flows in society. The bureaucracy is the protector of the status quo, rights to property and status, and economic individualism. It is the rule set that organizes the political economy. The colonial bureaucracy was a prebendal structure designed to benefit distant élites; in the postcolonial era it merely came to serve the interests of both distant and local ones. A new layer of élitism was added to the traffic economy, another level of extraction.

How did this happen with cadres who perhaps had a greater commitment to the people than the average bureaucrat? Again, in any revolutionary movement there are always petty bourgeois elements. Not all join with the same level of ideological commitment. There is always more to be gained through participation than the attainment of revolutionary ends. This was exacerbated by the fact that in the countryside, cadres had to operate with little direction from the top. Local cadres could and did develop small fiefs of power and wealth. They became big fish in small ponds. When these men were given posts in the new order, they continued their "**bigmanism**" on a new and larger playing field, with one privileged position replacing another.

The desire for personal gain and regional and ethnic interests began to undermine what unity PAIGC had achieved during the revolutionary years. This **particularism** began to weaken the capacity of the new government.

Guinea-Bissau became more like a proto-state, as defined by Jean Zigler. It emerged as a creation of imperialism and was designed to meet the needs of international capital, not the people. When I speak of imperialism I mean the planetary control of finance capital. Leaders within a proto-state have only fictional and illusory sovereignty, being almost entirely dependent on the dictates of a foreign metropole, and the increasingly mobile and electronic flow of finance capital. Hence, the proto-state remains dependent on capitalist-inspired financial strategies.

Of course, with the hindsight of **Bretton Woods Agreements**, structural adjustment programs (SAPs) and the heavy hand of IFIs in **HIPC** (Highly Indebted Poor Country) countries, we can now see that international control of nominally sovereign states in the South is an essential element in the spread of the global economy. Global capital feeds on extraction of wealth from the South, and profits from supplying markets there. Poor countries like Guinea-Bissau and others within the Economic Community of West African States (ECOWAS) lack industrial capacity and capital, and therefore are trapped by their needs for manufactured goods for which they must allow the exploitation of their raw materials and labor power.

This is clearly true of an HIPC, but it is also valid for wealthy Southern countries like Nigeria and *Côte d'Ivoire*, which also can be seen as peripheral states. Just as Guinea-Bissau was not able to formulate or implement a coherent economic plan after independence, other richer ECOWAS states found themselves negatively impacted by the ups and downs of the world economy, and the interference of the IFIs. Most West African countries are still caught in a web of unequal exchange, unequal power and unequal lifestyles. This is because the Northern metropole has a monopoly on industrial production, has unequal access to enormous amounts of credit and capital, and more or less controls the transport of goods worldwide.

One of my theses in this text is that corruption in West Africa is largely induced by external factors: the strictures placed on legal **accumulation** of capital by élites, and their restricted access to the means of production that could net them incomes commensurate with the **prebends** they derive from governance. Both the structures of colonialism and neocolonialism have effectively kept economic control in the hands of international firms. It is not only the lockout of West African élites *vis-à-vis* the means of production that is important, but also the cultural control of their minds. Part of the colonial vestige in West Africa is embedded in the bourgeois institutions of the state itself, including the courts, army, police, civic institutions, ideology, unions, etc. As Vergoupolos had said, "**primitive accumulation** is the reference to externals of all kinds." The cultural assumptions embedded in such idea sets, organizations and traditions create a climate of cultural domination that carries on the tradition of political domination by Westerners. The colonial culture of subjugation created a climate in which it was, and remains, exceedingly difficult for a West African to accumulate enough wealth to start any business of scale.

In other words, since West African élites are hampered in the normal human drive for status, wealth and power through commercial means, they seek the only alternative left open—high political and bureaucratic office. This is the only way for them to accumulate large amounts of capital, although, given the illegal nature of such capital, it cannot be used openly or reinvested in legitimate businesses in West Africa.

The political economy of colonialism also encumbered the peasant producer. Samir Amin and Kostas Vergoupolos comment that rural farmers are caught between the need to export and their desire for imports. This forces them to act very much like piece-rate workers in the factory system, that is, the more cash-crops they produce for the metropole, the more foreign-made goods they can buy.

In this neocolonialist climate, unproductivity prevailed. Both in the city and the backcountry of Guinea-Bissau, bureaucratic planners tried to implement a planned economy, but the relics of colonialism were too entrenched. So trapped, PAIGC operatives turned the state into an instrument to attract foreign aid. Like their counterparts elsewhere in West Africa, they found themselves ever more mired in the tentacles of international capital.

Speaking more broadly of Africa, Franz Fanon said:

> The setting up of the colonial system does not of itself bring about the death of the native culture. Historic observation reveals, on the contrary, that the aim sought is rather a continued agony than a total disappearance of the pre-existing culture. This culture, once living and open to the future, becomes closed, fixed in the colonials' status, caught in the yoke of oppression. . . . The apathy so universally noted among colonial peoples is but the logical consequence of this operation. The reproach of inertia constantly directed at "the native" is utterly dishonest. As though it were possible for a man to evolve otherwise than within the framework of a culture that recognizes him [as a peasant consumer] and that he decides to assume (brackets added).

I have tried to show the reader that the people of Guinea-Bissau were ensnared in a mummified cultural and economic frame, the remains of an imposed European tradition. Their actions, legal and otherwise, were influenced by that total inheritance from the colonial past. While the cadres had spoken of a new era, there never was a total detachment from the deeply embedded assumptions of the superiority of Western culture. Nor was there a sufficient understanding of the substantial similarity and affinity between traditional African collectivism and the Marxist-Leninist ideas of the cadres.

Real change in this situation was an uphill struggle. For example, in agriculture, a surplus continued to be taken from the peasant, even though liberal economists tried to portray him as a free producer for a free market. In reality, the yoke of both market and producer is complex and deeply hidden in the bourgeois culture of Western Europe, and in the economic and financial arrangements linking the periphery to the center.

In the end, the rural producer returned to old forms of resistance—in some cases peasants simply went back to subsistence production, which perhaps conveys a sense that these resisters knew that they were trapped in an exploitative circuit.

During the war years, the PAIGC was able to circumvent the international economy to an extent by creating a barter-based economy with people's markets. (Although a deeper analysis would show international financing behind the munitions and provisioning of the revolution). After taking power, this system faded away and the cadres encouraged peasants to produce more and more for the world market. In the urban areas, they planned to industrialize, their plans running far ahead of any real possibility of achievement.

Now they wanted more involvement with international capital, not less. They described this accelerated involvement with foreign markets as being in the national interest. Somewhat cynically Lopes notes that "The petty bourgeoisie commonly interprets what is of interest to it alone as national desires."

In the boom atmosphere after the revolution, the size of the state doubled. It created far too many projects and opened the school doors to all. It was a heady time. It was the time of "mobilization." In reality there was conflict between the needs of the people and the interests of state leaders. Peasants and **proletarians** alike resisted taxation. Farmers chaffed against a system of production for export. But the exuberant planners forged ahead, creating a myriad of schemes, projects and cooperatives such as state farms and parastatal fishing companies. Many failed, as has been the experience throughout West Africa. The cadres concentrated most of their development efforts in the capital Bissau, to the detriment of agriculture and rural improvement.

The capital city became cut off from the interior, the latter getting little development focus. In a moment of self-criticism, a national liberation movement internal planning document said "Guinea-Bissau in the early years directed itself for an economic *leap*, acquired factories, which necessitated foreign exchange, power stations which must be supplied, consumer goods beyond its means and non-essentials" (italics theirs). This document indicates that someone in the government had become aware that planners had totally unrealistic development goals.

Some of the naïveté of early planners can be seen in a partial list of their attempts to industrialize Bissau:

∗ The Blufo milk factories import milk powder from Europe and transform it into liquid milk for consumption in Bissau and for export, not for the rural people who could have made better use of it.
∗ The EGA car assembly plant assembles Citroen cars from parts produced in Europe. These cars are exported, or used by metropolitan élites.
∗ The plastics factory established in Bissau has never produced anything.
∗ The Pansau sponge factory operates on the average of only five minutes a day because of inefficiencies in supply of raw materials.

Unfortunately, the list is too long to reproduce here. Suffice it to say that the mistakes in Bissau have been multiplied many-fold throughout West Africa. Imitating industrial manufacturing perfected by the West has proved disastrously inefficient and expensive. The monies wasted in this attempt could have been used to develop appropriate technology and sustainable projects throughout the region—thus, the money and effort were doubly wasted.

In spite of these lofty goals, and partially because of them, the state was running a deficit by 1978. State receipts were 496 million pesos, while expenditures amounted to 922 million pesos. To finance this "leap" into modernity, the new state used four tactics. First, it printed more and more money, leading to high inflation. Second, it went into debt to IFIs. This is called **debt dependency**, where poor countries find it difficult even to pay the interest on the debts (**debt servicing**). Third, it sought foreign aid from whatever source it could find. The fourth tactic was unintended, though pragmatic: using the peasantry to generate income for the state. The state's revenues came largely from the transfer of the surplus value from the peasantry to the financial sector. The extroverted character of the national economy siphoned off value from the interior to the city and from Guinea-Bissau to the metropole.

In short, state functioning took precedence over party ideology. It is another unfortunate example of the old saw, "power corrupts." Manecas Santos placed the blame at the feet of human nature—the taste of authority, ambition and particularism, the tendency to support one's own against the masses. Whereas in wartime the cadres had the forced pressure of the field situation to constantly maintain their ideology, the new battleground of governance led to "**revolutionary formalism**," the inane retreat into radical rhetoric and slogans, the "Biblification" of the revolution, so to speak. This can most clearly be seen in the near deification of the *Combatentes da Liberdade da Pátria*.

The new governors of the state would make declarations of faith in public, and ignore them in private. They had become corrupt. Carlos Lopes said of this sad reversal, "Corruption in turn undermines mobilization. It disheartens consistent and capable militants and introduces discouragement and passivity."

But the state became more than just passive. It began to replicate the fascism against which the liberationists had fought. The use of the police and security forces to repress the people was a sad turn in the history of Guinea-Bissau. This is not an idle concept, but a historical reality in Guinea-Bissau. After the revolution, PAIGC leaders began to amass large farms and became the owners of factories. The PAIGC Central Committee was supposed to be able to prevent this from happening. Manecas Santos nicely referred to the Central Committee as the "Museum of the National Liberation Struggle." They had become a fragment of the rising privileged minority, the new prebendal élites.

In 1984 Guinea-Bissau adopted a constitution that established a new National Assembly, removed the post of Prime Minister and gave greater powers to the President. There were hopes that Guinea-Bissau could find its way back to mobilization toward responsibility to the people, but aggrandizement prevailed in Bissau. In November 1985 several ministers and officials were accused of plotting to overthrow the government and were subsequently executed in 1986.

At that time the state was inching toward an embrace of liberal economics. In November 1986, President João Bernado Vieira announced the continuation of economic liberalization reforms, and proposed to further reduce state controls over trade. At that time, the President was in profound conflict with General Ansumane Mane. To show the reader the insanity of such infighting (with little regard for the general welfare of the public) this conflict between two *grande homens* resulted in the planting of over 20,000 landmines, a terrible situation the government is still trying to figure out how to solve. Neither of the *grande homens* have been victims of the mines, but members of the public have.

In September 1990, the government adopted a document providing for a transition to a two-party political system. In May 1991, the Parliament approved a number of multiparty reforms, and in June of that year the constitution was amended to legalize opposition parties.

Portugal agreed to oversee the multiparty elections and President Vieira agreed that the PAIGC would hold a special congress to discuss constitutional amendments. On November 18, 1991, the Supreme Court legalized the opposition party—the Democratic Front led by Aristides Menezes, in effect ending the 17-year one-party rule. In December 1991, two further parties were also legalized.

On March 7, 1992, an approved opposition demonstration denouncing PAIGC corruption took place with some 30,000 people attending. The split between the people and the state seemed to widen. During 1992, as a result of the government's continued **privatization** of state enterprises and the freeing of prices, export-crop production rose by 19%. Simultaneously, there were large-scale army desertions due to appalling living conditions.

On March 17, 1993, an associate of President Vieira, Major Robalo de Pina was killed by another officer, an event that further delayed the planned elections. In May 1993 the leader of the Party for Renovation and Development was arrested amid claims of involvement in a planned March coup attempt, although he was later released. On July 10, 1993 President Vieira announced that the elections would be held on March 27, 1994. Such were the machinations of the former revolutionary government, now thoroughly in the camp of international capital, squabbling over the perceived rewards of power.

Not much has changed today, or to be frank, what change has occurred cannot be defined as progressive. There is still conflict between the people and the government, the military and the government and forces within the government are mightily contending with each other. In February 2000, President **Koumba Yala** was elected, but by November had come into direct conflict with General Ansumane Mane, who later died under suspicious circumstances. In spite of such doubts about the morality of the Yala government, the **Organization of African Unity (OAU)** has backed him and encouraged all to work with him to achieve stability in Guinea-Bissau.

While the OAU has only moral authority, the IMF has fiscal clout, and they used this to pressure government leaders. Guinea-Bissau had joined the IMF on March 24, 1977, and has been regulated by it and other IFIs since. Recently the IMF approved a three-year arrangement for Guinea-Bissau under the Poverty Reduction and Growth Facility (PRGF) in a total amount equivalent to US$18 million. This is to support the government's 2000–2003 economic program. In the neoliberal double-talk of the IMF they tout the program:

> The new three-year program provides a framework to restore economic growth, promote structural reform, and improve socioeconomic indicators. The program is based on an improvement of the fiscal and external situation, the removal of obstacles to economic development, and the implementation of a broadly-based strategy to reduce poverty. The program has been conceived within the context of increased regional integration under the West African Economic and Monetary Union.

> The priorities of the first annual program focus on strengthening fiscal policy, in particular through the adoption of a budget structure for reducing poverty, the reinforcement of revenue collection, and improvement in overall governance. The programs for military demobilization and civil service reform are key anchors in the proposed fiscal policy framework.

In this optimistic, new liberal world, the priorities of the first annual program (2001) focus on strengthening fiscal policy, in particular through the adoption of a populist budget and the reinforcement of revenue collection. At the same time, the authorities place key emphasis on measures to enhance the budget process, improve **transparency** in the fiscal accounts, and monitor the use of fiscal resources (including improvements in treasury management, a reform of the budget procurement system, public expenditure reviews, the publication of semi-annual budget execution reports, and the adoption of new budget regulations). The programs for military demobilization and civil service reform also are key anchors in the proposed fiscal policy framework, which will allow the reallocation of expenditures toward poverty-reduction activities.

That is the view from the outside. Inside Guinea-Bissau, it remains conflict as usual. On December 8, 2000, ten opposition parties held a press conference to denounce the human rights abuses of the Yala government, and demand a broad-based commission to investigate the death of General Mane. Guinea-Bissau is one of the 20 poorest countries in the world, and its leaders cannot agree on how to mobilize the power of the state to help the people. Rather they fight with each other over status, wealth and power.

How has this stagnation come about in a country that was founded by one of the great leftist thinkers and his cadres of revolutionaries? Let us realize that the inherited colonial legacy was filled with contradictions, and led to a myriad of possible choices by the new government. With such tough decisions to be made, two things happened to the state—its leaders moved to concentrate power, and to create a formalism. This elevated the head of state to the level of a traditional African chief, or what Lopes has called the "practice of tribalist methods in state government." This has happened elsewhere in West Africa, and may indicate the continuing importance of regard for the traditional big man, the strong and charismatic leader so common in precolonial West Africa.

On paper, and in public pronouncements, the state claimed to be democratic. This was part of the state formalism, which served the interests of the privileged few, the prebenders at the "trough" of state funds. It also served a psychological function. Forced with many possible futures, formalism afforded a safe haven for the leaders. Unfortunately such orthodoxy, coupled with the need to repress opponents, led to state abuses. In the end, the repressive actions of the government reproduced the structure of colonialism because of two factors. First, all the economic and financial relations linking Guinea-Bissau to Europe were still in place, and those who benefited from the functioning of such exchange relations had an interest in maintaining them.

Second, there were other powerful actors on the world stage that had similar interests. These were the IFIs that foster the views of the G-7 and international capital. As state leaders in Guinea-Bissau struggled to find a path toward the future, these actors could offer expertise, advice and financial backing. In short, they were able to co-opt government leaders and nudge them in the direction of a political economy of extraction and exploitation—a command economy not too dissimilar from the one Portugal had in place prior to the national liberation movement.

Guinea-Bissau's Position in the Global Economy

In the international economy of today, the G-7 constitute the core countries that benefit from the dependent status of other countries such as those in West Africa. Capitalist planners need to find new markets for its products, and it needs to produce those products at the lowest cost to maximize profits. It also needs a steady supply of the lowest cost raw materials and labor to do so. **Third World** Countries provide all these factors—cheap raw materials, low labor costs and product-hungry populations who quickly buy manufactured products sent by the core to the periphery. It is therefore axiomatic that for international capitalism to continue to expand, it must keep Third World Countries in a state of economic and political dependence.

These external forces of international capital penetrate countries like those in West Africa, co-opting the people through involvement in the cash economy, and by creating perceived needs for imported goods. Capitalists also interact with African metropolitan élites, who have an interest in such linkages because international capital provides their financing, both to run the state and to fund private ventures. To a certain extent, international capital uses the egos of West African politicos to foster larger-than-life development projects in the region, precisely the ones that do little to help the people, but do a lot for local politicians and foreign capitalists.

In Guinea-Bissau, the **Cumeré Agro-Industrial Complex** is a prime example. This multi-million dollar processing plant for groundnuts and rice was constructed with a capacity 70% greater than all the groundnuts or rice produced in Guinea-Bissau. Its construction lined the pockets of élites and did little to help the people. The Bissau-based Cumeré Agro-Industrial Complex, like so many scattered through the urban zones of West Africa, was a focal point of the twin circuits of appropriation. In the first, the West African State drains off peasant surplus. In the second, the core of international capital drains off wealth from the nation, leaving state functionaries with sufficient residue to keep them interested the next time around. In this way, prebendal élites have mortgaged the future of their people. The people's real interests are subjugated to the interests of the ruling class and foreign capitalists.

True development is not imitating the West. It is the evolution of a productive system lacking unbridled exploitation. It is one where the surplus is applied to human needs—food, shelter, health, education and meaningful work. True development does not try to be modern. It is not imitative. It looks to basic human needs and works up from there. It looks at the environment and determines what is possible with nature's cooperation in a non-damaging way. If capitalist development were ever to achieve this, it has a long way to go, in West Africa and elsewhere.

External Dependency and the Failure of Development

By the late 1970s and early 1980s Guinea-Bissau's economy had hit bottom, like so many others in West Africa. Its people were fleeing to nearby cities in Senegal and Guinea. Essential goods were scarce even in Bissau. Mario Murteira has shown that between 1976 and 1978 only 3.2% of foreign aid was actually spent in Guinea-Bissau. Furthermore, only about a quarter of it was spent on producer goods (often on useless projects) and the lion's share went to the purchase of consumer goods.

After a period of floundering in the **aid > loans > debt > dependency spiral**, Guinea-Bissau began to look to the IFIs and vice versa. With the fall of the Soviet Union, socialist countries like Guinea-Bissau lost much of their funding in that venue. But international capital has requirements—access to raw materials and new markets. Furthermore, like her fellow countries in West Africa, Guinea-Bissau has come under the strictures of SAPs that function to provide an environment in which capitalists more easily access raw materials and markets for their goods.

Thus, many West African countries have sunk deeper and deeper into debt and dependency. They now find themselves enmeshed in a SAP system that has taken away a degree of sovereignty. West African intellectuals now see that imitation of the West has had devastating consequences. Most of the capital-intensive projects constructed in West Africa since independence have amounted to little economic **integration** with the West, but have caused a great deal of economic dependence, following the dependency model developed by Hugues Bertrand for the Congo:

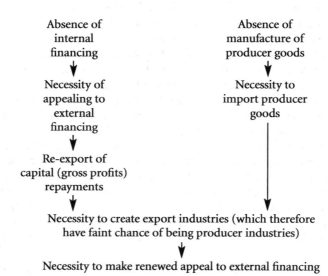

Absence of internal financing

↓

Necessity of appealing to external financing

↓

Re-export of capital (gross profits) repayments

↓

Absence of manufacture of producer goods

↓

Necessity to import producer goods

↓

Necessity to create export industries (which therefore have faint chance of being producer industries)

↓

Necessity to make renewed appeal to external financing

Of course, added to Bertrand's formulation above is that today, not only are West African countries caught in this spiral, but IFIs have got their hands into internal planning of state expenditures. In hindsight we can see how that happened. In Guinea-Bissau between 1978–79, the external debt tripled, growing to 11 times the 1975 total. During this period agricultural production fell off and the country was saddled with numerous failed *projetos colossal*. By 1980 the Central Bank of Guinea-Bissau was bankrupt.

I do not want to give the reader the impression that all the problems of the post-colonial period are due to foreign involvement in West Africa. It is much more complex than that. Carlos Lopes warns:

> To throw all the failure of the new African countries onto imperialism, colonialism and neocolonialism is an insult to the leaders of the new states. It is to attribute to them a passive role, defenseless victims of an historically predeter-

mined situation. All tendencies to dramatize the present by historical justification lead to decadence, to a simplistic interpretation of society.

On the other hand, to ignore the relatively uniform behavior of West African leaders, some of whom were revolutionaries and others clearly in the European camp, is to ignore sociohistorical causation, to reduce behavior to the whims of individuals. They all reacted in patterned ways to the forces with which they had to deal upon taking the reins of power. That those forces came mainly from the outside is not surprising, given the history of colonialism in the region, and its long history of involvement in trade with the West.

I do not present a mechanical explanation, but one that involves human sentient reaction to real sociohistorical forces, the most causative of which are economic. No matter how proactive and ideologically aggressive the postcolonial leaders were, their countries today are almost all in the same situation—they are being controlled, to varying degrees, by IFIs and international capital.

But to say that West African politicians merely respond to external forces is only part of the answer. They also carry within them the seeds of petty bourgeois sentiments, and ideas. Even the revolutionary cadres of the PAIGC revolutionary liberation movement carried these attitudes. These counter-revolutionary ideas were a result of their upbringing, education in European schools.

The idea of neocolonialism rests on the idea that petty bourgeois ideas were left over after the liberation movements of men like Kwame Nkrumah, Amílcar Cabral, Ahmed Sékou Touré and others. They were resident in two loci—in people and in institutions. The attitudes, values and aspirations of the petty bourgeoisie did not disappear when a new flag was raised over the capital; nor did the endless rules created by bourgeois colonialists. The structure and cultural attitudes of colonialism remained in place into the postcolonial period. Again, that is a static interpretation. All those rules could be ignored, or thrown out by new African leaders, but they were not. Part of the dynamic involved stems from the fact that the colonists didn't go very far, if they left at all. White politicians left, but the traders, entrepreneurs, financiers, and CEOs remained or visited frequently enough to manage the situation. They could finesse the situation because they had control of the technical expertise needed to run what little industry had been left behind, or that which was being proposed. They also had the financial clout.

Furthermore, a "state building" school of thought pervaded development planning at the time when most West African nations received their independence. That school was typified by the ideas of **Walter Rostow**, who saw the application of Western ideas and technology as essential for a "take-off" to modernity. It was popular to think that with a little tinkering, West African countries could be transformed into modern ones—politically and economically.

West African leaders did not react uniformly to this modernization school. Some chaffed against it. Some still do. Others wholeheartedly embraced it. Still others refused to participate. Despite this variation, the countries of West Africa today find themselves in a very similar situation. To different degrees, their economies, and increasingly their social services, are being controlled by IFIs and international capital. Thus, a common form of dependency exists across the ECOWAS countries today.

If we take it as an axiom of political sociology that the state always represents class interests, then we can add West Africa to a long list of empirical cases that supports this thesis. The West African states have been used as instruments of capitalist development, a postcolonial situation that has greatly benefited the core and impoverished the peripheral peoples of West Africa.

Certainly politicians of the West African State and bureaucrats of the adjoining administrations have assisted the penetration of their lands by the forces of the market and international capital, but they are not the only facilitators. Imperialism has crept in through the windows and side doors as well, through the market goods in every village and through radio and television. Today it slithers in through the Internet and, in general, through popular culture that arrives in West Africa embedded in books, magazines, popular music, videos and all sorts of avenues to the minds of the people.

According to this perspective, imperialism is embedded in Western culture, and especially in the products, services and advertising disseminated by the global market. Social scientists now know that the market has penetrated even the remotest of villages to some degree. It would seem, therefore, that modern and future politicians are going to have to learn to live with, or find ways to modify, the influence of this powerful force—global capitalism.

CRITICAL THINKING QUESTIONS

1. What did Professor Fage mean when he said that, "colonialism carried its own solvent"?
2. Discuss the role of education in the development of the anti-colonial movements.
3. What was the disagreement between Sékou Touré and Félix Houphouët-Boigny over the *Communité*? Given the way things have gone in postcolonial Francophone West Africa, which one do you think was correct?
4. What problems did the PAIGC revolutionaries face in trying to make the transition from freedom fighters to governors of the nation-state?
5. What is the problem for West African élites in the accumulation of capital to start capitalist enterprises or large-scale industries? Relate this answer to prebendalism and concepts of corruption in West African government.
6. What does the author mean when he says that the people of colonial and postcolonial West Africa have been "ensnared in a mummified cultural and economic frame"?
7. Running a budget deficit, the new government of Guinea-Bissau tried to finance a quick "leap" into modernity using what four tactics? What was the end result and why did this come about?
8. Be able to support or reject the thesis that imperialism is embedded in the process of global capitalist expansion, and that it is a force that the South will have to deal with for years to come.

KEY CONCEPTS

Acculturative impact of European culture **Antiquated bureaucracies**
Accumulation   **Cabral, Amílcar**
Aid > loans > debt > dependency spiral   **Césaire, Aimé**

Bigmanism
Bissau Seaman's Strike
Bourgeois mentality
Bourgeoisie
Bretton Woods Agreements
Communité
Convention Peoples Party (CPP)
Cumeré Agro-Industrial Complex
Debt dependency
Debt servicing
Dependency theory
G-7
HIPC
Houphouët-Boigny, Félix
Integration
International capital
Nkrumah, Kwame
Metropole
Neocolonialism
Nigerian Federal System
Organization of African Unity (OAU)
PAIGC
Pan-African Congresses
Pan-Africanism
Parallel economy

Particularism
People's National Assembly (ANP)
Periphery
Petty bourgeoisie
Prebendalism
Prebendal class
Prebends
Proletarians or Proletariat
Primitive accumulation
Privatization
Rassemblement Démocratique Africain (RDA)
Red Carnation Revolution
Revolutionary formalism
Shift to the Guinea-Bissau Peso
South
Third World
Touré, Ahmed Sékou
Transparency
Union of the Peoples of Guiné and Cape Verde (PAIGC)
United Cold Coast Convention (UGCC)
Walter Rostow
W.E.B. DuBois
Yala, Koumba

≋ SOURCES & SUGGESTED READINGS ≋

Amin, S. & K. Vergoupolos. 1978. *A questão camponesa e o capitalismo*. Lisboa: A Regra do Jogo.

Bertrand, Hugues. 1975. *Le Congo: Formation sociale et mode de développment économique*. Paris: Maspero.

Entralgo, Armando Szentes . 1979. *Africa-Sociedad*. Havana: Editorial de Ciêcias Sociales.

Fage, J. D. 1995. *A history of Africa*. London: Routledge. Chapter. 13

Fanon, Franz. 1967. *Toward an African Revolution*. New York: Monthly Review Press.

Gellar, Sheldon. 1995. The Colonial Era. In: Martin, Phyllis M. & Patrick O'Meara (eds.). *Africa* (Third edition). Bloomington: Indiana University Press, 135–155.

Lloyd, Christopher. 1973. *The search for the Niger*. London: Collins.

Lopes, Carlos. 1987. *Guinea-Bissau: From liberation struggle to independent statehood*. Trans. Michael Wolfers. Boulder: Westview Press.

Murteira, Mario. 1978. O desenvolvimento dos menos desenvolvidos: Reflexões sobre as economias da Guiné e Cabo Verde. *Economia e socialismo* 30 September, 3–17.

Shivji, Issa G. 1976. *Class struggles in Tanzania*. London: Heinemann.

Winchester, N. Brian. 1995. African politics since independence. In: Martin, P. & P. O'Meara (eds.). *Africa* (third edition). London: James Currey, 347–358.

Zigler, Jean. 1978. *Main basse sur l'Afrique*. Paris: Seuil.

16 THE POSTCOLONIAL ERA

> The old is dying, the new cannot be born: in this interregnum
> there arises a great diversity of morbid symptoms.
>
> —Antonio Gramsci, *Sections from the Prison Notebooks*

After successfully driving the imperialists from West Africa, African leaders and the people went through a naïve period of belief in modernization and progress. After 1970, events indicated that development was not working. Constitutional governments failed to meet the needs of their people, the military tried to govern and democracy was abandoned in an effort to streamline government. West African nations continued to slide into poverty and poor governance. Corruption became a way of life. Politics of the belly predominated. The region devolved into religious conflict and civil strife. Yet in spite of these problems and others, some seek an **African Renaissance**.

The Romance of Regaining Lost Freedom

The African Colin Legum characterizes Africa's political consciousness in three stages beginning with World War II:

1. The Romantic Period (1939–1970)
2. The Period of Disillusionment (1970–1985)
3. The Period of Realism (1988–present)

The Romantic Period was a period when modernization of West Africa seemed probable, even easy. The Period of Disillusionment came as Africans realized that something was wrong—modernity seemed illusive. After 1988, Africa entered a Period of Realism, where leaders began to face up to the fact that development was far more difficult than simple copying of Western ways.

With strong memories of oppression from the past and the presence of colonial overlords in their land, West African élites began to plan for a day when they could reclaim their freedom. It is remarkable that in West Africa this was accomplished with relatively little bloodshed. Certainly the post-World War II period was marked by mostly peaceful protests against colonial rule. The other remarkable aspect of the move to independence was the speed with which it proceeded in the post-war years. After the independence of Ghana in 1957, the domino effect took hold and most West African countries regained their liberty within a few years.

The men who pushed to regain sovereignty were a mixed lot. Conservatives like Félix Houphouët-Boigny of *Côte d'Ivoire* felt that West Africa was not ready for independence. Though he had started out a radical who flirted with Marxism, Houphouët-Boigny was an astute politician who spent most of his years in the halls of government in France. He and a handful of other conservatives believed that West Africans should move in a gradual way to build up a base of trained civil servants, politicians and technicians who could eventually take over from the Europeans.

Nevertheless, the dominant call was for "Freedom Now!"—the slogan of Kwame Nkrumah's CPP party in Ghana. He typified the fiery young radicals pushing for the expulsion of the imperialists. Others in West Africa were Dr. Nnamdi Azikiwe of Nigeria, Sékou Touré of Guinea, Modiba Keita of Mali and later, Amílcar Cabral of Guinea-Bissau. Some were simply nationalists, others were called "rhetorical Marxists," more prone to oratory than implementation of communist policies.

What united the new African leadership was that they were almost all **Western-educated modernizing élites.** Conservative or radical, they all looked to European political and administrative institutions as the means of governance with a separation of powers between an executive branch and parliament, bureaucratic administration, an independent judiciary, etc.

In the rush to independence, the state model was imposed on a people without any sense of national unity. The imposition of a foreign model of governance on West Africans disrupted the normal flow of life in the region. In this flux, modernizing élites proceeded according to their plans to lead the people into a modern and better way of life. Many in West Africa had bought into the idea that European civilization equaled progress. In this time of euphoria, the watchword was **African nationalism** and there were few detractors. It was a revolution of rising expectations set on the development of a modern way of life comparable to that in America and Europe. But governance and modernization failed in the postindependence era and Basil Davidson, in his book *The Black Man's Burden*, blames the wholesale adoption of the nation-state for this failure.

While the modern state in Europe grew out of an organic evolutionary process, forming nations over a long period of time, in West Africa, states were simply imposed, and often cut across ethnic and community boundaries. It is instructive that where state boundaries in Africa have coincided with previously existing nations—Swaziland, Botswana (Bechuanaland) and Lesotho (Basutoland)—governments have had relatively few problems.

Davidson and others indicate that in the early years of independence leaders failed to reform government to make it more appropriate for the African context. This led to problems, especially when the civil service clashed with the executive branch, which was often driven by party politics.

Many West African politicians resorted to what some have called "developmental dictatorship." This was a move toward autocracy—the one party state. Through extra-constitutional means, the party in power banned its competitors, repressed trade unions, newspapers, civil servants and university professors. Such curbing of freedoms was justified in the name of national unity and stability. Political leaders claimed that administrative expertise in West Africa was limited so multiparty democracy was inappropriate for the region. In order to have progress, it was purported, a single party needed tight controls to foster development.

In this move away from pluralism and freedom of expression, representative institutions such as the legislatures suffered a loss of power. The central committee of the single party extended its influence over the judiciary, civil service, police and the armed forces, using a combination of the carrot and the stick—they were bought off and threatened. Facing "unsettled" states, complex problems and shortage of trained personnel, aristocrats rationalized that such repression was warranted. It was no single state that used these tactics. Most West African nations used state power to eliminate political opposition. By the end of the 1960s only Gambia had a competitive multiparty system.

Single-party states did no better than democratic ones in dealing with the fundamental issues facing West Africa. This general failure led to the next stage in West Africa's political evolution—military rule.

Since politicians of one-party states tended to alienate students, professors, civil servants, the judiciary and trade unions, they were particularly vulnerable to violent takeovers. These significant segments of society were often ready for a change and, at least in the beginning of this period of disillusionment, tended to back militaristic regimes. The soldiers who led *coup d'états* sometimes did so out of personal ambition, but others did so with the best of intentions, citing such grievances as those outlined by N. Brian Winchester:

> unacceptably high levels of corruption and profiteering, government misman-
> agement and financial extravagance, the decision of political leaders to stay in
> power beyond their constitutionally mandated tenure, demands on the military
> to carry out distasteful policies such as strikebreaking on behalf of the politi-
> cians, and attempts by civilian governments to compromise or reduce the
> power, budget or perquisites of the military.

West African soldiers have found it easier to take power than to rule once in power. In fact, they have done no better than one-party rulers or democratic regimes. Lacking much experience at running a country, the military relied heavily on the civil service, which had become corrupt in many cases. Looking back on this period of recent *coup d'etats*, military rule did little to elevate public opinion toward government, and in most cases further contributed to a loss of faith in the state.

The intransigent problems facing West African states after liberation from colonial rule have not been effectively dealt with by any of the forms of government tried since independence—multiparty democracy, the one-party state or military juntas. At this writing, most West African states have reverted to some form of civilian rule. There are two reasons for this. First, there is a general preference by the people for this form of government, especially when there is more than one party to choose from, and second, lending bodies from the international domain, such as the IMF and World Bank, have actively pushed for such reforms.

In a number of countries in West Africa real efforts have been made to increase citizen participation in politics. In the late 1970s, President Senghor lifted the ban on political activity in Senegal, approving a modified multiparty system to replace the former one-party state he had headed. In January 1981 he decided to step down in favor of Prime Minister Abdou Diouf. In so doing he became a member of a select cadre of African leaders who have voluntarily relinquished power, the other in West Africa being General **Olusegun Obasanjo** of Nigeria, who has recently been re-elected to lead his country out of a decade of military rule and corruption.

In Burkina Faso, Ghana and Nigeria military regimes turned over power in 1978–79 to civilian rule. Parliamentary systems were instituted but eventually gave way to military rule in all three instances. However, by the new millennium, civilian rule was emerging. Today, most West African states have some form of democracy in place.

Things did not go well after independence, a fact that the great Nigerian novelist Chinua Achebé artistically showed in his novel *Things Fall Apart*. The region has suffered economic decline in the face of high expectation of development; accusations of cronyism, corruption and incompetent administration; and the rise and fall of military regimes. When compared to where most West Africans thought independence would take them, the period from 1970 to 1985 has been a rocky road indeed.

Colin Legum says of this period:

> The frequency of the military coup was symptomatic of the failure of the post-independence institutions which suffered from such weaknesses as inadequate checks and balances between the executive, legislative, administrative and judicial branches; a lack of accountability and transparency; and the absence of an influential countervailing civil society.

In the aftermath of failed military rule, West African states suffered from a lack of trained administrators and technicians, and those who were given the responsibility to administer state functions had their hands tied by political forces. As pointed out by Colin Legum, outstanding administrators like Robert Gardiner, Daniel Chapman and Yao Adu in Gold Coast (Ghana); Ivor Cummings in Sierra Leone; and Simeon Adebo in Nigeria early on came into conflict with the new political class over three principle issues. First, they insisted on maintaining a suitably defined relationship between ministers and civil servants. Second, the new monarchs tried to decolonize the civil service too fast. Finally, ministers wanted to install their supporters in civil service posts without regard to qualifications, thus further undermining a bureaucracy already weakened by colonial neglect.

Colonial control of economic base persisted and many of the problems in postcolonial West Africa are due to this retention by foreigners that led governmental ministers to act differently than if they had direct control over economic affairs. One example is the widespread emergence of parastatal corporations that, to an extent, has been a continuation of colonial policy. Throughout West Africa government officials moved to establish parastatal companies to gain some control over the private sector dominated by foreigners.

Kwame Nkrumah of Ghana forged ahead to establish a new industrial area at Tema, and sought to attract capital from entrepreneurs around the world. Many came, but as Colin Legum says, many of them "turned out to be crooks." These early schemes of the modernizing élites seem now to have been too ambitious. African leaders received substantial advice and aid from the developed world, but Mr. Legum, himself a Black African, nicely phrases the true nature of this seeming largesse of financial aid from the Core as "a poisoned chalice."

Another aspect of this early romantic period was the desire to carry through some of the ideals of Pan-Africanism. Kwame Nkrumah went so far as to advocate a **United States of Africa,** but in the end the Organization of African Unity (OAU) was formed, which in itself is a remarkable feat. It demonstrates an underlying commonality among African leaders who could agree on a format in spite of ideological differences, especially between the conservative Monrovia Group and the most radical members of the Casablanca Group.

There were conflicting sentiments among the new leaders, in spite of an overall belief in Africa. Some would say, however, that there is more unity among African leaders than between them and the people. In West Africa, members of the new ruling class and the growing bureaucracy set themselves above the general public. René Dumont, in his book *False Start in Africa*, criticized the new élites for their pomposity and avarice. He pointed out that in the first blush of independence a deputy or Member of Parliament earned as much in six weeks as did an average farmer in thirty-six years!

Dependency theorists attribute the failure of West African development to the stranglehold of economic ties established by Core Countries, the G-7 nations, primarily. I think dependency of this sort is the key reason for the relative backwardness of the region, but dependency goes deeper than mere economics. There is a **cultural dependency** in the area as well. West Africa is afflicted by a fascination with Western notions of progress as defined by materialism and consumerism. This was passed to acculturated West Africans through education, in the media and by powerful élites. One wonders about the impact on people without water in their village when the wife of the country's president imports a hot tub from America!

By the 1990s, West African autocrats, both civilian and military, were under "assault" by a combination of organizations from the civil sector of the region's cities — trade unionists, civil libertarians, human rights activists, students and professors from the universities, religious leaders and others. Such pressure was exerted on Benin's Mathieu Kérékou in February 1990. As supreme leader of his country, he was forced to convene a national conference, a referendum of sorts, to address the country's economic and political crises. Those who attended the conference were the élites of the country. Unexpectedly, they declared the conference to be sovereign and of a higher authority than the state ruled by Kérékou. They unilaterally suspended the constitution, dissolved the National Assembly and by the end of the ten-day conference, had stripped Kérékou of all power. Then the delegates chose an interim Prime Minister, Nicéphore Soglo, who was subsequently the winner in Benin's first free election in 17 years.

The **Benin Conference** became the rage, and other West African élites clamored to reassert the power of the people (at least through themselves as élites). Speaking of Africa in general, the political analyst Brian Winchester says:

> In the short space of two to three years, more than half of sub-Saharan Africa's governments were forced to respond to growing pressure for democratic reform "from the streets" and from external donors. The trend toward political liberalization may be widespread, but it remains fragile and incomplete.

A profound problem faced by West African countries is the artificiality of colonial boundaries. African leaders inherited states that encompass no common language, no unified culture and no collective history. They are rife with regional, ethnic and religious differences. The local civic culture of West Africans has been ignored, suppressed and co-opted by creating councils of chiefs to link local rulers to the national structure. But this has done little to help the local people, or to develop the capacity of West African governments to provide adequate social services. Dennis Austin in his book *Politics in Africa* summed up this postcolonial situation when he said that Africa was "governed by insecure regimes uneasily in control of unsettled societies."

The very "unsettled" nature of the new states was worrisome to national leaders, but they feared redrawing their inherited political maps for fear of losing their constituencies. Border disputes flared up periodically in the region. The OAU has ruled out any major restructuring of the colonial boundaries of African states and the only exception was the adjustment of the Nigeria-Cameroon border. The OAU is also against the use of force by one African nation on another; prohibits the meddling in the internal affairs of one African state by another; and it stresses the need for all to respect the sovereignty of nations. These policies have not been entirely successful.

Corruption

While West African leaders may not have been especially in need, the lesser bureaucrats often were, and this disparity has led to a culture of corruption in West Africa. It is said that even the idealist Kwame Nkrumah found it difficult to halt the corruption around him, so he tried to channel some of the monies to his causes by placing a 10% surcharge on all payoffs.

Corruption is fed by outside firms who shower those in power with enormous sums of money to help them accomplish their ends. I personally know one such European who regularly flies his private plane into African countries carrying suitcases of cash to bribe local government officials. These people come to meet him at the airport and the transactions take place without him ever needing to leave his plane. Although corruption is a part of industrialized and underdeveloped countries, it must be noted that not all African leaders are corrupt. Notable exceptions to the generalized are honorable men like Julius Nyerere, Nelson Mandela, Milton Obote, Kenneth Kaunda, Léopold Senghor, Jerry Rawlings and others.

Corruption is not the cause of decline, as many in the West would like to have it. I see the main cause of underdevelopment in the **articulation** of West African economies with the global economy, but there are internal causes as well. The first internal cause to consider is natural. West Africa was known as the White Man's Grave, but disease also affects the indigenes of the region, reducing their productivity. I have had Malaria on a regular basis while living in the region. I know how debilitating it is and how tired it leaves you when you enter an extended period of recovery, sometimes for days or even weeks after the onset of the attack. Unfortunately, Malaria is just one such endemic disease that acts in this fashion, and the reality of life in West Africa is that people are affected by a combination of such diseases that operate in tandem to limit a person's productivity.

There are also environmental factors such as West African soils, which are notoriously poor, limiting agricultural output. Then there are the recurrent droughts, ravages of insects, and the apparent creeping desiccation of the Sahara Desert dislocating whole communities in the Sahel region. These natural limits to agricultural output have been operating along with wide fluctuations in the world price of West African export crops. Furthermore, the switch to non-edible cash-crops such as cotton and cocoa, along with the environmental troubles enumerated above, has led West African nations to become food importers. The heavy expense of importing foodstuffs has contributed to the consumption of valuable foreign exchange, which could otherwise have been applied to development in the region.

Table 16.1 Commodity Prices	
Average Annual Growth Rate, 1960–1980 (%)*	
Copper	−5.5
Iron ore	−8.5
Bauxite	3.9
Phosphate rock	−0.2
Manganese ore	−6.4
Zinc	−0.7
Rubber	−2.3
Lead	1.6
Coffee	2.3
Cocoa	5.5
Sugar	−2.5
Tea	−3.4
Groundnuts	−1.7
Groundnut oil	−1.6
Beef	1.5
Palm oil	−2.0
Bananas	−4.0
Maize	0.2
Timber	0.7
Cotton	−1.0
Hides, skins	0

* After: World Bank, *Accelerated Development in Sub-Saharan Africa* , p.157.

Part of the **modernization approach** used by American development specialists involved loaning money to fuel development efforts in West Africa. The World Bank, other lenders, and foreign aid from governments, inundated the region with cash. The young governments were eager to take the aid and the loans were thought to be temporary. They would be paid back as soon as they produced more than the interest payments and redemption costs.

That never happened. The result was that by the end of the 1980s, most West African governments were forced to pay something between 40 and 80% of their foreign exchange earnings to service their debts. Thus, debt burden became one of the major obstacles to development.

Another external factor was and is the imbalance in world trade. With their economic clout, Core Countries can fix commodity prices to suit their own interests, along with managing world trade rules through the WTO and other international organizations (See Table 16.1). Shortly after independence the world economy changed, and there has been a steady drop in the world market price of most commodities exported by West African countries since.

The first blow was the tripling and quadrupling of oil prices in the mid-1970s. Imported machinery, fertilizer, pesticides, herbicides and improved seeds for agriculture shot up, as did imported consumer goods. With revenues falling, and foreign exchange reserves gone, the new leaders turned to foreign aid and loans.

With limited funds, these governments limited support to rural areas, focusing on the cities instead. In 1970, when I first went to Northern Ghana, for example, village primary schools instituted by Nkrumah were in operation. By the time I returned in 1975, the schools had been closed, cash-cropping was at a standstill and petrofarming was grinding to a halt for lack of fuel and spare parts for imported machinery.

This impoverishment of the rural areas led to a rapid increase in the number of urban migrants, increasing problems of underemployment, urban squalor, crowding and crime. Unemployment in Africa rose from 7.7% in 1978 to 22.8% in 1990. Today it hovers near 30% and threatens to go higher. The Economic Commission for Africa had forecast that its urban population will increase almost two and a half times in the next 25 years, reaching a staggering 470 million.

The last two decades of the 20th century were dismal ones for West Africa. Excessive dependence on a limited number of exports, which ran into a depressed foreign market, forced governments onto international handouts and credit. Military coups and authoritarianism were added plagues.

Professor Ade-Ajayi of Nigeria puts a sad epitaph on this period when he says:

> Failure to decolonize meant, in fact, failure to confront the past, make amends and make repairs. It implies a carry-over of the disabilities from the slave trade era to the colonial period, and from the colonial period into the period after independence. This often involved a loss of self-esteem, and undue willingness to substitute dependence on charity for self-confidence and self-reliance.

The spread of the global economy has brought the problem of corruption to the fore in what some have called the "corruption eruption." It is not that there is more corruption, but simply that it is held up to public scrutiny more. Demands for economic liberalization, democratic reforms and increasing global integration are combining to expose corruption and heighten awareness about its costs. As the corruption expert Kimberly Ann Elliot notes, "These trends, in turn, have sparked an anticorruption backlash that is spreading around the world."

The United States, which some have dubbed the "Lonely Boy Scout" in this regard, led the way with the passage of 1977 anticorruption legislation. The US Congress passed the Foreign Corrupt Practices Act (FCPA) making it a crime for any corporation or corporate official to make illegal payments to secure business in the international setting.

Generally, corruption is thought to have deleterious effects. Augustine Ruzindana lists some of them as economic waste and inefficiency, the persistence of underdevelopment and poverty, the stunting of development, an impediment to foreign investment and assistance and the distortion of official decisions. Corruption also frequently involves the payment of illegal funds. As they are monies that need to be hidden, they are more likely to remain hidden, in Swiss bank accounts for example, or to go into further illegal enterprises, since the funds cannot easily be laundered and brought into the realm of legitimate commerce.

The presence of widespread corruption in Peripheral Countries today cannot be divorced from the fact that most were colonies of Core Countries. In West Africa, these colonial regimes were authoritarian. Criticism of colonial policies by Africans was severely curtailed.

In this colonial atmosphere of seeming omnipotence, governors and officials were not held accountable by the West African people, except in a broad public opinion. In time, with African chiefs and monarchs folded into the colonial mix, everything became a privilege to be paid for. The rich could manipulate this system, leaving aside the majority of West Africans. Thus, it is not reasonable to lay the blame for corruption on Africans alone. It evolved out of the hybrid system of administration mixing traditional ways with imposed ones.

The hybrid nature of the system is important. It is a cross between traditional and imported ways. In the indigenous system, men exchanged "favors" in the spirit of mutual aid. When these practices were incorporated into European bureaucracies, they did not fit. Rose-Ackerman says "Widespread corruption is a sign that something has gone wrong in the relationship between the state and society." Witness the fact that the early Sudanic States to a large degree were built on the exploitation of trade passing through the region of the Niger Bend. Kings demanded first rights to goods at "state" prices, which then enabled them to turn a profit by selling those goods on the open market. West Africa has a long history of interplay between men in power and those in the commercial sector. To think that this would simply stop with the development of the nation-state and modern bureaucracies is naïve thinking. But it is important to see that the governmental structures taken over by West Africans were hybrids, a mixture of old and new ways, and this hybrid form of governance was already rife with contradictions that have led to widespread corruption in the region.

Since bribery and prebendalism (rent taking) are realities in the international marketplace, Core Countries are putting up resistance to criminalization of transnational bribery, because some companies are loath to eschew what they see as a useful and necessary tool in doing business overseas. According to the OECD, many Core Countries in effect encourage and contribute to corruption by making their bribes to foreigners tax deductible back home.

Also, the Cold War payments to puppet regimes can be considered a form of graft, and since the fall of the Soviet Bloc, this form of corruption is less tolerated in international circles. Glynn *et al* note this trend:

> The longevity of regimes such as those of Marcos in the Philippines, the Duvaliers in Haiti, Stroessner in Paraguay, and those of the many African tyrants who oppressed their citizens and looted their central banks was a concrete geopolitical expression of superpower rivalries. Foreign aid and military assistance continued to flow to these countries even though it was widely known that much of the time the titular destination was no more than a stopover en route to the private Swiss bank accounts of the ruling families and their cronies.

Corruption has distributive consequences in which wealth, information and opportunity are unfairly distributed to insiders. Corruption is part of privilege. As such, it is one more way to allow élites to communicate in ways that permit them to keep wealth, opportunity and information within a privileged class. Manzetti & Blake have shown that those with inside connections can more easily get government contracts or receive divested government assets under privatization schemes. Corruption, by preventing the free circulation of opportunity, maintains or even enhances class privilege.

Put another way, corruption and cronyism prevent full democracy by limiting the flow of wealth within a limited sphere and by limiting the flow of information. One of the major means of creating and maintaining stratification is the sequestering of information and opportunity, limiting it to a select network of "in-the-know" players. However, looking at corruption in this perspective raises some important questions about the nature of capitalism, which to an extent involves the secreting of information and opportunity. What is the line between legal and illegal? When is the hiding of information and opportunity just good business and when is it anti-democratic? Since corruption occurs at the interface between public and private sectors, and since it is clear that politics and economics go hand in hand, how does one go about defining the limits of discretionary behavior on the part of public and private individuals in interaction? Furthermore, how does one enforce constraints when such interactions can be held in private? It seems essential to answer these questions if a truly transparent form of democracy is to emerge in a time when more and more multinational firms are coming into contact with a greater number of public officials in the Periphery.

Corruption can lead to higher contract prices and shoddy workmanship, the costs of which are passed on to the general public. Society must pay for these consequences while the élites involved in the transactions enrich themselves and their cronies. In Sisalaland, wealthy farmers can bribe the GCC to plow large acreage for them, which means that poor farmers cannot get the tractors to plow their land. Or, their plowing is done late in the season, which means they will be late planting and may suffer accordingly in a farm economy dependent on seasonal rains. In other parts of West Africa where irrigation is practiced, rich farmers can pay irrigation officials for water, thus depriving downstream farmers of their livelihood.

These are micro-cases, but such deprivation can be seen at the macro-level as well. Take Nigeria as a case in point. Herbst & Olukoshi have shown that in this West African country with vast oil wealth much of it has been dissipated through corruption and other forms of rent seeking. After years of pumping, the oil companies and a few corrupt men are well off, while Nigeria remains the 17th poorest country in the world with per capita income statistics that have changed little.

The Nature of West African Politics

The following characteristics can be identified *vis-à-vis* West African political organizations:

* Politics of the belly, or clientelist (patronage) politics
* Ethnic politics
* Puppet politics
* Military authoritarianism
* **Authoritarian presidentialist regimes** or politics as personal rule

Politics of the belly simply means that it is common for politicians to use their offices to access wealth illegally. Sometimes they favor people of their ethnic background, providing government contracts to them. Puppet politics means that during the Cold War years, the two superpowers maintained stooges in Africa who would support their cause. Such puppets were not usually attentive to the needs of their people. Nor were the military dictators who used the power of the gun to subvert constitutional power. Finally, authoritarian presidentialist regimes were common in which the headman built up a cult of personality and ruled based on real or projected charisma.

Postcolonial Ghana provides one example of patronage politics. Kwame Nkrumah organized his constituents expeditiously by offering patronage to local big men who already had followings. Using this strategy, new politicos all over West Africa were able to recruit and maintain support long enough to gain national power, even though such clientelist formations proved to be highly destabilizing in the long run.

In another case, in Sierra Leone, the coalition formed by chiefly representatives and the Sierra Leone People's Party (SLPP), used their control over rural credit to reward key rural supporters with loans that were never repaid. Within such patronage systems the top man would pass valued resources along to local supporters as rewards for loyalty, and they in turn would pass them down the pipeline to lesser followers. Within the new governments and ruling parties clientelism bred corruption. This predated the 1950s, but expanded with great acceleration after independence.

As new wealth from abroad flowed into these "emerging democracies," ruling party leaders had access to large sums of money, which quickly became transformed into prebends — rewards for service in office, or for continued loyalty by local politicians and big men. Political decay began to set in with the rapid growth of political conflict and violence, abuse of human rights and graft.

As factionalism increased the formation of such ruling networks of patronage created a backlash. Not all categories of persons in the country could be included, so opposition parties began to organize the excluded persons, families, ethnic groups, churches or Islamic organizations using the same system of patronage. In this way, long-standing local, ethnic and religious conflicts became redrawn within national politics as hard-edged, sectional hostilities.

These conflicts were exacerbated by independence and became increasingly violent. Those in power began using force to maintain their hold, by harassing the opposition, rigging elections and later, resorting to banishments, beatings, jailings and even killings. Opposition forces retaliated and each side escalated the level of violence.

The spread of factionalism also began to eat away at party unity. Groups within the party began to vie for control over state resources. While some funds were still channeled to party loyalists in various localities throughout the country, larger and larger prebends found their way into the pockets of party activists — those with their hands on the purse strings. Within the officer corps of the military, big men began to use military forces to favor partisans. Also, greater and greater amounts of the military budget were funneled into private projects of corrupt officers.

The crisis of patronage governance was amended, though not resolved, in West Africa in two ways: by military takeover and by the establishment of one-party states. Sometimes military pressure failed even though its aim was to replace unstable systems with stable, authoritarian ones. These attempts to find more appropriate systems of government involved four key and overlapping elements. First, clientelism was retained, but brought under more control by the supreme leader. Second, power was centralized, vested in a president, who could therefore stand above factional maneuvering and control it to an extent. He had enormous power in controlling constitutional, military, financial and party resources as well as wide powers of appointment and dismissal in governmental and parastatal sectors. Third, the bureaucracy was able, to an extent, to take over as the main distributor of clientelist resources. Answerable to the president, bureaucrats were more controllable than the previous contestants for resources. Fourth, representative institutions in society were downgraded. Political parties, parliament, local government, the judiciary, trade unions and cooperatives suffered a curtailment of power or came to have only a symbolic presence.

These four overlapping changes are associated with a one-party system and a strong centralized presidency. It was thought that, in such a state, competition could be regulated, and resource allocation would be less vulnerable to clientelism.

Until the late 1980s, this approach worked for the most part. It even led to a peaceful transfer of power in Senegal when the president resigned. In Guinea, where the reforms were abused and the populace alienated in the dying years of Sékou Touré's rule, this led to a military takeover, the other major form of authoritarian rule in West Africa.

Most of the authoritarian presidentialist regimes were created in the early stages of the clientelist crisis, but a few were established after a series of coups. This type of rule proved to be a most unstable system, with regime changes, on average, every 18 months. In 1972, yet another *coup d'etat* put Mathieu Kérékou in power, and over the next few years he introduced reforms. Between 1974 and 1990 Benin remained stable, though by the late 1980s it had come under increasing challenges. Eventually it became one of the first regimes transformed by a wave of democratic struggles. Kérékou, who had ruled between 1974–1989, was reelected in 1996 with 52.6% of the vote.

Where clientelism could not be reigned in institutionally, **spoils politics** ruled the day, as seen in Nigeria, Sierra Leone, Liberia, Ghana, and Upper Volta (Burkina Faso) in the 1970s and 1980s. Sierra Leone subsequently became unstable, violent and was marked by intense civil war and a virtual collapse of the state. Spoils politics are characterized by eight interlocking features.

First, only the dominant political factions profit. They maintain control over resources by excluding other parties.

Second, there is widespread looting of the economy. Individuals use public office for private or factional gain.

Third, economic crises abound. These may be stimulated by external forces, such as changes of the price of commodities on the world market, or by internal neglect or disorganization. Throughout West Africa in the years from 1976 on, inflation has been extreme. The rate of inflation has, at times, exceeded 100% per year, causing rapid increase in poverty. Even oil-rich Nigeria was forced to rely on large external borrowing, austerity budgets and mass sackings.

Fourth, institutions break down. Politicians have no effective means of preventing mass dissatisfaction or of arbitrating between the nation-state and discontented groups. The situation in West Africa was marked by widespread strikes, withdrawal from production and sales of crops, riots, and even strikes by professional groups like the Ghana Bar Association.

Fifth, repression and violence increase in state-citizen relations and political activity. For example, in the1972 and 1977 Sierra Leone elections opposing candidates were eradicated, an opposition news office was blown up, voters were intimidated and votes were rigged. About the same time, Nigeria was a state "at war with its citizens," marked by an increased level of violent conflict, state repression and human rights abuses.

Sixth, factional activity plays an increasing role in national politics.

Seventh, instability becomes endemic, with continual attempts to overthrow sovereign governments, or a rapid sequence of regimes.

Finally, a general erosion of authority leads to alienation of the populace, a withdrawal from the state and, in some cases, populist revolt.

In West Africa, populist revolts have involved the overthrow of a regime by junior military and/or other groups such as urban workers, organized labor, student dissidents and even radicalized professional bodies. The push has been for the creation of democratic and accountable political systems. Such takeovers occurred in Ghana in 1979 and 1981, in Upper Volta (Burkina Faso) in 1984, Liberia and perhaps Gambia in 1981. More recently Nigeria has returned to civilian rule. Of course, G-7 nations have encouraged these moves, seeing them conjoined with SAPs and their pressure toward more accountability in West African governments.

These populist moves may indicate a search for an authentic African solution to spoils politics. Unfortunately, such movements do not seem to last. In Ghana, Rawlings' rather unorthodox behavior temporarily united a populist sentiment, junior officers, radical students, trade unionists and dissident élites. The Rawlings government was transformed into a centralized bureaucratic state, partly under pressure from structural adjustment, the SAP programs imposed on the region by IFIs. Reforms in Liberia rapidly reverted to a spoils system; in Burkina Faso attempts at reform declined into extreme factionalism that culminated in the assassination of the populist leader, Thomas Sankara.

During the 1980s, all West African nations suffered through a period of economic decline, though to varying degrees. This affected output, export revenues and capital inflows and resulted in massive and unserviceable debt burdens, the highest in relation to GNP anywhere in the Periphery.

With economies failing and debts rising, public services have also suffered. In an attempt to deal with this, the IMF, through SAPs, has implemented a rigid framework in most West African nations that reduces the government's control over the economy. The goal has been primarily to help West African states get their economic houses in order but this has also meant a reduction in wages and services provided to the poor. The Structural Adjustment Program, consequently, is unpopular with the general public, but Western economists deem it a necessity for West African governments. It has become virtually impossible to get foreign loans without following SAPs guidelines. Since foreign inflows of capital are the main source of revenue for these governments, especially with the decline in some major exports, West African states have had to comply.

Loan eligibility came to depend on political conditions as well. West African leaders had to comply with IMF regulations which required the development of formal institutions of a democratic nature, competitive elections, demonstration of accountability, the rule of law, administrative probity and good governance.

West African regimes have responded in different ways to these pressures. Some have made cosmetic reforms, implying democracy, whereas others have seen a reversal of constitutional gains. Most are still in a prolonged period of democratic struggle. Grave problems of war remain in Sierra Leone and Liberia, recently spilling over into Guinea. Nigeria has just come out of a dark period by electing Olusegun Obasanjo who is an apparent champion of democracy. Ghana went through a peaceful transfer of power as Jerry Rawlings stepped down. The jury is still out on the future of democracy in the region and the impact of SAPs and concomitant pressure from the Core.

Some regimes in West Africa have collapsed, only to be replaced by another no more competent to deal with the internal and external problems facing African governments today. Frequent, major challenges face these governments because nothing fundamental has been resolved by the previous regimes. Such is the stagnation that hovers over West Africa today.

It seems to this observer that West African states are jointly locked in a web of international forces that, to a large extent, ordain the future of the region. The fluctuations in the global economy, the lack of resources to cope with such falterings, the imbalance in trade between Core suppliers and West African buyers, the lack of capital in West Africa for nations to exploit their own natural resources, the heavy debt load borne by governments and the manipulation by Core agents promoting SAPs—all seem to indicate a continuation of "revolving governance." Effete regimes come and go with little effect on the neocolonialist grip on the region.

There are conflicting views of where West African governance is headed. Robert Kaplan portrays the region as a vanguard of the coming anarchy that presumably will engulf the entire planet—with scarcity, crime, overpopulation, tribalism and disease abounding. Optimists believe that democracy will prevail in the long run and that this will lead to development and good governance. Thus far, neither urging from the people below, nor external pressure by IFIs, has given rise to a democratic political system capable of surviving in West Africa. Chris Allen rather optimistically claims:

> If African states are to regain some of their autonomy, then there will have to be a second and more radical wave of innovation, this time directed at the production not of stable, authoritarian and centralised states, but towards stable decentralised and democratic systems, at regional, national, and subnational levels.

The problems of governance and lack of development in West Africa must be seen as the product of an interaction between externally imposed forces, the ambitions of West African élites and weak civil institutions. These are the same forces that have been in place throughout the contact period of West African history. Without a new force to alter this stagnation, one cannot be overly optimistic. If there is a glimmer of hope, it is in the fact that pressure from international and civil society is pushing in the same direction—toward a system of government that allows for the input of the people. On the other hand, a reason to be skeptical in this matter is that those same forces of international capital operate to keep West Africa dependent on the Core.

Religious Conflict in West Africa Today

In addition to corruption and bad governance, West African today is plagued by religious conflict between Muslims and non-Muslims. This is especially egregious in Northern Nigeria today and revolves around the encumbrance of *Shari'a* Law, an attempt to replace civil law in some northern states.

Box 16.1   Court Orders Hand Amputation for Boy

Wednesday July 25, 2001. 8:17 AM ET

LAGOS (Reuters)—A Muslim *Shari'a* court has ordered that a 15-year-old boy's hand be amputated in Nigeria's northwestern Birmin-Kebbi state, newspapers reported on Wednesday. The Birmin-Kebbi Upper *Shari'a* Court convicted Abubakar Aliyu of stealing 32,000 Naira ($286) from a businessman's home, the independent Guardian newspaper reported. His two accomplices, who confessed to helping plan the crime and holding the money for safekeeping, were sentenced to 50 lashes and 18 months in prison. The two were immediately given their lashes outside the court after they were sentenced on Friday. Birmin-Kebbi's implementation of the strict Muslim legal code has been more moderate than neighboring Zamfara state, which was the first state to adopt *Shari'a* law in October 1999. Zamfara attracted international outrage in Janu-

---

ary when it gave a pregnant 17-year-old girl 180 lashes for having pre-marital sex. The girl said she had been raped. The boy has the right to appeal the judgement in the *Shari'a* appeals court, the newspaper said. If his appeal fails the boy will be the first to have his hand amputated in Birmin-Kebbi since the state introduced the strict Muslim code in December. The boy's sentence must also be ratified by the state *Shari'a* Implementation Committee and the state governor's cabinet before his hand is cut off, the newspaper said.

Today, some Africans see Islam as progressive when compared to the animism of their forefathers. In 1998, I found that, among the Sisala, there was a gulf between the youth and the elders based on the former's adoption of Islam and the latter's adherence to traditional religion. The youth looked to a future filled with more positive changes. They said, "We are modern boys" with proud grins on their faces. Many had converted to Islam and had come to see themselves as explicitly *not* traditional, *not* old-fashioned like their Animist fathers and forefathers. Certainly, they contrasted the old with the new, traditionalism with modernity. I feel that it is this perceived modernity of recently introduced Islam that makes it attractive among the youth.

This is not a minor movement in Sisalaland. The oil-rich states of the Middle East are investing money in Sub-Saharan Africa to build mosques, hire village *Mallams*, finance literacy in Arabic, and make the Holy *Qur'an* available to locals. It appears to be working. In 1960 only 8.4% of rural Sisala were Islamic. By 1998 that figure had become 77.7%.

In some ways Islam has been divisive in West Africa, and in others it brings diverse peoples together by providing universal principles of living. The *Qur'an* regulates eating and drinking habits of believers, legislates rules of marriage, divorce and inheritance. It establishes a political community of believers that cuts across clan, family, ethnic or national groupings. This last aspect of Islam has been especially important in West Africa where peoples of disparate backgrounds and languages can find a common bond of allegiance to a central authority. While followers of the ancestral way of life of traditional African religion have no calling to carry their beliefs to others, followers of Allah are under obligation to convert the heathens.

Today in West Africa: A Renaissance?

A Renaissance is a rebirth or revival. Although some claim this is coming to Africa in this post-Mandela era, it is difficult to see even its beginnings. The continent has been growing poorer every year, governance is bad, corruption is everywhere, the HIV/AIDS pandemic threatens to further deepen the trough of despair and the continent faces widespread religious conflict. Already underemployment has risen to staggering heights. West Africa's city slums are teeming with people living cheek to jowl under the worst conditions imaginable. Children wander the streets hoping to make a few cents selling hankies or decals. Some sell their bodies.

But some note that violent crime has decreased, wars are less frequent, apartheid has been replaced nonviolently by the ANC, Mobutu Sese Seko died in defeat and disgrace, single-party and military regimes are diminishing and the IMF is predicting that (barring climatic disasters) "the average growth rate could be back to the average 6 percent growth of the immediate postcolonial period."

Liberal economists are encouraged by the fact that more than 100 parastatals have been privatized, African governments seem to be in compliance with IFI demands, and "a relatively free market system now operates throughout the continent." The Core powers are encouraged that countries like Nigeria and Ghana are moving towards "good governance," in spite of the fact that in West Africa only Senegal can be categorized as democratic, and even that is arguable. Certainly the recent elections in Nigeria and Ghana give us hope that what Crawford Young has called "patrimonial autocracies" are an artifact of the past. The majority of the ECOWAS countries must be labeled "transitional democracies."

But beneath the surface things look bleak. Most African countries are deep in debt, have few resources ready to market and are deeply dependent on foreign aid. Every year more capital flows out of Africa than in. Mining venture extraction and interest payments largely account for this outflow on the foreign debt.

This is a stage in history and perhaps West Africa will emerge on better footing. These nascent West African democracies are young. No democratic country on the globe has achieved democracy in such a short time span as the postcolonial era; it has been a rough forty years and some would say that more are ahead. Colin Legum notes that democracy is more than holding elections or making speeches about freedom. He cites the specific condition for achieving and maintaining democracy:

> There are at least eighteen conditions that characterize a democratic society and which need to be fulfilled to sustain it. First and foremost is a national constitution, negotiated and accepted by representative political parties and civic groups. Other conditions are enforceable guarantees for human rights, for free and regular elections, and freedom of political organizations; national institutions providing for checks and balance between executive, legislative and administrative powers; a truly independent judiciary, *habeas corpus*; freedom of movement and assembly; a free press; academic and religious freedom; independent trade unions; and an active civil society.

In hindsight, it seems that those who pushed for quick independence from European tyranny may have been hasty. The idea that democracy could just be transplanted and grow overnight seems naïve. The development of democracy involves much hard work in a slow political process with incremental change, not giant leaps. Yet one has to marvel at the minimal amount of conflict and bloodshed in West Africa in spite of the inappropriateness of colonial boundaries and the fact that various disparate ethnic groups were thrown together in imposed states. It is important for the reader to understand that what is portrayed in the media is not the whole picture. The news out of Africa is badly skewed away from what is truly African. Most people in West Africa are family-oriented individuals who worry about doing good work, caring for their children, want education for them and hope for a better life in each succeeding generation.

Yet what used to be called tribalism is a problem, one that will probably not disappear soon. How will West Africa be able to prevent ethnic diversity from impeding the move to a purer form of democracy? Many writers see Federalism as an answer.

In 2000, the presidents of South Africa, Nigeria and Algeria, Thabo Mbeki, Olesegun Obasanjo and Abdelaziz Bouteflika launched a drive to win support for the Millennium African Renaissance Plan, which they argue should help Africa escape its endemic conflict and poverty. According to Frank Chikane, a senior aid in Mbeki's office, "the Africa plan hopes to move away from the traditional aid concept whereby funds end up paying Africa's external debt service costs and make the continent an exporter of capital." The plan stresses the importance of restoring private sector confidence in Africa to spur investment. It also aims to give African countries greater control over economic reform programs. Mbeki said support for the initiative has already come from European governments and the UN as well as from the IMF and the World Bank.

More and more Africans are looking to African solutions. Note the words of Adebayo Adedeji, former UN Under-Secretary General, Executive Secretary of the Economic Commission for Africa (1975–1991) and now Executive Director of the African Center for Development and Strategic Studies:

> Africa will only be able to invent a future for itself that will bring rising prospects of prosperity through total commitment to its own programs and through their vigorous implementation. The politics of economic policy consist not only in their conceptualization, articulation, adoption and popularization, but also in total and unrelenting commitment to implementation. It is only by so doing that Africa, particularly Sub-Saharan Africa, can rediscover its self-respect and remold its image.

How much power do West African countries have to remake themselves? Standing alone, very little; in regional organizations like ECOWAS and the OAU they have much more power.

In *Africa Since Independence*, Colin Legum summarizes the daunting problems facing African nations at this time:

> Stripped of romanticism, the challenges that need to be confronted if there is to be a genuine African Renaissance are: weak and vulnerable states with regimes unable to maintain lawful order and to promote equitable economic development; ethnic conflicts; population and urban explosions; continuous decline of traditional rural life and a system of agriculture balanced between the production of food for local needs and for export cash-crops; religious fundamentalism; desertification and environmental degradation; stultifying economics; inadequate health services to cope with HIV/AIDS, tuberculosis, and other pandemics; poverty and unemployment; and **globalization**.

No clearer statement exists of the challenge ahead if West Africans are going have a standard of living that is adequate to sustain quality of life.

≋≋ CRITICAL THINKING QUESTIONS ≋≋

1. In West Africa, in postcolonial times, what forces kept the civil service and the government of the nation-state from functioning as it does in the West?
2. What evidence exists for an African Renaissance?
3. What are the sources of corruption in West Africa?

4. Why has there been so much ethnic and religious violence in the postcolonial era?
5. What are the different kinds of dependency in West Africa?
6. What do you see as the sources of instability in West Africa? What promise exists for an amelioration of these negative forces?
7. What led to the rise of so many soldier-politicians in West Africa? Relate your answer to the similarities and differences between this phenomenon and the advent of the one-party state. What were the justifications for both and why have they not held up?

KEY CONCEPTS

African nationalism
African Renaissance
Articulation
Authoritarian presidentialist regimes
Benin Conference
Coup d'état
Cultural dependency

Federalism
Modernization approach
Obasanjo, Olusegun
Spoils politics
United States of Africa
Western-educated modernizing élites

SOURCES & SUGGESTED READINGS

Ade-Ajayi, J. F. 1995. Africa's development crisis in perspective. In: Bade, Onimode & Synge. *Issues in African development.* Ibadan: Heinemann.

Austin, Dennis. 1978. *Politics in Africa.* Hanover, N.H.: Published for the University of Rhode Island by the University Press of New England.

Collier, Paul, in IMF. 1997. *Survey* 26, No. 23 (15 December).

Davidson, Basil. 1992. *The black man's burden: Africa and the curse of the nation-state.* New York: Times Books.

Dumont, René. 1966. *False start in Africa.* New York: Praeger.

Elliot, Kimberly Ann. 1997. Introduction. In: Elliot, Kimberly Ann (ed.). *Corruption and the global economy.* Washington DC: Institute of International Economics, 1–5.

Glynn, P., S. J. Korbin & M. Naim. 1997. The globalization of corruption. In: Elliot, Kimberly Ann (ed.). *Corruption and the global economy.* Washington DC: Institute of International Economics, 7–27.

Gray, John. 1998. *False dawn.* London: Granta Books.

Herbst, Jeffrey and Adebayo Olukoshi. 1994. Nigeria: Economic and political reform at cross purposes. In: Stephen Haggard and Steven B. Webb (eds.). *Voting for Reform: Democracy, political liberalization and economic adjustment.* New York:Oxford University Press for the World Bank.

Legum, Colin. 1999. *Africa Since Independence.* Bloomington: Indiania University Press.

Manzetti, Luigi and Charles Blake. 1996. Market reforms and corruption in Latin America: New means for old ways. *Review of international political economy* 3:4:662–697.

Mendonsa, Eugene L. 2000. What does anthropology have to offer in the solution of the world's problems—Are we kidding ourselves? *High Plains Applied Anthropologist* 20:2:185–192.

Reich, Robert. 1992. *The work of nations.* New York: Vintage.

Rose-Ackerman, Susan. 1997. The political economy of corruption. In: Elliot, Kimberly Ann (ed.). *Corruption and the global economy.* Washington DC: Institute of International Economics, 31–60.

Ruzindana, Augustine. 1997. The importance of leadership in fighting corruption in Uganda. In: Elliot, Kimberly Ann (ed.). *Corruption and the global economy.* Washington DC: Institute of International Economics, 133–145.

Sen, Amartya. 2000. *Development as freedom.* New York: Anchor Books.

Sutherland, Peter. 1998. *Time.* (February)

Winchester, N. Brian. 1995. African politics since independence. In: Martin, P. & P. O'Meara (eds.). *Africa* (third edition). London: James Currey, 347–358.

Young, Crawford. nd. Democracy and the Ethnic Question in Africa. Quoted in: Legum, Colin. 1999. *Africa Since Independence.* Bloomington: Indiana University Press, 56.

17 THE ECOWAS COMMUNITY

> This chapter presents statistics to illustrate the nature of economic underde-
> velopment and dependency of West African states on the Core Countries. It can
> be seen that the IFIs are actively involved in each country. In some cases they
> have gone so far as to interfere with the sovereign decisions of West African
> politicians. Yet, as the statistics clearly show, in spite of years of colonialism and
> neocolonial encroachment by Europeans, West African economies remain un-
> derdeveloped and political instability is widespread.

ECOWAS and the Definition of West Africa

The Economic Community of West African States (ECOWAS) is a regional group
of 16 countries, founded in 1975. Its goal is to promote economic integration in "all
fields of economic activity, particularly industry, transport, telecommunications, energy, agriculture, natural resources, commerce, monetary and financial matters, social
and cultural issues..." Its 16 republics include Benin, Burkina Faso, *Cabo Verde* (Cape
Verde Isles), *Cote d'Ivoire* (Ivory Coast), *Gambie* (Gambia), Ghana, *Guinee* (Guinea),
Guinee Bissau (Guinea Bissau), Liberia, Mali, *Mauritanie* (Mauritania), Niger, Nigeria, Senegal, Sierra Leone, and Togo.

The decision to consider these territories and not others as part of West Africa is
somewhat arbitrary, and I am following the lead of West African leaders who have made
this decision. However, other sovereign states such as Cameroon, Chad or the islands of
São Tomé and Príncipe in the Gulf of Guinea could have been included, as their history
relates to that of West Africa in general. The approach I will take is to bring their histories in where it sheds some light on the 16 member states of the ECOWAS union.

ECOWAS states cover the territory that was affected by European contact as the
Portuguese inched their way down the Guinea coast during their initial voyages. West
Africa has a common history of contact and trade with the Great Sudanic Kingdoms
and have all been influenced by Islam's penetration of the area. A common prehistory
and similarities of culture cause us to consider West African states as a bloc that, to an
extent, stands apart from other regions in the continent.

Yet it must be said that no region of Africa is completely isolated from what has occurred in other parts of the continent, just as the entire body of land is historically
linked to Europe and Asia through migration, trade and, in certain times and places,
military invasions.

Data on the Sixteen Countries

Below are detailed political, economic, demographic, and consumer data on each of the ECOWAS countries. These statistics are shown in a comparative context wherever possible, in contrast to other West African countries, former colonial powers, or other low-income countries in the world.

In what follows immediately, there are three kinds of tables interspersed with text. First, are tables showing economic variables such as the real growth rate, the GNP (Gross National Product) world ranking of the country, foreign aid received as a percentage of GDP (Gross Domestic Product), the average annual growth in exports (1970–1996) and energy use. The latter will be important throughout our story on West Africa, especially in the next chapter on development. I have also included a statistic on petrochemical fertilizer consumption in hundreds of grams per hectare of arable land, comparing the years 1979–81 with 1994–96. This is important because it shows how dependent a country is on outside petroleum supplies (See Photo 17.1). At present, the only world class supplier of oil is Nigeria. The rest must import petroleum, an expenditure that eats deeply into many budgets.

I have also included a list of interest payments for debt servicing. At present there is a debate raging between humanitarians on the left who want the IFIs and the G-7 to forgive such loans and Neoliberals on the right who resist such debt forgiveness saying that it is fiscally unsound to do so. This table, then, will help you understand where West African countries stand in this debate and how deeply enmeshed they have become in the spider web of debt dependency cast by the Core Countries. Data are also presented on revenues received by the state, their expenditures and specifically how much of that was spent on capital development as opposed to consumerism.

Most of the countries of ECOWAS are underdeveloped industrially. Agriculture, therefore, is quite important in our analysis of West African economies. Consequently, I give data on the percentage of a country's population working in agriculture, comparing the date of 1970 with 1996 to show trends in this regard. I also give statistics on agricultural production as a percentage of the total GNP for the same dates, as well as a percentage of growth relative to GDP. In this latter category, I include statistics on industrial production and services.

Since industrialization, or the lack of it, is an important subject in our analysis of West African economics, I include the changes in industry as a percentage of GDP from 1980 to 1996, which shows the degree to which a country is industrializing. This statistic indicates that for those West African nations on which we have data, more than half are de-industrializing, that is, their economies are moving more in the direction of agricultural production and the provision of services.

The final statistic in this table is irrigated land as a percentage of the total sq. km of land. West African agriculture is largely rainfed, thus most ECOWAS countries have low acreage under irrigation. Rainfed horticulture, as opposed to irrigated agriculture, is highly unreliable, given nature's variability, and this serves as a development barrier in the region.

The second series of tables I present is on consumer items owned and services provided. Ownership of high technology items such as cars, shows how integrated into the global economy a country has become, or perhaps the different decisions made by various ECOWAS countries regarding expenditures. While some of the data are about

Photo 17.1   Fueling an Imported Van with Imported Diesel.

exotic consumer goods like the cell phone, other goods such as an automobile or a fleet of trucks in West Africa is a much stronger indication of attachment to a distant economy that produces such expensive items.

The third kind of table gives demographic and social data ranging from religious preferences to mortality statistics. When analyzing the data on religion, we see a wide-ranging adherence to West Africa's three dominant categories of faith—traditional religions, Islam and Christianity.

The data on health care show a region plagued with problems. Infant mortality rates are among the highest in the world. The overall population growth rate is significant because, in spite of their high death rates, even war-torn areas like Sierra Leone and Liberia have high fertility rates. The regional growth rates hover around 3%, which tends to double a population about every 30 years.

Finally, as with health care provisioning, building a base of literacy and education is an investment in the future growth of a nation. The data presented show a region with a long way to go in providing both kinds of investment. Most are struggling just to deal with the present lack of sanitation and safe drinking water, let alone ethnic violence and wars that threaten the stability of the area.

The Republic of Benin

Benin, formerly known as Dahomey, became a French colony in 1902. It achieved independence in 1960. In 1972 military officers led by Mathieu Kérékou took power, proclaiming a " Marxist-Leninist" state and changing the country's name. By the end of 1989 Benin renounced Marxist policies and in the following year became a multiparty democracy.

In the March 1991 election Prime Minister Nicephere Soglo defeated Mr. Kérékou to become President. However, Mr. Kérékou was returned to office in the next election of 1996.

Recently, in accordance with a present trend in West Africa, Benin has embarked on a path of democracy. Presidential elections in both 1991 and 1996 saw a peaceful transfer of power. Increased freedom of the press and strengthening of civil institutions have strengthened the democratic process in Benin. Since 1996 the country has followed a Neoliberal, market-oriented economic approach, which seems to have a broad base of support in the country. Benin has a National Assembly that represents about 10% of the political parties in the country.

By world standards, Benin is a poor country, with an estimated yearly per capita income at US$380. However, with improved management and political stability Benin has been able to maintain around a 5% annual economic growth rate since 1995. Generally, Benin's economy is dependent on subsistence production of maize, yams, cassava, rice, fruits and beans. The country's principal exports are cotton, palm oil products, coffee, crude oil and cocoa beans. Recent years have seen an increase in exports of cotton and services related to transit trade, but the under-utilization and misuse of existing technical expertise hamper the country's productive ability. IFIs such as the World Bank claim that achieving higher levels of economic growth and development will require more opening up of the economy and improved public administration, including civil service reform and anti-corruption efforts.

Since the early 1990s, Benin has had relatively sound economic management and good economic growth prospects. Recent years have seen an increase in exports, a decrease in the fiscal deficit, and controlled inflation.

The World Bank currently has fourteen projects in Benin with a total commitment of US$207 million. According to that agency, these "projects support the consolidation of economic reforms, human development (especially girls' education), infrastructure improvements, rural development, and environment." Additionally, the International Finance Corporation has five projects in Benin.

As we will note for other ECOWAS countries, Benin is involved in a structural adjustment process, under programs referred to as Structural Adjustment Programs (SAPs). This is necessitated by the financial control exercised over her government by IFIs. This is largely dependent on incurred debts to international lenders—in 1998 Benin's foreign debt stood at a staggering US$1 billion, with a total debt service of

Table 17.1 Economic Variables: Benin	
% Real Growth Rate, 1998 (Est.).	4.4
GNP PPP World Ranking*	109
Aid as % of GNP (1996)	13.5
Average Annual Growth in Exports, 1965–96	3.7
	(Low-Income Countries = 5.9)
Trade as % of GDP, 1970 & 1996	50 > 57
Commercial Energy Use in kg of Oil Equivalent Units/Capita, 1995.	20 (USA=7,905)
Petrochemical Fertilizer Consumption/Hundreds Grams/Hectare Arable Land, 1979–81 > 1994–96	12 > 146
Debt Service as % of GNP	2.0 (1996)
1995 Revenues (Est.).	299 million US$
1995 Expenditures (Est.).	445 million US$
1995 Capital Expenditures (Est.).	14 million US$
Labor Force in Agriculture. As % of Total Labor Force, 1970/1996	81/64
Agriculture. value added as a % of GDP, 1970/1996	36/38
%GDP—Farming (% Growth)**	34 (3.7)
GDP—Industry (%)	14 (3.1)
GDP—Services (%)	52 (3.1)
Industry as % of GDP, 1980 > 1996	12 > 14
Irrigated Land in % of Total sq. km of Land	0.0009

* USA is the richest with a score of 1. Moçambique is the poorest with a score of 132.
** Average Annual % Growth, 1965–96

US$60.6 million.[1] Benin seems to be relatively stable economically at the moment, but her debt servicing has risen from 1.4 to 2.0% of her GNP. She is caught in the same financial web as other West African countries. Nevertheless, when compared to other **UDCs** (Underdeveloped Countries), both net private capital flows and direct foreign investment are low, though both doubled between 1990 & 1996.

Between 1991–1996, net official development assistance and official aid increased from US$268.4m to US$292.8m, but fell from US$55 to US$52 per person. Foreign aid as a percentage of GNP fell during the same time period from 14.5% to 13.5%. Japan and France are the major donors, with other **EU** countries contributing. Aid from the United States is low at 7%.

Table 17.1 below shows that Benin is on a moderate growth course, but has a high amount of foreign aid. Its growth in exports is well below the average of low-income countries. In the area of debt service as a percentage of GNP, its 2% payment is well below that of Ivory Coast's staggering 13.8% and just above the country with the lowest debt service payment, Burkina Faso at 1.9%.

1. See debt servicing in the glossary. This is the interest a country must pay just to keep payments current without reducing size of the debt.

Table 17.2 Consumables & Services: Benin	
Newspaper publishers per thousand persons (1994)	2
Radios per thousand persons (1995)	1461
Television sets per thousand persons (1996)	73
Mobile Phones per thousand persons (1996)	0
Fax Machines per thousand persons (1995)	0.1
Personal Computers per thousand persons (1996)	—
Web Hosts per thousand persons (1997)	0.02
# Motor Vehicles per thousand People, 1996	8
	(Low-Income Country = 8)

According to the number of motor vehicles in the country (Table 17.2), Benin is an average low-income country, though it has no mobile phones, few fax machines and little in the way of web presence.

Benin is unique in West Africa for its low rate of world religion adherents. The data in Table 17.3 show that 70% of its population is animist, followers of traditional African religions. Life expectancy at birth is only 54 years, worse than Cape Verde at almost 69 years and well below the former colonial overlord, France at over 78 years. At nearly 98 deaths per thousand live births, the child mortality rate is well above France at 5.62 per thousand, but below Guinea, which has the highest in West Africa at 126.32 deaths per thousand. Only 42% of the population has any access to health care and a quarter of the children younger than five years old are malnourished. Only a third of the people are literate and, while three-quarters of males are enrolled in primary school, only 43% of females have the opportunity. Official migration is nil, though Benin is a country with a very high rate of illegal smuggling across its eastern border into oil-rich Nigeria.

Table 17.3 Demographic Variables: Benin	
% Religion: Traditional, Muslim & Christian	70-15-15
Life expectancy at Birth	54.08
Infant Mortality Rate: Deaths per thousand Live Births1999 (Est.).	97.76
% (Est.) Population Growth Rate, 1999	3.3
Net Migration Rate, 1999*	0
Urban Population Growth as % of Total Population, 1970 & 1996	17 > 39
% Population with Health Care Access, 1993	42
% Child Malnutrition in children < 5 yrs., 1990–96	24
% Population with Sanitation Access, 1995	20
% Population with Safe Water Access, 1995	50
Net Primary School Enrollment % of Relevant Age Group—Male/Female, 1995	74/43
Literacy Rate (% of Population)	37.0

* Number of migrants per 1000 population, (Est.).

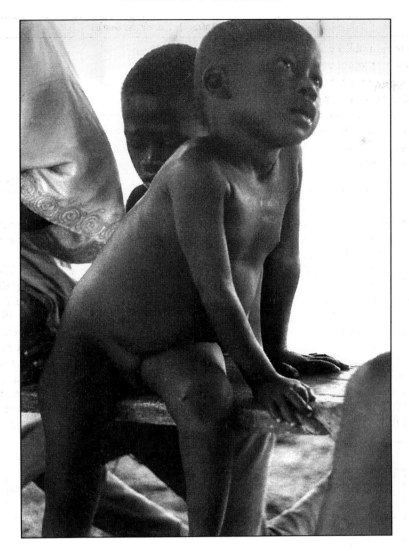

Photo 17.2   A Naked Child.

Burkina Faso

Burkina Faso has suffered in past years from political instability. Since independence in 1960, Burkina has remained one of the poorest countries in the world ranking 171 out of 174 countries in the United Nations Development Program's (UNDP) 1999 Human Development Index. Social indicators are very low: 45% of the population is below the poverty line, life expectancy at birth is 44 years, infant mortality is 99 per 1000, HIV/AIDS incidence is rising and gross primary school enrollment is only 40% (See Photo 17.2).

Situated at the heart of the Sahel, Burkina Faso is landlocked, though a rail line connects it to the port of Abidjan in *Cote d'Ivoire*. In contrast to some other West

Table 17.4 Economic Variables by Country: Burkina Faso	
% Real Growth Rate, 1998 (Est.).	6.0
GNP PPP World Ranking*	117
Aid as % of GNP (1996)	16.5
Average Annual Growth in Exports, 1965–96	3.5 (Low-Income Countries = 5.9)
Trade as % of GDP, 1970 & 1996	23 > 41
Commercial Energy Use in kg of Oil Equivalent Units/Capita, 1995.	16 (USA=7,905)
Petrochemical Fertilizer Consumption/Hundreds Grams/Hectare Arable Land, 1979–81 > 1994–96	26 > 69
Debt Service as % of GNP, 1996	1.9
1995 Revenues (Est.).	277 million US$
1995 Expenditures (Est.).	492 million US$
1995 Capital Expenditures (Est.).	233 million US$
Labor Force in Agriculture. As % of Total Labor Force, 1970/1996	92/92
Agriculture. value added as a % of GDP, 1970/1996	35/35
%GDP — Farming (% Growth)**	35 (2.6)
GDP — Industry (%)	25 (2.4)
GDP — Services (%)	40 (6.3)
Industry as % of GDP, 1980 > 1996	22 > 25
Irrigated Land in % of Total sq. km of Land	0.0007

* USA is the richest with a score of 1. Moçambique is the poorest with a score of 132.
** Average Annual % Growth, 1965–96.

African nations, Burkina is poorly endowed with natural resources. Rainfall is very limited — averaging about 350 mm in the north and 1000 mm in the southwest. Burkina Faso has tried to grow cotton and other export crops, but exports have hovered near a low 13% of GDP in 1998 and even fell to a low of 11.5% in 1999.

Table 17.4 shows that Burkina Faso is bouncing back economically. It had an estimated real growth rate of 6% in 1998, though its exports (3.5% growth) are below the low-income country level of 5.9%. Nevertheless, it is well above war-torn Sierra Leone at −5%, though nowhere near the extraordinary export growth spurt of Mali at over 7%. Burkina Faso is primarily an agricultural country with 92% of her people involved in farming. This number has changed little over time.

A semi-arid environment, lack of a seaport and politics have all played a large role in Burkina's economic backwardness. Since independence the governments efforts to develop the economy have met with little success. Following a series of short-lived governments, the nation-state emerged as the dominant actor in a more centralized economy during the Revolutionary period of 1983–1987.

The current government has been in power since October 1987, and has moved the nation steadily towards becoming a representative democracy. Since 1988 the country has organized several multi-party elections: presidential (1991, 1998), parliamentary (1992 and 1997), municipal (1995). However, political tension has increased since 1999 following the assassination of a leading journalist.

Photo 17.3   An Urban Drug Store.

Like other West African countries, Burkina has embarked on a stabilization and structural adjustment program supported by the IMF and the World Bank in 1991. Those organizations claim that an economic recovery in the 1990s was the result of major economic and institutional reforms. In 1999, despite some decline in cotton production, GDP growth rate was estimated at 5.2% in 1999, a drop from a high of 6.2% in the previous year.

Burkina benefits from broad-based donor support. The UNDP has played a role in organizing the donor community through roundtable discussions. The last one was organized in 1995. IFIs have coordinated budgetary support activities.

In spite of poverty and political instability, Burkina Faso has made determined efforts to address key social problems, such as primary education and basic health care. Over the past ten years, for instance, the share of the education budget allocated to basic education increased from 45% to about 58%. This reprioritization has been complemented by the construction of additional educational facilities, with an average of 800 classrooms added each of the past several years. Progress in the improvement of health indicators in Burkina Faso has been difficult with HIV/AIDS on the rise, though substantial steps forward have been made in building more health centers, training more health personnel and increasing the availability of essential generic drugs (See Photo 17.3).

Table 17.5 shows Burkina Faso to be a country with little Christianity and slightly more Muslims than followers of traditional religion. Its life expectancy (age 46) is not high by West African standards, but is consistent with its immediate neighbors of Mali at 47.5 years and Niger at nearly age 42.

Other demographics show that Burkina Faso is a substandard nation in terms of provision of social services. Child malnutrition stands at a third of the children under age five. Furthermore, its overall rate of literacy, at less than 20% of the population is well below neighboring Ghana's near 65%. In Burkina Faso, the 1995 estimate of edu-

Table 17.5 Demographic Variables: Burkina Faso	
% Religion: Traditional, Muslim & Christian	40-50-10
Life expectancy at Birth	45.89
Infant Mortality Rate: Deaths per thousand Live Births 1999 (Est.).	107.19
% (Est.) Population Growth Rate, 1999	2.7
Net Migration Rate, 1999*	−1.25
Urban Population Growth as % of Total Population, 1970 & 1996	6 > 16
% Population with Health Care Access, 1993	—
% Child Malnutrition in children < 5 yrs., 1990–96	33
% Population with Sanitation Access, 1995	18
% Population with Safe Water Access, 1995	78
Net Primary School Enrollment % of Relevant Age Group — Male/Female, 1980 & 1995	18/37::11/24
Literacy Rate (% of Population)	19.2

* Number of migrants per 1000 population, (Est.).

cated females stood at slightly over 9%. Former colonial power, France, claims 99% education for both males and females.

Burkina Faso has also devoted attention to implementing crucial economic reforms, with some good results. Despite deterioration in the terms of trade, real GDP between 1996 and 1999 grew on average by 5.6% annually, owing mainly to the 1994 monetary devaluation, a large public investment program, and financial and structural policies aimed at maintaining macroeconomic stability. In recent years inflation has dropped to 2%, and public finances have improved markedly, with government revenue increasing to 15% of GDP in 1999. It remains to be seen if these modest improvements can be translated into broad poverty reduction.

On July 11, 2000 The World Bank Group's International Development Association (IDA) and the IMF agreed that Burkina had satisfied the requirements to reach its completion point under the original Heavily Indebted Poor Countries Initiative, and thereby became eligible to begin receiving around $400 million in debt service relief, or $229 million in net present value (NPV) terms.

Burkina Faso was one of the initial countries to qualify for assistance under the original HIPC framework when it reached its decision point in September 1997. The IDA and the IMF also agreed that, based on its determined efforts in social and structural reform, the policy commitment presented in the Poverty Reduction Strategy Paper, and the implementation of IDA and IMF programs, Burkina Faso has qualified for additional assistance under the enhanced framework (adopted in September 1999) amounting to $300 million in debt service relief over time ($169 million NPV). The combined debt service savings from all Burkina Faso's creditors under the HIPC Initiative of $700 million effectively cuts in half Burkina Faso's debt service obligations over the coming years. It remains to be seen if such relief is translated into a reduction of poverty and improved living conditions for her people.

In spite of its efforts to reform, Burkina Faso is still one of the poorest countries in the world. Table 17.6 shows that automobile ownership is well below the low-income

Table 17.6 Consumables & Services: Burkina Faso	
Newspaper publishers per thousand persons (1994)	0
Radios per thousand persons (1995)	31
Television sets per thousand persons (1996)	6
Mobile Phones per thousand persons (1996)	0
Fax Machines per thousand persons (1995)	—
Personal Computers per thousand persons (1996)	—
Web Hosts per thousand persons (1997)	0.04
# Motor Vehicles per thousand People, 1996	5
	(Low-Income Country = 8)

country standard, and is dwarfed next to Ivory Coast's 32 cars per thousand, a country on which Burkina Faso is largely dependent for transport. Many Burkinans also work in Ivory Coast. Modern communications are almost nonexistent, with even the ubiquitous "wireless" (radio) standing at only 31 per thousand and televisions at a low six per thousand, compared to a high in West Africa of 73 per thousand in Benin and 147 per thousand for low-income countries.

Cape Verde

Cape Verde, or *Cabo Verde* in Portuguese, is a small archipelago of ten islands located 650 kilometers off the coast of Senegal. Only about one-tenth of the country's surface is arable. While the islands are home to about 400,000 Cape Verdeans, twice as many Cape Verdeans live abroad, but maintain close ties with their homeland.

Tourism is central to the economy of this island nation and the prospects for its expansion are most promising, which can be seen in the GDP figure on services from Table 17.7 below. Unlike most ECOWAS members, agriculture is the smallest part of Cape Verde's economy.

There is a prevailing conviction that within a few years hotel facilities in the country will be completely updated, which would also reflect greatly on the national economy by attracting more visitors from rich countries. At present, several investment projects are being implemented to take advantage of Cape Verde's image as a tropical paradise with an annual average temperature of 24 degrees Celsius and cool sea breezes.

Table 17.7 Economic Variables: Cape Verde	
% Real Growth Rate, 1998 (Est.).	5.0
%GDP—Farming*	13
GDP—Industry	19
GDP—Services	68
Irrigated Land in % of Total sq. km of Land	0.0007
* Average Annual % Growth, 1998.	

Table 17.8. Demographic Variables: Cape Verde	
% Religion: Traditional, Muslim & Christian	Roman Catholic (infused with indigenous beliefs); protestant (mostly Church of the Nazarene).
Life expectancy at Birth	68.91
Infant Mortality Rate: Deaths per thousand Live Births 1999 (Est.).	54.58
% (Est.) Population Growth Rate, 1999	3.35
Net Migration Rate, 1999*	−12.49
Literacy Rate (% of Population	71.6

* Number of migrants per 1000 population, (Est.).

Besides its climate, the islands present other favorable characteristics such as safety, tranquillity, and contrasting landscapes that vary from vast white sandy beaches with crystal clear water to magnificent volcanoes rising above the Atlantic.

The islands became independent in 1975 and Cape Verde has been one of the top economic performers in Sub-Saharan Africa in several respects. Commendable records of transparency and good governance have helped in shaping the country's economic and social development. Cape Verde has also used public resources to good purpose in its efforts to fight poverty and protect the environment. As the darling of the IFIs, Cape Verde was endorsed by the donor community in July 1998 when it presented its National Development Plan (1997–2000).

With the World Bank's support, policy reform efforts have progressed well. In 1998/1999, economic performance was satisfactory. In 1999, GDP growth was estimated at 8%, up from 5% in 1998. Estimated inflation in 1999 dropped to 4%, from 4.3% in the previous year. Privatization of the public enterprises and the divestiture transactions under the SAPs has been on track. According to the World Bank, public finance management reforms are on schedule. Nevertheless, there have been some problems with government performance that have led some international donors to withhold funds pending further evaluations.

On the political front, *Cabo Verde* is a functioning democracy, which has made impressive political reforms. Having emerged from a one-party system, the country held its first democratic general elections in 1991, and subsequent elections were held in 1996 and 2001.

The World Bank assumes a prominent role in SAPs and aid coordination in Cape Verde. Cape Verde's major bilateral donors are Portugal, Austria, Germany, the Netherlands, Sweden, Switzerland, with the EU and African Development Bank playing an important role.

Unlike other areas of West Africa, NGOs are not very visible in Cape Verde, but the government is trying to ensure that they become more actively involved in development efforts in the island nation. However, other IFIs such as the World Bank are active there. As of July 31, 2000, the Bank had extended fifteen credits to Cape Verde amounting to about US$149.4 million equivalent. Given the limited interest in Cape Verde, statistics about its use of consumables and services are difficult to find but data on demographics are shown in Table 17.8 below.

Since Roman Catholic Portugal was the colonizer in *Cabo Verde*, that religion dominates the island, though it has mixed with local beliefs in ways not unlike the syncretism found in Latin American Catholicism.

Note the high life expectancy at birth (68.91 years) compared with the next highest in West Africa of Liberia at nearly 60 and the lowest of Niger at almost 42 years of age. The Mediterranean climate, as opposed to the more heavily tropical climate of the mainland, may account for this difference but, as Basil Davidson has chronicled for the island nation, Cape Verde has had better than average governance by West African standards. This is also seen in the high literacy rate of 71.6% (males 81.4% and females 63.8%). Given the limited farming and fishing capabilities on the island, many Cape Verdeans migrate out.

Republic of The Gambia

The Gambia is a small riverine country in the Atlantic coast of Africa. Gambia often has the article before it, hence The Gambia. It became independent in 1965. The country's long tradition of democratic institutions was interrupted by an unsuccessful *coup d'etat* in 1981, and military take-over in July 1994. However, by early 1997, The Gambia returned to constitutional rule.

Being small, having limited natural resources and struggling with an underdeveloped human capital base have constrained both the diversification of the economy and its growth. At present, the government is pushing tourism, much like Cape Verde. But unlike that island nation where the GNP per capita is US$1,330, in The Gambia it is only US$340. Nevertheless, The Gambia attracts almost 100, 000 tourists each year, mainly from Europe. They come for the sunny climate, beautiful beaches and newly constructed hotel accommodations. In recent years, the Gambia has become increasingly popular among Africans of the diaspora and the International Roots Homecoming Festival takes place there.

None the less, The Gambia's economy remains highly vulnerable to adverse external and domestic shocks, in the absence of significant investment to help it diversify its narrow economic base. Its macroeconomic performance did not show much improvement in 1999, with inflation eating up much of the gains. As with many other West African countries, The Gambia operates with a high budget deficit and real interest rates remain very high.

Table 17.9 shows an estimated real growth rate of 3.8, but a 3.3% population growth rate will easily outstrip this. Foreign aid to The Gambia has fallen dramatically from 31.6% of GNP in 1991 to 13.4% five years later. Part of the tiny country's dependence on tourism and its meager economy can be seen in its 3.6% average annual growth in exports, compared to a low-income country average of 5.9 and 7.1 for nearby Mali. Nevertheless, trade as a percentage of GDP has doubled since 1970. However, the declining use of petrochemical energy in industry indicates a miniscule industrialized sector. This is supported by the fact that industry, as a percentage of GDP, has fallen. Add to that figures showing a decline in agriculture as a percent of GDP between 1970 and 1996 and we see an economy balanced precariously on tourism, which can be a fickle economic base. Additionally, the small 2.2% annual growth in agriculture will easily be wiped out by the 3.35% population growth rate.

Table 17.9 Economic Variables: Gambia	
% Real Growth Rate, 1998 (Est.).	3.8
GNP PPP World Ranking*	107
Aid as % of GNP (1996)	13.4
Average Annual Growth in Exports, 1965–96	3.6 (Low-Income Countries = 5.9)
Trade as % of GDP, 1970 & 1996	66 > 132
Commercial Energy Use in kg of Oil Equivalent Units/Capita, 1995	55 (USA=7,905)
Petrochemical Fertilizer Consumption/ Hundreds Grams/Hectare Arable Land, 1979–81 > 1994–96	132/49
Debt Service as % of GNP, 1996	2.0
1995 Revenues (Est.).	88.6 million US$
1995 Expenditures (Est.).	98.2 million US$
1995 Capital Expenditures (Est.).	—
Labor Force in Agriculture. As % of Total Labor Force, 1970/1996	87/82
Agriculture. value added as a % of GDP, 1970/1996	33/28
%GDP—Farming (% Growth)**	23 (2.2)
GDP—Industry (%)	13 (4.2)
GDP—Services (%)	64 (4.2)
Industry as % of GDP, 1980 > 1996	16 > 15
Irrigated Land in % of Total sq. km of Land	0.015

* USA is the richest with a score of 1. Moçambique is the poorest with a score of 132.
** Average Annual % Growth, 1965–96.

Table 17.10 does not show much that is different from other West African nations except the extraordinarily high ownership of motor vehicles (15) compared to a low-income country average of eight.

Table 17.11 shows The Gambia to be heavily Islamized, with Christianity being the second most frequent religion. Life expectancy there, at slightly over 54 years of age is

Table 17.10 Consumables & Services: Gambia	
Newspaper publishers per thousand persons (1994)	2
Radios per thousand persons (1995)	157
Television sets per thousand persons (1996)	—
Mobile Phones per thousand persons (1996)	3
Fax Machines per thousand persons (1995)	0.9
Personal Computers per thousand persons (1996)	—
Web Hosts per thousand persons (1997)	0
# Motor Vehicles per thousand People, 1996	15 (Low-Income Country = 8)

Table 17.11 Demographic Variables: Gambia	
% Religion: Traditional, Muslim & Christian	1-90-9
Life expectancy at Birth	54.39
Infant Mortality Rate: Deaths per thousand Live Births 1999 (Est.).	75.33
% (Est.) Population Growth Rate, 1999	3.35
Net Migration Rate, 1999*	3.34
Urban Population Growth as % of Total Population, 1970 & 1996	15 > 30
% Population with Health Care Access, 1993	—
% Child Malnutrition in children < 5 yrs., 1990–96	17
% Population with Sanitation Access, 1995	37
% Population with Safe Water Access, 1995	76
Net Primary School Enrollment % of Relevant Age Group—Male/Female, 1980 & 1995	66/64 :: 34/46
Literacy Rate (% of Population)	38.6

* Number of migrants per 1000 population, (Est.).

mid-range for continental West Africa. Again, the infant mortality rate of 75.33 falls in between Cape Verde's low of 54.58 and Guinea's high of 126.32. In the area of malnutrition, The Gambia scores the best in West Africa with only 17% of children under age five showing signs of malnutrition. Niger is the worst, with 43%. In access to safe water The Gambia is second from the top, at 76% of its population having access to potable water, while Guinea-Bissau is at the bottom with only 23%.

Educationally, The Gambia is not spectacular. In 1995, 64% of its school-age male population was enrolled in school, while only 46% of females were. With a total literacy rate of 38.6%, The Gambia is midway between Nigeria with a high of 57.1 and Burkina Faso. In contrast the former colonial powers of the region the United Kingdom and France show 99% of their population receiving education.

On the political front, The Gambia continues to work on institutional strengthening as a prerequisite for a functioning democracy and debt relief. The country is vulnerable to the political and social tensions of its region. The 1998/99 political and social tensions in Guinea-Bissau adversely affected this tiny nation which had to suffer large inflows of refugees.

The World Bank has been working with several development partners in The Gambia. Apart from the Bank's International Development Association (IDA), the largest traditional development partners of The Gambia are: the EU, African Development Bank, United Kingdom, Japan, and agencies of the United Nations organization.

Ghana

The country of the Black Star is a country of firsts. In 1957, Ghana became the first country in Sub-Saharan Africa to emerge from colonialism. After independence it experienced the highest GNP on the continent before an economic crisis in the late

1970s, and it suffered the trauma of military takeovers long before that became a trend in the region. It has also tentatively rebounded after launching one of the first and more stringent economic recovery programs in the region nearly 15 years ago. Ghana is very involved with the SAPs. It is now pioneering the "Comprehensive Development Framework" (CDF) as a new way of managing the development process. In the eyes of the Core Country developers, the Black Star is a "bright star."

With the first presidency and development ideas of Kwame Nkrumah, Ghana was on a path to create a just society that was in accordance with its collectivist civilizations of the past, but that was not to last.

Ghana enjoyed the highest per capita income in the region at independence, but its economy went into a tailspin in the 1970s. Ghana struggled under economic strain, drought and devastating crashes of world market prices of cocoa and other export products. Plant disease and mismanagement also despoiled cocoa plantations, the country's main export crop. By the early 1980s, per capita income had fallen by a third, and inflation was running at over 100%.

In 1983, the Government launched an aggressive program of stabilization and economic liberalization. According to the World Bank's view, it sought to reduce budget deficits and create a market-friendly environment. In the decade that followed, growth averaged 5% and physical and social infrastructure was somewhat rehabilitated. Nevertheless, the country still faces severe economic challenges. Although GDP growth for 1997–99 was over 4%, there is strong evidence that poverty continues to be a problem. This is true especially in the rural areas, although many urban youth cannot find adequate employment and are forced to work as street vendors selling handkerchiefs, decals, car products and other imported items from pushcarts or portable cases carried on their heads.

A series of governments have tried to cope, but found themselves ill-equipped to deal with the oppressive debts run up by previous regimes and the high cost of maintaining a bloated military and the depletion of the state's resources through malfeasance and poor administration.

Ghana's economy is mainly rural: cocoa, timber and pineapples are the main export crops; and mining (mainly gold) has become one of the biggest sources of foreign exchange. However, as Ghana enters the new millennium, it faces new challenges with the sharp decline in the international price of its two main exports of cocoa and gold. Like other West African countries, Ghana has little manufacturing infrastructure to show for its years of involvement in the global economy.

Table 17.12 shows a disappointing growth rate of 3.0, but it also shows a relatively modest 2.05% population growth rate, especially when compared to Liberia's phenomenal population explosion at nearly 5% per annum. Often referred to as the economic jewel of West Africa, Ghana has not lived up to its reputation of late. Nonetheless, in the GNP PPP rating, which is the gross national product converted into international dollars using purchasing power parity rates, Ghana has the best score in West Africa, 93 (1 being the best possible), while Sierra Leone has the worst at 130.

Being the pearl in the eye of many development agencies, Ghana receives foreign aid at the rate of 10.5% of its GNP, which is double that of Sub-Saharan Africa, but not close to the staggering 67.5% received by Guinea-Bissau. Its total debt service, as a percentage of GNP, is 7.6% compared to a West African high of 13.8% by the Ivory Coast and a low of 1.9% by Burkina Faso. Ghana's revenue figures show that in 1995, at least, it was spending more than it was producing, a sure sign of dependency on foreign aid and loans.

In the area of energy, Ghana is blessed with hydroelectric power, but it still became a major importer of petroleum in the 1980s and 1990s. In 1995, Ghana was one of the highest users in West Africa with 92 kg of oil equivalency per capita. The average for Sub-Saharan Africa is 238, and all West African countries fall below that, even Nigeria. To illustrate just how energy dependent and deficient West Africa is, the low-income country average is 393 kg. The oil-rich United Arab Republic uses a monumental 11, 567 kg per person and the United States rate is 7, 905.

Just after independence it seemed that Ghana's economy would take off, and its leaders invested heavily in high technology and the modernization approach. Its consumption of imported petrochemical fertilizer soared to 104,000 grams per hectare of arable land in the 1979–1981 time period, but by the late 1990s it had fallen to 43,000.

Ghana, like most other West African countries, has historically relied on agriculture to feed its people and to produce export crops. But again like other African nations, Ghana has become a food importer as food production fell from 1970 to 1996, along with agricultural output as a percentage of GDP. The percentage of growth in farming in the postcolonial era has been a paltry 1.2%. Farm output is more than overwhelmed by food demands brought on by urbanization, conversion to commercial farming and population growth. But if agriculture has been stagnant during this period, industrial growth at an inconsiderable 0.4 growth rate has been negligible.

Life expectancy and health could be better. Life expectancy is a little above 57 years and infant mortality, at a little over 76 per thousand live births, is in between Cape Verde's low of 54.58 and Guinea's high of 126.32.

For a country that was expected to shine in its postcolonial years, Ghana shows a disappointing health care situation. Only a quarter of its population has access to care, by 1993 figures. In the six years following 1990 over a quarter of its children under age five showed signs of malnutrition. The same amount had sanitation facilities and only slightly over half of the population had access to safe drinking water.

In terms of education, of the continental ECOWAS countries, Ghana is the best, with a 64.5% literacy rate. This is all the more remarkable since the country went through a bad period with regard to education after the fall of its first president and the termination of his socialist commitment to rural education. Many of the schools closed, only to be recently opened under the just retired Rawlings government.

Again, if we look at consumables and services Ghana seems relatively affluent by West African standards. Along with giant Nigeria, tiny Ghana has 18 newspaper publishers well over the Sub-Saharan African average of 11. Radios are everywhere, and Ghana sports many new FM Stations with a wide variety of programming. Television has reached some of the most remote towns, such as Tumu in the extreme north, but set ownership is still modest at slightly below the Sub-Saharan African standard of 43 per thousand persons. Mobile phones are becoming a fad in the cities. Communications centers can be found in competition in major cities with fax, telex, telephone and Internet capabilities (See Photo 17.4). Even small towns now have such centers. Motor vehicles clog the roads in urban areas, though ownership is well below the Sub-Saharan African level of 43 per thousand persons and equivalent to the low-income country standard of eight.

Under the guidance of Flight Lt. Jerry John Rawlings, a new constitution was introduced in 1992, and Ghana's first multiparty elections were organized shortly thereafter. In 1996, Ghana enjoyed a smooth second-term election, conducted with full participation of all political parties and of the Ghanaian electorate, strengthening democratic institutions.

Table 17.12 Economic Variables: Ghana	
% Real Growth Rate, 1998 (Est.).	3.0
GNP PPP World Ranking*	93
Aid as % of GNP (1996)	10.5
Average Annual Growth in Exports, 1965–96	3.6 (Low-Income Countries = 5.9)
Trade as % of GDP, 1970 & 1996	44 > 65
Commercial Energy Use in kg of Oil Equivalent Units/Capita, 1995	92 (USA=7,905)
Petrochemical Fertilizer Consumption/ Hundreds Grams/Hectare Arable Land, 1979–81 > 1994–96	104/43
Debt Service as % of GNP, 1996	7.6
1995 Revenues (Est.).	1.39 billion US$
1995 Expenditures (Est.).	1.47 billion US$
1995 Capital Expenditures (Est.).	370 million US$
Labor Force in Agriculture. As % of Total Labor Force, 1970/1996	60/59
Agriculture. value added as a % of GDP, 1970/1996	47/44
%GDP — Farming (% Growth)**	41 (1.2)
GDP — Industry (%)	14 (0.4)
GDP — Services (%)	45 (3.6)
Industry as % of GDP, 1980 > 1996	12 > 17
Irrigated Land in % of Total sq. km of Land	0.0003

* USA is the richest with a score of 1. Moçambique is the poorest with a score of 132.
** Average Annual % Growth, 1965–96.

President Rawlings, who has governed Ghana for most of the last two decades at the head of the National Democratic Congress (NDC), threw his support behind Vice President John Atta Mills. However, after the first round of the elections, John Agyekum Kufuor of the NPP (New Patriotic Party) polled 48.35% of total votes cast, while Mills of the NDC got 44.9%. Five other candidates shared the rest of the votes. A winner must have 50% plus one, so a runoff was called for, and in that subsequent ballot Mr. Kufuor won, making an orderly transition to power as he ousted the NDC from its long hold on power under Rawlings.

The new president and his party backers are facing a declining economic situation in Ghana. During the election, the government artificially held the price of petrol constant. When that hold is released, all prices are likely to skyrocket. Overall, Ghana's macroeconomic situation has deteriorated since mid-1999, reflecting a severe decline in its terms of trade and a shortfall in external assistance. The terms of trade fell by 10% in 1999 and by a further 16% in 2000, as the price of cocoa, the second main export, dropped by over 50% to a 20-year low, and imported oil prices tripled. This has led to a substantial run-down in international reserves and a rapid slide in the cedi, the local currency. The nominal exchange rate has depreciated by about 125% since September 1999, and gross international reserves are currently below 1.5 months of im-

Table 17.13 Demographic Variables: Ghana	
% Religion: Traditional, Muslim & Christian	38-30-24*
Life expectancy at Birth	57.14
Infant Mortality Rate: Deaths per thousand Live Births 1999 (Est.).	76.15
% (Est.) Population Growth Rate, 1999	2.05
Net Migration Rate, 1999**	−0.88
Urban Population Growth as % of Total Population, 1970 & 1996	29 > 36
% Population with Health Care Access, 1993	25
% Child Malnutrition in children < 5 yrs., 1990–96	27
% Population with Sanitation Access, 1995	27
% Population with Safe Water Access, 1995	56
Net Primary School Enrollment % of Relevant Age Group—Male/Female, 1980 & 1995	— Would be relatively highy *vis-à-vis* other West African countries
Literacy Rate (% of Population	64.5

* Ghana is the only West African country with a category called other, which had 8%.
** Number of migrants per 1000 population, (Est.).

ports. The Government has tightened fiscal and monetary policy to offset the adverse effects of the external shock.

As with other West African nations, the Ghanaian government is partially influenced by forces in the IFIs. Ghana is very dependent on foreign aid, the activity of NGOs and IFIs and has limited sources of income from taxation and other internal sources. The Ghana government is struggling against these recent downturns. In line

Photo 17.4   Sign for a Communications Center that Offers Telephone, Fax and More Recently, Internet Services.

Table 17.14 Consumables & Services: Ghana	
Newspaper publishers per thousand persons (1994)	18
Radios per thousand persons (1995)	Many, even in small villages
Television sets per thousand persons (1996)	41
Mobile Phones per thousand persons (1996)	1
Fax Machines per thousand persons (1995)	0.3
Personal Computers per thousand persons (1996)	1.2
Web Hosts per thousand persons (1997)	0
# Motor Vehicles per thousand People, 1996	8
	(Low-Income Country = 8)

with the 2000 program agreed to with the International Monetary Fund (IMF), Government increased the Valued Added Tax (VAT) rate from 10 to 12.5% and raised petroleum taxes. It has deferred some of its planned purchases and launched an aggressive program to significantly raise revenue through the sale of Government shares in major public enterprises.

Government officials are not entirely free to make decisions without input from IFI officials, a process that goes under the rubric of "Donor Coordination." Donor efforts are extensive. In addition to the World Bank, key donors in Ghana include Canada, Denmark, France, Germany, Japan, Netherlands, United Kingdom and the United States. What happens in these capitalist nations and the global economy in general has ripple effects in far away Ghana.

To show the student reader how such external control actually happens, I will explain the formation of the 1997 Consultative Group (CG) in Ghana. Advisors of the World Bank called a meeting between the Bank and the Government of Ghana. They set up a "Mini CG," which meets quarterly under the co-chairmanship of the Ghanaian Minister of Finance and the World Bank. This West African entity follows up on CG decisions, reviews the country's economic situation, and addresses key issues in donor coordination.

Part of the SAPs process has been a "partnering" of processes formerly under national sovereignty. IFIs have even become involved in the restriction of social services provision to the public. In Ghana "partner groups" perform similar functions for individual sectors, including health, education, roads, public finance management, community water supplies, governance, and decentralization. According to the World Bank, "The recent development of sector programs in roads, basic education, and health has enhanced donor coordination considerably."

The real situation contrasts with this statement. When I was in Ghana in 1998 many villages still lacked simple bore holes to provide unpolluted drinking water, the roads were generally in a state of severe deterioration, schools were without chalk, paper or books and health clinics lacked the basics of equipment, drugs and personnel. However, in the town of Tumu in Northern Ghana, the government had built an Olympic-size soccer stadium. It is hardly ever used, being taken over by weeds and the encroaching bush.

The reality is that in the century of colonial control and the postcolonial domination by Core interests, Ghana has progressed little. Indeed while the IMF and World Bank have been involved in the country, the index of the IFIs called the "Money and quasi money growth (annual %)" has fallen from 40.4 to 16.2. While global finance is sailing along, the average Ghanaian tries to live on US$390 per year or US$1.06 per day. In reality, these figures are averages that are elevated by the high incomes of élites. The real average is much, much lower. Many Ghanaians would love to have US$1.06 a day, and live on much less. While the global economy is doing fine, Ghanaians are not.

Guinea

Guinea covers 94,000 square miles and is divided into four regions: the coast of lower Guinea; the central, mountainous Futa Jalon; the savanna of upper Guinea; and the forest in the southeast. A complex process of migrations and invasion peopled the area.

Upper Guinea was part of the Ghana Empire in the 10th and 11th centuries, the Mali Empire until the 14th century, and the Songhai Empire until the 19th century. The Fulani moved into Guinea in the 17th century, bringing Islam with them and pushing the Soussou to coastal areas. French rule began in the 19th century.

After World War II, several labor parties were established, including the *Parti Democratique de Guinee* led by Ahmed Sékou Touré. In 1958, this party organized support to vote against Charles de Gaulle's proposed French community and then declared independence. Toure's regime was inward looking, but it was also shunned by other Western nations and, in this relative isolation, developed a strong national identity.

Touré ruled at the head of a single-party state and increasingly developed strong dictatorial tendencies. He survived several attempted *coup d'etats* and continued to rule Guinea until his death in 1984. It is interesting to note that Guinea is not worse off for having shunned international capital, when compared to nations like Ghana and Nigeria that have done the opposite.

Two weeks after the strongman died, the military took control of the government and established the Second Guinean Republic under Lansana Conte. Presidential and parliamentary elections took place in late 1993 and Lansana Conte was declared president. He again won the presidential elections in 1998 and is currently serving his final term in office.

Unlike Gambia, her northern neighbor, Guinea has abundant natural resources, including 25% of the world's known reserves of bauxite, along with diamonds, gold, and other metals. The country also has great potential for hydroelectric power. While bauxite and aluminum are currently the only major exports, the Guinean government plans to encourage the mining of other resources, further linking it with the international economy. Other industries include processing plants for beer, juices, soft drinks and tobacco.

As with most other West African nations, agriculture employs 80% of the nation's labor force. The new government encourages a free market economy and is determined to promote foreign investment, eschewing the isolationist policies of the autocrat Touré.

Moving toward a G-7 policy orientation, there is an ongoing privatization program, in line with the government's poverty-focused model of development, which reserves a key role for the private sector. Since 1984, a process of economic liberalization and integration with international capital has been underway in Guinea. Despite some positive overall results over the 1984–96 period (including a growth rate of 4% and single-digit inflation), performance was uneven, with successes alternating with policy reversals, especially in 1995. This has led to a degree of political insecurity in the region.

As with many West African countries, Guinea has a bloated military and the failed military coup in 1996 and the demands by the military for a 50% pay increase, had adverse fiscal consequences. Since July 1996, when a strong economic management team

Table 17.15 Economic Variables: Guinea	
% Real Growth Rate, 1998 (Est.).	4.9
GNP PPP World Ranking*	96
Aid as % of GNP (1996)	7.8
Average Annual Growth in Exports, 1965–96	—
Trade as % of GDP, 1996	41
Commercial Energy Use in kg of Oil Equivalent Units/Capita, 1995.	64 (USA=7,905)
Petrochemical Fertilizer Consumption/ Hundreds Grams/Hectare Arable Land, 1979–81 > 1994–96	19/16
Debt Service as % of GNP, 1996	3.0
1995 Revenues (Est.).	553 million US$
1995 Expenditures (Est.).	652 million US$
1995 Capital Expenditures (Est.).	317 million US$
Labor Force in Agriculture. As % of Total Labor Force, 1970/1996	92/87
Agriculture. value added as a % of GDP, 1996	26
%GDP—Farming (% Growth)**	24 (—)
GDP—Industry (%)	31 (—)
GDP—Services (%)	45 (—)
Industry as % of GDP, 1996	36
Irrigated Land in % of Total sq. km of Land	0.004

* USA is the richest with a score of 1. Moçambique is the poorest with a score of 132.
** Average Annual % Growth, 1965–96

was put in place, some progress has been made in the areas of macroeconomic management, fiscal discipline, budget elaboration and implementation, and addressing public sector corruption.

In 1997–98, real GDP grew at an average of about 4.7% and inflation averaged 3.5%. 1998 is estimated to be around 4.9%. The economy was apparently doing fine, but in 1999 its dependent status *vis-à-vis* the world economy caught up with it. The fall in global demand, drop in prices of bauxite and aluminum and the tenuous security situation in neighboring countries dragged down economic performance. Guinea's current growth levels, though encouraging, are considered by most observers to be below potential, especially in view of the country's tremendous natural resource endowments. Yet, like most poor countries, Guinea relies on foreign companies to develop those resources. The national economy is still relatively undiversified and preponderantly reliant on bauxite and mining revenue. Mining these reserves requires high technology from the developed world of the Core Countries, drawing Guinea further into the web of dependency.

Guinea is less dependent on foreign aid than many West African nations, but at 7.8% of its GNP, it is receiving more aid than the Sub-Saharan African average of 5.3%. Its debt servicing is also low at 3% of GNP. This is likely due to Guinea's isolationist stance of the past.

Table 17.16 Demographic Variables: Guinea	
% Religion: Traditional, Muslim & Christian	7-85-8
Life expectancy at Birth	46.5
Infant Mortality Rate: Deaths per thousand Live Births 1999 (Est.).	126.32
% (Est.) Population Growth Rate, 1999	0.82
Net Migration Rate, 1999*	−15.12**
Urban Population Growth as % of Total Population, 1970 & 1996	14 > 30
% Population with Health Care Access, 1993	45
% Child Malnutrition in children < 5 yrs., 1990–96	24
% Population with Sanitation Access, 1995	70
% Population with Safe Water Access, 1995	62
Net Primary School Enrollment % of Relevant Age Group—Male/Female, 1980 & 1995	—
Literacy Rate (% of Population	35.9

* Number of migrants per 1000 population, (Est.).
** At that time, this represented civil war refugees going home to Liberia and Sierra Leone.

Guinea's use of imported fertilizer has been falling and its commercial energy use per capita (64) for 1995 was well below the Sub-Saharan African average of 238 kg of oil equivalence. This is also reflected in a low number of motor vehicles (5 per thousand), compared to a Sub-Saharan African average of 20 (See Table 17. 17).

Largely Islamized, Guinea has one of the lowest life expectancies at birth (46.5 years) in West Africa. Only Burkina Faso is worse. At 126.32 deaths per thousand live births, Guinea is the worst in West Africa in child mortality, slightly worse off than Sierra Leone at 126.23 and Mali at 119.14. Less than half of the country's people have access to health care. About a quarter of the children under five suffer from malnutrition.

Clearly the government of Guinea has not been diligent in providing proper health care for its people. Additionally, in the area of education its 35.9% overall literacy rate is quite low, and only 21.9% of females can read and write.

Table 17.17 Consumables & Services: Guinea	
Newspaper publishers per thousand persons (1994)	—
Radios per thousand persons (1995)	76
Television sets per thousand persons (1996)	8
Mobile Phones per thousand persons (1996)	0
Fax Machines per thousand persons (1995)	—
Personal Computers per thousand persons (1996)	0.3
Web Hosts per thousand persons (1997)	0
# Motor Vehicles per thousand People, 1996	5
	(Low-Income Country = 8)

Government insecurity, strong populist challenges and reshuffles within the ruling party have not helped this situation. Furthermore, Guinea is surrounded by political instability. Guinea's geographical location presents significant risks of political spillover from outbreaks of crisis elsewhere in the sub-region (Liberia, Sierra Leone, and recently Guinea-Bissau). Incursions into Liberia's Lofa county by Liberian rebels based in Guinea and Liberia's claims of Guinean government complicity have strained relations between the two countries, although Guinea has vigorously denied the allegations. There have been moves to revive the Mano River Union (comprising Guinea, Liberia and Sierra Leone) to provide a forum for better cooperation and promoting peace and stability in the sub-region, although it remains to be seen whether such initiatives will survive the current heightened tensions between Guinea and Liberia. Guinea has suffered from the migration of some 650,000 refugees, mainly from Sierra Leone, Liberia and Guinea-Bissau, into their territory.

As yet, neither the efforts of international negotiators, nor those economic efforts of IFIs to rebuild Guinea's economy along capitalist lines have borne much fruit. The future of Guinea and the troubled sub-region surrounding it remain in question as of this writing.

It is interesting to note that in spite of Guinea's isolationist practices of the Touré years (or perhaps because of them) Guinea, when compared to the integrated country of Ghana, actually has a healthier economy in spite of the political instability of their sub-region. Whereas Ghanaians live on US$1.06 per day, Guineans fare slightly better at US$1.40 per day. This calls into question, at least in the short term, the benefits of becoming involved in the financial dealings with Core Countries.

Guinea-Bissau

Guinea-Bissau, a small country on the West African coast with about one million inhabitants, gained independence in 1974 after a protracted liberation war against Portugal. The war resulted in the dislocation of about one-fifth of the population and the destruction of important economic infrastructure. Yield from the country's main crops was reduced by over one-third. Assistance from the World Bank, the IMF, and other bilateral and multilateral donors, has played an important role in supporting Guinea-Bissau's social and economic development since then, particularly after 1983.

International capital is interested in Guinea-Bissau because it has good ports and fish, timber, phosphates, bauxite, unexploited deposits of petroleum, though its environment already suffers from the ravages of war and deforestation, soil erosion, overgrazing and over-fishing. One of the 20 poorest countries in the world, Guinea-Bissau depends mainly on fishing and farming, turning to export crops to shore up its depleted foreign exchange revenues. Growers have increased cashew crops in recent years, and the country now ranks sixth in cashew production. Guinea-Bissau exports fish and seafood along with small amounts of peanuts, palm kernels and timber. Rice is the major crop and staple food. Because of high costs, the development of petroleum, phosphate, and other mineral resources is not a near-term prospect. However, unexploited offshore oil reserves could provide much-needed revenue in the long run.

Guinea-Bissau's economic performance improved in 1997, but was severely disrupted by the political and social unrest that erupted in June 1998. Real GDP fell by

Table 17.18 Economic Variables: Guinea-Bissau	
% Real Growth Rate, 1998 (Est.).	3.5
GNP PPP World Ranking*	114
Aid as % of GNP (1996)	67.5
Average Annual Growth in Exports, 1965–96	2.2 (Low-Income Countries = 5.9)
Trade as % of GDP, 1970 & 1996	34 > 42
Commercial Energy Use in kg of Oil Equivalent Units/Capita, 1995.	37 (USA=7,905)
Petrochemical Fertilizer Consumption/ Hundreds Grams/Hectare Arable Land, 1979–81 > 1994–96	24/20
Debt Service as % of GNP, 1996	4.2
1995 Revenues (Est.).	—
1995 Expenditures (Est.).	—
1995 Capital Expenditures (Est.).	—
Labor Force in Agriculture. As % of Total Labor Force, 1970/1996	89/85
Agriculture. value added as a % of GDP, 1970/1996	47/54
%GDP—Farming (% Growth)**	54 (1.2)
GDP—Industry (%)	11 (2.5)
GDP—Services (%)	35 (9.2)
Industry as % of GDP, 1980 > 1996	20 > 11
Irrigated Land in % of Total sq. km of Land	0.0006

* USA is the richest with a score of 1. Moçambique is the poorest with a score of 132.
** Average Annual % Growth, 1965–96.

28% in 1998. The World Bank has moved in to provide quick relief through emergency loans to support demobilization and reintegration of ex-soldiers, settlement of sizable wage arrears, and improvement of public resource management.

As Table 17.18 shows, real growth was estimated to be 3.5% in 1998, which with the relatively low population growth rate of 2.3 may work to the benefit of the country, but the former Marxist nation-state is ranked near the bottom in the GNP PPP world ranking at 114. At 2.2% Guinea-Bissau's average annual growth in exports is well below the low-income country average of 5.9. On the other hand, trade as a percentage of GNP has risen since 1970 from 34 to 42.

Guinea-Bissau is severely underdeveloped as can be seen in the data on commercial energy use in Table 17.18. This can also be seen in the decline in fertilizer use. Apparently, in trying to recover from years of political and economic chaos (See chapter 16 for details), government leaders had deeply indebted the country with an astoundingly high aid/GNP ratio of 67.5%. The Sub-Saharan African average is 5.3 and the closest West African country to Guinea-Bissau is Mauritania with 26.4%.

For a country that was colonized by a Catholic country, Guinea-Bissau shows an extraordinarily low commitment to Christianity at only 5% with half of the population claiming traditional religion and 45% Islam.

Table 17.19 Demographic Variables: Guinea-Bissau	
% Religion: Traditional, Muslim & Christian	50-45-5
Life expectancy at Birth	49.57
Infant Mortality Rate: Deaths per thousand Live Births 1999 (Est.).	109.5
% (Est.) Population Growth Rate, 1999	2.31
Net Migration Rate, 1999*	0
Urban Population Growth as % of Total Population, 1970 & 1996	15 > 22
% Population with Health Care Access, 1993	—
% Child Malnutrition in children < 5 yrs., 1990–96	23
% Population with Sanitation Access, 1995	20
% Population with Safe Water Access, 1995	23
Net Primary School Enrollment % of Relevant Age Group—Male/Female, 1980	63/31
Literacy Rate (% of Population	53.9

* Number of migrants per 1000 population, (Est.).

The country's life expectancy at birth is about average for West Africa, as is access to sanitation and safe drinking water. Also, a quarter of children under five years have symptoms of malnutrition. While the literacy rate for the former colonial overlord, Portugal, is 85%, for Guinea-Bissau it is 53.9.

Table 17.20 shows a fairly high percentage of newspaper publishers for the tiny country, perhaps reflective of the influence of the colonial culture. It also reflects the focus on Bissau, the capital, and urban culture in general to the detriment of rural development, as does the high number of motor vehicles, well above the low-income country average. What development has gone into the country during its exploitative regimes was in the capital and much of it into roads, a form of development that favors wealthy metropolitan élites who own cars.

Following the disruption of political life in Guinea-Bissau during 1998/99, legislative and presidential elections took place in late-1999. Mr. Koumba Yala became the President of Guinea-Bissau following a free democratic election in November 1999. President Yala assumed office in February 2000. Yet, the political situation in Guinea-

Table 17.20 Consumables & Services: Guinea-Bissau	
Newspaper publishers per thousand persons (1994)	6
Radios per thousand persons (1995)	40
Television sets per thousand persons (1996)	—
Mobile Phones per thousand persons (1996)	—
Fax Machines per thousand persons (1995)	0.5
Personal Computers per thousand persons (1996)	—
Web Hosts per thousand persons (1997)	0.09
# Motor Vehicles per thousand People, 1996	12
	(Low-Income Country = 8)

Bissau has not stabilized. Continued tensions have been reported along the country's border with Senegal.

The World Bank has been a key donor in Guinea-Bissau, and has also played an active role in organizing the economy, using the familiar means of round table meetings. As of July 31, 2000, the World Bank had approved a total of 23 projects for Guinea-Bissau totaling about US$269.9 million equivalent. Total disbursements under these project as of July 31, 2000 amounted to the equivalent of about US$224.8 million.

As I write this, the political situation in Guinea-Bissau is still volatile. Contradictory reports are circulating in the capital, Bissau, about the circumstances surrounding the death of former military junta leader, Ansoumane Mane, killed along with three of his companions in a shootout with government forces. Mane was a man of immense renown, which came through his military feats during the liberation war. Later, he resisted Senegalese and Guinean intervention forces sent to protect Guinea Bissau's constitutional legitimacy, and succeeded in overthrowing President João Bernardo Vieira in 1999. The General had proclaimed himself Bissau's army chief of staff 20 November 2000, after challenging military promotions announced by President Kumba Yala. Prior to his death, Mane's close associates and his wife were reportedly arrested at the Quinhamel catholic mission, 40 km north-east of Bissau, an act which apparently led to a gun-battle between government troops and Mane's men.

Clearly, Guinea-Bissau is an example of a country where the military is still a powerful force and where the possible resort to violence to settle conflicts is never far away.

Ivory Coast

Cote d'Ivoire or Ivory Coast is an economic powerhouse in West Africa. In spite of a poor record on health care development, the Ivory Coast has a per capita GDP of US$710, giving Ivory Coast one of the highest per capita incomes in Africa.

Côte d'Ivoire became independent in 1960. The country's first President since independence, Félix Houphouët-Boigny, served as head of state for 33 years. Mr. Henri Konan Bédié succeeded him after his death in 1993. The Bédié Government was overthrown by a military *coup d'état* on December 24, 1999. In early January, 2000 former army chief General Robert Guéi formed an interim coalition government that was then reshuffled on May 18, 2000. The country has been in a state of unrest since.

Côte d'Ivoire has the biggest population as well as the largest economy of the West African Economic Monetary Union. The economy is largely dependent on agriculture; cocoa and coffee are the two main export crops providing over 40% of the gross domestic product (GDP) for the country. In addition, the country has developed other industrial crops including palm oil, rubber, cotton, sugarcane, pineapple and soya.

In spite of its integration into the world economy, the Ivory Coast seems in economic trouble, although as Table 17.21 shows, in 1998 the estimate was for 6% growth. By early 1999, the country had not received budgetary support for IFIs due to poor economic management performance and governance problems. This, along with a sharp deterioration of commodity prices (particularly cocoa), has led to a significant slowdown in growth in 1999.

Ivory Coast is relatively articulated with the global economy and external institutions, as can be seen in the 9.9% of GNP as foreign aid. This dependency is also evident in the extremely high percentage of motor vehicles (32) compared with a Sub-

Table 17.21 Economic Variables: Ivory Coast	
% Real Growth Rate, 1998 (Est.).	6.0
GNP PPP World Ranking*	100
Aid as % of GNP (1996)	9.9
Average Annual Growth in Exports, 1965–96	5.3 (Low-Income Countries = 5.9)
Trade as % of GDP, 1970 & 1996	65 > 83
Commercial Energy Use in kg of Oil Equivalent Units/Capita, 1995.	97 (USA=7,905)
Petrochemical Fertilizer Consumption/ Hundreds Grams/Hectare Arable Land, 1979–81 > 1994–96	261/224
Debt Service as % of GNP, 1996	13.8
1995 Revenues (Est.).	2.3 billion US$
1995 Expenditures (Est.).	2.6 billion US$
1995 Capital Expenditures (Est.).	640 million US$
Labor Force in Agriculture. As % of Total Labor Force, 1970/1996	76/60
Agriculture. value added as a % of GDP, 1970/1996	32/28
%GDP—Farming (% Growth)**	31 (2.2)
GDP—Industry (%)	20 (6.3)
GDP—Services (%)	49 (3.3)
Industry as % of GDP, 1980 > 1996	20 > 21
Irrigated Land in % of Total sq. km of Land	0.002

 * USA is the richest with a score of 1. Moçambique is the poorest with a score of 132.
** Average Annual % Growth, 1965–96

Saharan African average of 20. In fact, most West African countries have less than 15. Another indication is the 97 kg of oil equivalent units per capita, surpassed in West Africa only by Nigeria and Senegal, but also well below the Sub-Saharan African average of 238. Fertilizer use is also high, but has dropped of late. Also indicative of articulation with the Core is the highest total debt service as a percentage of GNP in West Africa, at 13.8, although this 1996 figure was down from the 1980 high of 14.6%.

The IMF has predicted the economy will grow by just 2% this year down from 4.5% in 1998. The IMF is blaming poor progress with economic reform and a build up of debt.

The Ivory Coast is still getting money from exports and also some money from tourism, but it became excessively dependent on foreign aid and loans, as have many of the other HIPC countries in West Africa. Part of its problem, also shared with other HIPCs, is that there is a small tax base.

Table 17.22 shows Ivory Coast to be heavily Islamic with the remaining 40% of the population almost evenly distributed between Christians and Traditionalists.

The health figures on this relatively prosperous country are sadly revealing of exploitation by metropolitan élites and foreign concerns. In spite of their comparative

Table 17.22 Demographic Variables: Ivory Coast	
% Religion: Traditional, Muslim & Christian	18-60-22
Life expectancy at Birth	46.05
Infant Mortality Rate: Deaths per thousand Live Births 1999 (Est.).	94.17
% (Est.) Population Growth Rate, 1999	2.35
Net Migration Rate, 1999*	−2.08**
Urban Population Growth as % of Total Population, 1970 & 1996	27 > 44
% Population with Health Care Access, 1993	60
% Child Malnutrition in children < 5 yrs., 1990–96	24
% Population with Sanitation Access, 1995	54
% Population with Safe Water Access, 1995	72
Net Primary School Enrollment % of Relevant Age Group—Male/Female, 1980 & 1995	—
Literacy Rate (% of Population	48.5

* Number of migrants per 1000 population, (Est.).
** Represents the Liberians who fled the civil war there returning home. As of September, 1998 only about 85,000 Liberians remained in country.

economic advantage, life expectancy at birth (46.05) is worse than in most West African countries. The infant mortality rate is at a shameful 94.17 deaths/live births. The health care access is the second highest in West Africa, but almost a quarter of the children under age five still exhibit malnutrition. Nearly half of the country is without sanitation facilities. Again, with all its wealth, less than half of Ivory Coast's people can read and write.

The rapid growth of urban population from 1970 shows a neglect of rural development, as does the decline in agricultural workers over the same time period. People are flocking to the cities. Their populations almost doubled in the last 30 years of the last century.

Table 17.23 shows many newspaper publishers, radios, television sets and a country beginning to use mobile phones. Surprisingly, it is very strong in computers and web access.

Table 17.23 Consumables & Services: Ivory Coast	
Newspaper publishers per thousand persons (1994)	7
Radios per thousand persons (1995)	Many
Television sets per thousand persons (1996)	60
Mobile Phones per thousand persons (1996)	1
Fax Machines per thousand persons (1995)	—
Personal Computers per thousand persons (1996)	1.4
Web Hosts per thousand persons (1997)	0.17
# Motor Vehicles per thousand People, 1996	32
	(Low-Income Country = 8)

In the year 2000, political uncertainty following the military coup in December 1999 was compounded by a fiscal crisis that caused the continuation of low commodity prices that further reduced Ivory Coast's short-term economic prospects. That such a wealthy country can have poverty indices among the worst in the region and continuing economic troubles again highlights the dangers of an extractive economy that favors foreign investors over local control

Liberia

Liberia is an unfortunate example of how modern warfare can ravage a beautiful land and displace millions of people. Liberia is located on the southern part of the West Coast of Africa. Its main ethnic groups include the Kru, Mandingo and Gola. There are also about 60,000 Americo-Liberians. The origins of the modern state of Liberia go back to the settlement in the nineteenth century of freed US slaves. This was done partly in an effort to address potential social tensions in the US between freed slaves and existing slave owners. Later, those rescued from illegal slave ships were resettled in Liberia as part of the drive to end slavery. By 1830, the population numbered a thousand people. The people united in 1839 to form the Commonwealth of Liberia under a governor appointed by the American Colonization Society and, in 1847, the Free and Independent Republic of Liberia was certified. In the 1930s, Americo-Liberians penetrated the interior and assimilated indigenous ethnic groups into the new nation.

President William Tolbert was inaugurated the tenth president of Liberia in 1972. Social troubles in the late seventies upset his government and resulted in populist riots in the capital city of Monrovia. Master Sergeant Samuel Doe overthrew Tolbert in 1980 in a military takeover. From 1980–1990, when Doe headed the government, corruption and economic mismanagement festered. In 1990, various rebellious factions mounted an uprising against Doe, setting in motion the civil war that would engulf the country for seven years. In 1997, an ECOWAS-brokered peace returned to Liberia. The former rebel Charles Taylor was elected in July of that year to head a civilian government for a term of four years.

The main challenges facing the Taylor Government were: to reconstruct Liberia's shattered economy; to rebuild its social fabric; to resettle and/or reintegrate vast numbers of refugees, displaced people and ex-combatants.

Before the outbreak of the Liberian civil war, agriculture provided a livelihood for about 70% of the population and accounted for roughly 40% of GDP. The rubber industry generated over US$100 million annually in export earnings and, directly and indirectly, provided employment for some 50,000 people. Important iron ore deposits had also attracted substantial foreign investment in the 1960s and the first half of the 1970s, encouraged by the government's "open door" policy. By 1975, Liberia had become the world's fifth largest exporter of iron ore. In spite of this extremely liberal approach to international capital, the country remains desperately poor. Only 31% of the population can read and write. Recently the life expectancy has fallen from a high near 60, to 47 years of age. With a just over a hundred deaths per thousand live births, Liberia has one of the highest infant mortality rates in West Africa.

The export-oriented concession sector—iron ore, rubber and timber—generated about one-quarter of the country's total output, most export earnings and about one-third of government revenue. However, Liberia's growth rates of 6% in the 1960s and

Table 17.24 Economic Variables: Liberia	
%GDP—Farming	30
GDP—Industry	36
GDP—Services	34
Irrigated Land in % of Total sq. km of Land	0.0002

4% in the 1970s, "characterized as growth without development" had relatively little impact on the overwhelming majority of Liberians, and mainly benefited a small urban élite. Liberia is a classic example of how a metropolitan nobility working with international capital can extract the wealth of a country for their benefit to the detriment of the majority of their countrymen.

The military coup that brought Samuel Doe to power in 1980 brought no relief. Liberia was so deeply indebted that it simply could not extricate itself from a severe slide into economic chaos. This eventually led to a breakdown of Liberia's relations with external creditors and donors during the latter part of the decade.

Furthermore, the seven-year civil war wreaked havoc on Liberia's economy, and caused most foreign businesses to flee the country. Tentative estimates put the 1996 GDP at between 25% to 50% of the pre-war level. Annual income was about a fourth of its former level of US$450. Many Liberians have been forced to live on about a third of one US dollar per day.

Liberia is a country that has been ravaged by war and social chaos for much of the last twenty years. The paucity of economic data in Table 17.24 indicates this disruption, but does show a struggling economy balanced between farming, industry and services.

Liberia's population is largely animist, with 20% Muslim and 10% Christian. Before the war, Liberians had an average life expectancy at birth of nearly 60 years of age, but with a high infant mortality rate of 100 or more, their population growth rate (nearly 5%) can only be sustained with a large number of births.

Health care statistics are not available, but a literacy rate has been calculated at 38.3%.

Because of the depletion of iron ore deposits, damage to mining sites, and the ravages of the war on rubber production, officially recorded exports plunged from US$440 million in 1988 to US$20 million in 1996. Real GDP is estimated to have doubled in 1997 with a post-war surge in agricultural production. Rice production is esti-

Table 17.25 Demographic Variables: Liberia	
% Religion: Traditional, Muslim & Christian	70-20-10
Life expectancy at Birth	59.88
Infant Mortality Rate: Deaths per thousand Live Births 1999 (Est.).	100.63
% (Est.) Population Growth Rate, 1999	4.92
Net Migration Rate, 1999*	18.77**
Literacy Rate (% of Population)	38.3

* Number of migrants per 1000 population, (Est.).
** Returning war refugees.

mated to have increased in 1999 to more than 90% of the pre-war level, while cassava production is estimated to have exceeded pre-war levels.

With direction from the World Bank, the government has undertaken several measures to restore fiscal discipline, and the budget for 1999 had a cash surplus of US$0.3 million. Liberia has again opened its doors to international business, this time hoping the result will be more auspicious.

Mali

Mali is a large landlocked Sahelian country with the desert covering 60% of its land area. It is vulnerable to drought, declining soil fertility, deforestation and desertification. Its population is estimated at 10.9 million in 1999 with 2.8% population growth rate per year. Mali is one of the poorest countries of the World, ranking 166 out of 174 countries in the 1999 Human Development Index prepared by the UNDP.

Social indicators are very low: 70% of the population is below poverty line, life expectancy at birth is 50 years, infant mortality is 123 per 1000 and illiteracy is 68%.

Economically, Mali's GNP PPP world ranking is near the bottom (126), but its average annual growth in exports between 1965 and 1996 (7.1%) was above the low-income country mean of 5.9%. Trade has also climbed significantly.

In the last two decades of the 20th century the total debt service as a percentage of GNP jumped from 1.0 to 4.5, but this is still low by West African standards. At 21 kg of Oil Equivalent Units/Capita, Mali is very low compared to a Sub-Saharan African average of 238, yet Mali's industry is growing. Its petrochemical fertilizer use was up in the same period from 60,000 to 83,000 grams/hectare of arable land, showing greater participation in the outside economy.

Demographically, Mali is mostly Muslim, with only 1% Christian and 9% animist.

Life expectancy in Mali is pretty average for West Africa, but infant mortality is high as is the percentage of children under age five with malnutrition—31%. Also, only about a third of the people in Mali have access to safe drinking water and sanitation facilities.

Nearly two-thirds of Mali's population cannot read or write. Slightly fewer than 20% of females attended primary school in 1995.

Consumables and services show a country that has fallen behind, even by West African standards.

Following independence in 1960, Mali was a one-party state. President Modibo Keita led the country on a path of socialism, with a heavy emphasis on control of the economy by a strong centralized government.

Mali entered the 1970s with a familiar West African pattern of political instability. Following a 1968 *coup d'etat*, Moussa Traoré ruled until his overthrow in 1991. The 1992 democratic elections ushered in the Third Republic under President Alpha O. Konaré. The last nine years have witnessed a profound political change in Mali. Competing interest groups had severely weakened the power of the state. Mr. Konaré's government has sought to find a balance between restoring the authority of the state and continuing to promote the democratization process. There have been four government reshuffles since June 1992; the next presidential election is due in 2002.

Table 17.26 Economic Variables: Mali	
% Real Growth Rate, 1998 (Est.).	4.6
GNP PPP World Ranking*	126
Aid as % of GNP (1996)	19.4
Average Annual Growth in Exports, 1965–96	7.1 (Low-Income Countries = 5.9)
Trade as % of GDP, 1970 & 1996	33 > 56
Commercial Energy Use in kg of Oil Equivalent Units/Capita, 1995.	21 (USA=7,905)
Petrochemical Fertilizer Consumption/ Hundreds Grams/Hectare Arable Land, 1979–81 > 1994–96	60/83
Debt Service as % of GNP, 1996	4.5
1995 Revenues (Est.).	730 million US$
1995 Expenditures (Est.).	77 million US$
1995 Capital Expenditures (Est.).	320 million US$
Labor Force in Agriculture. As % of Total Labor Force, 1970/1996	93/86
Agriculture. value added as a % of GDP, 1970/1996	66/48
%GDP—Farming (% Growth)**	49 (2.2)
GDP—Industry (%)	17 (2.6)
GDP—Services (%)	34 (6.2)
Industry as % of GDP, 1980 > 1996	13 > 17
Irrigated Land in % of Total sq. km of Land	0.0006

* USA is the richest with a score of 1. Moçambique is the poorest with a score of 132.
** Average Annual % Growth, 1965–96.

Since mid-1992 the Malian authorities have implemented an ambitious SAP program designed to achieve sustained economic growth and move Mali to financial viability over the medium term. Overall, under the 1992–1995 economic program, Mali made progress in reducing financial imbalances and liberalizing its economic growth.

The macro-economic objectives were broadly achieved, as the real GDP growth averaged approximately 3% annually over the period 1992–1994 and 4.6% over the period 1995–1999. Average annual inflation declined from 12.4% in 1995 to 2.5% in 1999. GDP growth in 1999 is estimated at some 5.5%, principally because of record food crop production.

With an abundant supply of domestic food products, the Consumer Price Index (CPI) declined by over 1% during 1999. Both the external account deficit and fiscal deficit were reduced and a prudent credit policy was pursued. Wide-ranging structural measures were implemented over the period, including price liberalization, the privatization, liquidation or restructuring of several public enterprises, and the implementation of agricultural sector reforms designed to reduce costs and expand and diversify production.

Progress in implementing reforms in the social sectors has been relatively slow and access to social services improved only marginally. Mali has an important agricultural

Table 17.27 Demographic Variables: Mali	
% Religion: Traditional, Muslim & Christian	9-90-1
Life expectancy at Birth	47.5
Infant Mortality Rate: Deaths per thousand Live Births 1999 (Est.).	119.14
% (Est.) Population Growth Rate, 1999	3.01
Net Migration Rate, 1999*	−0.87
Urban Population Growth as % of Total Population, 1970 & 1996	14 > 27
% Population with Health Care Access, 1993	—
% Child Malnutrition in children < 5 yrs., 1990–96	31
% Population with Sanitation Access, 1995	31
% Population with Safe Water Access, 1995	37
Net Primary School Enrollment % of Relevant Age Group—Male/Female, 1995	30/19
Literacy Rate (% of Population)	31.0

* Number of migrants per 1000 population, (Est.).

potential (cotton, rice and cereals, livestock) and has recently become the leading producer and exporter of cotton fiber in sub-Saharan Africa. Production has more than doubled since the devaluation of the CFA Franc in 1994 (the currency used in former French colonies). However, significantly lower production prospects are expected in 2000 and 2001.

Production of paddy rice in the *Office du Niger* zone has increased by a factor of five over the last 15 years. Livestock exports to neighboring countries are now more competitive and local rice is now able to compete with imports from Asia without recourse to excessively high levels of protection. The Niger River has large irrigation potential, and the Senegal River (Manantali) has important hydro-power potential. Of gold, phosphate, diamonds and copper deposits, only gold and phosphate are currently exploited. Indications of expansion in industrial activity are encouraging (cottonseed oil, textiles, vegetable oil).

Table 17.28 Consumables & Services: Mali	
Newspaper publishers per thousand persons (1994)	4
Radios per thousand persons (1995)	168
Television sets per thousand persons (1996)	11
Mobile Phones per thousand persons (1996)	0
Fax Machines per thousand persons (1995)	—
Personal Computers per thousand persons (1996)	—
Web Hosts per thousand persons (1997)	0.03
# Motor Vehicles per thousand People, 1996	4
	(Low-Income Country = 8)

The Islamic Republic of Mauritania or
Al Jumhuriyah al Islamiyah al Muritaniyah

Mauritania is a Sahelian country with a low population density of 2.4 persons per sq. km and which claims to have no arable land! In reality, about 10% of its land is irrigated. It is a sparsely populated country at the western extremity of the Saharan desert although, unlike Mali, Niger and Burkina Faso, this Sahelian country has a seacoast. More than 90% of the land surface is desert, with less than 200 mm rainfall per year. Only the southern edge supports rainfed vegetation and permanent pasturage for livestock. The population was estimated at 2.6 million in 1999, with a growth rate of 2.94% per year estimated for 2000, up from 2.7% the year before. The estimated birth rate is 3.36 births per 1,000 population, with a death rate of 13.97 deaths per 1,000 population (2000 est.)

At independence in 1960, Mauritania was essentially a nomadic society with only 5% of the population living in urban areas. In fact, more people in Mauritania lived in tents than in houses at that time. Much of West Africa has experienced heavy rural to urban migration since the 1960s, and Mauritania is no exception, with especially heavy migrations over the last decade. More than half the population now lives in urban centers.

Mauritania's ethnic mix reflects the country's geographical position, comprising about 50% Moors and 50% black Africans.

Social indicators (nutritional levels, food security, income, and access to water) confirm that 50% of Mauritania's people continue to live below the poverty line of one dollar a day.

A new constitution was approved in mid-1991 after which political parties were legalized and voters were registered. Presidential elections were held in early 1992 and Colonel Ould Taya was elected. He was re-elected for a further six-year term in December 1997 with 90% of the vote.

Table 17.29 Economic Variables: Mauritania	
Trade as % of GDP, 1970 & 1996	74 > 115

Although Mauritania's economy has become substantially liberalized since the early 1980s, the economic structure still presents a sharp contrast between a relatively small modern sector and traditional subsistence sectors. The country has a very narrow economic base, with an industrial sector dominated by mining and fishing, which together provide all export earnings, and a rural sector which employs an estimated 64% of the labor force.

The lack of statistics on Mauritania is an indication of its relative isolation from traditional sources of data collection. What data we do have on trade is encouraging, a move from 74% of GDP in 1970 to 115% by 1996.

Mauritania is the only country listed as entirely Islamic. Available data on consumables and services indicate average levels for West Africa, with one exception: personal computers are the second highest in the region behind neighboring Senegal.

Despite considerable changes since independence, Mauritania's economy remains vulnerable to external shocks, including climatic changes, plagues and fluctuations in world prices for its principal exports. In accordance with the push throughout ECOWAS toward engagement with international capital, Mauritania's development

Table 17.30 Demographic Variables: Mauritania	
Religion	100% Muslim
Life expectancy at Birth	50.76
Infant Mortality Rate: Deaths per thousand Live Births2000 (Est.).	78.15
% (Est.) Population Growth Rate, 1999	2.94
Net Migration Rate, 2000*	0

* Number of migrants per 1000 population, (Est.).

reform program is designed to reduce poverty through accelerated private sector-led growth. It hopes to accomplish this by encouraging a stronger response from the rural sector, developing basic urban infrastructure, promoting private sector development, encouraging employment creation and modernizing the public sector. The World Bank and other investors aid in this quest.

As with other West African countries, Mauritania faces a threat to its development plans from the scourge of HIV/AIDS. Some 10,000 AIDS cases have been officially recorded this year, where the prevalence rate among blood donors is put at 1.8%, marking a huge upsurge in the pandemic among the nation's estimated three million population.

Table 17.31 Consumables & Services: Mauritania	
Radios per thousand persons (1995)	188
Television sets per thousand persons (1996)	82
Fax Machines per thousand persons (1995)	0.1
Personal Computers per thousand persons (1996)	5.3
Web Hosts per thousand persons (1997)	0

Niger

The nation of Niger is another of the landlocked Sahelian countries with a desert-like environment. Since independence in August 1960 Niger has gone through a long period of political instability. A political deadlock in 1995 between the President, the Prime Minister, and Head of National Assembly culminated in a military coup in January 1996. Elections were held in July and General Ibrahim Maïnasara Baré won, but amidst charges of electoral irregularities. In the north and east of the country, armed rebel movements resisted repeated efforts to achieve peace agreements. Tension grew during the ensuing period of military rule, with opposition parties protesting increasing political malfeasance. Public anger mounted over probable fraud in municipal and district elections early in 1999, and increasing salary arrears in the public sector. Against this unrest, President Baré was assassinated on April 9th of that year. A military junta led by Major Wanke took power, vowing to restore civilian rule by the end of 1999.

A constitutional referendum held on July 18, 1999 was followed by Presidential and Legislative elections. The winning two-party coalition consisted of the MNSD

(*Mouvement Nigérien pour une Société de Développement*), which had ruled the country in the one-party regime of the 1980s, and the junior coalition partner CDS (*Convention Démocratique Sociale*), which had shared power in the former civilian government episode of 1993 to 1996. President-elect Tandja (MNSD) was sworn in on December 22, 1999, and the newly elected National Assembly was inaugurated on four days later. Finally, a new government headed by Hama Amadou (MNSD) was appointed on January 6, 2000, with the leader of the CDS, Mahamane Ousmane receiving the key position of President of the National Assembly. Since January 2000, the government has achieved political stability by ensuring that the civil service wage bill is paid, and by successfully underpinning peace accords with rebel movements in both the north and east.

Table 17.32 Economic Variables: Niger	
% Real Growth Rate, 1998 (Est.).	4.5
GNP PPP World Ranking*	118
Aid as % of GNP (1996)	13.2
Average Annual Growth in Exports, 1965–96	−0.6 (Low-Income Countries = 5.9)
Trade as % of GDP, 1970 & 1996	29 > 37
Commercial Energy Use in kg of Oil Equivalent Units/Capita, 1995.	37 (USA=7,905)
Petrochemical Fertilizer Consumption/ Hundreds Grams/Hectare Arable Land, 1979–81 > 1994–96	10/17
Debt Service as % of GNP, 1996	2.9
1995 Revenues (Est.).	370 million US$
1995 Expenditures (Est.).	370 million US$
1995 Capital Expenditures (Est.).	160 million US$
Labor Force in Agriculture. As % of Total Labor Force, 1970/1996	93/90
Agriculture, value added as a % of GDP, 1970/1996	65/39
%GDP—Farming (% Growth)**	40 (−0.1)
GDP—Industry (%)	18 (5.0)
GDP—Services (%)	42 (−0.4)
Industry as % of GDP, 1980 > 1996	23 > 18
Irrigated Land in % of Total sq. km of Land	0.0005

* USA is the richest with a score of 1. Moçambique is the poorest with a score of 132.
** Average Annual % Growth, 1965–96.

The growth record of Niger's rural-based and poorly diversified formal economy is, to a large extent, determined by factors such as the climatic conditions and the level of external assistance. Niger experienced a short-lived period of growth in the late 1970's, recording double-digit GDP growth rates in some years. This was based on integration into the world economy through a uranium boom. However, Niger found

Table 17.33 Demographic Variables: Niger	
% Religion: Traditional, Muslim & Christian	?-80-?
Life expectancy at Birth	41.96
Infant Mortality Rate: Deaths per thousand Live Births 1999 (Est.).	112.79
% (Est.) Population Growth Rate, 1999	2.95
Net Migration Rate, 1999*	0
Urban Population Growth as % of Total Population, 1970 & 1996	9 > 19
% Population with Health Care Access, 1993	30
% Child Malnutrition in children < 5 yrs., 1990–96	43
% Population with Sanitation Access, 1995	15
% Population with Safe Water Access, 1995	53
Net Primary School Enrollment % of Relevant Age Group—Male/Female, 1995	32/18
Literacy Rate (% of Population)	13.6

* Number of migrants per 1000 population, (Est.).

out what such integration can mean—volatility. Between 1983 and 1993, highly unstable real GDP growth averaged minus 0.6% as a result of declining demand for uranium, two severe droughts, the real overvaluation of the currency, market distortions and poor management of public finances. A state of underdevelopment and fragile dependency on the Core, coupled with the persistently high population growth, has been at the center of the country's deteriorating poverty situation over the last two decades.

In 2000, Niger was ranked 173rd out of 174 countries on the UNDP's Human Development Index since 63% of Niger's population lives on less than a dollar a day and per capita income was US$200 in 1999. Social indicators are correspondingly low, as seen in the rates of child mortality, life expectancy, literacy and primary school enrollment. In spite of all the efforts to the contrary, Nigeriens are much poorer today than they were 30 years ago: GDP growth has been negligible while the population has more than doubled.

Table 17.32 shows an estimated economic growth rate of 4.5, but also a dramatically low average annual growth in exports of minus 0.6, compared with 5.9 for low-income countries. Niger is a poor country, even by West African standards and aid is high at over 13% of GNP. Other data show a country articulated with the outside world, but not greatly benefiting from that connection. Industrial growth has done poorly in the last three decades; farming shows a decline of −0.1%; and services show an even greater decline at −0.4%. Agriculture, as a valued added percentage of GDP, also dropped dramatically between 1970 and the century's end. The labor force in agriculture also dropped, though less so.

Niger's demographics are not good, even by West African standards. Life expectancy at birth is slightly less than 42 years of age and infant mortality is high at almost 113 deaths per thousand live births. Less than a third of the population has access to health care, 43% of children are malnourished and only 15% of the population have access to sanitation facilities. Slightly over half the people have access to safe drinking water. Literacy and school enrollments are low.

Table 17.34 Consumables & Services: Niger	
Newspaper publishers per thousand persons (1994)	1
Radios per thousand persons (1995)	61
Television sets per thousand persons (1996)	23
Mobile Phones per thousand persons (1996)	—
Fax Machines per thousand persons (1995)	0
Personal Computers per thousand persons (1996)	—
Web Hosts per thousand persons (1997)	0.04
# Motor Vehicles per thousand People, 1996	6
	(Low-Income Country = 8)

The poverty of the country can be seen in its lack of consumables and services, with motor vehicle ownership slightly below the low-income country average of eight per thousand residents.

The CFA Franc devaluation of January 1994 restored some competitiveness to the economy. This helped to reinvigorate economic growth, which reached an annual average of 4.3% since the change in parity.

The primary sector, comprised of about 40% of GDP in 1999, is dominated by rainfed agriculture, while livestock production accounts for about a third of the value added in the sector. Of the national actively employed population, 84% of men and 97% of women are involved in growing crops or raising livestock, yet Niger continues to show negative figures *vis-a-vis* economic development. Agro-pastoral GDP grew at an annual average rate of only 1.1% in real terms in the period 1969–98, mainly from increasing area under cultivation. This has translated into an annual decline in per capita agricultural GDP by about two %, and an increase in the number of households lacking food security. Unlike other Sahelian countries, which have experienced productivity gains in cereals, yields of the Nigerian staples—millet and sorghum—are low and declining.

Nigeria

This is West Africa's giant. Nigeria has a population of 124 million people, over 250 ethnic groups and a diverse base of religious and political affiliations. The largest ethnic groups are the Hausa-Fulani in the North, the Igbo or Ibo in the Southeast, and the Yoruba in the Southwest. Regional, ethnic, and religious differences have contributed to great instability, and Nigeria's development will depend on the evolution of a political formula that takes into account the country's diversity.

Nigeria attained independence from Britain in 1960, but it has never stabilized. Starting with the disastrous secession of the Igbo people and the subsequent Biafran War, Nigeria slipped into a pattern of political, religious and ethnic conflict. A succession of military governments has controlled the country for 28 of its 40 years of independence.

Blessed with oil wealth, but unable to manage it effectively, Nigerian government officials are considered among the most corrupt in Africa. The malfeasance and political oppression became so bad in the 1990s that the international community literally turned their backs on Nigeria. Shortly after the heart attack that took General Abacha's life, elections brought back a former military leader, the widely respected President **Olusegun Obasanjo**. He assumed power on May 29, 1999.

Nigeria's economy is highly dependent on the oil sector that accounts for about 40% of GDP and about 85% of the country's foreign exchange earnings. We can learn something from Nigeria's "wealthy dependency" which is still a form of powerlessness, no matter how large the size of the dependent economy.

Table 17.35　Economic Variables: Nigeria	
% Real Growth Rate, 1998 (Est.).	1.6
GNP PPP World Ranking*	122
Aid as % of GNP (1996)	0.6
Average Annual Growth in Exports, 1965–96	2.2 (Low-Income Countries = 5.9)
Trade as % of GDP, 1970 & 1996	20 > 28
Commercial Energy Use in kg of Oil Equivalent Units/Capita, 1995.	165 (USA=7,905)
Petrochemical Fertilizer Consumption/ Hundreds Grams/Hectare Arable Land, 1979–81 > 1994–96	59/82
Debt Service as % of GNP, 1996	8.1
1995 Revenues (Est.).	13.9 billion US$
1995 Expenditures (Est.).	13.9 billion US$
1995 Capital Expenditures (Est.).	—
Labor Force in Agriculture. As % of Total Labor Force, 1970/1996	71/43
Agriculture. value added as a % of GDP, 1970/1996	41/43
%GDP—Farming (% Growth)**	33 (4.3)
GDP—Industry (%)	42 (6.0)
GDP—Services (%)	25 (3.4)
Industry as % of GDP, 1980 > 1996	41 > 25
Irrigated Land in % of Total sq. km of Land	0.011

* USA is the richest with a score of 1. Moçambique is the poorest with a score of 132.
** Average Annual % Growth, 1965–96.

Nigeria has never lived up to its potential. With its large reserves of human and natural resources, it has the potential to build a highly prosperous economy, to reduce poverty significantly, and to provide the health, education, and infrastructure services its population needs. Despite the country's relative wealth, poverty is shamefully widespread and Nigeria's basic indicators place it among the 20 poorest countries in the world.

Nigeria's GNP per capita, at about US$310 today, is below the level it was at independence 40 years ago and below the US$370 obtained in 1985. About 70% of the population now fall below the poverty line of roughly one U.S. dollar a day, compared to 43% in 1985.

Table 17.36 Demographic Variables: Nigeria	
% Religion: Traditional, Muslim & Christian	10-50-40
Life expectancy at Birth	53.3
Infant Mortality Rate: Deaths per thousand Live Births 1999 (Est.).	69.46
% (Est.) Population Growth Rate, 1999	2.92
Net Migration Rate, 1999*	0.31
Urban Population Growth as % of Total Population, 1970 & 1996	20 > 40
% Population with Health Care Access, 1993	67
% Child Malnutrition in children < 5 yrs., 1990–96	35
% Population with Sanitation Access, 1995	36
% Population with Safe Water Access, 1995	39
Net Primary School Enrollment % of Relevant Age Group — Male/Female, 1980 & 1995	—
Literacy Rate (% of Population)	57.1

* Number of migrants per 1000 population, (Est.).

The social and political chaos that has afflicted this huge and potentially rich country is evident in the statistics of the tables below. Nigeria's real growth rate in 1998 was estimated at 1.6% and today its GNP PPP ranking is 122, the third worst in West Africa.

The inefficient use of its wealth is evident in Nigeria's life expectancy at birth, which is not as good as tiny and less economically gifted neighboring Benin. At nearly 60 per thousand, its infant mortality rate is better than Benin's, however. As the most populated country in ECOWAS territory, Nigeria's 2.92 estimated population growth rate means a rapidly expanding citizenry and likely attendant problems.

While Nigeria claims that 67% of its people had access to health care in 1993, only one third of its people had access to safe drinking water and sanitation—a shocking statistic for a country with 13.9 billion US$ in expenditures. Such dismal figures underscore how a rising population in even resource-rich developing countries exacerbates its problems.

In the area of literacy Nigeria has done better. Its rate is 57.1 for the general population, and 67.3 for males, but only 47.3 for females.

Like Ghana, Nigeria has 18 newspaper publishers and together the two nations have more than all other West African nations combined. Given its overall potential for wealth and its relatively modernized cities, Nigeria's consumables and services show mediocrity relative to other West African states.

Part of the problem stems from its colonial legacy, beginning with the unfortunate formation of such a large country with little organic unity. Many of Nigeria's problems are also generated internally. Economic mismanagement, corruption, and the reluctance to diversify the economy have been the main reasons for the poor economic performance and rising poverty.

President Obasanjo's administration has identified corruption in governance as an issue that needs to be tackled forcefully in order to reverse the economic decline. This is a monumental task, as corruption pervades the society. The Anti-Corruption Bill,

Table 17.37 Consumables & Services: Nigeria	
Newspaper publishers per thousand persons (1994)	18
Radios per thousand persons (1995)	Many
Television sets per thousand persons (1996)	55
Mobile Phones per thousand persons (1996)	0
Fax Machines per thousand persons (1995)	—
Personal Computers per thousand persons (1996)	4.1
Web Hosts per thousand persons (1997)	0.01
# Motor Vehicles per thousand People, 1996	12
	(Low-Income Country = 8)

passed by the National Assembly, was recently signed into law by President Obasanjo. The government has also acknowledged the increase in widespread poverty and has embraced the need to adopt policies quickly to generate broad-based economic growth that can benefit the poor.

Nigeria is an important country in West Africa, accounting for 47% of the region's population and 41% of the GDP. It remains to be seen if Nigeria can exercise international leadership and pull its people out of poverty. In recent years, Nigeria has exercised a leadership role through the West African peacekeeping force, **ECOMOG**, the Monitoring Group of ECOWAS. They participated actively in restoring peace in Liberia and Sierra Leone, though that process is yet to be completed.

Because of Nigeria's economic and political importance in the region, and because its demise would bring untold suffering, the World Bank and other donors are working closely with officials there to cope with poverty, lack of economic diversity and corruption.

With somewhere between 2% and 4% of its population infected with the HIV/AIDS virus, Nigeria is also beginning to fight that battle, one which threatens a set-back for the country again, just as it seems to be committed to move toward true development. Unless government prevention programs work effectively in this most populous country in Africa, the death toll could be staggering.

Senegal

This is one of the wealthier countries in West Africa with a GDP per capita of US$510. It gained independence in 1960 from the French who had long used its capital of Dakar as the center of its colonial regime. After independence Senegal maintained a relatively stable political and social environment but, for the past several years, it has been confronted by a rebellion in the southern part of the country (the Casamance region).

In spite of being the darling of Francophone West Africa, until 1994 Senegal's economic performance was mediocre and the overvalued CFA Franc limited the effectiveness of the adjustment programs of the 1980s. The devaluation of the CFA Franc in 1994, as well as vigorous structural reform programs, have given some life to economic growth, which has averaged about 5.3% during 1996–1998.

Table 17.38 Economic Variables: Senegal	
% Real Growth Rate, 1998 (Actual)	5.7
GNP PPP World Ranking*	97
Aid as % of GNP (1996)	11.6
Average Annual Growth in Exports, 1965–96	3.2 (Low-Income Countries = 5.9)
Trade as % of GDP, 1970 & 1996	59 > 67
Commercial Energy Use in kg of Oil Equivalent Units/Capita, 1995.	104 (USA=7,905)
Petrochemical Fertilizer Consumption/ Hundreds Grams/Hectare Arable Land, 1979–81 > 1994–96	104/62
Debt Service as % of GNP, 1996	5.4
1995 Revenues (Est.).	885 million US$
1995 Expenditures (Est.).	885 million US$
1995 Capital Expenditures (Est.).	125 million US$
Labor Force in Agriculture. As % of Total Labor Force, 1970/1996	83/77
Agriculture. value added as a % of GDP, 1970/1996	21/18
%GDP—Farming (% Growth)**	19 (1.3)
GDP—Industry (%)	17 (3.9)
GDP—Services (%)	64 (2.4)
Industry as % of GDP, 1980 > 1996	21 > 17
Irrigated Land in % of Total sq. km of Land	0.004

* USA is the richest with a score of 1. Moçambique is the poorest with a score of 132.
** Average Annual % Growth, 1965–96.

However, recent economic developments are only satisfactory. Inflation has remained below 3% since 1996. Real GDP growth in 1998 was 5.7%, and is estimated at 5.1% in 1999. The external current account deficit has steadily improved from 9.2% GDP in 1994 to 6.9% in 1998.

In spite of its high real growth rate and PPP standing, Senegal is quite dependent on foreign aid at 11.6% of its GNP, compared to the Sub-Saharan African average of 5.3%. Dependency is also evident in its high use of imported oil, the second highest rate in West Africa behind Nigeria. This is used partially to fuel its high number of motor vehicles, which number 14 per thousand people compared to eight per thousand for low-income countries.

Senegal is largely Muslim. It has a high population growth rate of 3.35% per year. Only 40% of Senegal's citizenry had access to health care in 1993, 58% to sanitation facilities and half to safe water in 1995, in spite of the country's relative affluence within the ECOWAS community. About a fifth of the children below age five are malnourished. Only a third of the people are literate.

While the World Bank extols the virtues of their integrationist policies, they have had to admit that in Senegal "progress on the economic front has not been sufficient to make a dent on poverty." It is a familiar story: Senegal is caught in a web of underde-

Table 17.39 Demographic Variables: Senegal	
% Religion: Traditional, Muslim & Christian	6-92-2
Life expectancy at Birth	57.83
Infant Mortality Rate: Deaths per thousand Live Births 1999 (Est.).	59.81
% (Est.) Population Growth Rate, 1999	3.35
Net Migration Rate, 1999*	0
Urban Population Growth as % of Total Population, 1970 & 1996	33 > 44
% Population with Health Care Access, 1993	40
% Child Malnutrition in children < 5 yrs., 1990–96	22
% Population with Sanitation Access, 1995	58
% Population with Safe Water Access, 1995	50
Net Primary School Enrollment % of Relevant Age Group—Male/Female, 1980 & 1995	44/60 ::30/48
Literacy Rate (% of Population)	33.1

* Number of migrants per 1000 population, (Est.).

velopment and has been from the beginning of French domination of the area. With an economy oriented toward extraction of value, rather than its creation internally, poverty is bound to continue there.

But the Senegalese government is moving toward greater integration with the Core. Accordingly, it has launched a set of surveys on the quality of public services, the results of which will be used in the preparation of a National Consultation on Public Sector Reform.

On the political front, presidential elections were held in March 2000. Mr. Abdoulaye Wade, the third President of the Republic of Senegal, and the new cabinet members assumed office in April. The change in government was orderly and smooth, and the political situation in Senegal has remained stable.

The new government seems to be placing additional emphasis on economic and social development in the conflict-torn Casamance region where, since 1980, a rebellious militant group has led an armed struggle for independence.

Table 17.40 Consumables & Services: Senegal	
Newspaper publishers per thousand persons (1994)	6
Radios per thousand persons (1995)	Many
Television sets per thousand persons (1996)	38
Mobile Phones per thousand persons (1996)	0
Fax Machines per thousand persons (1995)	—
Personal Computers per thousand persons (1996)	7.2
Web Hosts per thousand persons (1997)	0.31
# Motor Vehicles per thousand People, 1996	14
	(Low-Income Country = 8)

Sierra Leone

This war-torn country is one of the disaster stories of West Africa. Despite great economic potential, the country has a life expectancy of only 37 years and an annual GDP per capita of US$130.

Table 17.41 Economic Variables: Sierra Leone	
% Real Growth Rate, 1998 (Est.).	0.7
GNP PPP World Ranking*	130
Aid as % of GNP (1996)	21.2
Average Annual Growth in Exports, 1965–96	−5.0 (Low-Income Countries = 5.9)
Trade as % of GDP, 1970 & 1996	62 > 43
Commercial Energy Use in kg of Oil Equivalent Units/Capita, 1995.	72 (USA=7,905)
Petrochemical Fertilizer Consumption/ Hundreds Grams/Hectare Arable Land, 1979–81 > 1994–96	58/62
Debt Service as % of GNP, 1996	6.4
1995 Revenues (Est.).	96 million US$
1995 Expenditures (Est.).	150 million US$
1995 Capital Expenditures (Est.).	—
Labor Force in Agriculture. As % of Total Labor Force, 1970/1996	76/67
Agriculture. value added as a % of GDP, 1970/1996	30/44
%GDP—Farming (% Growth)**	52 (3.2)
GDP—Industry (%)	16 (−0.7)
GDP—Services (%)	32 ((−0.2)
Industry as % of GDP, 1980 > 1996	21 > 24
Irrigated Land in % of Total sq. km of Land	0.015

* USA is the richest with a score of 1. Moçambique is the poorest with a score of 132.
** Average Annual % Growth, 1965–96

Never a formal colony, Sierra Leone became a republic in 1971, with Siaka Stevens as President for a five-year term. In 1978 it became a one-party state under Steven's party.

Military takeovers and the civil war have dominated the area's recent history. Yet Sierra Leoneans have also been caught up in the new trend toward integration into the global institutions. In early 1996, democratic, multi-party parliamentary and presidential elections were held. Sheikh Ahmad Tejan Kabbah became President, but stability was short lived. In May 1997, he was overthrown in a *coup d'etat* led by junior ranking officers, but was restored in March 1998, following a military offensive by ECOMOG forces.

Table 17.42 Demographic Variables: Sierra Leone	
% Religion: Traditional, Muslim & Christian	30-60-10
Life expectancy at Birth	49.13
Infant Mortality Rate: Deaths per thousand Live Births 1999 (Est.).	126.23
% (Est.) Population Growth Rate, 1999	4.34
Net Migration Rate, 1999*	14.5**
Urban Population Growth as % of Total Population, 1970 & 1996	18 > 34
% Population with Health Care Access, 1993	—
% Child Malnutrition in children < 5 yrs., 1990–96	29
% Population with Sanitation Access, 1995	11
% Population with Safe Water Access, 1995	34
Net Primary School Enrollment % of Relevant Age Group — Male/Female, 1980 & 1995	—
Literacy Rate (% of Population)	31.4

* Number of migrants per 1000 population, (Est.).
** Returning war refugees.

The civil war continued in the countryside. In January 1999, the rebel Revolutionary United Front attacked and held Freetown but was later repelled by ECOMOG and Government forces. This conflict is not just political. Diamond wealth lies at its heart. From their strongholds in the diamond-rich northern parts of the country, the rebels control the diamond fields and market diamonds to international buyers, giving them enormous wealth and power. The government strategy has rested on a dual-track approach, combining a military offensive with efforts to secure a negotiated settlement (with donor endorsement at the April 1999 London meeting of the Friends of Sierra Leone). Efforts to broker a peace settlement (in which ECOWAS countries, especially Nigeria and Togo, the UN and Liberia's President Charles Taylor played significant roles) led first to a cease-fire, then to the signing of the Lomé Peace Agreement on July 7, 1999.

Table 17.43 Consumables & Services: Sierra Leone	
Newspaper publishers per thousand persons (1994)	2
Radios per thousand persons (1995)	67
Television sets per thousand persons (1996)	17
Mobile Phones per thousand persons (1996)	—
Fax Machines per thousand persons (1995)	0.2
Personal Computers per thousand persons (1996)	—
Web Hosts per thousand persons (1997)	0
# Motor Vehicles per thousand People, 1996	6
	(Low-Income Country = 8)

Under the accord, a government of inclusion was formed with rebel nominees being appointed to ministerial and deputy ministerial positions. A general amnesty for

Photo 17.5 An Urban Street Scene.

the rebels and their allies was also provided. The Lomé Peace Accord was violated in May 2000, when the cease-fire was broken and the rebels held hostage some 500 UN peacekeepers. Since then, with support largely from Britain and an extended UN peacekeeping force, security has been generally restored to Freetown and its environs, and the key rebel leaders are in government custody.

Sierra Leone has substantial mineral, agricultural and fishery resources. By all accounts, it should be a jewel in the West African economy. Agriculture employs about two-thirds of the working population, with subsistence agriculture dominating the sector. The mining of diamonds, bauxite and rutile (a form of titanium) provides the major source of hard currency. Manufacturing is minimal, in keeping with the West African profile.

The five-year civil war dealt a severe blow to the economy, displacing nearly 1.5 million people (out of a total population of 4.7 million), and resulting in large-scale destruction of social and physical infrastructure. Mining and agricultural activities were particularly hard hit, as reflected in a decline in recorded merchandise exports from US$150 million in 1992 to only US$42 million in 1995.

Since the last quarter of 1999, the economy has been recovering, both through strong international support and the rehabilitation efforts of the government. Despite security setbacks, economic reforms have continued. Inflation has fallen from nearly 40% in 1999 to only 3.5% in 2000 and revenue is well above target.

With a 0.7 real growth rate and a –5% average annual growth in exports since 1965, Sierra Leone is among the poorest of the poor countries in West Africa. Foreign aid stands at 21.2% of its GNP, making Sierra Leone a classic example of a country that receives a lot of a help, but does little with it. This can be seen in the demographics in Table 17.42.

Consumables and services in Sierra Leone are average for West Africa, which is surprising for a country that has been ravaged by so much social unrest. Only a third of the country has safe drinking water, but there are a fair number of cars on the road and television sets in homes. Perhaps this speaks to the purchasing priorities of metropolitan élites even when their country is in chaos.

Togo

The last country I will consider in this survey is Togo. It gained independence from France in 1960. The first President, Sylvanus Olympio, was assassinated in 1963 and was succeeded by a provisional government led by Nicholas Grunitzky. This Government was subsequently overthrown in the 1967 *coup d'etat* led by General Gnassingbe Eyadéma, a clever, political strongman who has been in power since.

Table 17.44 Economic Variables: Togo	
% Real Growth Rate, 1998 (Est.).	3.8
GNP PPP World Ranking*	98
Aid as % of GNP (1996)	12.0
Average Annual Growth in Exports, 1965–96	3.8 (Low-Income Countries = 5.9)
Trade as % of GDP, 1970 & 1996	88 > 69
Commercial Energy Use in kg of Oil Equivalent Units/Capita, 1995.	45 (USA=7,905)
Petrochemical Fertilizer Consumption/ Hundreds Grams/Hectare Arable Land, 1979–81 > 1994–96	13/59
Debt Service as % of GNP, 1996	4.0
1995 Revenues (Est.).	232 million US$
1995 Expenditures (Est.).	252 million US$
1995 Capital Expenditures (Est.).	—
Labor Force in Agriculture. As % of Total Labor Force, 1970/1996	74/66
Agriculture. value added as a % of GDP, 1970/1996	34/35
%GDP — Farming (% Growth)**	32 (3.1)
GDP — Industry (%)	23 (2.9)
GDP — Services (%)	45 (1.5)
Industry as % of GDP, 1980 > 1996	25 > 23
Irrigated Land in % of Total sq. km of Land	0.0013

* USA is the richest with a score of 1. Moçambique is the poorest with a score of 132.
** Average Annual % Growth, 1965–96.

The economic reforms initiated in the late 1980s were not accompanied by a corresponding political transition, resulting in severe turbulence in 1992–93. Nevertheless President Eyadéma was re-elected in 1993 in voting boycotted by the opposition, and retained the presidency again in the disputed elections of 1998. Some have characterized his presidency as based on "the politics of smoke and mirrors," but no one can deny that he is one of the powerful West African leaders of the "old school" resisting the trend toward democratization.

Table 17.45 Demographic Variables: Togo	
% Religion: Traditional, Muslim & Christian	70-10-20
Life expectancy at Birth	59.25
Infant Mortality Rate: Deaths per thousand Live Births 1999 (Est.).	77.55
% (Est.) Population Growth Rate, 1999	3.51
Net Migration Rate, 1999*	0
Urban Population Growth as % of Total Population, 1970 & 1996	13 > 31
% Population with Health Care Access, 1993	—
% Child Malnutrition in children < 5 yrs., 1990–96	25
% Population with Sanitation Access, 1995	22
% Population with Safe Water Access, 1995	—
Net Primary School Enrollment % of Relevant Age Group—Male/Female, 1995	98/72
Literacy Rate (% of Population)	51.7

* Number of migrants per 1000 population, (Est.).

Togo experienced strong growth from 1960 to the mid-1970s with real gross domestic product (GDP) increasing by about 7% annually. After the boom in phosphate prices in 1975, Togo embarked on an ambitious investment program and created a multitude of public enterprises, many of which subsequently became a severe drain on the economy (no doubt partially because they were created as prebends for state officials).

Table 17.46 Consumables & Services: Togo	
Newspaper publishers per thousand persons (1994)	2
Radios per thousand persons (1995)	362
Television sets per thousand persons (1996)	14
Mobile Phones per thousand persons (1996)	—
Fax Machines per thousand persons (1995)	2.4
Personal Computers per thousand persons (1996)	—
Web Hosts per thousand persons (1997)	0.01
# Motor Vehicles per thousand People, 1996	27 (Low-Income Country = 8)

Togo's economy is heavily dependent on subsistence agriculture, which contributes 40% of GDP and employs 75% of the labor force although, as Table 17.44 shows, the percentage of workers in agriculture is falling. Cotton, coffee and cocoa are the main agricultural exports, generating about 35% of total export earnings. Phosphate mining is the most significant industrial activity. However, industry as a percentage of GDP declined in the last two decades of the 20th century.

This largely traditionalist country, with only 10% Muslims and 20% Christians, has an average demographic profile for West Africa, but with a rather high population growth rate of 3.51% per year. Like other ECOWAS countries, it is urbanizing fast—nearly tripling its urban population since 1970 (See Photo 17.5).

One fourth of the population under age five is malnourished and only a fifth of the people have access to sanitary facilities. However, Togo's literacy rate of nearly 52% is far better than neighboring Benin is at only 37%.

Togo's consumables and services are average for the region, except for the high number of motor vehicles at 27 per thousand, compared to a low-income country average of eight.

The government's economic reform efforts were severely hampered by the unrest in 1992–93. The modern sector collapsed, the tax base diminished, transit trade shifted to other countries, external aid virtually disappeared and GDP fell by 22% in just two years. In the aftermath of the political turmoil and the currency devaluation of the CFA Franc by 50%, Togo launched a comprehensive adjustment program in mid-1994 aimed at restoring sustained economic growth and achieving financial viability in the medium term. During the first two years of the program, considerable progress was made in reversing the deterioration of the 1991–93 period. By 1996, real GDP returned to its 1991 level, however, the economic situation deteriorated again in 1998, with the four-month energy crisis and the declining economic climate that accompanied the contested presidential election in June 1998.

Since that time, the political and economic situation has deteriorated and poverty indicators are on the rise. Also, the flow of public aid to the country declined significantly after the 1993 election, with several donors formally linking resumption of their cooperation to increased democracy and governmental transparency. Major donors are limiting their assistance to small social sector projects. Many international and local non-governmental organizations (NGOs) are active in the country, but, unlike many West African nations that are briskly moving to embrace democracy and a liberalization of their economies, Togo seems to be dragging its feet.

≋≋ CRITICAL THINKING QUESTIONS ≋≋

1. What was the logic of the author's placing the 16 countries in this chapter under the rubric of West Africa?
2. What similarities do you seem among the West African nations listed above? Given those transnational patterns, how are they different?
3. What are the IFIs and what are they doing in West Africa?

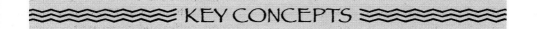

KEY CONCEPTS

ECOMOG
EU

Obasanjo, Olusegun
UDCs

SOURCES & SUGGESTED READINGS

BBC World Service, Bush House. October 30, 2000. Strand, London WC2B 4PH, UK.

Central Intelligence Agency (CIA). 2000. *The World Fact Book.*

Davidson, Basil. 1989. *The fortunate isles: a study in African transformation.* Trenton, N.J.: Africa World Press.

World Bank. 1998. *1998 World Development Indicators.* New York: World Bank.

World Bank. 2000. *Africa Home Page.* http:wbln0018.worldbank.org/afr/afr.nsf

18 DEVELOPMENT IN WEST AFRICA

Development in West Africa has failed. There are reasons for this to be found in its history, colonialism, inadequate methods and developers' attitudes of superiority. Nonsuccess is grounded in both internal and external factors. In fact, efforts to develop the region have largely enriched metropolitan élites and Western companies and underdeveloped the area. Recently, development efforts have taken a new turn toward more direct control by the Core Countries in West African governance. Nevertheless, development remains problematic today and will continue to falter until appropriate technology and sustainability are adopted by indigenes intent on developing their region.

Introduction — The Colonial Inheritance

The history of West Africa shows that indigenous governance was first overlooked, then altered and eventually superceded by the nation-state. Development became the responsibility, not of local leaders, but of colonial administrators. The development process in West Africa today still suffers from the colonial holdover. The legacy of colonization *vis-à-vis* development is not a beneficial one. This history reveals why modernization has been such a struggle in West Africa, why governance has been so difficult and why international capital continues to manipulate the political economy to their advantage. The colonials were reluctant to develop the region except where development enhanced extraction; they failed in what development efforts were made; and they frequently blocked indigenous efforts to modernize.

Colonials strongly pushed the production of export crops to gain revenue from the world market. They used two main coercive forces: taxation and mandatory participation in labor gangs. Both took workers away from their rural homes and immersed many of them in urban work. They labored on export-oriented plantations, mines or were drafted into the military, police force or worked on public works projects. Incentives were offered to encourage farmers to produce for overseas markets.

This labor drain placed an increased burden on the old people left in the villages and on women who had to pick up the slack in household production when men were taken or drawn away. Household and community reserves of food declined and increased vulnerability to malnutrition. Forced and induced labor migration disrupted the economic cycle of shared labor and reciprocal aid in farm work. Very much like the extraction of slaves before, pulling laborers away from the farms strained agricultural production and it increased the fragility of life in West Africa.

World War I brought rising malnutrition and an overall decline in public health to West Africa. It also brought a decline in real incomes. France took 100,000 West Africans to the Western Front and Britain took about a third of that number. When carriers and servants are added in, the total number of Africans taken in the war effort was about two million, which intensified an already serious drain on agriculture.

> World War II was to have an even greater impact in West Africa, but this time it led to rising expectations by indigenes that they would soon regain their freedom. The world economy was in a boom state, the demand for West African raw materials and export crops was at an all time high. It was a time of exuberant optimism. This "growth bubble" led to a renewed interest in the region by various European powers. Between 1947 and 1958 France doubled all the investment she had previously made in Francophone West Africa. Britain poured funds into creating large-scale mechanized farms in Northern Nigeria, though these later ended in dismal failure.

Independence came at the end of the postwar "growth bubble." While some West African countries like Ivory Coast, Ghana and Nigeria became relatively wealthy during this period, most did not, and certainly colonialism had not improved the lives of the majority of peoples in the villages spread over this vast region. The high ideals and rhetoric of nationalism came face to face with the reality that European colonialists had done little to prepare their colonies for a return to freedom—either economically or politically. Furthermore, freedom meant plunging into a starkly different political economic form for West Africans: the nation-state. This was supposedly a new and progressive unifying force—one that promised development of the region. However, the colonial institutions of wealth extraction did not change with political independence and the continued presence of these ties ensured that West Africa's wealth, in the main, would continue to flow out to Europe.

Furthermore, the new African leaders were not prepared to develop their new nations. They were members of an educated class that had been pressing for a return to independence, but they lacked the technical expertise to understand development. What was needed, but in conspicuously short supply, were middle-level technicians and trained officials to run the bureaucratic machinery of a nation-state.

> Buoyed by steadily rising export sales, agriculture, trade and manufacturing, all nations in West Africa tended to expand throughout the 1950s, based largely on the entrepreneurial spirit of the indigenous people. This success and optimism was about to end, but until it did, it fueled a revolution in rising expectations among West Africans. Many are still asking, "what went wrong?"

Force majeure in the Failure of West African Development

There are several major forces, or ***force majeure***, behind West Africa's failure to develop. They include a tropical environment with poor soils, disease, uneven rains,

Table 18.1 Growth of Real GDP per Capita* (Average Annual Percentage Change)			
Group	1965–73	1973–80	1980–89
Industrialized countries	3.7	2.3	2.3
East Asia	5.3	4.9	6.2
Sub-Saharan Africa	2.1	0.4	– 1.2

* After World Bank, *World Development Report 1991*, Table 1, p. 3.

devastating pests and population increase. These are formidable barriers to development and development planners are troubled. African countries are among the poorest of the poor: they have, in fact, fallen on such hard times that many now have to import food, in spite of ample land and manpower to enable Africans to feed themselves, as they did in precolonial times. Not only are there food shortages, but poverty has increased since independence. Relative to the economic growth in the rest of the world, Africa is less developed today than it was in the past (See Table 18.1).

First, the tropical environment is hostile to improvement and both agriculture and herding have suffered. When the rains and the resultant forage failed in the late 1960s and early 1970s, herders' vulnerability was exacerbated. Pastoralists moved their herds ever southward in search of grass and water, putting extra pressure on the grasslands of agriculturists there. Nonetheless, the drought took the lives of hundreds of thousands of cattle and it is estimated that a quarter of a million herders perished.

A second *force majeure* category of problems is disease, which derives from the tropical climate in West Africa. Until the 20th century, the burden of disease and low agricultural productivity in West Africa kept population densities among the lowest in the world. Pests and diseases wreaked havoc with crops, people and herds. Torrential rains alternating with periods of drought have also devastated the area. The data for 1965–1990 suggest that tropical Africa suffered a geographical penalty compared with temperate-zone countries. Sachs says, "Sustained agriculture-led development…has always been a temperate-zone affair."

Modern medicine has helped to an extent, but many people in West Africa suffer from malaria and other endemic tropical diseases that weaken them and cut into economic productivity. Such debilitation has also, of late, been coupled with falling food consumption and rising nutritional problems, especially in the poverty-stricken rural areas. And now there is an even greater threat from illness with the recent rise in HIV/AIDS cases. According to the World Bank, 2.4 million Africans died of AIDS in 2000 alone and another 25 million are infected with the virus. This disease threatens to further reduce West Africa's ability to gain enough population density to stimulate economic growth. In much of rural West Africa, human labor forms the primary source of agricultural energy. Any reduction in the number of strong workers will be devastating, and this is precisely the demographic cohort affected by AIDS. If this disease hits farming communities with any force, it will reduce an already limited labor pool even more.

A third *force majeure* is related to demographics. Population has risen because of improvements to health based on modern medicine. Where populations have grown drastically, the land has come under pressure, leading to outmigration, as people escape to the cities.

The last hundred years in West Africa has seen an exodus from the rural areas. Since World War II this has accelerated. It is estimated that within ten years, half the population of some West African countries will live in the cities, many of them in their capital cities. Cities are attractive for a variety of reasons. Generally cities have better services and rural people see better economic opportunities, better life chances there. Population pressure and urban migration combine to make development more difficult.

A fourth *force majeure* is globalization itself. Hazel Henderson defines globalization in this way:

> Globalization today involves the increasing interdependence of national economies, financial markets, trade, corporations, production, distribution, and consumer marketing. This globalization process is driven by two main-springs. The first is technology which has accelerated innovation in telematics, computers, fiber optics, satellite, and other communications; their convergence with television, global multimedia, electronic courses for trading stocks, bond, currency, commodities, future options, and other derivatives; and the global explosion of e-commerce and the Internet. The second is the fifteen-year wave of deregulation, privatization, liberalization of capital flows, opening of national economies, extension of global trade, and the export-led growth policies that followed the collapse of the Bretton Woods fixed currency-exchange regime in the early 1970s.

In the post-war boom, West African governments greatly increased spending in an effort to modernize. An economic decline began almost immediately after independence in the late 1960s and 1970s as world demand for its products diminished. Africa was especially disadvantaged because of its limited infrastructure. As export prices fell in world markets, and as competition from other parts of the world rose, the region became increasingly vulnerable to swings in far away markets. In the realm of cash-cropping, many West African nations were growing one major export crop, which made the impact from market fluctuations even more severe.

After independence, the general infrastructure fell into disrepair. Roads were filled with potholes, bridges became unsafe, government buildings were not painted, the plumbing could not be repaired, communications lines went down, and spare parts could not be found for tractors and government vehicles.

These and other problems have made West Africa a high-risk zone for foreign investment. Since there are many areas of the globe where investors can make profits more safely, capital flight has become a problem that further exacerbates West Africa's underdevelopment. Today, more capital flows out of Africa than in.

Some efforts have been made to develop the region, but with little success. Since the 1960s there has been a steady decline in the standard of living for West Africans, in spite of the massive amounts of money and personnel invested in modernization. Ernest Stern, former Vice President of Operations at the World Bank said:

> We...have failed in Africa, along with everybody else. We have not fully understood the problems. We have not identified the priorities. We have not always designed our projects to fit the agro-climatic conditions of Africa and the social, cultural, and political frameworks of Africa countries...We, and everybody else, are still unclear about what can be done in agriculture in Africa.

Although this statement was made in 1984, it is just as valid today.

The *force majeure* issues I have discussed are part of the reason for continuing pessimism, but there have also been many mistakes made, which I will discuss below. In closing this section let me say that the economy in West Africa has been on the decline since the 1960s. The reasons for this decline, though debated by scholars, generally include the disorganization brought on by slavery and colonialism, the fluctuations in West African export prices and the 1970s OPEC price hike, the environmental problems of drought and disease, the population explosion, the mismanagement of the political economy and the stranglehold on the economy by outside forces. Let us now turn to some of these issues in detail.

Improper Development Policies

Both Africans and foreign planners have been striving to make rural agricultural production a market-oriented activity. Subsistence farming is defined as primitive, yet little thought is given to the long-term **sustainability** of modern techniques. Furthermore community needs are ignored or superceded by national needs in too many modernization plans. Export crops are given preference over home consumption, which is sometimes even portrayed as unpatriotic and selfish. In the process, urban élites and bourgeois planners minimize rural needs. Furthermore, planners define development in monetary terms, which has caused misdirected focus on the export of cash-crops.

Development specialists have felt that by using Western technology, agriculture could be improved, infrastructures created and repaired and industry established on West African soil. Such policies are based on top-down plans devised by financial planners with little or no knowledge of West African environment, culture or economic methods.

Development philosophies have been changing throughout the last half of the 20th century. In the 1950s and 1960s, Keynesian models predominated. These posited the need for a strong state with centralized planning to promote economic development. Today, *laissez faire* economics dictates a minimal role by the state, privatization and development by foreign NGOs. Whether West Africa is assaulted with **Keynesianism** or Neoliberalism, the result has been the same—underdevelopment, poverty and stagnation. Let's look at some reasons why this is the case.

Arrogance and Top-Down Planning

Perhaps the most widespread cause of failure in agricultural development projects in West Africa is **top-down planning** by individuals and organizations that do not understand the nature of farming in the various environments and eco-niches in which they try to implement their plans. This is exacerbated by ignorance of local customs or social organization so vital for proper implementation of any development project. This lack of local knowledge, often coupled with indifference toward local people who do possess essential ecological lore, has been disastrous in West Africa. Centralized, top-down planning seeks little grass roots input, allows little community control of projects and does not seek to empower local farmers.

Anthropologists have come to know that local people have a vast ecological knowledge, which is crucial to the functioning of any development project in their area. Ignoring such knowledge can lead to environmental disaster. For example, in the 1950s and 1960s a series of wells were dug in the West African Sahel in an effort to give herders and their cattle access to water. In the new scheme the pastoralists were expected to sell their cattle to traders who would sell the meat and hides to metropolitan centers and foreign buyers. For a while, this went according to plan. But other, unexpected things happened. The permanent water supplied attracted so many herders that the grass surrounding the waterholes was soon overgrazed so that both people and cattle had to search far beyond for sufficient pasturing. In the traditional roaming of the herders, the land is given a chance to regenerate. The permanent sinkholes may have seemed a good idea to planners who had never lived with pastoralists, but they resulted in disaster, causing unpredicted problems. When the rains and the resultant forage failed in the late 1960s and early 1970s the situation worsened. Pastoralists moved their herds southward in search of grass and water. The drought ultimately took the lives of hundreds of thousands of cattle and an estimated quarter of a million herders. In desperation, the remaining pastoralists sold off their herds to get money to buy food, but nature and man had conspired to drastically reduce the amount of food available for purchase. While the drought crippled agricultural output, governments had been encouraging farmers to switch from food production to cash-crops. The end result was very short food supplies and high prices.

If local people are involved in planning, such failures can be reduced. For example, in Hausaland, when the British completed the railway from the coast, local entrepreneurs responded. Hausa traders created massive purchasing schemes that stimulated local farmers to grow cotton and peanuts as never before.

Inappropriate Technology & the Modernization Approach

The modernization approach of the last four decades of the 20th century has focused on the importation of modern machinery. It was thought that by using tractors, petroleum and scientifically improved seeds and chemicals to work the fields, yields would rise (See Photo 18.1).

In the immediate post-independence period, West Africans thought it would be possible to increase agricultural production and sell their products on the world market. There was an early rush to buy tractors, but these had to be imported at high cost, as did spare parts and petroleum. These machines quickly broke and there was a dearth of spare parts. Furthermore, West Africans had limited knowledge about maintaining such machinery.

High transport costs were also a factor. West Africa is distant from modern agricultural equipment suppliers and most farms lie at some distance from the ports where fuel, fertilizer, chemicals and machinery arrive. Thus, rural farmers are burdened by excessive shipping costs. Furthermore, when there are problems in the supply chain, producers ship to the zones nearer the point of production, cutting off distant lands.

The one part of the Green Revolution package that has worked is improved maize strains that have caused many farmers to switch from millet to maize production. By growing more maize for urban areas, these peasants have gained access to a new and significant source of wealth. Such peasant production by women has given them an important new source of wealth and, consequently, power in the household. An NGO

Photo 18.1   Imported Modern Farming Technology.

named Ghana SG 2000 has been able to increase maize yields in the region by about 40% using a high-technology package of improved seed and imported fertilizer and chemicals. While this brings short-term benefits to peasants and female farmers, it continues to make them dependent on such inputs.

Development thinkers need to focus on appropriate technology and sustainability, not what is "modern" and dependent on industrial production. A whole new mode of thought is necessary. Inappropriate technology — tractors, petrofuel, chemicals and petrochemical fertilizers — have been pushed by states for two reasons: First, they appear to be "modern" solutions. West African administrators sometimes reason, "What's good for the West is good for us." Or again, "Why should we use "inferior" technology, when farmers in Iowa or Germany plow their lands with giant machines?" Secondly, Core Countries profit from continued use of such farming technology, even though it is unsuitable for the West African context.

Sustainability is development that can be maintained indefinitely by local people using local inputs and energy and does not harm future generations. Appropriate technology is that which fits the local environment and purchasing power of local farmers. It does not create undue dependence on far-away suppliers or energy sources. In **Natural Capitalism**, Hawken, Lovins & Lovins give us a new vision of industrial life, one that takes living systems into account. Their version includes the following fundamental assumptions:

✴ The environment is not a minor factor of production but rather is "an envelope containing, provisioning, and sustaining the entire economy;"
✴ The limiting factor to future economic development is the availability and functionality of *natural capital*, in particular, life-supporting services that have no substitutes and currently have no market value;
✴ Misconceived or badly designed business systems, population growth, and wasteful patterns of consumption are the primary causes of the loss of natural capital, and all three must be addressed to achieve a sustainable economy;
✴ Future economic progress can best take place in democratic, market-based systems of production and distribution in which *all* forms of capital are fully valued, including human, manufactured, financial, and natural capital;

✷ One of the keys to the most beneficial employment of people, money, and the environment is radical increases in resource productivity;

✷ Human welfare is best served by improving the quality and flow of desired services delivered, rather than by merely increasing the total dollar flow;

✷ Economic and environmental sustainability depends on redressing global inequities of income and material well being;

✷ The best long-term environment for commerce is provided by true democratic systems of governance that are based on the needs of people rather than business.

If this natural model perspective has merit for the future, and I think it does, then we can see that petrofarming and large-scale development projects in West Africa appear all the more inappropriate.

The Impact of Export Crops on Food Production

Cash-crops are important sources of revenue for local farmers, middlemen and the nation-state. But, in Africa, the emphasis on export crops has been linked to famine and the inability of Africa to feed herself today. This is not a process that came about in a benign way. Some decision-makers in Core Countries actually advocate using food as a weapon to politically coerce Peripheral Countries. For example, former Vice President Hubert Humphrey, speaking of the U.S. Food for Peace program, said:

> I have heard...that people may become dependent on us for food. I know that was not supposed to be good news. To me, that was good news, because before people can do anything they have got to eat. And *if you are looking for a way to get people to lean on you and to be dependent on you*, in terms of their cooperation with you, it seems to me that *food dependence would be terrific* (emphasis added).

And again in 1980, John Brock said during confirmation hearings as Secretary of Agriculture in the United States:

> Food is a weapon but the way to use it is to tie countries to us. That way they'll be far more reluctant to upset us.

These comments sadly reflect the results of much foreign aid to Africa. Although altruistic motives may prevail, the end result of food aid has been to create dependence. Today, after years of shipping wheat grains to Africa, there is a new market there for wheat. West Africans, especially in the cities, have developed a taste for bread, and now expect it as part of their daily fare. In many West African cities like Lomé, Abidjan, or Conakry, bread has become a staple. Urban tastes have become influenced by foreign imports. Above all else, such sophisticated consumers demand diversity in their diets, and West African farmers simply cannot supply that range of food products. The African specialist Bill Rau has said of this issue:

> It is at this point of decisions within African countries to minimize the contributions of rural producers to meet food security requirements and of policies

within the U.S. and the European Community to export at subsidized rates their agricultural surpluses, that the rationale develops to speak of Africa's food crisis and to justify policies that retain countries' orientation toward external markets.

Many involved in agricultural development in Peripheral Countries now see food as a distribution problem, one that is exacerbated by planting the wrong crops. Cash-crops bring revenues for governments and producers. The shift away from food production has had negative consequences. With the introduction of cash-crops, total crop diversity was reduced as commodity crops took labor away from food production. Additionally, growers quickly realized that in the intensified labor-short situation they had to move toward maize and cassava production because both took less time than millet, sorghum and Guinea corn. Bill Rau says of this situation:

> Malnutrition as it is known today, based on structural deprivation among producing households, only emerged in African societies in the early stages of the colonial era. Although food production remained the central concern of rural households, vulnerability to hunger occasioned by slight changes in the economic or natural environment affected millions of people. Variations in household food production could be affected by such factors as out-migration of male workers, sickness at critical times in the production cycle, and rains that arrived too late or were too heavy, flooding fields.

What little research in agriculture is being carried out goes not so much to food production, but to export crops. Agricultural research has made little headway in facilitating food crops like yams, cassava, cocoyams or millet. Frances Moore Lappé wrote a well-known book on development with the title, *Food First: Beyond the Myth of Scarcity*. Its thesis is that food shortages are politically created. Export crops bring foreign exchange into state treasuries, but set back food production at the very time when cities are growing. Where possible food is trucked into cities, but storage is a problem. During harvest months, in rural areas, food is more plentiful and cheaper, but as time passes urban scarcities develop and the prices rise. If there were adequate storage facilities for maize, millet and guinea corn, either at the site of production or in the cities, farmers could make better profits on their crops, even taking into account the transport costs they would have to pay.

With the introduction of cash-cropping, West Africans work harder and have access to a wider array of goods and services. In Northern Ghana, for example, women have recently entered the agriculture labor force partly to gain access to more cloth, wigs, household utensils, clothes and to pay for their children's education. Income from cash-crops has given them a sense of pride and more power in their households. A cost-benefit analysis of cash-cropping is a complicated issue. For example, in Sisala-land in Northern Ghana, I found that the Ghana Cotton Corporation (GCC) has had an equalizing effect, at least in the short term. It has given subordinate men and women an opportunity to earn cash, giving them more power *vis-à-vis* their elders. The GCC helps women by giving them fertilizer that allows them to work depleted farms abandoned by men. This has given women more power in society and has allowed young men to achieve independence earlier.

Those engaged in growing cash-crops may produce more food too. Overall, Sisala farmers appear to be producing more cash-crops *and* more food, since maize is now bringing such high prices in urban markets, and farmers, male or female, regularly use fertilizer on their maize crops that is supposed to go on cotton. To say that cash-cropping is bad is too simplistic. Its effects are diffuse and variable and they can have varied interpretations depending on one's perspective.

Cash-cropping has also exacerbated social stratification in rural areas, by placing profits in the hands of wealthy middlemen and corporations. For example, when the railway was completed between the coast and Kano in 1912, it led to a ten-fold increase in marketed groundnut production between 1912–1913. This increase was at the expense of food production that contributed to the 1913–1914 famine in the area. Again, wealthy Hausa merchants profited twice from the production of cash-crops. When the government encouraged people to grow export crops, food prices skyrocketed, causing poor farmers to go into debt to the rich merchants. When the famine was over, the poor had to go back into cash-crop production in order to try to extricate themselves from debt.

Agricultural production in West Africa today is intricately tied up with global markets, but again, in a way that creates unequal exchange to the benefit of the Core. To counter this situation for Peripheral Countries, India is proposing adoption of a concept called a "Food Security Box," which would grant developing countries sufficient flexibility to address their food security needs. The idea is that developing countries, lacking sufficient resources and infrastructural capacity to manage their geographic and economic vulnerabilities, are at a disadvantage *vis-à-vis* their developed country competitors. According to the Indian proposal, only the combined benefits of both subsidized agriculture and unimpeded market access to developed countries.

The Problem of Credit

West African farmers find it difficult to capitalize efforts to expand production because of a lack of credit. At present, there are four sources of loans: 1) Official channels like banks, government, large firms, IFIs and foreign loans. 2) Local moneylenders who practice usury, lending money at 25–30% interest. 3) Small private companies like the GCC provide a service that gives people collateral-free credit to acquire farm inputs. This stimulates local entrepreneurship by providing individuals with the incentive to increase their production. But here is an example of a rational peasantry—the farmers often put most of the fertilizer designated for cotton onto their maize crops. Clearly you can eat maize and not cotton, but beyond that maize requires less labor and brings greater profits to the farmer on the open market. He must sell his cotton to the GCC, but he can hold his maize and sell it when the market is high, or he can eat it—in short, he can do with it what he wants, when he wants. 4) High government officials: because there are large profits to be made by lending money in the informal sector, those in office such as bureaucrats, police or military often lend money because they can avoid the high default rate facing other lenders. They do this by using "official" enforcement to retrieve bad debts. It is a simple matter to send round the police or a squad of soldiers and most recalcitrant borrowers will pay their debts.

According to traditional West African legal principles, individuals don't own land, so the can't use it for collateral to secure loans. Farmers are sitting on ample and valuable land, but that value is not formally represented in a legal way. Part of the problem exists because African farmers are articulated to a Western capitalist system that could provide capitalization for farming, but they are not fully integrated into the system. The reason is the contradiction between African customary law and Western contract law. In Northern Ghana, it would be possible for a villager to have a thousand acre farm, but he could not get a loan for agricultural inputs to work that farm using it as collateral, because it is not represented in a universally accepted conversion system as being worth anything. It is wealth, but not capital.

This has been a great problem for entrepreneurs wanting to get ahead in the commercial world. They might have access to land, but they don't own it in a legal sense, according to a system of law accepted in the international marketplace. I have walked along pristine sandy beaches in Africa that those living in many Core Countries would pay a local fortune to have. But this real estate is not marketable because there is no legal way to transfer ownership from one lawful owner to another since nobody owns it.

Wealth is unrealized capital. A house or farm in a village is not capital because it cannot be represented as such through a humanly-created and universally accepted symbol system. Capital, on the other hand, is wealth that can produce other wealth. The reason it can replicate itself is the fact that it is enmeshed in a conversion system. For example, the house can be represented abstractly to cost $1,000, while the farm is equivalent to $2,000. Thus, symbolically in the accepted system of conversions, this farm represents two such houses. Worth can be calculated and communicated over time and space. A person living a thousand miles away can understand the value of the farm. Another person, five years after it is given a representative value, can ascertain its worth, according to the rise or fall in values over time.

West African governments have failed to provide many critical public goods, including a legal system that can efficiently transform *de facto* assets into *de jure* property. Without such a system, the reality of property rights becomes primarily a function of the political power of the property holder. Unless an asset can be turned into marketable property, there will be limited opportunities to use it to capitalize economic expansion. An owner of capital can borrow against it. A bank may be willing to give a farmer a loan of 60% of its value against his farm. Hernando De Soto shows that in spite of the fact that many of the poor of the world are literally sitting on great wealth—land and houses—they cannot utilize it to make more wealth because it is most frequently unrepresented in any legal system.

The work of Hernando de Soto underlines the importance of legal regimes in facilitating economic growth and equitable wealth distribution. In *The Other Path*, De Soto studied Peru's informal sector and came to the conclusion that mass empowerment through entrepreneurism was being stifled by élite-dominated mercantilist states. More recently, in *The mystery of capital*, De Soto defends the creation of a system of rules in the West that protected property and created from that wealth the possibility of capital, giving rise to the industrial revolution and capitalism. De Soto describes for the Old West a situation that exists today in Africa:

> Most people worked on the land, which was owned by a very few big landlords, some of them indigenous oligarchs, others colonial planters. Cities were small and functioned as markets and ports rather than industrial centers; they were dominated by tiny mercantile elites *who protected their interests with thick wrappings of rules and regulations.* (my italics)

Not only does the lack of a formal system of land tenure laws inhibit acquisition of development funds by farmers and entrepreneurs, it also leads to capital drain. A country that lacks a functional intellectual property system will produce few patents. That does not mean that the people in such a place lack useful ideas for technological innovation; It does mean that they cannot transform those ideas into property to increase the capital base of their society.

The Role of the Nation-State

It is clear that the nation-states in West Africa have failed to develop rural areas and agriculture, which is not to say that they have been successful at developing urban areas or an industrial infrastructure. I am merely saying that agricultural development has been sorely overlooked or corrupted by state involvement. In his classic treatise *The Political Economy of West African Agriculture*, Hart asserts that the structure of the nation-state is not working. For it to become a tool for development will require decades of hard work. Nevertheless, Hart advocates that the state take control of agriculture. On the other hand, Barry Munslow sees the nation-state as an *inappropriate* development agent, feeling that its role should be relegated to that of facilitating encouraging "the self-help process at the base."

Hart's state-sponsored farms would surely face two main problems in the West African context. First, land is still held by families across the region. To try to increase agricultural output by creating huge state-run farms would mean a massive appropriation of land by the state. This would run counter to local customs and create a tremendous backlash on the part of civil society, as well as alienate international donors who espouse democratic control of land or private property.

The future role of the nation-state in agricultural development is still unclear. As HICPs, West African nations are seriously involved in SAPs and have had to open their doors to NGOs and **BINGOs**. Future development programs are unlikely to be funded by local sources without massive intervention of Core help. It would seem, then, that if development of rural areas and agriculture were to proceed in West Africa, it would have to come about through the cooperation of the nation-state, IFIs, foreign MNCs, NGOs, BINGOs and perhaps a host of yet unknown participants in this developmental alphabet soup.

In many cases the state has tried to operate through local chiefs. Chiefs have often acted as brokers for the state by supplying labor gangs to work on government projects or on the farms of prominent officials.

Despite their aggrandizing behavior local governments and officials in rural areas can be more effective than dealing with high-level bureaucrats. Chiefs are still influential in West Africa and can be helpful to developers or block their plans. As important interstitial players, chiefs could be key players in future development plans.

Many ineffectual development schemes have come and gone in West Africa and most farmers are quite skeptical about "development" projects. In Northern Ghana some locals call them "disappearing" projects. Local farmers see how the state uses projects for their extractive value. Such schemes have given the government a chance to enter the agricultural economy of the village. With such development projects, government agents begin to distribute agricultural inputs, and attempt to set themselves up as the principal sources of local credit. They also establish government agencies as the primary or only buyer of farm produce—especially cash-crops. This has often been done with little thought for local consequences, even at times of famine. One West African government was negotiating with the World Bank at the time of the mid-1970s famine for a $20 million loan to expand ground-nut production. The project ran from 1974–1978. During this time the government extracted over $12 million from farmers by fixing low prices and by imposing export taxes.

Élites at all levels find ways to collaborate and extract value from the work of rural peoples. With the backing of local chiefs and big men as supporters, government officials become active political agents in the lives of villagers. Today, under SAP pressure, parastatals performing these functions have been forced to privatize, but I am doubtful whether that has really changed the structure of exploitation much. We might ask, "who owns the new companies?" In my experience, it is often the same cadre of élites who were part of the parastatal experience.

I found that among the Sisala of Northern Ghana farmers are benefiting from such companies, nonetheless. The privatized Ghana Cotton Corporation gives loans to farmers against their cotton crop. The inputs are supposed to be used primarily for cash-crop production, but many cotton farmers divert them into maize production, which is actually easier to grow and brings more profit. While this is an imperfect way of getting development funds into the hands of the farmers, it is one of the only available sources of credit in the region.

In some cases, large-scale plantation-like projects have been attempted. State-backed farms or projects have been failing in West Africa though, because there is little labor commitment by workers (many simply leave to return to their small farms), the bureaucracy is large, corrupt and inefficient, and inappropriate methods and technology have been employed. Keith Hart rightly impales these farm cooperatives by saying:

> If the government cannot derive substantial revenues from direct control over the basic conditions of production, the next best thing is to organize farmers in such a way that they must pass over a portion of their product to the government. These initiatives are normally called "cooperatives," but West Africans know what they are: a source of employment for government workers, a nexus of indebtedness to rival the Lebanese storekeeper [who used to act as money-lenders], a means of transferring part of their labor to the state, a monopoly distributor who sells dear and buys cheap, a political payoff to the government's supporters, and a general agent of the state in the local community of farmers [brackets are mine].

The basis of agribusiness and their representative BINGOs is a strategy of "contract farming" or plantations. To increase production of crops they desire, agribusiness has refined the "Green Revolution" package to include bio-engineered seeds and plants, petrochemical technology and utilizes these inputs on large farms using contract labor. This approach fills the needs of global capital, with crops such as pineapples, bananas, spices and even flowers. Since contract farms find it hard to attract laborers, they rely on hi-technology farming methods, which make this approach profitable as long as relatively inexpensive petroleum is available in West Africa. This seems an unlikely long-term strategy.

In Ghana one of the largest contract farmers is Lever Brothers Ghana, a subsidiary of Unilever. Another is Nestle. These are powerful companies with annual operating budgets greater than any West African nation. Others beginning to move in are the giants in biotechnology, Monsanto, DuPont, AgriBiotech, Norvatis and Advanta. The strong financial position of these giants allows them tremendous leverage in dealing with local farmers, and with representatives of the national government from whom they are able to extract concessions. For example, while urban warehouse space may be limited, many have been able to establish storage facilities at international airports in the capital cities. In this way, they can easily and speedily move goods in and out, providing them with rapid air linkage to suppliers and markets throughout the globe. By co-opting West African politicians and bureaucrats, they also get tax waivers, special rights to retain foreign exchange. This is done by the traditional "dash," or by giving them paid advisory positions in the enterprises.

Another limiting factor to rural development is the lack of adequate transport. Maize is in high demand in cities. Many farms are very far from main transport arteries and urban areas. They are at a great disadvantage because formal transport is minimal. It is not uncommon to see private automobiles and NGO vehicles buying food crops in such areas and transporting them back to the cities to sell at great profit.

Also, there is a link between the lack of urban industrial capacity and the failure of modern farming in West Africa. Even where small firms have been created to produce industrial products locally, most West African countries lack sufficient populations to provide markets for all but the cheapest products. In most cases the fledgling companies find it prohibitive to try to compete in the world market. Even where there is a heavy concentration of people, as in Nigeria or Ghana, much of the population is too poor to purchase anything but "penny products." The lack of production in West Africa of high technology has meant that nation-states must import it, at a great expense. This has limited the development of the inappropriate technology. On the other hand, too little has been done to develop more appropriate forms of agricultural technology.

Internal Reasons for Underdevelopment

I have said that arrogance and top-down planning are problems for development specialists, and this is also true of West African politicians and bureaucrats. From the beginning of nationalist movements, the leaders were educated urban élites, for the most part. Throughout West Africa's latter history, metropolitan élites have been cut off from the core of civic life in rural Africa. Their ties with the countryside have been minimal. They live in a world of relative luxury between the Western world and the common people. Why is there so much wealth among a limited class of persons in this poor region? Why does the Mercedes Class exist in a sea of misery? These élites are building a capital base for themselves. Within their networks, their assets are more or less integrated, fungible and protected by formal property systems inherited from the West. They are a privileged few who can afford to hire lawyers, accountants and tax specialists. They have insider connections, personalistic leverage in the bureaucracy and ties with powerful operators in the external economy.

Bourgeois upbringing and education have brought exceptional opportunities to West Africa. Sometimes this has led to class formation and capital accumulation and it has also fomented a brain drain. Bourgeois children, who gain extraordinary skills, say in computers or science, find that they have more opportunities to exercise their knowledge in Europe or the United States. Élitism and a loss of skilled people to the world marketplace help prevent the development of a strong middle class and national civic institutions. Those left behind compete for a limited number of jobs and opportunities. Competition for employment is further narrowed by ethnic identity and religious affiliation. Since wealth and power are so limited and channeled, skills are not distributed on open competition. In short, development suffers as resources are held by the privileged few who are not necessarily the gifted few.

Neocolonialism: Development Blocs from Outside Forces

This neocolonialist system—metropolitan élites in league with wealthy foreigners—continues the dependencies created through European imperialism and colonial domination of the past. It is a system that claims to aim at integration and development, but which in fact impedes them. Here I want to follow Samir Amin in his *Neo-colonialism in West Africa* in which he takes the view that much, if not most, of the backwardness of West Africa is due to external influences, first *via* the impact of *Pax Colonia*, then through neocolonialism. In each phase, Europe has dominated the economy of West Africa, both in terms of the extraction of value from the region, and by creating markets for European products. According to Amin and many others, this *economic* domination was and is more significant than the short period of *political* domination by Europeans in West Africa. More important is the sense that it retarded development of indigenous industries, both those that could have benefited from exports and those that have been dwarfed by European imports.

Neocolonialism is a dominating force that ties the region to the vagaries of the global marketplace. Should there be a sharp downturn in the global economy, consumer products, petroleum, fertilizer and agricultural chemicals simply stop coming. West Africa is heavily dependent on importing goods that it does not produce itself. These goods can only be purchased with foreign exchange. There are three ways governments in West Africa get such hard currency: by selling exports in the world market, by using foreign assistance monies or by taking out loans.

Those who note the debilitating influence of neocolonialism point to a number of obstacles from outside the region. These external blockages can be clarified under the following labels:

* Core domination of commerce, both imports and exports
* Lack of developmental capital investment in the region
* Structural Adjustment Programs (SAPs)
* Debt stranglehold
* The security vacuum leading to capital flight and brain drain

In the main, Core forces of the global economy have imposed these blockages, even the security vacuum which is exacerbated by sales of weapons to the military. The machinery of *direct* external control has shifted in the years since West African independence to economic and political control by *indirect* means—through influence exerted by Core diplomats or companies. Today pressure points have moved to multilateral bodies and NGOs. These G-7-sponsored organizations are even more distant from popular control and accountability than are national West African governments. Furthermore, they are more opaque in their maneuverings. To the people, their mandates from on high come as if out of a dark and distant fog.

Neither long-term viability of political organization nor sustainability in economics are fostered by neocolonial interests. True sustainability means being in control of the technology needed to produce the basics of life. This is easier to do in a West African village than it is in Detroit or London, for one simple reason—the needs of the villagers are only minimally materialistic. If West Africans can find the roots of their communalistic past and revive cooperation at the local level, creating a sustainable infrastructure would be possible.

Outside Aid and Dependency

There are two competing views on aid. One says it is absolutely needed to jumpstart an impoverished region like West Africa. Proponents of aid usually take the moral high ground and claim that to withhold aid from starving people or nations in trouble would be worse than callous. Opponents of aid say that foreign aid, charity donations and loans keep the poor in a state of dependent poverty.

Giving economic aid is part of the foreign policy of the G-7 nations and Islamic proselytizers. Both also claim humanitarian grounds for such help. In principle, the benefits of aid are hard to deny, especially in times of famine, when children are seen wasting away on television sets around the world. But there is another, disturbing view of such seemingly charitable gestures. Food aid to famine-stricken peoples may be the wrong response. In an important study entitled, *Famine that Kills, Darfur, Sudan, 1984–85,* Alexander De Waal found that susceptibility to disease was of greater significance than a lack of food in the battle for survival in famine-stricken areas. He said "there is little evidence that the food relief had any [positive] impact on mortality." It may be that many more people would survive if their villages had proper water supplies, sanitation facilities, health clinics, immunization programs and simple public health services.

It is not the élites who die in such camps. Bill Rau comments on famine in Africa:

> Famine is very much a class issue and those classes affected by famine have been determined by the course of history. Those most affected are predominately rural poor, pastoralists, small farmers, and agricultural labourers who have lost the ability to raise or purchase food. People who are already poor are (and have been) those most likely to have inadequate resources to respond to further hardships. Their positions are already so marginal, their edge of survival already so narrow, that drought, civil war, loss of land to "development" projects, adverse government policies and declining world commodity prices all can precipitate famine.

Foreign aid, famine relief and excessive loans are three examples of a neocolonialist system that saps West Africa's strength. True development comes when people begin to develop themselves. To the extent that the Core Countries help in development, it should be through the provision of appropriate technology and sustainable means.

IFIs and Underdevelopment

Since the 1970s, the United States, Europe and other G-7 powers have increasingly tended to secure their economic interests in West Africa through IFIs and through their influence over international trade regimes such as the WTO. This indirect approach to control reflects the declining interest of the G-7 in West Africa, where trade, loans and investment flows have declined. IFIs support Neoliberalism, the philosophy of international capital. The evolution of neoliberal doctrine can be traced in publications of the World Bank following the collapse of its own state-led modernization model in the 1970's. The importance of macroeconomic fundamentals, and thus structural adjustment in Africa, is outlined in "Accelerated Development in Sub-Saharan Africa: Agenda for Action" (1981) and "Sub-Saharan Africa: From Crisis to Sustainable Growth" (1989). *The 1990 World Development Report* (WDR) reemphasized the importance of public investment in basic services and infrastructure (public goods). The 1991 WDR canonized the "market-friendly approach" to development that combines macroeconomic stability (SAPism) with global integration (open international markets), a domestic climate that facilitates efficient private investment (microeconomic liberalization), and public "investment in people" (health and education as the bases for human capital formation). The 1999/2000 WDR adds that enabling institutions, including those that form functional political and judicial systems, are critical to making markets work efficiently and for the benefit of the majority.

Events in the world have changed the approach to Africa and created a drift to the right by policy makers. In the 1980s IFIs tried to strengthen the nation-state, now neoliberal programs try to weaken it. For West African countries experiencing economic decline, two IFI policy documents changed the nature of development planning in the region—the "1981 Accelerated Development in Sub-Saharan Africa" and the "1989 Sub-Saharan Africa, From Crisis to Sustainable Growth." These documents provided the policy framework for SAPs. Both negatively assessed the role of West African states in agricultural development.

It is important to realize that SAPs are new, and are *experimental* procedures intended to compensate for the failure of IFI programs in the 1980s. They tend to weaken the power of the state in both commerce and in the area of service delivery. The aim of SAPs is to privatize economic functions of the state, and to make the nation-state more socially responsible according to policies devised by Core interests. Whether West African governments continue to give in to such pressure, or unite in supra-national blocs to fight back remains to be seen.

SAPs and other IFI programs are about control. In association with the World Bank, IMF economists and advisors have laid down requirements for West African governments that amount to direct control of the internal affairs of these developing countries. SAPs can be seen as a form of neocolonialism by increasing direct control of funding to West African governments and the disposition of their loan funds. But they are more than that—SAPs also now dictate social policies, telling governments where to spend their money and how much to put into different sectors of society. The IMF effectively acts as an agent for all international creditors. It can dictate economic policy to the poorest countries, impose economic austerity programs, undermine fledgling democracies and withhold assistance. Politicos in West Africa are under pressure to conform to the dictates of the West. Again Bill Rau:

> For the majority of rural people well being, if not survival, became more dependent on the interaction between national élite and international financiers, policy-makers and development planners. In...Niger, the government was required by its chief donors to sell off its major grain reserves (maintained against possible shortages) in order to repay its debts to French banks.

The pressure on the nation-state has been intense. Most West African governments have relented. However the SAPs have initially hurt the already weakened African economies, creating hardships and social protests in West Africa. There have been sharp declines in real income, hitting urban populations hardest, as they were most dependent on food imports and the largest users of foreign manufactured goods.

The watchword of the New Consensus of the Neoliberals has become **Conditionality**. The new pressure on African governments to conform to IFI dictates came in the form of making both short-term balance-of-payments credits and long-term development loans conditional on adoption of the structural adjustment policies advocated by international capital. Whereas SAPs may have started out as suggestions, they have been laden with stipulations. Conditionality has locked West African governments into new forms of dependent relationships with Core Countries. Tony Binns says:

> Not since the days of colonialism have external forces been so powerfully focused in shaping Africa's economic structure and the nature of its participation in the world system.

Specific SAP policies have involved such measures as currency devaluation, major expenditure cuts and a reorientation towards agriculture, rehabilitation of corrupt structures and maintenance of good governance. Taxes on consumer goods have risen, wage increases restricted, price controls reduced and producer prices for cash-crops increased. Government-owned assets have been privatized and attempts have been made to improve the efficiency of remaining governmental institutions. Increased competition and flexibility have been introduced into agricultural marketing.

The significance of conditions imposed by the IMF is twofold. First, in the hierarchy of international financial institutions the IMF ranks highest. Compliance with IMF conditions enables governments to receive the "seal of approval" that permits access to other international creditors and investors. Thus IMF conditions weigh especially heavily upon borrowing governments. Second, it is quite common that World Bank loans have, as their first requirement, compliance with certain IMF conditions. This is known as cross conditionality. Where the IMF goes, so follows the World Bank.

There is a ray of hope at present. Social protests around the world by activists and grassroots groups represent an awakening cognizance of the problem of IFI interference in the internal affairs of sovereign nations in the Periphery. As yet, in Africa, only countries with strong civic cultures like South Africa, are voicing such objections. In February, 2001 representatives of 4,000 NGOs, churches, the media and community organizations met with World Bank delegates to discuss the Global Development Gateway project. They voted to oppose the GDG initiative and to work towards a more appropriate development network in its place. The Global Development Gateway project had the stated objective of promoting local community organizations and their information initiatives. Civil society spokespersons disagreed, saying that its true intention was to control the development information discourse to promote its own particular aims. After decades of World Bank interference in community life, these opposition groups took action. They defined the World Bank as interfering with community life and attempting to dominate it.

Even Neoliberals like Jeffrey Sachs have seemingly turned around and are calling for a radical reform of IFIs. Sachs has said:

> The World Bank needs to do less country lending and more to create and disseminate knowledge for development... the IMF should get out of development altogether and go back to monitoring global financial markets... [They should stop] lecturing poor countries about weak governance, while providing precious little money for technological advance, public health and other needs... [my brackets].

Debt Dependency

Many Peripheral Countries have fallen deeply into debt to foreign lenders and IFIs. The more severely indebted are called HIPCs, or Highly Indebted Poor Countries. Most if not all ECOWAS countries are so classified. In the 1980s a combination of factors led to worsening trade and West African governments were forced to borrow more and more, with soaring interest payments. In 1984, for example, the external debt of the Ivory Coast was equal to 90% of their annual GNP. The debt burden became so staggering that most of their earnings from exports went right back to the West in the form of interest payments on loans. Sara Berry says:

> From 1985 to 1990, Sub-Saharan Africa paid out more, in interest and debt repayment, to the IMF and the World Bank combined than it received from them in the form of grants and loans.

Africa is the world's most aid-dependent and indebted region. Loan forgiveness is essential if Africa is to grow rapidly while increasing consumption to reduce poverty. Excluding private inflows, the savings gap for a typical country is about 17% of GDP, and other regions show that private flows cannot be sustained at more than 5% of GDP without risk of crisis. But aid, particularly when delivered in a weak institutional environment by large numbers of donors with fragmented projects and requirements, can weaken institutional capacity and undermine accountability.

Quite understandably, bankers and lending organizations insist that loans are not gifts, and need to be repaid. The African perspective is quite different. Most African governments say the continent will only be able to develop if the billions owed to the World Bank and IMF are unconditionally forgiven. Some of the poorest countries in Sub-Saharan Africa spend a quarter of their revenues servicing foreign debt. If the IFIs forgave the debt and gave out no more ill advised loans, the HIPCs automatically would have 25% more working capital and would not need to go further in debt just to get by.

In June 1999, G-7 leaders were embarrassed by protests. The clamor for change was taken up again at Jubilee 2000, where millions around the world rallied behind the call for an end to the extraction of value from the poor through debt servicing. G-7 leaders were forced to respond with a pledge to write off $100 billion of poor country debts "within a matter of weeks." As of this writing, little has been done to fulfill this promise.

Little relief has been forthcoming in Africa. By June 1999, only 2.6% of the debts of 41 indebted countries had been written off—Uganda and Moçambique being the only two African countries on the list. However, their gains were quickly wiped out by rising interest payments required by the World Bank. One hand gives, the other takes away. The total debt of the HIPCs remained unchanged: $216 billion in 1996 and $216 billion in 1998. Also, debt service paid by the most indebted nations of the world (the poorest), rose from $25 billion a year to $28 billion in 1998.

As of now the only West African country to receive any debt relief has been Mauritania, a 31% reduction. It will now only have to pay $80 million a year in interest payments! This, in spite of the fact that 50% of Mauritania's people continue to live below the poverty line of one dollar a day.

It is likely that creditors will continue to dominate the lending process unless an independent international arbiter is set up to serve as a watchdog organization in this regard. Needed are a new partnership and a revised regulatory framework for monitoring credit relations between poor nations and their public and private creditors. When debts become unpayable, such arbiters should have the authority to require accountability from both sides. They should function to encourage public scrutiny of lending operations, participation and accountability by wealthy creditors and poor governments alike, and prevent the ongoing cycle of high levels of recurring debt and default.

Jubilee 2000 has suggested one possible framework to make these things happen. It is an independent Debt Review Body (DRB) based on the concept of arbitration, which would guarantee transparency and the participation of civil society in the process. This could be channeled through the United Nations or the International Court of Justice. A country with debt problems could apply for an independent review of its debt, and for debt cancellation. During the review, the debt payments would go to finance the proceedings. The DRB would act as a binding arbitration panel. They would work with the debtor government, lenders and civil society to draw up documents concerning the dispersal of any debt relief funds.

The Move to NGOs and BINGOs

Although new forms of NGOs aligned with the private sector (BINGOs, see below) are emerging, the old-style NGOs are still out there and they are speaking out about neocolonialist practices. For example, Christian Aid says that there are many cases where fledgling African industries are drowned by cheap imports because of SAPs and enforced liberalization. They complain that the requirement to open West African markets to international competition is hurting people of the region. Liberalization is causing some small businesses in West Africa to go under, for example, in the poultry business: "Excess exports of poultry from the United States or the EU are dumped into Africa at subsidised prices" reported the BBC, "undermining local livelihoods and destroying local domestic industries."

While some NGOs protest neocolonialism by the IFIs, others are favored by them. While IFIs push for privatization of public services, they often take a direct approach by pulling an end run on West African governments. They fund NGOs, missions, European-based organizations, foreign donors and those they deem to be more efficient. To cite one example in the field of health care: much of the finance of, and policy control within, this sector is external to West Africa. Even control of health has been taken away. One can see why many West African politicians are decrying the usurpation of sovereignty by international agencies.

Based on Core definitions of governmental failure in West Africa, IFIs have also turned to NGOs to implement agricultural development projects instead of governmental agencies. Certainly government did not do a great job, but NGOs do not have a great track record either. IFI planners see NGOs as closer to the people and therefore able to avoid the pitfalls of top-down planning carried out by West African government agencies. But from another perspective, NGOs can be seen as part of the underdevelopment process. There is no reason to believe that they are suddenly going to make a big difference in the neocolonialist venture. As self-perpetuating bureaucratic organizations, they can be seen as part of the problem, not the solution.

Even worse are BINGOs. They are for-profit NGOs or those closely aligned with commercial interests under the new privatization guidelines of the IFIs. They are interested in export crops, commercializing farming and in species and genetic material capable of being patented. The move away from state control of agriculture has increased reliance on BINGOs at international, national and local levels. As agents for the private sector, these organizations have taken over the role of the state in several areas of the agricultural sector in order to sustain it. The intensity of NGO involvement in West African agriculture since the 1980s has been unprecedented. This can be seen in the dramatic increase in their numbers, and in their shift in focus, under IFI prompting, toward commercial concerns.

IFIs are now trying to work out a new adjustment strategy where NGOs, BINGOs and nation-states can work together, which if you think about it, is circumventing the stated neoliberal ideals of *laissez faire* and an open marketplace. We don't know how this new political economy will work, but if it follows suit, it will provide opportunities for **rent taking** by metropolitan élites and will greatly enhance the commercial foothold of international capital in West Africa.

The nation-state and NGOs have had an uneasy relationship in the past. The state is not enamored with the rising power of NGOs as they are seen to threaten ownership of programs and sovereignty. Their motivation to support agricultural research and development must be stimulated if the region is ever going to be able to feed itself again. Progress in this field will depend on a shift away from export crops such as cotton and cocoa and toward food crops for internal consumption. Export of food should occur only if a surplus is achieved. This is unlikely without a radical turnaround of the IFI/G-7 commitment to privatization and the extractive measures already in place. A policy change will necessitate more state-NGO cooperation and a reduction in the tension in that relationship. In short, it is not probable that there will be any sharp deviation from the privatization undertaking moving NGOs in the direction of greater involvement in commerce.

States have made mistakes but the NGOs are not entirely blameless. They consistently produce reports and television programs that portray Africans as being inherently weak, dependent, passive and needy recipients of outside aid, incapable of confronting their own problems. The implication is that this is an intrinsic condition of the African people, or the fault of African governments. In reality, famines and food dependence are at least partially a result of the network of trade ties between exploiting foreign companies and their transnational allies, the WTO, IMF and World Bank, as well as a host of NGOs and relief agencies. NGO workers are sometimes accused of being spies, operating as they do with a certain degree of secrecy. Furthermore, sometimes in their role as advocates or critics, NGOs highlight the failings of the state. In another sense, funds that go to NGOs are not flowing through the hands of state operatives. Yet again, NGOs are often seen by state bureaucrats as an alternative power base, and hence a threat to power holders within the state apparatus. By helping the disadvantaged members of society, or strengthening the institutions of civil society, NGOs could be building up a revolutionary power base.

In conclusion, with the "NGOization" of the development process, we can expect a continuation of the unequal power/dependence relation between the forces of international capital and West Africa. The shift to NGOs and BINGOs is likely to lead to a move away from issues of equity and poverty eradication, except through so-called "trickle down" measures resulting from the growth of commerce, such as they might *someday* be (See **Trickle down economics** in the glossary).

Corporations, Privatization and Development

IFI policy is to encourage governments to divest themselves of direct government control of commercial ventures. What heavy industry exists is primarily foreign-owned. Given the lack of a strong industrial infrastructure and a largely unskilled labor force, West Africa is mainly attractive for mining and drilling operations that rely on a small cadre of highly-skilled expatriates. One of the new thrusts of privatization is contract farming to grow cut flowers, pineapples, shea nuts, bananas and cashews as export crops to supplement revenues from traditional crops such as cocoa, groundnuts and cotton. Certainly IFIs have created a neoliberal "open-arms" environment for commerce, though it remains to be seen how much actual development this produces.

For reasons of environmental and political instability, corporations have viewed West Africa with skepticism. Corporations manage risk, and given the fluidity of the global marketplace today, they do not need to make long-term investments in places that are perceived to pose problems. Some large corporations already have established roots in the region—Shell Oil, Kaiser Aluminum, Firestone Rubber, Nestles and UAC, for example. Corporations do try to limit their risks and maximize their gains. One of the factors they evaluate is the political stability of a state, as well as things like proximity to production facilities, the skill level of in-country labor and the buying power of the populace for their products. West Africa comes up short in such analyses and many MNCs have avoided investment in West Africa.

MNCs directly interact with nation-states. To an extent, sovereign states control MNCs, are controlled by them, and MNCs exercise their ingenuity in eluding state jurisdiction. This is the typical interaction of sovereign states and business in the late twentieth century. In West Africa, then, nation-states are under outside pressure from both IFIs and MNCs, and have to deal increasingly with NGOs and the new transformation, BINGOs. This is the climate of the political economy in West Africa. The state is not free to act alone, constantly having to deal with these outside forces, but neither are the other actors entirely free, though taken collectively MNCs, IFIs, NGOs and BINGOs are a formidable penetrating force in the region.

From the very beginning in West Africa, adventurers and traders operated outside the law and bent what rules there were in the favor of European traders. To varying degrees, this continues today. As with days of old, MNCs today are not very concerned with social progress. The actions of Kaiser Aluminum in Ghana or Firestone Rubber in the

Ivory Coast are no different than corporations around the globe—profits and the bottom line drive thinking. One blatant example of crass disregard for human life and environmental integrity is the piratical actions of Royal Dutch Shell in Nigeria. Nigerian newspapers are awash with stories claiming that Shell Oil actually secretly and privately imported weapons into Nigeria. News stories claimed that this was to ensure their continued ability to exploit the Niger Delta region in the face of opposition by local peoples who believe that the European company is destroying the environment, while raping their valued resources with little benefit to them. The wealth and power of such bandit organizations enables them to corrupt national and local officials and police to get them to aid in such exploitation. What men like George Goldie started, these pirates continue.

On March 26, 2001 BBC News Online reported that Shell was to be sued in a New York court. The United States Supreme Court ruled that families of two environmental activists executed in Nigeria could sue the MNC. The families brought the case against oil exploration by Shell in the Ogoni region of Nigeria. The suit alleges that the corporation took land without paying proper compensation, polluted the atmosphere and paid for local police to suppress opposition. The torture and execution of two of the activists opposing Shell, the famed author Ken Saro-Wiwa and John Kpuinen, led to Nigeria's suspension from the Commonwealth. The suit alleges that Royal Dutch Petroleum, and its sister company Shell Transport and Trading, fabricated evidence to support murder charges against the two men.

Shell fought the suit but the Supreme Court rejected Shell's argument that United States federal courts lack jurisdiction over alleged violations of international law that occur abroad. Under United States law, claims can be made against companies on human rights grounds and many Nigerians consider Shell to be a blatant privateer with little regard for human rights or environmental integrity.

In spite of these allegations, the company is firmly entrenched in Nigeria. Shell is the largest oil operator in Nigeria, with the oil coming from the Niger Delta providing most of Nigeria's export earnings and government income. The company has tremendous power in the region. The local Ogoni people feel they are getting little back from the company's exploitation of their natural resources. Their anger at Shell has become a major source of tension in the region. Local rage was most famously mobilized by the late Mr. Saro-Wiwa, but in all parts of the Niger Delta protesters have blocked access roads, occupied production platforms and, on occasion, sabotaged pipelines. It is reported that armed Ogoni gangs openly do battle with heavily armed Shell-sponsored gangs.

Taken as a whole, foreign interests in the region have been exploitative and have shown little regard for the environment or the health and welfare of the local people. Capitalism both creates and destroys, but such frontier zones have tended to ignore the long-term environmental and social costs of their behavior.

Falling Aid and Trade in Africa

Of late both foreign aid to Africa and international trade with the region has fallen off drastically. Since the late 1960s Africa's loss of world trade has cost it almost $70 billion a year, reflecting a failure to diversify into new, dynamic products as well as a falling market share for traditional goods. The ease of capital movement is partly to blame for the fall in trade. The global economy is clearly moving to a different level, with more fluidity of capital and more interdependence between local, regional and national economies. In this new economic environment, profit can be had with quick movements of capital from one part of the globe to another. Capital is fleeing Africa for other domains. Whereas West Africa needs patient, long-term investment to build up a manufacturing base, and to enhance its agricultural infrastructure, international capital has sought profits in global zones seen as less risky and/or more profitable.

Investment funds and trade are going to the NICs, the former Soviet Union, the old Iron Curtain countries and to the newly democratized Republic of South Africa (RSA). With the economic prosperity of East Asia, Africa has fallen even farther behind. In globalization, trade, manufacturing and financial markets have been changing, as fixed rates have given way to variable ones. The volume of international capital movements has grown astronomically, dwarfing output from international production of goods and services. This fluidity has hurt trade in Africa.

David Dollar of the Development Research Group of the World Bank has been conducting a research project on "Aid and Reform in Africa." The aim of the project was to arrive at a better understanding of the links between foreign aid and policy reforms in Africa. Recent cross-country evidence has shown that foreign aid has a strong, positive effect on a country's economic performance *if* the country has embarked on policy and structural reforms. Paradoxically, the evidence also shows that countries with good policies receive less assistance than countries with poor or mediocre policies. The juxtaposition of these two findings has led to the assertion that "aid cannot buy reform." The aim was to analyze the reform processes rather than the results. To achieve their objective, researchers undertook a series of country case studies in Africa. Each case study examined the nature of external assistance and the causes and paths of reforms in different policy areas, and attempted to trace a relationship between the two. The project included *Côte d'Ivoire*, the Democratic Republic of Congo, Ethiopia, Ghana, Kenya, Mali, Nigeria, Tanzania, Uganda and Zambia. The final report, published March 27, 2001, shows that aid to governments that are not interested in reforming their institutions is wasted money. It demonstrates that foreign aid is unlikely to help poor countries, and may even hurt them, unless they have already decided on and begun serious policy reforms on their own.

What is also paradoxical about this report is that just when SAPs have been implemented in Africa, and when some African countries such as Ghana are struggling to make adjustments, bilateral per capita aid to Africa has diminished. What is happening? Not only has aid to Peripheral Countries in general fallen off of late, but also help to Sub-Saharan Africa has become almost nonexistent relative to lending to other poor countries. As the OECD's *Development Cooperation Report 1997* shows, not a single Sub-Saharan African country was listed in the top ten largest recipients of bilateral development assistance (1995–96). Aid funds are limited and they have been flowing to other hot spots around the world, some of which are deemed more strategically important to G-7 countries.

Solutions to Underdevelopment

While development economists still debate the pros and cons of SAPs, West African governments are deeper in debt, the people have no greater control of modern production, foreign firms are doing better than ever and West Africans are more dependent on the importation of goods by foreign companies. Diminishing the role of the nation-state, while good in some respects, has merely opened the way to more direct control by international capital, which has not led to improvement in social security or development of the region.

Neoliberals see the market as the main driver of globalization and development. They advise all nations to open their doors by dropping tariffs and any blocks to free trade. They see the nation-state playing less of a role in the future, with globalization unfolding freely without government "interference." They believe that, initially, opening West African markets to competition from other countries may hurt people and reduce the delivery of social services but that, in the long run, wealth will "trickle down" and all will benefit from "free" trade. To Neoliberals the nation-state should step aside and let the market define globalization's path. Development should be a result of allowing market forces into a country, most of it being performed by private enterprise.

Neoliberals are hostile to state provisioning and state funding. Privatization of aid has been accomplished by decreasing funds to governments, while increasing them to NGOs and BINGOs and by using SAPs to pressure governments to divest themselves of marketing boards and other rent seeking agencies. It is thought that this will limit government influence, licit and illicit. Of course, this policy overlooks the fact that managerial élites are in limited supply in West Africa, and many of the people who dominated government-sponsored boards and parastatals are the same people running privatized companies.

On the other side of the ledger, there are Statists. They claim that the nation-state is a strong player in the globalization process and, ultimately, it is the main actor in controlling it. Their philosophy fell from favor with the rise of Neoliberalism, but is gaining a comeback. Now they believe that a strong state is necessary to guide development. Statists point to the success of the NICs of East Asia where the state is strong. They claim that the NICs have risen in economic power *because* of their strong states. Historical Structuralists agree with the Neoliberals that the market is the main driver of globalization, but also see state decisions as important determinants of development policy.

What if the pundits such as John Naisbitt are right in predicting the demise of the nation-state? He says:

> The nation-state is dead. Not because nation-states were subsumed by superstates, but because they are breaking up to smaller, more efficient parts—just like big companies.

If nation-states have been "hollowed out" to the extent that they are worthless, Africa's reification of the nation-state as the quintessential mode of governmentality is behind the times. It should move forward to develop at least stronger regional economic blocs and perhaps follow the suggestion of Kwame Nkrumah and Mu'ammar Gadhafi to develop a United States of Africa.

In my opinion, even though the West African state has been wounded by globalization, it is likely to remain as a mediating structure (and a prebendal one too). It will continue to act as a transactional agent between IFIs, MNCs, NGOs and civil society. The latter is mainly a minor player, even a benchwarmer, in the competitive game being played today. Some seek basic resources (oil, minerals, wood), some markets and others the attention of the citizenry.

The prestige of the nation-state was up, then down and now it seems to be rising again, at least in the eyes of the agencies fostering SAPs. In March 2001 the IMF Executive Board met to discuss allegations that the agency had overstepped its bounds in mandating policy to peripheral governments, thereby short-circuiting national decision-making. The loss of sovereignty issue has arisen out of IFI moves into areas of governance for which they have doubtful expertise. An IMF spokesperson said: "the aim of streamlining should be to leave the maximum possible scope for countries to make their own policy choice...." If he had stopped there, it would have made some happy, but he continued: "while ensuring that the Fund's financing is provided only if those policies that are essential to the purpose of the Fund continue to be implemented." Assuredly, Fund bureaucratic interests are never far from policy decisions.

Conclusions

Let's assume that West African politicians can do something to develop their states further. What should they do? Given the enormous power of the global economy, this really is asking if they should open up their economies to international capital, or not. But it is more complicated than that. What if the raging bull of global capitalism suddenly dies? What if the world is not destined to have a universal capitalistic system, but several different kinds? The question then shifts to asking what kind of capitalism does West Africa want, or even, will there be a singular type of capitalism for all of West Africa, or will Togo have a sort that is different from Senegal's style and which is yet again different from Nigeria's oil-rich format, and so forth. Could there be a regional ECOWAS style? Again, if some form of governance is going to be necessary in the future, what will be its international nature? Will it be a federalist system with decentralized pockets of diversity, or could we see the rise of strong centralized states to cope with the problems of the future?

Recent World Bank estimates show African economies improving in 2002 from about 2.5% growth to 3.5%. That's the good news. The bad news is that those gains will be more than eaten up by a rapidly rising population that will double the continent's population by 2025. It seems that unless something is done, Africa is in for more of the same economic stagnation.

Campaigners from around the world, from both Core and Periphery, are increasingly calling for a more just, independent and accountable process for managing relations between peripheral debtors and their public and private creditors. Transparency is a key issue. It is clear that the creditors cannot continue to play the role of plaintiff, judge and jury. They cannot be allowed to continue to make the rules behind closed doors. To prevent future crises, there must be a brake on capital flows that serve to corrupt governments in poor countries. More discipline and transparency in the process is necessary, but will probably not be possible without pressure from a stronger civil society and a free press, both of which tend to be weak in West Africa.

Another strategy is withdrawal or protectionism—closing the doors to WTO measures and the interference of the IFIs. Neoliberals dominate macroeconomic policy today and they deride any attempts at protectionism as antediluvian. Jeffrey Sachs advocates opening up West African economies to the outside world but cautiously:

> The current pattern of the rich countries—to provide financial aid to tropical Africa while blocking Africa's chances to export textiles, footwear, leather goods, and other labour-intensive products—may be worse than cynical. It

may in fact fundamentally undermine Africa's chances for economic development. The advice of the World Bank may also have to be rethought. Integrated rural development may sound equitable and effective, but it can be wishful thinking. If disease, poor soil, unreliable rainfall, pests, and other tropical ills so deeply harm tropical agricultural in large parts of Africa, then priority should go to industrial zones, ports, warehousing and customs facilities, and other infrastructural needs of manufacturing exporters.

Contra protectionism, the idea behind **Trade Liberalization**, is to dismantle costly and largely ineffective government controls on commerce, to reduce élite access to prebendal siphoning from development funds. Neoliberal economists would have us believe peripheral countries like Mauritania and The Gambia will do better if they join the globalization movement. But, these economists ignore the fact that this has not worked so far.

One of the key questions is whether West Africa, or any nation of the region, can do it alone. Can development proceed as a purely internal matter? Historically, during colonialism and in what I have termed a neocolonialist era, Africans have looked to the outside world for help. They have sought Western technology, loans and financial aid from nations, agencies or NGOs. They have even wistfully hoped that African-Americans and others of the African diaspora would be interested in helping. The angst over what little support has been forthcoming from this quarter is painfully summed up in the title of an article I ran across in a journal recently—"Waiting for Oprah." Of course, the problem in getting outside help is the lack of control of how much help, what kind of help and when the help is given or stopped.

We have to ask: what are the consequences of the imposition of outside help? To answer such a question, it is important to be aware of what is happening today in the larger global economy. Good or socially-responsible capitalism fosters social cohesion; **Bad Capitalism** breaks forms of social organization apart. Unfortunately, **Good Capitalism** is not cost-effective in the short-run. Bad Capitalism easily out-competes it, but destroys society in the process, so its long-term benefits are lost. International capitalism is a snake eating its own tail. If these kinds of effects are being generated in New Zealand and Mexico, how much more vulnerable are places like Cape Verde or Niger? When the environmentally damaging effects of slash-and-burn capitalism are added into the equation, pulling out would seem to be the sensible thing. If capitalist companies are voracious consumers of nature and polluters to boot, it does not seem rational to link up with such a system.

Furthermore, Historical Structuralists such as myself do not think that the choice is between "integrate" or "don't integrate" into the global economy. Rather we see Peripheral Countries as being articulated with and feeding the Core. We say that capitalism is able to grow by integrating some outside economies into it, but also by keeping others on the Periphery. Marginal economies may just provide value to capitalism without actually becoming capitalist. Whatever the future direction of this articulation, the present state of marginal countries is that they are being greatly influenced by the world system, but their legal structures have not yet been converted in such a way as to allow true capitalism in their regions.

So another question presents itself to leaders of Peripheral Countries: "do we want to be involved in unequal exchanges with the more powerful Core Countries?" Most West African politicians have answered that already—they have wholeheartedly embraced adjustment programs of the IFIs. Beginning in the 1980s the IFIs stepped in to link foreign aid to economic liberalization. By the 1990s they were making official grants and loans that were conditioned on replacing authoritarian governments with multiparty democracy. Some military dictatorships have been replaced by multiparty systems while others, such as Gnassingbé Eyadéma of Togo, have maneuvered within the context of seemingly democratic institutions to hold onto anti-democratic means of governance. But today Eyadéma is the exception that proves the rule. Most West African leaders tend to cooperate according to IFI rules.

Yet, logically, given the long history of dominating and underdeveloping forces at work in West Africa, there are two reasons to pull out of involvement with IFIs and the Neoliberal Program. First, it has led to, and continues to lead to, exploitation and unequal exchange that has resulted in ongoing backwardness, not development. Second, there are thinkers who see the rapid expansion of international capitalism as a short-term phenomenon. They do not believe the Enlightenment credo that Western culture will engulf diverse cultures. For example, John Gray believes that the 21st century will see a decline in Western influence, especially that by the United States. He envisions a world of declining hegemony, where old monoliths such as East and West no longer apply. He says:

> We have entered an era of Occidental twilight. It is not an era in which all Asian countries will prosper and all western countries decline. It is an age in which the identification of "the West" with modernity is being severed. The very idea of "the West" may already be archaic—the old polarities of East and West do not capture the diversity of cultures and regimes in the world today.

The inexorable development of a global market does not necessarily advance a universal civilization, but it makes the interpenetration of cultures a dominant feature of our global circumstance.

I am dubious about Neoliberal Optimism. All universalistic reformers—be they communist or capitalist, secular or religious are seemingly convinced that a rational world is possible. I am not so sure. The core of the Soviet system was based on the idea that human beings, especially peasants and the bourgeoisie, must be reshaped to fit the needs of a "rational" economy. Likewise, the goal of the agents of Neoliberalism is to homogenize populations everywhere, to Americanize them—turning them into consumers of the first order. Both plans seem overly buoyant to my mind.

In thinking about the future, two widely diverse views exist. On the one hand, is the economic argument *a la* Julian Simon's *The ultimate resource*, which gleefully states that capitalist expansion can continue forever because as we approach production-created problems, the profits to be derived from fixing them technologically will drive capitalism to repair itself. Thus, as an economic system it is self-healing. On the other hand, environmental thinkers and many social scientists tend to regard this view as ludicrous. Rather, they see capitalism being halted by a lack of raw materials (primarily petroleum) and by its tendency to concentrate wealth in the hands of a few, which eventually reaches a point where social cohesion breaks down and capitalism's base falls away. That such diverse views of capitalism's future exist should give pause to those tied to it in dependent ways.

Whatever the future holds for West Africa, some form of governance will be required. I am going to recommend that the reader thinks about different options—family firms on the Asian model, a federalist system as Nigeria is attempting to use, or as was implemented in Taiwan. Perhaps a regional or federal system could redirect inputs to local governments so that they could be used to develop agriculture and small businesses. Taiwan serves as a model of what can be done in this vein. Gray notes that in the middle decades of the last century, Taiwan "implemented a far-reaching land reform in which farmland was redistributed to create a rural economy of small farms." Any student of West Africa knows that the region is already dotted with small farms, so such a step is unnecessary. In Taiwan, from the 1950s onwards, state-owned enterprises were fazed out. Again, this has been proceeding in West Africa under SAPs. The ground is fertile for the development of this next organizational form—the family farm and the family firm. It worked in Taiwan. With such a decentralized economy Taiwan has averaged around 9% growth during the post-World War II period.

Another option would be a strong centralized nation-state, as one finds among some of the NICs of East Asia. The East Asian and Japanese model of capitalist development demonstrates that development can result from a nation-state active in economic affairs. There seems to be a better fit between African civilization and that in Asian societies than exists between Africa and the culture of her former colonists.

Perhaps West Africa would do better to abandon its fascination with things western, and look inward to its own civilized strengths—family, community and trading skills, taking a pointer from Asia. A more socially-oriented and humane variant of capitalism is alive and well in East Asia. It is based on values and social forms common to West Africa. Just as in Japan, West Africans build trading linkages based on kinship relations and trust. Whereas Western capitalism has seen a separation of community and market, in Japan, business is far less disconnected from the structure of their surrounding communities than American corporations. According to Gray, "Their relations with the institutions of the state are close and continuous. The ethical life which Japanese capitalism expresses is not individualist and shows no signs of becoming so."

Neoliberals in IFIs are encouraging reform, but on a Western model. Perhaps West Africans need to find an alternate path to renew their ties with their own past. Given disastrous record of underdevelopment since independence, now is the time for reform. The new century offers a window of opportunity to reverse the marginalization of its people—and of its governments, relative to donors, in the development agenda. Political participation has increased sharply in the past decade, paving the way for more accountable governments, and there is greater consensus on the need to move away from the failed models of the past. With the end of the Cold War, Africa is no longer an ideological and strategic battleground where "trusted allies" receive foreign assistance regardless of their record on governance and development. Globalization and new technology, especially information technology, offer great potential for Africa, historically a sparsely populated, isolated region. Though these factors also pose risks, including that of being left further behind, these are far outweighed by the potential benefits.

As one trained in the empirical field methods of anthropology, I would recommend starting with what West African entrepreneurs are actually doing. Homegrown capitalism is alive and well in the **parallel economy**. Basil Davidson and Barry Munslow cite the case of flourmills in Nigeria. Most work to capacity, but most of the produce disappears from official ledgers, going into the parallel economy. They comment: "If this is happening, why can't we say let it happen? Let us assist it to happen and open all of the gates. If you do that, then if it works it works." Rather than trying to stamp out "illegal behavior" West African leaders should recognize entrepreneurship for what it is—initiative. They should embrace it and model the economy on it. Managerial élites find this difficult to do. Many of the problems in development efforts derive from the haughtiness of élites, the government officials and development planners who think they know more than the people. By imposing plans that have been developed according to élite interests, and not those of the people, they create systems that eventually fail. Paper plans mean nothing if the interests of the people are not involved in their formation. As Andrzej Rapacznski says, "individuals have an incentive to follow their own interests, regardless of any paper constraints." Beyond this, so-called experts rarely ask members of the target community to get involved in the planning process. Thus, the paper plans don't fit the reality on the ground.

It is not the illegal behavior of people practicing entrepreneurship in the parallel economy that is the problem, but their recognition that corruption in high places makes their clandestine activities necessary. Corruption and cronyism in high places in much of West Africa has prompted social disintegration and a disparity between extralegal strategies and legal rules. Most West Africans have now come to realize the formulas for modernization have been better at lining the pockets of élites than those of those who sorely need help. This has led some people to vote with their feet and go abroad. Those who cannot, vote by working around the government in a variety of informal and extralegal ways. This rise in smuggling and extralegal behavior indicates that the state in places like Benin, Nigeria and Senegal have lost credibility in the peoples' eyes. The transformation of a large part of the economy into "illegal" profiteering and various petty strategies to survive does little to provide West African governments with needed tax revenues. All they are getting from the people are complaints and demands, and little to relieve the growing headache of debt burden and a shrinking revenue base. By embracing the way the effective economy actually works, West African leaders could begin to tax it and learn from it.

Shigeto Tsuru has reminded us of John Stuart Mill's observation that "a stationary condition of capital and production need not be a stationary state of human improvement." In other words, if Africa can find her core and develop a form of socially-oriented capitalism, perhaps focusing on regional trade and internal development, it need not be isolationist defeatism. It could prove to be a better form of capitalism than the brand being volunteered by the Washington Consensus.

African leaders need to ask some fundamental questions:

* What is our approach to personhood?
* What is our approach to society?
* What is our approach to the environment?

I think that in looking to their ancestral ways, Africans will find a sustainable path to the future. It is a path with signposts that say:

* The person only develops when the whole group develops.
* Society comes first.
* Society cannot develop without a respect for the environment.

Such values will have to be operationalized through some form of governmentality. Two models seem attractive for West Africa. First is a federalist system that gives maximum freedom to and support of local governments. This would put government closer to the people, giving them more direct control over decision-making. Second is a regional government of oversight to deal with external affairs, maintenance of regional order and so forth. These two approaches could work in tandem and both are presaged in the parallel economy that crosses national borders and has its basis in the people, not in élite economic plans.

Whatever form of government develops in West Africa, even if it is the likely continuation of the inherited nation-state, development planners should strive to create an economy that is founded on two great underpinning principles: 1) Sustainability of an economy that can last through time using local resources in ways that do not harm the environment or future generations; and 2) Maximum equity where wealth should be allocated first to the creation of proper health and social services.

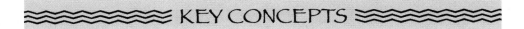

CRITICAL THINKING QUESTIONS

1. What similarities and differences are there between the development approach under colonialism and in the post-independence era?
2. To what extent has the lack of development been due to acts of God, or to human error?
3. Discuss the relation between arrogance by élites and top-down development planning.
4. According to the author, what is the difference between inappropriate technology and appropriate technology and how do they relate to the concept of sustainability?
5. How do export crops impact food production in West Africa?
6. Why can't farmers or entrepreneurs easily get credit for development purposes in West Africa? What is De Soto's perspective on this?
7. Discuss the various ways élites take rents in West Africa.
8. Discuss the role of NGOs and the variant forms of them in the development process in West Africa.
9. What is Neocolonialism?
10. What is Neoliberalism?
11. Compare and contrast Good Capitalism with Bad Capitalism and relate them to macroeconomic theories discussed in this chapter.

KEY CONCEPTS

BINGOs
Bad Capitalism
Conditionality
Good Capitalism
Keynesianism

Natural Capitalism
Rent taking
Sustainability
Trade Liberalization
Trickle down economics

SOURCES & SUGGESTED READINGS

Amin, Samir. 1973. *Neo-colonialism in West Africa.* Translated from the French by Francis Mc-
   Donagh. Harmondsworth: Penguin.
Berman, Harold J. 1983. *Law and revolution: The formation of the Western legal tradition.* Cam-
   bridge: Harvard University Press.

Berry, Sara. 1995. Economic change in contemporary Africa. In: Martin, P. & P. O'Meara (eds.). *Africa.* (Third Edition). London: James Currey, 359–374.

Binns, Tony. 1994. *Tropical Africa.* London: Routledge.

Castaneda, Jorge G. 1995. *The Mexican shock: Its meaning for the U.S.* New York: New Press.

Chomsky, Noam. 1992. *Manufacturing Consent: Noam Chomsky and the Media.* Film in 2 parts. Distributor: Zeitgeist Films. See also: Achbar, Mark [ed]. 1998. *Noam Chomsky and the media.* London: Black Rose Books, Ltd.

Cohn, Theodore H. 2000. *Global Political Economy: Theory and practice.* New York: Longman.

Cornia, Andrea *et al* (eds.). 1987–88. *Adjustment with a human face.* Oxford: Clarendon.

Davidson, Basil. 1992. *The black man's burden: Africa and the curse of the nation-state.* New York: Times Books.

Davidson, Basil & Barry Munslow. 1990. The crisis of the nation-state in Africa. Review of African political economy 17:49:9–21.

De Soto, Hernando. 1986. *The other path: the invisible revolution in the Third World.* New York: Harper & Row.

De Soto, Hernando. 2000. *The mystery of capital: Why Capitalism Triumphs in theWest and Fails Everywhere Else.* New York: Basic Books.

Development Assistance Committee Report. 1998. *Development Cooperation Report 1997.* Paris:OECD.

De Waal, Alexander. 1989. *Famine that kills: Darfur, Sudan, 1984–1985.* Oxford: Clarendon Press.

Eames, Elizabeth A. 1997 (1985). Navigating Nigerian bureaucracies. In: Spradley, James & D. W. McCurdy (eds). *Conformity and conflict* (9th edition). New York: Longman, 290–298.

Figes, Orlando. 1996. *A people's tragedy: The Russian revolution, 1891–1924.* London: Jonathan Cape.

Fieldhouse, David. 1986. *Black Africa, 1945–1980: Economic decolonization and arrested development.* London: Allen & Unwin.

Frank, Andre Gunder. 1980. *Crisis in the world economy.* New York: Holmes & Meier Publishers,.

Fukuyama, Francis. 1992. *The end of history and the last man.* New York: Free Press.

Giddens, Anthony. 1990. *The consequences of modernity.* Cambridge: Polity Press.

Gray, John. 1998. *False dawn: The delusions of global capitalism.* New York: New Press.

Hampden-Turner, Charles & Alfons Trompenaars. 1993. *The seven cultures of capitalism: value systems for creating wealth in the United States, Japan, Germany, France, Britain, Sweden, and the Netherlands.* New York: Doubleday.

Hawken, Paul, Amory Lovins, and Hunter Lovins. 1999. *Natural capitalism : creating the next industrial revolution.* Boston : Little, Brown and Co.

Held, David *et al.* 1997. The globalization of economic activity. *New political economy* 2:2:257–77.

Held, David *et al.* 1997. *Global flows, global transformations: Concepts, theories and evidence.* Cambridge: Polity Press.

Henderson, Hazel. 1999. *Beyond globalization: Shaping a sustainable global economy.* West Hartford, Connecticut: Kumarian Press for the New Economics Foundation in association with Focus on the Global South.

Hirst, Paul & Graham Thompson. 1996. *Globalization in question.* Cambridge: Polity Press.

IMF. 2001. www.imf.organization/external/np/secretary/pn/2001/pn0128.htm

Lappé, Frances Moore. 1977. *Food first: beyond the myth of scarcity.* Boston : Houghton-Mifflin.

Marx, Karl. 1930 [1867]. *Capital, Vol. I.* Trans. E. Paul & C. Paul. London: Dent.

Mendonsa, Eugene L. 1980. The failure of modern farming in Sisala-land, northern Ghana. *Human organization* 39:275–279.

Mendonsa, Eugene L. 2000. What does anthropology have to offer in the solution of the world's problems—Are we kidding ourselves? *High Plains Applied Anthropologist* 20:2:185–192.

Mendonsa, Eugene L. 2001. *Continuity and Change in a West African Society: Sisala Elders, Women and Youth.* Durham: Carolina Academic Press.

Merton, Robert King. 1957. *Social theory and social structure.* Glencoe, Ill.: Free Press.

Morel, E. 1911. *Nigeria: Its People and Problems.*

Naisbitt, John. 1995. *Global paradox.* London: Nicholas Brealey Publishing.

Ohmae, Kenichi. 1995. *The end of the nation-state: The rise of regional economics.* London: HarperCollins.

Payne, John C. 1961. In search of title: Part I. *Alabama Law Review* 1.

Pettifor, Ann. 2000. Debt cancellation, lender responsibility & poor country empowerment *Review of African political economy* 27:138–144.

Perrin, Noel. 1979. *Giving up the gun: Japan's reversion to the sword, 1543–1879.* Boston: Nonpareil Books.

Piot, Charles. 1999. *Remotely global: Village modernity in West Africa.* Chicago: University of Chicago Press.

Rau, Bill. 1991. *From feast to famine: Official cures and grassroots remedies to Africa's food crisis.* London: ZED Books.

Rapaczynski, Andrezej. 1996. The roles of the state and the market in establishing property rights. *Journal of economic perspectives* 10:Spring.

Redding, S. G. 1990. *The spirit of Chinese capitalism.* New York: W. de Gruyter.

Rostow, W. W. 1965. *The economics of take-off with sustained growth.* London: Macmillan.

Sachs, Jeffery. 1997. Nature, nurture and growth. *The Economist* (US). June 14th, 343:8021:19–21.

Sachs, Jeffrey. 2000. A new Map of the world. *The Economist* (22nd June).

Schumacher, Ernest. 1973. *Small is beautiful.* New York: Harper Collins.

Sen, Amartya. 2000. *Development as freedom.* New York: Anchor Books.

Simon, Julian L. 1981. *The ultimate resource.* Princeton, NJ: Princeton University Press.

Snow, Donald M. 1993. *Distant thunder : Third World conflict and the New International Order.* NY: St. Martin's Press.

Strange, Susan. 1986. *Casino capitalism.* Oxford: Blackwell.

Szeftel, Morris. 2000. Between governance & underdevelopment: Accumulation & Africa's 'catastrophic corruption' *Review of African political economy* 84:287–306.

Thomas-Emeagwali, Gloria. 1995. *Women pay the price: structural adjustment in Africa and the Caribbean.* Trenton, N.J.: Africa World Press.

Timberlake, Lloyd. 1985. *Africa in crisis.* London: Earthscan.

Tsuru, Shigeto. 1993. *Japan's capitalism.* Cambridge: Cambridge University Press.

Umehara, Takeshi. 1992. Ancient Japan shows post-modernism the way. *New progressive quarterly* 9:Spring.

Wall Street Journal. 1995. 24 October.

Walworth, Arthur. 1946. *Black ships off Japan.* New York: Alfred Knopf.

Wallerstein, Immanuel. 1974. *The modern world-system: Capitalist agriculture and the origins of the European world-economy in the sixteenth century.* New York: Academic Press.

Weissman, Robert. 2000. Stop the IMF. http://lists.essential.org/mailman/listinfo/stop-imf

Winchester, N. Brian. 1995. African politics since independence. In: Martin, P. & P. O'Meara (eds.). *Africa* (third edition). London: James Currey, 347–358.

World Bank. 2000. Online Media Briefing Center at http://www.worldbank.org/html/extdr/forjourn.htm.

World Bank. 2000. *World Development Report on Poverty.* Oxford: Oxford University Press.

19 CONCLUSION

The future is always inextricably tied to the historico-material world of the past and present. Forces emanating from the larger world dominated West Africa in the past, politically and economically. This continues today and is likely to be projected into the future. Any African Renaissance will be predicated on finding a balance between these poleconomic forces and the region's civilization, rooted in its ancestral codes of the past.

West Africa's Past, Present and Future

West Africa is a region with a foot in two worlds. Both its history and its modern condition are fraught with contradictions, social disruption and upheaval. This turbulence began slowly with the rise of the great states of the Niger Bend and the arrival of Islam, but it was greatly accelerated with the advent of European trade in the 15th century and the eventual imperialism of European colonists.

This contact with the West led to a clash of cultures and exploitation by the West. Both cultural confusion and an extractive political economy prevail in the region today, reminders of this early and fateful collision. Since the 15th century West Africa has been under continual influence from European culture. At times this contact with the Core led to economic and political domination, conditions that waxed and waned throughout the region's history. Today many see West Africa as mired in poverty, poor governance and as being a region with little development potential.

I would submit that this is largely because West Africans have been derailed by European contact. They have forgotten their deep roots in an indigenous African civilization. Many West Africans have looked to the West for a new model, but found it lacking. It has not led to good governance and modernization. Instead, it has impoverished a once proud people.

In their haste to modernize, African leaders ignored the democratic nature of traditional culture (See Table 19.1).
The African Takyiwaa Manuh says it well in discussing the varieties of political experiments after independence:

> What was remarkable about these experimentations was that in their haste to modernize, few African states saw the wisdom of building constitutions, which borrowed from existing traditional institutions. These better reflect African

Table 19.1 Comparative Economic Freedom in West African Nations, 1996*		
Borderline to Freedom (Score 5.0)	Mostly Unfree (Score 5.0–4.0)	Repressed (Score Under 4.0)
	Ghana	
		Benin
	Mali	Côte d'Ivoire
	Senegal	Niger
	Sierra Leone	Nigeria
		Togo

* Compiled from *The Economist*, 13 January 1996, 22.

conceptions of the accountability of rulers to the ruled, provide against arbitrary rule, and are accepted by the majority of the population where they exist. While modern governments have come and gone, in many countries traditional political authority and institutions have shown tenacity even in the face of governmental attempts to curb their power. This is an important point to keep in mind in the present period, when many African states reconsider new directions for their societies and for relations between ruler and ruled, either because their citizens demand it or because it has become conditional for assistance from the World Bank, the International Monetary Fund, and Western governments.

Since contact with Europeans, West Africans have adopted Western ways and looked to the Core Countries for development funds, ideas, technology and models of governance. In so doing, they have lost sight of the fact that they already had a better model of good governance. In accepting the imposition of the nation-state, modern constitutional law and now the mandates of the International Financial Institutions they have adopted a false modernism, a chimera of development.[1]

I have noted that West Africa's geographical location below the forbidding Sahara and its uninviting coastline discouraged exploration until the 15th century. The forest areas of the region were dense and filled with diseases that proved deadly to foreigners. Furthermore, Africans tried to keep newcomers away from the sources of gold, exotic products and slaves. This combination of environmental barriers and middleman kings held the traders on the coast, as Africans brought raw materials and slaves to exchange for imported goods.

Slowly, over centuries, European language, religion and values affected coastal Africans. The strong, egalitarian civic culture so characteristic of African societies began to bend under the weight of European influence. Kings became more powerful and wealthy as an élite class formed based on their newly found trading links. Peoples living on the coast began a process of acculturation and accommodation, but Europeans did not significantly penetrate the interior. These interior peoples had retained a civilization that was egalitarian, humanitarian, group-oriented and which provided a generally peaceful way of life. This changed, however, as the armed bands of slave raiders began to invade the interior. War and carnage became commonplace as the

---

1. What some are beginning to realize is than neoliberalist promises are a form of exploitation that has bedeviled the region since contact with the West.

spread of firearms and butchery brought an unprecedented level of disruption. The weak fled for their lives, were captured or were killed. Whole villages were wiped out. Others were left with few strong workers to maintain the farms. Whole societies were placed under tributary status by powerful states demanding slaves as payment, which meant they had to raid their neighbors to meet such demands. Evil rippled across the land. The communalistic and humanitarian civilization groaned under its weight.

Before these wars, indigenous peoples of the region participated in a culture in which older men controlled dependents using the linked structures of kinship and religion. It was a culture with a social order grounded in conformity to the ways of the ancestors. It was oriented to the past where, in ancient and traditional conditions, people saw themselves as subject to the will of a variety of spirits. This human-spirit relation was codified and acted out in ritual and a belief system that was animist and polytheistic. West Africans stuck to their particularisms—life was local and revolved around kin, neighbors and the ancestor cult. For them, the influences to come from various World Religions were still centuries away—first from Islam, and later from Christianity.

Before the Europeans arrived, West Africa was limited in its industrial expertise. Most people were simple farmers, fishers or herders. They were blacksmiths who produced some iron tools, but large-scale manufacturing did not exist. However, trade was a common feature of the region's economy, so naturally it was logical to exchange the region's raw materials for foreign manufactures. And these imports were very attractive, having the added patina of being foreign and therefore exotic. Those first exchanges of gold for goods, of people for firearms or precious wood for brightly colored cloth established an extractive pattern that still plagues the area today.

This extractive process soon took an ominous form: chattel slavery. European demand for slaves started a process of dehumanization and social disorder from which West Africa has never entirely recovered. While the Portuguese professed an interest in proselytizing in *Guiné*, they were largely interested in commerce and increasingly became involved in slaving. In this they were quickly joined by other European nations who recognized the economic potential in *Guiné* and who began to compete for access to suppliers and profits. In time, the Portuguese were largely pushed aside—replaced by the British, French and Dutch. As Europeans competed with each other for resources, they manipulated West Africans in ways that set some ethnic groups against others and encouraged powerful states to raid weaker ones for slaves.

The slaving years saw many crimes against humanity fomented by the triangular system of the Atlantic Slave Trade. Slaving required the participation of Africans who did most of the raiding, then traded their captives to Europeans. The latter then shipped the slaves to the New World.

The arrival of the Europeans not only had a profoundly disorganizing effect on the economy of the region, but also altered politics. The burgeoning trade in raw materials and slaves gave existing monarchs greater power and wealth than ever before and the previous democratic principles of such kingdoms were severely weakened. States grew in power and complexity while accountability of leaders lessened. A wealthy and privileged class emerged, their new political economy built on the riches of trading and slaving. But their power lay in bolstering customary ways with newfound military hardware.

Some Africans benefited from the European presence; others did not. Armed resistance movements emerged, but the superior firepower of the foreigners eventually allowed them to dominate West Africans militarily. European-organized regiments such as the Frontier Force, the Hausas and the *Tiralilleurs Sénégalais* were too powerful for freedom fighters and resistance movements.

In the Proto-Colonial Period (1880–1885) European domination moved from an informal governmental backing of traders in the area to formal colonization. After the Berlin Conference, a period of formal administration began that lasted into the late 1950s and early 1960s.

Colonialism was an era in which Europeans used cumbersome bureaucracies, military officers and native troops to bring large numbers of West Africans under their dominion. Lord Lugard's now famous Dual Mandate claimed that colonialism would the benefit European traders and as part of the *mission civilisatrice*, would eventually benefit Africans by bringing modern development into their lives. Lugard was also the architect of Indirect Rule whereby a handful of British administrators used local chiefs and native councils to run the colonies. The British took a "separate but equal" approach to development, while the French were very authoritarian. But the French held up the promise of assimilation and citizenship to those few who would actively learn their language and manners. The Portuguese took a similar approach to the French, but were even more dictatorial in their administration. By whatever guise, colonialism did little to enhance the lives of the vast majority of interior peoples. What little infrastructure was constructed served to transport African raw materials to the coast and load them on ships bound for Europe.

European missionaries did, however, build schools and these had an enormous impact on a few students who would pass on to college and foreign universities. Men such as Kwame Nkrumah, Félix Houphouët-Boigny, Amílcar Cabral and Léopold Senghor achieved great heights, eventually toppling the colonial regimes in their respective regions.

Using forced labor in some cases and the inducement of wages in others, colonials began to construct a new bureaucratic and urban-centered way of life. Some Africans were moved from the interior to coastal capitals and port cities to work, while others were attracted to these areas by the promise of jobs and a better way of life. Children went to what schools were available in hopes of getting a position in the new administrative order or in one of the few European businesses that were set up in the region.

As West Africans became more educated and involved in urban life, most tried to adapt and participate in what development existed. However, some began to be disenchanted with colonial regimes. Discontent was initially limited to a few well-placed attorneys and educated Africans. Many belonged to voluntary associations that gathered to discuss their perceptions of colonial inequities and what could be done about them. As they began to press for change, colonials responded with limited accommodation, such as establishing legislative councils that gave Africans some say in government. Labor unions were also formed in which union leaders organized to push for better wages and working conditions among the urban proletariat.

Colonial primary and secondary schools in West Africa taught little that was of practical use to locals, as the curricula were mainly filled with liberal arts courses. The system turned out few engineers and medical practitioners, but many attorneys and men conversant with Shakespeare, the Bible and European literature. Nevertheless, this kind of education exposed such Africans to revolutionary ideas in vogue in America and Europe. Nkrumah was impressed with the Pan-Africanism of W.E.B. DuBois, Senghor with the *Négritude* of Aimé Césaire—a Martinican poet, playwright and political leader—and Cabral became enamored with Karl Marx.

African intellectuals were attracted to the many Pan-African congresses that were influential in formulating ideas about Africanity and the need for a revolution in Sub-Saharan Africa. Especially significant was the 1945 congress held in Manchester, England, attended by Kwame Nkrumah and many other Africans who would soon take power. While they started out with radical ideas, many were to become fixtures in the prebendal class. Others died with their ideals or were overthrown by successors who corrupted the political order — kleptocrats who cared more for power and wealth than a moral political order.

West Africa went through some bad times after independence. Leaders made mistakes, were corrupt or became dictatorial. When elected officials failed, the military tried to govern, but with doleful results.

At the same time, various international institutions were being developed that would have ramifications for West Africans. The Bretton Woods Conference of 1944 produced the idea that the developed nations had an obligation to help advance those who were less affluent.

However, much of the modernization effort in Africa (indeed, throughout the world) had been grounded upon assumptions from Enlightenment philosophies, premises that are summed up in the word "Progress." In the era of positivism, post-Bretton Woods bureaucrats believed that West Africans needed to adopt a Western way of life in order to become "modern." In so doing, they ignored the costs of modernization, summed up in this statement by Brian Fagan:

> Progress has brought many things: penicillin, the tractor, the airplane, the refrigerator, radio, and television. It has also brought the gun, nuclear weapons, toxic chemicals, traffic deaths, and environmental pollution, to say nothing of powerful nationalism and other political passions that pit human being against human being, society against society. Many of these innovations are even more destructive to non-Western societies than the land grabbing and forced conversion of a century and a half ago.

In the flush of independence the World Bank, the IMF and NGOs became active in every West African nation, intent on modernizing them. This began an era of intensive modernization efforts based largely on the ideas of the development thinker, Walter Rostow. He advocated breaking the ties to traditionalism by adopting advanced industrial technology that would enable less-developed peoples to pursue their dreams of progress. Development planners pushed quickly with large-scale projects. But foreign technology required an underpinning infrastructure. Tractors, petrochemical fertilizers and hydroelectric dams were impossible to repair and maintain in West Africa's underdeveloped condition. Additionally, these efforts to impart technology were profitable to foreign firms and a few local élites, but actually undermined development in West Africa by making it dependent on Core Countries, keeping West Africans from developing along their own organic lines. On their part, West Africans believed in European "superiority," at least in technological and economic matters. They assumed that technology from the West would function in the African context. It did not, and they were frequently left with rusting hulks of useless machinery and giant projects that were non-functional.

When it became apparent that development was failing, West African politicians sought and received increasing aid from the West in the form of loans. They invested these finances into more of the same — big projects and imported industrial machinery. Still, development was elusive and most West African nations became mired deep in debt.

IFI bureaucrats responded with Structural Adjustment Programs or SAPs. Since many West African nations were caught in the trap of debt dependency, IFI officials set conditions that required them to make changes in the way they ran their countries. This caused much consternation about the "loss of sovereignty," but African leaders simply had little choice but to comply. Recently the World Bank has revised its approach to structural adjustment. It had tried more or less to bypass government by giving development funds almost exclusively to NGOs. The thinking was that NGOs were closer to the people and used a more "grass roots" approach to development than governments. They were expected to be less inclined to divert funds to private use than government officials would.

Two problems have arisen with this approach. First, NGO workers need government help in order to carry out their in-country work. Second, many prebendalists in government simply became involved in the management of NGOs in order to gain access to the flow of wealth coming from abroad. IFIs have now reintegrated government into the process, albeit with a watchful eye on fiscal matters and a continued interest in regulating social policy.

On a larger scale, West Africa is a "proving ground" for Neoliberalism. Advocates of the Washington Consensus believe that African countries should remove all regulatory impediments to free trade. In effect, this means that Africans should allow even more foreign firms to compete with their already weak manufacturing and agricultural base. Critics of this approach see Neoliberalism as an extreme form of Neocolonialism. It seems a way to give powerful foreign commercial interests an even stronger foothold in the region. Critics of the Washington Consensus assert that since independence, Africans have remained in a quagmire of dependency and that neoliberal economic policy is just another mechanism of keeping them there. This debate continues as of this writing.

The processes of centralization, urbanization, commercialization and stratification were all present beginning in the 6th century AD in the great Niger Bend states of Ghana, Mali and Songhai, as well as many other societies of ancient West Africa. But history did not allow their organic progression. New, intrusive forces altered their course—foreign trade, world religions and the imposition of a bureaucratic way of life in the form of the nation-state. These forces have created layers of contradictions in West African society, ones that are still generating new institutional forms and new conflicts in society.

There are three distinct and contradictory perspectives at work in West Africa today. These ideological positions are: (1) Traditionalism, (2) Islam and (3) Westernism. These views raise profound questions for the future of West Africa. Should life be based on customary ideas based in kinship and animistic orders? Should the foreign ideas of *Shari'a* Law predominate? Is constitutional democracy the correct way to govern the land? Is the nation-state a viable form of governance, or have West Africans missed some alternative way that has yet to emerge? Should politicians be involved in acceding to the demands of Core Countries that maintain self-interests in the extractive commerce of the region? Is there a possibility of regional development in a world heading for globalism? Does destiny lie in the strict order of fundamentalist religion? Is unbridled freedom the course to take? These are just some of the questions that come to mind when contemplating the plight of one of the world's most underdeveloped regions, the home of some of the world's poorest people.

Let's look at these three stands—Tradition, Islam and Liberalism—in light of an ongoing issue in geopolitical events: the status and treatment of women. Each perspective has a different point of view. Traditional African culture sees women as having a status that is complementary to men, albeit a relatively subordinate one. Nevertheless, under traditional morality, most women had a secure place and highly valued roles in society. Though women could not be chiefs in most traditional polities, they could be strong queen mothers or "chiefs of the women," influencing a complementary domain in social life.

In Islam, the roles of man and women are also seen as complementary, though women are in a subaltern position to men. In extreme forms of the religion, women are cloistered, dressed in ways that conceal their appearance. They are prevented from pursuing education or work outside the home. This fundamentalist approach is rare in West Africa, but at present, street clashes and riots in West African cities attest to the fact that some Muslims do hold fundamentalist views. Many Muslims today take a less extreme position on women, but in general do not consider gender equality entirely appropriate.

Finally the tenets of liberal democracy formulated in the West consider all human beings as equal. Men and women should have equal rights under the law. Women should be given similar access to education and the workplace and their rights should be protected by the constitution of the nation-state.

Having no formal church, Islam exists in a variety of forms and can adapt to a myriad of local situations. The *Qur'an* does provide a stabilizing force, albeit one open to diverse interpretations. Christianity, on the other hand, has various organizations that operate to formalize the religious life of their congregates. Some West Africans have also spawned new versions of Christianity—the so-called Newgeneration Churches. Some of these tend to be based on emotion and are extremely evangelical. Extremism from both Muslims and Christians has created deadly confrontations in modern-day West Africa. Adherents to traditional animist religions are scorned by both, but do not get involved in the fracas.

Finally, we must ask ourselves where West Africa is going. What is the future for this region? Is an African Renaissance possible? Africa's future is tied to G-7 powers, now under attack by radical fundamentalists. It is unlikely that African leaders can successfully extricate their economies from the vagaries of global affairs. However, international capitalists will always need raw materials and that provides some leverage for African leaders. West Africans have a source of strength. It lies in their indigenous ways. It could become a solution to political instability and underdevelopment in the region. Ultimately, its elaboration could lead to real independence and full integration into the global economy. Perhaps West Africans *will* turn to their roots to rediscover the truly valuable civilization of their ancestry. Happily, it is not very far away.

≋ SOURCES & SUGGESTED READINGS ≋

Fagan, Brian. *Clash of cultures*. New York: W. H. Freeman.
Manuh, Takyiwaa. 1995. Law and society in contemporary Africa. In: Martin, P. & P. O'Meara (eds.). *Africa* (third edition). London: James Currey, 330–343.

GLOSSARY — TERMS

In parenthesis at the end of each entry below is the number of the chapter in which the term is bolded and first referenced.

Acculturative impact of European culture – throughout West Africa most who took over control of the postcolonial political structures were acculturated élites with bourgeois educations obtained in the West. Thus, it is not surprising that they have largely replicated a middle-class lifestyle and European-like form of administration in West African governments. (15)

Accumulation – in a broad sense, the acquisition of wealth. See also: Primitive Accumulation. (15)

Acephalous peoples – peoples without centralized political forms—no chiefs, kings or emirs. In West Africa commonly have segmentary lineage systems, but may have looser forms of kinship groupings that function politically and/or sodalities. (3)

Acheullean tools – Paleolithic stone implements that show a progression of skill from early tools that are crude and unpolished to later tools with fine flaking that are polished. Named after the type station at St. Acheul, in France. (8)

Affines – in-laws. Affinity is the opposite of kinship or descent. It is a relation created by marriage, almost always with non-kin. (2)

Affinity – in-law relations or the condition of being those marrying into a group. (2)

African Association— In 1788, British politicians, philanthropists, clergymen, military men, and members of the nobility founded this association that was to employ explorers to find the full course of the Niger. In 1831, this association was folded into the Geographical Society. (13)

African Nationalism – the belief that Africans had to govern themselves before they could begin to develop and modernize. (16)

African Renaissance – a hopeful belief that having gone through a long period of devolution and failed development, Africa is about to enter an era of rebirth. (16)

Afro-Portuguese Ivories – ivory pieces carved in European motifs. Collected by European aristocracy as curiosity pieces. Thought to be so well done that Africans could not have carved them, so they were sometimes attributed to Asian origin. (6)

Age-set – a corporate group based on age grading or the principle of age. Typically such groups have formal rites of passage from grade to grade and hold joint rights and duties as members of each grade. An age grade is a non-corporate cohort of persons of more or less the same age. (5)

Aggrandizer – a go-getter, someone with an intense desire to "get ahead" or become "big." (5)

Agriculture – farming using intensive methods e.g., irrigation and often associated with the use of the plow. (4)

Ahiato – lower class in Asante society. See also: *Ahiato, Sikapo* and *Sikapo-Ahiato* ranking. (12)

Aid > loans > debt > dependency spiral – many West African countries, as well as others in the South, have become dependent on foreign aid and international loans just to run their governments. This has given the IFIs great leverage over them. See: IFIs. (15)

Akwanshi phallic statues – large Basalt rock penises found in the Cross Rivers area of Nigeria today inhabited by the Ekoi peoples. Most likely fertility related of an ancient and vanished people. (6)

Aladura Churches – specifically prayer churches among the Yoruba, but more generally a form of Christian church that adapts Christianity to African ways of thinking and behaving. Generally called newbreed or newgeneration churches. (3)

al-Kunti, Sidi Mukhtar – (1729–1811) created a widespread spiritual alliance that spread across the Western Sahelian zone. He also made treaties and alliances with the militant Tuareg, acting as a mediator in disputes with blacks. He was builder, rather than a destroyer. He was also a scholar, authoring over 300 treatises on Islam. (9)

Amazon women – King Agaja (c. 1673–1732) of the Fon Kingdom of Dahomey established a corps of women soldiers (known to the Europeans as Amazons). They were concubines, farmers and warriors thought to be especially loyal to the king. (4)

Amradofo – Asante bureaucracy. Bureaucrats were selected from all parts of the empire who owed their allegiance to the king, not to their local factions. (12)

Ancestor veneration – the ancestral spirits form a focal point for community ritual and reverence. Ancestors remain an integral part of the extended family by afflicting living members when they deviate from customs. To alleviate misfortune, the living must placate the ancestors through blood sacrifice on ancestral shrines. (2)

Animatism – according to R. R. Marret, a basic form of religion based on the belief in a universal life force in the cosmos. (3)

Animism – according to Sir E. B. Tylor, a basic form of religion based on the "belief in spirit beings." Commonly used to describe traditional West African religions. See animists. (3)

Animists – pagans or practitioners of animism or the worship of local gods and spirits. Commonly used to describe traditional West African religions. See animism, *kaffir*. (3)

Anthropophagy – see cannibalism.

Antiquated bureaucracies – many of today's bureaucracies in West Africa were put in place in the latter part of the 19th century before government administrations were modernized. They have tended to be replicated as such, in fact, in most cases, they have become even more bloated and cumbersome with time due to the tendency toward nepotism and filing posts with clients from a big man's home district. (15)

Apical ancestor – progenitor at the top of a genealogical hierarchy. Founder of the descent group. (2)

Articulation – being marginalized, on the edge of the industrial economy. Not integrated as equal partner in the benefits of industrialization, but locked into an unequal exchange. See also: Integration, dependency theory. (16)

Artisanship – West Africans recognize that some people have special craft specialties, skills over and above farming or cattle herding. Common crafts are carving, pottery production, artist, musician, blacksmith and basketmaker. (6)

Asantehene – King of the Asante or the Akan Empire. (11)

Asiatic Mode of Production – Marx's concept of a mode of production that saw the state as a class, as central to the economy, forming a political economy. This assumption implies a form of State that appears as a primary and determinant reality in opposition to the strictly epiphenomenal status to class that State occupies in the Marxist orthodoxy. (4)

Assimilados – in Portuguese territory, the locals who could read or write Portuguese, "owned" (private) property, exercised a profession, had done their military service and who did not practice *fetichismo* or traditional religion. Often involved in trade. (14)

Atlantic Slave Trade – with the discovery of the New World, Europeans started plantations and needed laborers. The would sail to West Africa with trade goods, exchange them for slaves, take the slaves to the New World, pick up agricultural goods and ship them back to Europe, to complete the Triangular Trade. (5)

Authoritarian rule – just as rule in Europe was liberalizing, colonialism swept over West Africa and rule there became authoritarian and paternalistic towards the indigenous people. This governance was founded on the concept that Europeans had the truth (both science and religion) and therefore the right to rule as they saw fit. (13)

Authoritarian presidentialist regimes – in the postcolonial era West Africa was plagued with one-party states under the dictatorial rule of strong rulers. (16)

Authority – legitimized power or socially-accepted power, often deriving from holding a formal office. See influence. (2)

Autochthons – original inhabitants of the land. Aboriginals or natives of the land. (3)

Avunculocal residence – living with one's mother's brother. (2)

Bad Capitalism – American or Neoliberal brand of socially irresponsible capitalism that feels that stakeholders in society (essentially the people or organizations representing the people) have no right to the benefits of business – only stockholders. Companies do not waste money investing in a safety net and social services. See also: Good Capitalism, Capitalism. (18)

Bagre myth – 11,000-line myth of the Dagara people of northwest Ghana. (3)

Baikie, William Balfour – credited with discovering the prophylactic effects of quinine on malaria. (13)

Band – comprise of households of foragers that clustered in groups of about 50 or 100 individuals. (5)

Barth, Henry – a German doctor and adventurer who crossed the Sahara in Muslim disguise visiting Kanem-Bornu, the emirates of Northern Nigeria and Timbuktu. (13)

Bantu migration – population movements from an area near the Nigeria-Cameroon border in a south, south-easterly direction. It likely occurred before 5000 B. C. (8)

Battuta, Ibn – (1304–1369?) traveled both to East Africa and to Mali. Born in Tangier of a family of *qadis* (religious judges) was perhaps the most widely traveled man of his age — surpassing Marco Polo, writing his book *Rihlah*, still an important source of the early history of Africa. (9)

Bedouin – (Arab. *Badawi*, "dwellers in the desert"), nomadic Arabs inhabiting the deserts of the Middle and northern Africa. (9)

Begho – it was a trading town that emerged at the edge of the rain forest in the Akan region of modern-day Ghana. It came to thrive on the north-south trade. It was founded by Iron-Age agriculturists in the third millennium BP. These early West Africans occupied the site continuously until about nine hundred years ago. (8)

Benin Conference – by the 1990s, West African autocrats, both civilian and military, were under "assault" by a combination of organizations from the civil sector of the region's cities — trade unionists, civil libertarians, human rights activists, students and professors from the universities, religious leaders and others. Such pressure was exerted on Benin's Mathieu Kérékou. He was forced to convene a national conference, a referendum of sorts, to address the country's economic and political crises. Those who attended the conference were the élites of the country. Unexpectedly, they declared the conference to be sovereign and of a higher authority than the state ruled by Kérékou. They unilaterally suspended the constitution, dissolved the National Assembly and by the end of the ten-day conference, had stripped Kérékou of all power. Then the delegates chose an interim Prime Minister, Nicéphore Soglo, who was subsequently the winner in Benin's first free election in 17 years. Subsequently, this phenomenon spread to other West African countries. (16)

Ber, Sunni Ali – Songhai king who expanded the kingdom using Niger River vessels as war machines. (9)

Berlin Conference – 1884–1885. European powers meet to draw up a colonial map of Africa effectively dividing up the continent.

Big man – the idea that by having many followers, being generous and having wealth a man can acquire prestige. In some societies women can also achieve this status, usually after her child-bearing years are over. See also: Rank, Big woman Bigness, Bigmanism. (8)

Big woman – women, often in urban contexts or in societies where when dominate the economy, who follow the idea that by having many followers, being generous and having wealth she can acquire prestige. See also: Rank, Big man, Bigness, Bigmanism. (2)

Bigmanism – the idea in West Africa, perhaps partially derived from traditional culture, that a leader should exhibit strength and generosity in ruling, a concept that has led to autocracy and military rule in many cases. See also: Big Man, Rank, Big woman and Bigness. (15)

Bigness – idea of being elevated above others socially and in terms of prestige or the possession of some symbols thereof. Existed in pre-stratified societies e.g., stateless societies. See also: Rank, Big Man, Bigmanism. (5)

BINGO – "business and industry non-governmental organization." New form of NGO that is set up by corporations to further their commercial concerns. Also called FPNGO, "for profit NGO." (18)

Bissau Seaman's Strike – 1959 strike organized by the PAIGC in Portuguese *Guiné* where the Portuguese killed 50 and wounded over a hundred seamen. Caused Amilcar Cabral to rethink his nonviolence. (15)

Black gold – aphorism for slaves. See also: Black Ivory. (5)

Black ivory – aphorism for slaves. See also: Black Gold. (10)

Blacksmiths – artisans who work with metal in West Africa. Thought to be mystically dangerous and powerful magically. May also be carvers. (8)

Blood Men – an organization of slaves in the Calabar region of present-day Nigeria which formed to protect themselves against abuses, and forced the freeborn to respect their human rights. (11)

Boserup Hypothesis – claims that shifting cultivation favors polygyny and that with the introduction of the plow and more intensive forms of agriculture the need for multiple marriage declines. My Sisala data contradict this, as both animal-traction plowing and plowing with tractors have allowed women to more fully participate in farming. (4)

Bourgeoisie – members of the wealthy or property-owing class as opposed to the working class in Marxist theory; or more generally, the middle-class. See: Bourgeois mentality, Petty bourgeoisie. (15)

Bourgeois mentality – a mindset based on middle-class values. Ideas, attitudes and behavior marked by conformity to the standards and conventions of the property-owning class. See: Bourgeoisie. (15)

Brasileiros – overall term for marginal people in the slaving days of West Africa including *Criolas* (Creoles), *lançados* (often mulattos) and *Senhoras* or *Senares*. They were called *Brasileiros* because some of them had been returned to West Africa from slavery in Brazil. (11fn)

Bretton Woods Agreements – name commonly given to the United Nations Monetary and Financial Conference, held July 1–22, 1944 at Bretton Woods, New Hampshire in USA. The conference resulted in the creation of the International Monetary Fund, to promote international monetary cooperation, and of the International Bank for Reconstruction and Development. By December 1945, the required number of governments had ratified the treaties creating the two organizations, and by the summer of 1946 they had begun operation. See also: SAPs, IMF and IFIs. (15)

Brideservice – customary work done by groom for his brides father or her people prior to marriage and often throughout the life of the marriage. (2)

Bridewealth – payments of goods and services (See: Brideservice) to the bride's people by the groom in return for rights to the woman's domestic capacities, sexual access and the legitimization of the offspring of the marriage. (2)

Brigandage – violent aggrandizement by men intent on taking slaves, seizing booty and sometimes establishing themselves as political rulers over vanquished peoples. (5)

Brotherhood of the Virgin of the Rosary – a slave organization that existed in Lisbon by 1460. They were African reformers who resisted the excesses of slavery in Portugal. (11)

Cabral, Amilcar – (1924–73) head of the PAIGC liberation movement in Portuguese *Guiné* and a brilliant political theorist. Returning from exile (1956), he founded Guinea-Bissau's nationalist movement. By 1959, Portuguese repression prompted Cabral to adopt guerrilla tactics. By 1973 when he was assassinated, the PAIGC controlled half of Portuguese Guinea. When Guinea-Bissau became independent (1974), Cabral's brother, Luis, became president (1974–80). (15)

Caliphate – a political organization in Islam headed by a ruler called a *Caliph*, (Arabic *Khalifah* or successor) e.g., Sokoto Caliphate. (13)

Calendrical rites – rituals, usually of the intensification variety, performed on a regular basis, according to some schedule. (3)

Call-response form of music – typically the lead singer will sing a few lines and the audience or chorus will repeat it. This reflects the African emphasis on the group as opposed to the European tradition of the audience passively listening to an individual perform music. This participatory form can also be seen in Newbreed churches in West Africa, as well as in many "Black" churches in the Diaspora. (7)

Cannibalism – humans eating human flesh. (3)

Cape Bojador – the southern tip of modern-day Western Sahara which juts out into the Atlantic. This was the first major hurdle, which was passed by Gil Eannes in 1434. (10)

Capital – as opposed to simple wealth, are assets that can be exchanged through legally recognized property system and which can produce further wealth. When used with the modifier, international—as in "international capital" it can mean capitalists in the global sphere. When coupled with the word, venture—as in "venture capital" it means wealth risked. Wealth, as opposed to capital, is unrealized capital or assets that cannot be exchanged through legally recognized property system. See also: capitalism. (4)

Capitalism – an economic system in which the means of production and distribution are privately or corporately owned and development is proportionate to the accumulation and reinvestment of profits gained in a "free" market. Free is in quotes because while that is the ideal version of the story, many political thinkers have come to realize that in the real world, some operators have privileged access to wealth and power that favor their operations in the economy. See: Political economy, Good Capitalism, Bad Capitalism. (1)

Caravel – a Portuguese innovation in a sailing ship that brought an advance in exploration. The caravel's chief excellence lay in its capacity for sailing to windward. It was also capable of remarkable speed. A typical caravel was a broad-beamed vessel of between 50 and 160 tons. About 75 feet long, the typical caravel had two or three pole masts, lateen-rigged (i.e., with triangular sails). Later versions added a fourth mast with square sail for running before the wind. (10)

Castelo São Jorge da Mina – the Castle of Saint George of the Mine. First outpost established on the Gold Coast by the Portuguese in 1482. The Portuguese held it till it was captured by the Dutch in 1637. They abandoned it in 1882 to the British. Presently called Elmina. (10)

Centralized polities – political systems that have developed chiefs, kings or other formal leaders that act as the head of a larger society. (8)

Césaire, Aimé – West Indian poet and essayist. After studying in Paris he concerned with the plight of blacks in what he considered a decadent Western society. With Léopold Senghor and Léon Damas he formulated the concept of *négritude*, which urges blacks to reject assimilation and cultivate consciousness of their own racial qualities and heritage. See: Négritude. (15)

Chattel slavery – condition under which human beings are treated like cattle, to be put to hard labor and bought and sold like commodities without regard to their humanity or human sentiments. (11)

Chiefdom – political system with a chief viz., a headman over many descent groups or families, one that unites a relatively large number of people under his rule, but which lacks a well-developed bureaucratic structure characteristic of later kingdoms. (5)

Cicisbeism – practice of a husband hiring a genitor or man to impregnate his wife. (2)

Cire perdue **method** – the "lost wax" method of making bronze statues by first making a clay mold, firing it, then filling it with molten bronze and re-firing it. When the clay mold is broken, a unique statue in bronze is left. (6)

Civic culture – the moral order of a people or the ideas about how society should be organized and people should behavior towards each other. (1)

Civilization – a common set of ideas about how to organize society in a moral manner. In the West African context, the cultural patterns developed that contain a high degree of humanitarianism and a focus on municipality i.e., the need for people to value each other and to form cooperative communities. (2)

Civilizing mission – some Europeans felt the need to carry Christianity to West Africa to bring to the people the benefits their perceived to be part of their civilization and Christianity itself. West Africans were seen as having souls and were therefore capable of being "saved", but they had not yet seen the light of Christ. In French it is called *mission civilisatrice*. (14)

Clan – members of a descent group that reckon a genealogical link to a common ancestor, though they may not be able to demonstrate the entire genealogy. A totemic clan taboos a common thing. (2)

Clitoridectomy – a ritual operation similar to male circumcision where the clitoris of the girl is extracted and sometimes some of the labia as part of a *rite de passage*. Westerners sometimes condemn this practice as barbaric, terming it FGM or female genital mutilation. (3)

Cocoa holdup – a protest by cocoa farmers in 1939 against the exploitation they felt was being perpetrated by the Cocoa marketing boards of the European powers. (14)

Codification process – operations by which men create ideas that form the basis of their world, their sociocultural formations. (2)

Cognatic (bilateral or ambilateral) descent – tracing one's lineage through both mother and father. (2)

Columbus, Christopher – 1492 he discovered the Americas, thus opening up vast lands for plantations, the owners of which needed cheap labor, a condition that led to the Atlantic Slave Trade. Since West Africa was closest to the Americas and to Europe, it was hardest hit in the slave trade. (10)

Comey – the dues or tariffs paid by European traders who came to the Niger Delta area of modern-day Nigeria. In paying such "comey" dues, Europeans reinforced the political power of big men *cum* kings in the area. (4)

Communitas – a sense or feeling of collective unity held by members of a community. (2)

Communalism – a collectivist or group-oriented approach to economics and life. Group is more important than the individual. Individuals should submerged their interests into the group interest. Collective ownership and participation in production, distribution and consumption. Emphasis on sharing and collective responsibilities. (5)

Communal land tenure – collective ownership of land where a corporate group e.g., a clan owns the land, but nobody holds rights *in rem* over it, thus rights to sell the land. Those who work the land only have rights *in usufruct*, or usury rights. When not in use, it reverts to the corporate group. (4)

Communité – the Francophone West Africa community of nations, similar to the British Commonwealth, proposed by Charles de Gaulle as a federated solution to independence. Favored by Léopold Sédar Senghor and opposed by Félix Houphouët-Boigny who preferred to take on France single handedly, each new nation going it alone. (9, 15)

Complimentary filiation – the other way of reckoning descent in a unilineal society e.g., matrilineal in a patrilineal society, patrilineal in a matrilineal society. Relatives in the line other than the primary one used for organizing inheritance and succession. (2)

Composite tools – two tools or tool-elements conjoined to form a more effective tool. See microliths. (8)

Consanguinity – the idea of a blood relationship between people and the fundamental principle of descent group organization. (2)

Constructionist approach – the social theory that states that all sociocultural formations are humanly fabricated. Such constructions give meaning to life and allow the generations to be connected by commonly understood traditions. (2)

Contagious magic – the idea that two things once in intimate contact with each other retain a connection with and force over each other e.g., when a magician collects a person's hair or a piece of clothing worn by a person over which to work a magical spell. (3)

Convention Peoples Party (CPP) – founded by Kwame Nkrumah in the Gold Coast, a party that swept him to the first presidency of Ghana in 1957. See: Kwame Nkrumah. (15)

Conversionist ideology – held by World Religionists that "others" should be converted to their way of thinking. In West Africa this proselytizing fervor is found among Christians and Muslims, not animists. (3)

Cool funeral – among the Sisala of Northern Ghana, funerals are divided into hot funerals, for those who die before old age, which tend to be short and sad, and cool funerals, for people who lived long lives, which tend to be longer, gayer and more musicalized. (7)

Core or Core Countries – G-7 countries or the Core Countries of the industrialized world. Also called the North or the First World. Contrasted to the Periphery or Peripheral Countries. See also: G-7, Western Civilization, Periphery. Dependency Theory. (1)

Core Countries – See Core. (1)

Corporation, principle of – that a group can have collective rights and duties that outlast the lives of the group members. The group as a legal entity, as with a single person and can hold property and rights over people through time. (2)

Corporation sole – the idea that the corporation is a legal person. It outlasts its members, and is a property-holding entity through time. (5)

Corvée labor – laborers obtained by a monarch from his subjects by decree or established custom. (5)

Coste de dentes – old Portuguese name meaning "Coast of the Teeth", after the abundance of elephant teeth. Later this area became known as Côte d'Ivoire. (10)

Counter-magic – magical means used to fight aggressive magic, witchcraft or sorcery. Sometimes called protective magic. (3)

Cowry shells or cowries – small seashells brought in by ship and caravan to West Africa from the Maldive Isles in the Indian Ocean. Used as currency and in artwork and in formal exchanges e.g., bridewealth. (3)

Coup d'etat – French for a takeover, usually military, of the state. A common occurrence in West Africa in postcolonial times leading to the development of a Military Statesman complex and much tension between the military and those advocating civilian rule. (16)

Crowther, Bishop Samuel Ajayi – (c. 1809–1891) a Yoruba, he was sold into slavery at the age of 12, he was rescued in mid-passage by a British cruiser and landed at Sierra Leone, where he was educated in a mission school and baptized. In 1842 he went to the Church Missionary College in London, and received holy orders. Back in the Yoruba country, Crowther worked among his people as a missionary from 1843 to 1851. In 1864 he became the first African to be to be ordained by the Church Missionary Society. (13)

Cultural dependency – the idea that in addition to poleconomic dependency, Africans have also become enamoured with European culture and have come to feel it to be the only avenue to development. Some feel that this reliance on European ways obscures the use of African ways to develop an organic African system of governance. (16)

Cultural imperialism – pushing a foreign culture onto others who have different ways and who may not necessarily wish to embrace another culture. (3)

Cultural monism – the idea that there should be one culture. See ethnocentrism, cultural imperialism. (3)

Cultural presupposition – an assumption of reality made by people of a society who share a common culture. (2)

Cultural schizophrenia – a crisis of identity suffered by some West Africans who partly identify with the "White" way and the African way. To a degree, they are caught between two worlds. (3)

Cumeré Agro-Industrial Complex – an example of an inappropriate development project. This multi-million dollar processing plant for groundnuts and rice was constructed with a capacity 70% greater than all the groundnuts or rice produced in Guinea-Bissau. Foreign construction firms made great profits building it, even though it was not needed. An example of development by *projeto colossal* – large albatrosses hanging around the necks of poor people in poor countries. (15)

Dash – a gratuity often paid at the end of any economic transaction in West Africa e.g., if you buy rice from a market lady she will ladle out the amount you purchased then add a small cup at the end, which is your dash. It can also be given to kick off a business relationship. (4)

Debt Dependency – the state of dependency brought about by falling into debt. These countries are called HIPCs, or highly indebted poor countries. See also: Dependency theory, HIPCs and debt servicing. (15)

Debt servicing – the monies spent on paying the ongoing interest on outstanding foreign loans. This places a heavy burden on many West African nations, some of which pay as high as almost 14 percent of their GNP to pay this interest. See also: Dependency theory. HIPCs and debt dependency. (15)

Democracy – a system in which the people of a country rule through any form of government they choose to establish. In West Africa the sociocultural formations of village life were accreted over time, not by any despot, nor by any outside force, but by the people — hence democratically. (2)

Dependency theory – political paradigm that states that most political and economic power emanate from the core of international capital, which dominates the more peripheral and weaker political economies of the countries of the South or Third World (those in Africa, Asia and Latin America). See also: Debt dependency. (15)

Descent – a genealogical reckoning of kin, often based on consanguinity that connects one generation to the other in a systematic way and which determines certain rights and obligations across generations. See: Descent group. (2)

Descent group – a group organized genealogically around the principle of descent. Descent groups can be traced through both sexes (that is, ambilaterally or cognativel — See: Double descent) or through only the male or the female link (unilaterally). In unilaterally traced groups the descent is known as patrilineal if the connection is through the male line or matrilineal if it is through the female line. See: Descent. (5)

Direct capture – in the early stages of slaving Europeans would use force to capture coastal peoples in Guinea, but soon found that it was easier and safer to buy them from chiefs and African traders. (11)

Divination – method to communicate with the spirit world, often mechanical, but also by possession of a spirit in the body of the diviner. (3)

Domestic mode of production – production carried out by a domestic group e.g., the lineage mode of production. In West Africa, this is usually farming or herding or a combination of each, with supplemental foraging of the bush. (4)

Domestic slavery – also called household slavery or the house system. Slaves worked in the household or on the family farms and were treated not unlike family members. Very common in West Africa prior to the Atlantic Slave Trade. The key difference between a slave and a West African kinsmen, however, lies in the fact that the former cannot have ancestors, shrines to them and s/he will not be given a normal funeral and burial. (11)

Double descent – rights passed in patriline for some purposes (usually fixed wealth and political office) and in the mother's line for others (usually moveable property and ritual office). (2)

Dual Mandate – Lord Lugard's concept of having both rule by local leaders and the British. This was to benefit both, that is Europe would be able to develop trade in the area and West Africans would benefit from the imports from Europe, as well as the industrialization of their lands. In the ideal, this was to be mutually beneficial; in reality, the British were able to profit greatly and when they were eventually forced out of West Africa they left behind little development for the locals. (14)

Dual urban residential pattern – many ancient West African towns had a section for the aboriginal residents and one for newcomers or strangers, called a *zongo*. See *zongo*. (8)

DuBois, W.E.B. – an American black intellectual who founded the Pan-African Congresses and the movement called Pan-Africanism. See: Pan-African Congresses and Pan-Africanism. (15)

Dutch East India Company – another example of a European trading company that profited from the slave trade to enrich Europe. Between 1637–1642 this trading company occupied the *Mina* forts of Elmina (*Castelo São Jorge da Mina*), Gold Coast Castle, Axim and Shama, and they built even more. From Senegal to the Congo the Dutch and others traded in human beings from the mid-17th century through the middle of the 19th. (11)

ECOWAS – the Economic Community of West African States is a regional group of sixteen countries, founded in 1975. Its goal is to promote economic integration in "all fields of economic activity, particularly industry, transport, telecommunications, energy, agriculture, natural resources, commerce, monetary and financial matters, social and cultural issues…" Its sixteen republics include Benin, Burkina Faso, *Cabo Verde* (Cape Verde Isles), *Cote d'Ivoire*, *Gambie* (Gambia), Ghana, *Guinee* (Guinea), *Guinee Bissau* (Guinea Bissau), Liberia, Mali, *Mauritanie* (Mauritania), Niger, Nigeria, Senegal, Sierra Leone, and Togo. (1)

ECOMOG – the Monitoring Group of ECOWAS, the peacekeeping force. (17)

Egalitarianism – democratic condition in pre-political phase of history wherein foragers held relative equality amongst themselves, with a simple sexual division of labor and minor age grading. Lack of significant ranking or stratification. (5)

***Ekine* society** – secret society of the Kalabari Ijo, an ethnically clustered group of thirty or so villages in the tidal zone of the Niger Delta in Nigeria. They have elaborate masks and masquerades involving the water spirits. (6)

***Ekpe* Trading Association** – organized by the New Men of the Delta States to control the slave trade in the area. If Europeans misbehaved, they were able to close down trade in the region. (11)

Elohim – the Biblical name for God, the equivalent of Allah in Islam. (3)

Embeddedness – principle that some functions can be achieved through institutions that overtly do not appear to serve such ends e.g., when economic functions are buried in the structure of a kin group. (4)

Emic – the native point of view. (2)

Envoutement – a combination of homeopathic and contagious magic e.g., when a magician sticks a pin in a doll that has been dressed in tiny garments made from the clothes of the person he wishes to harm. (3)

Equiano, Olaudah – the slave who escaped in the Americas in 1789 wrote an autobiography in which he counseled to treat West Africans as customers, not as merchandise. (11)

Equipment clause – during the naval blockade of the Guinea Coast by British vessels, they passed a law stating that any ship found to have slave shackles and other equipment for securing slaves aboard ship would be seized. This was to prevent the practice by slave captains of throwing their human cargo overboard upon encountering the British anti-slaving fleet. (11)

***Esie* statues** – in Nigeria, a large group of soapstone statues, most of them seated on stools. Found in the Rain Forest. Number over eight hundred, ranging from 20 cm high to a full meter. (6)

Ethos – a society's set of values. (3)

Etic – the outsider's point of view. (2)

EU – European Union. (17)

Exogamy – prescribed marriage outside the group. (2)

Extended family – a domestic group based on parents, their married children and their wives and their children, or three generations of family members and their spouses and offspring living together. (2)

Extensive farming – normally using the slash-and-burn method working a plot for a few years, then abandoning it to lie fallow. Associated with low population density and amble land. (4)

Extractive infrastructure – the roads, railways, bridges, quays, harbors and the like built by Europeans were constructed mainly to get out West Africa's raw materials and to bring in manufactured goods to sell to locals. Little non-commercial base was set in place. (13)

EU – European Union including Belgium, Denmark, Germany, Greece, Spain, France, Ireland, Italy, Luxembourg, The Netherlands, Austria, Portugal, Finland, Sweden, and the UK.

Eurasia – Europe and continental Asia, those connecting areas of the land mass to the north and east of Africa. (2)

European materialism – the focus on possessions, a devotion to material wealth and possessions at the expense of spiritual or intellectual values. While Europe had been developing materially and technologically and economically, West Africans had been working on their social relations and intellectual ideas to support a collectivist way of life. (13)

European rivalries – the real basis of the scramble for Africa, not any missionary zeal, though that was used as a post-facto rationale. Europe was in Africa to get territory and to prevent their rivals from getting too much. (10)

Evangelical mobility – the efforts of those seeking education in mission schools to further themselves by getting a good education. They saw this as a means of finding a good position in the colonial bureaucracy. Thus, to some religion was a means of socioeconomic mobility. (14)

Exogamy – marriage outside a defined group, in West Africa usually a descent group. The opposite is endogamy, marriage within a defined group, though this is not practiced in the region. (2)

Extractive infrastructure – the roads, railways, bridges, quays, harbors and the like built by Europeans were constructed mainly to get out West Africa's raw materials and to bring in manufactured goods to sell to locals. Little non-commercial base was set in place. (13)

Fabrication of rules – the process whereby aggrandizers construct rules that are deemed to be socially good, but which may also be turned to particularistic use. (5)

Faidherrbe, Governor – the expansionist governor based in St. Louis, Senegal who was favored by the French commercial class to rule because he wanted to expand French hegemony through treaty, but also by military force if necessary. (13)

Fairies – beings of the wild or bush. They are spiritual beings that represent the forces of nature, and who often act as go-betweens with the supreme being, or as tutelary spirits for those with knowing the techniques to call and control them. See: *kantongoo*. (3)

Federalism – the system of governance that allocates power to states or regions under the umbrella of an overseer national government. (16)

Female father – in Dahomey in West Africa the practice of a big woman, a woman of wealth and high prestige, who pays the bridewealth for another woman, hires a male to impregnate her and thus holds legal rights over the offspring. (2)

Fetish – a Portuguese term and common West African nomenclature for a shrine, amulet or any object thought to have supernatural power. (3)

FGM – see clitoridectomy. (3)

Fictive kinship – assigned kinship status to someone who is not an actual blood relative. (2)

Filiation – the primary bond between parents and children. Anthropologists say that descent can be considered an extension of filiation as found in the nuclear family. (2)

Firearms – the importation of guns into West Africa changed the balance of power. Those small polities that got guns first were able to dominate those around them and were successful in slaving, becoming larger, wealthy and powerful in the process. (11)

Fission – the process of a social group breaking into two segments due to population pressure on resources, or over conflict between members. See fusion. (3)

Fodio, Usman dan– (1754–1817) Called *Shehu*, a Fulani leader who led a *jihad* in Northern Nigeria. A scholar, and teacher who founded the Sokoto sultanate. (9)

Foragers – people in a pre-political phase or operating under an egalitarian condition that relied mainly on hunting and gathering to survive. (5)

Fostering – a common West African practice where children are housed with friends or relatives who perhaps need labor in the household, or who have some advantage for the children or their parents e.g., close proximity to school. (2)

Forced labor – beginning with the use of forced labor in Asante at the end of the 19th century, the British and other colonials systematically rounded up young men to work on road gangs, to mine ore and to carry out the construction of the infrastructure of extraction of West Africa's wealth. (12)

Formal sector – wage labor employment in companies or in the government. See informal sector. (4)

Francophone – generally means French or of France. Francophone West Africa consists of the former colonies of France—Mauritania, Mali, Niger, Burkina Faso, Chad, Benin, Togo, Ivory Coast, Guinea and Senegal. (13)

Free Trade – in the 1400s, Portugal wanted the backing of Rome to keep Spain and other European nations out of Guinea, claiming the whole area by right of discovery. Spain countered with the argument that Portugal had no inherent rights to African territory and all nations should be free to exploit the area. The issue then, as it is now in much of the world, the conflict between the principle of Free Trade or Open Waters (*mare abertum*) and that of Closed Waters (*mare clausum*) or monopoly of certain seas by a given nation. Today, free trade is an issue for neoliberal economics of the Washington Consensus who want West Africa to drop trade barriers and allow unfettered access to their markets. See: *Mare abertum* and *Mare Clausum*, Neoliberalism (9)

Fronbenius' Theory of Mediterranean Origin – the European Fronbenius found many marvelous bronze heads at Ife in Yorubaland, Nigeria in 1910. He did not believe that blacks could have produced such fine art work and attributed them to diffusion from the Mediterranean. (6)

Frontier Force – the British formed this military garrison to police for them in West Africa. This shows that some West Africans were willing to cooperate with the Europeans against their own. See also: *Tiralilleurs Sénégalais*. (13)

Futa Jalon or Fouta Djalon – an area in present-day Guinea, the site of the 1725 uprising of the Muslim Fulbe against their pagan overlords. (9)

G-7 – USA, UK, Germany, Japan, Italy, Canada and France. While Japan is not a Western country, it is successfully capitalist. When the Former Soviet Union (FSU) is added in, this amalgam of powerful countries is called the G-8. (15)

GCC – the Ghana Cotton Corporation. Operates in place of old Cotton Development Board, a colonial marketing board. Offers farmers front end financing of farm inputs and guaranteed prices if they will grow at least one acre of cotton. (4)

Gendered dualistic complementarity – in West African art men and women are depicted as having complementary roles, as they should in the political economy created by men. (6)

Genderization of musical instruments – often in Africa musical instruments are assigned male or female qualities such as a male drum and a female one. (7)

Generalized reciprocity – give and take between kith or kin wherein no exact accounting is kept or time frame placed on repayment, though it is generally expected that a giver can become a receiver at some future time. (4)

Generation – a common West African principle of organizing and classifying members of a community, that is, all more-or-less of the same age. Members of such a cohort are thought to have a special bond with each other. (2)

Gerontocracy – rule by the elders. (2)

Go cult – the Dan-Kran's secret society with a masking and masquerading tradition. (6)

Golden stool – among the Asante of Ghana, the *sike gwa* of the *Asantehene* is not only a symbol of the power of the sovereign, but is thought to be the very repository of the nation's soul. It is so sacred that even the king does not sit on it. The myth of origin for the *sike gwa* tells of a time in the reign of Osei Tutu when there was a great storm, with much thunder and lightening. At one point the skies opened and the sacred stool descended to earth and landed in the lap of the *Asantehene*. (6)

Goldie, George (Sir) – a British commercialist given broad powers of governance in West Africa in 1886 through his Royal Niger Company. See: Informal Empire and Royal Niger Company. (13)

Gomes, Fernão – King Alfonso V of Portugal granted him, a wealthy Lisbon merchant, a charter to explore the coast of Guinea beyond Sierra Leone, which was to prove very profitable for both Gomes and the government of Portugal as this led to the discovery of the Gold Coast. As part of the agreement, Gomes has to explore 100 leagues of coastline every year or about 400 miles. In total, Gomes' people explored some 2000 miles of coastline. It is interesting to note that after a lifetime of exploitation of the riches of West Africa, though he never went there, the Crown awarded him a knighthood. On his coat of arms he had a silver shield embossed with the figure of three Negro chiefs wearing gold rings and gold collars. (10)

Global economy – worldwide economic system which began ca. 1500 with the rise and spread of commercialism and has evolved into an expanding system of industrial capitalism. See also: Globalization, Hyperglobalization. (1)

Globalization – involves the increasing interdependence of national economies, financial markets, trade, corporations, production, distribution, and consumer marketing. See also: Global Economy, Hyperglobalization. (16)

Good Capitalism – European and Asia brand of socially responsible capitalism that feels that stakeholders in society (essentially the people or organizations representing the people) have a right to the benefits of business as do stockholders. Companies invest in a safety net and social services. See also: Bad Capitalism, Capitalism. (18)

Gonçalves, Antam – first European to return from the Guinea Coast with a load of slaves, 1441. (10)

Grain Coast – home of the Malagueta Peepers or Guinea grains, hence the appellation Guinea Coast. See also: Malagueta coast and Guinea Grains. (10)

Green Revolution – development approach using high technology and improved seeds. Part of the modernization approach popular in the 1960s. (4)

Griots – bards who sing songs of praise to notables of society or those who have died. They often are charged with the responsibility to keep the oral histories of a people. (7)

Guggisburg, Gordon (Sir) – served as governor of the Gold Coast from 1919–1927. He was unique in at least having the foresight to see the importance of husbanding the human and natural resources of the colony. He wanted to build railways, roads, schools and colleges, and the Gold Coast did become a showcase for colonial infrastructure, if not breath-taking social progress. (14)

Guiné – the Portuguese word for Guinea or West Africa. See Guinea. (1)

Guinea – name given by Portuguese to West Africa. Also referred to as the Guinea Coast. The Portuguese borrowed the Moroccan Berber term, *Guineus*, and referred to the Western Africans as Guineans, residents of Guinea. Presently, the name of one of the ECOWAS countries, a former French colony. See *Guiné*. (10)

Guinea grains – Malagueta Peppers from the Malagueta Coast. (10)

Guinea season – time when Europeans could sail to and from West Africa without encountering sweltering heat or without being becalmed on the return trip. Approximately October to May. (10)

Hamitic hypothesis – Sub-Saharan African material accomplishments were often explained by Europeans as being due to the movement south of light-skinned Hamites who had wandered into Sub-Saharan Africa to construct such wonders. (2)

Henrician tradition – Prince Henry the Navigator of Portugal wanted gold and a trade route to India, but he also had two other ideas. The first was a military idea, to get in contact with Prestor John. He thought this mythical Christian king might be the king reported to have so much gold in "Melli." By linking up with him, the Prince hoped to box in the Moors in North Africa. Secondly, a devout Catholic, the Prince was sincere about wanting to Christianize the natives of Africa. (10)

Heritability – the idea that goods and important offices should be passed on to successive generations in an orderly fashion. (5)

Heterarchy – political power organized as a lateral distribution of authority. A non-hierarchical political order. (5)

High Life – a modern form of band music that originated in Ghana during the Colonial Era. (7)

Hijra – Islamic concept of strategic withdrawal in battle. Based on the retreat to Medina made by Muhammad from conflict in Mecca. (13)

HIPC – acronym for Highly Indebted Poor Country, used by the United Nations and International Financial Institutions to refer to the poorest of the poor countries of the South. (15)

Homeopathic or imitative magic – technique that is like a desired end e.g., throwing a pan of water in the air to bring falling rain. Frazer called it the principle of "like produces like." (3)

Horticulture – farming without irrigation or the plow. (4)

Houphouët-Boigny, Félix – prominent independence leader in Francophone West Africa. In 1946 associated with the radical party called the RDA or *Rassemblement Démocratique Africain* (which was affiliated with the international communist party).

Served as head of state in Ivory Coast for 33 years (1960–1993). Died in office. See, *Rassemblement Démocratique Africain.* (15)

Hot funeral – see cool funeral.

Household production system – production, distribution and consumption by those who live in a common house or compound. (5)

Human sacrifice – slaves and criminals were often publicly sacrificed in Asante (as they were elsewhere in Africa). When the British got wind of this, they used such behavior to justify their aggression toward a people they defined as "savage." (12)

Ibeji **dolls** – twin dolls. A woman loosing a twin will have a doll carved to replace the dead twin. She will do everything for the doll that she does for the live twin. When the twin grows up, s/he will often carry on the tradition. (6)

IFIs – International Financial Institutions. In the West African context, primarily the World Bank and the IMF, or International Monetary Fund. They are running the SAPs, or Structural Adjustment Programs in West Africa today. (14)

IMF – International Monetary Fund, one of the International Financial Institutions set up supposedly to help poor countries, but which actually functions to further the integration of those countries into the global market and furthers the goals of the G7 and the spread of international capitalism. (14)

Imperialism – broadly: the extension or imposition of power, authority, or influence. Traditionally, this has been the policy, practice, or advocacy of extending the power and dominion of a nation especially by direct territorial acquisitions or by gaining indirect control over the political economic life of other areas. More recently, imperialism is the planetary control of finance capital. No longer do imperialists move into a country with troops or colonial administrators. Today it is done with International Financial Institutions such as the IMF, World Bank under the direction of the G7 through the World Trade Organization. (3)

Imperialistic proselytizing – aggressive form of missionary work where the evangelist propagandizes and pushes the potential convert to accept the "true gospel." This form of aggressive evangelism is creating social conflict in contemporary West Africa, and has led to protests, riots and death. (3)

Indirect Rule – the brainchild of Lord Lugard a British administrator in Nigeria. His idea was to co-opt African leaders to rule for the British. In this way, the Europeans could dominate large tracts of land with few soldiers or administrators. (5)

Influence– the informal ability to persuade others to do what they might otherwise wish not to do. Often based on acquired prestige rather than authority that derives from holding a formal office. See authority. (2)

Informal empire – idea of the British that in the early phases of a move to dominate West Africa, they would not establish formal colonial structures, but rather rule through traders and trading companies in the region such as the Royal Niger Company. (13)

Informal sector – off-the-record economy of the streets. Hawkers buy goods and resell them from head carriers or sometimes pushcarts or small roadside stands or kiosks. Similar to Sol Tax's concept of Penny Capitalism. See formal sector. (4)

Integration – being joined to industrial economy in a beneficial way. Folded in as equal partner that receives the benefits of industrialization. Not articulated or marginalized. See also: Articulation. (15)

Intensive farming – when population density rises and people cannot fallow land, they begin to farm all the land using fertilization, irrigation, intercropping, green manuering and other intense methods of cultivation. (4)

International Financial Institutions – See: IFIs.

International capital – the core political economy of capitalists. The center of power in the world economy held by wealthy capitalists. Can also mean finance capital in a broad sense i.e., the capitalist system of the modern global economy. (15)

Islam – a religion founded by Muhammad in Arabia in the 7th century. Its followers of Allah, the one true god, are called Muslims. Islam came to West Africa during the time of the Great Sudanic Kingdoms and gradually was accepted first by kings, then by common people. See also Qur'an. (1)

Iwo Eleru – a 12,000 year old rock shelter in modern-day Nigeria. (8)

Jaja (1821–1891) – an ex-slave of origin who had broken away from the ancient trading state of Bonny to found his own state in 1869 at Opobo. A brilliant modernizer, he came to be seen as a threat to British trade. He was tried on trumped up charges and exiled from his native land. (13)

Jihad – holy war concept where violence against infidels is justified if the war is undertaken with the idea of converting the enemy. In West Africa this concept was used to justify some slave raiding and empire-building. (2)

Jizya – or tribute levied against non-Muslims under Islamic rule. (12)

Joint family – a domestic group based on siblings and their wives, usually composed of two generations, parents and children. Can be patrilineal, where the siblings are brothers; or matrilineal, where the siblings share a common mother with whom they reside. (2)

Joking relations – almost all West Africans stand in a joking relation to some other people in certain generational standing, usually alternate generations e.g., grandsons and grandfathers; or those who are members of groups with a history of joking with each other e.g., the Sisala traditionally joke with members of the Kasena tribe and *vice versa*. (2)

Juju – A West African term for magic. (3)

Jural relations – the relational rights and duties *vis-à-vis* material goods, labor, or ancestor shrines held by two people or corporate groups. (2)

Kaananke-Jooro **relationship** – among the Jelgoji Fulani the *Kaananke* is the secular chief imposed from the outside by strangers; the *Jooro* is the "master of the *wuro*" (basic homestead) and is called the *Jom Muro*, or more frequently by its contraction, *Jooro*. He is a little chief or headman. He is in power, but does not need to exercise power. As an authoritative headman, he has only the power of influence with the *wuro*. He is an arbiter, advisor and represents the community in dealings with outsiders. (5)

Kaffir – non-believer in Allah as the one true god, according the Muslim belief. (3)

Kanton family – a family in Tumu, Sisalaland that became powerful and wealthy through the appointment of Kanton I as paramount chief over the Sisala, when traditionally they had no formal chiefs, let alone a paramount chief. Kanton I and later chiefs used their connection to British power to enrich themselves. (14)

Keita, Sundiata – the first king of Mali, ruling the empire from about 1240 until his death in 1255 AD. He built the kingdom by promoting agriculture over war; by taking control of trans-Saharan trade and by mining of gold. (9)

Kenke – cassava flour dough balls common in the rain forest of West Africa. (4)

Kente cloth – Asante multicolored cloth often made of woven strips of cotton and silk. (8)

Keynesianism – or Keynesian economics after the ideas of Lord Keynes. He believed that the hills and valleys of economic variation could be controlled through government planning and adjustment of key variables in the economy.

Khaldun, Ibn – (1332–1406), a Tunisian was perhaps the first social historian, analyzing the rise and fall of states and postulating universal conflict between nomads and urban peoples. (9)

King Coffee – the *Asantehene* Kofi Kakari was dubbed by the British as "King Coffee." He was not a wise ruler, given to excess and debauchery. He had the unfortunate habit of lavishing gold on his paramours, thus he was known by several unflattering nicknames, one of which was *osape,* "one who scatters gold." In his scattering Kofi Kakari managed to mightily run down the royal treasury. He fought General Sir Garnet Wolseley. He abdicated in 1874 after Wolseley sacked Kumase. (12)

Kingdom – political system with a king viz., a headman over many descent groups or families, one that unites a relatively large number of people under his rule, and which reins atop a well-developed bureaucratic structure. More stratified than a chiefdom. See: Stratification. (5)

Kinship – the idea that people have a natural affinity with each other based on a common genealogical connection or birthright. Human relations based on biological descent. The links between blood relatives that are assigned certain legal, political, and economic significance. (2)

Kin terms – designations people use for relatives. Terms of address, when speaking to them; terms of reference when speaking about them with others. (2)

Komfo – a priest in the Fante culture of Southern Ghana. Presides over a possession cult. (13)

Kleptocracy – a political system that has as a central function the theft of state funds. One in which prebendal élites or kleptocrats siphon off funds for their own use or those of their political supporters. See prebendalism. (12)

Kotoko – 18-member Inner Council directly below the *Asantehene* in power, but which had strong veto power over inappropriate behavior by the *Asantehene*. (12)

Kuoro (kuoroo) – chiefs imposed by the British on the Sisala of Northern Ghana. (3)

Kwadro, Osei – (1764–1777) the *Asantehene* who created the first professional bureaucracy in the kingdom, wherein bureaucrats owed their allegiance only to the King. (12)

Lagos Company, The – Lagos is a town in the Algarve, the southern part of Portugal. In 1444, the Portuguese Crown sanctioned the formation of The Lagos Company, which constructed a staging facility on Arguin Island just south of Cape Blanco, which had been discovered in 1443. The founding entrepreneurs of the company made huge profits in slaves and gold, between 50 and 800 percent on investment. The Crown usually took a fifth of the profits. This was the first of many venture capitalist companies to exploit the resources of West Africa. (4)

Lançados – a Portuguese word referring to the early Portuguese traders who flourished in the slave trade, some based in the Cape Verde Islands, and who tended to marry African women who became known as the *Senhoras* or *Senares*. It literally means those who launch something. (10)

Lander, Richard – credited with mapping the course of the Niger River. (13)

Legislative Councils – assemblies established in Lagos, the Gold Coast, Sierra Leone and the Gambia. Each had some elected West African members. The idea was to give West Africans some political representation, however limited. (14)

Leveling mechanism – socially accepted devices such as gossip, shunning and ridicule that impress a deviant with the group's consensus. (5)

Liminality – betwixt and between. That social space in a rite of passage where the ritual participant is not in any status, but is in the process of leaving one and attaining a new role in life. (3)

Lineage – a segment of a larger descent group whose members feel a close affiliation with each other because of their decent from a known common ancestor. Sometimes anthropologists distinguish a lineage from a clan by noting that in the former, the members may be able to trace their actual links back to the ancestor, while this may be more difficult in the clan. In the segmentary lineage system, the lineage may be an important residential and corporate group. (2)

Little chief – a man who is similar to a big man who has prestige and power, but no true formal heritable authority. He may rule in his lifetime, but does not pass a conventional office on to the next leader. More earned by achievement than acquired through ascription. (5)

Long-distance trade – the north-south routes brought in goods from the Mediterranean and Levant; while the east-west routes brought cowries from the Maldive Isles in the Indian Ocean. Often involved with the movement of high prestige items. Control of long-distance trade allowed formation of the Great Sudanic States. (8)

Maghrib – an area in northwest Africa that anciently influenced the Great Sudanic States. Maghrib means west in Arabic and also refers to the fifth *salah* or prayer of the day, the "sunset" prayer. (1)

Magic – incantations or acts thought to automatically bring about a desired effect in the material world without recourse to a sentient spiritual being. (3)

Mahdi – in Arabic it means "divinely guided one." In Islamic eschatology, a messianic deliverer who will fill the Earth with justice and equity, restore true religion, and usher in a short golden age lasting seven, eight, or nine years before the end of the world. (13)

Malagueta Coast – the area along present-day Senegal, Gambia, Sierra Leone and Liberia. Known for its peppers, which became known as "Guinea Grains." (10)

Mallam – originally an Islamic cleric who accompanied traders to the Savannahh zone. Also, a local holy man who makes a living teaching, preaching and making magically-protective amulets. (3)

Manillas – bronze or brass bracelets imported by Europeans. Locals used them as body ornaments, money and to melt down to be reshaped into other objects. (4)

Mansfield decision of 1772 – the law which freed slaves in Great Britain. (9)

Manumission – freeing a slave at the end or a term or when s/he pays a release fee. (11)

Marabout – a holy man of Islam. Technically members of an ascetic Muslim order in North Africa residing in *ribats*, or monasteries, and held in veneration by the Berbers. They are successors to the powerful Almoravids, who ruled Morocco, part of Algeria, and Spain in the 11th and 12th centuries. Sometimes interchanged in West Africa with the term *Mallam*. See: *Mallams*. (3)

Mare abertum – open water or free trade. That any nation should have the right to exploit West Africa by sea. Position taken by Spain and other nations who wanted to cut in on Portugal's rich finds in West Africa. See: Free Trade vs. Government Regulation. (10)

Mare clausum – closed water or unfree trade. That no nation should have the right to exploit West Africa by sea except that country that first planted its flag on the territory. Portugal's position to the Papacy. See: Free Trade vs. Government Regulation. (10)

Market economy – capitalist market based on supply and demand to set prices. Often portrayed as a free market, with open opportunity, but the reality of political and economic control of the market is often overlooked by advocates of free trade. Tends to treat all inputs as commodities with a price. (5)

Marketing Boards – governmental purchasing organizations set up originally during colonial times with the stated purpose to help the farmer but guaranteeing that he could sell his crops at a set price. In reality, these were prebendal structures that enabled the state to extract rents from peasants. See Prebendalism; rent taking. (9)

Marriage – an affinal (See: affines) relationship established between a woman and one or more persons. (2)

Matriarchy – a legendary political order in which women dominated men. There is no historical or ethnographic evidence that this was ever the case, nor do any contemporary matriarchies exist. (5)

Matrifocal family – a family or domestic group focused on the mother, often in matrilineal societies. (2)

Matriliny – descent, inheritance and succession to office reckoned in the mother's line. See matriarchy. (2)

Matrilocal – postmarital residence with one's mother, usually to the exclusion of one's father who lives in a different household. (2)

Mbari **House** – an art house with elaborately painted walls and painted mud statues inside. Southeastern Nigeria. Villages compete with each other to have the best one. (6)

Mbira – a hand piano often made of hollowed wood with metal keys. (7)

Maclean, George (Capt.) – one of the only British administrators in *Mina* to rule with compassion and understanding toward the people. There was peace during his 16 years in power. As a great tribute to Maclean the Asante referred to him as "The White Man in whose time all slept soundly." (12)

Means of destruction – weapons, military organizational knowledge and means of transporting soldiery. (5)

Mercedes Class – a common street term in West Africa for rich people or the upper class. (4)

Merchant Council – in *Mina* a council of merchants that was sometimes empowered to govern the area on and off with more official governors from Britain. This is an example of how the economics and politics of European expansion overlapped. (12)

Metropole – often used as a synonym for the core countries, but can also mean the urban élite who control capital flows. Broadly, the capitalist system. See also: Core, periphery, dependency theory. (15)

Microliths – small chip-like or flakes of stone that were often embedded in wood or bone to make composite tools. See composite tools. (8)

Middle Niger Zone – an area at the bend of the Niger River in present day Mali that anciently was filled with swamps and standing water, which made it remarkably fertile, but it lacked stone (for querns and smithing tools), copper or iron ore. The area did produce ample crops and had abundant fish. Its early cities had a strategic location along a navigable river in a productive floodplain lacking raw materials. This stimulated exchange. Initially trade networks developed that allowed the people of Jenné-Jeno, Gao and Timbuktu to market their produce and exchange them for ore and stone. With the coming of Arab traders, local kings came to control their commercial activities. (8)

Middle passage – the journey by slaving ship from West Africa to the New World. Conditions were terrible for the captives on board. It is estimated that 1 of every 6 slaves died along the way. (11)

Mina Coast – Portuguese established *Castelo São Jorge da Mina* there in 1482. An area of intense European interest because of the prevalence of gold to be had. Later known as the Gold Coast, then Ghana at independence in 1957. Sometimes simply referred to as *Mina*. (10)

MNC – Multinational Corporation. Also called a TNC or Transnational Corporation. A company that has bases in various nations and/or does business internationally. (4)

Mode of production – A patterned way of making a living. (4)

Modernization approach – advocates use of modern technology to drive the development process. See also: Walter Rostow, Green Revolution. (16)

Mogoho Naba – king of the Mossi of Burkina Faso. (5)

Monogenism – monogenists believed that all humans were descended from a single creation event or a single origin; that human groups had degenerated since the original event, which accounted for differences between groups and resulted in the existence of different races of humankind; and, finally, that some races had degenerated more—fallen further from grace—than others, which explained the natural superiority or inferiority of various peoples. See polygenism. (11)

Mosque Arabic – more literate form of Arabic taught in *Qur'anic* schools, as opposed to Market Arabic, a common form of the language used in everyday life in West Africa, principally among Muslim traders. (3)

Muhammad, *Askia* – emperor/general of Songhai till 1529 AD. He made Songhai the largest empire in the history of West Africa. He restored the tradition of Islamic learning to the University of Sankore, made Islam the court religion, and made his own spectacular *hajj* to Mecca where he was appointed as *Caliph* of western Sudan by the ruler of all Islam. (9)

Mujaddid (pl. *mujihaddin*) – in the *Tijaniyya* movement, thought to be a reformer or great leader who will come and lead a *jihad* establishing a theocracy based on the *Qur'an*. (12)

Musicalization of social events – social events tend to be accompanied by music in Africa—social events such as rites of passage, funerals, marriages and village festivals. (7)

Muslim/Christian Youth Dialogue Forum – the Christian evangelist James Wuye and Imam Muhammad Nurayn Ashafa jointly founded and coordinate this forum in Kaduna, Northern Nigeria. Their organization holds forums and has published literature and books in an attempt to mediate the conflict between the two religious camps.

They have toured several countries outside of West Africa to find ways to resolve such tensions and antagonisms. Their most well known work is *The Pastor and the Imam Responding to Conflict*. (3)

Musa, Mansa – (1312–1332 AD) *mansa* (meaning emperor) Malian Emperor who made a *hajj* (pilgrimage) to Mecca (1324 AD). Under his control, the kingdom doubled in size through conquest. He financed his *hajj* with about ninety camel-loads of gold dust. He gave away so much gold that he depressed its price in North Africa. (9)

Mythology or myth – mythology is the study and interpretation of myth and the body of myths of a particular culture. In general, myth is a narrative that describes and portrays in symbolic language the origin of the basic elements and assumptions of a civic culture. For the people themselves, their myth is an unquestionable reality, a social charter for the moral code by which they should live their lives. A truth system. (2)

Na – common term for chief in Northern Ghana. Often those who conquered the original inhabitants of an area. (3)

Natural Capitalism – book advocating using nature as a model to reform the wasteful linear process of capitalism by creating within capitalism itself recycling of matter and energy. (18)

Negerplastik – book on African sculpture written in 1915 by Carl Einstein. (6)

Négritude – an idea developed by Léopold Sédar Senghor in his book, *Négritude and Humanism* (1975), a reaffirmation of the values of traditional African culture and the concept that peoples of Sub-Saharan Africa and the African diaspora share a common understanding of life. (2)

Neocolonialism – the postcolonial condition in which the economic power established under colonialism remains in place even though West Africans have been given back their political independence. Given the reality of the international political economy, this concept implies that West African politicians are really hampered by their dependence on international capital i.e., their political sovereignty is largely symbolic. International capitalists pull the strings through the International Financial Institutions. (15)

Neoliberalism – followers of Adam Smith who advocate *laissez-faire* capitalism with no trade regulations, open markets and unbridled competition in the global marketplace. (9)

Neolithic Revolution – in the Near East, circa 12,000 B. P.–8,000 B. P. the domestication of plants and animals leading to a storable surplus and sedentary living. In West Africa, about four thousand years ago we begin to see evidence of domestication and a move away from simple foraging and into an age of cultural flowering. (4)

Neolocal residence – when the newly married couple lives together apart from their parents. In West Africa this is common among acculturated people and urban élites. (2)

Newbreed Churches – syntheses of Christianity and African philosophy that often become radically opposed to pagan practices, but turn to emotional or pentecostal rites in church to evoke strong emotions in the congregation. They are often fundamentalist and highly aggressive in their approach to non-believers. Sometimes called Newgeneration Churches. See *aladura*. (3)

New Men – aggrandizing entrepreneurs in coastal areas where slaving allowed them to acquire tremendous wealth and thus power to threaten the traditional political order. (4)

NGO – a non-governmental organization e.g., charities, for example. (4)

Nigerian Federal System – because of the extraordinary ethnic diversity of the colony, the British settled on a federal system, a form of political organization that continues today in Nigeria. (15)

Niger Delta – that area of the Guinea Coast in present-day Nigeria where the great Niger River meets the sea. (11)

Niger-Congo –The dominant language family of West Africa, including Bantu. This family includes two subfamilies, Niger-Congo and Kordofanian. (1)

Nkrumah, Kwame – educated in the United States, he returned to the Gold Coast to found the CPP, the Convention People's Party. Became the first president of Ghana in 1957. Strong Pan-Africanist who advocated the development of a United States of Africa. See: Convention People's Party. (15)

Nuclear family – a man, his wife and their children. As a domestic group in West Africa it is most often associated with urban living and/or neolocal residence after marriage. (2)

Obasanjo, Olusegun – elected to office on May 29, 1999 as head of Nigeria. In office as of this writing. A former general in the army. (16)

Occult power – widespread belief in West African religion that a preternatural power exists. It can be harnessed and directed for good or evil by those who know the techniques. It is the life force that makes things alive and work in the cosmos. See occult realm. (3)

Occult realm – widespread belief in West African religion that a preternatural and un-seen world exists where spirits live and operate. Sometimes called the supernatural or extrahuman realm. See occult power. (2)

Organization of African Unity (OAU) – a continent-wide watchdog organization similar to the United Nations now called AU, African Union. (15)

Otherizing process – mental process of perceiving a fellow human being as being an "other", being something less that human. Making fellows seem subhuman because of different characteristics or traits. (3)

Otiose high god – in West Africa the supreme being was a creator of all things, but then he withdrew from the affairs of humans, for the most part. These matters are mostly handled by intermediary spirits or demi-gods. (3)

Paganism – generally, from the Christian or Muslim standpoint, any practice that seems outside the realm of the worship of the Supreme Being. Practitioners of animism, totemism and "fetishism" are sometimes labeled such. Generally applied to any traditional African religious practice. (3)

PAIGC – See, *Union of the Peoples of Guiné and Cape Verde.* (15)

Palm oil plantations – some West Africans attempted to replace the revenues lost from slaving by exporting palm oil to Europe which was in great demand at that time. (11)

Pan-African Congresses – organized by W. E. B. DuBois. The First Pan-African Congress, convened in London in 1900, was followed by others in Paris (1919), London and Brussels (1921), London and Lisbon (1923), and New York City (1927). At first these congresses were attended by the black intelligentsia of the African diaspora, but did not propose immediate African independence. Rather they favored gradual self-govern-ment and interracialism. In 1944, several African organizations in London joined to form the Pan-African Federation, which for the first time demanded African autonomy and independence. The Federation convened (1945) in Manchester the Sixth Pan-African Congress, which included such future political figures as Jomo Kenyatta from Kenya, Kwame Nkrumah from the Gold Coast, S. L. Akintola from Nigeria, Wallace Johnson from Sierra Leone, and Ralph Armattoe from Togo. See: Pan-Africanism. (15)

Pan-Africanism – a general term for various movements in Africa and the African diaspora that had as their common goal the unity of Africans and the elimination of colonialism and white supremacy from the continent. See: Pan-African congresses. (15)

Parallel economy – or black market. Smuggling of contraband considered illegal by government, but it is common in West Africa. (15)

Paramountcy – political supremacy over other rulers e.g., the paramount chief over village chiefs. (14)

Park, Mungo – In 1794, the African Association chose the 23-year old Scottish medical doctor as a "geographical missionary" to find the source of the Niger River. Park made two trips, finally drowning in the river on his second attempt to chart the river's course. (13)

Particularism – as opposed to universalistic interests of a broad nature, particularistic interests are confined to one's own, small sphere—say a village or ethnic group. In the West African context, particularism usually refers to the tendency of the powerful to funnel jobs and contracts toward their own as opposed to allowing them to be awarded according to universal selection criteria. (15)

Pastoralism – herding mode of production. Having herds of animals as a store of wealth. As a way of life it often involved following the growth of grasses dependent on the seasonal rains in different places, thus a nomadic way of life; but some pastoralists stay on one area, thus are more sedentary. (4)

Patriliny – descent, inheritance and succession to office reckoned in the father's line. (2)

Patrilocal residence – postmarital residence with the groom's father, though usually the groom's mother lives in or near the same household. The bride leaves her kin to live with her affines. (2)

Penny capitalism – Anthropologist Sol Tax's idea of an informal economy wherein petty traders sell small quantities of goods. See: Informal Sector. (4)

People's National Assembly (ANP) – the revolutionary legislative body proclaimed by the PAIGC in the hills of Boé in Portuguese *Guiné* in 1973. (15)

People without history – those tribes encountered by Europeans who were thought to be without a discernable past. In their narrow view, Europeans saw only the great civilizations of Eurasia as having had a real past. (2)

Periphery – those marginalized countries and regions dependent on the Core Countries of the industrialized world. Also called the South and the Third World. See also: Core, metropole, Third World, dependency theory. (15)

Personalistic theory of causation – the etiological system that attributes events in the world, especially misfortunes, to the will of sentient beings, alive or dead, of this world of the occult world. (3)

Petrofarming – a form of farming using high-tech, petrochemical fertilizers, imported goods made possible by the used of a petrol-driven transport system. In short, a form of farming dependent on the cheap availability of petroleum. (4)

Petty bourgeoisie – the lower middle-class, including minor businesspeople, tradespeople, and craftworkers. Also called the petite bourgeoisie. See also: Bourgeois mentality, bourgeoisie. (15)

Piacular rites – rituals intended to appeased angered spirits and right the balance in society disturbed by that anger. Also called expiatory rites. (3)

Plantation system – Because sugar cane is very labor intensive to grow, the owners needed laborers who could survive in the tropical climate of the Caribbean. West Africans fit this bill and West Africa was close to both the Americas and Europe. See: Sugar Plantations, palm oil plantations. (10)

Poleconomic – my conjunction of the term "political economy" to make it a modifying adjective e.g., poleconomic processes refer to those that constitute the processes going on in a given political economy. (5)

Policy of *assimilation* – French policy that began in 1870 when France extended limited citizenship rights to residents of the four *communes* of Senegal: Goreé, St. Louis, Rufisque and Dakar. In the ideal, any African in Francophone West Africa could become a citizen of France, though in reality few ever did. (14)

Political authority – the socially legitimized ability to force someone to do what they do not want to do. This is power that society recognizes and condones. (5)

Political economy – a tangle of institutions and relations involving political powers and related economic endeavors in a country or region. In most behavioral arenas, politics and economics go hand in glove. Politicians work with wealthy patrons and influential barons of industry, each influencing the other. More and more social scientists are realizing the fundamental importance of this complex as a driving force behind behaviors that heretofore were spoken of as separately – political or economic, not both in combination. (5)

Political power – the ability to force someone to do what they do not want to do. It can be legitimized (See: Authority) or not, remaining simply raw power. (5)

Political system – that form of institutional organization dealing with governance and the exercise of power. (5)

Polygenism – Polygenists claim that different races are the result of separate creation events or separate evolutionary trajectories and, hence, there is no biological connection from one race to another. See monogenism. (11)

Polyrhythmic music – African music is composed of complex combinations of different rhythms, all played at once. Dancers move various parts of the body to the different rhythms. (7)

Polygyny – a polygamous union between one man and more than one wife. (2)

Positivism – Positivists attempt to find and uncover obdurate truth, and see themselves as engaged in a discovery process. They believe that a bedrock reality exists that can be ascertained by the scientific method. (2)

Possession – the entry of a spirit into a human body taking over the thought, speech and behavior of the person. Thought to be a form of augury or divination. Often part of cult activity. (13)

Post-marital residence rules – norms governing where the couple will live after marriage. Can be patrilocal, with father; virilocal, with father's people; matrilocal, with mother's people; or neolocal, apart from either matrilineal or patrilineal relatives (rare in West Africa, though increasing with urbanization). Avunculocal residence is living with one's mother's brother. See matrilocal, patrilocal, virilocal, avunculocal and neolocal. (2)

Prebendal class – a prebend is a stipend drawn from the endowment or revenues of an organization, originally limited to a church by a presiding member of the clergy. Today it is applied to governments in the periphery because state functionaries can use structure of the state to access funds for personal use. The prebendal class, then, is that rank of political élites that governs. See also: Prebends, metropole, prebendalism, rent taking, kleptocracy. (15)

Prebendalism – taking rents through legitimate structures e.g., government marketing boards. See also: rent taking, prebendalism, prebendal class, marketing boards. See Prebends, metropole, prebendalism, rent taking. kleptocracy. (15)

Prebends – originally meant a grant of money given to a cleric but in terms of the governments of the Periphery, it refers a fund used illegally or by shady means within the government. See also: rent taking, prebendalism, kleptocracy and prebendal class. (15)

Prempeh, Agyemon – put in power by his mother, Yaa Akyaa, in 1888 after a time of civil war in Asanteland, and officially enstooled in 1894. In 1896 he was captured by General Maxwell and Colonel Scott in Kumase. He lived in exile there till 1924, when he returned to head up his nation once more, ruling till his death in 1931. (12)

Prestor John – mythical Christian King that was supposed to have lived in "Ethiopia" and who Prince Henry the Navigator though might be *Mansa* Musa of "Melli." Part of Henry's plan in exploring the West Coast of Africa was to get in contact with Prestor John to pull off a pincher movement on the Moors in North Africa. (10fn)

Primitive – the idea that some peoples were less developed in civilizational terms. Backward. Savage. Childlike. (2)

Primitive accumulation – the first acquisition of capital to begin to build a capitalist enterprise or industrialize. See also: Accumulation. (15)

Proletarians or Proletariat – in Marxian theory, the working class. (15)

Protectorates – a relationship of protection and partial control assumed by the self-proclaimed superior powers over West African dependent regions. (5)

Primitive – idea that some people are socially or mentally behind other more advanced or civilized peoples. This concept has been disproved by anthropology. (2)

Primitive mentality – idea put forward by Lucien Lévy-Bruhl (1857–1939). He was an intellectual force in European thought, particularly known for his research on the mentality of preliterate peoples, writing numerous studies, including *How Natives Think* in 1910. (3)

Prince Henry the Navigator – the third son of King John I of Portugal. He attended the siege against the Moors at Cueta. When the Portuguese took control of Cueta, Henry became the first governor of the territory. While there, he began to hear tales from Arab traders of Bilad Ghana, a kingdom near a great river, governed by a mighty king who had access to large quantities of gold. Gave financial and political backing to navigators who began to explore the Guinea Coast. (9)

Privilege – the idea that some people should have favored access to socially valued rewards. (5)

Privatization – Neoliberal program to reduce state involvement in economics. States in Peripheral Countries often have to divest themselves of state-owned enterprises and parastatal companies. (15)

Proletarians or Proletariat – in Marxian theory, the working class. (4)

Protectorates – a relationship of protection and partial control assumed by the self-proclaimed superior powers over West African dependent regions. (13)

Purdah – the seclusion of women from male sight under Islamic law. (9)

Qur'an (English, Koran) – the official religious text of Islam, revelations made from Allah to Muhammad at the founding of Islam after 610 AD. Holy Scriptures of Islam. See also Islam. (1)

Rainfed horticulture – simple farming that relies on rainfall and nature's seasons, rather than more intensive irrigated agriculture, which is not much practiced in West African farming. (1)

Rain forest – the jungle or heavily forested tropical zone running along the 10_ N in West Africa. (1)

Rank – idea of being elevated above others socially and in terms of prestige or the possession of some symbols thereof. Existed in pre-stratified societies e.g., stateless societies. See also: Bigness. (5)

Ranked Societies – societies formed around the principle of a limited number of informal positions of bigness or high rank. See: Big Man. (5)

Rassemblement Démocratique Africain (**RDA**) – founded by Félix Houphouët-Boigny of the *Cote d'Ivoire* ca. 1946. Affiliated with the communist party. (15)

Rawlings, Jerry John – recent president of Ghana. A former flight lieutenant, he took over in a coup the 1970s. In September 1979 he stepped down in favor of an elected civilian president, a Sisala, Hilla Limann (1934–98). When economic conditions worsened, Limann was deposed in a second coup led by Rawlings on Dec. 31, 1981. Worked under SAPs to try to privatize the economy. Replaced in the elections of December 2000. (3)

RDA – See: *Rassemblement Démocratique Africain.*

Red Carnation Revolution – on the 25th of April 1974, the Portuguese Armed Forces Movement (AFM) and hundreds of thousands of workers crowded the streets of Lisbon to celebrate the overthrow of the hated Caetano regime, some placing long-stemmed red carnations down the gun barrels of the left-leaning soldiers. Portugal had suffered decades of injustice under the fascist dictator Salazar. In 1974 these army units were disillusioned with the carnage and injustice of the wars in Africa, as well as the fascism of Caetano who had followed in the footsteps of Salazar. This revolution hastened the liberty of Guinea-Bissau. (15)

Redistributive mode of production – stage between a purely egalitarian society and an extractive one wherein a headman assumes the privilege of collecting the group's surplus and doles it out throughout the year. A herd of animals under the control of a senior herdsman functions similarly. (4)

Redistributor ruler – a ruler who takes goods and services from the people, but who maintains power by giving away about as much as he receives, thus becoming a support to the people and functioning to redistribute wealth more evenly in the polity. (5)

Redundancy – repetition of behavior, somewhat analogous to tradition. (2)

Rent taking – extraction of value from subordinates. See also: Prebendalism. (18)

Revolutionary formalism – tendency for the members of the revolution to become idols and their ideas to be enshrined as axiomatic and unquestionable, in spite of changing circumstances that call for a fresh approach. (15)

Rights *in genetricem* – legal or jural rights over the offspring of a marital union. Reproductive rights. (2)

Rights *in rem* – rights to use something and to sell it. Usually held over private property. (4)

Rights *in usufruct* – rights to use something, but not to sell it. Usually held over communal property. (4)

Rights *in uxorem* – legal or jural rights over the sexual (not reproductive) and domestic rights of a marital union. (2)

Rites of reversal – rituals performed to indicate the ambiguity of a role or to highlight some aspect of the role or transition from one role to another. (3)

Rites of passage – rituals performed when a person or social cohort passes from one social status to another e.g., warriors to adults. (3)

Ritual – redundant religious acts usually performed at some crisis in life, or to ward off an anticipated calamity, or to renew the power of a shrine or to connect with the occult world at a time of passage from on social status to another. See rites of passage, rituals of intensification. (3)

Rituals of intensification – usually performed at some crisis in life, or to ward off an anticipated calamity, or to renew the power of a shrine. (2)

Riverine – land alongside a river i.e., a riverine area. (4)

Rostow, Walter – a development theorist of the modernization school of the 1960s who advocated modernization through adoption of the growth model of the West and their technology. He believed that by injecting enough technological infrastructure into an backward country, they would reach a plateau from which "take off" to industrialization could occur. History has shown this to be false for most of the South. (15)

Royal Niger Company – company headed by a British commercialist, Sir George Goldie, which was given broad powers of governance in West Africa in 1886. See: Informal Empire and George Goldie. (13)

Sacralizing – The process whereby men attach sacred ideas to mundane processes, events or places. See also: Mythologizing. (3)

Sacrifice – in a general sense any ritual that causes the sacrificer to give up something, but in the West African context this is usually a blood sacrifice where an animal is killed as an offering to a spirit or supernatural power. (3)

Sahara Desert – The great desert area of northern Africa extends from the Atlantic Ocean eastward past the Red Sea to Iraq. The entire desert, the largest in the world, is about 1610 km (about 1000 mi.) wide and about 5150 km (about 3200 mi.) long from East to West. The total area of the Sahara is more than 9,065,000 sq. km (more than 3,500,000 sq. mi.), of which some 207,200 sq. km (some 80,000 sq. mi.) consist of partially fertile oases. The boundaries are not clearly defined and have been shifting for millennia. (1)

Sahel – the area lightly covered with scattered trees and desert between the Sahara Desert to the north and the Savannah to the south. Means, "coast" in Arabic i.e., the edge of the desert. (1)

Salaga – a major trading town in north-central Ghana that grew wealthy on its middleman status. Both legitimate trade goods and slaves passed through this entrepôt. (11)

Salia Bujan – the author's Sisala name. (4)

Samory Touré – the Mandingo slaver and state-builder who proclaimed a *jihad*, spreading death and destruction across West Africa starting in Senegambia until he was finally captured by the French in the early 20th century. French called him "The Black Napoleon of the Sudan." See: *Sofa* army. (9)

SAPs – Structural Adjustment Programs based on the principles first laid down in the Bretton Woods Agreements which state that it is the responsibility of the developed countries to aid in the maturation and development of the poor countries of the South or Third World. See: Bretton Woods Agreements. (3)

Saro – Christian missionaries in Yorubaland who were of mixed racial background, Creoles from Sierra Leone. (13)

Savannah – the area covered in orchard bush between the Sahel to the north and the rain forest to the south. (1)

Scramble for Africa – most texts refer to this as the rush for territory by European powers at the end of the 19th century. I divide this scramble into two parts: the first scramble took place after Portugal's discovery of Guinea, when other European nations like Spain tried to get in on the riches being made there. The second scramble indeed came much later when European nations were feeling the need to formalize their hegemony in Africa. (13)

Scorpion ordeal – a judicial and social control method. The lineage headman in Sisalaland informs all that the scorpion (under the direction of the ancestors) is about to ferret out the thief. It is not uncommon for the truant to step forward and confess to a crime (e.g., stealing grain from a granary) at this point, thereby avoiding the pain of the sting and possible death from the trauma. If not, the headman places the scorpion on the arm of each family member until it stings someone. (5)

Secret society – a voluntary association either the membership of which is secret, or it has secrets that cannot be divulged to the public at large. A form of a sodality. See: Sodality, Voluntary association. (3)

Sedentism – settling down from a migratory way of life. Living in towns. This followed the Neolithic Revolution when domestication of plants and animals led to the development of urban dwelling. (8)

Segmentary lineage system – organizationally based on the principle of opposition between segments of a larger descent group. By fission one segment becomes two and stands in opposition to its opposite. By fusion two can merge to become one. (2)

Senares – French for the women who married European traders and became wealthy off their interstitial position in trading exchanges. In Portuguese called *senhoras*. (4)

Sénégambia – ancient region encompassing Senegal and The Gambia and environs where Mandinka (Mandingo) kingdoms were established prior to contact. (5)

Senghor, Léopold Sédar – first president of Senegal (1960–80), a poet and an intellectual. He was educated at the University of Paris. First elected to the general council of Senegal in 1946, he worked for Senegalese independence. He also served as a Socialist member of the French National Assembly from Senegal from 1946 to 1958. Called

Africa's leading intellectual, Senghor published both poetry and articles on literature and politics. His first volume, *Chants d'ombre* (Shadow Songs), was published in Paris in 1945 to critical acclaim. Among his works published in English are *Selected Poems* (1964), *On African Socialism* (1964), *Ethiopiques* (1975), and *Négritude and Humanism* (1975), a reaffirmation of the values of traditional African culture. In 1984 he was named to the French Academy, the first black person ever to receive that honor. He favored a federalist position in Francophone West Africa rather than total independence from France, as opposed to the ideas of Félix Houphouët-Boigny. (2)

Senhoras – See: *senares*. (4)

Shamans – part-time healers, curers and those who use magic or medicines for good purposes. (3)

Shari'a **Law** – *Qur'anic* law or religious law of Islam that claims superiority over civic law. Some Muslim fundamentalists today are trying to impose this law on West Africans who do not practice Islam and this has led to civil strife e.g., in Northern Nigeria. (3)

Sharpe, Granville – an abolitionist and humanitarian in England, led a fight against re-exportation of slaves. Also instrumental in founding Freetown in Sierra Leone in 1787 as a place to return freed slaves. This started out as a private venture, but the British government took over running the settlement after it made the slave trade illegal in 1807. In 1808 the coastal settlement became a British colony. (13)

Shift to the Guinea-Bissau Peso – after independence, the new government needed to replace the Portuguese Escudo with a new Peso, but lacked the expertise to plan and manufacture the new notes. They had to contract this out to Algeria, which got the contract and benefited rather than any firm within Guinea-Bissau. (15)

Shifting cultivation – extensive farming that uses slash-and-burn techniques to clear and farm a plot, then moves on to new land once the soil is depleted, leaving the old farmland to lie fallow and regenerate itself as the bush reclaims it. See slash-and-burn, extensive farming. (4)

Sickle-cell trait – this adaptive genetic trait is found in populations of people exposed to malaria for long periods of time. It affected the composition of the red blood cells allowing them to more effectively fight off the affects of the disease. In a small portion of such a population a deleterious form of the trait emerges called sickle-cell anemia. This is not a feature tied to race so much as to populations living in areas with endemic malaria. (1)

Sikapo – wealthy class in Asante society. See also: *Ahiato*. (12)

Sikapo-ahiato **ranking** – wealthy class vs. lower class in Asante society. See also: *Ahiato* and *Sikapo*. (12)

Silent barter – an ancient custom wherein the exchange of goods occurred without speaking. This allowed trade before trade languages developed. Goods would be left in a designated spot, and then the trader would withdraw to await the coming of another trader. The second man would place the amount of exchangeable goods next to the first pile of goods. If the first trader accepted the amount offered, he would advance and take them, leaving his own goods behind for the second trader. If not, he would wait till the second trader added more or went away with his goods. (4)

Sipaalaaraa – aggrandizers and little chiefs or big men who rose to power through control over armies of men who defended their settlements initially, but who also came to operate protection schemes for passing traders and who also engaged in brigandage. (5)

Slash-and-burn cultivation – extensive farming wherein farmers use techniques to clear, burn and farm a plot, then move on to new land once the soil is depleted, leaving the old farmland to lie fallow and regenerate itself as the bush reclaims it. See shifting cultivation, extensive farming. (4)

Slave Coast – the coast along the Gulf of Guinea from Accra on the West to Lagos on the East. Many strong city-states emerged in this area built on the wealth derived from trading slaves e.g., Ouidah, Grand Popo, Jakin, and immediately behind them Great Ardrah (Allada). (11)

Slippage – the sometime minute and imperceptible changes in tradition as it is passed on from generation to generation. This is due to different perceptions by members of different generations and by a loss of memory when one generation dies out. (2)

Social banking – the exchanges one makes to establish and cultivate important labor relations. Investing in people, see: Wealth in People System. (4)

Social control – usually informal means of directing people's behavior e.g., through non-governmental means such as divination or membership in a sodality. However, social control functions are also part of state systems, but they become more formalized in a system of administration. (5)

Sociocultural formation – also called institutions, social structure, social formations. All are ideas. All are constructed by people to give meaning to their lives. (2)

Sodalities – associations of fellowship or comradeship e.g., age-sets, voluntary associations, cult and secret societies. (2)

Sofa army – the *sofas* were Samory Touré's troops. See: Samory Touré. (13)

Somatic compliance – a biophysical shut down of life giving process in the body induced by a firm belief in magical practices aimed at the person by a magician. (3)

Sorcery – the use of herbal or medicinal means to do harm to others. Sometimes, like witchcraft, called black magic. See witchcraft. (3)

Sororal polygyny – marriage of one man to sisters. (2)

South – politically correct terminology to replace the older Third World. Poor countries of Africa, Asia and Latin America, many of whom lie in the Southern Hemisphere. See also: Third World, periphery, North. (15)

Specific reciprocity – not part of traditional West African culture, but a form of exchange brought in by Europeans wherein exact amounts or time frames for repayment are specified e.g., wage labor. (4)

Spirit possession – form of divination where a spirit is thought to enter a medium and which takes over the consciousness of the person, often speaking through the medium. *Jine-ton* is a form of this that occurs in Muslim West Africa. (3)

Spoils politics – also called politics of the belly wherein politicos use political office to line their own pockets. See prebendalism, prebendal class, rent taking, kleptocracy. (16)

State – a stratified society with a paramount chief or king at the head of a royal descent group and/or ruling bureaucracy. Commonly considered to be advanced chiefdoms, kingdoms and empires. (5)

Steatite – soapstone, a soft metamorphic rock composed mostly of the mineral talc, has been a favorite medium for carvers throughout West African history. (6)

Storable surplus – grains and domesticated herds allowed humans a form of wealth that could be saved and exchanged, a big step toward the concentration of wealth in the hands of "haves", creating "have nots' and social stratification. (5)

"Storyed" houses – usually two-story houses in West Africa are the sign of bigness, having made it wealth wise. (8)

Stratification –hierarchy or layers of ranked cohorts in society. Position in these strata determined prestige and privileged access to the resources. (5)

Structural Adjustment Programs – see SAPS. (3)

Sub-Saharan Africa – the area in Africa below the Sahara Desert, generally those countries including and below Mauritania, Mali, Niger, Chad, Sudan and Ethiopia. Sometimes referred to as Black Africa. (1)

Succession to high office – rules that allocate the political economy of the office holder to an heir. (5)

Sudanic Zone – the Savannah belt that runs east-west across the top of the rain forest and just south of the Sahara Desert. Includes the Savannahh and the Sahel. (8)

Sugar plantations – the Portuguese and others were looking for ways to fill the new sweet tooth acquired by Europeans who had discovered the joys of sugar. The Portuguese tried plantations on the Canaries, Fernando Po, São Tomé and Principe, then later in the Americas. Because sugar cane is very labor intensive to grow, the owners needed laborers who could survive in the tropical climate of the Caribbean. See: the Plantation System. (10)

Surplus value of labor – in Marx's theory of capitalist exploitation it is the difference between a fair market price and wages paid to the worker. Thus, if the capitalist is making exorbitant profits and paying low wages, he is exploiting the surplus labor value of the workers. (4)

Sustainability – a quality inherent in some development techniques that can be maintained indefinitely by local people using local inputs and energy and that do not harm future generations. (18)

Syncretism – the attempted reconciliation or union of different or opposing principles, practices, or parties, as in philosophy or religion. In the West African context, often refers to syncretistic cults, sects and churches that have blended Christianity with other African forms of worship. (3)

Taboo – something to be avoided, often because it is considered ritually sacred e.g., when the Crow clan prohibits killing and/or eating of that bird. (2)

Tagharza – place between the Niger Bend and the Maghrib where salt has been mined for centuries. (9)

Tendana – common term for the custodian of the earth, a ritual leader of those in Northern Ghana who were the original inhabitants of the area. (2)

Third World – politically incorrect terminology replaced the newer, South. Poor countries of Africa, Asia and Latin America, many of which lie in the Southern Hemisphere. See also: Periphery, South. (15)

Tigare Cult – "Tiger" anti-witchcraft cult started in Ghana but now widespread in West Africa (Note: There are no real tigers in Africa). (3)

Tijaniyya – a dominant religious brotherhood in the western half of West Africa. Anyone leaving the brotherhood is considered an infidel equivalent to a *kaffir*. (9)

Tiralilleurs Sénégalais – regiment of African soldiers organized by the French. Like the British counterpart, the Frontier Force, this shows that some West Africans collaborated with the Europeans against their fellow West Africans. See: Frontier Force. (5)

Totem – a totem is the identifying insignia of a kin group e.g., the crocodile of the crocodile clan. It may be an animal or any other symbol of group unity. Members of the group taboo the use of the totem, for example Crocodile clansmen cannot kill or eat a crocodile. When the totem is a living species, for example crows, crow clansmen may believe that the fate of the species is intricately tied up with the fate of the members of the clan. See totemism. (2)

Totemism – an organizational system in which plants, animals, objects or other phenomena are associated with a descent group. The totem is the identifying insignia, e.g., the crocodile of the crocodile clan. (2)

Touré, Ahmed Sékou – a leader in the struggle for the liberation of Guinea from the French. He was a trade unionist organizer and member of the RDA also opposed the breakup of the RDA. Under Touré's leadership, Guinea became the only colony to vote against the constitution of the French Community in 1958 and to opt for complete independence, which was achieved on Oct. 2, 1958. France retaliated by severing relations and withdrawing all financial and technical aid. Guinea cultivated close relations with the Soviet Union. He advocated African unity. In 1966, when Ghana's President Kwame Nkrumah was deposed, Touré welcomed him to Guinea as joint president. Under Sékou Touré, who held the presidency from the date of independence until his death in 1984, Guinea was a one-party Marxist-socialist republic. (15)

Traffic economy – one in which goods are not produced locally or regionally, but which requires the export of raw materials out to pay for manufactured goods coming in. It presupposes the lack of development in the region, except for that infrastructure needed to move goods in and out. (4)

Trade Liberalization – opening markets, reducing tariffs and rules preventing a free flow of trade between countries. See also: Neoliberalism. (18)

Tradition – customs from the past. Similar to sociocultural formation. The whole accumulation residue of previous generations' codification of ideas, but it is always received imperfectly, due to slippage in intergenerational transmission, and it is reworked by living people to meet their present needs. (2)

Trans-Saharan Trade – routes connecting Sub-Saharan Africa with the Maghrib to the north and the Levant to the northeast across the Sahara Desert. First slaves from West Africa to Europe went along these routes. (1)

Trans-Saharan Slave Trade – along the many routes across the desert, Arab traders took Black Africans to Europe and the Middle East as slaves. Compared to the Atlantic Slave Trade, very few Sub-Saharan Africans were taken as slaves along these routes. See: Trans-Saharan trade routes, Atlantic Slave Trade. (11)

Transparency – ability to see and hear the decision-making process within an organization. (15)

Triangular Slave Trade – See: Atlantic Slave Trade. (11)

Tribalism – the feared ethnic conflict that has arisen in some parts of West Africa. Some see this as being inherent in Africa due to precolonial tribes with long standing hatred for each other, but some analysts see it as a result of improper colonial boundaries and inappropriate systems of governance brought on by Europe's imperialism. (2)

Tribes – congeries of kin groups and supra-band social organizations that developed after the Neolithic Revolution but before the rise of states. (5)

Tsetse Fly – common name for any of several African bloodsucking insects of the genus *Glossina*. Tsetses are found abundantly in rain forests and along the edges of lakes and rivers in West Africa. Commonly causes *Trypanosomaiasis* or sleeping sickness. Some varieties infect humans and others just bovines. Mostly found in the rain forest, the tsetse prevented the use of cavalry and transport by horse through this zone. (1)

Treaty of Alcaçovas – ended the war between Spain and Portugal over rights to Guinea (1475–1479). (10)

Trickle down economics – Neoliberal idea that even though the wealthy get rich off of unbridled competition, profits will eventually diffuse throughout all levels of society. (18)

Tutelary figures – statues or masks representing spirits with whom a person has a special relationship, usually being able to call upon the spirit to help her, him or others with special supernatural powers. (6)

Tutu, Osei – was the first such supreme ruler of the Asante (*fl. ca.* 1680–?1717). He is credited with directing a war of liberation against the Denkyira, with some military backing from Akwamu, where he had been a prince in residence for a number of years. (12)

Twin governance – in many parts of traditional West Africa autochthonal leaders held ritual control of the land, while invading political leaders held chiefships and ruled in a secular sense. (3)

Tyi wara – a half man/half snake figure in Bambara culture that taught humankind the art of horticulture. The *tyi wara* masks are stylized depictions of an antelope venerated in honor of the legendary culture hero. (6)

UDCs – Underdeveloped Countries, or those of the South, or countries of the Third World. (17)

'Ulama – the learned of Islam, those who possess the quality of *'ilm*, "learning," in its widest sense, those who are versed theoretically and practically in the Muslim sciences. From this rank comes the religious teachers of the Islamic community—theologians (*mutakallimun*), canon lawyers (*muftis*), judges (*qadis*), professors—and high state religious officials like the *shaikh al-Islam*. In a narrower political sense, *'ulama* may refer to a council of learned men holding government appointments in a Muslim state. (9)

Umar, Al-Hajj – (1794–1864), a Tukolor cleric-warrior from Futa Toro. As a member of the *Tijaniyya* order, he was a fundamentalist who believed in using any means to establish *Shari'a* and a just theocracy. He waged a *jihad* establishing an empire from the French outpost of Medina on the River Senegal to Timbuktu in the Niger Bend, an area almost as large as the Songhai Empire. He fought against French incursion into the area. (9)

Unanimist fallacy – idea that tradition is more or less bounded and fixed through time. (3)

Underdeveloped capitalism – a limited form of capitalism based on the traffic economy in West Africa and the fact that most industry, control and benefit from this economy belongs to the core countries of the North. See, Traffic economy. (1)

Unilineal descent – a reckoning of lineage through either one's father or one's mother. Inheritance and succession to important offices pass from father to son in patrilineal societies, and from mother's brother to sister's son in matrilineal ones. (2)

Union of the Peoples of Guiné and Cape Verde (PAIGC) – the military liberation movement in Portuguese *Guiné*, modern-day Guinea-Bissau. (15)

United Cold Coast Convention (UGCC) – founded by the West African lawyer J. B. Danquah in the Gold Coast. He was appointed by the British to draft a constitution. Kwame Nkrumah considered the UGCC to be too conservative and advocated a more radical approach than Danquah was willing to pursue. (15)

United States of Africa – Kwame Nkrumah's dream of a pan-African system of governance that would transcend nationalism and the colonial inheritance. See: Nkrumah, Kwame, Convention People's Party. (16)

University of Sankore – 14th century university established at Timbuktu by as-Saheli who distinguished himself by building at the behest of *Mansa* Musa. (9)

Urban development bias – begun under colonialism the undo focus of development was in the cities, to the exclusion of the countryside. This continues today to the detriment of rural peoples and agricultural development. It is part of the reason for the massive rural-urban migration of recent years in West Africa. (14)

Urbanization – process of the growth of cities often accompanying state-building and the centralization of power. (9)

Virebaling – in the lineage mode of production of the Sisala, the central big or male granary in which traditionally the lineage headman stored millet. It is both a functional crib and a *vene* shrine, a ritual focal point of the lineage group. (5)

Virilocal residence – postmarital residence with the groom's father's people, though not necessarily in the same household as the groom's father. (2)

Vodoun – an active religion in Ouidah (Uidah) in the country of Benin. Likely the ancestor of Voodoo as practiced in the African diaspora. (6)

Voltaic Region – that area of West Africa around the Volta River which runs through present-day Burkina Faso and Ghana. (2)

Wattle and daub –mud and sticks or grass mixed to produced a building material. (4)

Wealth in People System – the WIP system wherein people invest in social relations to carry out economic processes i.e., production, distribution and consumption. In labor-short West Africa, people to help with weeding, harvesting and other labor intensive tasks are crucial. Social banking is the exchanges one makes to establish and cultivate such important relations. See: Social Banking. (4)

Western-educated modernizing élites – those who led the independence movements were most often those who had advanced through education to challenge the colonial powers. They were committed to moving away from indigenous ways to modernize West Africa. (16)

White man's grave – because of the hot tropical climate and high incidence of disease in West Africa, many Europeans died even aboard ship off the coast, but in even greater numbers once they went ashore. It got a bad reputation, especially when compared to more temperate climatic zones where White settlers predominated, in East and Southern Africa. (2)

Witchcraft – belief in evil as practiced by witches who have the magical capacity to harm, either by intent or absentmindedly. Sometimes called black magic. See sorcery. (2)

Wolseley, General Sir Garnet – a racist put in charge at *Mina* who was intent on destroying the Asante. Sacked Kumase in 1874. (12)

World Bank – an international leading organization of the United Nations. Its official name is the International Bank for Reconstruction and Development. Plans were laid at the Bretton Woods Conference. The bank not only makes loans to member nations, but, under government guarantee, to private investors, for the purpose of facilitating productive investment, encouraging foreign trade, and discharging burdens of international debt. All members of the bank must also belong to the IMF. The bank is self-sustaining and has maintained a profit on its lending activities. See: Bretton Woods, IMF. (14)

World Religions – Christianity and Islam, as well as other widespread religions that proselytize and take an exclusive approach to other points of view. (3)

Yala, Koumba – present president of Guinea-Bissau. (15)

Yaw, Osei – the only *Asantehene* that could be considered to have been belligerent toward the British. (12)

Zongos (sing. ***Zongo***) – strangers' quarters in a town, a place where non-residents live in the town. See dual urban residential pattern. (8)

GLOSSARY — PEOPLE, CITIES, STATES & EMPIRES

Almoravids – Berber dynasty based in modern-day Morocco that ruled in Africa and Spain in the 11th and 12th centuries. Between 1053 and 1061, a large part of northwestern Africa was subjugated by the Muslim religious military brotherhood known as the hermits (Arab. *al-murabit*). In 1076 AD their army attacked Ghana, and led it into a period of internal conflicts and disorganization. (9)

Arma – descendants of Moorish soldiers from the Maghrib who attacked and defeated the Songhai Empire, but who married local girls and settled down in the Western Sudan. See also Maghrib, Songhai Empire. (9)

Asante – originally an offshoot of the Denkyira, a kingdom in the rain forest centered around Kumase in modern-day Ghana. Noted for trade in kola nuts and gold. Known in medieval Europe as Akaney, a gold-rich kingdom of the blacks. Whole empire also referred to as the Akan Empire. (8)

Baule – of the Ivory Coast give the most utilitarian objects a touch of art. Objects such as bobbins, spoons, bombs, hairpins, combs, stools, doors and diviner's boxes are produced by artists with a flair for elaboration. (6)

Benin City – Ancient Yoruba city-state in the modern-day Nigerian rain forest. It began about a thousand years ago and reached its greatest extent in the 15th century when European seafarers reached the city. It was the center of a divine kingship ruled by the *Oba*, the principle political and religious leader of the nation. (8)

Dahomey – an ancient kingdom founded in the 17th century, in present-day Benin, based on the Fon people. Became wealthy on slave trade. In the 19th century King Ghézo (r. 1818–1858) came close to being a despot under an Asiatic Mode of Production system when he used slaves to clear and farm plantations of oil palm for export to Europe. Coquery-Vidrovitch points this out when she says that through a carefully maintained confusion between the "lands of the kingdom" and the "lands of the king" the monarch was able to privately appropriate land and its product.

Dan or **Dan-Kran** – people of Ivory Coast known for the beautiful masks.

Denkyira – people of *Mina* who began to become wealthy through contact with Europeans and who expanded northward, eventually giving rise the to the Asante Empire. (11)

Dogon – Malian cliff dwellers who have an elaborate cosmology and produce much artwork. The *Tellem* figures found archaeologically in their area are likely associated with contemporary Dogon ancestral figures. (6)

Denkyira – people of *Mina* who began to become wealthy through contact with Europeans and who expanded northward, eventually giving rise the to the Asante Empire. (11)

Fante Federation of States – an organizational attempt by the Fante peoples to stave off the growing aggression of their northern neighbors, the Asante. The Fante often sided with the British against the Asante. (12)

Fon Kingdom – a kingdom traditionally tributary to Oyo that arose directly above the city states along the Slave Coast. Since their capital was called Abomey, this kingdom is commonly known as Dahomey, which became the name of the French colony established in that area, although the name has since been changed to Benin. (11)

Fulani – the pastoralists or cattle herders of West Africa, many of whom have become urbanized and converted to Islam. Rulers of the Emirates of Northern Nigeria, for example. (5)

Ghana, Empire of – (6–12 CAD). First of the Great Sudanic Kingdoms of the Niger Bend area in the Savanna. See also: Mali, Songhai, Great Sudanic Kingdoms. (8)

Great Sudanic Kingdoms – (6th–17th century) Ghana, Songhai and Mali arose in the Niger Bend areas as they traded with the Levant and Mediterranean across the formidable barrier of the Sahara Desert. They also have all, in varying degrees, been influenced by the history of Islam's penetration of the area. See also: Ghana, Mali, Songhai, Sundiata Keita, *Mansa* Musa, Great Sudanic Kingdoms, Sunni Ali Ber, *Askia* Muhammad and the University of Sankore.

Ife – City in modern-day Nigeria thought to be the site of the origin of the Yoruba people. It is probably their oldest town. Considered by the Yoruba to be a holy city and the legendary birthplace of humankind, it is held to have been founded by a son of the god *Oduduwa*. Ife was the capital of a well-established kingdom by the early 11th century. By the late 12th or early 13th century, its artisans were producing the naturalistic terracotta heads and bronze pieces made by the lost-wax process for which the Ife kingdom is now well known. (8)

Igbo-Ukwu – excavation of an archaeological site in Nigeria and dated at about 1,200 BP. contains the oldest known African use of the lost wax method. (8)

Jenné-Jeno – (which means "old Jenné) show a trading town that began about 2,250 BP and lasted over 1,600 years. It reached its height about 1,200 years ago and began to decline around 350 years later to be abandoned by 600 BP. (8)

Kanem-Bornu – an Islamic state that formed around Lake Chad about 1,300 BP. It was instrumental in spreading Islam in the Central Sudan and into Nigeria, especially among the Hausa states. (9)

Kintampo Culture – Ghana's prehistorical culture with stone tools found in conjunction with clay works – pottery, figurines and the famous and mysterious terracotta "cigars", which may have been rasps, but they exact function is still unknown. Additionally, there were arm rings, beads and arrowheads. (8)

Kumase – ancient capital of Asanteland and presently a major city in Ghana. Alternate spelling is Kumasi. (11)

Mali, Empire of – second kingdom in the Niger Bend after Ghana and before Songhai. By 1087 AD this Mandinka kingdom rose to power at a time when Islam was filtering into the area. Sundiata Keita was the first king of Mali, ruling the empire from circa 1230 until his death in 1255 AD. Perhaps the most well known ruler was *Mansa* Musa (1312–1332 AD) who made a *hajj* (pilgrimage) to Mecca (1324 AD) spreading around so much gold that its valued dropped in the area. Under his control, the kingdom doubled in size through conquest. He also established the University of Sankore at Timbuktu. Mali began to decline after 1400. See also: Ghana, Sundiata Keita, Songhai, *Mansa* Musa, Great Sudanic Kingdoms and the University of Sankore. (9)

Nok Culture – (ca. 2,900–1,800 B. P.) originated in a valley in West Africa between the Niger and the Benue Rivers. They have produced the oldest sculptures in Sub-Saharan Africa. They left behind a strong legacy of fine art, terracotta statues and metalworking. (6)

Oyo Empire – Ancient Yoruba city-state in modern-day Nigeria located to the northeast of Ife. Militarily dominated outlying provinces and towns. Replaced Ife as Yorubaland's political center. When the Portuguese first arrived in the late 15th century, it was Oyo that controlled trade in peppers and slaves. (8)

Sisala – a people of Northern Ghana studied by Dr. Mendonsa. (1)

Songhai, Empire of – in 1468 AD, the army of Sunni Ali Ber defeated the largely Tuareg contingent at Timbuktu and captured the city. Ali Ber extended the Songhai empire by controlling the Niger River with a navy of war vessels. His death in 1492 AD created a vacuum which his son was unable to fill, and was soon deposed by Mamadou Touré who ascended the throne in 1492 AD under the name *Askia* Muhammad. During his reign which ended in 1529 AD, he made Songhai the largest empire in the history of West Africa. He restored the tradition of Islamic learning to the University of Sankore, made Islam the court religion, and made his own spectacular *hajj* to Mecca where he was appointed as Caliph of western Sudan by the ruler of all Islam. After 1528 AD the empire entered a long period of decline with attacks my Moroccan troops. See also: Ghana, Sundiata Keita, Mali, *Mansa* Musa, Great Sudanic Kingdoms, Sunni Ali Ber, *Askia* Muhammad and the University of Sankore. See also Arma. (9)

Soninke – a people (also called Sarakole, Seraculeh, or Serahuli) who were located in present-day Senegal near Bakel on the Senegal River. Today some Senegalese Soninke have migrated to Dakar, but the people in the Bakel area remained millet farmers. The Soninke, by first controlling local trade then the trans-Saharan trade flowing through the area, became the founders of the great Soninke Empire of Ghana (1400 to 600 BP). See also Ghana, the empire of. (9)

Tekrur – perhaps the earliest state in West Africa and precursor of the Tukolor Empire in modern-day Senegal. Established about 1,200 years ago, it continued till the tenth century. First known state to accept Islam. See Also: Tukolor. (9)

Tichitt-Oualata State – an early state (4,000–2,800 BP) in Mauritania. (8)

Tukolor Empire (Tukolor) – Tijani state in the Futa Jalon founded by al-Hajji Umar. In the 9th century the Tukolor settled in the Senegal River valley dominating eastern Senegal from the 11th to the 14th century. By the 15th century a pattern of Wolof and Serer states was well established there. Until far into the 18th century the decentralized Wolof empire near the coast retained nominal suzerainty over the other Wolof states, including those of Baol, Wale, and Cayor. (9)

ACRONYMS

AD	After Christ.
AFM	Armed Forces Movement (Portugal).
ANC	African National Congress (RSA).
BINGO	Business and Industry Non-Governmental Organization.
BC	Before the birth of Christ.
BP	Years before present.
Ca.	*Circa* or about. Used with dates e.g., *ca.* 500 AD.
CG	Consultative Group of the World Bank.
CEA	Centre for African Studies (Lisbon).
CIA	Central Intelligence Agency, a spy agency on the US government.
CPI	Corruption Perception Index.
CUF	*Companhia União Fabril,* a company in Portuguese *Guiné.*
ECA	The UN Economic Commission for Africa.
EDF	European Development Fund.
EU	European Union.
Est.	Established.
DRB	Debt Review Body proposed by Jubilee 2000.
FCPA	Foreign Corruption Practices Act of the United States.
FPNGO	For Profit Non-Governmental Organization.
GCC	Ghana Cotton Corporation.
GDP	Gross Domestic Product.
GNP	Gross National Product.
GNP PPP	World ranking of countries in terms of Gross National Product.
HIPC	Highly Indebted Poor Country.
HIPCI	Highly Indebted Poor Country Initiative launched in 1996 by the World Bank.
HRAF	Human Relations Area Files.
IDA	International Development Association established by the World Bank.
IFIs	International Financial Institutions e.g., the IMF and World Bank.
IMF	International Monetary Fund.
ISI	Import Substitution Industrialization.
kg	Kilogram.
km	Kilometer.
NDC	National Democratic Congress, a political party in Ghana.

NIC	Newly Industrialized Countries.
NPP	New Patriotic Party, a political party in Ghana.
NPV	Net Present Value.
OECD	Organization of Economic Cooperation, a UN agency.
OAU	Organization of African Unity, a UN-like organization in continental Africa.
PRGF	Poverty Reduction & Growth Facility (Guinea-Bissau effort sponsored by the IMF).
RSA	Republic of South Africa.
SLPP	Sierra Leone People's Party.
sq.	Square.
UDC	Underdeveloped Country.
UNDP	United Nations Development Program.
USAID	United States Agency for International Development.
VAT	Value Added Tax.
WB	World Bank.
WDR	World Development Report of the UN.
WTO	World Trade Organization.

INDEX